A Dictionary of the

ANCIENT

GREEK

WORLD

A Dictionary of the

ANCIENT GREEK WORLD

David Sacks

Historical Consultant:
Oswyn Murray,
Fellow of Balliol College and
Lecturer in Ancient History at Oxford University

Original drawings by Margaret Bunson

Oxford University Press
New York   Oxford

Oxford University Press

Oxford   New York
Athens   Auckland   Bangkok   Bombay
Calcutta   Cape Town   Dar es Salaam   Delhi
Florence   Hong Kong   Istanbul   Karachi
Kuala Lumpur   Madras   Madrid   Melbourne
Mexico City   Nairobi   Paris   Singapore
Taipei   Tokyo   Toronto

and associated companies in
Berlin   Ibadan

Library of Congress Cataloging-in-Publication Data
Sacks, David.
[Encyclopedia of the ancient Greek world]
Dictionary of the ancient Greek world / David Sacks ; historical
consultant, Oswyn Murray : original drawings by Margaret Bunson.
p.   cm.
Previously published under title: Encyclopedia of the ancient
Greek world.
Includes bibliographical references and index.
ISBN 0-19-511206-7 (Pbk.)
1. Greece—Civilization—To 146 B.C.—Dictionaries.   I. Murray,
Oswyn.   II. Title.
DF16.S23   1996   96-32023
938'.003—dc20

1 3 5 7 9 10 8 6 4 2
Printed in the United States of America
on acid-free paper

This book is for
Rebecca and Katie Sacks.

CONTENTS

AUTHOR'S ACKNOWLEDGMENTS

There are several people to whom I am most grateful for help. My former teacher Oswyn Murray, fellow of Balliol College and lecturer in ancient history at Oxford University, vetted the manuscript with the same patience and receptiveness that distinguish his tutorial sessions. I owe him a great deal, not only for the book's preparation but also for my wider fascination with the ancient world. Two other scholars kindly donated their time to read sections and make comments: Gilbert Rose, professor of classics at Swarthmore College, and Christopher Simon, currently a visiting assistant professor of classics at the University of California, Berkeley. (Any factual errors here remain my own, however.)

I wish to thank my parents, Louis and Emmy Lou Sacks, for their unstinting encouragement. Ditto my good friend Jeffrey Scheuer. My thanks to Facts On File editor Gary Krebs, who kept the door open while the manuscript came together. Especially I must thank my wife, Joan Monahan, who brought home the family's bacon, day after day, during the four years consumed by this project.

Mainland Greece, the Aegean Sea, and Western Asia Minor

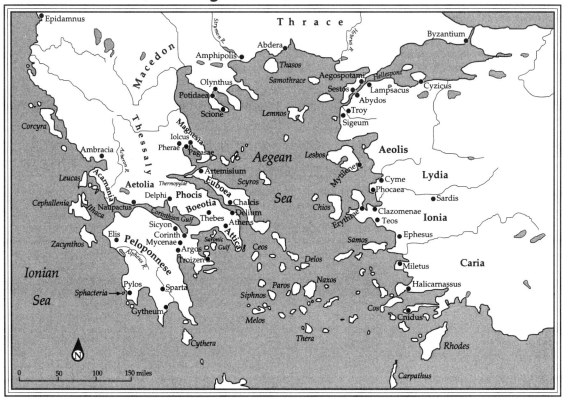

INTRODUCTION

About 2100 B.C. a migrant, cattle-herding, pony-riding people made their way into the Mediterranean land mass that today is called Greece. They entered overland from the north, probably the Danube Basin, but their origins may have lain farther northeast, for they spoke a language of the Indo-European linguistic family. Modern philologists believe that the ancestral Indo-European language—whose modern descendants include English, German, Gaelic, French, Farsi, Hindi, and modern Greek—evolved in the fourth millennium B.C. on the plains of southern Russia. This mother tongue then branched into different forms, carried in all directions by nomadic tribes. The group that reached Greece circa 2100 B.C. brought with it an early form of the Greek language. These people can be called the first Greeks.

The land that they invaded was held by farmers who had probably immigrated centuries earlier from Asia Minor, a place with which they perhaps remained linked via an eastward trade network that included the Aegean island of Crete. This settled, non-Greek people apparently knew seafaring and stone masonry—two skills that the nomadic Greeks did not yet have.

But the Greeks were the stronger warriors. They took over the country, probably by violence in the most desirable locales, but elsewhere perhaps by intermarriage (as may be reflected in the many Greek myths in which the hero marries the foreign princess). One apparent sign of conquest is the wrecked remnant of a pre-Greek palace that modern archaeologists call the House of the Tiles, at Lerna on the plain of Argos. Destroyed by fire circa 2100 B.C., this may have been the home of a native ruler who led an unsuccessful defense of the fertile heartland of southern Greece. Yet at certain other sites, archaeologists have found no clear signs of violence—only continued habitation and the abrupt emergence of a new style of pottery, betokening the Greeks' arrival.

The region that the Greeks now took over—and that would henceforth be their homeland—is a huge, jagged, southward-pointing peninsula, with a coastline stretching nearly 2,000 miles. Beyond its shores, particularly to the southeast, are islands that beckon to sea travelers and traders. Through the peninsula's center, from north to south, runs an irregular line of mountain ranges, whose slopes in ancient times held forests of oak, beech, and fir—timber for generations of house builders and shipwrights. In a later era, the limestone formations in these mountains would yield marble for sculptors and architects. But the mountains also occupied most of the mainland's total area, leaving only 20 percent as arable land.

Aside from scattered pockets, the farmland lay mainly in three regions: the plains of Argos, Boeotia, and Thessaly, in southern, central, and northern Greece, respectively. These territories were destined to become early Greek centers of power, especially the region of Argos, with its capital at Mycenae.

The soil of much of Greece is red or orange from clay deposits, which served centuries of potters and sculptors. In ancient times the farmed plains and foothills produced wheat, barley, olives, grapes, figs, and pomegranates—crops that could survive the ferociously hot, dry Greek summer. Summer, not winter, is the barren season in Greece, as in other parts of the Mediterranean. Winters are relatively mild—cool and rainy, but far rainier on the mainland's western side. The eastern regions, although traditionally densely populated, are blocked by the central mountains from receiving the westerly rainy weather. Athens gets only about 15 inches of rainfall a year; Corfu, on the west coast, has three times that much.

In such a country, where farmland and water supplies were precious, the Greek invaders of circa 2100 B.C. found most of the best locales already settled. The Greeks took over such settlements but kept their pre-Greek names. For that reason, the names of most ancient Greek cities do not come from the Greek language. Names such as Athens, Corinth, and Mycenae are not etymologically Greek; their original meanings are lost in prehistory. Relatively few ancient mainland sites have recognizably Greek names, among them Pylos ("the gate"), Megara ("the great hall"), Chalcis ("bronze city"), and Marathon ("fennel").

Eventually the Greeks acquired the civilizing arts of the people they had conquered. The Greeks learned shipbuilding, seamanship, and stoneworking—skills at which they excelled. More significantly, they borrowed from the non-Greeks' agrarian religion, which perhaps involved the worship of a mother goddess and a family of fertility deities. Non-Greek goddesses and beliefs, imported into Greek religion, served to complement and refine the warrior Greeks' Indo-European–type worship of a sky father and male gods. A new spirituality was born.

Thus in the centuries after 2100 B.C. came the creative fusion of two cultures—one primitive Greek, one non-Greek. To these two elements was added a third: the example and influence of the dynamic, non-Greek, Minoan civilization of Crete. By 1600 B.C. such factors had produced the first blossoming of the Greeks, in the Bronze Age urban society called the Mycenaean civilization.

For reasons never adequately explained, the Greeks of the next 15 centuries showed a spiritual and intellectual genius that expressed itself in religious awe, storytelling, poetry, sports, the material arts, trade, scientific studies, military organization, and in the governments of their self-contained city-states, particularly Athens. Their legacy to modern global society is immense. The Greeks invented democracy, narrative history writing, stage tragedy and comedy, philosophy, biological study, and political theory. They introduced the alphabet to European languages. They developed monumental styles of architecture that in the United States are used for museums, courthouses, and other public buildings. They created a system of sports competitions and a cult of physical fitness, both of which we have inherited. In sculpture, they perfected the representation of the human body. In geometry, they developed theorems and terminology that are still taught in schools. They created the idea of a national literature, with its recognized great writers and the libraries to preserve their work. And (perhaps what most people would think of first) the Greeks bequeathed to us their treasure trove of myths, including a hero who remains a favorite today—Heracles, or Hercules.

The early Greeks learned much about art and technology from Near Eastern peoples such as the Egyptians and Phoenicians. But more usually the Greeks became the teachers of others. They were an enterprising, often friendly people, and—as sea traders, colonists, mercenary soldiers, or conquerors—they traveled the world from southern Spain to Pakistan. Everywhere they went, they cast a spell through the magnetic appeal of their culture and style of life.

Their most fateful protégés were the Romans, a non-Greek people of Italy. Influenced by imported Greek goods and ideas from the 700s or 600s B.C. onward, the Romans modeled their religion largely on the Greeks', using Greek deities to shape their native Roman gods. This early stage was followed by a more elaborate copying—of Greek coinage, architecture, and other arts—starting in the 300s B.C. When the Romans sought to create their own national literature, they naturally turned to Greek models in epic and lyric poetry, history writing, rhetoric, tragedy, and comedy. They also became important patrons of Greek artists and craftsmen.

But meanwhile Roman armies were capturing Greek cities and kingdoms—first in Italy and Sicily (300s–200s B.C.), then in mainland Greece, Macedon, and Asia Minor (100s B.C.), and finally in Syria and Egypt (first century B.C.). Roman generals and governors plundered centuries' worth of Greek sculptures and other art treasures, removing them from temples and public squares and shipping them to Rome. In most locales, the inhabitants became tax-paying subjects of the Roman Empire. The Romans more or less put an end to the Greek achievement, even as they inherited it. The Roman poet Horace found a more hopeful phrasing for this when he wrote, about 19 B.C., "Captive Greece took mighty Rome captive, forcing culture onto rustic folk."

The Romans went on to conquer a domain that, at its greatest extent, stretched from Scotland to Mesopotamia. Their borrowed Greek culture became part of the permanent legacy of Europe and the eastern Mediterranean. Today we speak automatically of our "Greco-Roman" heritage. But there was no necessary reason for the Romans to imitate the Greeks (the two did not even speak the same language), except that the ambitious Romans saw these people as superior to them in the civilizing arts.

The Romans were by no means the only ones to fall under the Greek spell. Another such people were the Celts. Extant Celtic pottery and metalwork clearly show that the "La Tène" culture, emerging circa 500 B.C. in Gaul (modern France, Switzerland, and Belgium), was inspired by Greek goods and influences, undoubtedly introduced up the Rhone River by Greek traders from Massalia (modern Marseilles, founded by Greeks circa 600 B.C.). By the first century B.C. the Celts of Gaul were writing in the Greek alphabet and had learned from the Greeks how to grow olive trees and grape vines (the latter mainly for winemaking). The creation of the French wine industry is a legacy of the ancient Greeks.

Similarly, from the 200s B.C. onward, the powerful African nation of Nubia, in what is now northern Sudan, traded with Greek merchants from Ptolemaic Egypt. In time the Nubian upper class adopted certain Greek styles of life: for instance, queens of Nubia were using the Greek name Candace down to the 300s A.D.

Nor were the Jews immune to Greek influence, especially after the conquests of Alexander the Great (334–323 B.C.) created a Greco-Macedonian ruling class in the Near East. In religion, Jewish monotheism was not much affected by Greek paganism. But in society and business, many Jews of Near Eastern cities adapted enthusiastically to the Greek world. They attended Greek theater, exercised publicly in Greek gymnasiums, and used the Greek language for commerce and public life. In Egyptian Alexandria (although not everywhere else), Greek-speaking Jews forgot their traditional languages of Hebrew and Aramaic. For the benefit of such people, a Greek translation of the Hebrew Bible began being produced in Alexandria during the 200s B.C. Thus, for many assimilated Jews of this era, Judaism was preserved in Greek form. Today a Jewish house of worship is known by a Greek word—synagogue (from *sunagoge*, "gathering place")—which is but one reminder of the Jews' fascination with the Greeks.

This encyclopedia attempts to give all the essential information about the ancient Greek world. Aimed at high-school and college students and general readers, the book tries to convey the achievements of the Greek world, while also showing its warts. (And warts there were, including slavery, the subordination of women, brutal imperialism, and the insanely debilitating wars of Greek against Greek.)

The encyclopedia's entries, from "Abdera" to "Zeus," range in length from about 100 to 3,000 words. The entries embrace political history, social conditions, warfare, religion, mythology, literature, art, philosophy, science, and daily life. Short biographies are given for important leaders, thinkers, and artists. Particular care is taken, by way of several entries, to explain the emergence and the workings of Athenian democracy.

The book's headwords include the names of real-life people (for example, Socrates), mythical figures (Helen of Troy), cities (Sparta), regions (Asia Minor), and institutions (Olympic Games), as well as many English-language common nouns (archaeology, cavalry, epic poetry, marriage, wine). Supplementing the text are more than 70 ink drawings, based mainly on photographs of extant Greek sculpture, vase paintings, architecture, and metalwork.

My research has involved English-language scholarly books and articles, ancient Greek works in translation, and many of the ancient Greek texts themselves. (I have used my own translations for quotations from Greek authors.) In writing this encyclopedia, I have tried to be aware of recent archaeological finds and other scholarly developments. My manuscript has been vetted by an eminent scholar. However, I have chosen and shaped the material for the general reader, not the scholarly one.

I have assumed that the reader knows nothing about the ancient Greeks and that he or she wants only the "best" information—that is, for any given topic, only the main points, including an explanation of why the topic might be considered important in the first place. I have tried to keep my language simple but lively and to organize each entry into a brisk train of thought. Although facts and dates abound in this book, I hope they only clarify the bigger picture, not obscure it.

In choosing the entries, I have had to abbreviate or omit much. Names or topics that might have made perfectly good short entries—Antaeus, grain supply, or Smyrna— have been reduced to mere cross-references in the text or to listings in the index. The reader is therefore urged to consult the index for any subject not found as an entry.

In time frame, the encyclopedia covers over 2,000 years, opening in the third millennium B.C. with the beginnings of Minoan civilization and ending with the Roman annexation of mainland Greece in 146 B.C. Occasionally an entry will trace an ongoing tradition, such as astronomy, beyond the cutoff date. And short entries are given for a few Roman-era Greek authors, such as Plutarch (circa A.D. 100) and the travel-writer Pausanias (circa A.D. 150), because their work sheds important light on earlier centuries. But most Greek personages and events of the Roman Empire, including the spread of Christianity, are omitted here as being more relevant to the Roman story than the Greek.

Within its 2,000-year span, the encyclopedia gives most attention to the classical era—that is, roughly the 400s and 300s B.C., which produced the Greeks' greatest intellectual and artistic achievements and most dramatic military conflicts. The 400s B.C. saw the Greeks' triumphant defense of their homeland in the Persian Wars, followed by Athens' rise as an imperial power. This was the wealthy, democratic Athens of the great names—the statesman Pericles, the tragedians Aeschylus, Sophocles, and Euripides, the historian Thucydides, the sculptor Phidias, and the philosopher Socrates. In these years the Parthenon arose and the fateful Peloponnesian War was fought, ending in Athens' defeat. The 300s B.C. brought the rise of Macedon and the conquest of the Persian Empire by the Macedonian king Alexander the Great. This was the time of the philosophers Plato and Aristotle, the historian Xenophon, the orator Demosthenes, and the swashbuckling Macedonian prince Demetrius Poliorcetes. Many of the topics that will bring readers to a book about ancient Greece fall within these two centuries.

In a book of this scope written by one person, certain preferences are bound to sneak in. I have tried always to be thorough and concise. But I have allowed slightly more space to a few aspects that I consider more likely than others to satisfy the general reader's curiosity. When I studied Greek and Latin at graduate school, my happiest hours were spent reading Herodotus. He was an Ionian Greek who, in the mid 400s B.C., became the world's first historian, writing a long prose work of incomparable richness about the conflict between the Greeks and Persians. And I find, with all humility, that I have favored the same aspects that Herodotus tends to favor in his treatment—namely, politics, personalities, legends, geography, sex, and war.

David Sacks

Mainland Greece and Neighboring Regions

A

Abdera Important Greek city on the north Aegean coast in the non-Greek region known as THRACE. Located on a coastal plain near the mouth of the River Nestos, Abdera served as a depot for TRADE with local Thracian tribesmen and as an anchorage on the shipping route between mainland Greece and the HELLESPONT. After a failed beginning in the 600s B.C. due to Thracian attacks, Abdera was reestablished by Greek colonists circa 544 B.C. These settlers came from Teos—a city in the Greek region of western ASIA MINOR called IONIA—which they had abandoned to the conquering Persians under King CYRUS (1). Among the Tean settlers was a young man, ANACREON, destined to become the most famous lyric poet of his day.

Like other Greek colonies of the northern Aegean, Abdera prospered from Thracian trade, which brought GOLD and SILVER ore, TIMBER, and SLAVES (available as war captives taken in Thracian tribal wars). These goods in turn became valuable Abderan exports to mainland Greece and other markets. Local wheatfields and fishing contributed to prosperity. The disadvantages were periodic Thracian hostility and the northern climate (cold and wet by Greek standards).

Lying directly in the path of the Persian invasion of the spring of 480 B.C., Abdera submitted to the Persian king XERXES and hosted him at legendary expense. After the Persian defeat (479 B.C.), Abdera became an important member of the Athenian-controlled DELIAN LEAGUE (478 or 477 B.C.). In 457 B.C. wealthy Abdera was paying an annual Delian tribute of 15 TALENTS (as much as BYZANTIUM and more than any other state except AEGINA).

Although other Greeks considered the Abderans to be stupid, the city produced at least two important thinkers of the middle and late 400s B.C. the sophist PROTAGORAS and the atomist philosopher DEMOCRITUS. In these years Abdera, like other cities of the silver-mining north Aegean, was famous for the beauty of its COINAGE. The city's symbol on coins was an ear of wheat.

Abdera passed briefly to Spartan influence after Athens' defeat in the PELOPONNESIAN WAR (404 B.C.), but by about 377 B.C., Abdera was a member of the SECOND ATHENIAN LEAGUE. Seized by the Macedonian king PHILIP II circa 354 B.C., Abdera remained within the Macedonian kingdom over the next 180 years. Sacked by Roman troops in 170 B.C. during the Third Macedonian War, Abdera recovered to become a privileged subject city in the Roman empire.

The ancient site, excavated since the 1950s, has yielded the outline of the city wall and the admirably precise grid pattern of the city's foundations.

(See also COLONIZATION; PERSIAN WARS; ROME.)

Abydos See SESTOS.

Academy The Akademeia was a GYMNASIUM and park about a mile outside ATHENS, sacred to the local hero Akademos. In around 386 B.C., PLATO bought land and buildings there and set up a school of PHILOSOPHY, which can be counted as the Western world's first university.

Plato's aim was to train future leaders of Athens and other Greek states. Students at the early Academy did not pay fees, and lessons probably took place in seminars similar to the disputations portrayed in Plato's written *Dialogues*. Teachings emphasized MATHEMATICS and the Platonic reasoning method known as dialectic. In its breadth of inquiry, the Academy of 386 B.C. was distinct from all prior Greek schools of advanced study, which taught only RHETORIC, poetry, or the argumentative techniques of the SOPHISTS.

Two great students of the early Academy were the mathematician-astronomer Eudoxus of CNIDUS and the philosopher ARISTOTLE. Aristotle was considered Plato's possible successor as president, but after the master's death Academy members voted Plato's nephew Speusippus as head (347 B.C.). Aristotle evetually set up an Athenian philosophical school of his own, called the LYCEUM.

Under Speusippus and his successors, the Academy's curriculum became more mathematical and abstract, until Arcesilaus of Pitane (president circa 265–242 B.C.) redirected it toward philosophical SKEPTICISM. Arcesilaus and his distant successor Carneades (circa 160–129 B.C.) both were known for their criticisms of the rival school of STOICISM.

After the Romans annexed Greece (146 B.C.), the Academy attracted students from all over the Roman—and later the Byzantine—Empire. The Academy survived more than 900 years from its founding, until the Christian Byzantine emperor Justinian closed it and the other pagan philosophical schools in A.D. 529.

The school's name has produced the English common noun *academy*, meaning a place of rigorous advanced study.

(See also EDUCATION.)

Acarnania A region of northwest Greece between the Gulf of Patras (to the south) and the Gulf of AMBRACIA (to the north). Although largely mountainous, the region contains a fertile alluvial plain along the lower Acheloüs River. Acarnania was inhabited by rough Greek "highlanders" who in the 400s B.C. were still known for carrying weapons in public. Their main town was named Stratos, and their political structure was a loose-knit union of rural

1

cantons (later, of towns). Acarnania was bordered west and east by hostile neighbors—the Corinthian colonies of the seaboard and the inland people of AETOLIA. Because of these threats, the Acarnanaians sought alliances with several great states of the Greek world.

As allies of ATHENS in the PELOPONNESIAN WAR, Acarnanian troops under the Athenian general DEMOSTHENES (2) wiped out most of the army of the Corinthian colony of Ambracia in three days (426 B.C.). In 338 B.C. Acarnania (with the rest of Greece) passed to the control of the Macedonian king PHILIP II. The Acarnanians were staunch allies of King PHILIP V in his wars against Aetolia and shared his defeat in the disastrous Second Macedonian War against ROME (200–196 B.C.). Thereafter, Acarnania passed into Roman hands.

(See also ALCMAEON (1)).

Achaea   For most of ancient Greek history, the place-name Achaea was applied to two different regions of Greece: (1) the hilly northwest corner of the PELOPONNESE, and (2) a small area in THESSALY. The Peloponnesian Achaea (the more important of the two) was at some early date organized into a 12-town Achaean League, with shared government and citizenship. In the late 700s B.C., Achaean colonists founded or cofounded important Greek cities in south ITALY, including CROTON and SYBARIS.

Under the commander Aratus of SICYON (active circa 250–213 B.C.), the Achaean League emerged as the strongest power of mainland Greece. By tapping the Greeks' hatred of Macedonian overlordship, Aratus united the northern Peloponnese against MACEDON (and in defiance of the rival Peloponnesian state of SPARTA). For a few years the democratic league was the last hope for that unfulfilled dream of Greek history: the creation of an independent, federal state of Greece.

But the maneuverings of two greater powers, Macedon and ROME, made it impossible for the league to survive alone. As a Roman ally (198 B.C. and after), the Achaean League encompassed most of the Peloponnese, including the important city of CORINTH. However, resistance to Roman interference led to the disastrous Achaean War of 146 B.C., in which the Romans sacked Corinth, dissolved the league, and made Achaea part of a Roman province.

(See also ACHAEANS.)

Achaeans   The word Achaioi (Achaeans) is one of the terms used by the poet HOMER (circa 750 B.C.) as a general name for the Greeks. In this, Homer probably preserves a usage of the Mycenaean Age (circa 1600–1200 B.C.), when Achaioi would have been the Greeks' name for themselves. As a result, modern scholars sometimes use the name Achaeans to mean either the Mycenaeans or their ancestors, the first invading Greek tribesmen of about 2100 B.C.

Intriguingly, a place-name pronounced Ahhiyawa has been deciphered in the cuneiform annals of the Hittite people of ASIA MINOR (1300s–1200 B.C.). In the documents, the name indicates a strong foreign nation, a sea power, with which the Hittite kings were on polite terms. Possibly this foreign nation was the mainland Greek kingdom ruled from the city of MYCENAE. The Hittite rendering Ahhiyawa

may reflect a Greek place-name, Achaiwia or "Achaea," meaning the kingdom of Mycenae.

In later centuries, the Greek place-name ACHAEA came to denote a region of the northwestern PELOPONNESE, far from Mycenae.

(See also MYCENAEAN CIVILIZATION.) Probably that name arose because surviving Mycenaeans took refuge there after their kingdom's downfall.

Achilles   Preeminent Greek hero in the legend of the TROJAN WAR. Achilles (Greek: Achilleus, perhaps meaning "grief") was son of the hero PELEUS and the sea goddess Thetis. He figured in many tales, but received his everlasting portrait as the protagonist of HOMER's epic poem the Iliad (written down circa 750 B.C.). At the story's climax, Achilles slays the Trojan champion HECTOR in single combat, fully aware that his own preordained death will follow soon.

To the Greek mind, Achilles embodied the old-time heroic code, having specifically chosen a brief and glorious life over one that would be safe and obscure. Achilles recounts the terms of this choice in a well-known passage in the Iliad:

> My goddess mother says that two possible destinies bear me toward the end of life. If I remain to fight at Troy I lose my homecoming, but my fame will be eternal. Or if I return to my dear home, I lose that glorious fame, but a long life awaits me [book 9, lines 410–416].

The Iliad's announced theme is "the anger of Achilles" (book 1, lines 1–2). Opening in the war's 10th year, the poem portrays Achilles as a glorious individualist, noble and aloof to the point of excessive pride. Still a young

Achilles—the most formidable of all Greek warriors who sailed against Troy—waits at a temple of Apollo to ambush the Trojan prince Troilus, in a black-figure scene on a cup from Laconia, circa 550 B.C. Achilles is shown driving away the temple's guardian serpents.

man, he has come to the siege of TROY from his native THESSALY at the head of a contingent of troops, his Myrmidons ("ants"). After quarreling justifiably with the commander-in-chief, King AGAMEMNON, over possession of a captive woman named Briseis, Achilles withholds himself and his men from the battlefield (book 1). Consequently, the Greeks suffer a series of bloody reversals (books 8–15). Achilles rebuffs Agamemnon's offered reconciliation (book 9) but relents somewhat and allows his friend PATROCLUS to lead the Myrmidons to battle (book 16). Wearing Achilles' armor, Patroclus is killed by Hector, who strips the corpse.

Mad with grief, Achilles rushes to battle the next day wearing wondrous new armor, forged for him by the smith god HEPHAESTUS at Thetis' request (books 18–20). After slaying Hector, he hitches the Trojan's corpse to his chariot and drags it in the dust to the Greek camp (book 22).

His anger thus assuaged, Achilles shows his more gracious nature in allowing Hector's father, the Trojan king PRIAM, to ransom the body back (book 24). At the *Iliad's* end Achilles is still alive, but his death has been foretold (for example, in book 19, lines 408–417). He will be killed by the combined effort of the Trojan prince PARIS and the god APOLLO, patron of the Trojans.

Greek writers later than Homer provide details of Achilles' life before and after the *Iliad's* events. At Achilles' birth his mother tried to make him immortal by dipping him into the River Styx (or into fire or boiling water, in other versions). But she was interrupted or otherwise forgot to immerse the baby's right heel, and this later proved to be the hero's vulnerable "Achilles' heel."

Knowing at the Trojan War's outset that her son would never return if he departed, Thetis arranged with Lycomedes, king of the island of Scyros, to hide Achilles, disguised as a girl, in the WOMEN's quarters of the king's palace. There Achilles fathered a son with Lycomedes' daughter Deidameia; the boy was named NEOPTOLEMUS. The Greeks, having heard a prophecy that they could never take Troy without Achilles' help, sent ODYSSEUS and other commanders to find Achilles, which they did.

At Troy, Achilles showed himself the greatest of warriors, Greek or Trojan. Among the enemy champions he slew were, in sequence: Cycnus, TROILUS, Hector, Queen Penthesilea of the AMAZONS, and the Ethiopian king MEMNON. At last Achilles himself died, after his vulnerable heel was hit by an arrow shot by Paris and guided by Apollo. (Either the arrow was poisoned or the wound turned septic.) In Homer's *Odyssey* (book 11), Odysseus meets Achilles among the unhappy ghosts in the Underworld. But later writers assigned to Achilles a more blissful AFTERLIFE, in the Elysian Fields.

(See also FATE; PROPHECY AND DIVINATION.)

Acragas (Greek: Akragas, modern Agrigento) The second most important Greek city of SICILY, after SYRACUSE. Today the site of ancient Acragas contains some of the best-preserved examples of Doric-style monumental Greek ARCHITECTURE.

Located inland, midway along the island's southern coast, Acragas is enclosed defensively within a three-sided, right-angled mountain ridge. The city was founded in about 580 B.C. by Dorian-Greek colonists from the nearby city of GELA and the distant island of RHODES. Acragas lay close to the west Sicilian territory of the hostile Carthaginians, and the city soon fell under the sway of a Greek military tyrant, Phalaris, who enlarged the city's domain at the expense of the neighboring native Sicans, circa 570–550 B.C. (Notoriously cruel, Phalaris supposedly roasted his enemies alive inside a hollow, metal bull set over a fire.)

Acragas thrived as an export center for grain to the hungry cities of mainland Greece. Local WINE, olives, and livestock added to the city's prosperity. Under the tyrant Theron (reigned 488–472 B.C.), Acragas became the capital of a west Sicilian empire. Theron helped defeat the Carthaginians at the Battle of HIMERA (480 B.C.) and used Carthaginian war captives as labor for a grand construction program at Acragas. Among Theron's works was a temple of ZEUS, never finished but intended to be the largest building in the Greek world.

After ousting Theron's son and successor, Thrasydaeus, the Acragantines set up a limited DEMOCRACY (circa 472 B.C.). Associated with this government was Acragas' most illustrious citizen—the statesman, philosopher, and physician EMPEDOCLES (circa 450 B.C.). In Empedocles' time, Acragas underwent a second building program, whose remnants include the temples that stand today along the city's perimeter ridge, as if guarding the site. The most admired of these is the beautifully preserved Temple of Concord (so-called today, perhaps really a temple of CASTOR AND POLYDEUCES).

Captured and depopulated by the Carthaginians in 406 B.C., Acragas was resettled by the Corinthian commander TIMOLEON (circa 338 B.C.) but never recovered its former greatness. By about 270 B.C. the city was again a Carthaginian possession. As a strategic site in the First Punic War between CARTHAGE and ROME (264–241 B.C.), Acragas was twice besieged and captured by Roman troops. In 210 B.C. it was again captured by the Romans and soon thereafter repopulated with Roman colonists.

(See also DORIAN GREEKS; ORPHISM; TYRANTS.)

acropolis The "upper city," or hilltop citadel, was a vital feature of most ancient Greek cities, providing both a refuge from attack and an elevated area of religious sanctity. The best-known acropolis is at ATHENS, where a magnificent collection of temples and monuments, built in the second half of the 400s B.C., remains partially standing today; the most famous of these buildings is the PARTHENON, the Temple of the Virgin ATHENA. In terms of natural setting, the highest and most dramatic Greek acropolis was on the 1,800-foot mountain overlooking ancient CORINTH.

Most primitive societies naturally concentrate their settlements on hilltops. In Greece, the hilltop citadels of pre-Greek inhabitants were attacked and captured by Greek-speaking tribesmen in around 2100 B.C. On the choicest of these hills arose the royal palaces of MYCENAEAN CIVILIZATION (1600–1200 B.C.). The Mycenaean Greeks favored hilltops close to farm plains and not too close to the sea, for fear of pirate raids. Typical Mycenaean sites include MYCENAE, Athens, and Colophon (meaning "hilltop"), a Greek city in ASIA MINOR. Of the great classical Greek

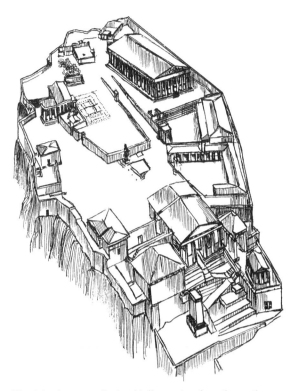

The Athenian acropolis, in a bird's-eye view from the north-west, circa 400 B.C. On the highest part of the summit stood Athena's most glorious temple, the Parthenon, *rear right*. The Erectheum, *rear left*, was a temple housing several patriotic cults. The acropolis entrance was in the west, through the col-onnades and roofed gateway of the Propylaea, *front center*. The little temple of Athena Nike stood perched outside the Propylaea, *front right*.

cities, only SPARTA—a post-Mycenaean settlement—had a puny, unfortified acropolis. Rather than rely on a defensive citadel, Sparta relied on its invincible army and on the mountain ranges enclosing the region.

The Athenian acropolis is a limestone-and-schist forma-tion, rising about 300 feet above the lower town. The hill's association with the goddess Athena probably dates from Mycenaean times (circa 1200 B.C.), when the king's palace stood there. ARCHAEOLOGY reveals that the acropolis' upper sides were first enclosed in a man-made wall circa 1200 B.C.; a later wall from ancient times still encloses the upper rock face today.

Like other Greek citadels, the Athenian acropolis played a role in its city's turbulent politics. CYLON (circa 620 B.C.) and PISISTRATUS (circa 560 B.C.) each began an attempted coup by seizing the acropolis; later, as dictator (546–527 B.C.), Pisistratus beautified the site with marble temples to the gods. But these were burned down by the occupying Persians of 480–479 B.C.

The remarkable monuments now standing on the Athen-ian acropolis—a focus of international tourism in the an-cient world, as today—derive from the building program prompted in around 448 B.C. by the Athenian statesman PERICLES and supervised by the sculptor PHIDIAS. To cele-brate a peace treaty with PERSIA and to glorify the city, the Athenians voted to erect temples to replace those destroyed by the Persians 30 years before. The resulting group in-cludes the small, Ionic-style temple of Athena Nikē (Athena of Victory), the Ionic-style Erectheum (which housed the cults of Athena, POSEIDON, and the legendary king Erectheus), and the monumental Propylaea (gateway). But the pride of the group is the Parthenon.

Financing for the acropolis building program came from tribute paid by Athens' allies within the DELIAN LEAGUE. The fact that other Greek states paid for Athens' beautifica-tion caused angry debate at that time, both among the allies and within Athens itself.

(See also ARCHITECTURE; CALLIAS; PERSIAN WARS; THUCYD-IDES (2).)

Adonis   A beautiful mortal youth who was a lover of the goddess APHRODITE. According to the usual version of the MYTH, Adonis was the son of a Cypriot or Syrian princess who had fallen in love with her own father and became impregnated by him. Growing up, Adonis became the beloved of both PERSEPHONE and Aphrodite. When the two rival goddesses appealed to ZEUS, he decreed that Adonis should spend part of the year with each. (This myth resem-bles the similar tale of DEMETER and Persephone).

Out hunting one day in the mountains of what is now Lebanon, Adonis was gored to death by a wild boar—the disguised form of the jealous god ARES, Aphrodite's occasional lover. Roses or anemones sprang from the dying youth's blood; these scarlet flowers recall Adonis' beauty and mortality.

At ATHENS and other cities of classical Greece, the death of Adonis was commemorated each summer in a WOMEN'S festival lasting about eight days. At the culmination, women of all social classes would stream out of the city in a mourning procession, wailing for the slain Adonis and carrying effigies of him to be thrown into the sea. For this occasion, women would cultivate "gardens of Adonis"—shallow baskets of earth in which seeds of wheat, fennel, and flowers were planted, to sprout quickly and then die and be thrown into the sea. While probably symbolizing the scorched bleakness of the eastern Mediterranean sum-mer, this strange rite also invites a psychological interpreta-tion—as a socially permitted emotional release for Greek women, amid their repressed and cloistered lives.

The worship of Adonis is a prime example of Greek cultural borrowing from non-Greek peoples of the Near East. According to modern scholars, the Greek cult of Adonis derived from a Phoenician festival of the mother goddess Astarte and her dying-and-reborn lover Baalat or Tammuz. The center of this worship was the Phoenician city of BYBLOS. Around the 700s B.C., Greek or Phoenician merchants brought this worship from Byblos to Greece perhaps by way of the Greco-Phoenician island of CYPRUS. In the Greek version of the myth, the sex-and-fertility goddess Astarte becomes the love goddess Aphrodite.

The name Adonis is not Greek, but rather reflects the Phoenician worshippers' ritual cry of *Adon*, meaning "lord." (Compare Hebrew *Adonai*, "the Lord.")

Adrastus See SEVEN AGAINST THEBES.

adultery See MARRIAGE.

Aegean Sea The approximately 80,000-square-mile section of the eastern Mediterranean stretching between Greece and ASIA MINOR, bounded on the north by the coast of ancient THRACE and on the south by the island of CRETE. The Aegean contained or bordered upon most of the important ancient Greek states. The sea was supposedly named for the mythical King Aegeus, father of the Athenian hero THESEUS; Aegeus was said to have drowned himself in this sea. But its name may in fact come from the Greek word *aigis*, "storm."

(See also CHIOS; CYCLADES; GREECE, GEOGRAPHY OF; LESBOS; RHODES; SAMOS.)

Aegina Small island state in the Saronic Gulf, in southeast-central Greece. Only 33 miles square, the triangular island lies 12 miles southwest of the Athenian coast and five miles northeast of the nearest point on the Argolid. Aegina's capital city, also called Aegina, stood in the northwest part of the island, facing the Argolid and Isthmus.

In prehistoric times, Aegina was inhabited by pre-Greek peoples and then by Mycenaean Greeks before falling to the invading DORIAN GREEKS in circa 1100–1000 B.C. The unfertile island gave rise to merchant seamen who claimed descent from the mythical hero Aeacus (son of ZEUS and the river nymph Aegina). In the late 600s and the 500s B.C., Aegina was a foremost Greek sea power, with a Mediterranean TRADE network rivaling that of CORINTH. In the 400s B.C., however, the island became a bitter enemy of nearby ATHENS. The Athenian statesman PERICLES (mid-400s B.C.) called Aegina "the eyesore of Piraeus"—a hostile presence on the sea horizon, as viewed from Athens' main harbor.

The Aeginetans' trade routes have been difficult to trace, because they were simply the middlemen in the selling of most wares. Specifically, they manufactured no POTTERY of their own for modern archaeologists to find in far-off locales. But we know that Aeginetan trade reached EGYPT and other non-Greek Near Eastern empires. Circa 595 B.C. Aegina became the first Greek state to mint coins—an invention probably learned from the kingdom of LYDIA, in ASIA MINOR. Made of SILVER and stamped with the image of a sea turtle, Aegina's COINAGE inspired other Greek states to start minting.

The 500s B.C. were Aegina's heyday. Relations with Athens had not yet soured. Aeginetan shippers brought Athenian black- and red-figure pottery to the ETRUSCANS of western ITALY; they probably also brought WINE, metalwork, and textiles. In exchange, the Etruscans gave raw metals such as silver and tin.

Aegina's prosperity is reflected in the grand temple of the goddess Aphaea (a local equivalent of ATHENA or ARTEMIS), built of local limestone soon after 500 B.C. Located near the island's northeast coast and still partly standing today, this Doric-style structure is the best-preserved early temple in mainland Greece. The building's pediments contained marble figures of mythical Greek heroes fighting at TROY; these important archaic SCULPTURES were carted off in A.D. 1811 and now are housed in a Munich museum.

Hostility with Athens flared in the late 500s B.C. The two states had become trade rivals, and Athens feared Aegina's navy, the largest in Greece at that time (about 70 ships). Hatred worsened when Aegina submitted to envoys of the Persian king DARIUS (1), the enemy of Athens (491 B.C.).

By about 488 B.C., Aegina and Athens were at war. The Athenians, urged by their statesman THEMISTOCLES, built 100 new warships, doubling their navy's size. But this Athenian navy fought alongside the Aeginetans in defending Greece against the invasion of the Persian king XERXES (480 B.C.).

After the Persians' retreat, Aegina joined SPARTA's alliance for protection against Athens. Nevertheless, in 459 B.C. the Athenians defeated an Aeginetan fleet, landed on the island, and besieged the capital. Defeated, Aegina was brought into the Athenian-controlled DELIAN LEAGUE and made to pay the highest tribute of any member, 30 TALENTS. Probably at this time Athens settled a garrison colony on the island. Aegina's anger and defiance in these years are suggested in certain verses by the Theban poet PINDAR, who had friends there.

According to the Thirty Years' Peace, agreed to by Athens and Sparta in 446 B.C., the Athenians were supposed to grant Aegina a degree of self-determination (*autonomia*). This promise was never kept. The resentful Aeginetans continually urged the Spartans against Athens until, at the outbreak of the PELOPONNESIAN WAR (431 B.C.), Athens evicted the Aeginetans and repopulated the whole island with Athenian colonists. The Aeginetans, resettled by Sparta, eventually were reinstalled on Aegina by the triumphant Spartan general LYSANDER (405 B.C.).

After some renewed hostility toward Athens in the CORINTHIAN WAR (395–386 B.C.), Aegina fades from history.

(See also NAUCRATIS; PERSIAN WARS; PIRAEUS; WARFARE, NAVAL.)

Aegospotami Aigospotamoi, "goat's rivers," was a shoreline on the European side of the HELLESPONT, opposite the city of Lampsacus, where the strait is about two miles wide. There in September 405 B.C., the final battle of the PELOPONNESIAN WAR was fought. At one swoop, the Spartan commander LYSANDER eliminated the Athenian fleet and left the city of ATHENS open to blockade and siege. Within eight months of the battle, Athens had surrendered.

The battle was waged over possession of the Hellespont. In the summer of 405 B.C., Lysander slipped into the Hellespont with a fleet of about 150 warships. There he captured the Athenian ally city Lampsacus and occupied its fortified harbor. In pursuit came 180 Athenian warships—almost the entire Athenian navy—led by six generals drawn from a depleted Athenian high command.

The Athenians encamped opposite Lampsacus, on the open shore at Aegospotami. The next morning they rowed out toward Lampsacus to offer battle. But Lysander kept his fleet inside the harbor's defenses, which the Athenians were unwilling to attack. Returning late in the day to Aegospotami, the Athenians beached their ships and went ashore for firewood and food. Lysander sent out a few fast ships to spy on them.

This procedure continued for several days. The Athenian generals did not withdraw to the nearby port city of SESTOS, where a fortified harbor could offer defense; apparently they thought a withdrawal would allow Lysander to escape.

On the fifth evening the Athenian crews beached their ships as usual at Aegospotami and went ashore. This time the Spartan scout ships signaled back to Lysander's fleet—which immediately rowed out from Lampsacus and attacked. The Athenians were completely unprepared: many of their ships still lay empty as the Spartans reached them. Only one Athenian leader, CONON, got his squadron away; the other 170 or so Athenian ships were captured, with most of their crewmen. The Spartans collected their prisoners—perhaps 5,000 Athenians and allies—and put to death the 3,000 or so Athenians among them.

(See also WARFARE, NAVAL.)

Aeneas In Greek MYTH, Aeneas (Aineias) was a Trojan hero of royal blood, the son of the goddess APHRODITE and the mortal man Anchises. Aeneas' earliest appearance is as a minor character in HOMER's epic poem the *Iliad* (written down circa 750 B.C.). He is shown as a respected figure, pious to the gods (who protect him in his overambitious combats with the Greek champions DIOMEDES and ACHILLES). The god POSEIDON prophesies that Aeneas will escape Troy's doom and that his descendants will rule future generations of Trojans (book 20).

Over later centuries, partly in response to Greek exploration and COLONIZATION in the western Mediterranean, there arose various non-Homeric legends describing how, after the fall of Troy, Aeneas voyaged westward, establishing cities in SICILY, ITALY, and elsewhere. In the first century B.C. the Roman poet Vergil amalgamated these tales in his patriotic Latin epic poem, the *Aeneid*. Vergil's Aeneas endures hardships and war in order to found the city of Lavinium and initiate a blood line that will eventually build the city of ROME. Aeneas was thus one of the very few Greek mythological figures who was more important in the Roman world than in the Greek.

(See also TROJAN WAR.)

Aenus Rich and important Greek trading city on the northeastern Aegean coast, in the principally non-Greek region known as THRACE. Aenus (Greek: Ainos) was founded circa 600–575 B.C. by colonists from CYME and other AEOLIAN GREEK cities of ASIA MINOR. The city lay advantageously at the mouth of the Hebrus River, in the territory of the powerful Odrysian Thracians. Like its distant Greek neighbor ABDERA, Aenus prospered from TRADE with the Thracians, who brought TIMBER, SLAVES, SILVER ore, and other precious resources for overseas export to the major markets of Greece.

Circa 477 B.C. Aenus became an important member of the Athenian-controlled DELIAN LEAGUE. Around this time Aenus was minting one of the most admired silver coinages in the Greek world; the Aenian coins showed the head of HERMES, god of commerce. The city remained an Athenian ally during the PELOPONNESIAN WAR (431–404 B.C.), and it came under Spartan rule after Athens' defeat. Later Aenus passed to the region's dominant powers: MACEDON, PERGA-

MUM, and, in the 100s B.C., ROME. A late tradition connected the founding of Aenus with the mythical Trojan-Roman hero AENEAS.

(See also AEOLIS; COINAGE.)

Aeolian Greeks Ethnic branch of the ancient Greeks, distinct from the two other main groups, the IONIAN GREEKS and DORIAN GREEKS. The Aeolians spoke a dialect called Aeolic and claimed a mythical ancestor, Aeolus (not the ruler of the winds in the *Odyssey*, but another Aeolus, son of the first Greek man, HELLEN).

During the epoch of MYCENAEAN CIVILIZATION (circa 1600–1200 B.C.), the Aeolians seem to have been centered in central and northeastern Greece. But amid the Mycenaeans' violent end (circa 1100–1000 B.C.), displaced Aeolians migrated eastward across the AEGEAN SEA. First occupying the large eastern island of LESBOS, these people eventually spread along the northwest coast of ASIA MINOR, in the region that came to be called AEOLIS.

By the 600s B.C. Aeolian Greeks inhabited Lesbos and Aeolis (in the eastern Aegean) and BOEOTIA and THESSALY (in mainland Greece). The strong poetic traditions of Aeolian culture reached their peak in the poetry of SAPPHO and ALCAEUS, written at Lesbos in the early 500s B.C.

(See also GREEK LANGUAGE; LYRIC POETRY.)

Aeolic dialect See GREEK LANGUAGE.

Aeolis Region inhabited by AEOLIAN GREEKS on the northwest coast of ASIA MINOR. Extending from the Hermus River northward to the HELLESPONT, Aeolis was colonized by Aeolians in eastward migrations between about 1000 and 600 B.C.; the nearby island of LESBOS apparently served as an operational base for these invasions. The major city of Aeolis was CYME.

Aeolis prospered from east-west TRADE. However, the loose confederation of Aeolis' cities never achieved international power in the Greek world, and Aeolis was dwarfed in importance by its southern Greek neighbor, the region called IONIA.

Aeolus See ODYSSEUS.

Aeschines Athenian orator who lived circa 400–320 B.C. and who is remembered mainly as a political enemy of the famous orator DEMOSTHENES (1). In 346 B.C., when the Macedonian king PHILIP II was extending his power by war and intimidation throughout Greece, Aeschines and his mentor, Eubulus, belonged to an Athenian party that sought a negotiated peace with Philip; Aeschines served on two Athenian embassies to Philip that year. Aeschines' conciliatory speeches in the Athenian ASSEMBLY brought him into conflict with Demosthenes, who staunchly advocated war.

Soon Philip's flagrant expansionism had borne out Demosthenes' warnings, and Demosthenes brought Aeschines to court twice (346 and 343 B.C.) on charges that he had advised the Athenians irresponsibly, acting as Philip's paid agent. Although the bribery charge was probably false, Demosthenes' second prosecution nearly succeeded, with Aeschines winning the jury's acquittal by merely one vote.

Thirteen years later Aeschines struck back with a charge against an associate of Demosthenes named Ctesiphon, who had earlier persuaded the Athenians to present Demosthenes with a golden crown, in gratitude for his statesmanship. By a procedure known as *graphē paranomon*, Aeschines accused Ctesiphon of having attempted to propose illegal legislation in the assembly. Demosthenes spoke in Ctesiphon's defense; his speech, *On the Crown*, which survives today, is considered to be Demosthenes' masterpiece of courtroom oratory. Defeated and humiliated, Aeschines retired to the island of RHODES.

Three of Aeschines' speeches are extant, each relating to one of his three court cases against Demosthenes. In the speech *Against Timarchus* (346 B.C.), Aeschines successfully defended himself by attacking Demosthenes' associate Timarchus, who was coprosecuting. Invoking an Athenian law that forbade anyone of bad moral character from addressing the court, Aeschines argued persuasively that Timarchus had at one time been a male prostitute. The speech is a valuable source of information for us regarding the classical Greeks' complex attitudes toward male HOMO-SEXUALITY. Aeschines' speech *Against Ctesiphon* (330 B.C.) also is interesting, for it gives a negative assessment of Demosthenes' career.

(See also LAWS AND LAWCOURTS; RHETORIC.)

Aeschylus Earliest of the three classical playwrights of fifth-century-B.C. ATHENS. (The other two were SOPHOCLES and EURIPIDES.) He wrote 90 plays, of which only seven survive under his name; and of these, *Prometheus Bound* may not really have been written by him. Like other Athenian tragedians, Aeschylus wrote mainly for competition at the annual Athenian drama festival known as the City Dionysia, where three playwrights would each present three tragedies and a satyr play. Among Aeschylus' extant plays is the only complete Greek tragic trilogy to come down to us, the *Oresteia*, or *Oresteian Trilogy*—one of the greatest works of Greek literature.

Aeschylus' place in Western culture is due to his solemn vision of divine justice, which orders events on earth. He drew largely on MYTHS for his stories, and described his plays as morsels from the banquet of HOMER. He was also a pioneer of stage technique at a time when Greek drama was still crude and was a spokesman for the big, patriotic emotions that had been aroused by Athens' victory in the PERSIAN WARS (490–479 B.C.). Aeschylus won first prize at the Dionysian competition 13 times; after his death, his plays came to be seen as old-fashioned in theme and language.

Aeschylus was born in 525 B.C. into an aristocratic family of Eleusis, a city in Athenian territory. His father's name was Euphorion. Little is known of Aeschylus' life, but as a teenager he would have witnessed two great public events: the expulsion of the dictator HIPPIAS (1) (510 B.C.) and the institution of Athenian DEMOCRACY as fashioned by the reformer CLEISTHENES (1) (508 B.C.). In 490 B.C. Aeschylus took part in the single most important moment in Athenian history, fighting as a soldier in the Battle of MARATHON, which repulsed a Persian invasion (and in which his brother Cynegeirus was killed). Aeschylus also may have fought 10 years later at the sea battle of SALAMIS

(1), where a much larger Persian invasion was defeated. His participation in these great events shaped his patriotism and his faith in an ordering divinity—themes that echo throughout his plays. These were beliefs shared by his audiences in the 480s–460s B.C.

One anecdote from Aeschylus' early years mentions a competition circa 489 B.C. to choose the official epitaph for the Athenian dead at Marathon. Aeschylus' submitted poem was not selected, although he was an Athenian who had fought at the battle; the judges, finding that his poem lacked sympathy of expression, preferred the poem submitted by the poet SIMONIDES of Ceos. A modern scholarly reconstruction of the two poems has shown that Simonides' poem characterized the dead men as saviors of Greece, but Aeschylus' as saviors of Athens. The episode is significant in showing Aeschylus' pro-Athenian outlook and his inclination toward the grand vision rather than the human details. Both of these traits tend to contrast Aeschylus with the younger tragedian Euripides, and it is no coincidence that the comic playwright ARISTOPHANES fictionally showed Aeschylus and Euripides competing in his comedy *Frogs* (405 B.C.).

Aeschylus presented his first tragedies in around 499 B.C. and won his first festival victory in 484 B.C., with a trilogy whose name we do not know. His tragedy *The Persians* was presented in 472 B.C. as part of a trilogy that won first prize, and its *chorēgos* (paying sponsor) was the rising young politician PERICLES. *The Persians* apparently is modeled somewhat on *The Phoenician Women*, by the tragedian PHRYNICHUS. It is unusual in that its subject matter is drawn not from myths but rather from a recent events—namely, the Persian disaster at Salamis, as seen from the Persian viewpoint. The play's title describes the chorus (a group of Persian councillors), and the protagonist is Atossa, mother of the Persian king XERXES. In the simple plot, arrival of news of the calamity is followed by an invocation of the ghost of the great Persian king DARIUS (1), Xerxes' father. The Persians are presented theatrically, but with pathos and dignity, as victims of Xerxes' insane HUBRIS.

Shortly afterward, Aeschylus traveled to SICILY, to the wealthy court of the Syracusan tyrant HIERON (1) (patron also of such poets as Simonides and PINDAR). It was probably at this time that Aeschylus wrote a new play, *Women of Aetna* (now lost), to commemorate Hieron's founding of a city of that name, near Mt. Etna. Aeschylus returned to Athens to compete at the City Dionysia of 468 B.C., but he lost first place to a 28-year-old first-time contestant named Sophocles.

Of Aeschylus' other extant work, the *Seven Against Thebes*—a pageant centering on the Theban king Eteocles' decision to meet his brother, Polynices, in combat to defend his city—was presented in 467 B.C. Another play, *The Suppliants*—about the Danaid maidens' flight from their suitors, the sons of Aegyptus—dates from around 463 B.C. The three plays of the *Oresteia*—*Agamemnon*, the *Libation Bearers*, and the *Eumenides*—were performed in 458 B.C.

Perhaps alarmed by growing class tensions at Athens, Aeschylus traveled again to Sicily, where he died at the age of 69 (456 B.C.). *Prometheus Bound*, if it is in fact by Aeschylus, may have been presented in Sicily in his final years. He was buried at GELA. Aeschylus' brief verse epitaph, which he supposedly prepared himself, ignored his many literary honors and mentioned only that he had fought at Marathon.

The Oresteian trilogy, Aeschylus' greatest work, describes the triumph of divine justice working through a series of horrific events on earth. In the first play, *Agamemnon*, the vainglorious Agamemnon, fresh from his victory in the TROJAN WAR, is so misled by pride that he cannot see that his wife, the adulterous CLYTAEMNESTRA, plans to murder him. After the killing, their son, ORESTES, must avenge his father by slaying his mother in the trilogy's second play, the *Libation Bearers* (*Chōephoroi*). But this act in turn incites the wrath of supernatural fiends, the FURIES (Erinues), whose divine function is to avenge a parent's blood. In the third play, the *Eumenides*, Orestes is pursued by the chorus of Furies to Athens, where he is cleansed of his curse with the help of ATHENA and APOLLO. Tried for his murder before the Athenian law court of the AREOPAGUS, Orestes is acquitted, and his persecutors are invited to stay on at Athens as protective spirits—the "Kindly Ones" of the play's title. The *Eumenides* is simultaneously a bit of Athenian nationalism and a profound vision of civilized society as a place where the old, violent code of blood vengeance has been replaced by law.

Aeschylus was responsible for many innovations that soon became standard on the Athenian stage. He developed the use of lavish costumes and introduced a second speaking actor, thereby greatly increasing the number of possible speaking roles (since each actor could "double" or "triple" on roles). Aeschylus had a fondness for visual affects and wild, demonstrative choral parts, which his successors found crude. Yet in places his language has a spellbinding solemnity, and in the scenes leading up to the murders in the *Agamemnon* and *Libation Bearers*, he is a master of suspense.

His later life saw a period of serious political strife at Athens, between radical democrats and more right-wing elements. The brilliant left-wing statesman THEMISTOCLES was ostracized (circa 471 B.C.) and forced to flee to PERSIA to avoid an Athenian death sentence, but his policies eventually were taken up by the young Pericles and his comrades. It is evident that Aeschylus was a member of this democratic party, not only from his 472 B.C. association with Pericles, but also from the plays he wrote. The Athenian navy is indirectly glorified in *The Persians*; there are muted, approving references to Themistocles in *The Persians* and *The Suppliants*; and a major aim in the *Eumenides* (458 B.C.) is to dignify the Areopagus, which in real life had recently been stripped of certain powers by left-wing legislation.

But Aeschylus' work was never partisan in a petty way: plays such as *The Suppliants* and the *Eumenides* end with hopeful reconciliation between opposing forces, and in this we can see the lofty, generous spirit of an artist who sought out the divine purpose in human affairs.

(See also DIONYSUS; ELECTRA; EPHIALTES; PROMETHEUS; SEVEN AGAINST THEBES; THEATER.)

Aesop Supposed author of a number of moralizing fables, many involving animals as characters. According to legend, Aesop was a slave on the island of SAMOS in the 500s B.C. In fact, Aesop may have been no more than a name around which certain folktales gravitated.

One of the best known of Aesop's fables tells of the race betwen the tortoise and the hare. The overconfident hare, stopping to nap in midrace, loses to his slower but steadier opponent.

Animal parables also occur in extant verses by ARCHILOCHUS (circa 650 B.C.), whose writings may have inspired some of the tales that we know as Aesop's.

Aetolia Mountainous region of central Greece, north of the Corinthian Gulf, bordered on the west by ACARNANIA and on the east by the Mt. Parnassus massif. Interior Aetolia contained good farmland, but the southern mountains blocked Aetolia from the gulf and from outside influences. Through the 400s B.C. the Aetolians remained rugged Greek "highlanders," divided by tribal feuds and known for carrying weapons in public for self-defense.

During the PELOPONNESIAN WAR, Aetolia was invaded by the Athenian general DEMOSTHENES (2), who hoped to seize the eastward mountain route into enemy BOEOTIA. But the Aetolians, arrayed as javelin-throwing light infantry, defeated the cumbersome Athenian HOPLITES in the hills (426 B.C.).

In the late 300s B.C. Aetolia emerged as a force in the Greek resistance to the overlordship of MACEDON. By now the Aetolians had united into a single federal state—the Aetolian League. Aetolian towns shared a common citizenship, representative ASSEMBLY, and a war captain, elected annually; the capital city was Thermon. By the late 200s B.C. the aggressive league dominated most of central Greece, with alliances extending to the PELOPONNESE. Aetolia fell into conflict with its southern rival, the Achaean League, as well as with Macedon. In 218 B.C. the dynamic Macedonian king PHILIP V invaded Aetolia and sacked Thermon.

Aetolia was a natural ally for Philip's enemy, the imperialistic Italian city of ROME. Allied to Rome in the Second Macedonian War, the Aetolians helped defeat Philip at the Battle of Cynoscephalae (197 B.C.). However, disappointed by the mild Roman peace with Macedon, the Aetolians allied with the Seleucid king ANTIOCHUS (2) III against Rome (192 B.C.). After the Romans had defeated Antiochus, they broke the Aetolian League's power and made it a Roman subject ally (189 B.C.).

(See also ACHAEA; WARFARE, LAND.)

afterlife Throughout ancient Greek history, nearly all Greeks believed in some form of life after death. Only the philosophy called EPICUREANISM (after 300 B.C.) maintained unequivocally that the human soul died with the body. Because Greek RELIGION had no specific doctrine on the subject, beliefs in the afterlife varied greatly, from crude superstition to the philosopher PLATO's lofty vision (circa 370 B.C.) of an immortal soul freed of its imperfect flesh and at one with absolute reality in another world.

The primitive concept that the dead somehow live on in their tombs never disappeared from Greek religion. The shaft graves at MYCENAE—datable to 1600–1550 B.C., at the dawn of MYCENAEAN CIVILIZATION—were filled with armor, utensils, and even pets and SLAVES, killed in sacrifice, to comfort the deceased in the afterlife. This practice may have been inspired by the burial rites of Egyptian pharaohs, but the general idea seems to have survived in Greece for over 1,000 years. Greeks of the 400s and 300s B.C. were still offering food and drink at graveside, as nourishment for the dead.

Another belief was that the souls of the dead traveled to an Underworld, the realm of the god HADES and his wife, PERSEPHONE. Unlike the modern concept of Hell, this "House of Hades" (as the Greeks called it) was not primarily a place of punishment. It was, however, a cold and gloomy setting, where the souls—after being led from the living world by the messenger god HERMES—endured a bleak eternity.

The earliest extant description of Hades' kingdom comes in book 11 of HOMER's epic poem the *Odyssey* (written down circa 750 B.C.), when the living hero ODYSSEUS journeys there by ship to seek prophecy. The site is vaguely described as a grim shoreline of OCEANUS, at the edge of the living world. (Later writers tended to situate it underground.) There Odysseus recognizes the ghosts of some of his family and former comrades. He also sees the torments of three sinners—Tityus, TANTALUS, and SISYPHUS—who had betrayed the friendship of the gods. The only people to be excused from Hades' realm were those who had been granted divinity and who now resided with the other gods on Mt. OLYMPUS. These lucky few included HERACLES and the twins CASTOR AND POLYDEUCES.

Gradually, concepts of reward and punishment were enlarged. Poets wrote of a place called Elysium (*Elusion*) where certain souls, chosen by the gods, enjoyed a happy afterlife. Also known as the Islands of the Blessed, this locale is described by the Theban poet PINDAR (476 B.C.) in terms of shady parklands and athletic and musical pastimes—in other words, the ideal life of the living Greek aristocrat. Post-Homeric sources placed ACHILLES there with other heroes, including the Athenian tyrannicides of 510 B.C., HARMODIUS AND ARISTOGITON.

Similarly, legend began to specify a lowermost abyss in Hades' realm, a place called Tartarus. This was the scene of punishment for the evil TITANS and for the worst human sinners. (Post-Homeric sources add the DANAIDS and IXION to the group.) Typical punishments require the prisoner to endure eternal frustration of effort (Sisyphus, the Danaids) or desire (Tantalus).

Greek writers such as Plato began to describe the mythical judges who assigned each soul to Elysium, Tartarus, or the netherworld. These judges were MINOS and Rhadamanthys (who were brothers) and Aeacus, all of whom had once been mortal men. The concept of eternal judgment contains an obvious ethical message—a warning to act justly in this life—that resembles the later Christian view.

The well-known rivers of the Underworld are best described in Vergil's Latin epic poem, the *Aeneid* (circa 20 B.C.). But the idea of rivers or lakes in Hades' kingdom goes back at least to the Greek poet HESIOD's *Theogony* (circa 700 B.C.). The Greeks associated these Underworld waters with actual rivers of mainland Greece, apparently believing that the waters continued their course underground. The Styx ("hated") was an actual river in ARCADIA.

The Acheron ("woeful") flowed in EPIRUS, near an oracle of the Dead. The Underworld's other rivers were Lethe ("forgetting"), Cocytus ("wailing"), and Pyriphlegethon or Phlegethon (burning). These dire names probably referred to Greek FUNERAL CUSTOMS rather than to any punishment for the souls.

Legend usually described the Styx as the Underworld's boundary. New arrivals were brought across by the old ferryman Charon, and Greek burial rites often included placing a coin in the corpse's mouth, to pay for this final passage. The monstrous many-headed dog CERBERUS stood watch on the Styx's inner bank, preventing the souls from leaving.

This grim Greek picture of the common man's afterlife eventually inspired a reaction: A number of fringe religious movements arose, assuring their followers of a happy afterlife. These were called mystery cults or mysteries (*mustēria*, from *mustēs*, "an initiate"). While centering on a traditional deity such as DIONYSUS, DEMETER, or Persephone, the mysteries claimed to offer the correct beliefs and procedures for admittance into Elysium. In Greek tombs of southern ITALY from about 400 B.C., archaeologists have discovered golden tablets inscribed with precise directions for the soul entering the Underworld: The soul is warned not to drink from the attractive spring of forgetfulness— "seen on the right, where the white cypress grows"—but from the lake of remembrance, beyond.

One mystery faith, ORPHISM, emphasized reincarnation (also known as transmigration). According to this belief, each person's soul passed, at death, into a newborn body, whether human or not. The new assignment was based on the person's conduct and belief in the prior life; bad souls descended through criminals, slaves, and animals, but a right-living soul ascended to kings and heroes, eventually gaining admittance to Elysium. This concept was adapted by the philosophers PYTHAGORAS (circa 530 B.C.) and EMPEDOCLES (circa 450 B.C.), who influenced Plato.

(See also ELEUSINIAN MYSTERIES; HELLENISTIC AGE; PROPHECY AND DIVINATION.)

Agamemnon   In MYTH, the king of MYCENAE and ARGOS, son of ATREUS, husband of CLYTAEMNESTRA, and commander of the allied Greek army in the TROJAN WAR. Agamemnon's earliest appearance in literature is in HOMER's epic poem the *Iliad* (written down circa 750 B.C.), where he is portrayed negatively. Contrary to his name, which means "very steadfast," Agamemnon is shown to be an irresolute, arrogant, and divisive leader. His quarrel with the Greek champion ACHILLES over possession of a female war captive provokes Achilles to withdraw from the fighting and sets in motion the *Iliad*'s tragic plot.

The events leading up to Agamemnon's command are told by Homer and later writers. The Greek-Trojan conflict began when Helen, wife of MENELAUS (Agamemnon's brother) was seduced by the Trojan prince PARIS and eloped with him. Agamemnon organized an expedition against TROY to recover Helen, but incurred Clytaemnestra's hatred by sacrificing their daughter IPHIGENIA as a blood offering to the hostile goddess ARTEMIS, who was sending contrary winds to prevent the Greek ships' departure.

After the Greeks sacked Troy, Agamemnon sailed for home with his war booty, which included the captured Trojan princess CASSANDRA. But on the very day that they stepped ashore, Agamemnon and Cassandra were murdered by henchmen of Agamemnon's treacherous cousin Aegisthus, Clytaemnestra's illicit lover. (This is Homer's version in the *Odyssey*; in later tales the king dies while emerging from his bath, stabbed by Aegisthus or axed by Clytaemnestra.) It was left to Agamemnon's son ORESTES and daughter ELECTRA to avenge his murder.

Agamemnon's downfall is the subject of Athenian playwright AESCHYLUS' tragedy *Agamemnon* (458 B.C.), the first play in the Oresteian Trilogy.

(See also HELEN OF TROY)

Agathocles   Ruthless and flamboyant ruler of the Sicilian Greek city of SYRACUSE from 316 to 289 B.C. Agathocles was the last of the grandiose Syracusan TYRANTS. He challenged the mighty African-Phoenician city of CARTHAGE and captured most of SICILY from Carthaginians and fellow Greeks. His imperial reign in the Greek West was inspired partly by the example of ALEXANDER THE GREAT'S successors in the East.

Agathocles did not come from the ruling class. Born in 361 B.C. in Thermae, in the Carthaginian-controlled western half of Sicily, he was the son of a Greek manufacturer of POTTERY; enemies later derided Agathocles as a mere potter. Emigrating to Syracuse, he came to prominence as an officer in the Syracusan army. In 316 B.C. he overthrew the ruling Syracusan OLIGARCHY and installed himself as *turannos*, or dictator, with the common people's support.

Many adventures followed. Suffering a major defeat in battle against the Carthaginians, Agathocles was besieged by land and sea inside Syracuse (summer 311 B.C.). But he solved this predicament with an amazingly bold action: In August 310 B.C., when the Carthaginians briefly relaxed their naval blockade, Agathocles sailed from Syracuse harbor with 60 ships and a mercenary army of about 13,000 to invade Carthage itself.

His was the first European army to land in Carthaginian North Africa. But despite his victories over Carthaginian armies in the field, Agathocles failed to capture the city. Meanwhile, in Sicily, Syracuse held out against the Carthaginians; but a Sicilian-Greek revolt against Agathocles induced the tyrant to abandon his African army under his son Archagatus and return to Sicily. Eventually Archagatus and his brother were murdered by the army, which evacuated North Africa.

Agathocles made peace with the Carthaginians, giving up territories in west Sicily (306 B.C.). But he soon became the sole ruler of Greek-held eastern Sicily. In 304 B.C., patterning himself on Alexander the Great's heirs who were reigning as supreme monarchs in the East, Agathocles adopted the absolute title of king (*basileus*).

He then extended his power to Greek south ITALY and western mainland Greece. Circa 300 B.C. he drove off the Macedonian king CASSANDER, who was besieging CORCYRA. Agathocles took over Corcyra and gave it, twice, as a dowry for his daughter Lanassa's two influential MARRIAGES, first to the Epirote king PYRRHUS (295 B.C.) and

then to the new Macedonian king, DEMETRIUS POLIORCETES (circa 291 B.C.). The aging Agathocles himself married a third wife, a daughter of the Greek Egyptian king PTOLEMY (1). But his hope of founding a grand dynasty faded when his son Agathocles was murdered by a jealous relative.

The elder Agathocles died at age 72, probably from jaw cancer (289 B.C.). Although he had thwarted the Carthaginian menace, he left no legacy of good government for Sicily. However, his military exploits were influential in demonstrating that mighty Carthage was susceptible to invasion. The Romans would invade Carthage more effectively during their Second Punic War (202 B.C.).

Agathon   Athenian tragic playwright of the late 400s B.C., considered by the Athenians to be their fourth greatest tragedian after AESCHYLUS, SOPHOCLES, and EURIPIDES. Less than 40 lines of his work survive; these show a clever, polished style, influenced by the contemporary rhetorician GORGIAS and by the SOPHISTS. Agathon won his first drama competition at the annual festival known as the City Dionysia, in 416 B.C., with a tragic trilogy whose titles have not survived.

We know little of Agathon's life. But we do know that in 407 B.C. he left Athens—as Euripides had done—for the court of the Macedonian king Archelaus, and there (like Euripides), Agathon died, circa 401 B.C.

From references in ARISTOTLE's *Poetics* we know that Agathon was an innovator. He often removed the chorus from the story's action, reducing the choral odes to mere interludes. In his day he was noteworthy for his tragedy *Antheus*, of which he invented the entire plot himself, rather than drawing on MYTH or history. His plots were overinvolved; Aristotle once criticized him for having crammed the entire tale of the TROJAN WAR into one play.

Agathon had personal beauty and apparently an effete manner. He appears as a fictionalized character in ARISTOPHANES' comedy *Thesmophoriazusae* (411 B.C.) and is burlesqued for his effeminacy—but not for his writing, which Aristophanes calls "good" (*agathos*). Agathon also appears as a character in the philosopher PLATO's dialogue the *Symposium* (circa 370 B.C.), which is set at a drinking party at Agathon's house to celebrate his 416 B.C. competition victory.

(See also THEATER.)

Agesilaus   Spartan king who reigned 399–360 B.C., leading SPARTA's brief phase of supremacy after the PELOPONNESIAN WAR. Although a capable battlefield commander, Agesilaus steered Sparta into a shortsighted policy of military domination in Greece. Eventually this policy provoked the rise of a challenger state, THEBES.

The Athenian historian XENOPHON was a friend of Agesilaus' and wrote an admiring biography of him, as well as including his exploits in the general history titled *Hellenica*. These two extant writings provide much of our information about Agesilaus.

Born in 444 B.C., a son of King ARCHIDAMUS of Sparta's Eurypontid royal house, Agesilaus was dynamic, pious, and lame in one leg. He became king after the death of his half brother, King Agis II. In 396 B.C. he took 8,000 troops to ASIA MINOR to protect the Spartan-allied Greek cities there from Persian attack. Marching inland through Persian-held west-central Asia Minor, Agesilaus defeated the Persians in battle before being recalled to Sparta (394 B.C.). His raid probably helped inspire the future conquests of ALEXANDER THE GREAT.

Agesilaus had been summoned home to help his beleaguered city in the CORINTHIAN WAR. Bringing his army overland through THRACE and THESSALY, he descended southward into hostile BOEOTIA, where he narrowly defeated a coalition army of Thebans, Argives, Athenians, and Corinthians at the Battle of Coronea (394 B.C.). Wounded, and with his army now too weak to occupy Boeotia, Agesilaus withdrew to Sparta. He commanded subsequent Spartan actions against ARGOS (391 B.C.), CORINTH (390 B.C.), ACARNANIA (389 B.C.), and defiant Thebes (378–377 B.C.).

His hostility toward the Theban leader EPAMINONDAS at a peace conference resulted in renewed war and a disastrous Spartan defeat at the Battle of LEUCTRA (371 B.C.). In the disarray that followed, Agesilaus helped lead the defense of the Spartan homeland, culminating in the stalemate Battle of MANTINEA (362 B.C.).

After peace was made, the 82-year-old king sailed to EGYPT with 1,000 Spartan mercenary troops to assist an Egyptian prince's revolt against the Persians. (The expedition's purpose was to replenish Sparta's depleted revenues.) The revolt went awry, and Agesilaus died on the voyage home (360 B.C.).

(See also EURYPONTID CLAN.)

Agiad clan   The Agiads (Agiadai) were the senior royal family at SPARTA, which had an unusual government in that it was ruled simultaneously by two kings. The Agiads, "descendants of Agis," traced their ancestry back to a legendary figure who was one of the sons of HERACLES. As the senior house, the Agiads enjoyed certain ceremonial privileges over their partners, the EURYPONTID CLAN. Notable Agiad kings include the brilliant CLEOMENES (1) and Leonidas, the commander at the Battle of THERMOPYLAE.

agora   The open "place of assembly" in an ancient Greek city-state. Early in Greek history (900s–700s B.C.), free-born males would gather in the agora for military duty or to hear proclamations of the ruling king or COUNCIL. In the more settled centuries that followed, the agora served as a marketplace where merchants kept open-air stalls or shops under colonnades.

Classical ATHENS boasted a grand agora—the civic heart of the city that dominated Greece. Under the Athenian dictators PISISTRATUS and HIPPIAS (1) (second half of the 500s B.C.), the agora was cleared to a rectangular open area of about 600 by 750 yards, bordered with grand public buildings. Devastated by the occupying Persians in 480–479 B.C., the agora was rebuilt in the later 400s to include temples, government buildings, and several colonnades, of which the best known was the Stoa Poikilē (painted colonnade).

Today the ancient Athenian agora has been partly restored. The pride of the reconstructed buildings is the Doric-style temple of HEPHAESTUS (previously misidentified as a temple of THESEUS), built circa 449 B.C.

(See also ARCHITECTURE; ASSEMBLY; DEMOCRACY; OSTRACISM; PAINTING; STOICISM.)

agriculture   See FARMING.

Ajax (1)   In the legend of the TROJAN WAR, Ajax (Greek Aias) was king of SALAMIS (1) and son of Telamon. After ACHILLES, he was the bravest Greek warrior at Troy. In HOMER's epic poem the *Iliad*, Ajax engages in many combats—for example, dueling the Trojan hero HECTOR to a standoff (book 7) and leading the Greeks in defense of their beached ships (book 13). Giant in size, stolid, and slow-spoken, Ajax embodies the virtue of steadfastness. He carries a huge oxhide shield and is often called by the poetic epithet "bulwark of the Achaeans." Homer implicitly contrasts him with his chief rival among the Greeks, the wily ODYSSEUS. Although the stronger of the two, Ajax loses a WRESTLING match to Odysseus' skill (*Iliad* book 23).

As described by Homer in the *Odyssey* (book 11), Ajax's death came from his broken pride over this rivalry. After Achilles was killed, Ajax and Odysseus both claimed the honor of acquiring his wondrous armor. The dispute was arbitrated by Trojan prisoners of war, who agreed that Odysseus had done more to harm the Trojan cause. Maddened with shame, Ajax eventually killed himself with his sword. This tale is the subject of the extant tragedy *Ajax*, written circa 450–445 B.C. by the Athenian playwright SOPHOCLES. Sophocles' Ajax is brought down by his flaws of anger and pride—and by a deep nobility that prevents him from accepting a world of intrigue and compromise, personified by Odysseus.

(See also ACHAEANS; HUBRIS.)

Ajax (2)   Greek warrior—son of Oileus and leader of troops from LOCRIS—in the legend of the TROJAN WAR. Often known as the Lesser Ajax, he was brave, swift-footed, arrogant, and violent. His savage behavior at the sack of TROY, unmentioned by the poet HOMER, is described by later writers. Finding the Trojan princess CASSANDRA in sanctuary at the goddess ATHENA's altar, Ajax pulled her away and raped her. He was hated by Athena, but his death, as described in Homer's *Odyssey* (book 4), occurred at POSEIDON's hands. On the homeward voyage from Troy, Ajax's ship was wrecked; he reached shore safely but sat atop a cliff declaring hubristically that he had beaten the gods. Poseidon, enraged, blasted him back into the sea.

(See also HUBRIS.)

Alcaeus   Lyric poet of the city of MYTILENE on the island of LESBOS. Born in about 620 B.C. into an aristocratic family, Alcaeus was a contemporary and fellow islander of the poet SAPPHO. Like her he wrote love poems, but unlike her, he also wrote of his involvement in great events, such as the civil strife between Mytilene's traditional ARISTOCRACY and ascendant TYRANTS. Better as a poet than as a political analyst, Alcaeus was a spokesman for the old-fashioned aristocratic supremacy, which in his day was being dismantled throughout the Greek world.

Although no one complete poem by him has come down to us, the surviving fragments show his talent and give a dramatic biographical sketch. When Alcaeus was a boy in around 610 B.C., his elder brothers and another noble, PITTACUS, expelled the local tyrant. Soon Alcaeus was fighting under Pittacus' command in Mytilene's war against Athenian settlers in northwest ASIA MINOR. Alcaeus threw away his shield while retreating and (like ARCHILOCHUS, an earlier Greek poet) wrote verses about it.

When another tyrant arose in Mytilene, Alcaeus went into exile until the tyrant died. Alcaeus may have gone home—but only for a brief time—because soon his former comrade Pittacus was ruling singly in Mytilene, and Alcaeus and many other nobles were expelled. In his poetry Alcaeus raved against Pittacus as a "low-born" traitor and expressed despair at being excluded from the political life that was his birthright.

Apparently Alcaeus went to EGYPT, perhaps as a mercenary soldier. (Meanwhile, his brother joined the army of the Babylonian king Nebuchadnezzer and took part in the campaign that captured Jerusalem in 597 B.C.) At some point Alcaeus and his friends planned to attack Mytilene and depose Pittacus, but the common people stood by their ruler. Supposedly Pittacus at last allowed Alcaeus to come home.

Like Sappho, Alcaeus wrote in his native Aeolic dialect and used a variety of meters. A number of his extant fragments are drinking songs, written for solo presentation at a SYMPOSIUM. Even by ancient Greek standards, Alcaeus seems to have been particularly fond of WINE. He wrote hymns to the gods, including one to APOLLO that was much admired in the ancient world. In accordance with the upper-class sexual tastes of his day, he wrote love poems to young men.

More than 550 years after Alcaeus' death, his poetry served as a model for the work of the Roman poet Horace.

(See also GREEK LANGUAGE; HOMOSEXUALITY; HOPLITE.)

Alcestis In MYTH, the wife of King Admetus of Pherae in THESSALY. She became Admetus' wife after he was able, with the god APOLLO's help, to fulfill her father Pelias' onerous precondition of yoking a lion and wild boar to a chariot and driving it around a racecourse.

Alcestis is best known for the story of how she voluntarily died in her husband's place. Apollo, discovering from the Fates that his mortal friend Admetus had only one day to live, arranged that Admetus' life be spared if a willing substitute could be found; the only one to consent was Alcestis. In EURIPIDES' tragedy *Alcestis* (438 B.C.), this old tale of wifely duty is recast as a disturbing account of female courage and male equivocation.

(See also FATE.)

Alcibiades Athenian general, politician, and social figure who lived circa 450–404 B.C and strongly influenced the last 15 years of the PELOPONNESIAN WAR between ATHENS and SPARTA. The mercurial Alcibiades embodied the confident Athenian spirit of the day. Although brilliant as a leader in battle, he was prone to dangerously grandiose schemes in war strategy and politics. His fellow citizens repeatedly voted him into high command, yet they mistrusted him for his private debaucheries and for his ambition, which seemed aimed at seizing absolute power at Athens. After his political enemies organized the people

against him (415 B.C.), Alcibiades spent three years as a refugee turncoat, working for the Spartans (414–412 B.C.). Pardoned by Athens in its hour of need, he led the Athenians through a string of victories on land and sea (411–407 B.C.) that could have saved the city from defeat. But the Athenians turned against him once more, and he died in exile, murdered at Spartan request, soon after Athens surrendered.

As a flawed genius of tragic dimensions, Alcibiades is vividly portrayed in extant Greek literature. His Athenian contemporaries, the historians THUCYDIDES (1) and XENOPHON, describe him in their accounts of the Peloponnesian War. A biography of Alcibiades comprises one of PLUTARCH's *Parallel Lives*, written circa A.D. 100–110. A fictionalized Alcibiades appears in dialogues written by the philosopher PLATO in around 380 B.C.

Alcibiades was born into a rich and powerful Athenian family during the Athenian heyday. His mother, Deinomache, belonged to the aristocratic Alcmaeonid clan. After his father, Cleinias, was killed in battle against the Boeotians (447 B.C.), Alcibiades was raised as a ward of Deinomache's kinsman PERICLES, the preeminent Athenian statesman. Breeding and privilege produced a youth who was confident, handsome, and spoiled, and he became a rowdy and glamorous figure in the homosexual milieu of upper-class Athens; Plutarch's account is full of gossip about men's infatuated pursuit of the teenage Alcibiades. Later he also showed a taste for WOMEN, especially for elegant courtesans. He married an Athenian noblewoman, Hipparete, and they had two children, but Alcibiades' conduct remained notoriously licentious. We are told that he had a golden shield made, emblazoned with a figure of the love god EROS armed with a thunderbolt.

In his teens Alcibiades became a follower of the Athenian philosopher SOCRATES, who habitually tried to prompt innovative thought in young men bound for public life. This is the background for the scene in Plato's *Symposium* where a drunken Alcibides praises Socrates to the assembled drinkers: According to Plato's version, the middle-age Socrates was in love with Alcibiades but never flattered the younger man or had sexual relations with him, despite Alcibiades' seductive advances.

Alcibiades reached manhood at the start of the Peloponnesian War. At about age 18 he was wounded in the Battle of POTIDAEA (432 B.C.) while serving as a HOPLITE alongside Socrates. (Supposedly Socrates then stood guard over him during the combat.) Alcibiades repaid the favor years later at the Battle of Delium (424 B.C.): On horseback, he found the foot soldier Socrates amid the Athenian retreat and rode beside him to guard against the pursuing enemy.

Although an aristocrat, Alcibiades rose in politics as leader of the radical democrats, as his kinsman Pericles had done. He was only about 30 years old when he was first elected as one of Athens' 10 generals. Meanwhile, he pursued fame with scandalous extravagance, sponsoring no less than seven CHARIOTS at the OLYMPIC GAMES of 416 B.C.—the most ever entered by an individual in an Olympic contest. His chariots took first, second, and fourth places, and inspired a short poem by EURIPIDES. Many right-wing Athenians were alarmed by this flamboyance, so reminiscent of the grandiose TYRANTS of a prior epoch.

Alcibiades' political leadership was similarly reckless. In 420 B.C. he helped to sabotage the recent Peace of NICIAS (which had been meant to end Spartan-Athenian hostilities), by convincing the Athenians to ally themselves with Sparta's enemy, the city of ARGOS. The outcome was a Spartan field victory over an army of Argives, Athenians, and others at the Battle of MANTINEA (418 B.C.).

In 415 B.C. Alcibiades led the Athenian ASSEMBLY into voting for the most fateful undertaking of Athenian history—the expedition against the Greek city of SYRACUSE. (This huge invasion—by which Alcibiades hoped eventually to conquer SICILY and CARTHAGE—would later end in catastrophe.) Not trusting Alcibiades as sole commander, the Athenians voted to split the expedition's leadership between him and two other generals, including the cautious Nicias. But the force, with 134 warships, had barely reached Sicily when Athenian envoys arrived, summoning Alcibiades home to face criminal charges of impiety.

One accusation (possibly true) claimed that on a prior occasion Alcibiades and his friends had performed a drunken parody of the holy ELEUSINIAN MYSTERIES. A second accusation concerned a strange incident that had occurred just before the Sicilian expedition's departure: An unknown group had gone around overnight smashing the herms (hermai, marble figures of the god HERMES that stood outside houses throughout Athens), perhaps to create a bad omen against the invasion. Alcibiades was charged with this mutilation—although this charge was certainly false.

Knowing that these accusations had been orchestrated by his enemies to destroy him, Alcibiades accompanied the Athenian envoys by ship from Sicily but escaped at a landfall in southern ITALY. Crossing on a merchant ship to the PELOPONNESE, he sought refuge at Sparta, where his family had ancestral ties. The Athenians condemned him to death in absentia and confiscated his property.

In Alcibiades the Spartans found a most helpful traitor. At his urging, they sent one of their generals to Syracuse to organize that city's defense; within two years the Athenian invasion force was totally destroyed. Also on Alcibiades' advice, the Spartans occupied Decelea, a site about 13 miles north of Athens, to serve as their permanent base in enemy territory (413 B.C.). By now Athens had begun to lose the war.

In 412 B.C. Alcibiades went on a Spartan mission to the eastern Aegean to foment revolt among Athens' DELIAN LEAGUE allies and to help bring PERSIA into the war on Sparta's side. Yet the Spartans soon condemned Alcibiades to death—they mistrusted him, partly because he was known to have seduced the wife of the Spartan king Agis. With Sparta and Athens both against him, Alcibiades fled to the Persian governor of western ASIA MINOR. From there he began complex intrigues with commanders at the Athenian naval base on the nearby island of SAMOS in hopes of getting himself recalled to Athenian service.

His chance came in June 411 B.C., after the government at Athens fell to the oligarchic coup of the FOUR HUNDRED, and the Athenian sailors and soldiers at Samos defiantly proclaimed themselves to be the democratic government-in-exile. Alcibiades was invited to Samos and elected general. After the Four Hundred's downfall (September 411 B.C.), he was officially reinstated by the restored DEMOC-RACY at Athens, although he stayed on active duty around Samos.

Then about 40 years old, Alcibiades began a more admirable phase of his life. The theater of war shifted to Asia Minor's west coast and to the HELLESPONT seaway, where Spartan fleets, financed by Persia, sought to destroy Athens' critical supply line of imported grain. Alcibiades managed to keep the sea-lanes open. His former ambition and recklessness now shone through as bold strategy and magnetic leadership. (For example, he once told the crews of his undersupplied ships that they would have to win every battle, otherwise there would be no money to pay them.) His best victory came in 410 B.C. at CYZICUS, where he surprised a Spartan fleet of 60 ships, destroying or capturing every one. In 408 B.C. he recaptured the strategic but rebellious ally city of BYZANTIUM. In 407 B.C., at the height of his popularity, he returned ceremoniously to Athens to receive special powers of command. Then he sailed back to war, destined never to see home again.

In 406 B.C. a subordinate of Alcibiades was defeated in a sea battle off Notium, near EPHESUS, on Asia Minor's west coast. The fickle Athenian populace blamed Alcibiades and voted him out of office. Alarmed, he fled from his fellow citizens a second time—only now he could not go to Sparta. He eventually settled in a private fortress on the European shore of the Hellespont. But, with Athens' surrender to Sparta in 404 B.C., Alcibiades had to flee from the vengeful Spartans, who now controlled all of Greece.

He took refuge with Pharnabazus, the Persian governor of central Asia Minor. But too many people desired Alcibiades' death. The Spartan general LYSANDER and the Athenian quisling CRITIAS feared that Alcibiades would lead the defeated Athenians to new resistance. At Spartan request, Pharnabazus sent men to kill him. Legend says that Alcibiades was abed with a courtesan when he awoke to find the house on fire. Wrapping a cloak around his left arm as a shield, he dashed out naked, sword in hand, but fell to arrows and javelins. The woman escaped and later had him buried.

So died the foremost Athenian soldier of his day. The historian Thucydides sums up the dual tragedy of Athens and Alcibiades: "He had a quality beyond the normal, which frightened people. . . . As a result his fellow citizens entrusted their great affairs to men of lesser ability, and so brought the city down." The Athenians' puzzlement over him is suggested in ARISTOPHANES' comedy Frogs, staged in 405 B.C., the year before Alcibiades' death. The play involves a poetry contest in the Underworld; the final question to the contestants is: "What do you think of Alcibiades?"

(See also ALCMAEONIDS; HOMOSEXUALITY; PROSTITUTES.)

Alcmaeon (1)   In MYTH, a hero of the city of ARGOS. After his father, Amphiaraus, was killed in the exploit of the SEVEN AGAINST THEBES, Alcmaeon led the expedition of the Epigoni (Descendants) and captured THEBES. Then, in accordance with a prior vow to Amphiaraus, Alcmaeon murdered his own mother, Eriphyle, for her treacherous role in convincing Amphiaraus to join the doomed expedition. The dying Eriphyle cursed her son, wishing that no land on earth might welcome him.

Tormented by the FURIES for his crime, Alcmaeon fled from home. On advice he journeyed to ACARNANIA, where a recent strip of alluvial shore from the River Acheloüs supplied a "new" land, unaffected by Eriphyle's curse. There Alcmaeon received absolution.

The story is similar to the myth of ORESTES, who was also compelled by duty to kill his mother. The horror and legalistic dilemma of this situation appealed to the classical Greek mind. Alcmaeon was the subject of at least two tragedies by the Athenian playwright EURIPIDES (late 400s B.C.).

Alcmaeon (2)   See CROTON.

Alcmaeonids   The Alkmaionidai (descendants of Alcmaeon) were a noble Athenian clan, active in politics in the 600s–400s B.C.. The family claimed descent from a certain Alcmaeon (not the same as the Argive hero ALCMAEON or the physician Alcmaeon of CROTON). Although the Alcmaeonids were aristocrats, a few of them played major roles in the Athenian DEMOCRACY of the late 500s–mid-400s B.C. These included CLEISTHENES (1) and (by maternal blood) PERICLES and ALCIBIADES.

As a group, the Alcmaeonids were not greatly trusted by other Athenians. They were suspected of plotting to seize supreme power, and they were considered to be living under a hereditary curse from the days when an Alcmaeonid commander had impiously slaughtered the conspirators of CYLON (632 B.C.).

The Alcmaeonids were thought to be responsible for the treasonous heliographic signal—the showing of the shield—that accompanied the Battle of MARATHON (490 B.C.). In the rash of OSTRACISMS of the 480s B.C.—aimed against suspected friends of the fallen tyrant HIPPIAS—two Alcmaeonid figures were expelled: Cleisthenes' nephew Megacles and XANTHIPPUS, who had married into the clan and was Pericles' father.

Pericles gained the people's trust by disassociating himself from the family; he avoided Alcmaeonid company and aristocratic gatherings in general. In 431 B.C., on the eve of the PELOPONNESIAN WAR, the hostile Spartans demanded that the Athenian people "drive out the curse," that is, by expelling Pericles. But the demand was ignored.

(See also ARISTOCRACY; HARMODIUS AND ARISTOGITON; TYRANTS.)

Alcman   Famous poet of SPARTA, circa 630 B.C. A plausible later tradition says Alcman was an Ionian Greek who had immigrated from ASIA MINOR; he was notorious for his supposed gluttony. Only a few fragments of his work have come down to us, but they include the earliest surviving example of a choral ode—a type of poem sung by a chorus of girls or men, to musical accompaniment, at a religious festival or other event. Choral poetry was in those years a distinctly Spartan art form, and the Doric Greek dialect of Sparta was the language of the genre.

Alcman's 101-line fragment presents the final two thirds of a *partheneion*, a "maiden song." The fragment begins by recounting one of the adventures of the hero HERACLES, then abruptly switches topic and starts praising by name the individual teenage girls who are singing the words.

Certain passages seem intended for delivery by half choruses in playful rivalry. The poem obviously was composed for a specific occasion, perhaps a rite of female adolescence connected with the Spartan goddess ARTEMIS Orthia. Alcman's technique of layering mythology and personal references seems to anticipate the work of the greatest Greek choral poet, PINDAR (born 508 B.C.).

Intriguing for a modern reader are the emotionally charged statements that Alcman wrote for public recitation by these aristocratic girls. ("It is Hagesichora who torments me," the chorus says, referring to the beauty of a girl who may have been the chorus leader.) The nuances are sexual, and presumably the verses commemorate genuine emotions within this exclusive girls' group. In the surviving fragments of another *partheneion*, Alcman seems to be addressing the same topic. The situation resembles the female-homosexual style of life later described by the poet SAPPHO (circa 600 B.C.).

In other extant verse, Alcman celebrates simple aspects of the natural world: birds, flowers, food. His buoyant, sophisticated poetry reflect a golden phase of Spartan history—the period of the city's triumph in the hard-fought Second Messenian War, before Sparta had completely become a militaristic society.

(See also GREEK LANGUAGE; HOMOSEXUALITY; IONIAN GREEKS; LYRIC POETRY; MESSENIA.)

Alexander the Great   Macedonian king and conqueror who lived 356–323 B.C. Alexander was the finest battlefield commander of the ancient world, and when he died of fever just before his 33rd birthday he had carved out the largest empire the world had ever seen, stretching 3,000 miles from the Adriatic Sea to the Indus River.

His principal achievement was the conquest of the empire of PERSIA, an event that remade the map of the ancient world. For 200 years previously, the Persian kingdom had been a menacing behemoth on the Greeks' eastern frontier. With Alexander's conquests, Persia ceased to exist as a sovereign power. The Persians' former territory—including their subjugated regions such as EGYPT and Mesopotamia—became Alexander's domain, garrisoned by Macedonian and Greek troops.

Alexander's sprawling realm quickly fell apart after his death, and there arose instead several Greco-Macedonian kingdoms of the East, including Ptolemaic Egypt, the SELEUCID EMPIRE, and Greek BACTRIA. These rich and powerful kingdoms carried Greek culture halfway across Asia and overshadowed old mainland Greece, with its patchwork of relatively humble city-states. Historians refer to this enlarged Greek society as the Hellenistic world.

At the start of his reign, the 20-year-old Alexander was the crowned king only of MACEDON—a crude Greek nation northeast of mainland Greece—and some of the credit for his triumphs must go to his father, King PHILIP II. When the tough, hard-drinking Philip fell to an assassin's knife in 336 B.C., he himself was preparing to invade Persian territory. Philip had devoted his reign to building a new Macedonian army, invincible in its CAVALRY and its heavy-infantry formation known as the PHALANX. He bequeathed to Alexander troops, home-base organization, and propaganda program needed for the Persian campaign.

Alexander the man. The conqueror's yearning and determination, as well as a certain premature aging, are conveyed in this marble bust ascribed to the workshops at Pergamum, circa 180 B.C. The likeness may be based on a bronze portrait statue, apparently sculpted not long before Alexander's death (323 B.C.).

Alexander conquered to rule, not to plunder. Whereas most Greeks despised non-Greeks as barbarians (*barbaroi*, meaning "those who speak gibberish"), Alexander planned to introduce the Persian ruling classes into his army and government. This plan is sometimes referred to as Alexander's fusion policy.

Still, the man had serious flaws. He neglected his kingdom's future by exhausting himself in warfare while he delayed in fathering a royal successor. He was capable of dire cruelty when opposed. His heavy drinking led to disastrous incidents and hastened his death. His lack of long-range planning is shown by his conquest of the far-off Indus Valley (327–325 B.C.)—how could he have hoped to manage such an immense domain? It has been said that Alexander died just in time, before he could see his empire collapse.

Knowledge of Alexander comes mainly from the surviving works of four ancient authors who lived centuries after him: Arrian, PLUTARCH, DIODORUS SICULUS, and the first-century A.D. Roman writer Curtius Rufus. Arrian, the most reliable of the four, was an ethnic Greek Roman citizen who served in the Roman government in the 120s–130s and devoted his retirement to writing. His thorough account of

Alexander's campaigns, written in Greek, is believed to derive from the now-vanished campaign memoirs of Alexander's friend and general PTOLEMY (1). Plutarch's biography of Alexander, written circa A.D. 110, is one of his *Parallel Lives* (paired short biographies comparing noble Greeks with noble Romans); here, Alexander's life story is paired with that of Julius Caesar.

Alexander (Alexandros, "defender") was King Philip's eldest legitimate child. His mother, Olympias, came from the ruling clan of the northwestern Greek region called EPIRUS. The tempestuous Olympias remained for 20 years the foremost of the polygamous Philip's wives. But the royal MARRIAGE was unhappy, and mother and son sided together against Philip.

As a mystical follower of the god DIONYSUS, Olympias was said to sleep with a giant snake in her bed as a pet and spiritual familiar. Apparently she convinced the young Alexander that in conceiving him she had been impregnated not by Philip but by ZEUS, king of the gods. This divine parentage would have put Alexander on a par with the noblest heroes of MYTH.

Such childhood influences gave Alexander a belief in his preordained greatness, a need to surpass his father and all other men, and an imperviousness to danger, pain, and fatigue. Ancient writers describe Alexander's yearning for adventure and exploration. He modeled his behavior on two legendary heroes—the world-civilizing HERACLES and the great soldier ACHILLES.

Alexander was fair-skinned, fair-haired, and not tall. Although a dedicated soldier, he disliked all SPORT except hunting. He was sexually abstemious, once remarking that sleep and sexual intercourse both made him sad since they reminded him that he was mortal. When he did pursue

Alexander the god. A generation after his death, Alexander is shown with the ram's horns of the Greek-Egyptian deity Zeus-Ammon, on this silver tetradrachm, or four-drachma coin, minted circa 300 B.C. The coin comes from the north Aegean region of Thrace, where one of Alexander's followers, Lysimachus, ruled after the conqueror's death.

love, he tended in his youth to prefer males: His lifelong intimate friend was Hephaestion, a Macedonian noble. Later in life, Alexander had sexual relations with WOMEN; when he died he left behind two wives, one of whom was pregnant with his son. Alexander's bisexual development was in keeping with Greek upper-class custom.

Legend claims that at about age nine Alexander tamed the stallion Bucephalus (*Boukephalas*, "ox head"), after its trainer failed to do so. Bucephalus became Alexander's war-horse, carrying him into each of his major battles over the next 20 years.

To tutor the teenage Alexander, King Philip brought the Greek philosopher ARISTOTLE to Macedon. Between about 343 and 340 B.C. Aristotle taught Alexander political science and literature, among other subjects. For the rest of his life, Alexander is said to have kept with him Aristotle's edited version of HOMER's *Iliad*. Also, in future years King Alexander supposedly sent specimens of unfamiliar plants and animals from Asia to his old tutor, to assist Aristotle's biological studies at the LYCEUM.

At age 16 Alexander held his first battlefield command, defeating a Thracian tribe on Macedon's northern frontier. Two years later, in 338 B.C., he commanded the Macedonian cavalry at the Battle of CHAERONEA, in which King Philip won control over all of Greece. (In all his battles, even as king, Alexander remained a cavalry commander, personally leading the charge of his 2,000 elite mounted assault troops known as the Companions.)

With Greece subjugated, King Philip next planned to "liberate" the Persian-ruled Greek cities of ASIA MINOR— and to seize the fabled wealth of Persian treasuries. For propaganda purposes, Philip arranged the creation of a federation called the Corinthian League, representing all the major mainland Greek states, except resistant SPARTA. League delegates dutifully elected Philip as war leader. But before Philip could invade Persian territory, he was assassinated in Macedon (summer 336 B.C.).

The killer, an aggrieved Macedonian nobleman, was slain as he tried to escape. The official verdict claimed that he had been bribed by the Persian king, Darius III. Yet suspicion also lights on Alexander and his mother, who had both recently fallen from royal favor. After Philip's death, Alexander was immediately saluted as the new Macedonian king.

The invasion was delayed for two more years. First Alexander was elected as the Corinthian League's new war captain, empowered to raise troops from mainland Greece and to make war against Persia, in revenge for the Persian king XERXES' invasion of Greece over 140 years before. But despite this pretence of alliance, the Greek city of THEBES revolted (335 B.C.). Alexander—who feared a Greek rebellion as the worst threat to his plans—angrily captured the city and destroyed it. Six thousand Thebans were killed; 30,000, mostly women and children, were sold as SLAVES.

Leaving behind a regent, ANTIPATER, to guard Greece and Macedon and organize reinforcements, Alexander invaded Persian territory in the spring of 334 B.C. He sailed across the HELLESPONT to northwestern Asia Minor with a small Macedonian-Greek force—about 32,000 infantry, 5,100 cavalry, and a siege train. His second-in-command

was the 60-year-old Parmenion, who had been Philip's favorite general.

The events of the next 11 years, culminating in Alexander's conquest of Persia and the Indus Valley, can only be summarized here. Alexander's first battle victory came within a few days, at the River Granicus, where he defeated a smaller Persian army commanded by local Persian governors. The central action was a cavalry battle on the riverbank, after Alexander had led a charge across the river.

The Granicus victory opened Asia Minor to Alexander. There he spent the next year and a half, moving methodically south and east. Local Persian troops fell back to a few strongholds. The fortress of Sardis surrendered without a fight. The Persian garrisons at MILETUS and HALICARNASSUS resisted but succumbed to siege.

As local Greek cities opened their gates to Alexander, he set up democratic governments and abolished Persian taxes. But in Asia Minor's non-Greek territories, he merely replaced Persian overlordship with a similar system of obligation toward himself. Most non-Greek cities continued to pay tribute, now to Alexander. His governors were chosen either from his staff or from cooperative local gentry.

By the spring of 333 B.C. he had reached the province of Phrygia, in central Asia Minor. At the Phrygian capital of Gordium stood an ancient wagon supposedly driven by the mythical king MIDAS. The wagon's yoke carried a thong tied in an intricate knot, and legend claimed that whoever could untie the Gordian Knot was destined to rule Asia. According to the most familiar version, Alexander sliced the knot apart with his sword.

In November 333 B.C. Alexander defeated a second Persian army, this one commanded by King Darius himself. The battle took place in a seaside valley on the Gulf of Issus—the geographic "corner" where Asia Minor joins the Levantine coast—about 15 miles north of the modern Turkish seaport of Iskendrun. The mountainous terrain presents a string of narrow passes; it was a natural place for the Persians to try to bottle up Alexander.

At the Battle of Issus, Alexander had about 40,000 troops; Darius had about 70,000. Although half of Darius' army was inferior light infantry, they could have won the battle had not Darius fled in his chariot when Alexander and his Companion Cavalry charged into the Persian left wing. Darius' retreat caused most of his army to follow.

Darius had lost more than a battle. The captured Persian camp at Issus contained the king's wife (who was also his sister) and other family, who now became Alexander's hostages. Ancient writers emphasize that Alexander not only refrained from raping Darius' beautiful wife, as was his due, but he also became friends with Darius' captive mother!

Oddly, rather than pursue the beaten Darius, Alexander chose to let him go. (Upon reaching Mesopotamia, Darius began raising another army.) Alexander turned south to the Levant, to capture the Persians' remaining Mediterranean seaboard. Most of PHOENICIA submitted. But the defiant island city of Tyre provoked an immense siege, which lasted eight months (332 B.C.). The siege's turning point came when the Greeks of CYPRUS rebelled from Persian rule and declared for Alexander, sending him 120 badly needed warships. Lashing these ships into pairs as needed, Alexander equipped some with catapults and others with siege ladders. When the ships' catapults had battered down a section of Tyre's wall, he led his shipborne troops inside. With exemplary cruelty, Alexander sold most of the 30,000 inhabitants into slavery.

Envoys from Darius offered peace: Darius would give his daughter in marriage to Alexander and cede all territory west of the Euphrates River. When the Macedonian general Parmenion commented that he would accept such terms if he were Alexander, the young king replied, "So would I, too, if I were Parmenion." Alexander dismissed the envoys.

In Egypt in the fall of 332 B.C., he received the Persian governor's surrender and was enthroned by the Egyptians as their new pharaoh (as Persian kings had customarily been). In the spring of 331 B.C., west of the Nile's mouth, he founded a city destined to be one of the greatest of the ancient world, ALEXANDRIA (1).

The final campaign against Darius came in the fall of 331 B.C. Alexander marched northeast from Egypt. King Darius, with a huge army levied from all remaining parts of the empire, awaited him east of the northern Tigris, near Gaugamela village, not far from the city of Arbela (modern Erbil, in Iraq).

The Battle of Gaugamela, also called the Battle of Arbela, was a huge, clumsy affair that has defied modern analysis. Alexander was greatly outnumbered. Against his 7,000 cavalry and 40,000 foot, the Persians had perhaps 33,000 cavalry and 90,000 foot. The Persians remained weak in the quality of their infantry, most of whom were Asiatic light-armed troops. But Darius intended a cavalry battle.

Darius launched a massive cavalry attack against both wings of Alexander's army. Somehow the cavalry's departure left Darius' own center-front infantry open to attack; Alexander led his Companion Cavalry charging across the open ground between the two armies' center fronts and struck the Persian infantry there. The melee brought the Macedonians close to Darius—who turned and fled in his chariot, just as at Issus. Soon all Persian troops were in retreat, despite having inflicted heavy losses on Alexander's men.

With his kinsman Bessus, Darius fled into the mountains toward Ecbatana (modern Hamadan, in Iran). For the second time, Alexander turned away from a defeated Darius and marched south, into Mesopotamia.

Alexander now declared himself king of Asia. At Babylon he received the submission of the Persian governor and appointed him as *his* governor there. This move is the first sign of Alexander's fusion policy. Soon he would reappoint other such governors and organize well-born Persian boys into units of cadets, to train for a Macedonian-Greek-Persian army.

From Babylon, Alexander headed southeast, overcoming some fierce resistance, into the Persian heartland. The royal cities of Susa and Persepolis surrendered, opening to him the fantastic wealth of the Persian kings. In April 330 B.C., at Persepolis, Alexander burned down the palace complex designed by King Xerxes. (Its impressive ruins are visible today.) According to one story, Alexander—usually so respectful of Persian royalty—set the fire during a drunken revel.

Alexander's claim to the Persian throne was confirmed by Darius' death (July 330 B.C.). Stabbed by Bessus' men in the countryside near what is now Tehran, Darius died just as Alexander's pursuing cavalry arrived. Alexander is said to have wrapped his cloak around the corpse. Bessus fled farther east and declared himself king, but Alexander had him hunted down and executed.

Still Alexander did not rest. The years 330–327 B.C. saw him campaigning in Bactria (northern Afghanistan) and Sogdiana (Uzbekistan and Tajikistan), where rugged mountain dwellers and horsemen had lived semi-independent of any Persian king. Subduing these people, Alexander took one of them as his bride—Roxane, the beautiful daughter of a Sogdian baron. No doubt the marriage helped to pacify the defiant region. But it is puzzling that the 29-year-old conqueror did not choose a marriage of wider political advantage.

By then he had won the entire domain over which his adversary Darius had ruled. Alexander's northeast frontier became dotted with garrison towns named ALEXANDRIA (2). But these years brought worsening relations between Alexander and certain Macedonian nobles who resented his solicitude toward the defeated Persians and his adoption of Persian customs. Between 330 and 327 B.C. several of Alexander's associates were executed for suspected treason. These included the 70-year-old Parmenion and the army's official historian, Callisthenes, who was Aristotle's nephew. History does not record Aristotle's reaction.

In the summer of 327 B.C., Alexander led his army across the Hindu Kush Mountains and down into the plain of the Indus River (called India by the Greeks but today contained inside Pakistan). This region had at one time been part of the Persian Empire. Alexander's conquest required three arduous years, during which he encountered a fearsome new war machine—the Indian elephant, employed as "tank corps" by local rulers.

A battle fought in monsoon rains at the River Hydaspes (an Indus tributary, now called the Jhelum) was Alexander's military masterpiece. There he defeated his most capable adversary, the local king Porus. The captured Porus was confirmed as Alexander's governor of the region (May 326 B.C.).

In fall 326 B.C., at the Beas River, Alexander's men mutinied, refusing to continue east to the Ganges River. Angrily and reluctantly, Alexander turned west and south. The army had reached its easternmost point and was now on a roundabout route home.

At the resistant fortress of the Malloi (perhaps modern Multan, in Pakistan), Alexander's siege ladder collapsed behind him as he went over the enemy wall. Trapped inside, he was hit in the lung by an arrow. Although rescued, he nearly died. The damaged lung surely hastened his death, now less than two years away.

After a disastrous march west through the southern Iranian desert (325 B.C.), Alexander returned to the Persian royal cities. At Susa in 324 B.C. he held his famous marriage of East and West. Although he already had a wife, he now also married Darius' daughter Barsine, and 90 other Macedonian and Greek officers married high-born Persian women.

That year Alexander sent messages to the mainland Greeks requesting that they honor him as a living god. This request was granted but was met with derision at ATHENS and elsewhere—the Greeks of that era did not generally deify living people. If Alexander had a political purpose in this, it failed. By now he may have been losing his grip on reality.

At Ecbatana in the late summer of 324 B.C., Alexander's close friend Hephaestion died from fever and drinking. Alexander, frantic with grief, ordered a stupendously extravagant monument and funeral. He himself was drinking heavily. Reportedly, in these last days, the brooding Alexander would go to dinner dressed in the costumes of certain gods, such as HERMES or ARTEMIS.

Planning a naval expedition to Arabia, Alexander traveled in the spring of 323 B.C. to Babylon (which is humid and unhealthy in the warmer months). After several nights of drinking, he fell ill. He died 10 days later, on June 10, 323 B.C., in the palace of Nebuchadnezzar. The story that he was poisoned by Antipater's sons CASSANDER and Iolas—to preserve their father's power—is probably false. Legend claims that the dying Alexander, when asked to name his successor, replied, "The strongest."

Of his two widowed wives, Barsine was murdered by order of the pregnant Roxane, who gave birth to Alexander's only legitimate son, also named Alexander. Cassander, as ruler of Macedon, later murdered Roxane, her son, and Olympias. The empire broke into warring contingents under Alexander's various officers, known as the DIADOCHI, or Successors.

(See also ANTIGONUS (1); HELLENISTIC AGE; HOMOSEXUALITY; RELIGION; WARFARE, LAND; WARFARE, NAVAL; WARFARE, SIEGE.)

Alexandria (1)   Major Mediterranean port of EGYPT, in ancient times and still today. Alexandria was founded in 331 B.C. by ALEXANDER THE GREAT, one of the many Eastern cities that he established. Located 20 miles west of the Nile's westernmost mouth, the city was immune to the silt deposits that persistently choked harbors along the river. Alexandria became the capital of the hellenized Egypt of King PTOLEMY (1) I (reigned 323–283 B.C.). Under the wealthy Ptolemy dynasty, the city soon surpassed ATHENS as the cultural center of the Greek world.

Laid out on a grid pattern, Alexandria occupied a stretch of land between the sea to the north and Lake Mareotis to the south; a man-made causeway, over three-quarters of a mile long, extended north to the sheltering island of Pharos, thus forming a double harbor, east and west. On the east was the main harbor, called the Great Harbor; it faced the city's chief buildings, including the royal palace and the famous Library and Museum At the Great Harbor's mouth, on an outcropping of Pharos, stood the lighthouse, built circa 280 B.C. Now vanished, the lighthouse was reckoned as one of the SEVEN WONDERS OF THE WORLD for its unsurpassed height (perhaps 460 feet); it was a square, fenestrated tower, topped with a metal fire basket and a statue of ZEUS the Savior.

The Library, at that time the largest in the world, contained several hundred thousand volumes and housed and employed scholars and poets. A similar scholarly complex was the Museum (Mouseion, "hall of the MUSES"). During Alexandria's brief literary golden period, circa 280–240 B.C., the Library subsidized three poets—CALLIMACHUS, APOLLONIUS, and THEOCRITUS—whose work now represents the best of Hellenistic literature. Among other thinkers associated with the Library were the mathematician Euclid (circa 300 B.C.), the inventor Ctesibius (circa 270 B.C.), and the polymath Eratosthenes (circa 225 B.C.).

Cosmopolitan and flourishing, Alexandria possessed a varied population of Greeks and Orientals, including a sizable minority of JEWS, who had their own city quarter. Periodic conflicts occurred between Jews and ethnic Greeks.

The city enjoyed a calm political history under the Ptolemies. It passed, with the rest of Egypt, into Roman hands in 30 B.C., and became the second city of the Roman Empire.

(See also ASTRONOMY; HELLENISTIC AGE; MATHEMATICS; SCIENCE.)

Alexandria (2)   Name of several cities founded by ALEXANDER THE GREAT on his conquests eastward (334–323 B.C.). Among these were:

1. Modern-day Iskenderun (previously known as Alexandretta), in southeastern Turkey. Founded after Alexander's nearby victory at Issus (333 B.C.), the city guarded the mountain passes linking ASIA MINOR with the Levantine coast.
2. Modern-day Herat, in northwest Afghanistan.
3. A city at or near modern-day Kandahar, in southeast Afghanistan.

The grandiose Greek city recently excavated at the site called Aï Khanoum, in northern Afghanistan, may have been the Alexandria-in-Sogdiana mentioned by ancient writers.

(See also COLONIZATION.)

Al Mina   Modern name for an ancient seaport at the mouth of the Orontes River, on the Levantine coast in what is now southern Turkey. In around 800 B.C. the town was settled as an overseas Greek trading depot—the earliest such post-Mycenaean venture that we know of—and it seems to have been the major site for Greek TRADE with the East for several centuries. Al Mina was surely the main source for Eastern goods that reached Greece and the islands during the "Orientalizing" period, roughly 750–625 B.C. This seaport is not mentioned in ancient Greek literature and was discovered purely by ARCHAEOLOGY in A.D. 1936.

The first Greeks must have arrived with permission of the Armenian-based kingdom of Urartu, which then controlled the Al Mina region. From types of POTTERY found at the site, we can guess that Greeks from EUBOEA predominated, with Cypriot Greeks and Phoenicians also present. Being a place where East and West mingled, Al Mina is the most probable site for the transmission of the Phoenician ALPHABET to the Greeks (circa 775 B.C.).

Al Mina apparently remained important until about 300 B.C., wher it was displaced by nearby ANTIOCH and its seaport, Seleuceia.

(See also CHALCIS; ERETRIA; PHOENICIA.)

alphabet   The Greek alphabet, containing 24 to 26 letters (depending on locale and era), originated by being adapted from the 22-letter alphabet of the ancient Phoenicians, sometime between 800 and 750 B.C. Prior Greek societies had relied on cumbersome syllabic scripts, in which each character represented a whole syllable: e.g. in modern English, one symbol for "pen," two for "pencil." (Although simple in concept, a syllabic system needs several dozens or even hundreds of symbols to accommodate the various sounds in a language.) The genius of the alphabet is that it reduces the number of symbols by assigning each symbol a precise sound, not an entire syllable. These alphabetic symbols (we call them letters) can be used flexibly in innumerable combinations, to fit different languages.

Presumably, the Greeks first learned about the Phoenician alphabet from observing the record keeping of Phoenician traders. This observation may have taken place at the north Levantine seaport of AL MINA, where Greeks and Phoenicians mingled from about 800 B.C. on. Alternatively, CYPRUS, CRETE, or mainland Greece may have supplied the point of contact. We know that one of the earliest forms of the Greek alphabet was written by the Greeks of CHALCIS (who were also prominent at Al Mina); by 700 B.C. many regional versions of the Greek alphabet had emerged. The Ionic version, as later adopted and modified at ATHENS, is the ancient form most familiar today.

The Greeks imitated the general shapes, names, and sequence of the Phoenician letters. Phoenician ⨍ (*aleph*, "an ox") became Greek Λ and was renamed *alpha*. Phoenician ᘔ (*bayt*, "a house") became Greek *beta*, Β, and so on. All of the Phoenician letters represented consonantal sounds, and most of these were retained by the Greeks—Greek Β imitates the "b" sound of Phoenician ᘔ, for instance. But the Greeks changed the meaning of seven of the letters, so as to supply vowels. Thus Greek Λ represented the vowel sound "a," replacing the *aleph*'s glottal stop.

The Phoenician alphabet is loosely preserved in the modern Arabic and Hebrew alphabets. The ancient Greek letters live on in modern Greek, but were also adapted by the ETRUSCANS and the Romans to produce a Roman alphabet (circa 600 B.C.) that is the direct ancestor of our English alphabet, among others.

(See also PHOENICIA; ROME; WRITING.)

Amazons   In Greek MYTH, a tribe of female, horse-riding warriors imagined as dwelling in northeast ASIA MINOR, or along the east coast of the BLACK SEA, or at other locales on the northeast fringe of the known world. Beneath layers of poetic elaboration, the Amazon myth may owe something to travelers' tales of real-life Scythian male shamans, who dressed as women but worked and fought as men. Alternatively, the myth may recall Hittite armed priestesses in Asia Minor in the second millennium B.C.

Whatever its origin, the Amazon story exerted a strong influence on the Greek imagination. Amazon society was thought of as savage and exclusively female. To breed, the Amazons periodically mated with foreign males, and they discarded or crippled any resulting male babies. The Amazons wore clothes of animal skin and hunted with bow and arrow; to facilitate use of the bow, they would sear off their young girls' right breasts—hence their name, "breastless" (Greek: *amazoi*).

Appropriately, the Amazons worshipped ARTEMIS, virgin goddess of the hunt, and ARES, the war god. In Greek art, Amazons usually are shown wearing Scythian-style trousers, with tunics that reveal one breast; they are armed with bow, sword, or ax and carry distinctive crescent-shaped shields.

In HOMER's epic poem the *Iliad* (written down circa 750 B.C.) the Amazons are mentioned as a distant people, previously warred upon by the Trojan king PRIAM and the Greek hero BELLEROPHON.

Later writers give the Amazons a role in the TROJAN WAR. The beautiful Amazon queen Penthesilea led a contingent of her tribeswomen to Troy to aid the beleaguered city after HECTOR's death; she was slain by the Greek champion ACHILLES, who then grieved over her death. Other tales develop the sexual overtones; for his ninth Labor, HERACLES journeyed to the Amazons' land and fought them to acquire the belt (often called the "girdle") of their queen, Hippolyta. Similarly, the Athenian hero THESEUS abducted the Amazon queen Antiope; when her outraged subjects pursued them back to Athens and besieged the city, Theseus defeated them and (Antiope having been killed) married their leader. This Amazon bride, also named Hippolyta, bore Theseus' son, HIPPOLYTUS.

Certain tales associated the Amazons with the founding of EPHESUS and other Greek cities of Asia Minor. A later legend claimed that an Amazon queen met the real-life Macedonian king ALEXANDER THE GREAT on his Eastern campaign and dallied with him, hoping to conceive his child (circa 330 B.C.).

Surely the Amazons were in part a reverse projection of the dowdy, housebound lives of actual Greek WOMEN, most of whom were excluded from the men's world, bereft of both political power and sexual freedom. Imaginary "male women" apparently were both fascinating and frightening to Greek men. On the one hand, the Greeks found tall, athletic women generally attractive, and the legend of hard-riding, overtly sexual Amazons seems designed in part to provide an enjoyable male fantasy.

On the other hand, the Amazons represented the kind of foreign, irrational power that was felt to threaten life in the ordered Greek city-state. A favorite subject in Greek art was the Amazonomachy, the battle between Greeks and Amazons; by the mid-400s B.C. the Amazonomachy had come to symbolize the Greeks' defeat of Asian invaders in the PERSIAN WARS. An Amazonomachy is portrayed among the architectural marble carvings of the Athenian PARTHENON.

Ambracia   Corinthian colony of northwestern Greece, located north of the modern Gulf of Ambracia. The city was founded in around 625 B.C. as part of a string of northwestern colonies along CORINTH's trade route to ITALY.

Ambracia soon came into conflict with its non-Corinthian Greek neighbors in ACARNANIA and Amphilochia. In the PELOPONNESIAN WAR (431–404 B.C.), Ambracia fought as a Corinthian ally against ATHENS, but Ambracia was effectively neutralized in 426 B.C., when most of its army was wiped out by the brilliant Athenian general DEMOSTHENES (2).

In 338 B.C. Ambracia was occupied by troops of the Macedonian king PHILIP II. In 294 B.C. the city passed into the hands of King PYRRUS of EPIRUS, who made it his capital. As a member of the Aetolian League, Ambracia was besieged and captured by the Romans in 189 B.C. It later became a free city of the Roman empire.

(See also AETOLIA; PERIANDER.)

Amphiaraus   See SEVEN AGAINST THEBES.

Amphictyonic League   Confederation of different peoples in central Greece, organized originally around the temple of DEMETER at Anthela (near THERMOPYLAE) and later around the important sanctuary of APOLLO at DELPHI. The league's name derives from the Greek *amphictiones*, "dwellers around." The 12 member states included THESSALY, BOEOTIA, LOCRIS, and PHOCIS. The league maintained its two sanctuaries, holding regular meetings of members' delegates and raising and administering funds. It was the league, for instance, that managed Delphi's PYTHIAN GAMES.

Amphipolis   Athenian colony near the north Aegean coast of the non-Greek region known as THRACE. Located about three miles inland, Amphipolis ("surrounded city") stood on a peninsula jutting into the Strymon River. Originally a Thracian town had occupied the site. The Athenian colony was established in 437 B.C., after a failed attempt in 462 B.C., when native Thracians massacred the settlers.

Amphipolis controlled the local bridge across the Strymon and hence the east-west route along the Thracian coast, as well as the north-south riverine route to the interior. As a local TRADE depot, Amphipolis was an important source of certain raw materials exported to ATHENS. Among these were GOLD and SILVER ore (mined from Thrace's Mt. Pangaeus district) and probably SLAVES, purchased as war prisoners from the feuding Thracian tribes. Shipbuilding TIMBER was another valuable local product, and it seems that Athenian warships were constructed right at Amphipolis.

In 424 B.C., during the PELOPONNESIAN WAR, the city was captured without a fight by the brilliant Spartan commander BRASIDAS. In 422 B.C., at the Battle of Amphipolis, Brasidas and the Athenian leader CLEON were both killed as the Athenians tried unsuccessfully to retake the city. Thereafter Amphipolis remained beyond Athenian control. Captured by King PHILIP II of MACEDON in 357 B.C., it became a Macedonian city and coin-minting center. After ROME's final defeat of Macedon in the Third Macedonian War (167 B.C.), Amphipolis passed into Roman hands.

(See also THUCYDIDES (1).)

amphora   See POTTERY.

Anacreon   Celebrated Greek lyric poet of the late 500s B.C., active at SAMOS and ATHENS but born circa 565 B.C. at Teos, a Greek city of western ASIA MINOR. Witty, decadent, and evidently bisexual, Anacreon was the poet of pleasure. His sophisticated verses celebrate WINE, WOMEN, boys, and song—the vital ingredients at the SYMPOSIUM, or upperclass drinking party. Anacreon exemplified the wealth and sophistication of his native region of IONIA, which during the poet's own lifetime fell disastrously to Persian invasion.

Anacreon was in his teens or 20s when he joined the evacuation of Teos to escape the attacking Persians, circa 545 B.C. Sailing north to the coast of THRACE, these refugees founded the city of ABDERA; one poem by Anacreon, presumably from this period, is an epitaph for an Abderan soldier slain in local fighting.

Before long, however, Anacreon had emerged at one of the most magnificent settings in the Greek world—the court of the tyrant POLYCRATES of Samos. There (where another great poet, IBYCUS, was installed) Anacreon won fame and fortune and became a favorite of the tyrant. In keeping with upper-class taste (and with Polycrates' own preference), Anacreon wrote many poems on homosexual themes, celebrating the charms of boys or young men.

In around 522 B.C., when the Persians killed Polycrates and captured Samos, Anacreon went to Athens. According to one tale, he escaped the Persian onslaught aboard a warship sent expressly by Hipparchus, the brother and cultural minister of the Athenian tyrant HIPPIAS (1). Anacreon thrived at Hippias' court (where the poet SIMONIDES was another guest). By the time of Hippias' downfall (510 B.C.), Anacreon had found new patrons among the aristocrats of THESSALY. Soon, however, he was back in Athens, where he seems to have been welcome despite his prior association with the tyrant.

His Athenian friends of these years include XANTHIPPUS (later the father of PERICLES) and a young man named Critias (the future grandfather of the oligarch CRITIAS and an ancestor of PLATO), to whom Anacreon wrote love poems. Anacreon seems to have created a cultural sensation at Athens; a red-figure vase circa 500 B.C. shows a symposium scene with a figure labeled "Anacreon" wearing an Asian-style turban and playing an Ionian-style lyre. Surely Anacreon's long stay in Athens helped to introduce Ionian literary tastes, thus contributing to the city's grand cultural achievements in the following decades. He probably died at Athens, perhaps in around 490 B.C.; legend assigns to him an appropriate death, from choking on a grape seed. In later years the Athenians set up a statue of him on the ACROPOLIS.

Most of Anacreon's surviving poems are short solo pieces for lyre accompaniment, written to be sung at a symposium. In simple meters and simple Ionic language, these verses combine yearning with merriment. Whereas a poet like SAPPHO (circa 600 B.C.) might earnestly describe love as a fire under the skin, Anacreon writes of love as a game of dice or a boxing match. "Boy with the virginal face," he writes, "I pursue you but you heed me not. You do not know you are the charioteer of my heart."

One poem (later imitated by the Roman poet Horace) compares a young woman to a frisky colt who needs the right fellow to mount her gently and break her in. Another poem clearly presents the poet's sophisticated world: "Now golden-haired Love hits me again with a purple ball and tells me to play with the girl in colored sandals. But she comes from Lesbos, a cosmopolitan place, and finds fault with my gray hair. And she gapes at someone else— another girl!"

Among his other surviving work are hymns to ARTEMIS, EROS, and DIONYSUS. The corpus also includes 60 anonymous poems, not written by Anacreon but penned centuries after his death, in imitation of his style. These verses, called Anacreonta, had great literary influence in the Roman era.

(See also GREEK LANGUAGE; HOMOSEXUALITY; LYRIC POETRY; MUSIC.)

Anaxagoras   Greek philosopher (circa 500–428 B.C.), born in Clazomenae but active at ATHENS. Coming from the intellectually advanced region called IONIA, in Greek ASIA MINOR, Anaxagoras played a vital role in introducing the study of PHILOSOPHY at Athens. As such, he was an important forerunner of the philosopher SOCRATES.

A teacher and friend of the Athenian statesman PERICLES, Anaxagoras is said to have lived at Athens for 30 years, probably circa 480–450 B.C. Supposedly he taught philosophy to the tragic playwright EURIPIDES. Eventually, however, Anaxagoras was charged with the criminal offense of impiety (asebeia, the same charge that would destroy Socrates 50 years later). The supposed offense was Anaxagoras' theory that the sun is really a huge, red-hot stone—an idea that would logically deny the existence of the sun god, HELIOS—but probably the accusation was meant to harm Pericles. Anaxagoras fled Athens, apparently before the case went to trial, and was condemned to death in absentia. He settled at Lampsacus, in Asia Minor, near the HELLESPONT, where he founded a philosophical school and lived as an honored citizen.

Anaxagoras carried forth the Ionian tradition of natural philosophy—that is, of theorizing about the natural world. He is said to have written only one book (now lost). Our knowledge of his work comes mainly from sometimes contradictory references by later writers. He seems to have accepted PARMENIDES' doctrine that reality is unchanging and eternal, but he also was influenced by the atomist theories of DEMOCRITUS and LEUCIPPUS to the extent that he pictured a system of various "seeds" that bunch together in different combinations to constitute different material. Behind the movements of these seeds is "Mind" (nous), the universe's animating force, which is infinite and aloof, but which is somehow reflected in human intelligence and other phenomena. These concepts help to explain Anaxagoras' best-remembered (although enigmatic) statement: "In everything there is a portion of everything except Mind. And there are some things in which there is Mind also."

An important figure in early Greek ASTRONOMY, Anaxagoras followed ANAXIMENES' theory that the earth is flat and suspended in air, with the heavenly bodies rotating around it. Anaxagoras guessed that the moon is closer to us and smaller than the sun, and that its light is reflected from the sun. His belief that the sun, moon, and stars are really huge stones was probably influenced by the fall of a large meteorite in the Hellespont district in 467 B.C.

(See also ANAXIMANDER; PERSIAN WARS; THALES; THUCYDIDES (2).)

Anaximander   Early brilliant scientist and philosopher of the 500s B.C. A pupil of THALES, Anaximander lived between about 610 and 545 B.C. in MILETUS, in the flourishing Greek region called IONIA, in western ASIA MINOR. In modern opinion, Anaximander is the most distinguished of the three thinkers who comprised the Milesian School of natural philosophers. (The third is ANAXIMENES.) Anaximander also can be called the West's first astronomer and geographer.

Anaximander wrote the earliest known Greek prose work, a theoretical description and history of the natural world. This treatise has not survived, but a number of later ancient writers refer to it. It contained the first Greek map of the heaven and the earth, and described the movements of the constellations. It was probably the first written attempt in the West to substitute SCIENCE for MYTH in explaining the universe.

Anaximander pictured the earth as a cylinder suspended upright, with the flat ends at top and bottom; humans live on the top surface, surrounded by the heavens. While Thales had theorized that the earth floats on water, Anaximander believed that the earth is suspended in air, equidistant from all other heavenly bodies. This idea looks remarkably like a guess at the celestial law of gravity.

According to Anaximander, the primal element in the universe is not water, as Thales believed, but a more mysterious substance that Anaximander refers to as the apeiron, the "boundless" or "indefinite." He apparently imagined this apeiron as partaking of characteristics more usually ascribed to the gods. The apeiron is immortal, indestructible, the source of creation for the heavens and the earth, and also the receptacle that receives and recirculates destroyed matter. Although abstruse, Anaximander's theory seems to point toward a pantheistic or monotheistic notion of a life force animating the universe; it also anticipates modern chemistry's discovery that basic matter is never really destroyed but only undergoes change.

Anaximander seems to have guessed at the biological process of evolution. He is recorded as having believed that humankind originally emerged from fishes to step forth onto land. He is also credited with constructing the first sundial in the Greek world, probably based on Babylonian examples.

Anaximander is said to have died around 545 B.C., the same year in which the proud, accomplished Ionian Greek cities were conquered by the Persian armies of King CYRUS (1).

(See also ASTRONOMY; PHILOSOPHY.)

Anaximenes   Early Greek philosopher and scientist. He lived between about 585 and 525 B.C. at MILETUS, a prosperous Greek city in the region called IONIA, in western ASIA MINOR. Following his two greater predecessors, THALES and ANAXIMANDER, Anaximenes was the last important member of what is called the Milesian School of natural philosophers. Nothing is known of his life except that he wrote a book in "simple and unpretentious Ionic language," as one later writer described it. Although the book is lost to us, enough of it is paraphrased by other authors to give an idea of its message.

Like Thales and Anaximander, Anaximenes sought to identify a single, primal substance that is the basic element in the universe. Thales had said that this primal substance is water. Anaximenes, apparently observing that water is itself part of a larger process of condensation and evaporation, identified the universal element as *aër*—"air" or "mist."

The air, he said, is infinite and eternally moving. As it moves, it can condense into different forms: into wind, which produces cloud, which creates rain, which can freeze into ice. Contrarily, air can rarify itself to form fire. Cold is a result of condensation; heat, of rarefaction. This is why a person puffs through compressed lips to cool down hot food, but puffs through open lips to heat cold hands.

Anaximenes believed that the earth was flat and floated on air in the cosmos. He considered air to be the divine, ordering force in the universe; it is said that he did not deny the existence of the gods, but claimed that the gods arose from air. Although much of Anaximenes' theory seems to derive from his two forerunners, his commonsensical attempt to explain material change was to have great influence on later philosophers, particularly on the atomist DEMOCRITUS.

(See also PHILOSOPHY; SCIENCE.)

Andocides Athenian political figure and businessman who lived circa 440–390 B.C. and whose adventures were associated with the downfall of his city in the PELOPONNESIAN WAR (431–404 B.C.). Four speeches are preserved under his name, although one of these "Against Alcibiades," is considered a later forgery.

Andocides was born into a prominent aristocratic family at ATHENS. As a member of a right-wing club, he was named as one of the conspirators in the Mutilation of the Herms in 415 B.C. To gain immunity from prosecution, Andocides confessed and named his co-conspirators—whether truthfully or not is unclear. Departing from Athens, he prospered elsewhere as a merchant, supplying needed oars at cost to the Athenian fleet at SAMOS.

Unluckily, Andocides' return to Athens in 411 B.C. coincided with the oligarchic coup of the FOUR HUNDRED, which brought to power men from the right-wing circles that had been harmed by his confession of four years before. He was then thrown into prison. Released, he left Athens again and resumed his trading. Eventually he was reinstated at Athens, after defending himself against certain charges in his speech "On the Mysteries" (circa 400 B.C.).

As an Athenian ambassador to SPARTA in 392 B.C., during the CORINTHIAN WAR, Andocides helped negotiate a proposed Athenian-Spartan peace treaty, the terms of which are preserved in his speech "On the Peace."

Unfortunately, the Athenians rejected the terms and prosecuted the ambassadors, whereupon Andocides left Athens yet again. He died soon after.

(See also OLIGARCHY; RHETORIC.)

Andromache In Greek MYTH, a princess from southeastern ASIA MINOR who became the wife of the Trojan prince HECTOR. During the 10-year TROJAN WAR, her father, brothers, and husband were slain by the Greek hero ACHILLES. Her son, Astyanax, was executed by the Greeks after their capture of TROY, and Andromache became the slave of Achilles' son, NEOPTOLEMUS. She accompanied him home to EPIRUS and bore him a son, Molossus, ancestor of the royal Molossian tribe. She ended her days in Epirus, as wife of the refugee Trojan prince Helenus.

In HOMER's epic poem the *Iliad*, she appears as a gracious and stalwart lady whose future misery is clearly foreshadowed. As an embodiment of female suffering at the hands of conquerors, Andromache was a natural subject for the intellectual Athenian playwright EURIPIDES; his tragedy *Andromache* (presented circa 426 B.C.) survives today, and Andromache also is prominent among the characters in his *Trojan Women* (415 B.C.).

Andromeda See PERSEUS (1).

Antaeus See HERACLES.

Antalcidas See KING'S PEACE, THE.

Antigone Mythical princess of the central Greek city of THEBES. A daughter of the incestuous union of OEDIPUS and Jocasta, Antigone is the heroine of an extant tragedy by the Athenian playwright SOPHOCLES. His *Antigone* (performed circa 442 B.C.) examines the conflict between law and moral obligation. Although Sophocles was drawing on an existing MYTH, most of the information available to us about Antigone comes from his play.

Antigone had two brothers, Eteocles and Polynices. In the disastrous expedition of the SEVEN AGAINST THEBES, Polynices led a foreign army to Thebes in an attempt to depose Eteocles, who, contrary to prior agreement, was monopolizing the kingship. The two brothers killed each other in single combat. The new Theban ruler, Creon, decreed that the invader Polynices' corpse go unburied, thereby—according to Greek belief—denying Polynices' ghost a resting place in the Underworld. But Antigone chose her obligations of KINSHIP and RELIGION over her obligations as a citizen, and she covered the body with dust and did honors at the graveside. As punishment, Creon sentenced her to be sealed alive in a vault. After being warned prophetically that he was offending the gods, Creon relented: too late, for Antigone had killed herself. This brought calamity to Creon's house, in the suicides of Creon's son Haemon (who had been betrothed to Antigone) and of his wife, Eurydice.

Antigone was the subject of a lost play by EURIPIDES that seems to have followed a familiar folktale pattern. In this version, the condemned Antigone is handed over to Haemon for execution; instead he hides her in the countryside, and they have a son. Unaware of his royal lineage, the boy eventually makes his way to Thebes, where adventures and recognition follow.

(See also AFTERLIFE; FUNERAL CUSTOMS.)

Antigonus (1)   Macedonian general and dynast who lived circa 382–301 B.C. and ruled ASIA MINOR and other parts of the Greek world in the tumultuous years after the death of ALEXANDER THE GREAT (323 B.C.). Antigonus is counted as one of the DIADOCHI, who carved up—and fought over—Alexander's vast domain. Antigonus and his son, the dynamic soldier DEMETRIUS POLIORCETES, came close to reconquering and reknitting Alexander's fragmenting empire. But Antigonus died in battle at the hands of a coalition of his enemies (301 B.C.). Much of our information about him comes from the later writer PLUTARCH's short biography of Demetrius.

Born in about 382 B.C., Antigonus was nicknamed One-eyed (Monophthalmos), possibly from a war injury. Serving as one of Alexander's generals in the East, Antigonus was appointed governor of Phyrgia (central Asia Minor), circa 333 B.C. His ascent truly began in 321 B.C., when the Macedonian regent ANTIPATER appointed him chief commander in Asia. In the next two decades, Antigonus' ambition of reuniting the empire brought him and his son into wars on land and sea against the four secessionist Diadochi—PTOLEMY (1) (who claimed EGYPT as his domain); CASSANDER (who claimed MACEDON and Greece); LYSIMACHUS (who claimed THRACE); and SELEUCUS (1) (who, having deserted from Antigonus' command, claimed vast tracts in Mesopotamia and the Iranian plateau).

Based at Celaenae, in southern Phrygia, Antigonus and Demetrius fought against the allied Diadochi over two periods, 315–312 B.C. and 307–301 B.C., in Syria, Asia Minor, Greece, and the Mediterranean. After Demetrius' spectacular naval victory over Ptolemy near Cyprian Salamis (306 B.C.), Antigonus adopted the title king (*basileus*)—that is, king of Alexander's empire. Soon after, each of the other Diadochi took the title king as well.

The downfall of Antigonus, aged about 80, came from a concerted campaign against him. With Ptolemy and Cassander helping elsewhere, Seleucus marched an army west out of Asia and joined Lysimachus in northern Phrygia. The Battle of the Kings was fought at Ipsus, in central Phrygia, in 301 B.C. Antigonus and Demetrius, with an army allegedly of 70,000 infantry, 10,000 cavalry, and 75 elephants, opposed Seleucus and Lysimachus' force of 64,000 foot, 10,500 horse, and 480 elephants. Demetrius, leading his cavalry, was drawn too far forward in the field and was cut off by the enemy's elephants. Antigonus was surrounded and killed; his last recorded words were: "Demetrius will come and save me." Demetrius survived the battle and fled to EPHESUS, to fight another day. Antigonus' kingdom was divided between Seleucus and Lysimachus.

Antigonus (2)   See MACEDON.

Antioch   Rich and important Greek city on the northern Levantine coast, situated beside the Orontes River, about 15 miles inland from the Mediterranean Sea. King SELEUCUS, (1) creator of the SELEUCID EMPIRE, founded Antioch in 300 B.C. to be his Syrian provincial capital. He named it for his son, Prince Antiochus. The city thrived, eventually replacing Seleuceia-on-the-Tigris as the empire's capital. Antioch's port was another city named Seleuceia, at the Orontes' mouth.

Antioch profited from its fertile plain and especially from its position on the age-old TRADE route between Mesopotamia and the Mediterranean. Militarily, it gave access north to ASIA MINOR, west to the Mediterranean, and east to the Asian continent. Antioch was the second city of the eastern Mediterranean, after Egyptian ALEXANDRIA (1); like Alexandria, it had an international population, including a large minority of JEWS.

Along with the remaining Seleucid domain, Antioch became a Roman possession in 63 B.C.

(See also HELLENISTIC AGE.)

Antiochus (1)   See ANTIOCH; SELEUCID EMPIRE.

Antiochus (2) III   Capable and ambitious king of the SELEUCID EMPIRE (reigned 223–187 B.C.). Surnamed "the Great," Antiochus reconquered prior Seleucid holdings in the Iranian plateau and eastward, but came to grief on his western frontier against the expansionism of ROME. The Romans were alarmed by Antiochus' conquests in the Levant at the expense of Ptolemaic EGYPT (202–198 B.C.), by his invasion of THRACE (196 B.C.), and finally by his invasion of Greece at the invitation of the Aetolian League (192 B.C.). In the Romans' Syrian War (192–188 B.C.), Antiochus was defeated in Greece and western ASIA MINOR and at sea. His peace treaty with Rome prohibited any further Seleucid military activity on the Mediterranean seaboard. This Treaty of Apamaea (188 B.C.) was a major step toward Rome's absorption of the Greek East. Antiochus died the following year.

(See also AETOLIA.)

Antipater   Macedonian general who lived 397–319 B.C. During King ALEXANDER THE GREAT's eastern campaigns (334–323 B.C.), Antipater served as Alexander's regent over MACEDON and the conquered land of Greece. He destroyed two Greek rebel uprisings: one in 331 B.C., led by the Spartan king Agis III, and the second in 323–322 B.C., when ATHENS and other states arose at news of Alexander's death.

With the Macedonian royal house in disarray, Antipater became nominal regent of Alexander's whole empire in 321 B.C. In his last years' struggle to keep the vast domain together, Antipater was aided by his friend ANTIGONUS (1), whom he made chief commander in Asia. But on Antipater's death, his own son CASSANDER seized Macedon and Greece, in defiance of Antigonus.

(See also DIADOCHI.)

Antiphon   Athenian orator who lived circa 480–411 B.C. and who masterminded the abortive right-wing coup of the FOUR HUNDRED in 411 B.C. at ATHENS. After the coup's failure, Antiphon chose to remain behind when most of his co-conspirators fled. Arrested, he was condemned for treason and executed. The historian THUCYDIDES (1) knew Antiphon and describes him as one of the most capable

Athenians of the day. Antiphon rarely spoke in public, before the ASSEMBLY or law courts, preferring instead to advise or to compose speeches for clients. His speech in his own defense at his treason trial was, according to Thucydides, probably the best courtroom speech ever made.

Antiphon's work survives in three rhetorical exercises for courtroom-speaking practice, plus two or three speeches written for actual court cases. The exercises are known as tetralogies, from their four-part structure—two speeches each by both prosecution and defense. The best known of the tetrologies concerns an imagined criminal case, apparently popular among contemporary thinkers, in which a boy at the GYMNASIUM has been killed accidentally by a thrown javelin. Who is guilty, the speech inquires: the one who hurled the weapon, or the weapon itself?

(See also OLIGARCHY; PROTAGORAS, RHETORIC.)

Aphrodite Goddess of love, sex, regeneration, and bodily beauty. She is one of several deities (along with ZEUS, ATHENA, and APOLLO) whose earthly influence is most celebrated in Greek art and poetry.

At some time between about 1200 and 900 B.C. Aphrodite's cult arrived in mainland Greece, probably imported from the island of CYPRUS, which had attracted Greeks in the copper TRADE. In MYTH, Cyprus was said to be Aphrodite's birthplace, and in historical times the Cyprian city of Paphos had an important temple of the goddess.

The early Aphrodite of Cyprus may have been adapted from a non-Greek, Phoenician fertility goddess named Astarte. Among the Greeks she came to personify sexual urge and pleasure, and was devoutly worshipped as a universal force. Aphrodite oversaw the mating and reproduction of animals. She was a protector of seafarers (a trait perhaps derived from mercantile Cyprus). In some locales she was

The goddess Aphrodite teaches her son Eros how to use his bow and arrow, in this scene incised onto a bronze mirror cover, 300s B.C. The goddess wears only a pair of slippers.

a war goddess (which may be the background of her mythical association with the war god ARES). Not surprisingly, Aphrodite was also the patron deity of PROSTITUTES. Her temple at CORINTH was famous for its official harlots, whose fees helped enrich the goddess. (This feature, unique in a Greek cult, may have owed something to tradeborne Syrian-Phoenician influence in the 700s B.C.) Among Aphrodite's other cult centers was the island of Cythera, off the southern Peloponnesian coast.

In myth, Aphrodite was married to the smith god HEPHAESTUS but had Ares as a frequent lover. Her human paramours included the Trojan prince Anchises (their union produced the hero AENEAS) and the Cypriot youth ADONIS, whom jealous Ares eventually killed.

The origin of the name Aphrodite is unknown; the Greeks fancifully explained it as meaning "foam-born." A passage in HESIOD's epic poem the *Theogony* (circa 700 B.C.) tells the best-known version of her birth: how the primeval god CRONUS cut off the genitals of his father, Uranus, and threw them into the sea, where they generated a white foam (Greek: *aphros*). From this the goddess arose and stepped ashore at Cyprus. But in HOMER's *Iliad* and *Odyssey*, written down perhaps 50 years before Hesiod's time, Aphrodite is described as the daughter of Zeus and Dione, an Oceanid.

Homer's Aphrodite is an oddly undignified character. In the *Iliad*, she tries to protect the Trojans and her Trojan son, Aeneas, but she ignominiously flees the battlefield after being wounded by the Greek hero DIOMEDES, whereupon Zeus reminds her that her province is love, not war (book 5). An episode in the *Odyssey*'s book 8 tells how Aphrodite's cuckolded husband, Hephaestus, used a chain-link net to trap her and Ares together in bed, then dragged the ensnared pair before the assembled gods on MT. OLYMPUS.

Later legends made Aphrodite the mother (by Ares) of the boy-god EROS and also the mother (by the god HERMES) of Hermaphroditus, a creature with the sex organs of both genders.

Aphrodite's attributes included the dove, the myrtle leaf, and the woman's hand mirror; in later centuries these traits, like the rest of Aphrodite's worship, were borrowed by the Roman goddess Venus. Aphrodite's titles included Pandemos (of the whole people), Ourania (celestial), and Philommeides (laughter-loving or genital-loving).

Naturally enough, Aphrodite was the subject of some of the most ambitious and inspired ancient artwork. The marble statue known today as the Venus de Milo, displayed in the Louvre in Paris, France, is a second-century-B.C. Aphrodite found on the Greek island of MELOS; apparently it is a copy of a lost original from the 300s B.C. The finest statue of the ancient world was said to be the Aphrodite of CNIDUS, carved by PRAXITELES in around 365 B.C., which shows the goddess standing naked, having disrobed for her bath.

(See also OCEANUS; PHOENICIA.)

Apollo Important Greek god who embodied certain high ideals of ancient Greek society. Apollo's association with human intellect, musical harmony, religious purity, and male beauty have led him to be called (in one modern scholar's phrase) "the most Greek of the gods."

According to MYTH, Apollo and his twin sister, the goddess ARTEMIS, were offspring of the demigoddess Leto and the great god ZEUS. The Greeks imagined Apollo as partaking of his father's wisdom and authority, but in a young form. Greek SCULPTURE and PAINTING portrayed him as muscular, handsome, and (often) in his late teens—at manhood's threshold but still wearing his hair long in a boy's fashion.

Apollo personified Greek male citizen youth. The name Apollo (Greek: *Apollōn*) may mean "god of the assembly," and it seems connected with the annual Greek festival of the Apellaia, at which 17-year-old males were initiated into the community.

The god was believed to oversee several facets of civilized life. As patron of MEDICINE and physicians, he could cure human illness or, contrarily, bring it on. As lord of MUSIC, poetry, and the MUSES, he inspired human bards and was often shown in art holding the bard's stringed instrument, the lyre. He was associated with Greek mathematical discoveries and philosophical thought. He was a patron of shepherds and archers. Along with the lyre, Apollo's most usual attribute was the archer's bow; the arrows with which he killed his enemies might be either solid or intangible and "gentle," bringing disease.

Apollo oversaw human religious purification and atonement. One myth, most famously retold in AESCHYLUS' tragedy *Eumenides* (458 B.C.), described how the god personally exonerated the hero ORESTES of blood guilt. In real life, certain priests of Apollo could provide rituals or advice intended to cleanse a person or place of religious pollution.

This giving of advice was related to Apollo's most famous aspect, the giving of prophecies. Through various oracles—that is, priests or priestesses who supposedly spoke for the god—Apollo might reveal the future and the will of his father, Zeus. Although Apollo was not the only Greek god of prophecy, one of his oracular shrines became the Greek world's most influential religious center—DELPHI, in central Greece.

Oracles of Apollo existed at other Greek locales, including CUMAE (in western ITALY), Didyma and Claros (on the western coast of ASIA MINOR), and sites along Asia Minor's southern coast. Delphi's preeminence was due to its role as religious adviser to the great colonizing expeditions that sailed from Greece in the 700s through 500s B.C. The god of Delphi was protector of colonists; one of Apollo's many cult titles was Archagetēs, "leader of expeditions."

The lord of harmony was linked with human restraint and moderation. Apolline ideals were expressed in two famous proverbs carved on the Delphi temple wall: "Nothing in excess" and "Know thyself" (meaning "Know your human limitations").

After Delphi, Apollo's second-most important sanctuary was the tiny Aegean island of DELOS, his mythical birthplace. Although adorned with architectural splendors, Delos had no oracle in historical times. Two other prominent, non-oracular shrines of Apollo were at Amyclae (near SPARTA) and at THEBES.

Modern scholars believe that Apollo's cult, like that of APHRODITE, entered Greek RELIGION relatively late—in the centuries after the collapse of MYCENAEAN CIVILIZATION circa 1200 B.C. Apollo may have emerged from the fusion of two older deities: 1) a god of shepherds, brought south-

ward by the invading DORIAN GREEKS of about 1100–1000 B.C. and 2) a non-Greek, Semitic god of plague, imported from PHOENICIA circa 1000–800 B.C. via the island of CYPRUS, where Greeks and Phoenicians mingled. If the primitive Dorian god was associated with tribal animal totems, this could help explain Apollo's many sacred animals, including the wolf, stag, swan, and dolphin. Apollo's familiar title Phoibos, often translated as "shining," more probably meant "fox god."

Similarly, Apollo's Near Eastern ancestry may be reflected in his Asia Minor cults and his mythical association with the non-Greek city of TROY, in Asia Minor. According to Greek legend, Apollo helped to found that city and in the TROJAN WAR he fought for Troy against the Greeks, shooting arrows of plague into the Greek camp (*Iliad* book 1) and later guiding the Trojan arrow that killed the Greek champion ACHILLES.

Contrary to some modern belief, Apollo was not a sun god. Although a Greek philosophical theory of the 400s B.C. associated him with the sun, this never became a sincere religious concept. Instead, the sun had its own mythical character, named HELIOS.

(See also APOLLONIA; ASCLEPIUS; BASSAE; BOXING; CASSANDRA; COLONIZATION; CYRENE (1); CYRENE (2); EPIC POETRY; HERACLITUS; HOMER; HOMOSEXUALITY; HYACINTHUS; ION (1); LYCEUM; LYRIC POETRY; NIOBĒ; PROPHECY AND DIVINATION; PYTHAGORAS; PYTHIAN GAMES.)

Apollonia   Several Greek cities bore this name, in honor of APOLLO, god of colonists. The most important Apollonia was located inland of the eastern Adriatic coast, in a non-Greek territory that is now Albania. The city was founded circa 600 B.C. by colonists from CORINTH and perhaps also from CORCYRA, as part of a Corinthian TRADE network extending westward to ITALY.

Other Greek cities named Apollonia included one on the Aegean island of Naxos, one on the western BLACK SEA coast, and one that was the port city of CYRENE (1).

(See also COLONIZATION; EPIDAMNUS; ILLYRIS.)

Apollonius   Greek poet and scholar of ALEXANDRIA (1), in EGYPT, who lived circa 295–230 B.C. His surviving epic poem, the *Argonautica*, presents the legend of JASON (1) and the Argonauts in their quest for the Golden Fleece. Impressive in its verbal beauty and presentation of character, the *Argonautica* is the only Greek epic to be preserved from the HELLENISTIC AGE (300–150 B.C.). The poem's scholarly subject matter, its often playful tone, and its concern with male and female sexual feelings all reveal the values of the Alexandrian literary movement. Apollonius—along with his rival, CALLIMACHUS—epitomizes this sophisticated movement.

Although probably born in Alexandria, Apollonius is often known by the surname Rhodios (of RHODES), referring to the Greek island city where he spent the last part of his life. According to various sources, he began as the pupil of the established poet Callimachus, but the two men became antagonists in a famous literary feud. This bitter quarrel—which the poets also pursued in their verses—was perhaps based partly on literary tastes. (The experimental Callimachus objected to the writing of Homeric-style EPIC POETRY, with its familiar subject matter and long plot.)

Another cause of enmity may have been King PTOLEMY (2) II's appointment of Apollonius as director of the great Library at Alexandria (circa 265 B.C.). This prestigious job made Apollonius the most influential person in the Greek literary world and incidentally placed him in authority over Callimachus, who also was employed at the Library (and who may have been passed over for the directorship).

Whether the disruptive feud played a part or not, Apollonius resigned from the Library post and withdrew to Rhodes, in order to write, or rewrite, his *Argonautica*. This relatively short epic—5,834 dactylic hexameter lines, in four books—skillfully combines traditional MYTH, scholarly erudition, and romance. The first two books describe the outward voyage from THESSALY to Colchis, at the eastern shore of the BLACK SEA; the admirable third book describes the Colchian princess MEDEA's self-destructive love for the hero Jason and the exploits relating to the fleece's capture; the last book recounts the Argonauts' escape homeward by way of a fantastical route that calls forth much geographical lore from the poet. The poem's flaw is a lack of cohesion in theme and tone, but it is noteworthy for being the first Greek epic to include psychological descriptions of a woman in love (possibly inspired from the stage tragedies of EURIPIDES). In this and other aspects, the *Argonautica* had a great affect on subsequent poetry, particularly on the Roman poet Vergil's epic work, the *Aeneid* (circa 20 B.C.).

Apollonius also wrote prose treatises, epigrams, and scholarly poems on the foundations of certain cities, according to the literary taste of the day. Other than one extant epigram attacking Callimachus, these writings survive only in fragments.

(See also LYRIC POETRY; WOMEN.)

Aratus (1)   See ACHAEA.

Aratus (2)   Greek poet and philosopher of the mid-200s B.C., best known for his long poem about ASTRONOMY, titled the *Phaenomena*. Born circa 315 B.C. in the city of Soli in southeastern ASIA MINOR, Aratus studied at ATHENS under the Stoic founder Zeno. There he met the future Macedonian king Antigonus II (reigned circa 276–239 B.C.). Aratus became a court poet to Antigonus in MACEDON.

The *Phaenomena* survives today. It combines religious and philosophical lore with the astronomical theories of Eudoxus of CNIDUS (active circa 350 B.C.) in explaining the heavenly bodies' movements. The poem was immensely popular in the ancient world, and later generations regarded Aratus as one of the four great Hellenistic poets, alongside CALLIMACHUS, APOLLONIUS, and THEOCRITUS. But the *Phaenomena*'s abstruse subject matter leaves it virtually unread today.

(See also HELLENISTIC AGE; STOICISM.)

Arcadia   The mountainous, landlocked, central portion of the PELOPONNESE, bordered on the south by the territory of SPARTA and on the northeast by that of ARGOS. Arcadia was inhabited by a rugged breed of highlanders who claimed to have inhabited their mountain glens since before the moon was born. The poverty and hardiness of the Arcadians is shown in their ancient reputation for eating acorns. Serving as HOPLITES, they were formidable warriors, and by the 400s B.C. they were producing mercenary soldiers for wars abroad.

Arcadia had few cities aside from the important group of TEGEA, MANTINEA, and Orchomenus in the eastern plains, and (later) Megalopolis in the west. The area's history in the 500s–300s B.C. mostly involves feuding between Tegea and Mantinea and periodic resistance to Spartan domination. The Theban statesman EPAMINONDAS liberated Arcadia from Sparta and founded Megalopolis (circa 365 B.C.) after his victory over the Spartans at LEUCTRA (371 B.C.).

The Arcadians' dialect bore resemblance to that of the distant island of CYPRUS; scholars believe that this shared, unique dialect goes back to the language of the MYCENAEAN CIVILIZATION (circa 1600–1200 B.C.). Both Arcadia and Cyprus seem to have been points of refuge for the Mycenaeans, whose civilization was destroyed by internal wars and by the invading DORIAN GREEKS of 1100–1000 B.C. Corroboratively, archaeological evidence reveals little settlement in Arcadia before about 1000 B.C.

In the cosmopolitan circles of the Hellenistic and Roman worlds (and later, in the European Renaissance), Arcadia was romanticized as the home of rustic virtues amid a mythical Golden Age. The Sicilian-Greek poet THEOCRITUS (circa 265 B.C.) imagined Arcadia as an idyllic haunt of lovelorn shepherds and shepherdesses.

(See also HELLENISTIC AGE.)

archaeology   The systematic study of the past through recovery and interpretation of material remains, including building debris, metal weapons and utensils, clay utensils, human and animal skeletons, and inscriptions in stone or fired clay. Typically these items are preserved by being buried protectively underground or by lying undisturbed for centuries on the sea floor.

POTTERY, widespread in ancient use and surviving up to 10,000 years in the ground, provides by far the single most common source of archaeological data. Likewise stone, in building and SCULPTURE, is nearly indestructible underground, but many ancient structures have disappeared because they were quarried for materials in later antiquity or the Middle Ages. Moisture plays a major role in the deterioration of wood, textiles, and papyrus. Only in the dry sands of EGYPT and other southern and eastern Mediterranean sites have a few such materials been preserved from ancient Greek times.

The specific study of Greek and Roman antiquities is traditionally called classical archaeology. It had its origins in art collecting, going back at least to the London-based Society of Dilettanti (founded A.D. 1733), which financed a series of expeditions to Italy for the sketching, written description, and purchase of visible remains. The practice of excavation had begun by 1738, when Queen Maria of Naples sponsored the dig that discovered the ancient Roman city of Herculaneum. Many archaeological treasures reached Western Europe in these early years, as French, British, and German enthusiasts purchased excavation rights at sites in the Eastern Mediterranean, then stole whatever they could find. Today, increasingly sophisticated host countries such as Greece and Turkey monitor digs to ensure that all discovered items remain government property.

The most spectacular archaeological discoveries regarding the ancient Greek world took place in the later 19th century. Using intuition and reliance on descriptions in HOMER's *Iliad*, the wealthy German businessman and amateur archaeologist Heinrich Schliemann discovered and excavated the site of ancient TROY (1871–73). Schliemann next turned his attention to the mainland Greek city of MYCENAE (whose location was already known). Digging just inside the famous Lion's Gate in summer of 1876, Schliemann discovered the group of treasure-filled, second-millennium tombs now known as Grave Circle A. Schliemann also excavated at Boeotian ORCHOMENUS and at TIRYNS. His work proved the historical basis of the Homeric poems and established the existence of a previously unsuspected Greek prehistory, circa 1600–1200 B.C.—the MYCENAEAN CIVILIZATION. Similarly, starting in A.D. 1900, excavations by the British scholar Sir Arthur Evans at CNOSSUS and other sites in CRETE brought to light the earliest great Aegean culture, the MINOAN CIVILIZATION.

In the century since Evans, archaeology has benefited from advanced technology, including aerial photography and electromagnetic search. Aerial viewing of terrain from aircraft at several thousand feet can reveal variations in the color of topsoil or of ripening crops that indicate the presence of buildings underneath. Electromagnetic search—typically conducted on foot, with hand-held equipment—can reveal the presence of buried material by indicating an obstruction to the soil's natural conductivity of electrical flow. Similarly, buried items of IRON or burned clay create a perceptible distortion in the area's natural magnetic field.

Modern underwater equipment such as submersible vessels, scuba gear, and the vacuum cleaner–like suction dredger have opened the sea floor to archaeology since the mid-20th century. The most dramatic Aegean find of recent years is the sunken ancient trading ship lying off the island of Dokos, near the Argolid, in southern Greece. Possibly a remnant of the pre-Hellenic inhabitants of Greece, circa 2200 B.C., this very early find testifies to those people's shipbuilding skill and overseas TRADE routes—assets later taken over by the conquering Greeks.

Despite modern equipment, archaeology still relies much on "low-tech" tools as the trowel, brush, sieve, and icepick-like piolet. After removing the area's topsoil and sifting it for displaced remains, the archaeological team might divide the site into numbered quadrants, indicated by a gridwork of strings held aloft on poles. As digging proceeds with trowel, piolet, and brush, the team keeps records regarding the depth at which each discovered item was found. With some variation, earlier items tend to be located deeper underground, later items nearer the surface.

Perhaps the greatest modern advance has been scholars' ability to assign a time frame to recovered items. Until recently, dates were assigned largely on the basis of associated information, such as excavation level, or how the item's shape compared with similar ones of known date. But recent technology allows for dating on the basis of some items' molecular structure. For example, carbon-14 dating measures the radioactive type of carbon that occurs in all living matter. Thermoluminescence reveals the number of loose electrons in certain material. Both methods can give approximate dates to some archaeological remains.

The most fruitful archaeological sites are ones that are no longer inhabited. For instance, much of our information about housing and town planning in the 300s B.C. comes from OLYNTHUS, a north Aegean Greek city abruptly destroyed by war in 357 B.C. and never reoccupied. Conversely, archaeology at ATHENS has been greatly restricted by the problem of how to requisition excavation sites in the middle of the modern Greek capital city. THEBES and PIRAEUS are two examples of modern Greek cities sitting atop ancient layers that remain largely untouched and inaccessible.

Among the more successful classical archaeological projects of recent years has been the excavation of the original city of Smyrna, near the modern Turkish seaport of Izmir. The site—containing remnants of houses, a temple of the goddess ATHENA, and an encircling wall—provides the best surviving example of a Greek city-state of the early 500s B.C.

(See also DELOS; DELPHI; EPHESUS; EPIDAURUS; LEFKANDI; LINEAR B.)

Archidamus   Dynastic name among the Eurypontid kings of SPARTA. The best known was King Archidamus II, who reigned from about 469 to 427 B.C. His reign was clouded by Spartan-Athenian hostility, culminating in the PELOPONNESIAN WAR. Impressed by Athenian sea power and wealth, Archidamus unsuccessfully urged his fellow Spartans to vote against war in 431 B.C. He predicted (correctly) that they would be bequeathing the war to their children.

After hostilities began, the aged Archidamus led the Spartan invasion of Athenian territory in 431, 430, and 428 B.C. and the attack on PLATAEA in 429 B.C. The war's first decade, from 431 to the Peace of NICIAS in 421 B.C., is often known as the Archidamian War.

(See also EURYPONTID CLAN.)

Archilochus   One of the earliest and greatest Greek lyric poets. Archilochus, who lived from about 680–640 B.C., was the bastard son of Telesicles, an aristocrat of the island of Paros, and a slave woman. Archilochus emigrated with a colonizing expedition that his father led to the northern Aegean island of THASOS (in a GOLD- and SILVER-mining region). There Archilochus served as a soldier, defending the colony against native Thracians. At some point he may have taken work as a mercenary to fight elsewhere. He is said to have died in battle.

As a poet, Archilochus was an innovative genius, the first person in Western culture to write movingly about his own experiences and emotions. There had been lyric poets before him, but he gave to his verses the kind of strong personal content that is considered to be the identifying feature of more modern poetry. Later generations of Greeks revered him.

Archilochus' work survives in some 100 items, most of which are fragments of once-longer poems, quoted by later writers. His favorite verse forms are iambic meters (which he pioneered as a form for satire) and the elegy (generally composed to be sung or recited to flute accompaniment). The personality that emerges in these verses is cynical, angry, proud, and vigorously heterosexual. Archilochus' illegitimate birth and adverse life seem to have given him an outsider's sardonic view of the world, yet he could also feel intense passions.

Archilochus writes of his love for and anger with the woman Neoboule and of his tender seduction of her younger sister. Other subjects include shipwreck, war, WINE, and the male organ. One famous fragment describes with jovial regret how he had to abandon his (expensive but heavy) shield in order to run away from the Thracians: "Let the shield go,' the fragment ends, "I'll get another just as good.' The antiheroic tone sounds almost modern and sets Archilochus apart from other voices of his age. Greek society frowned on a soldier's retreat and loss of shield, but that did not stop Archilochus from writing about it. Among later Greeks he had a reputation for being abusive in verse. According to legend, when Neoboule's father, Lycambes, reneged on his promise to give her in MARRIAGE to Archilochus, the infuriated poet circulated such withering satirical verses that Lycambes, Neoboule, and the rest of the family hanged themselves out of shame.

See also COLONIZATION; HOPLITE; LYRIC POETRY.

Archimedes Inventor and mathematician from the Sicilian Greek city of SYRACUSE, circa 287–211 B.C. Archimedes' discoveries in geometry and hydrostatics (the study of the properties of standing water) were monumental, and represent a high point of Greek achievement.

A friend and advisor of King Hieron II, Archimedes was famous for his inventions, which included the Archimedes screw, still used today for drawing a continuous flow of water upward. Yet he dismissed engineering feats as pandering to a vulgar public and was prouder of his work in geometry, particularly his discovery that a sphere contained inside a cylinder will always have an area two-thirds that of the cylinder.

Regarding the weight-displacing abilities of the lever, Archimedes made the famous statement, "Give me a place to stand and I will move the world." But his best-remembered utterance concerns his discovery of the principle of specific gravity, after he was asked by King Hieron to determine whether a golden crown had been adulterated by baser metal. Pondering the problem in his bath at the GYMNASIUM (the story goes), Archimedes suddenly realized that he could compare the amount of water displaced by the crown with that displaced by an equal weight of pure GOLD. Delighted with his discovery, he ran naked through the street shouting "I have found it!—*heurēka!*" (or, as we render it today, "eureka").

During the Roman siege of Syracuse (213–211 B.C.), he constructed elaborate devices of defense, including a giant glass lens that focused sunlight on Roman warships in the harbor and set them afire. When the Romans captured the city, Archimedes was killed, supposedly because he enraged a Roman solider by commanding "Don't disturb my circles" as the man found him pondering diagrams in the sand.

Of his written work, nine treatises survive in Greek and two others in later Arabic translation. Most of these deal with geometrical inquiries, particularly regarding circles, spheres, and spirals.

(See also MATHEMATICS; SCIENCE.)

architecture Perhaps the most visible legacy from ancient Greece is the three famous architectural "orders," or styles, that the Greeks developed in stone in the 600s–300s B.C. These orders—whose most distinctive feature was the use of stone columns to hold up a solid entablature (upper structure)—were known as the Doric, the Ionic, and the Corinthian. These architectural styles can be seen today on the exteriors of such modern neoclassical public buildings as banks, museums, libraries, and city halls.

The Doric and Ionic orders (both older than the Corinthian) were developed specifically for the construction of temples of the gods. Of course, temples were being built long before these orders appeared, and the orders themselves seem to have emerged, in the 600s B.C., as imitations in stone of existing woodworking techniques. Unfortunately, because wood decays, no wooden structures survive from ancient Greece for us to compare with their stone successors. But certain purely ornamental details of the

The Doric order of architecture emerged with the limestone temple of Artemis at Corcyra, built circa 600–580 B.C. Little of the building remains today. Pictured here is an artist's conception of the western facade. The pediment's center shows the running figure of the demon Medusa with her son Chrysaor, flanked by panthers. A few panels of the pediment—including the carved limestone Medusa, over 9 feet tall—are preserved today in the Corfu Museum. Medusa supplied a favorite Greek artistic motif, used to scare away evil-wishers.

The Ionic order reached its zenith in the temple of the goddess Artemis at Ephesus, shown here in a side view through the entrance porch. Built between the mid-500s and mid-400s B.C., this marble temple was the biggest in the Greek world at that time—180 × 380 feet—and was counted as one of the Seven Wonders of the World. The drawing is conjectural: Little of the temple remains today. The scene conveys the lushness of Ionic architecture, with its scroll-like column capitals and other decorative patterns, borrowed (probably) from Near Eastern architecture.

Doric style are best understood as preserving (in stone) the shapes of wooden beams and pegs that had been necessary elements of earlier, wooden temples. Also, the fluting of Doric and Ionic columns surely commemorates the grooving done by adze in the tree-trunk pillars of earlier temples.

The Doric order emerged in mainland Greece. The name (Dorikē archē in Greek) refers to the style having originated at such prosperous Dorian-Greek cities as CORINTH and the Corinthian colony of CORCYRA. The earliest all-stone building that we hear of was the goddess ARTEMIS' temple at Corcyra, completed circa 590 B.C.; it was built of carved limestone (cheaper and softer than marble, which later became the stone of choice). Although only the temple's foundations and parts of its western pediment survive today, modern scholars have re-created the building's probable appearance. The heart of the temple was a walled, rectangular, roofed structure (the *naos,* or cella) that housed

the cult statue of the deity. The cella's single doorway was typically in the east, perhaps with two columns in the entranceway. The roof extended on all four sides around the cella and was supported on each side by at least one row of columns. At Corcyra—as at the most famous Doric temple, the Athenian PARTHENON (completed by 438 B.C.)—the proportions of these outer columns are eight across front and back, with 17 along each side (counting the corner columns twice).

A temple's sloped roof had a triangular gable, or pediment, at front and back. These pediments were often adorned with SCULPTURES that were fastened to the wall behind. The figures often showed a scene from MYTH, and Greek sculptors used great ingenuity in devising arrangements that would accommodate the pediment's narrowing height at the outside edges. The sculptures were painted, to project the flesh, hair, clothing, and weaponry, and the pediment's background was also painted, usually a solid blue or red. Similarly, painting would enliven the carved reliefs of the panels known as metopes—or "intervals"—that ringed the outside of the entablature, alternating with unadorned, corrugated panels known as triglyphs.

Meanwhile the Ionic order emerged at such wealthy Ionian-Greek cities as EPHESUS and MILETUS, on the west coast of ASIA MINOR. Lighter but more ornate than the Doric order, the Ionic employed certain distinctive details, the most obvious of which were the scroll-like volutes (or curls) at four corners of the capital (or head) of each column; this lovely design may derive from the Tree of Life motif on Near Eastern architecture, known to the Ionians through their trading contact with Oriental kingdoms of Asia Minor and the Levant. A forerunner of the

A Corinthian-style capital, from inside the rotunda at Asclepius' shrine at Epidaurus, circa 330 B.C. The Corinthian column, basically an elaboration of the Ionic type, was invented in the later 400s B.C. The Corinthian capital shows acanthus leaves and small volutes (curls).

Ionic capital may be the treetoplike shape of the Aeolic capital, which survives in a carved stone form of the 600s B.C. from the Greek island of LESBOS (near the Asia Minor coast).

Ionic columns were more slender than their Doric counterparts. Other distinctive Ionic features included the use of a column base and the absence of Doric-style metopes and triglyphs along the frieze beneath the roof and pediments; unlike the Doric structure, the Ionic entablature could show continuous carvings around the frieze. The most glorious building in the Ionic order was the huge temple of Artemis at Ephesus, constructed circa 550–450 B.C. and considered to be one of the SEVEN WONDERS OF THE WORLD. Unfortunately, it and most other Ionic temples have disappeared over the centuries; among the few Ionic structures standing today are the Erechtheum and the temple of Athena Nike, both on the Athenian ACROPOLIS.

The Corinthian order arose in the 400s B.C. as an ornate variant on the Ionic form, using stylized acanthus leaves around the column capital. Early use seems to have been confined to the interiors of certain structures in southern Greece. Beginning as a single capital inside the Doric temple of APOLLO at BASSAE (circa 430 B.C.), the Corinthian design was employed in the 300s B.C. at the rotunda of ASCLEPIUS' temple at EPIDAURUS and at the temple of ATHENA at TEGEA. Later the design was thought to communicate imperial splendor, and became a favorite of the Romans.

(See also DORIAN GREEKS; IONIAN GREEKS; RELIGION.)

archon   Meaning "leader" or "ruler," the archon was a political executive in numerous ancient Greek states. In the democratic ATHENS of the mid-400s B.C. and later, the archonship was a prestigious but relatively narrow job, with executive and courtroom duties. Nine archons were selected annually by lot, from the Athenian upper and middle classes.

The three senior Athenian archons were the archon *basileus* (or king), the *polemarchos* (war leader), and the archon *eponumos* (eponymous). The *basileus* oversaw state religious functions and any related lawsuits. Religious and judicial duties also were assigned to the *polemarchos* (whose role as a military commander was discontinued soon after 490 B.C.). The *eponumos* had jurisdiction over cases of inheritance and other property rights. The man who served as archon *eponumos* also gave his name to the calendar year— that is, the year was henceforth known as that in which so-and-so had been archon.

A man (WOMEN were ineligible) might be an archon only once at Athens. After the end of his office, barring any disqualifying offense, he was enrolled for life in the judiciary council known as the AREOPAGUS.

(See also DEMOCRACY; LAWS AND LAW COURTS.)

Areopagus   In the democratic ATHENS of the mid-400s B.C. and later, the Areopagus was a special law court of 200–300 members, comprised of former ARCHONS. With regard to its origin, the Areopagus (Areiopagos means "hill of ARES," indicating the site where the court's building stood) was a remnant of Athens' old-time aristocratic government.

In the days of aristocratic rule, circa 900–600 B.C., the Areopagus probably ran the city, acting as a legislative body and high court. As Athens developed in stages toward DEMOCRACY, however, the Areopagus gradually was shorn of power. Under SOLON (circa 594 B.C.), a new COUNCIL preempted the Areopagus' legislative-executive duties, and a newly created court of appeals made the Areopagus' legal decisions no longer final.

As the job of Athenian archon became less exclusive and demanding (500s–400s B.C.), so did the Areopagus cease to function as a right-wing bastion. In 462 B.C. the radical reforms of EPHIALTES deprived the Areopagus of most of its important legal jurisdictions and distributed these among the citizens' ASSEMBLY, the council, and the other law courts. The Areopagus henceforth heard only cases of deliberate homicide, wounding, and arson.

In its capacity as a homicide court, the new, diminished Areopagus is celebrated in AESCHYLUS' tragedy the *Eumenides* (458 B.C.). In the second half of this play, actors portray the ancient Areopagus sitting in judgment over the mythical hero ORESTES for the murder of his mother. Aeschylus wrote the *Eumenides* during the period of civil turmoil following Ephialtes' reforms, and one of his intentions was to soothe the class strife of his fellow citizens.

(See also ARISTOCRACY; LAWS AND LAW COURTS.)

Ares   The Greek god of war. Ares was one of the 12 principal gods, but he never stood in the Greek mind as a benevolent guardian figure, as did his Roman counterpart, Mars. Ares was a god with little moral aspect—he seems to have been mainly a personification of war. His cult was never neglected, but it was of second rank. Only in THEBES was Ares' worship important.

Ares was associated with the land of THRACE and may have been Thracian in origin, although his name seems to be Greek. In MYTH he was the son of ZEUS and HERA, and the adulterous lover of the goddess APHRODITE. A picturesque passage in HOMER's epic poem the *Odyssey* (book 8) describes how the two lovers were surprised and trapped in a chain-link net sprung by Aphrodite's husband, the smith god HEPHAESTUS. This irreverent tone is typical of much of Ares' treatment in myth and poetry; one passage in the *Iliad* (book 5) mentions that Ares was subdued by the demigods Otus and Ephialtes, and imprisoned in a metal casket.

Fierce and impetuous, Ares had unhappy associations. Disguised as a wild boar, he jealously killed Aphrodite's lover, the beautiful youth ADONIS. Ares' children by various mortal women included such violent characters as the Thracian Diomedes and the outlaw Cycnus, both slain by HERACLES. Ares and Aphrodite were the parents of EROS and of Harmonia, who became CADMUS' wife.

(See also ATHENA.)

Argonauts   See JASON (1).

Argos   Major city of the eastern PELOPONNESE, located three miles inland, on the western rim of the Argive plain, at the neck of the large peninsula known as the Argolid. The city's patron deity was the goddess HERA, whose Argive cult was very ancient, going back to the pre-Greek mother goddess worshipped there. In its early days, Argos was one of the foremost cities of Greece. But after about 600 B.C. SPARTA displaced Argos in the control of the Peloponnese, and thereafter Argos' story was one of decline and subordination, despite flashes of ambition.

With its farmland and twin citadels, Argos was a fortress and cult center well before the first Greek invaders arrived (circa 2100 B.C.). The Greeks' conquest of the region may perhaps be shown by local ARCHAEOLOGY in the burned remnants of the House of the Tiles at Lerna, near Argos. During the Greek MYCENAEAN CIVILIZATION (circa 1600–1200 B.C.), Argos shared preeminence with the overlord city of MYCENAE, just across the plain, and with nearby TIRYNS.

Argos' importance in this era is suggested by the city's prominent role in Greek MYTH, as the home of PERSEUS (1), of ATREUS and his royal family, and of many other heroes. In general, Argos seems to have supplanted Mycenae in later folk memory (or perhaps Mycenae was once called Argos). In the epic poems of HOMER, the term *Argive*—along with *Achaean* and *Danaan*—simply means "Greek."

During the Dorian-Greek invasion of about 1100–1000 B.C., Argos became a Dorian city and the Dorians' base for their conquest of southern Greece. Thereafter Argos remained supreme in the Peloponnese for over 400 years until the rise of Sparta, farther south. In the mid-600s B.C. Argos enjoyed a brief peak of power under its dynamic King PHEIDON, who defeated the Spartans at the Battle of Hysiae (669 B.C.) and extended his rule across the Peloponnese. But soon Sparta and CORINTH had become the great southern Greek powers, while Argos withdrew into isolation, occasionally emerging to fight (and lose to) Sparta. Argos' worst defeat came at the Battle of Sepeia (494 B.C.), at the hands of the Spartan king CLEOMENES (1). This disaster brought the Spartans right up to the walls of Argos (where, according to legend, the Argive poet Telesilla rallied her fellow citizens and led a counterattack of armed Argive WOMEN).

During the Persian king XERXES' invasion of Greece (480–79 B.C.), Argos alone of the Peloponnesian states remained neutral, in effect siding with the Persians. Internal strife, possibly caused by the trauma of Sepeia, now resulted in the OLIGARCHY's overthrow and the rise of a DEMOCRACY on the Athenian model. Argos allied itself to ATHENS in 461, 420, and 395 B.C., but did so without realizing its potential as a rival to Sparta.

(See also DORIAN GREEKS; PELOPONNESIAN WAR; THEMISTOCLES.)

Ariadne   See THESEUS.

Arion   Greek lyric poet active at CORINTH, at the wealthy court of the tyrant PERIANDER, circa 620 B.C. Arion was born on the Aegean island of LESBOS—where strong artistic traditions produced other poets of this era, including SAPPHO, ALCAEUS, and TERPANDER—and he became famous as a performer who sang his own verses, as well as other poets', while accompanying himself on the cithara (a type of lyre). The Greek historian HERODOTUS described Arion as "the best singer in the world."

Arion is credited with imposing artistic order on the dithyramb, a song sung by a chorus in honor of the god DIONYSUS. Apparently he systematized the performance so that the singers stood stationary, grouped in a circle; he may have assigned a specific subject to each song. These developments would later contribute to the emergence of Greek stage tragedy. None of Arion's compositions survives today.

But Arion is best remembered for the charming legend that he rode on a dolphin's back through the sea. According to the tale told by Herodotus, Arion—returning from a lucrative performance tour of the Greek cities of SICILY and ITALY—took passage on a ship from Italy to Corinth. But he was forced to jump overboard when the crew decided to steal his money. As the ship sailed on, Arion was picked up at sea by a dolphin—an animal sacred to the god APOLLO, who was also the patron of poets. Carried to Cape Taenarum, on the southern coast of the PELOPONNESE, Arion made his way back to Corinth, arriving ahead of the ship. When the ship's crew reached Corinth, they were confronted by Arion and the ruler, Periander.

The legend may have a kernel of truth. According to modern scientific studies, the sea-mammals known as dolphins and porpoises are the only wild animals to be attracted to humans. It is not unusual for dolphins to flock around a human swimmer at sea.

(See also MUSIC; LYRIC POETRY; THEATER.)

Aristides   Athenian soldier and statesman (circa 530–465 B.C.) who was one of the founders of the Athenian empire. Aristides (or Aristeides) was instrumental in creating the Athenian-controlled alliance of Greek states known as the DELIAN LEAGUE. He was surnamed "the Just" for his reputedly fair dealings in politics and in diplomacy with other Greek states.

According to the later Greek writer PLUTARCH, Aristides was one of the Athenian generals at the Battle of MARATHON (490 B.C.). Yet in 482 B.C. the Athenians voted to ostracize him—amid a rash of OSTRACISMS in the 480s B.C. This might have been an outcome of Aristides' political conflict with THEMISTOCLES.

As required by the ostracism law, Aristides withdrew from ATHENS, expecting to be in exile for 10 years. However, two years later he was recalled to help against the Persian king XERXES' invasion of Greece. Elected as a general by the Athenians, he served alongside his former enemy Themistocles. Aristides fought at the Battle of SALAMIS (1) (480 B.C.) and, reelected as general for the following year, commanded the Athenian contingent at the land BATTLE OF PLATAEA (479 B.C.).

As a general again in 478 B.C., Aristides led the Athenian squadron in the allied Greek naval liberation of BYZANTIUM and much of CYPRUS. When the arrogance of the Spartan commander Pausanias alienated the other Greeks, Aristides began his diplomatic efforts to secure a mutual-defense alliance between Athens and the eastern Greek states. When the resulting Delian League was formed, in the summer of 478 or 477 B.C., Aristides won admiration for his fair assessment of the annual contribution due from each member state.

Aristides seems to have been widely contrasted with the wiliness and rapacity of Themistocles. At the performance of AESCHYLUS' tragedy SEVEN AGAINST THEBES in Athens in 467 B.C., when certain lines were spoken concerning the hero Amphiaraus' wisdom and righteousness, the entire audience turned to look at Aristides in his seat.

Aristides is said to have died poor, having refused to enrich himself dishonestly through office.

aristocracy (*aristokratia***)** "Rule by the best," an early form of government in some Greek city-states whereby power was shared by a small circle whose membership was defined by privilege of noble birth. This ruling circle—often confined to one clan—tended to monopolize wealth, land, and military and religious office as well as government. The typical instrument of aristocratic rule was the COUNCIL (*boulē*), a kind of omnipotent senate in which laws and state policies were decided.

Aristocracies arose to supplant the rule of kings, after the fall of MYCENAEAN CIVILIZATION circa 1200–1100 B.C. (Some Greek states, such as ARGOS and SPARTA, seem to have retained kings who were merely the first among aristocratic equals.) By the 600s B.C., however, growth in TRADE and revolutionary developments in warfare had resulted in the breakup of the old aristocratic monopoly, as a new class of citizen—the middle class—acquired wealth and military importance. In some cities, such as CORINTH, conflict between aristocrats and commoners produced revolutions that placed popular TYRANTS in power; elsewhere, the new middle class gradually was granted political power. In these cases, the aristocracy became an OLIGARCHY (rule by the few—the mass of poorer citizens still were excluded from power). Although oligarchies resembled aristocracies in certain ways, such as the council, they notably lacked the old requirement of noble blood. (See also HOPLITE; POLIS.)

Aristogiton See HARMODIUS AND ARISTOGITON.

Aristophanes Athenian comic playwright who lived circa 450–385 B.C. In antiquity, Aristophanes was recognized as the greatest classical Athenian writer of comedy. Eleven of his 30 or so plays have survived in their entirety. These 11 plays supply our only complete examples of fifth-century-B.C. Athenian "Old Comedy" and show the highly political nature of that art, with plots and jokes devoted to current events. Aristophanes' work provides valuable information about Athenian public opinion during the PELOPONNESIAN WAR (431–404 B.C.).

As suggested by his name (meaning "noblest showing"), Aristophanes probably came from an aristocratic family. On the basis of a reference in Aristophanes' play *Acharnians,* some scholars believe that the playwright owned land on the Athenian occupied island of AEGINA. The satirical spirit of his comedies provides no clear proof of Aristophanes' own political beliefs, but he probably identified with the intellectual, anti–left-wing, and basically antiwar Athenian noble class (the class that provided the military's CAVALRY and that is sympathetically portrayed in Aristophanes' play *Knights*). Without being fully antidemocratic, Aristophanes' comedies mock the excesses of Athenian DEMOCRACY: namely, the people's fickle abuse of power and the political pandering and vulgarity of the demagogues.

But any aspect of Athenian life was fair game for Aristophanes, whose weapons were parody, burlesque, and comic exaggeration. Against members of his own leisured class, he derides the dishonest quibbling of the SOPHISTS, and the abstruse brainwork of the philosopher SOCRATES and the tragedian EURIPIDES. These men and many of his other targets were Aristophanes' contemporaries, who might be found in the audience at a play's performance.

Athenian comedy was performed at two state-sponsored festivals: the Lenaea, in midwinter, and the grander holiday called the City Dionysia, in early spring. Each play was part of a three-way competition.

By a convention of the era, most of Aristophanes' plays are titled according to the group character of the onstage chorus. His earliest play, *Banqueters* (427 B.C.), was presented when he was probably in his early 20s. Neither that work nor his comedy of the next year, *Babylonians*, has survived, but we know that *Babylonians* daringly portrayed the Greek subject allies of the Athenian empire as SLAVES, grinding at the mill. Coming at a moment when ATHENS was relying heavily on allied loyalty against the Spartan enemy in the Peloponnesian War, the play provoked the powerful left-wing politician CLEON to prosecute Aristophanes. (We do not know the exact charge.) The prosecution failed, and Aristophanes' mocking pen was eventually turned against Cleon.

Acharnians, performed at the Lenaea of 425 B.C., is Aristophanes' earliest surviving work. The plot involves an Athenian farmer who makes a private peace with the Spartans while the Athenian military fights on. The play's pro-peace message foreshadows the more urgent antiwar themes of Aristophanes' *Peace* (421 B.C.) and *Lysistrata* (411 B.C.). Without being defeatist, *Acharnians* spoke to a city disillusioned in its hopes of an early victory, and the play received first prize.

Knights, performed at the 424 B.C. Lenaea, is Aristophanes' most political play: It amounts to a vicious attack on the politician Cleon, who at that time was standing for election to Athens' board of generals. In *Knights*, Cleon clearly appears in the character of a flattering, scheming slave named Philodemos ("lover of the people"). Philodemos' foolish and elderly master is Demos ("the people"), and the plot involves Philodemos' vulgar competition with a sausage vendor for Demos' affection. The Athenians approved of Aristophanes' mockery of Cleon, and *Knights* received first prize. However, the real-life Cleon still won the election.

Clouds ridicules the real-life Socrates as a crackpot scientist and corrupt teacher of sophistry and RHETORIC. The play won only third prize at the 423 B.C. City Dionysia, being defeated by CRATINUS' masterpiece, *The Bottle*. The next year saw the *Wasps*, which parodies Athenian litigiousness and the elderly Athenians' enthusiasm for jury duty. Like *Knights*, this play contains liberal mockery of Cleon (who had sponsored a law increasing jury pay). Cleon's death in battle in 422 B.C. deprived Aristophanes of his favorite comic butt.

Peace was presented at the City Dionysia of 421 B.C., just a few days before or after the Peace of NICIAS was concluded, which supposedly ended the Peloponnesian War. The plot involves the rescue of the goddess Peace from her prison pit. Despite its topical subject, *Peace* received only second prize.

Aristophanes' comedies of the years 420–415 B.C. have not come down to us. By the time of his next extant work, *Birds* (414 B.C.), the playwright had begun to move away from political topics in favor of themes more generally social. In *Birds,* two Athenians, in despair over the city's litigiousness, fly off and create a bird city in the sky, Cloud-cuckoo-land (Nephelokokkugia). *Birds* contains some of Aristophanes' finest theatrical effects, particularly in its onstage chorus of birds. The play won second prize at the City Dionysia.

The year 411 B.C. brought two comedies about WOMEN's issues. *Thesmophoriazusae* (women celebrating the Thesmophoria festival) amounts to a satire on the tragedies of Euripides; the story involves a scheme by the Athenian women to destroy Euripides on account of his plays' revealing portrayal of women. *Lysistrata* imagines the Athenian women organizing a sex strike to compel the men to make peace in the Peloponnesian War (which by now was turning disastrously against Athens). The comedy combines bawdiness with a sincere, conciliatory, antiwar message.

Frogs, which won first prize at the Lenaea in 405 B.C., is considered Aristophanes' masterpiece. The comic protagonist is the god DIONYSUS, who journeys to the Underworld to fetch back the tragedian Euripides (who in fact had died the previous year). But, once in the Underworld, Dionysus is compelled to judge a contest between Euripides and AESCHYLUS (died 456 B.C.), as to who was the greater tragedian. Deciding in favor of Aeschylus, the god brings *him* back, instead, to save Athens. Part of *Frogs'* appeal is its pathos: Performed barely a year before Athens' final defeat in the war, the play conveys a giddy sense of desperation.

Aristophanes' career continued after the war's end for perhaps 20 years, but we have only two plays from this final period. *Ecclesiazusae* (women in the assembly) was presented in 392 or 391 B.C.. In this play, the Athenian women, tired of the men's mismanagement, take over the government and proclaim a communist state.

Wealth (388 B.C.) is Aristophanes' latest surviving comedy. Plutus, the god of wealth, is blind, which explains why riches are inappropriately distributed in the world. But when Wealth regains his sight in the story, attempts at redistribution create social chaos. *Wealth* clearly belongs to the less political, more cosmopolitan "comedy of manners" of the 300s B.C.

(See also ASSEMBLY; EUPOLIS; MENANDER; THEATER.)

Aristotle   Greek philosopher and scientist who lived 384–322 B.C. A man of immense learning and curiosity, Aristotle (Aristoteles) can be seen as the most influential Western thinker prior to the 19th century A.D. After spending 20 years as a student of the great Athenian philosopher PLATO, Aristotle rejected Plato's otherworldly doctrines, partly because he was fascinated by the multifaceted material world around him. Aristotle was as much interested in defining problems as in finding answers, and he more or less established the scholarly tradition of systematic research, creating categories—including "logic," "biology," and "physics"—that are still in use today. The Athenian scholarly community that he founded, the LYCEUM, was

Aristotle's combination of mental power and compassion is apparent in this likeness, from a Roman marble bust. The bust is thought to be copied from a bronze portrait statue made by the Greek sculptor Lysippus, circa 330 B.C.

one of the greatest centers for advanced study in the ancient world.

His chief accomplishment in PHILOSOPHY was in devising the first system of logic—the system now known as Aristotelian syllogistic, which provided a cornerstone of logic studies for centuries. In SCIENCE his work was epoch-making. He pioneered the studies of biology and zoology (among others), and he divorced science from philosophy, setting scientific method on its future course of empirical observation.

Of his many writings, less than one-fifth have survived—about 30 treatises. Yet these few works came to dominate European higher learning during the Middle Ages and Renaissance. Among his other accomplishments, Aristotle was one of the first political scientists, cataloguing and analyzing the various forms of government in the Greek world and beyond. His extant treatise *Politics* is now probably his most widely read work, having become a virtual textbook for college political science courses.

Although he spent more than half his adult life in ATHENS, Aristotle was never an Athenian citizen. He was born in a minor town named Stagirus (later Stagira), in the Greek colonial region called CHALCIDICĒ, on the northwest Aegean coast near the Greek kingdom of MACEDON. Aristotle's father, Nicomachus, was the court physician to the Macedonian king Amyntas III. Aristotle's career was destined to be shaped by both the Macedonian connection and by the medical tradition's emphasis on observation and diagnosis. The family was probably rich; hence Aristotle's ability to travel and to devote himself to study.

After Nicomachus' death, 17-year-old Aristotle was sent to Athens to join Plato's philosophical school, the ACADEMY (367 B.C.). Eventually recognized as Plato's foremost pupil and possible successor at the Academy, Aristotle remained there for 20 years until Plato's death (347 B.C.). In the election of the Academy's new president, Aristotle was passed over—which may be why he then left Athens with a number of friends and followers. They traveled to northwest ASIA MINOR, where they set up a school at the town of Assos at the invitation of Hermias, a local Greek ruler who was a Persian vassal. Evidently Aristotle became a close friend of Hermias, for he married Hermias' adopted daughter, Pythias. But when Hermias was arrested and executed for some unknown reason by the Persians, Aristotle and his followers sailed to the nearby Greek island of LESBOS, and stayed in the city of MYTILENE. By then Aristotle's group included a well-born man of Lesbos named Theophrastus, who became his protégé and later his successor as head of his philosophical school.

At the landlocked lagoon of Pyrrha, in central Lesbos, Aristotle conducted many of the observations of marine animals recorded in his zoological writings. His method of field observation and documentation—an innovation in his own day—was destined to set the pattern for all future biological study.

In around 343 B.C. the 41-year-old Aristotle accepted an invitation from King Philip, by then the most powerful man in the Greek world, to go to Macedon to tutor Philip's 13-year-old son, Alexander (who was destined to conquer the Persian Empire and be known to history as ALEXANDER THE GREAT). Aristotle spent about three years providing a higher education for the prince and some of his retinue. The curriculum probably included political science—Aristotle wrote two (lost) treatises for Alexander, *On Kingship* and *On Colonists*—as well as studies in literature and biology. Aristotle gave Alexander an edited version of HOMER's *Iliad* that the young warrior supposedly carried with him for the rest of his life. According to legend, King Alexander would later send Aristotle specimens of unfamiliar Eastern plants and animals to study. Beyond this, however, Aristotle's influence on Alexander was not profound, and the teacher probably went home to Stagirus after Alexander began serving as regent for his father, in 340 B.C.

In 335 B.C., after Alexander had inherited the throne, Aristotle returned to Athens to establish his own philosophical school there. He opened the school in rented buildings outside the city, on the grounds of a GYMNASIUM known as the Lyceum ([Lukeion], named for its grove sacred to the god APOLLO in his cult title Lukeios). Aristotle's Lyceum period (335–323 B.C.) is the third and most important phase of his life.

The Lyceum enjoyed special resources and status—Alexander supposedly donated the immense sum of 800 TALENTS—and was protected by the local Macedonian authorities. Without doubt, the Lyceum provided Aristotle with the means to engage in the encyclopedic array of inquiries for which he is remembered. The school resembled a modern university in some ways, with general courses alongside "graduate" research projects under the master's guidance. Among such delegated projects was a description of the individual governments (or "constitu-

tions") of the 158 most important Greek cities; of these 158 analyses, only one survives today—the *Constitution of Athens* (*Athenaion Politeia*), our major source of information for the workings of the Athenian DEMOCRACY.

Supposedly, Aristotle would lecture to general audiences in the morning and to the advanced scholarly circle in the afternoon. It is said that he had a habit of walking around (*peripatein*) while lecturing and that his listeners walked with him—which gave to the community its title of the Peripatetic School. (However, the name may come from the roofed courtyard, *peripatos*, that was a physical feature at the Lyceum or at a later site.) In personal demeanor, Aristotle is said to have dressed elegantly or even foppishly and to have spoken with an upper-class lisp.

During these years at Athens, Aristotle's wife, Pythias, died, and he lived with a common-law wife, Herpylla. Aristotle had two children: a daughter named Pythias, after her mother, and a son, Nicomachus, by Herpylla. Nicomachus is remembered in the title of Aristotle's *Nicomachean Ethics*, so called because the son supposedly edited the work after his father's death.

With Alexander's sudden death in the East (323 B.C.), anti-Macedonian feeling erupted at Athens, and a criminal charge of impiety was lodged against Aristotle. The 61-year-old scholar fled, supposedly remarking that he was saving the Athenians from committing a second sin against philosophy (a reference to their execution of SOCRATES for impiety in 399 B.C.). Aristotle took refuge at the nearby city of CHALCIS, where his mother had been born and where a Macedonian garrison was in control, and there he died in the following year (322 B.C.).

As previously mentioned, less than one-fifth of Aristotle's writings are represented in the 30 works that have come down to us. The vanished work—bits of which survive as quotations cited by later ancient authors—included poems, letters, essays, and Platonic-style dialogues. Many of these were polished literary pieces, intended for a general readership: In a later century, the Roman thinker Cicero described Aristotle's writing style as "a river of gold." This praise would not be appropriate for the 30 surviving items, which often make for difficult reading.

Ironically, most of these extant writings probably were never meant for publication. Many seem to be Aristotle's lecture notes for his more advanced courses of study. These "treatises" or "esoteric writings," as they are sometimes called, contain passages that are notoriously difficult—either overly condensed or repetitive—with apparent cross-references to works now lost. The titles and sequence of these preserved treatises are not Aristotle's choice, but rather are the work of ancient editors after Aristotle. However, the 30 treatises do provide a good sampling of Aristotle's mature thought, covering logic, metaphysics, ethics, scientific inquiries, literary criticism, and political science.

Aristotle's six treatises on logic (*logikē*, meaning "the art of reasoning") are sometimes mentioned under the collective title Organon, or "tool"—that is, of thought. Of these works, the best known is the one titled *Prior Analytics*, which contains Aristotle's system of syllogistic. (A syllogism is a form of reasoning consisting of two premises and a conclusion. The classic form of syllogism is: [1] Socrates is a man. [2] All men are mortal. Therefore, [3] Socrates is mortal.) The *Prior Analytics* examines the various forms of syllogistic thought.

Other extant treatises include studies of the natural world: *Physics, On the Heavens, Meteorology, Generation of Animals,* and the admired *History of Animals* (so called traditionally, although *Zoological Researches* would better translate the Greek title), which presents many careful descriptions of different species. The very notions of genus and species—general type, specific type—are among the categories devised by Aristotle.

Aristotle's theory of reality is found in his *Metaphysics,* or "Beyond Physics" (a title created by an ancient editor, originally signifying only that the book followed the *Physics* in sequence). Here—in a criticism and radical adaption of Plato's theory of Forms—Aristotle explains how universal qualities are rooted in particulars. For example, a specific dog partakes of universal "dogness" along with all other canines, yet this dogness has no existence apart from the world's flesh-and-blood dogs. Book 12 of the *Metaphysics* presents Aristotle's well-known picture of God as the unmoved mover—pure intelligence, uninvolved in the world's day-to-day occurrences.

In book 1 of the *Nicomachean Ethics,* Aristotle identifies the attainment of happiness as the highest good, and he defines happiness as an activity of the soul in conformity with virtue (*aretē*). Book 2 is famous for defining virtue as the mean (*mesotēs*) between two extremes of behavior: Courage, for example, falls between cowardice and recklessness; generosity falls between stinginess and extravagance.

In the *Rhetoric,* Aristotle examines the art of public speaking in terms of its desired goal, persuasion. The *Poetics* analyzes the nature of literature and offers the famous Aristotelian observation that stage tragedy provides a cleansing (*katharsis*) of the audience's emotions of pity and fear.

(See also ASTRONOMY; EDUCATION; MEDICINE.)

Aristoxenus   See MUSIC.

armies   See ALEXANDER THE GREAT; CAVALRY; HOPLITE; PELOPONNESIAN WAR; PERSIAN WARS; PHALANX; WARFARE, LAND.

arms and armor   See CAVALRY; HOPLITE; WARFARE, LAND.

art   See ARCHITECTURE; PAINTING; POTTERY; SCULPTURE.

Artemis   Greek goddess of wilderness, wild animals, and the hunt, also associated with childbirth and the moon. Although her worship was of secondary rank in most cities of mainland Greece, she was a principal deity for many Greeks of ASIA MINOR. At EPHESUS, in Asia Minor, she was honored with a huge temple, begun in the mid-500s B.C. and counted as one of the SEVEN WONDERS OF THE WORLD.

In MYTH, Artemis was the twin sister of the god APOLLO; their parents were the great god ZEUS and the demigoddess Leto. Impregnated by Zeus, Leto fled from Zeus' jealous wife, HERA, and found refuge on the island of DELOS, in the AEGEAN SEA. There she gave birth to the divine twins. Artemis and Apollo grew to be skilled archers. With their

arrows, they slew a number of Leto's enemies, including the children of the arrogant NIOBĒ. Artemis also shot the enormous hunter ORION, whose body now hangs as a constellation in the sky.

Like ATHENA and HESTIA, Artemis was a virgin goddess. Imagined as a lithe young woman, she was said to roam mountain forests and uncultivated lands, hunting the beasts and, contrarily, overseeing their safety and reproduction. Her most famous title, mentioned by the poet HOMER (circa 750 B.C.), was Potnia Theron, "lady of wild animals." In art she often was shown accompanied by deer, bears, or similar beasts, and myths told of her retinue of NYMPHS—female creatures embodying the spirit of wilderness places. Among her human devotees described in myth were the Athenian prince HIPPOLYTUS and the female warriors known as AMAZONS. Two regions dear to Artemis were the mountains of CRETE and ARCADIA.

In the classical Greek mind, Artemis' virginity probably suggested the sanctity of wilderness places. A legend tells how the Theban prince Actaeon, while out hunting with his hounds, accidentally found Artemis bathing naked in a stream. Enraged to have her modesty compromised, the goddess changed Actaeon into a stag, whereupon his own hounds mauled him to death.

Although she had no children of her own, Artemis was concerned with birth and offspring among both animals and humans. One of her titles was *Kourotrophos* ("nurse of youths"). Like the goddess HERA, Artemis watched over WOMEN in labor: They would call on her in their distress, remembering the birthing pains of Leto. Women who died in childbirth, or who died suddenly from other natural causes, were said to have been killed by Artemis' arrows.

The goddess Artemis, with her emblematic bow and arrows, commands the hounds of the Theban prince Actaeon to maul their master to death. This red-figure scene was painted circa 475 B.C. on an Athenian vase of the type known as a bell krater.

The puzzle of why the Greeks would have a virgin fertility goddess can perhaps be explained. Artemis may combine two different heritages, of which the fertility concept is the older. The name Artemis seems not to come from the Greek language, and scholars believe that this goddess—like Athena and Hera—was not originally Greek. Rather, Artemis represents a religious survival from the non-Greek peoples who inhabited the Aegean region before the first Greek invaders arrived circa 2100 B.C. A goddess of mountains and beasts is portrayed on surviving gemstones and other artwork of the second millennium B.C. from Minoan Crete. This unnamed goddess, or series of goddesses, is shown walking with a lion and standing between rampant lions. She appears to be a deity of wilderness abundance. Presumably the conquering Greeks appropriated this regal Lady of Animals into their own RELIGION, during the second millennium B.C., changing her into Zeus' daughter. This origin would explain the Greek Artemis' ties to Crete. Artemis' virginity could have been an aspect created by the Greeks, perhaps because the original fertility-Artemis had no husband in the mythology.

Even in historical times, certain cults of Artemis emphasized fertility over virginity. The Artemis worshipped at Ephesus was a mother figure, influenced by the contemporary cult of the goddess Cybele, from interior Asia Minor. The Ephesian Artemis' cult statue, of which copies survive today, portrayed a crowned goddess with at least 20 breasts—very unlike the boyish huntress of mainland Greek religion.

Another peculiar cult existed at SPARTA. At the annual festival of Artemis Orthia (the surname's meaning is lost to us), Spartan boys endured a public ordeal of whipping as they tried to steal cheeses from the goddess' altar. This brutal rite, dating at least from the 400s B.C., had deteriorated into a tourist attraction by the days of the Roman Empire.

(See also MINOAN CIVILIZATION.)

Artemisia See HALICARNASSUS.

Artemisium Harbor and ship-beaching site on the north shore of EUBOEA, off the eastern coast of Greece, named for a local temple of the goddess ARTEMIS. The site overlooks a six-mile-wide channel whose opposite shore lies along the Magnesian peninsula of THESSALY. In this channel, during the PERSIAN WARS, the allied Greek navy first opposed the invading navy of King XERXES (summer 480 B.C.). The Battle of Artemisium was fought nearly simultaneously with the land battle of THERMOPYLAE, 40 miles away, and was part of a Greek strategy to block the Persian southward advance at two neighboring bottlenecks, on land and sea, north of central Greece. Like Thermopylae, Artemisium was a marginal Persian victory that neverthless helped to boost Greek morale.

The allied Greek fleet had about 380 warships, with the largest contingent supplied by ATHENS (180 ships). The Persian ships—which in fact were manned by subject peoples, such as Phoenicians, Egyptians, and IONIAN GREEKS—may have numbered 450 or more. This fleet recently had been reduced, from perhaps 600 ships, by storms off Thessaly.

The battle began when the Persian fleet left its base on the channel's Thessalian shore and rowed out in an enveloping crescent formation against the Greeks. In its Phoenician contingent, the Persian side had the better sailors and faster vessels, but these advantages were reduced in the chaotic press of battle.

The fight was something of an infantry battle on the water. The Persians preferred boarding tactics to ramming: They fought by bringing their ships alongside the Greeks' and sending over the thirty Persian foot soldiers who rode aboard each ship. The Greeks fought back with their own ships' soldiers, about 40 per vessel. After substantial mutual damage, the two fleets returned to their harbors. But upon receiving news of the Greek defeat at Thermopylae, the Greeks withdrew southward.

Artemisium contributed to the strategic Greek naval victory at SALAMIS (1), about three weeks later. The Artemisium losses weakened the Persian fleet and narrowed Xerxes' options for using it; he decided against sending a squadron to raid Spartan territory (which might have been successful in breaking up the Greek alliance). For the Greeks, Artemisium supplied a lesson. It probably helped convince the Greek commanders that, to offset the enemy fleet's better maneuverability, they would have to offer battle in a narrower channel than the one at Artemisium—a channel such as the one at Salamis.

In modern times, the Artemisium waters have yielded up one of the finest artworks of the ancient world: a larger-than-life BRONZE statue of the god ZEUS, from about 455 B.C. Lost with an ancient shipwreck and recovered by underwater ARCHAEOLOGY in the 1920s, the statue now stands in Athens' national museum.

(See also SCULPTURE; WARFARE, NAVAL.)

Asclepius Mythical Greek physician-hero who was eventually worshipped as a god of MEDICINE. The cult of Asclepius blossomed in the 300s B.C., partly in response to a new spirit of individualism, which sought a more personal RELIGION. Asclepius' cult was centered on his sanctuary at EPIDAURUS, in the northeastern PELOPONNESE. Sick people flocked there to acquire, for a fee, cures supposedly provided by the god.

The myth of Asclepius is told in a choral ode by the poet PINDAR, performed circa 470 B.C. At this time Asclepius was still regarded as a mortal hero who had lived and died long before. He was the son of APOLLO and the Thessalian woman Coronis, but was brought up by the centaur Chiron after Apollo destroyed Coronis for her infidelity. Medicine was one of Apollo's arts, and his son, taught by Chiron, came to excel as a physician. Unfortunately, Asclepius overstepped the boundary of human knowledge when, at the plea of the goddess ARTEMIS, he resurrected a previously dead man (HIPPOLYTUS, a favorite of Artemis'). The high god ZEUS, recognizing Asclepius' skill as a threat to natural order, immediately killed both men with a thunderbolt.

In the latter 400s B.C., Asclepius became associated with divine healing. It is unclear why he should have grown to rival his mythical father, Apollo, as patron of physicians, but in any case Asclepius began to be worshipped as a god. His cult center at Epidaurus became a shrine for invalid pilgrims, comparable to that of Lourdes, in France.

The Epidaurus cult was based on a process known as incubation, whereby a worshipper who sought a cure would spend a night in a dormitory associated with the temple, and be visited by the god in a dream. The next morning, perhaps, the god's priests would interpret the dream and dispense specific medical advice. Many existing inscriptions attest to this procedure's success, whether the explanation lies in the worshippers' autosuggestion or in pious fraud on the part of priests who might impersonate the nocturnal god. But Epidaurus and other Asclepian shrines contained genuine health-promoting facilities, such as baths and GYMNASIUMS. Major Asclepian sanctuaries, established through the Epidaurus priesthood, arose at ATHENS (420 B.C.), PERGAMUM (300s B.C.), and the Italian, non-Greek city of ROME (291 B.C.). At Rome, the god's name was latinized to Aesculapius.

Asclepius' totem was a sacred snake; a snake normally lived at each of his shrines. Greek art often portrayed the Asclepian snake as wrapped around another of the god's emblems, the physician's staff. Asclepius' snake and staff survive today as the symbol of the modern medical profession.

(See also CENTAURS; HIPPOCRATES.)

Asia   See EUROPE and ASIA.

Asia Minor   Peninsular landmass, 292,260 miles square, forming a western subcontinent of Asia. Also known as Anatolia, this territory now comprises much of Turkey. In Greek and Roman times, Asia Minor contained important Greek cities, particularly in the central west coast region called IONIA.

The name Asia Minor (lesser Asia) came into use among the Romans not long before the birth of Jesus; for the Greeks of prior centuries, the region was simply called Asia. At its northwest corner, Asia Minor is separated from the European continent by the narrow BOSPORUS and HELLESPONT waterways and the SEA OF MARMARA. The hospitable west coast—fertile, temperate, with fine harbors—opens onto the AEGEAN SEA; large inshore islands include (from north to south) LESBOS, CHIOS, SAMOS, and RHODES. Asia Minor's southern coast faces the greater Mediterranean; its north coast faces the BLACK SEA. North and south coasts give rise to steep mountains. The Pontic Range, alongside the north coast, offered TIMBER and raw metals in ancient times. The Taurus Range, in the south, intrudes on the shoreline and limits the number of harbors and habitable sites. Stretching eastward, the long Taurus chain also restricts land travel between southeast Asia Minor and northern Syria, narrowing the route to a series of mountain passes, such as the Cilician Gates, north of Tarsus. Inland of the mountains, Asia Minor is an often-arid plateau.

By the early second millennium B.C., before the first Greeks arrived, Asia Minor was controlled by the Hittites, who ruled out of the north-central interior. Probably with the Hittites' permission, Mycenaean Greeks set up trading posts along the west coast in around 1300 B.C. (as we can guess from the troves of Mycenaean POTTERY found at

MILETUS and other sites). The Greeks were looking for raw metals—copper, tin, GOLD, and SILVER, all mined in the Asia Minor interior—and for luxury goods, such as carved ivory, available through TRADE routes from Syria and Mesopotamia. The legend of the TROJAN WAR surely reflects (distortedly) the Mycenaean Greeks' destruction of an actual, non-Greek fortress town in northwest Asia Minor, a town we call TROY, which evidently was interfering with inbound Greek shipping in the Hellespont (circa 1200 B.C.).

After the Hittite Empire collapsed (circa 1200 B.C.), central Asia Minor came under control of an Asian people called the Phrygians. Their name survived in the central region, known as Phrygia. In these years the new technology of IRON-working, previously monopolized by the Hittites, spread from Asia Minor to mainland Greece (before 1050 B.C.). Greek legend claimed that the world's first ironworkers were the Chalybes, a mountain people of northeastern Asia Minor.

Asia Minor's west coast then came under steady Greek invasion, amid the migrations accompanying the downfall of Myceneaen society in mainland Greece. By 1000 B.C. Greeks of the Ionian ethnic group had settled in the region thereafter called Ionia; the foremost states here were Miletus, Samos, Chios, and EPHESUS. Greeks of the Aeolian type, using Lesbos as their base, colonized Asia Minor's northern west coast, thereafter called AEOLIS (circa 1000–600 B.C.). Greeks of Dorian ethnicity occupied sites around the southern west coast (circa 900 B.C.), including HALICARNASSUS, CNIDUS, and the islands of Cos and Rhodes. Seizing the best harbors and farmlands, the arriving Greeks ejected the non-Greek peoples. One such people were the Carians, who survived in the southwestern region called Caria.

Greek settlement spread to Asia Minor's northern and southern coasts during the great age of COLONIZATION (circa 750–550 B.C.). In the north, CYZICUS, on the Sea of Marmara, and SINOPE, midway along the Black Sea coast, were among the colonies founded by Miletus in an attempt to control the Black Sea trade route. On the south coast, the principal Greek cities were (from west to east) Phaselis, Perge, Aspendus, and Side.

The Greek settlements prospered along their sea routes and caravan routes. The cities of Ionia produced the poet HOMER (circa 750 B.C.) and the earliest Greek achievements in SCIENCE, PHILOSOPHY, and monumental ARCHITECTURE (600s–500s B.C.). But there were also non-Greek nations of the interior to contend with. The marauding Cimmerians overran Phrygia and besieged Ephesus (circa 600 B.C.). The kingdom of LYDIA dominated the west coast (by 550 B.C.) and then fell to the Persian king CYRUS (1) (546 B.C.).

By the late 500s B.C. all of Asia Minor was under the jurisdiction of the Persian king, who ruled and collected tribute through governors called satraps. The two chief satraps of western Asia Minor were based at the former Lydian capital of Sardis and at Dascylium, on the Sea of Marmara. At the end of the PERSIAN WARS, the Greek naval counteroffensive liberated most of Asia Minor's western Greek cities (479–477 B.C.). Persian puppet governments were expelled in favor of Athenian-style DEMOCRACY, and the Greek cities became tribute-paying members of the Athenian-dominated DELIAN LEAGUE. Passing to Spartan control by the end of the PELOPONNESIAN WAR (404 B.C.), these cities were ignominiously handed back to PERSIA by the terms of the KING'S PEACE (386 B.C.).

ALEXANDER THE GREAT's invasion of Asia Minor (334 B.C.) reliberated the Greek cities and brought them into a suddenly enlarged Greek world. Alexander restored local democracies and abolished tribute. After his death (323 B.C.), Asia Minor became a battleground for his warring successors. ANTIGONUS (1) ruled from his Phrygian citadel of Celanae, but upon his death at the Battle of Ipsus (in Phrygia, in 301 B.C.), Asia Minor was parceled out between LYSIMACHUS and SELEUCUS (1). Seleucus destroyed Lysimachus at the Battle of Corupedium (in Lydia, in 281 B.C.) and brought Asia Minor into the sprawling SELEUCID EMPIRE. But the emergence of the city of PERGAMUM, inland on the middle west coast, created a local rival for power (mid-200s B.C.). By the early 100s B.C., Pergamum was one of the most beautiful and prosperous Greek cities.

The Pergamene kings cooperated with the encroaching nation of ROME, and—after helping a Roman army defeat the Seleucids at the Battle of Magnesia (189 B.C.)—Pergamum obtained control of most of Asia Minor. The entire region passed into Roman hands with the death of the last Pergamene king (133 B.C.). Later the non-Greek kingdom of Pontus arose against Roman authority.

(See also AEOLIAN GREEKS; BRONZE; DIADOCHI; DORIAN GREEKS; HELLENISTIC AGE; IONIAN GREEKS; MYCENAEAN CIVILIZATION.)

Aspasia   Common-law wife of the Athenian statesman PERICLES. After divorcing his legal wife, Pericles lived with Aspasia from about 450 B.C. until his death in 429 B.C.

Aspasia was an immigrant from MILETUS and thus was a resident alien at ATHENS. Pericles, being an Athenian citizen, was prohibited from marrying her (according to a law of 451 B.C., which he himself had sponsored). Historians traditionally have theorized that Aspasia was either herself a prostitute (*hetaira*) or that she at least managed a "house" of *hetairai*, but some modern scholars dismiss this information as being a daring joke of Athenian stage comedy. Contemporary comic playwrights such as CRATINUS, EUPOLIS, and ARISTOPHANES made vicious public fun of Pericles' liaison with Aspasia.

Witty and well educated, Aspasia seems to have had a captivating personality. She is said to have given lessons in RHETORIC, and the Athenian philosopher SOCRATES supposedly enjoyed conversing with her.

The 430s B.C. at Athens saw a rash of politically motivated prosecutions indirectly aimed at Pericles; the immediate targets included Aspasia and Pericles' friends PHIDIAS and ANAXAGORAS. Aspasia was accused of impiety (*asebeia*)—a common charge against intellectuals—and she also may have been accused of procuring freeborn Athenian ladies for Pericles' pleasure. At trial she was acquitted after Pericles made a personal appeal to the jurors, during which he uncharacteristically burst into tears.

She and Pericles had a son, also named Pericles. Although ineligible for Athenian citizenship because his mother was alien, the younger Pericles was enrolled as a citizen at his dying father's request, circa 429 B.C. In 406 B.C. the younger Pericles was one of six Athenian generals executed by public order for failing to rescue Athenian

survivors after the sea battle of Arginusae, during the PELOPONNESIAN WAR.

Aspasia provides an example of the kind of success that an ambitious woman might find in a society that excluded WOMEN from power and wealth. Although further disadvantaged by being alien, she achieved a degree of influence and security by attaching herself to a powerful man.

(See also EDUCATION; MARRIAGE; METICS; PROSTITUTES.)

assembly   The word used to translate the Greek word *ekklēsia*—the official gathering of citizens in a Greek DEMOCRACY for the purpose of public debate and vote. At democratic ATHENS in the 400s and 300s B.C., the assembly was the sovereign body of government.

Admission to the Athenian assembly was open to all male citizens over age 18 (in theory about 30,000–40,000 men; in practice about 5,000). Under the radical democracy there were no property requirements for admission, and the 300s B.C. saw the introduction of a small payment for attendance, comparable to our modern jury pay.

The Athenian assembly met at least 40 times per year, with extra meetings as called for by the COUNCIL or by the board of generals. In the 400s B.C. the usual place of meeting was the Pnyx ("Packing Place"), a smoothened hillside west of the ACROPOLIS. There the people might vote on issues by show of hands; if written balloting was required—such as in an OSTRACISM vote—then the AGORA would be used. In debate, any Athenian had the right to address the assembly; a chairman of the day presided; and rules of order were maintained. Foreign ambassadors and other noncitizens might be allowed to address the assembly on issues of state.

Usually the assembly could debate and vote only on those topics placed on the agenda by the council; however, the assembly could (by vote) require the council to list a certain topic for the next meeting. Like other instruments of Athenian government, the assembly enjoyed courtroom powers. For example, it had the final verdict in certain serious criminal cases. By its vote the assembly passed laws, declared war, made peace, inflicted individual sentences of death or exile, and elected the army's generals and other important executives. The power of the assembly during Athens' imperial heyday can be seen in the Mytilenean Debate—described in THUCYDIDES' (1) history of the PELOPONNESIAN WAR (book 3)—where the fate of every man, woman, and child of the rebellious city of MYTILENE was decided in public debate at Athens in 427 B.C.

astronomy   The ancient Greeks pioneered the study of astronomy in the Western world, cataloguing the stars and identifying five of the planets (besides the earth). Most important, they developed several geometric models that tried to explain the movements of the heavenly bodies in terms of concentric spheres and other orbital paths. Unfortunately, the Greeks incorrectly placed earth at the center of the universe. This geocentric theory was brought to a false perfection by Ptolemy of ALEXANDRIA (1), circa A.D. 135; with Ptolemy's revisions, the geocentric model seemed to account for all heavenly motion observable to the unaided eye. (The Greeks possessed no telescopic lenses, only crude sighting devices.)

Ptolemy's system was so persuasive that it remained canonical in late antiquity and the Middle Ages, before it was finally ousted in A.D. 1543 by Copernicus' heliocentric model, which correctly placed the sun at the center of the solar system. Ironically, the ancient Greek astronomer Aristarchus of SAMOS (circa 275 B.C.) had produced a simple heliocentric model, but this had been bypassed in favor of the more apparently promising geocentric one.

Like other ancient peoples lacking precise calendars, the earliest Greeks relied on the rising and setting of the constellations in order to gauge the FARMING year. The poet HESIOD's versified farming almanac, *Works and Days* (circa 700 B.C.) mentions certain duties as signaled by the stars—for instance, grapes are to be picked when the constellation ORION has risen to a position overhead, in early autumn.

In the verses of HOMER (circa 750 B.C.) and other early poets, the earth is imagined as a disk surrounded by the stream of Ocean (*Okeanos*). The early philosopher-scientist THALES of MILETUS (circa 585 B.C.) elaborated on this concept, picturing a world that floats like a log on a cosmic lake of water. Thales' successor ANAXIMADER (circa 560 B.C.) devised the first, crude astronomical theory; he saw the world as a cylinder or disk suspended in space, with the cylinder's flat top constituting the inhabited world and the visible sky comprised of a series of fitted rings forming a hemisphere. The sun, moon, and stars are holes in these rings, through which we glimpse a distant celestial fire.

An obvious weakness of Anaximander's theory is its inability to explain the puzzling movements of the planets. The five planets known to the Greeks were Mercury, Venus, Mars, Jupiter, and Saturn (to use modern names). To the naked eye they look like bright stars, but their individual, looping progress through the night skies earned them the Greek name *planētai*, or "wanderers."

The planets' movements were first plausibly explained by the brilliant mathematician Eudoxus of CNIDUS, who was a student of PLATO at the ACADEMY at ATHENS (circa 350 B.C.). Eudoxus held that all heavenly movements are caused by the circular rotations of 27 concentric spheres, with the earth at their center. All of the proper stars exist on the single, outermost sphere (according to Eudoxus), but each planet employs no fewer than four concentric spheres, which spin along different axes to produce the planet's irregular course. Similarly, sun and moon are governed by three spheres each. Greater precision seemed to be achieved when more spheres were added by Eudoxus' younger contemporary Callipus of CYZICUS and by the great ARISTOTLE (both circa 330 B.C.).

Another astronomer of this Athenian intellectual heyday was Heraclides Ponticus (like Eudoxus, a younger associate of Plato at the Academy). Using the geocentric model, Heraclides suggested that the earth itself rotates on its axis. All of these thinkers approached astronomy as a challenge in geometry, not physics; there seem to have been no theories regarding what mechanical forces would cause the spheres to move. Understandably, the Greeks had no knowledge of astrophysics; topics such as gravity or the chemical compositions of stars were largely unexplored.

Aristarchus of Samos was a follower of the Aristotelian Peripatetic School at Athens, circa 275 B.C. Rejecting the

Eudoxan model, Aristarchus invented the heliocentric theory, which correctly posited that the earth and planets revolve around the sun and that the earth spins on an axis. Like prior astronomers, Aristarchus imagined the stars as spread along a vast outer sphere—but thought that this sphere was stationary. He also correctly believed that the stars' apparent movement is an illusion created by the earth's orbit. Few of Aristarchus' writings survive, and we know of his theory mainly from later authors.

This heliocentric theory was not accepted in antiquity for two reasons. First, it ran counter to prevailing religious-philosophical beliefs by removing humankind from the center of creation. Second, it failed to account satisfactorily for the absence of stellar parallax—in other words, if the earth moves through space, then the stars should be seen to slide sideways in their progress overhead, which they do not seem to do. (In fact, the stars do shift their angles minutely as the earth orbits past, but their immense distance from the earth makes this variation invisible to the naked eye.)

The next great name in Greek astronomy is Apollonius of Pergē (a Greek town in southern ASIA MINOR), who was active at Alexandria circa 200 B.C. A mathematical genius, Apollonius revolutionized the geocentric theory by abandoning Eudoxus' cumbersome spheres in favor of two different models explaining celestial movement in terms of irregular orbits called eccentrics and epicycles. For example, the epicyclical theory imagined a planet shooting around in a small circle while at the same time orbiting in a much larger circle around the earth.

One of antiquity's few practical astronomers was Hipparchus of Nicaea (a Greek city in western Asia Minor). Active at RHODES circa 135 B.C., Hipparchus invented or improved the sighting device known as the dioptra, and was the first to map and catalogue approximately 850 stars.

The work of Apollonius and Hipparchus laid the groundwork for the greatest astronomer of the ancient world, Claudius Ptolemaeus, usually known as Ptolemy (but not a member of the Macedonian-Egyptian royal dynasty that used that name). A Greek-blooded Roman citizen of Alexandria, Ptolemy was active circa A.D. 127–140, under the Roman Empire. His written masterpiece was the *Almagest*, which has survived in medieval Arabic translation. (That title is the Arabic form for the unofficial Greek title *Megistē*, "the greatest," i.e. textbook.) In 13 books, the *Almagest* presented the sum total of astronomical knowledge of the day, as enlarged by Ptolemy's own work on the geocentric model. Aided by his pioneering use of the sighting device known as the armillary astrolabe (the forerunner of the medieval astrolabe), Ptolemy also enlarged Hipparchus' star map, among his many other achievements.

(See also ARATUS (2); MATHEMATICS; OCEANUS; PYTHAGORAS.)

Astyanax   See ANDROMACHE; HECTOR.

Atalanta   In MYTH, an Arcadian or Boeotian heroine of the athletic, forest-ranging, virginal type (in the pattern of the goddess ARTEMIS and of the AMAZONS). Beloved by the hero Meleager, Atalanta joined him in the CALYDONIAN BOAR HUNT. But the best-known legend about Atalanta concerns her MARRIAGE. Unwilling to be wed, she declared that she would submit only to the man who could beat her in a footrace. According to one version, she would follow the racing suitor with a spear and stab him as she overtook him. She was finally won by a suitor named Melanion (or Hippomenes) who, with the goddess APHRODITE's help, had acquired three golden apples. During the race he dropped these treasures one by one in Atalanta's way; pausing to acquire them, she lost the contest. Their son was named Parthenopaeus ("born of the virgin").

Athena (often Athene) Important Greek goddess, guardian of the city of ATHENS—whose name she shared—and patron of wisdom, handicraft, and the disciplined aspect of war. Athena was worshipped on the ACROPOLIS at several Greek cities, including ARGOS and SPARTA. But her most significant shrine was on the Athenian acropolis, where a succession of temples culminated, in 438 B.C., in the building that is the gem of ancient ARCHITECTURE: the PARTHENON, or Temple of Athena the Virgin.

The name Athena, like the name Athens, is not actually Greek; the ending -na belongs to the language of the non-Greek people who preceded the Greeks as the inhabitants of mainland Greece. In her pre-Greek form, Athena was probably a patron deity of kings, whose hilltop palaces she

The head of Athena, from a Roman marble bust copied from a classical Greek work. Scholars dispute whether this head portrays the famous Lemnian Athena—a bronze statue by the great Athenian sculptor Phidias, circa 440 B.C. Regardless, the face conveys the sternness and intelligence of the goddess of wisdom, handicraft, and military strategy.

guarded as an idol shown clad in armor; in her ultimate origins she may be related to armed goddesses of the ancient Near East, such as the Mesopotamian Ishtar. After about 2100 B.C., when ethnic Greek invaders began taking over the land of Greece, Athena became incorporated into the developing Greek RELIGION (as did other pre-Greek goddesses, including HERA and ARTEMIS). Keeping her armor and her association with the hilltop, Athena entered Greek MYTH as the daughter of the great god ZEUS. This transition was under way by the Mycenaean era (1600–1200 B.C.), as is suggested by the mention of a "Lady of Atana" on a surviving Mycenaean clay tablet, inscribed in LINEAR B script and dated by archaeologists to 1400 B.C.

The charming myth of Athena's birth from the head of Zeus is told by the poets HESIOD (circa 700 B.C.) and PINDAR (467 B.C.). It seems that Zeus swallowed his first wife, Metis, when she was pregnant. He did this because a prophecy had warned him that Metis would otherwise bear a son destined to depose his father. But Zeus soon felt a terrible headache. And when the smith god HEPHAESTUS helpfully split open Zeus' skull, the goddess Athena sprang out—adult, in full armor, giving a war shout. This tale surely contains a primitive religious-political motive: namely, it shows absolutely that the goddess is Zeus' daughter and hence subordinate to him. The story also symbolizes how Zeus and Athena both partake of cleverness (Greek: *mētis*). The birth scene is a favorite subject on surviving Greek vase paintings from the 600s B.C. onward.

As goddess of organizational wisdom, Athena was thought to guide the typical Greek city-state (not only Athens). Her cult titles included Boulaia, "goddess of the COUNCIL," and Polias, "goddess of the city." In these functions she resembled Zeus, who was god of cosmic order and whose titles included Poleios, "lord of the city." In later centuries she naturally became associated with the academic wisdom of PHILOSOPHY.

As a protector of civilized Greek life, Athena was prominent in myths of order versus chaos. She was imagined as fighting gallantly in the gods' primeval war against the rebellious GIANTS: A famous section of the Great Altar of PERGAMUM, sculpted circa 180 B.C. and now in Berlin, shows Athena hauling the subdued Giant leader, Alcyoneus, by his hair. In other myths she repeatedly appears as a counselor to heroes struggling against monsters and villains: She helps HERACLES with his Twelve Labors, ODYSSEUS with his homecoming, and PERSEUS (1) with the killing of MEDUSA.

As a war goddess, Athena overlapped with the war god ARES. But where the brutal Ares embodied war's madness and waste, Athena tended to represent the more glorious aspects—strategy, discipline, national defense. She was said to have introduced such military inventions as the ship, the horse bridle, and the war chariot. In HOMER's epic poem the *Iliad* (written down circa 750 B.C.), she is the Greeks' staunch ally against the Trojans: She accompanies her Greeks into battle; intervenes to aid her favorite, DIOMEDES; and, in the poem's climactic section, helps ACHILLES to slay the Trojan HECTOR. Yet early in the poem she restrains Achilles from an act of violence against the Greek commander, AGAMEMNON, for she is also a deity of reason and control.

In poetry and art, Athena's war gear includes a breast-plate, helmet, spear, and shield of some sort. Sometimes her shield is the supernatural aegis (*aigis*), associated also with Zeus. Homer describes the aegis as a fearsome storm cloud, but by the mid-600s B.C. vase painters were picturing it as a goatskin mantle on Athena's left arm, tassled with live snakes and showing the vanquished Medusa's face. Later the aegis became styled as a round metal shield, embossed with Medusa's image.

Among peaceful duties, Athena was said to have invented weaving, spinning, and other domestic crafts performed by WOMEN in the ancient Greek world. She was also the patron of carpenters, potters, and (like the god Hephaestus) of metalworkers. Her relevant title was Erganē, "worker woman."

The Athenians credited her with introducing the cultivation of the olive, a staple of the ancient Greek diet and economy. Legend said that Athena and the god POSEIDON had competed publicly over who would become the Athenians' patron deity. Poseidon stabbed his trident into the acropolis summit, bringing forth a saltwater well; but alongside it Athena planted the first olive tree, and so was judged the winner by the people. The saltwater well and sacred olive tree were features of the Athenian acropolis in historical times.

Athena was pictured as stately and beautiful, although stern. In Homer's verses, Zeus calls her by the fond nickname *glaukopis*, "gray eyes" or "bright eyes." Her virginity—a trait she had in common with the goddesses Artemis and HESTIA—may perhaps harken back to her primeval form as a defender of the citadel: She is inviolate, like the fortress that she oversees. Her famous Athenian cult title was Parthenos, "the virgin," and her very old title Pallas was likewise understood as meaning "virgin." In myth, the Palladium (Palladion) was an image of Athena, sent down from heaven and worshipped by the Trojans.

By the late 400s B.C. Athena had two sanctuaries atop the Athenian acropolis. One was the Parthenon, housing a 35-foot-tall, GOLD-and-ivory statue of Athena Parthenos; the other was the Erectheum, housing a smaller, immemorably old, olivewood statue of Athena Polias. This simple wooden idol was revered at the midsummer festival of the Panathenaea ("all Athens")—considered to be Athena's birthday—when the people ceremoniously brought a new woolen gown (*peplos*) up to the goddess. An especially large celebration, held every fourth year, was called a Great Panathenaea. At another festival, in early summer, the Polias statue was carried down to the sea to be washed.

The Greeks identified their gods with certain animals; Athena was associated with snakes and, particularly, owls. Folklore claimed that owls were wise, like their goddess. Modern scholars believe that Athena's links with the owl, snake, and olive tree were all survivals of her primitive, pre-Greek cult, dating back to the third millennium B.C.

(See also FARMING; MINOAN CIVILIZATION; PARIS; PHIDIAS.)

Athenian democracy See DEMOCRACY.

Athens Foremost city of ancient Greece, and one of the three most important ancient cities that shaped Western

civilization, along with ROME and Jerusalem. The culture produced by the rich and confident Athens of the mid-400s B.C.—in THEATER, ARCHITECTURE, SCULPTURE, and PHILOSOPHY—provides a cornerstone of our modern society. Most important, Athens was the birthplace of DEMOCRACY (*dēmokratia*, "power by the people").

The physical city, beautified by the wealth of empire, was a marvel to the ancient world—as it is today for the tourists and scholars who visit Athens (now the modern Greek capital). With some justification the Athenian statesman PERICLES described his city as "the greatest name in history . . . a power to be remembered forever." Defeat in the PELOPONNESIAN WAR (431–404 B.C.) broke Athens' imperial might, but the city remained politically important for the next century and culturally influential for the rest of antiquity.

An advantageous site helped make the city great. Located in southeast-central Greece, in the peninsular landmass called ATTICA, Athens lies amid the region's largest plain, where grain and olives were grown in historical times. The site's specific attraction was a 300-foot-tall, rock-formed hill (later known as the ACROPOLIS). This defensible position dominated the plain and, being four miles inland of the Saronic Gulf, gave access to the sea without inviting naval attack.

The locale was inhabited long before the first Greek-speaking tribesmen arrived circa 2000 B.C.: Archaeological excavations at Athens have yielded artifacts datable prior to 3000 B.C. The name Athens (Athenai) is pre-Greek and is associated with the city's patron goddess, ATHENA, who is likewise pre-Greek. Evidently the early Greek invaders appropriated these two related names (whose original meanings are lost to us). During the flourishing Greek MYCENAEAN CIVILIZATION (1600–1200 B.C.), Athens was a second-rank power—overshadowed by MYCENAE, THEBES, and other centers.

Greek MYTH claims that the unification of Attica under Athenian control was brought about by the Athenian king THESEUS. This legend probably recalls a real-life event of the late Mycenaean era. In later centuries this unification (*sunoikismos*, "synoecism") was celebrated at an annual Athenian festival called the Sunoikia. Among the resources of the Attic countryside that then passed to Athenian control were the fertile plain of Eleusis, the marble of Mt. Pentelicus, and, most important, the raw SILVER of Mt. Laurium. In a later era, Laurium silver would provide the Athenian COINAGE and help finance the social and military programs of the democracy.

A united Attica was able to resist the invading DORIAN GREEKS who swept southward through Greece after the collapse of Mycenaean society (circa 1100 B.C.). Legend tells how the last Athenian king, Codrus, sacrificed his life to save Athens from Dorian capture. Other legends describe Athens as a rallying point for Greek refugees whose homes in the PELOPONNESE had been overrun by the Dorians. These refugees, of the Ionian ethnic group, migrated eastward to establish cities on the ASIA MINOR coast that in later centuries retained cultural and political ties to Athens.

Following the depressed years of the DARK AGE (1100–900 B.C.), Athens emerged as a mainland commercial power, alongside CORINTH, CHALCIS, and a few other cities. In the

800s–700s B.C., Athenian workshops produced a widely admired Geometric-style POTTERY eventually imitated throughout Greece. At Athens, as at other prosperous Greek cities, there arose a monied middle class—mainly manufacturers and farmers—who resented being excluded from political power.

Like other Greek states, Athens at this time was governed as an ARISTOCRACY. A small circle of noble families monopolized the government and judiciary and owned most of the land. The general population was unrepresented, its political function being mainly to pay taxes, serve under arms, and obey the leaders' decrees. The emergence of democracy involved a drastic revamping of Athens' government in the 500s and 400s B.C., to the point where the citizens' ASSEMBLY comprised the sovereign, decision-making body.

This process required improvization, compromise, and bloodshed. In about 632 B.C. an adventuring nobleman named CYLON tried to exploit middle-class unrest to make himself tyrant of Athens, but the coup failed. Popular demand for a permanent, written law code was left unsatisfied by the aristocratically biased legislation of DRACO (circa 624 B.C.), but SOLON's radical reforms (circa 594 B.C.) averted revolution and laid the foundations for Athenian democracy. In foreign affairs, Athens defeated its nearby rival MEGARA (1) for control of the island of SALAMIS (1). Athenian COLONIZATION in the HELLESPONT district—at Sigeum and the CHERSONESE—foreshadowed Athens' imperial control of that region in future years.

Despite Solon's legislation, class tensions remained keen enough for PISISTRATUS to seize power as tyrant (mid-500s B.C.). Under his enlightened rule, Athens advanced commercially and artistically. Supplanting Corinth as the foremost mainland mercantile power, Athens monopolized the pottery market, exporting Athenian black-figure ware throughout the Mediterranean. Athens became a cultural center, as Pisistratus and his son and successor, HIPPIAS (1), attracted poets, sculptors, and other craftsmen from throughout the Greek world.

The expulsion of Hippias in 510 B.C. brought on the birth of democracy. The reforms of CLEISTHENES (1) (508 B.C.) broke the aristocracy's residual influence by means of administrative changes based on the redivision of the population into 10 new tribes. A citizens' COUNCIL of 500 became the guide and executive for the popular assembly, which in practice numbered about 5,000 men. The assembly held regular meetings in the Pnyx ("packing place"), a hollowed-out hillside about 500 yards west of the acropolis. In around 507 B.C. the Athenians repulsed an attack by the Spartan king CLEOMENES (1) that was aimed at dismantling the fledgling democracy. The optimism of the following years helped the Athenians to repel a Persian invasion force at the Battle of MARATHON, outside Athens (490 B.C.).

By 500 B.C., the physical city had begun to take on its classical layout. Probably by then a surrounding wall had been built (although only later walls have survived in remnants). Atop the acropolis, which was sacred to Athena and the other gods, old temples of wood or limestone were being replaced by marble structures. At the acropolis' southeast base stood an open-air THEATER dedicated to the god DIONYSUS, where performances of the newborn

The goddess Athena mourns, in an Athenian marble bas-relief, probably a funerary stone, circa 460 B.C. The short column at the lower right may represent a list of Athenian war dead. Showing all the grace and simplicity of the Early Classical style, this 21-inch-tall carving dates from the height of the Athenian Empire, when an overconfident Athens was leading its Delian League allies against the Persians in Cyprus and Egypt, and—closer to home—against the Spartans, Corinthians, Boeotians, and other Greeks. Eventually Athenian aggression would bring on the start of the Peloponnesian War (431 B.C.).

Athenian art-forms of tragedy and comedy were held. Northwest of the acropolis lay the AGORA—the city's commercial center. Some distance northwest of the agora, beyond the Dipylon Gate, stood an industrial suburb, the Ceramicus (*Keiramikos*, or "potters' quarter"), at the outer edge of which lay the aristocratic families' elaborate graveyards, still visible today.

Under leadership of the left-wing statesman THEMIS-TOCLES, the Athenians developed PIRAEUS as a seaport and amassed the biggest navy in Greece, 200 warships. This navy played a paramount role in defending Greece against the invasion of the Persian king XERXES (480 B.C.). Athens was evacuated before the advancing Persians—who burned and sacked the empty city twice, in 480 and 479 B.C.—but the Athenians fought on in their warships and helped destroy the Persian navy at the sea battle of Salamis.

The defeat of Xerxes' invasion created an outpouring of confidence—and an influx of money—that made Athens into the cultural capital of the Greek world. First the city wall, torn down by the Persians, was rebuilt and enlarged, despite Spartan objections (479 B.C.); remnants of this four-mile-long "Themistoclean Wall" survive today. In the Greek naval counteroffensive against Persian territories, Athens now took the lead, organizing the Greek city-states of the AEGEAN SEA and the Asia Minor coast into an Athenian-controlled coalition, the DELIAN LEAGUE (478 or 477 B.C.). The league's most prominent officer was the conservative Athenian statesman CIMON. Delian member states paid dues—in the form of silver or military service—which in time came to be used strictly for Athens' advantage.

Athenian aggressions in mainland Greece—against AE-GINA, BOEOTIA, PHOCIS, and Corinth—brought Athens into intermittent conflict with those states' powerful ally, Sparta (459–446 B.C.). Meanwhile the left-wing statesman Pericles became heir to Themistocles' policies of sea empire and resistance to Sparta. Pericles tightened Athens' control over the Delian allies, and he built the LONG WALLS, connecting Athens to its naval base at Piraeus in a continuous fortification (461–456 B.C.). After arranging peace with PERSIA, he initiated a building program (448 B.C.) to replace the temples destroyed in 480–479 B.C. This program, supervised by the sculptor PHIDIAS, turned Athens into the grandest city of the Greek world. Among the famous constructions still standing today are the PARTHENON, Propylaea, Erectheum, and Temple of Athena Nikē (all on the acropolis), and the admirably preserved temple of the god HEPH-AESTUS in the agora.

The middle and late 400s B.C. saw the Athenian high noon. The tragic playwrights AESCHYLUS, SOPHOCLES, and EURIPIDES, the painter Polygnotus, the intellectual movement of the SOPHISTS, the comic playwright ARISTOPHANES, the historian THUCYDIDES (1), and the West's first great ethical philosopher, SOCRATES, all lived in Athens during these years. From other Greek cities craftsmen, poets, and businessmen flocked to Athens, swelling Attica's population to over 200,000 (including SLAVES) and making the city fully dependent on imports of Ukrainian grain, supplied by Pericles' far-reaching naval program.

Fear of Athenian expansionism led Sparta, Corinth, and Boeotia to start the Peloponnesian War (as we call it), in 431 B.C. Despite the outbreak of plague (430 B.C. and later), the Athenian navy and maritime network could have brought the city safely through the conflict, had the citizens not wasted lives and resources in a vainglorious attempt to conquer SYRACUSE, in Greek SICILY (415–413 B.C.). This calamitous defeat threw Athens on the defensive, while the Spartans, with the help of Persian money, were able to develop a navy, subvert Athens' Delian allies, and attack the Athenian lifeline in the Hellespont. With their fleet destroyed (405 B.C.), the Athenians surrendered after an eight-month siege (404 B.C.). The victorious Spartans pulled down the Long Walls. Despite urgings from the Thebans and Corinthians to destroy Athens, the Spartans spared the city, installing the short-lived dictatorship of the THIRTY TYRANTS .

Athens quickly recovered, joining another war against Sparta (395–387 B.C.) and organizing another maritime coalition, the SECOND ATHENIAN LEAGUE (377 B.C.). In spite of the eloquent harangues of the statesman DEMOSTHENES (1), the Athenians proved ineffectual against the military-diplomatic campaigns of King PHILIP II of MACEDON. After sharing in the defeat at CHAERONEA (338 B.C.), Athens received lenient treatment as Philip's subject city; the league, however, was disbanded. Athens revolted against Macedonian rule after the death of ALEXANDER THE GREAT (323 B.C.), but defeat brought an end to Athens' foreign policy ambitions, and a Macedonian garrison was then installed at Piraeus (322 B.C.). Under the Macedonian king CASSANDER, Athens was governed by the enlightened Demetrius of Phalerum (317–307 B.C.). Liberated by the warrior prince DEMETRIUS POLIORCETES, Athens reverted periodically to Macedonian control, until the coming of ROME broke Macedon's power (167 B.C.).

The 300s B.C. marked the greatest days of Athenian philosophy, starting with the establishment of PLATO's school of higher learning, the ACADEMY (circa 385 B.C.). In 335 B.C. Plato's former pupil ARISTOTLE opened a rival school, the LYCEUM. Among other influential philosophical movements to emerge at that time at Athens were EPICURE-ANISM (circa 307 B.C.) and STOICISM (circa 300 B.C.). Athens still retained a foremost position in the arts, producing, among other talents, the sculptor PRAXITELES (circa 350 B.C.) and the playwright MENANDER (circa 300 B.C.).

But Athens' creative output had begun to diminish by the early 200s B.C., as the HELLENISTIC AGE produced new centers of wealth and patronage, such as ALEXANDRIA (1). Under Roman rule, Athens remained a prestigious center of EDUCATION.

(See also CORINTHIAN WAR; PAINTING; PERSIAN WARS; POLIS; TRADE; TYRANTS.)

Atlantis The legend of Atlantis ("island in the Atlantic") first appears in two dialogues, the *Timaeus* and the *Critias*, written circa 355 B.C. by the Athenian philosopher PLATO. Plato describes Atlantis as a vast, wealthy island or continent that used to exist, 9,000 years earlier, in the Atlantic Ocean. This domain was an ideal society, inhabited by an advanced and virtuous people who conquered eastward to Europe and Africa. But their greed for power grew, until the angry gods sent a deluge to submerge the island.

Despite our modern-day fascination with this legend, it seems clear that Atlantis never existed as described. Plato probably made up the tale as a parable of self-destructive pride. Or, Plato's story may possibly record some 1,100-year-old folktale telling of the decline of MINOAN CIVILIZA-TION in the Aegean region. ARCHAEOLOGY indicates that in around 1480 B.C. the mighty island of CRETE was devastated by earthquakes and tidal waves. Plato's Atlantis may be a disturted memory of Crete's downfall, projected beyond the Mediterranean world.

(See also HUBRIS; THERA.)

Atlas In MYTH, one of the TITANS (the race of demigods that ruled the universe before the emergence of the Olympian gods). After the Titans' overthrow by the gods, Atlas was condemned by ZEUS to hold up the sky on his shoulders for eternity. The Greeks associated Atlas with the far West. By the mid-400s B.C. he was identified with the Atlas mountain range in North Africa, and his name had been given to the Atlantic Ocean (Greek Atlantikos, "of Atlas").

Atlas was said to be the father of the HESPERIDES (daughters of Evening), who tended the fabled garden in the West where golden apples grew. When the hero HERACLES arrived to fetch a few such apples for his twelfth Labor, Atlas offered to get them for him if he would kindly support the sky in the meantime. Returning with three golden apples, Atlas intended to leave Heracles holding up the celestial canopy, but Heracles was able to trick Atlas into resuming his assigned burden. The incident is portrayed on a famous marble carving from the temple of ZEUS at OLYMPIA.

(See also OLYMPUS, MT.)

Atreus Mythical king of MYCENAE. Atreus was the father of the heroes AGAMEMNON and MENELAUS, who in poetry are often referred to as the Atridae (Atreidai), the sons of Atreus.

Atreus and his brother Thyestes labored under a hereditary curse received by their father, PELOPS. The events of their own lives perpetuated this curse. Thyestes offended Atreus by seducing his wife and stealing a golden ram, a token of the kingship. Atreus banished his brother, but then, pretending to be reconciled, invited him to a banquet. At the feast, Atreus treacherously served the cooked flesh of Thyestes' own children, which the unwitting guest ate. Upon realizing the horror, Thyestes invoked a curse on his brother and departed. This curse was fulfilled when Thyestes' surviving son Aegisthus helped murder Agamemnon after the latter's return from the TROJAN WAR. The banquet of Atreus and Thyestes was a favorite reference in later Greek and Roman poetry. The Roman statesman-

philosopher Seneca (circa A.D. 60) wrote a tragedy *Thyestes*, presenting the monstrous events onstage.

(See also CLYTAEMNESTRA; ORESTES.)

Attalus See PERGAMUM.

Attica Territory of ATHENS. Named perhaps from the Greek word *aktē*, "promontory," Attica is a triangular peninsula in southeast-central Greece, extending southward into the AEGEAN SEA. The peninsula's neck is bordered by BOEOTIA (to the north and northwest) and by the territory of MEGARA (1) (to the northwest). Attica's western sea is the Saronic Gulf, containing the islands SALAMIS (1) and AEGINA, among others.

With 1,000 square miles, Attica is about half the size of Massachusetts. The mountainous terrain reaches four separate peaks: Mt. Hymettus in the southwest (near Athens); Mt. Pentelicus halfway up the east coast; Mt. Parnes in the north-central area; and Mt. Laurium at the southern tip.

Attica's natural resources played vital roles in making Athens a major commercial power, starting in the 500s B.C.; particularly significant was the SILVER mined at Laurium. An admired marble was quarried at Pentelicus and Hymettus, and the superior clay in the Attic soil was obviously important for Athens' domination of the Greek POTTERY market in the 800s–700s and 500s–400s B.C..

The mountains and hills of Attica enclose four discrete farming plains, which from prehistoric times determined the groupings of settlement. There is (1) the large plain of Athens, (2) the southern plain of the Mesogeia ("midland"), (3) the small northeastern flatlands of MARATHON and Aphidna, and (4) the one truly fertile plain, at Eleusis in the west. The prominence of Eleusis as a food source is reflected in the ancient, state-run ELEUSINIAN MYSTERIES, which celebrated the goddess DEMETER's gift of grain to humankind. Other crops grown in the rather thin Attic soil included vines, figs, and olives.

Among other important locales was Sunium, at Attica's southern tip, where a famous temple to Poseidon was built in the 440s B.C..

(See also ATHENA; CLEISTHENES (1); DEME; DEMOCRACY; PELOPONNESIAN WAR; PERSIAN WARS; PIRAEUS; THESEUS.)

B

Bacchae See EURIPIDES; MAENADS.

Bacchus See DIONYSUS.

Bacchylides Greek lyric poet from the island of Ceos, circa 520–450 B.C. His work survives mainly in the form of 20 choral poems—14 victory odes and six dithyrambs—discovered in an Egyptian papyrus in A.D. 1896. He is known to have written many other verses for choruses, including hymns that survive in a few fragments. Despite his lack of genius, Bacchylides showed genuine artistic virtues, including clarity of expression and a talent for narrative.

Bacchylides was the nephew (sister's son) and protégé of the famous poet SIMONIDES, and it was to Simonides' sponsorship that Bacchylides owed much of his worldly success. He seems to have followed his uncle's footsteps from early on and to have been employed by some of the same patrons. Like Simonides, Bacchylides wrote dithyrambs for poetry competitions at ATHENS. (The dithyramb, a precursor of Athenian stage tragedy, was a narrative poem on a mythological subject; it was sung in public performance by a chorus, one of whose members would take on a solo role in character.) Two of Bacchylides' extant dithyrambs present imaginative episodes from the life of the Athenian hero THESEUS. In around 476 B.C., Bacchylides accompanied the 80-year-old Simonides to the court of HIERON (1), ruler of the Sicilian-Greek city of SYRACUSE. There Bacchylides and Simonides are said to have been engaged in an unfriendly rivalry with the Theban poet PINDAR, who was visiting Sicily in those years and was probably close to Bacchylides' age.

Bacchylides and Pindar both composed victory odes for Hieron. Hieron's victory in the horserace at the OLYMPIC GAMES (476 B.C.) is commemorated in Bacchylides' Ode 5 as well as in Pindar's Olympian Ode 1; similarly, Hieron's victory in the chariot race at the PYTHIAN GAMES (470 B.C.) produced Bacchylides' Ode 4 and Pindar's Pythian 1. But when Hieron won his coveted Olympic chariot victory in 468 B.C., it was Bacchylides, not Pindar, who was assigned to write the celebratory ode.

This poem, Ode 3, is Bacchylides' most successful work. It addresses a rich dictator who, although at his peak of prestige, was in failing health, with only a year to live. The poem is full of sad reminders of human transience, couched in terms that are lovely despite being wholly conventional: *Life is short and troubled*, the poet says, in essence, *and hope is treacherous. Be ready for death tomorrow or 50 years hence. The best a mortal man can do is worship the gods and live a good life.* The poem is spun around the central legend of the Lydian king CROESUS, who fell from wealth and power to defeat, before being saved by the god APOLLO. The ode's consolation in the face of death and its muted warning against the sin of pride may have proved poignant to Hieron. In closing, the poet refers to himself as "the nightingale of Ceos"—a charmingly modest and apt self-description.

(See also HUBRIS; LYRIC POETRY; THEATER.)

Bactria Corresponding roughly to what is now northern Afghanistan, Bactria was an important province of the Persian Empire in the mid-500s to mid-300s B.C. In 330 B.C. the region was captured by the Macedonian king ALEXANDER THE GREAT, during his conquest of the Persian domain. Bactria's significance for Greek history is that, after being assigned heavy settlements of Alexander's veteran soldiers, the region developed into a far-eastern enclave of Greek culture.

Following Alexander's death (323 B.C.), Bactria passed into the east Greek SELEUCID EMPIRE, but by 255 B.C. it had revolted under a leader named Diodotus, who became its first king. Prospering from its central Asian TRADE routes, this Greek kingdom lasted for over a century and enveloped what is now southern Afghanistan, western Pakistan, southern Uzbekistan, and southeastern Turkmenistan. The Bactrian kings—of which there seem eventually to have been two rival dynasties, reigning out of different capitals—minted a superb COINAGE, stamped with royal portraits. Today surviving Bactrian coins provide some of the most realistic portraiture from the ancient Greek world.

Among the principal Bactrian cities were two named ALEXANDRIA (2)—modern Kandahr and Herat, in Afghanistan. The remarkable remnants of a Greek-style GYMNASIUM and temple discovered at Aï Khanoum, in northern Afghanistan, mark the site of another city—probably also named Alexandria—that thrived under Bactrian kings. But by 100 B.C. Bactria had fallen, overrun by Asian nomads.

(See also HELLENISTIC AGE.)

Bassae Site, in southwest ARCADIA, of a remarkable temple to APOLLO, now reconstructed. Bassae (meaning "ravines") is located on the remote slopes of Mt. Cotilion. The austere Doric-style temple was begun in about 450 B.C. and completed perhaps 30 years later. It was designed by Ictinus, the architect of the Athenian PARTHENON, and it almost certainly predates the Parthenon (begun 447 B.C.).

Built atop a narrow mountain ridge, the temple necessarily has a north-south orientation (as opposed to the typical east-west). Its most famous feature is the single Corinthian-style column that stands in one part of the interior. The column's original capital disappeared in the 19th century A.D. but was previously noted and sketched as having acanthus-leaf decorations on four sides. This makes it the earliest known example of a Corinthian column.

The temple's architectural SCULPTURES, stripped off and carted away in the 19th century, now stand in the British Museum in London. They portray battles between Greeks and AMAZONS and between Lapiths and CENTAURS—two favorite subjects of Greek temple carving, conveying the theme of (Greek) order versus (barbarian) chaos, and appropriate to a Greek god of culture such as Apollo. Similar scenes existed among the sculptures of the Parthenon.

(See also ARCHITECTURE.)

Bellerophon   Mythical Corinthian hero. Bellerophon came to be associated with a flying horse named Pegasus, but Pegasus is not mentioned in the earliest surviving references to Bellerophon, in HOMER's *Iliad* (written down circa 750 B.C.).

Like HERACLES and other Greek heroes, Bellerophon was assigned a series of impossible-seeming tasks, which he accomplished. His adventures began when he resisted the advances of Anteia (or Stheneboea), the wife of King Proteus of ARGOS (or TIRYNS). Humiliated, she claimed he had tried to seduce her, and so Proteus sent him away with an encoded letter for the king of Lycia, in ASIA MINOR. The letter requested that the king kill the bearer. Obligingly, the king sent Bellerophon to fight the Chimera and the AMAZONS, among other hazards. But the hero triumphed and eventually married the king's daughter; Philonoë.

Later versions of the MYTH—such as in the poet PINDAR's 13th Olympian ode (466 B.C.)—had Bellerophon assisted by the winged Pegasus, which the goddess ATHENA helped him to capture. Pegasus appeared as a symbol of Corinth on the city's COINAGE.

Bion   See CYNICS.

birth control   See PROSTITUTES.

Black peoples   The ancient Greeks were acquainted with people of Negro race. During the second and first millennia B.C. the Greeks had periodic contact with EGYPT, culminating in ALEXANDER THE GREAT's conquest of the land in 322 B.C. Although most Egyptians were of Semitic blood, some were of Negro blood, with also an intermingling of the two races. As is the case in Egypt today, many inhabitants may have had dark skin, with Semitic or Negro physical features in varying degrees. People of black African descent played important roles as soldiers, administrators, priests, and sometimes pharaohs.

Moreover, the Greeks knew about Egypt's southern neighbor—the powerful nation called Nubia or Kush (also spelled Cush). Located along the Nile in what is now northern Sudan, Nubia was inhabited by black Africans, with possibly an admixture of Semitic blood. Nubia was a trading partner and periodic enemy of the pharaohs' Egypt; during the third to first millennia B.C. the two nations warred intermittently over a shared, shifting frontier that lay south of the first Nile cataract (modern-day Aswan). Nubia was an important supplier of GOLD ore to Egypt, and Nubian troops often served as mercenaries in Egyptian service.

By the mid 700s B.C. the Nubians had reorganized themselves and had begun a large-scale invasion of Egypt, the conquest of which was completed in around 715 B.C. by the Nubian ruler Shabako (or Shabaka). The period from about 730 to 656 B.C., when Nubian pharaohs ruled part or all of Egypt, is called by modern historians the 25th Egyptian Dynasty. But Assyrian invaders toppled the dynasty, and Egypt passed to other hands.

In the early 500s B.C. Nubia came under military pressure from a resurgent Egypt. The Nubians removed their capital southward to Meroë, situated between the fifth and sixth Nile cataracts (about 120 miles north of modern-day Khartoum). This "Meroitic" Nubian kingdom flourished for 900 years as an African society independent of Egypt and of Egypt's successive conquerors—the Persians, the Greco-Macedonian Ptolemies, and the Romans.

Among the Greeks, such facts became the stuff of legend. HOMER's epic poems, the *Iliad* and *Odyssey*, written down circa 750 B.C., make reference to a people known as *Aithiopes* (Greek: "burnt-face ones"). Beloved of the gods, they dwelt far to the south, in the land called *Aithiopia*. It was the force of the southern sun, the early Greeks believed, that crisped these people's faces. Greek MYTH told of an Aithiopian king, MEMNON, who led an army northward to help defend TROY during the TROJAN WAR but was killed in single combat with the Greek hero ACHILLES. This episode (not described by Homer) was recounted in a now-vanished Greek epic poem usually called the *Aethiopis*. It is not known whether this legend contains any kernel of historical truth.

Homer and other early writers give no clear location for Aithiopia. But by the early 400s B.C. the Greeks had come to equate it specifically with the nation of Nubia, south of Egypt. The Greek historian HERODOTUS, visiting Egypt circa 450 B.C., heard tales about Aithiopia-Nubia. According to Herodotus, the Aithiopians were said to be "the tallest and most attractive people in the world" (book 3). Herodotus also mentions that Aithiopian troops, armed with spear and bow, served in the Persian king XERXES' invasion of Greece in 480 B.C. (Although not part of the Persian Empire, Nubia seems to have been enrolled as a diplomatic friend of PERSIA.)

In modern times, the place-name Aithiopia (latinized to Ethiopia) has been applied to an African nation located far southeast of ancient Nubia. Confusingly, however, modern historians of the ancient world sometimes use the terms Ethiopia and Ethiopian in the old, Greek sense, to denote ancient Nubia. Egypt's 25th Dynasty is often referred to as the Ethiopian Dynasty.

As a result of contact with black people of Egypt and Nubia, ancient Greek artists began portraying blacks in statuary, metalwork, vase paintings, and the like; the earliest surviving examples date from the 500s B.C. One of the finest pieces is an Athenian clay drinking cup, realistically shaped and painted to represent the head of a black youth (circa 525 B.C.). The hero Memnon appears on several extant vase paintings; usually he is shown with distinctly Negro facial features.

Another black man in Greek art was the evil Busiris. According to Greek legend, Busiris was an Egyptian king, a son of the god POSEIDON; capturing any foreigners who entered Egypt, he would sacrifice them on the altar of the god ZEUS. But at last the Greek hero HERACLES arrived and—in a scene popular in vase paintings—killed Busiris and his followers. This odd tale may distortedly recall Greek relations with Egypt amid the downfall of the 25th (Nubian) Dynasty in the mid 600s B.C.

Alexander the Great's conquest of the Persian Empire brought Egypt into the Greek world, thus opening Nubia and other parts of West Africa to Greek exploration and TRADE. Circa 280–260 B.C. Egypt's king PTOLEMY (2) II sent explorers and merchants sailing along the Red Sea coast as far as modern-day Somalia, and up the Nile to Nubian Meroë and beyond. Ptolemy's goal was the acquisition of gold and other goods, particularly live African elephants for military use. Subsequent Ptolemies maintained these African trading and diplomatic ties, which incidently brought Greek influences to the ruling class in Nubia. We know, for example, that the Greek name Candace was used by Nubian queens from this era until the 300s A.D.

(See also NAUCRATIS; POTTERY; XENOPHANES.)

Black Sea Modern name for the 168,500-square-mile oblong sea bordering ASIA MINOR on the south and Ukraine and southwestern Russia on the north. Attractive for its access to Asia Minor's metal TRADE and Ukraine's vast wheatfields, the Black Sea became ringed by Greek colonies, from circa 700 B.C. onward. The Greeks called it Pontos Euxeinos, "the hospitable sea." But this name was intentionally euphemistic, insofar as fierce native inhabitants and a cold and stormy climate might make the region distinctly inhospitable.

The Black or Euxine Sea was opened up by explorers from the Greek city of MILETUS, on the west coast of Asia Minor. The Milesians' first goal was to acquire copper, tin, GOLD, and other raw metals of interior Asia Minor, and one of their early colonies was SINOPE, located halfway along the southern Black Sea coast. In the next 100 years, colonies from Miletus (and a few other east Greek cities) arose around the entire Black Sea.

Along the northern coastlines, the principal Greek cities were Olbia (meaning "prosperous"), at the mouth of the River Bug, and PANTICAPAEUM, on the east coast of the Crimean peninsula. These sites offered the very valuable resource of grain, grown as surplus by farmers in the interior and purchased by the Greeks for export to the hungry cities of mainland Greece. By 500 B.C. the north Black Sea coast was a major grain supplier, especially for ATHENS. This shipping route placed strategic importance on two narrow waterways—the BOSPORUS and the HELLESPONT—that help connect the Black Sea to the AEGEAN SEA.

(See also AMAZONS; COLONIZATION; HECATAEUS; HERODOTUS; JASON (1); SHIPS AND SEAFARING.)

Boeotia Northwest-southeast–elongated region of central Greece, bordered by PHOCIS to the northwest, by the Straits of EUBOEA to the northeast, and by the Corinthian

Gulf to the southwest. Central Boeotia consists of a mountain-girt plain that provided rich FARMING and the raising of horses. In the plain's southeast corner lay the major Boeotian city, THEBES. The second city was ORCHOMENUS, in the plain's northwest corner, opposite Thebes.

South of Thebes, Boeotia shared an ill-defined border with the Athenian territory, along the east-west line of Mt. Parnes and Mt. Cithaeron. The historically important Boeotian town of PLATAEA lay just north of Cithaeron. Farther northwest stood Boeotia's tallest mountain, Helicon (about 5,800 feet).

The Boeotian heartland comprised one of the centers of MYCENAEAN CIVILIZATION (circa 1600–1200 B.C.)—as suggested by Thebes' prominent place in Greek MYTH. The name Boeotia refers to the raising of cattle (*boes*) and specifically commemorates the Boiotoi, a Greek people who invaded the region, migrating south from THESSALY circa 1100 B.C. The Boeotians of historical times spoke a form of the Aeolic dialect, related to the dialect of Thessaly and that of the east Aegean island of LESBOS. Boeotians were reputed to be boorish and ignorant, although prosperous. "Boeotian pig" was a Greek epithet. But Boeotia's literary tradition produced the poets HESIOD, PINDAR, and Corinna.

With the exception of Plataea, the Boeotian towns followed Thebes as enemies of ATHENS, starting in the late 500s B.C. Boeotia was a target of Athenian expansionism, and the Athenians actually occupied Boeotia for a decade, 457–447 B.C. Soon thereafter the towns formed a Boeotian League, under Theban dominance, for mutual defense and a jointly decided foreign policy. The Boeotian army then emerged as one of the best in Greece, distinguished by a large CAVALRY force in addition to strong infantry. At the Battle of Delium in 424 B.C., during the PELOPONNESIAN WAR, the Boeotians defeated the invading Athenians and ended their hope of reconquering the region. Later, under the Theban commander EPAMINONDAS, the Boeotian League broke the might of SPARTA (371 B.C.) and became the foremost power in Greece, before falling to Macedonian conquest (338 B.C.).

Boeotia's central location and flat interior often made it a battleground—"the dancing floor of War," Epaminondas called it. Famous Boeotian battlefields included Plataea (479 B.C.), LEUCTRA (371 B.C.), and CHAERONEA (338 B.C.).

(See also GREECE, GEOGRAPHY OF; GREEK LANGUAGE; MUSES; PERSIAN WARS; PLATAEA, BATTLE OF; WARFARE; LAND.)

Bosporus (or Bosphorus) Narrow, zigzagging, 18-mile-long channel flowing southwestward from the BLACK SEA to the SEA OF MARMARA. Beyond the Marmara, the current continues south and west through the HELLESPONT channel to the AEGEAN SEA. Like the Hellespont, the Bosporus borders part of northwestern ASIA MINOR; it was considered to be a dividing line between EUROPE AND ASIA.

Shorter and generally narrower and swifter-flowing than the Hellespont, the Bosporus ranges in width from 2.5 miles to 400 yards. Its name, "cow ford" or "ox ford," was in ancient times said to refer to the mythical wanderings of IO, a woman loved by the god ZEUS and transformed into a cow by Zeus' jealous wife, HERA. But the name may refer to a more mundane cattle crossing.

Around 513 B.C., the Persians under King DARIUS (1)—preparing to cross from Asia to Europe for their invasion of Scythia—spanned the Bosporus with a pontoon bridge consisting of about 200 ships anchored in a row. This was a remarkable engineering feat in the ancient world, although not as amazing as the Persians' bridging of the Hellespont, a wider channel, 30 years later. In modern times the Bosporus, now a part of Turkey, was not bridged until 1973.

The Bosporus and Hellespont were the two bottlenecks along the shipping route between the Black Sea and the Aegean. This route had become crucial by about 500 B.C., when ATHENS and other cities of mainland Greece were becoming dependent on grain imported from the northern Black Sea coast. As a natural site where shipping could be raided or tolled, the Bosporus, like the Hellespont, offered wealth and power to any state that could control it. This, combined with the excellent commercial fishing in the strait and its value as a ferry point, helps to explain the prosperity of the Bosporus' most famous city, BYZANTIUM, located at the southern mouth. Athens controlled the Bosporus in the 400s B.C. by holding Byzantium as a subject ally.

(See also THRACE.)

boulē See COUNCIL.

boxing Important SPORT among the ancient Greeks, although less popular than the two other combat sports, WRESTLING and PANKRATION.

Our knowledge of Greek boxing comes mainly from extant literature, artwork, and inscriptions (on tombs and religious offerings). Because HOMER's epic poem the *Iliad* describes a boxing match in book 23, we know that the Greeks were practicing boxing by at least the mid-700s B.C., when the Homeric poems were written down. Possibly the early Greeks learned the sport from MINOAN CIVILIZATION of the ancient Aegean region (2200–1400 B.C.). A surviving fresco from Minoan THERA, painted circa 1550 B.C., shows two boys engaging in what appears to be a stylized form of boxing.

The sport's patron god was APOLLO, a deity of the civilizing arts. During historical times boxing was the sort of discipline that a wealthy young man in a Greek city-state might practice at a local GYMNASIUM. Like other Greek sports of the pre-Roman era, boxing was purely an amateur pastime. The best boxers could hope to compete in the men's or boys' category at the OLYMPIC GAMES or at one of the other great sports festivals.

The Greeks had no boxing rings; official contests might take place on an unfenced sand floor in an outdoor stadium, where the referee would keep the two opponents in a fighting proximity. More brutal than today's sport, Greek boxing did not recognize different weight classes; the advantage tended to go to the heavier man. The match had no rounds, but continued until one man either lost consciousness or held up a finger, signaling defeat. Boxers were allowed to gouge with the thumb but were forbidden to clinch or grab. Certain vase paintings show a referee using his long stick to beat a clinching boxer.

Down through the 400s B.C. boxers often wore protective rawhide thongs wrapped around their hands. During the 300s B.C. the thongs developed into a heavier, more damaging form, with a hard leather knuckle pad. For practice only, boxers might use soft gloves similar to our modern boxing gloves. Boxers tended to attack the face—ancient artwork and inscriptions commemorate broken noses and damaged eyeballs. It was not unusual for a boxer to die from injuries.

Although champions came from all over the Greek world, boxing was particularly associated with the grim discipline of SPARTA. The Athenian philosopher PLATO's dialogue *Gorgias* (circa 386 B.C.) mentions "the boys with the cauliflower ears," referring to the antidemocratic, upper-class Athenian youth who practiced boxing in imitation of Spartan training.

(See also EDUCATION; OLIGARCHY.)

Brasidas Dynamic Spartan general of the PELOPONNESIAN WAR. His successes against Athenian holdings on the north Aegean coast in 424–422 B.C. helped to offset Athenian victories elsewhere and bring about a mood of stalemate, resulting in the Peace of NICIAS. Brasidas' great triumph was his capture of the vital Athenian colony of AMPHIPOLIS (early 423 B.C.). He died at the Battle of Amphipolis, successfully defending the city from an Athenian army under CLEON (422 B.C.).

Brasidas saw that the way to attack an impregnable ATHENS was to destroy its northeastern supply lines. His northern campaign was an early, crude, land-bound version of the strategy that would later win the war for SPARTA, in the naval campaigns of 413–404 B.C.

(See also THUCYDIDES (1).)

bronze Alloy of copper and tin, usually in a nine-to-one ratio. Bronze supplied the most useful metal known during the third and second millennia B.C., replacing prior uses of copper in weaponry, tools, and artwork throughout the Near East and Mediterranean.

Fortified by its measure of tin, bronze is harder than copper, but it melts at the same relatively low temperature—2,000 degrees Fahrenheit. Molten bronze can be intricately shaped by casting—that is, by being poured into a mold. Once cooled, the bronze item can be sharpened or shaped further.

This technology was invented in the Near East before 3000 B.C. and had spread to Minoan CRETE by around 2500 B.C. Whether the first arriving Greek tribesmen of about 2100 B.C. already had their own bronze weapons is unknown, but in the centuries after they occupied mainland Greece they steadily increased their bronzeworking skill, especially for warfare. As shown by ARCHAEOLOGY, bronze was providing the Greek MYCENAEAN CIVILIZATION with swords and spear-points before 1500 B.C., and by 1400 B.C. Mycenaean metalsmiths had mastered the technique of casting bronze plates, then hammering them out to make helmets and body armor. The Mycenaeans used bronze plowshares, sickles, ornaments, and vessels for drinking and cooking.

The potential disadvantage of bronze was that one of its two component metals, tin, could be difficult for the Greeks to acquire. Whereas the Greeks mined copper on the islands of EUBOEA and CYPRUS, tin had to be purchased through expensive, long-range TRADE with ASIA MINOR and western Europe. Tin was mined intensively by native peoples in what is now Cornwall, in southwest England; it then traveled overland—brought by non-Greek middlemen—to trade outlets on the Mediterranean.

The collapse of Mycenaen society and the invasion of mainland Greece by the DORIAN GREEKS (circa 1100–1000 B.C.) temporarily destroyed the tin routes. Compelled to find a replacement for bronze, the Greeks began mining and working IRON. Just as bronze had supplanted copper, so iron now replaced bronze in many objects, such as plowshares and sword blades. But bronze-working returned, alongside ironworking, once the tin supplies were renewed. In ancient technology, bronze was far more malleable than iron, and bronze remained essential wherever shaping or thinness was required.

During the great trading expansion of the 800s–500s B.C., the mainland Greeks imported and copied the artful bronzework of cauldrons, hand mirrors, and other artifacts from the Near East. Bronze helmets, breastplates, and shield facings were standard equipment for Greek HOPLITE armies (circa 700–300 B.C.). The foremost Greek city of about 700 B.C. was CHALCIS, whose name probably refers to bronze (Greek: *chalkos*). Now and later, bronze provided a favorite material for SCULPTURE; one technique was to pour the molten metal into a wax mold that had a clay or plaster core, to produce a hollow statue.

Tin supplies were always a concern. The lure of tin brought Greek traders into the western Mediterranean by 600 B.C., when the Greek colony of MASSALIA was founded. A major tin supplier was the Celtic kingdom of Tartessus, in southern Spain. (Perhaps none of this tin was mined locally; it may all have come from Cornwall.) Competition over metal supplies brought the western Greeks into conflict with similarly aggressive traders—the Carthaginians. Circa 500 B.C. the Carthaginians probably destroyed Tartessus, but by then the Greeks had found new tin suppliers, in ITALY and what is now France.

(See also BRONZE AGE; CARTHAGE; SINOPE; WARFARE, LAND.)

Bronze Age   Term used by modern archaeologists and historians to describe the phase of Asian and European human prehistory that falls roughly between 3500 and 1000 B.C. Coming after the Neolithic or New Stone Age, the Bronze Age is considered to have spread from the Near East to various other regions over several centuries. The era was marked by improved metallurgy that produced the alloy BRONZE as the prime substance for tools of war, agriculture, and industry. For the kings and lords who could produce or buy it, bronze replaced copper, obsidian, and flint. IRON—destined to replace bronze for many uses—was not yet in use.

The Bronze Age saw the birth of the earliest great civilizations of the Near East and the eastern Mediterranean. These include the Sumerian kingdom in Mesopotamia (which arose circa 2800 B.C.), the Egyptian Old Kingdom (circa 2660 B.C.), the MINOAN CIVILIZATION in CRETE (circa 2000 B.C.), the Hittite kingdom in ASIA MINOR (circa 1650 B.C.), and the MYCENAEAN CIVILIZATION of mainland Greece (circa 1600 B.C.).

By scholarly convention, the Bronze Age in mainland Greece is divided into three phases, called Early Helladic (circa 2900–1950 B.C.), Middle Helladic (circa 1950–1550 B.C.), and Late Helladic (circa 1550–1100 B.C.), with each phase subdivided into stages I, II, and III. Much of Early Helladic covers an epoch prior to the Greeks' appearance on the scene, when mainland Greece was still inhabited by a non-Greek people (who used bronze, although not extensively). The violent arrival of the first primitive Greeks is usually placed between Early Helladic II and III, circa 2100 B.C. The flowering of Greek Mycenaean culture corresponds to the Late Helladic era. The Mycenaeans' downfall marks the end of the Bronze Age and the advent of the DARK AGE in Greece.

Bucephalus   See ALEXANDER THE GREAT.

building   See ARCHITECTURE.

burial   See FUNERAL CUSTOMS.

Byblos   Greek name for the northernmost of ancient PHOENICIA's three major seaports. (The other two were Sidon and Tyre.) Today the site of Byblos is about 26 miles north of Beirut, in Lebanon.

Called Gebal ("citadel") by the Phoenicians, Byblos was one of the earliest cities of the Near East. In the Phoenician heyday of the 900s–700s B.C., Byblos was the nation's capital, with a powerful navy and TRADE routes extending to Greece and EGYPT.

Contact between Greek and Bybline traders, at such ports as AL MINA, in Syria, and Citium, in CYPRUS, was a crucial factor in transmitting certain Near Eastern advantages to the emerging Greek culture, including the ALPHABET (circa 775 B.C.). Byblos at this time was the major export center for papyrus (primitive "paper" made from the pith of Egyptian water plants and used as a cheap substitute for animal skins in receiving WRITING). Byblos' monopoly in this trade is commemorated in the early Greek word for papyrus, *biblos*. That word, in turn, yielded Greek *biblion*, "book," and *bibliotheka*, "library," which survive in such familiar words as Bible, bibliophile, and French *bibliothèque* ("library").

Byblos' political fortunes in the era 700–300 B.C. followed those of greater Phoenicia, and the city quickly faded in importance after the founding of the nearby Seleucid-Greek city of ANTIOCH (300 B.C.).

(See also ADONIS.)

Byzantium   Celebrated Greek city on the European side of the southern mouth of the BOSPORUS channel. Byzantium is now the Turkish metropolis of Istanbul.

Founded in the mid-600s B.C. by Greeks from MEGARA (1), the city was called Buzantion in Greek. Supposedly it took its name from the colonists' leader, Buzas; more probably, it was the name of a preexisting settlement of native Thracians. The Greek city thrived amid Thracian tribes hungry for Greek goods.

Byzantium enjoyed a superb location on a peninsula jutting between the Bosporus mouth and the SEA OF

MARMARA. Alongside the peninsula's landward base lay the mouth of the Golden Horn River, providing rich fishing and access to the interior. More important, Byzantium controlled the Bosporus. Greek merchant ships—full of precious grain from the BLACK SEA coast, bound for cities of mainland Greece—would sail south through the channel. Byzantium's navy was able to impose tolls on this passing traffic.

Byzantium was held as a strategic point by successive imperial powers: PERSIA (circa 513–478 B.C.), ATHENS (478–404 B.C.), and ROME (mid-100s B.C. onward). As a member of the Athenian-dominated DELIAN LEAGUE in the 400s B.C., Byzantium played a vital role in Athens' control of the Black Sea grain route. We know that in 457 B.C. wealthy Byzantium was paying a relatively high yearly Delian tribute—15 TALENTS. The city revolted unsuccessfully against Athens twice (440 and 411 B.C.).

Passing to Spartan influence at the end of the PELOPON-NESIAN WAR (404 B.C.), the Byzantines soon became disenchanted with their new masters. By about 377 B.C. they were again Athenian allies. The Macedonian king PHILIP II unsuccessfully besieged Byzantium in the winter of 340–339 B.C.

Amid the wars of the DIADOCHI in the late 300s B.C., Byzantium was able to keep its independence. The city suffered attacks from the CELTS, who invaded much of the Greek world in the early 200s B.C., and eventually Byzantium seems to have paid ransom to keep them away. The city went to war in 220 B.C. against the emerging naval power of RHODES over the issue of Byzantium's Bosporus tolls.

In A.D. 330 Byzantium became a foremost city of the world when the Roman emperor Constantine made it the eastern capital of his empire and renamed it Constantinople.

(See also THRACE.)

C

Cadmus In Greek MYTH, Cadmus (Greek: Kadmos) was a prince of the Phoenician city of Tyre and founder of the Greek city of THEBES. Young Cadmus' sister at Tyre was EUROPA, whom the god ZEUS abducted in the shape of a bull. Cadmus was assigned by his father, King Agenor, to find the vanished Europa. Leading a band of men to central Greece, he consulted the god APOLLO through the oracle at DELPHI. Apollo advised Cadmus to abandon the search and instead follow a cow that he would find outside the temple; he should establish a city wherever the cow lay down to rest. Accordingly, the cow led Cadmus to the future site of Thebes, about 50 miles away. There Cadmus built the Cadmea, which became the citadel of the later city.

Several adventures accompanied this foundation. To gain access to the local water supply, Cadmus had to slay a ferocious serpent, the offspring of the war god ARES. When Cadmus consecrated the dead monster to the goddess ATHENA, she appeared and told him to sow the serpent's teeth in the soil. Immediately there sprang up a harvest of armed men to oppose him, but Cadmus cleverly threw a stone into their midst, thereby setting them to fight one another. The surviving five of these warriors joined Cadmus' service and became the ancestors of the Theban nobility, known as the Sown Men.

After enduring eight years' servitude to Ares in expiation for having killed his serpent son, Cadmus was allowed to marry Harmonia, daughter of Ares and APHRODITE. As a wedding gift, Harmonia received a wondrous necklace that bestowed irresistible attraction on its wearer; this necklace would play a role in the next generations' misfortunes, in the adventure of the SEVEN AGAINST THEBES.

Reigning as king of Thebes, Cadmus civilized the crude local Greeks by teaching them how to write. He and Harmonia had four daughters, all of whom suffered unhappy fates: Semele (later the mother of the god DIONYSUS); Ino (who was driven mad by the goddess HERA); Agave (whose son PENTHEUS would be destroyed by Dionysus); and Autonoë (whose son ACTAEON would be destroyed by the goddess ARTEMIS). In old age, Cadmus and Harmonia emigrated to the northwest, where they ruled over the Illyrians and eventually were changed into serpents.

The Cadmus legend—a Phoenician prince civilizing and ruling part of Greece—presents an odd combination. Although the Greeks had extensive contact with the Phoenicians in the 900s–700s B.C., this myth seems to commemorate an earlier period of Greek contact with the Near East, possibly during the Mycenaean era (circa 1200 B.C.).

(See also ALPHABET; ILLYRIS; MYCENAEAN CIVILIZATION; PHOENICIA.)

Callias Athenian nobleman and diplomat, active in the early and mid-400s B.C. Callias' family was the richest in ATHENS, renting out slave labor to the state SILVER mine at Laurium. Despite his upper-class background, Callias became a political follower of the radical democrat PERICLES. During Pericles' preeminence, Callias was the foremost diplomat for Athens.

Callias made at least one embassy to King Artaxerxes I of PERSIA, circa 461 B.C. Most modern scholars accept the theory, previously disputed, that circa 449 B.C. Callias negotiated an end to the Greek-Persian hostilities known as the PERSIAN WARS. Apparently the Peace of Callias in part protected the Athenian-allied Greek cities of western ASIA MINOR, prohibiting the Persians from sailing or marching west past certain set boundaries. For their part, the Athenians may have agreed to dismantle the fortifications of the Asia Minor Greek cities.

(See also DELIAN LEAGUE; IONIA; SLAVES.)

Callimachus The most admired lyric poet of the HELLENISTIC AGE. Born in the Greek city of CYRENE (1) in North Africa, Callimachus (Greek: Kallimachos) lived circa 310–240 B.C. and wrote at Egyptian ALEXANDRIA (1) during the brief literary golden age under King Ptolemy II (reigned 285–247 B.C.). Of Callimachus' voluminous output—a reported 800 scrolls' worth—only six hymns and some 60 epigrams survive whole. Several dozen fragments of other poems exist, and more of his verses are being discovered in the sands of Egypt. (One sizable fragment was published from papyrus in 1977.) Callimachus' best-known work, now lost, was the *Aetia* (Origins), a narrative elegy of about 7,000 lines; this erudite and digressive poem presented MYTHS and descriptions explaining the origins of places, rites, and names throughout the Greek world.

Callimachus was the Alexandrian poet par excellence: witty, scholarly, and favoring brief forms and cerebral topics. He was an "in" poet, composing for an "in" group of sophisticated readers or, more accurately, *listeners*, to whom he would read aloud. His work remained immensely popular in later literary circles; 200 years after his death, his style and values were influencing such Roman poets as Catullus, Propertius, and Ovid. Callimachus also is remembered for his bitter rivalry with his former pupil and intimate, the poet APOLLONIUS. Their dispute, based partly on differing poetic tastes, was the most famous literary quarrel of the ancient world.

Emigrating from Cyrene to EGYPT, the young Callimachus began his career as a schoolteacher in a suburb of Alexandria. Eventually attracting royal patronage, he was installed at Alexandria's famous Library, with the huge job of cataloguing the several hundred thousand books there. His resultant catalogue supposedly ran to 120 volumes and must have taken 10 years; it would have included lists of titles, biographical sketches of authors, and literary criticism. Apparently it was an admirable piece of scholarship, and it testifies to the scholarly, cataloguing urge that also infused his poetry.

Callimachus never reattained the prestigious post of director of the Library, but rather was passed over in favor of Apollonius after the retirement of the director Zenodotus. This development sparked or fueled the two men's quarrel. The enmity was part of a larger literary dispute between the writers of lengthy, narrative EPIC POETRY, based on HOMER's *Iliad* and *Odyssey*, and poets such as Callimachus, who considered epic irrelevant to modern society. "A big book is a big evil," Callimachus wrote. Although he did compose certain lengthy poems toward the end of his life, he seems to have objected specifically to the continuous plot and familiar subject matter of the Homeric-style epic; rather, Callimachus' longer poems were innovative and episodic.

Callimachus' epigrams have been praised for their sincere emotion and their charming word use; they include epitaphs and expressions of sexual desire. The most admired epigram poignantly describes the writer's feelings on learning of the death of his fellow poet Heraclitus. Of Callimachus' five surviving hymns, Hymn 1 describes the mythical birth and rearing of the god ZEUS. Famous in antiquity, this Hymn to Zeus set a standard of court poetry by drawing subtle parallels between the king of the gods and King Ptolemy II.

No information exists regarding a wife or children for Callimachus. He seems to have been one of those strictly homosexual Greek men who shunned MARRIAGE. Of his surviving epigrams, every one of the erotic poems celebrates the charms of boys. He lived to about age 70, highly esteemed and enjoying the patronage of Ptolemies; certain of his verses, such as his poem on Queen Arsinoë's death (270 B.C.), sound like the public presentations of a court poet laureate.

(See also HOMOSEXUALITY; LYRIC POETRY.)

Callinus One of the earliest Greek lyric poets whose work (in part) has come down to us. Callinus lived in the mid-600s B.C. in the Greek city of EPHESUS in ASIA MINOR, and wrote patriotic verses encouraging his countrymen in their defense against the Cimmerians, a nomadic people from southwestern Russia who were ravaging Asia Minor in those years. In the single substantial fragment by him that survives, Callinus reminds his audience how honorable it is to fight for city and family and how death finds everyone eventually.

Callinus is the first known writer of the verse form known as the elegy, which was intended for recital to flute accompaniment.

(See also LYRIC POETRY, MUSIC.)

Calydonian Boar Hunt One of many Greek MYTHS recounting the destruction of a local monster. King Oeneus of Calydon (a region in AETOLIA) offended the goddess ARTEMIS by forgetting to sacrifice to her. In retaliation, she sent a monstrous boar to ravage the countryside. To hunt the beast, Oeneus' son Meleager collected a band of heroes, including the virgin huntress ATALANTA, with whom Meleager was in love. After much effort, the heroes succeeded in killing the creature, the honor of the first spear thrust going to Atalanta. At Meleager's insistence, she then received the edible portions of the boar. But this insulted Meleager's maternal uncles, who were part of the hunt, and in the ensuing fight, Meleager slew them.

Upon hearing the news, Meleager's mother, Althaea, took vengeance on her son. She had in her possession a half-burned log, with the following significance: years before, just after Meleager's birth, Althaea had been visited by the three goddesses of FATE, the Moirai, who informed her that her baby son would live only until the log then on the fire should be burned away. Subverting the prophecy, Althaea had quenched the fire and preserved the half-burned log in a chest. Now, in anger at her brothers' murder, she threw the log on the fire, and Meleager died.

The boar hunt was a favorite subject in vase painting and other artwork. Among surviving representations is a panel on the Athenian black-figure François vase (circa 570 B.C.).

(See also POTTERY.)

Calypso A beautiful nymph who played a role in the MYTH of ODYSSEUS, as told in HOMER's epic poem the *Odyssey* (book 5). The name Kalupso means "concealer." A daughter of ATLAS and the sea goddess Thetis, she lived alone on a remote island, where she received the shipwrecked Odysseus. As Odysseus' lover, she detained him for seven years, promising to make him immortal if he stayed; but he insisted on returning to his wife and kingdom. At ZEUS' command, Calypso helped him build a boat on which to put to sea.

In the structure of the *Odyssey*, Calypso supplies a benevolent doublet to the sinister CIRCE (who also detains Odysseus seductively, for one year). Odysseus' seven years with Calypso can be interpreted as representing the distractions of pleasure versus the duties of leadership.

(See also NYMPHS; WOMEN.)

Cappadocia See ASIA MINOR.

Caria See ASIA MINOR.

Carthage Major non-Greek city of North Africa, located about 10 miles from the modern city of Tunis. Carthage was founded by Phoenician settlers from Tyre circa 800 B.C. to be an anchorage and trading post for Phoenician merchant ships in the western Mediterranean. The Phoenician name Kart Hadasht means "New City"; the Greeks called it Karchedon and the Romans, Carthago.

Governed as an OLIGARCHY under two presiding officials called shophets, Carthage thrived by commerce. It became a foremost power of the ancient world, with a feared navy to protect its trading monopolies in the western

Mediterranean. The Carthaginians maintained trading bases such as Gades and Malaca (modern Cadiz and Malaga, both in southern Spain), from which they acquired valuable raw metals. The Carthaginians traded with the Greeks, as indicated by the troves of Corinthian POTTERY discovered at Carthage by modern archaeologists. But Carthage is important in Greek history mainly as an enemy and occasional overlord of the western Greeks, particularly in SICILY.

Greeks and Carthaginians first came into conflict when the Greeks intruded into Carthaginian trading waters. Circa 600 B.C. a Carthaginian fleet was defeated by Phocaean Greeks in the vicinity of MASSALIA (modern-day Marseille, in southern France). About 60 years later a joint fleet of Carthaginians and ETRUSCANS successfully drove the Greeks away from Corsica. Carthage also dominated Sardinia and most of western Sicily.

For the next 300 years, Greeks and Carthaginians fought for control of Sicily, whose coast lies about 130 miles from Carthage. Carthage's greed for Sicily eventually brought on conflict with the rising Italian city of ROME. The resulting three Punic Wars (264–241 B.C., 218–201 B.C., and 149–146 B.C.) ended in the complete destruction of Carthage by the Romans.

Prosperous Carthage won the admiration of the philosopher ARISTOTLE (mid-300s B.C.), whose treatise *Politics* contains a remarkable section that favorably compares the Carthaginian government with that of certain Greek cities. But another Greek writer describes—and ARCHAEOLOGY confirms—the gruesome Carthaginian custom of sacrificing upper-class children in time of public crisis, to ensure the god Baal-Ammon's care of the city.

(See also AGATHOCLES; BRONZE; DIONYSIUS (1); GELON; HIMERA; PHOCAEA; PHOENICIA; SILVER; TRADE.)

caryatid The Greeks' name for their type of decorative pillar represented as a clothed woman, holding up a ceiling structure with her head. The most famous caryatids are the six in marble from the south porch of the Athenian Erectheum (built 421–406 B.C.); the best preserved one of these is now in the British Museum in London.

Supposedly the name caryatid referred to the region of Caryae in LACONIA, where WOMEN traditionally danced with baskets on their heads. In any case, the sight of women carrying water pitchers or laundry baskets in this way was a familiar one in the ancient Greek world and certainly contributed to the design. The male equivalents of caryatids were called Atlantes, from the mythological figure ATLAS, who held up the heavens with his head.

(See also ARCHITECTURE.)

Cassander Macedonian general and ruler, one of the several DIADOCHI (Successors) who carved up the empire of ALEXANDER THE GREAT after the latter's death in 323 B.C. Born circa 360 B.C., Cassander (Greek: Kassandros) was son of the Macedonian general ANTIPATER, who served as regent in MACEDON during Alexander's eastward campaigns (334–323 B.C.). Cassander joined Alexander's army in Asia in 324 B.C. He and the king seem to have disliked each other bitterly, and Cassander is mentioned by ancient writers as a suspect in theories that Alexander died from

poisoning. After Antipater's death (319 B.C.), Cassander seized control of Macedon and most of Greece. He executed Alexander's mother, Olympias, Alexander's widow, Roxane, and Alexander's young son, Alexander III.

In the following years Cassander joined the other secessionist Diadochi—SELEUCUS (1), PTOLEMY (1), and LYSIMACHUS—in resisting the efforts of ANTIGONUS (1) to reunite Alexander's empire. Cassander died circa 297 B.C., and his dynasty in Macedon lasted only a few years before falling to the descendants of Antigonus.

Cassandra In MYTH, a daughter of King PRIAM of TROY. She is mentioned in HOMER's *Iliad* simply as the loveliest of Priam's daughters, but later writers—particularly the Athenian playwright AESCHYLUS, in his *Agamemnon* (458 B.C.)—present her in pathetic terms. Cassandra was beloved by the god APOLLO, who wooed her by offering her the power of prophecy. She accepted the gift but still refused his advances. Apollo could not revoke his gift, but he decreed vindictively that no one would ever believe her predictions.

In the TROJAN WAR, the Trojans ignored Cassandra's frantic plea not to take the Greeks' giant wooden horse into the city. When the Greeks emerged from the horse to sack Troy, Cassandra was dragged away from the altar of the goddess ATHENA and raped by AJAX (2) the Locrian. Afterward, Cassandra was allotted as concubine to the Greek grand marshal, King AGAMEMNON. On her arrival with Agamemnon at his kingdom of MYCENAE, Cassandra and Agamemnon were murdered by Agamemnon's wife, CLYTAEMNESTRA. Naturally, Cassandra foresaw her own and Agamemnon's death.

Our modern expression "to be a Cassandra" or "to play Cassandra" is applied to someone who habitually predicts that bad things will happen.

(See also PROPHECY AND DIVINATION.)

Castor and Polydeuces Mythical twin Spartan heroes, worshipped as gods. The cult of Castor and Polydeuces was important at SPARTA and other Dorian-Greek cities, and was an early cultural export to the Romans, who latinized the youths' names to Castor and Pollux.

The distinction between mortal hero and immortal god played a central role in the MYTH. According to the story, the Spartan king Tyndareus had a wife, LEDA, whom the god ZEUS raped or seduced. Leda bore two pairs of twins: the girls CLYTAEMNESTRA and Helen (later known as HELEN OF TROY) and the boys Castor and Polydeuces. One version says that both boys were the immortal sons of Zeus— hence they were called Dioscuri, or Dios kouroi, "the youths of Zeus." But a different tradition says that only Polydeuces was Zeus' child and thus immortal, while Castor, fathered by Tyndareus, was doomed to die like other humans.

The boys grew up inseparable and devoted to each other. Polydeuces became a champion boxer, Castor a famous horseman. They had three major adventures: they raided Athenian territory to rescue their sister Helen after she was kidnapped by the Athenian king THESEUS, sailed with the Argonauts under the Thessalian hero JASON (1) to capture the Golden Fleece, and abducted the two daughters of the Messenian nobleman Leucippus, who sent in pursuit his nephews Idas and Lynceus (to whom the young women had been betrothed). In the ensuing fight, Idas, Lynceus, and Castor were all killed. But Polydeuces prayed to his father, Zeus, who resurrected Castor on the condition that the twins thereafter divide their lot, living together one day among the gods and the next day in the Underworld. HOMER's epic poem the *Odyssey* mentions that "the grain-giving earth holds them, yet they live . . . One day they are alive, one day dead" (book 11).

Like HERACLES (another hero turned god), the Dioscuri were thought to be sympathetic to human needs and were worshipped widely by the common people. As patron gods of seafarers, they averted shipwreck, and their benevolent presence supposedly was indicated by the electrical phenomenon that we call St. Elmo's fire (whereby the mast and rigging of a sailing ship would seem to sparkle during a thunderstorm). They also were identified with the constellation known as the Twins (Gemini).

Often pictured as riding on white horses, the Dioscuri embodied the spirit of military youth. At the Battle of the Sagras River (late 500s B.C.), the divine twins were believed to have appeared in person to aid the army of LOCRI (a Dorian-Greek city in south ITALY) against the army of CROTON (a nearby Achaean-Greek city). This miracle was copied by the Romans, who claimed that the Dioscuri helped them to win the Battle of Lake Regillus, against the Latins (circa 496 B.C.).

(See also AFTERLIFE; BOXING; DORIAN GREEKS; ROME; SHIPS AND SEAFARING.)

Catana Greek city on the east coast of SICILY, at the foot of volcanic Mt. Etna. Set at the northeastern rim of a large and fertile plain, this site is now the Sicilian city of Catania. The locale was seized circa 729 B.C. by Greek colonists from the nearby city of NAXOS (2), who drove away the region's native Sicels. This attack was part of the Greeks' two-pronged capture of the plain; the other captured site was Leontini.

Catana (Greek: Katanē) possessed one of the Greek world's first law codes, drawn up by a certain Charondas, probably in the early 500s B.C. As an Ionian-Greek city, Catana took part in ethnic feuding between Ionians and DORIAN GREEKS in Sicily. By 490 B.C. the city had fallen under the sway of its powerful Dorian neighbor to the south, SYRACUSE. In 476 B.C. Syracusan tyrant HIERON (1) emptied Catana, exiling its inhabitants to Leontini, and repopulated the site with his Greek mercenary troops. The "new" city, renamed Aetna, was celebrated by the visiting Athenian playwright AESCHYLUS in a play (now lost), titled *Women of Aetna*. But after Hieron's death, the former Catanans recovered their city by force and gained independence (461 B.C.).

Catana provided the Athenians with a base against Syracuse in 415 B.C., during the PELOPONNESIAN WAR. In 403 B.C. Catana was recaptured by the Syracusans under their tyrant DIONYSIUS (1). For the next 150 years, despite moments of independence provided by such saviors as the Corinthian commander TIMOLEON (339 B.C.) and the Epirote king PYRRHUS (278 B.C.), Catana remained a Syracusan possession. Seized by the Roman in 263 B.C., during the First Punic War, Catana become an important city of the Roman Empire.

(See also COLONIZATION; IONIAN GREEKS; LAWS AND LAW COURTS; ROME.)

cavalry Ancient Greek warfare emphasized the foot soldier over the horse soldier. It took the tactical genius of the Macedonian kings PHILIP II and his son ALEXANDER THE GREAT (mid-300s B.C.) to raise cavalry to even a prominent secondary position. One reason for cavalry's inferior status lay in the mountainous terrain of mainland Greece, which was resistant to the strategic movement of horsemen and to horse-breeding itself; in most regions, only the very rich could afford to raise horses.

During the 700s to 300s B.C., when Greek citizen-soldiers supplied their own equipment, a city's cavalry typically consisted of rich men and their sons. Cavalry contingents were therefore small in most Greek armies. Only on the horse-breeding plains of THESSALY, BOEOTIA, and Greek SICILY did large cavalry corps develop.

In those days, cavalry was not so effective a "shock" troop as it would become in later centuries. The Greeks knew nothing of the stirrup—a vital military invention that enables a rider to "stand up" in the saddle and lean forward strenuously without falling off. (The stirrup probably came out of Siberia circa A.D. 550.) Nor had the horseshoe or the jointed bit yet been invented. The Greeks knew only small breeds of horses prior to the late 300s B.C. (when Alexander's conquests introduced larger breeds from the Iranian plateau). Therefore, in battle, cavalry was not usually strong enough to ride directly against formations of infantry. The juggernaut charges of medieval Europe's armored knights were still 1,500 years in the future.

Ancient Greek artwork and certain writings—such as the historian XENOPHON's treatise *On Horsemanship* (circa 380 B.C.)—suggest what a horse soldier looked like. He might wear a corset of linen or leather, with a BRONZE helmet (open-faced, to leave his vision clear). He probably carried no shield, or at most a small wooden targe attached to his left forearm. The Greek cavalry weapon was a spear for jabbing (not usually for throwing); unlike the long lance of a medieval knight, this spear was only about six feet long.

Cavalry in action against infantry, in a painted scene on a vase from the Greek city of Gela, in Sicily, circa 490 B.C. The horsemen are perhaps overtaking an enemy in retreat.

The Athenian cavalry received its basic training in organizations of cadets—wealthy young men who supplied their own horses and who drilled at local riding tracks and in countryside maneuvers. This vivid marble carving from the Parthenon frieze, circa 432 B.C., shows Athenian cadets riding in procession to the acropolis, at a sacred festival of the goddess Athena.

We know from battle scenes in Greek art that the horseman used his spear for a downward thrust, often overhand from the shoulder: the spear was not couched in the armpit for the charge, since the impact probably would have knocked the stirrupless rider off his horse. If the spear was lost, the horseman would rely on the IRON sword tied into a scabbard at his waist. As in other eras of military history, the preferred cavalry sword was a saber—that is, it had a curved cutting edge, designed to slash downward rather than to stab.

Horsemen of the 500s and 400s B.C. were needed for scouting and supply escort, and in combat they had the job of guarding the vulnerable infantry flanks. When one side's infantry formation began to dissolve into retreat, the cavalry of both sides might have crucial roles to play, either in running down the fleeing enemy, or (on the other side) in protecting the foot soldiers' retreat. Descriptions of ancient battles make clear that a disorderly retreat could become a catastrophe once the withdrawing infantry was overtaken by enemy horsemen. Among such examples is the plight of Athenian HOPLITES pursued by Boeotian cavalry after the Battle of Delium (424 B.C.), during the PELOPONNESIAN WAR.

The kingdom of MACEDON had a strong cavalry in its horse-breeding barons, whom King Alexander I (circa 480 B.C.) organized into a prestigious corps of King's Companions. The subsequent innovations of Philip and Alexander brought cavalry into the heart of battle. Cavalry became the offensive arm, to complement the more defensive role of the heavy-infantry PHALANX. The Macedonian phalanx would stop the enemy infantry attack and rip gaps in its battle order, and the cavalry would then attack these vulnerable gaps before the enemy could reorganize. In this case cavalry could charge against massed infantry, since the charge was directed not against the enemy's waiting spear-points but against open ground. Into such a gap Alexander led the Macedonian cavalry at the battles of CHAERONEA (338 B.C.) and Gaugamela (331 B.C.). Prior to Alexander's conquests, the Persians possessed the most numerous and formidable cavalry known to the Greeks. All noble-born Persian boys were taught to ride and shoot with the bow.

The HELLENISTIC AGE (300–150 B.C.) saw Greek kings in the eastern Mediterranean experimenting with such Persian-influenced cavalry as mounted archers and javelinmen, and horse and riders protected by chain-mail armor and known as *kataphraktai*, "enclosed ones." These cataphracts pointed the way toward the Parthian heavy cavalry of the Roman era and the armored knights of the Middle Ages.

(See also PERSIA; WARFARE, LAND.)

Celts   Race of people speaking an Indo-European language who emerged from central Europe in a series of invasions after about 750 B.C. Among the places they occupied were France, Spain, and Britain. Today Celtic languages and culture still exist in Ireland, Scotland, Wales, and Britanny (in France), and the Celts are commemorated in place names such as Galicia (in modern Spain) and Gaul (Gallia, the Roman name for ancient France). The Celts (Greek: Keltoi) were known for their physical size and beauty, their natural spirituality, and their undisciplined fierceness in battle. The distinctive Celtic armament was the long, oblong shield.

Celtic society was tribal and agricultural, with walled towns for commerce and defense, but few cities. Although not a literary people (at that time), they developed an admirable material culture, especially in metallurgy. Early Celtic culture reached maturity circa 400–100 B.C., in the La Tène style of art and metal design (named for an archaeological site in Switzerland).

By 600 B.C. Greek merchants in the western Mediterranean were dealing with Celtic peoples in Spain and France, to acquire metals such as tin and SILVER. The Spanish Celtic kingdom of Tartessus had friendly dealing with Greek merchants from PHOCAEA. From the Phocaean colony at MASSALIA (modern Marseille), Greek goods and culture slowly spread inland among the Celts of Gaul, and prompted the subsequent emergence of the La Tène civilization.

But the Greeks and Celts collided in the 200s B.C., when Celtic tribes descended the Danube, invaded mainland Greece from the north, and overran the sanctuary at DELPHI (279 B.C.). Another column of invaders crossed the HELLESPONT to attack ASIA MINOR, where they were contained after being defeated in battle by the Seleucid king Antiochus I (circa 273 B.C.). The valor and brutishness of these invaders is portrayed in Greek statues like the Dying Gaul, commissioned by the people of PERGAMUM and known to us from later Roman copies.

Settling in north-central Asia Minor, immigrant Celts formed the kingdom of Galatia. Amid the neighboring Greeks and Phrygians, the Galatians maintained Celtic customs and language for centuries. In the first century

A.D. Galatia contained an early Christian community, and these Galatians are commemorated in the New Testament, as recipients of a letter from St. Paul.

(See also BRONZE; CARTHAGE; TRADE; WINE.)

centaurs Legendary tribe of creatures who were part human, part horse. A centaur was usually imagined as having a male horse's body with a male human torso and head emerging above the horse's chest. This shape is portrayed on the earliest surviving likeness of a centaur— a baked-clay figurine from the 900s B.C., decorated in Geometric style, discovered at LEFKANDI, in central Greece. However, certain other early images in art show human forelegs, with a horse's body and rear legs. The original meaning of the Greek word *kentauros* is not clear to us.

In Greek MYTH, centaurs had occupied the wild regions of THESSALY and ARCADIA in the old days; they represented the uncivilized life, before the general establishment of Greek laws and city-states. Although capable of wisdom and nobility, they were fierce, oversexed, and prone to drunkenness. The best-known myth about the centaurs, mentioned in HOMER's *Iliad* and *Odyssey*, is their battle with the Lapiths, a human tribe of Thessaly. The gathering began as a friendly banquet to celebrate the wedding of the Lapith king Pirithous, but the centaurs got drunk on WINE and tried to rape the Lapith women. In the ensuing brawl the centaurs were defeated. As a symbol of savagery versus civilization, this battle was a favorite subject of Greek art. It appeared, for instance, in the architectural SCULPTURES on the Athenian PARTHENON and on the Temple of ZEUS at OLYMPIA (mid-400s B.C.).

Another myth tells how a centaur named Nessus offered to carry HERACLES' second wife, Deianira, across a river but then tried to rape her. Heracles shot the creature with poisoned arrows, but before Nessus died he gave to Deianira the poisoned blood-soaked garment that would later cause Heracles' death. A more benevolent centaur was Chiron, or Cheiron, the wise mountain-dweller who served as tutor to heroes, including JASON, ASCLEPIUS, and ACHILLES.

(See also AMAZONS; GIANTS.)

Cerberus In MYTH, a monstrous dog that guarded the inner bank of the River Styx, at the entrance to the Underworld. Cerberus (Greek: Kerberos) had 50 heads, according to HESIOD's epic poem the *Theogony*. A later, more familiar version gave him three heads and outgrowths of snakes. Cerberus would fawn on the ghosts arriving at the infernal kingdom, but became vicious toward anyone who tried to leave.

Cerberus was the target of HERACLES' eleventh labor. The hero visited the Underworld and won permission from the god HADES to bring the dog temporarily to the upper world. Dragging Cerberus to the city of TIRYNS, Heracles mischievously frightened his taskmaster, King Eurystheus. This was a favorite scene in ancient Greek artwork. One famous Athenian black-figure vase (530s B.C.), now in the Louvre, shows the timid king hiding inside a storage jar as the hound of Hell is led in.

(See also AFTERLIFE.)

Chaeronea Northernmost town of BOEOTIA, located in the Cephissus River valley, on the main route between central and northern Greece. There in the summer of 338 B.C. the Macedonian king PHILIP II defeated an allied Greek army, to make Greece a subject state of MACEDON.

The decisive Battle of Chaeronea was one of the most consequential fights of ancient history—not only for politics, but for the development of battlefield tactics. The Greek army, comprised mainly of contingents from Boeotia and ATHENS, had a slight advantage in numbers: 35,000 HOPLITES (heavily armed infantry) against Philip's 30,000, with about 2,000 CAVALRY on each side. The allied Greeks comfortably guarded the route southward—their battle line filled the valley side to side, from the town's citadel on their left, to the river on their right. The Athenian hoplites, 10,000 strong, occupied the army's left wing; in the center were various levies and a company of 5,000 mercenaries; and on the right wing were 12,000 Boeotians, including the men of THEBES, the best soldiers in Greece. The position of honor, on the extreme right wing, was given to the Theban Sacred Band, an elite battalion of 300, consisting entirely of paired male lovers.

Philip, on horseback behind his army's right wing, brought his men southward through the valley in an unusual, slantwise formation, which was destined to become a model Macedonian tactic. The Macedonian PHALANX was angled so that the right wing advanced ahead of the center and the center ahead of the left wing. Holding back on the Macedonian left wing was the cavalry, commanded by Philip's 18-year-son, Prince Alexander (later known to history as ALEXANDER THE GREAT).

Philip's battlefield plan was a refinement of tactics used by the Thebans themselves at LEUCTRA more than 30 years before. Like the Thebans at Leuctra, Philip planned to hit his enemies at their strongest point: their right wing. But Philip's inspired innovation was to precede this blow with a disruptive feint against the enemy's left wing in the hope of creating a gap along the long line of massed Greek soldiery.

According to a statement by a later ancient writer, it is possible that Philip staged a retreat of his right wing during the battle. Presumably the Macedonians withdrew by stepping backward in good order, with their 13-foot-long pikes still facing forward. The disorganized Athenians followed, in deluded triumph. But in fact, the overexcited Athenians were drawing their army's left wing forward, with the Greek troops in the center following suit. Eventually gaps appeared in the Greek battle line, as various contingents lost contact with one another. On the Greek far right, the Theban Sacred Band stood isolated from the rest of the army. It was then that Prince Alexander led his cavalry charging down the valley, followed by the reserve Macedonian infantry.

The Sacred Band was surrounded and overrun by Alexander's cavalry. Meanwhile Philip, off on the Macedonian right, ordered an end to his false retreat. His men pressed forward against the Athenians, who scattered and fled. The Macedonians pursued, killing 1,000 Athenians and taking 2,000 prisoners. Among the fugitives was DEMOSTHENES (1), the great Athenian orator and enemy of Philip's.

After the battle, the corpses of the Sacred Band lay in the serried ranks of their disciplined formation. Of their 300 men, only 46 had survived. The rest were buried on the battlefield, where their 254 skeletons were discovered by archaeologists in the 20th century. Today the site is marked by a marble lion, sculpted in ancient times, overlooking the Sacred Band's graves and the burial mound of the Macedonian dead.

(See also HOMOSEXUALITY; WARFARE, LAND.)

Chalcedon See BYZANTIUM.

Chalcidicē Northwestern coast of the AEGEAN SEA, located in what eventually became Macedonian territory, north of Greece proper. Chalcidicē is distinguished by three peninsulas, each about 30 miles long, jutting into the Aegean and providing harbors and natural defense. These three, west to east, were called Pallene, Sithonia, and Acte (meaning "promontory" in Greek).

Originally inhabited by Thracians, the region was colonized in the latter 700s B.C. by Greeks from the city of CHALCIS; they established about 30 settlements and gave the region its Greek name, "Chalcidian land." Among later Greek arrivals were Corinthians who, circa 600 B.C., founded the important city of POTIDAEA on the narrow neck of the Acte peninsula. Another prominent city was OLYNTHUS, founded in the 400s B.C., north of Potidaea.

Chalcidicē offered precious TIMBER, SILVER ore, and SLAVES, and controlled the coastal shipping route to the HELLESPONT. The prosperous Chalcidic towns had become tribute-paying members of the Athenian-dominated DELIAN LEAGUE by the mid-400s B.C., but in the spring of 432 B.C. Potidaea revolted unsuccessfully against the Athenians. More revolts followed the arrival of the Spartan general BRASIDAS in 432 B.C., during the PELOPONNESIAN WAR. The town of Scione, recaptured by the Athenians in 421 B.C., was treated with exemplary cruelty: All men of military age were killed and the WOMEN and children were sold as slaves.

Chalcidicē endured a generation of Spartan rule after SPARTA's victory in the Peloponnesian War (404 B.C.), yet meanwhile the Chalcidic towns organized themselves into a federation, with a shared citizenship and government and with Potidaea as the capital (circa 400 B.C.). In the 370s B.C. this Chalcidic League joined the SECOND ATHENIAN LEAGUE. But renewed Athenian interference with Potidaea drove the Chalcidic Greeks to make an alliance with the ambitious Macedonian king PHILIP II (356 B.C.). Resistance to Philip led to war, in which Philip captured and destroyed Olynthus and Potidaea (348 B.C.). Henceforth the region was ruled by MACEDON.

Chalcidicē revived under the Macedonian king CASSANDER (reigned 316–298 B.C.). He built a grand new city, Cassandreia, on the site of the ruined Potidaea.

(See also ARISTOTLE.)

Chalcis Important city midway along the west coast of the large inshore island called EUBOEA, in east-central Greece. Chalcis was strategically located on the narrow Euripus channel, so as to control all shipping through the Euboean Straits. Inland and southward, the city enjoyed the fertile plain of Lelanton.

Inhabited by Greeks of the Ionian ethnic group, Chalcis and its neighbor ERETRIA had emerged by about 850 B.C. as the most powerful cities of early Greece. Chalcis—its name refers to local copper deposits or to worked BRONZE (both: *chalkos*)—thrived as a manufacturing center, and its drive for raw metals and other goods placed it at the forefront of Greek overseas TRADE and COLONIZATION circa 800–650 B.C. Seafarers from Chalcis and Eretria established the first Greek trading depot that we know of, at AL MINA on the north Levantine coast (circa 800 B.C.). A generation later, in western ITALY, they founded the early Greek colonies PITHECUSAE and CUMAE.

Around 735 B.C. the partnership of Chalcis and Eretria ended in conflict over possession of the Lelantine plain. Chalcis apparently won this LELANTINE WAR (by 680 B.C.), and the city and its new ally CORINTH then dominated all Greek westward colonization. Among the westward colonies founded by Chalcis in this era were RHEGIUM, in southern Italy, and NAXOS (2) and ZANCLĒ, in SICILY. In the late 700s B.C., Chalcis also sent colonists to the north Aegean region eventually known as CHALCIDICĒ (Chalcidian land). But by the mid-600s B.C. Chalcis was being eclipsed in commerce by Corinth.

According to tradition, Chalcis' last king was killed in the Lelantine War, after which the city was governed as an ARISTOCRACY led by the *hippobotai* (horse-owners), Chalcidian nobles. In 506 B.C. these aristocrats, with help from nearby BOEOTIA, made war on ATHENS and its newly democratic government. Chalcis was completely defeated, and a portion of the *hippobotai's* land was confiscated for an Athenian garrison colony.

Chalcis contributed 20 warships to the defense of Greece in the PERSIAN WARS (480–479 B.C.). Soon after, Chalcis and all the other Euboean cities were compelled to join the Athenian-led DELIAN LEAGUE. In 446 B.C. Chalcis led a Euboean revolt from the league, but Athens crushed this harshly, exiling the *hippobotai*. A successful revolt followed later, amid the Delian uprisings of the later PELOPONNESIAN WAR (411 B.C.). However, after a bitter taste of Spartan overlordship, Chalcis joined the SECOND ATHENIAN LEAGUE (378 B.C.).

The Macedonian king PHILIP II conquered the Greeks in 338 B.C. and placed a garrison in Chalcis. For the next 140 years or more, Chalcis served as a Macedonian stronghold—one of the Macedonians' four "fetters" of Greece.

In 194 B.C. the Romans ejected the Macedonian garrison; however, as a member of the anti-Roman Achaean League, Chalcis was besieged and captured by the Romans in 146 B.C. The city recovered, to play a role in the empire of ROME.

(See also ACHAEA; ALPHABET; GREECE, GEOGRAPHY OF; IONIAN GREEKS; MACEDON.)

chariots The chariot—an axled, two-wheeled vehicle typically pulled by horses—played a small but picturesque role in Greek history. Circa 1600–1200 B.C. the kings of the MYCENAEAN CIVILZATION kept fleets of war chariots, as indicated by archaeological evidence (including an extant Mycenaean tomb-carving and texts of LINEAR B tablets listing inventories of chariots and chariot parts). The Mycenaean chariot probably was made of wood plated with BRONZE, with upright sides and front. It was drawn by two horses and carried two soldiers—the driver and a passenger armed with spears or arrows.

Although the chariot would have served well for display and for sportsmanlike Mycenaean battles on the plains of ARGOS, BOEOTIA, and THESSALY, it must have had very limited use elsewhere, in the hilly Greek terrain. Modern scholars believe the Mycenaeans copied the chariot's use from Near Eastern armies—either from the Hittites of ASIA MINOR or the New Kingdom Egyptians—without themselves having a clear tactical need for such a vehicle. Evidently the Mycenaeans were attracted to the machine's pure glamour.

Mycenaean chariots are commemorated in HOMER's *Iliad* (written down circa 750 B.C. but purporting to describe events of circa 1200 B.C.). Homer describes chariots as two-horse, two-man vehicles that bring aristocratic heroes such as ACHILLES and HECTOR to and from the battle. For actual fighting, the warrior leaps to the ground while the driver whisks the chariot to the sidelines. Modern scholars doubt that this poetic picture is accurate. Homer, presumably without realizing his mistake, has represented Mycenaean chariots as being used exactly as horses were used in his own day—to carry noble champions to battle. In fact (says the modern theory), like their Hittite and Egyptian counterparts, Mycenaean chariots seem to have taken part directly in combat—in charges, sweeps, and similar tactics—with an archer or spearman stationed inside each vehicle.

After the destruction of Mycenaean society and the ensuing DARK AGE (circa 1100–900 B.C.), the Greek chariot became used purely for SPORT, in races held at the great religious-athletic festivals. Because of this new function, the chariot evolved a new design. They were usually a one-man vehicles drawn by four horses or, sometimes, by four mules. During the 700s–100s B.C., the most prestigious competition in the entire Greek world was the race of horse chariots at the OLYMPIC GAMES. Coming last in the sequence of Olympic events, this race involved dozens of chariots in 12 laps around the stadium's elongated track, for a total distance of almost nine miles. Like the later chariot races of imperial ROME, the Greek sport offered considerable danger of collisions and other mishaps. For instance, at the PYTHIAN GAMES of 482 B.C., the winning chariot finished alone in a starting field of 41 vehicles.

The official competitors in a chariot race were not usually the drivers (who were professionals), but the people sponsoring the individual chariots. It was a sport for the rich, requiring large-scale breeding and training of horses. For Greek aristocrats and rulers, an Olympic chariot victory was the crowning achievement of public life. To help celebrate such a triumph, a winner might commission a lyric poet such as PINDAR (circa 476 B.C.) to write a victory song.

Among the more famous chariot owners was the flamboyant Athenian politican ALCIBIADES. For the Olympic Games of 416 B.C., he sponsored no less than seven chariots, which finished first, second, and fourth.

(See also ARISTOCRACY; PELOPS; WARFARE, LAND.)

Charon   See AFTERLIFE; FUNERAL CUSTOMS.

Charybdis   See SCYLLA.

Chersonese   The Chersonēsos ("peninsula") was a 50-mile-long arm of the northeastern Aegean coast, alongside northwestern ASIA MINOR. The peninsula's eastern shore forms the western side of the HELLESPONT—the 33-mile-long strait that was a crucial part of the ancient TRADE route to the BLACK SEA. To control the Hellespont, great powers such as ATHENS and MACEDON sought to hold the Chersonese. In modern times this region is known as Gallipoli, the scene of bloody fighting in World War I.

Although part of the non-Greek land of THRACE, the Chersonese began receiving Greek colonists from LESBOS and MILETUS by the 600s B.C. Athenian settlers arrived in the early 500s B.C. The elder Miltiades, an Athenian, ruled most of the Chersonese as his private fief (mid-500s B.C.). His nephew and successor, the famous MILTIADES, abandoned the area to Persian invasion.

After the PERSIAN WARS, the Chersonese settlements were dominated by Athens through the DELIAN LEAGUE. In 338 B.C. the region passed to the Macedonian king PHILIP II. Thereafter it was held by various Hellenistic kingdoms, until the Romans conquered Greece and Macedon in the mid-100s B.C..

The Chersonese had two chief cities, both Greek: SESTOS, which was the commanding fortress of the Hellespont; and Cardia, on the peninsula's western side.

Chilon   Spartan EPHOR who lived in the mid-500s B.C. and who is credited with certain developments in SPARTA's government and foreign policy. Apparently, Chilon increased the ephors' power to counterbalance the two Spartan kings, and he probably launched Sparta's policy of hostility to TYRANTS throughout Greece. He also organized Sparta's individual alliances with other states—including CORINTH and SICYON—into a permanent network of mutual defense, which modern scholars call the Peloponnesian League.

Revered at Sparta after his death, Chilon was counted as one of the SEVEN SAGES of Greece. His political heir was the Spartan king CLEOMENES (1), who reigned circa 520–489 B.C..

Chios   Large Aegean island, 30 miles long and 8–15 miles wide, lying close to the coast of ASIA MINOR. The main city, also named Chios, was situated on the island's east coast (five miles across from the Asian mainland) and was one of the foremost Greek city-states.

Occupied circa 1000 B.C. by IONIAN GREEKS from mainland Greece, Chios thrived as a maritime power whose exports included a renowned WINE as well as textiles, grain, figs, and mastic (a tree resin used for varnish). Chios figured prominently in the cultural achievements of the east Greek region known as IONIA. The island is said to have been the birthplace of the poet HOMER (born probably circa 800 B.C.); in later centuries a guild of bards, the Homeridae, or sons of Homer, were active there. Chios was also known as an international slave emporium, supplying the markets of Asia Minor and itself employing many SLAVES for FARMING and manufacturing.

During the Greek wars of the 700s–600s B.C., Chios tended to ally itself with MILETUS, against such nearby rivals as Erythrae and SAMOS. In government, the emergence of certain democratic forms at Chios is shown in an inscription (circa 560 B.C.) that mentions a "People's Council"—possibly a democratically elected COUNCIL and court of appeals. This democratic apparatus may have been modeled on the recent reforms of SOLON at ATHENS.

Like the rest of Ionia and Asia Minor, Chios fell to the conquering Persian king CYRUS (1) in around 545 B.C. In the ill-fated IONIAN REVOLT against Persian rule, Chios contributed 100 warships, which fought gallantly at the disastrous Battle of Lade (494 B.C.). Later the avenging Persians devastated Chios.

Following the liberation of Ionia during the PERSIAN WARS (479 B.C.), Chios became a prominent member of the Athenian-dominated DELIAN LEAGUE. Chios chose to make its Delian annual contributions in warships rather than in SILVER—one of the few league members to do so. For 65 years Chios proved the most steadfast of any Athenian ally. The Athenians paid Chios the compliment of coupling its name with that of Athens itself in public prayer at each Athenian ASSEMBLY. But in 412 B.C., with Athens' power dissolving during the PELOPONNESIAN WAR, Chios initiated the revolt of the Delian subject cities. Chios staved off the vengeful Athenians, and by 411 B.C. the island was firmly controlled by Athens' enemy, SPARTA.

After 30 years of Spartan domination, the Chians joined the SECOND ATHENIAN LEAGUE, but in 354 B.C. revolted from Athens again. During the 200s B.C., in resistance to the SELEUCID Empire's designs, Chios joined the Aetolian League. The island passed to Roman control in the next century.

(See also AETOLIA; DEMOCRACY.)

choral poetry   See LYRIC POETRY.

chorus   See LYRIC POETRY; THEATER.

Cilicia   See ASIA MINOR.

Cimon   Athenian soldier and conservative statesman in the 460s B.C. who lived circa 505–450 B.C. Cimon briefly dominated Athenian politics but succumbed to the failure of his pro-Spartan policy. He was the political enemy of the radical democrats, and his decline after 462 B.C. marked the rise of the young left-wing politician PERICLES. In foreign policy, Cimon was the last great Athenian enemy of PERSIA, and his death ushered in a Greek-Persian peace treaty that officially concluded the PERSIAN WARS.

Cimon (Greek: Kimon) was born into a rich and eminent family, the Philaïds. His father was the Athenian soldier MILTIADES; his mother, Hegesipyle, was daughter of a Thracian king. By the 470s B.C., Cimon was regularly being elected to the office of general. He assisted ARISTIDES in the organization of the DELIAN LEAGUE (circa 478 B.C.), and from 476 to 462 B.C. he was the premier Athenian soldier, leading the league's expeditions against the Persians. He became known particularly as a sea commander.

Cimon's height of success came in 469 or 466 B.C. (the exact date is unknown) when, with 200 league warships, he totally destroyed a Persian fleet and army at the River Eurymedon, midway along the south coast of ASIA MINOR. In purely military terms, the Eurymedon was the greatest

Greek victory over Persia prior to the campaigns of ALEXANDER THE GREAT (334–323 B.C.).

At home, this success established Cimon in Athenian politics. Gracious and well-connected (his first or second wife, Isodice, was of the powerful Alcmaeonid clan), Cimon now emerged as leader of the conservative opposition. He blocked left-wing reforms and advocated an old-fashioned policy of hostility toward Persia and friendship with SPARTA. He even gave one of his sons the striking name Lacedaemonius, "Spartan."

Cimon's downfall came after he persuaded the ASSEMBLY to send him with an Athenian infantry force to assist the Spartans against their rebellious subjects, the Messenians (462 B.C.). This expedition ended in fiasco; the Spartans—fighting a serf rebellion—apparently found the Athenian soldiers' pro-democratic sentiments alarming and sent the Athenians home. Humiliated, Cimon now saw his conservative party swept out of power by democratic reforms sponsored by EPHIALTES and Pericles. In the following year, 461 B.C., the angry Athenians voted to ostracize Cimon.

Although the OSTRACISM law allowed a victim to return home after 10 years, this event ended Cimon's power and policies. Soon Athens began a full-fledged war against Sparta and its allies (460 B.C.). In 457 B.C., when the Athenian army was about to battle the Spartans near Tanagra, in BOEOTIA, the exiled Cimon arrived, asking permission to fight alongside his countrymen. Permission was refused but, according to one story, Cimon was specially recalled to Athens soon after.

In 450 B.C. he died while leading Athenian troops against the Persians in CYPRUS. He was remembered for his nobility and bravery, but his policies were at odds with Athens' destiny as a radical democracy that would dominate the rest of Greece.

(See also ALCMAEONIDS; CALLIAS; MESSENIA; WARFARE, NAVAL.)

Circe   In MYTH, a beautiful goddess and witch, daughter of the sun god HELIOS and his wife, Perse. Circe dwelt on a magical island in the West, in a stone house with enchanted wolves and lions. Her name (Greek: Kirkē) seems derived from kirkos, "hawk."

Circe plays a sinister but exciting role in Homer's epic poem the *Odyssey* (book 10). When the homeward-bound Greek hero ODYSSEUS brings his ship to her island and sends half his crew ashore to scout, she welcomes them with a magic drink that turns them into pigs. Odysseus goes to their rescue, armed with a magical herb called moly (*molu*)—the gift of the god HERMES—that makes him immune to Circe's spells. Odysseus forces her to restore his men's human shapes. Then, at her invitation, he lives with her for a year as her lover, but finally demands that she give him directions for his continued voyage home. Circe's advice (book 12) enables Odysseus to resist the deadly SIRENS and avoid other dangers. Circe is one of two supernatural women who become Odysseus' lovers during his wondrous voyage; the other is CALYPSO.

Generations of Greeks after Homer elaborated Circe's story. Her home was sometimes identified with Monte Circeo, a promontory midway along the west coast of ITALY. According to one story, she bore Odysseus' son Telegonus, who later unwittingly killed his father. In APOL-

LONIUS' epic poem, the *Argonautica*, Circe welcomes JASON (1) and MEDEA after their escape from the kingdom of Colchis.

city-state   See POLIS.

Cleisthenes (1)   Athenian statesman of the late 500s B.C., usually considered to be the father of Athenian DE-MOCRACY. Cleisthenes began his career as a privileged aristocrat in a political arena of TYRANTS and aristocrats; but, whether through pure ambition or genuine convictions, he used his influence to reorganize the government to enlarge the common people's rights.

Born circa 560 B.C. into the noble Athenian clan of the ALCMAEONIDS, Cleisthenes (Greek: Kleisthenes) was son of the politician Megacles and of Agariste, daughter of the Sicyonian tyrant CLEISTHENES (2). The younger Cleisthenes served as ARCHON (525 B.C.) under the Athenian tyrant HIPPIAS (1), but was later banished with the rest of the Alcmaeonids, on Hippias' order.

After Hippias' ouster (510 B.C.), Cleisthenes returned to Athens and became leader of one of two rival political parties. When his opponent Isagoras was elected archon (508 B.C.), Cleisthenes struck back. According to the historian HERODOTUS, writing some 70 years later, Cleisthenes "took the common people (*dēmos*) into partnership." Cleisthenes proposed, in the Athenian ASSEMBLY, certain radical reforms to increase the common people's rights at the expense of the aristocrats. This program made Cleisthenes the most powerful individual at Athens, with all the common people behind him. His reforms continued a process begun by the lawmaker SOLON nearly 90 years prior and transformed Athens into a full democracy, the first in world history.

Cleisthenes' changes were extensive and complicated. The enabling first step was to improve the rights of the mass of poorer citizens (the laborers and peasants, called *thetes.*) The *thetes* were disadvantaged by the traditional system of four Athenian tribes (*phulai* or phylae). These tribes, which supplied the basis for public life in the city, were traditionally dominated by aristocratic families. Cleisthenes overhauled the tribal system, replacing the four old phylae with 10 new ones. Each new tribe was designed to include a thorough mix of Athenians—farmers with city dwellers, aristocrats and their followers with middle-class people and *thetes*. The effect was to reduce greatly the influence of the nobles within each tribe.

To create his new, "mixed-up" tribes, Cleisthenes reorganized the political map of ATTICA, the 1,000-square-mile territory of Athens that included all Athenian citizens. It was now, if not earlier, that Attica became administratively divided into about 139 DEMES—*dēmoi*, "villages" or local wards. By means of Cleisthenes' complicated gerrymandering, each new tribe was made to consist of several demes (an average of about 14, but the actual numbers varied between six and 21). Typically these tribal-constituent demes were unconnected by geography, traditional allegiances, and the like. The new tribes thus were relatively free from aristocratic domination and from the localism and feuding associated with aristocratic domination. Across the map of Attica, the traditional pockets of local-family influence were, in effect, broken up.

With his 10 tribes as a basis, Cleisthenes democratized other aspects of the government. The people's COUNCIL was enlarged from 400 to 500 members, now consisting of 50 citizens from each tribe, chosen by lot from a pool of upper- and middle-class candidates. The Athenian citizens' assembly received new powers, such as the judicial right to try or review certain court cases. But these radical changes did not go unchallenged. Cleisthenes' rival Isagoras appealed to the Spartan king CLEOMENES (1), who marched on Athens with a small Spartan force. Cleisthenes and his followers fled (507 B.C.). But when Cleomenes attempted to replace the new democracy with an OLIGARCHY consisting of Isagoras and his followers, the Athenian populace rose in resistance. Cleomenes and his army were besieged atop the Athenian ACROPOLIS, then were allowed to withdraw, taking Isagoras with them.

Cleisthenes returned to Athens, but soon his prominence was over. He may have involved himself in diplomatic overtures to the Persian king DARIUS (1), and if so he would have been disgraced in the ensuing anti-Persian sentiment. But when Cleisthenes died (circa 500 B.C.), he received a public tomb in the honorific Ceramicus cemetery, just outside Athens. His democratization of Athens would be taken further by the radical reforms of EPHIALTES and PERICLES, in the mid-400s B.C..

(See also KINSHIP; OSTRACISM.)

Cleisthenes (2)   Tyrant of the Peloponnesian city of SICYON and maternal grandfather of the Athenian statesman CLEISTHENES (1). Cleisthenes ruled Sicyon from about 600 to 570 B.C., when the city was one of the foremost commercial and military powers in Greece. He extended his influence to DELPHI by leading a coalition against PHOCIS in the First Sacred War (circa 590 B.C.) and crowned his achievements with a chariot victory at the OLYMPIC GAMES (circa 572 B.C.). His wealth and prestige are apparent in the historian HERODOTUS' tale of how Cleisthenes hosted his daughter Agariste's 13 suitors at his palace for a year, observing their aristocratic qualifications for marrying his daughter. The suitors came from various parts of the Greek world, but Cleisthenes favored two Athenians: Megacles, son of Alcmaeon of the clan of the ALCMAEONIDS, and Hippocleides, son of Teisander of the Philaïd clan.

On the day appointed to announce his choice, Cleisthenes held a great feast, at which the suitors competed in two final contests, lyre-playing and public speaking. Hippocleides, who outshone the others, was the one whom Cleisthenes had by now secretly chosen. But as more WINE was drunk, Hippocleides requested a tune from the flute-player and boldly began to dance. Then he called for a table and danced atop it, while Cleisthenes watched with distaste. And when Hippocleides started doing handstands on the table, beating time with his legs in the air, Cleisthenes cried out, "O, son of Teisander, you have danced away your wedding!" To which the young man replied, "Hippocleides doesn't care" (*ou phrontis Hippokleidei*).

The story became proverbial as an example of aristocratic detachment and *joie de vivre*. Agariste's hand in MARRIAGE went to Megacles, and their son was Cleisthenes, the Athenian statesman (born circa 560 B.C.).

(See also MUSIC; TYRANTS.)

Cleomenes (1)   Dynamic and ambitious king of SPARTA who reigned circa 520–489 B.C.. Cleomenes' efforts to expand Spartan power beyond the PELOPONNESE, along with his resistance to Persian encroachment, mark him as one of the dominant personalities of the late 500s B.C. Unfortunately, our major source for his reign, written by the historian HEROTODUS (circa 435 B.C.), is tainted by Spartan official revisionism that tries to diminish Cleomenes' importance.

The son of King Anaxandridas of the Agiad royal house, Cleomenes (Greek: Kleomenēs) was awarded the kingship in victorious rivalry against his half brother Doreius. Soon Cleomenes was taking aim against the Athenian dictator HIPPIAS (1). Cleomenes wanted to end Hippias' reign in order to bring ATHENS into the Spartan alliance. In addition, Hippias' diplomatic overtures to the Persian king DARIUS (1) had made Cleomenes fear that Hippias was maneuvering to assist a Persian invasion of mainland Greece. In 510 B.C. Cleomenes entered Athens with an army, ejected Hippias, and withdrew. But Cleomenes was mistaken in expecting that this would result in an Athenian OLIGARCHY friendly to Sparta. Instead, there occurred peaceful revolution, producing the Athenian DEMOCRACY (508 B.C.).

Cleomenes returned with an army in 508 or 507 B.C., intending to overthrow the new government. He captured the Athenian ACROPOLIS but found himself besieged there by the Athenian populace and withdrew under truce. His later attempt to organize a full Spartan-allied attack on Athens was blocked by the other Spartan king, Demaratus, and by Sparta's ally CORINTH (which at that time was still friendly with Athens).

Despite a request from the Greek city of MILETUS, Cleomenes wisely declined to send Spartan troops overseas to aid the IONIAN REVOLT against the Persians (499 B.C.). He had an enemy nearer home to attend to—Sparta's Peloponnesian rival, ARGOS. In 494 B.C., at the Battle of Sepeia, on the Argive plain, Cleomenes obliterated an Argive army and marched his Spartans to the walls of Argos. But the city withstood Cleomenes' siege, a failure that later was to be used against him by his enemies at Sparta.

In around 491 B.C. Persian envoys went to Sparta asking for earth and water, the tokens of submission to PERSIA. Probably at Cleomenes' prompting, the Spartans threw the Persians down a well, telling them they would find plenty of earth and water there. But other states, notably AEGINA, did submit. When Demaratus blocked Cleomenes' desired retaliation against Aegina, Cleomenes decided to rid himself of this uncooperative partner. He persuaded Demaratus' kinsman Leotychides to claim the kingship on grounds that Demaratus has been an illegitimate child, and he bribed the oracle at DELPHI to support this claim. Demaratus was deposed and succeeded by Leotychides.

Circa 490 B.C. Cleomenes was in THESSALY. According to Herodotus, the king was in hiding because his disgraceful intrigues against Demaratus had been exposed. However, it seems more likely that Cleomenes was still at the height of power and working to organize Greek resistance to Persia. He then visited ARCADIA, a Peloponnesian region traditionally under Spartan control. By then he may have been aiming at an ambitious goal—to resist the Persians by creating a unified Peloponnesian state, under his personal dictatorship. Possibly he even tried to gain support from the Spartan serfs known as HELOTS, promising them freedom in exchange.

After returning to Sparta, Cleomenes died violently. According to the official version, he took his life in a fit of insanity. But it looks as if he were assassinated by conservative Spartan elements. His successor was his half brother, Leonidas, who was fated to die at the Battle of THERMOPYLAE (480 B.C.), resisting the Persian invasion that Cleomenes had tried to prevent.

(See also AGIAD CLAN; CLEISTHENES (1); PERSIAN WARS.)

Cleomenes (2)   See SPARTA.

Cleon   Athenian demagogue (rabble-rouser) of the early PELOPONNESIAN WAR. For seven years after the death of the statesman PERICLES (429–422 B.C.), the left-wing Cleon was the foremost politician in ATHENS. Although not really a soldier, he was the one person at the time who—by his bold planning and determination—could have won the war for Athens. But he was killed in battle in 422 B.C., and the Athenian war leadership passed temporarily to the cautious NICIAS.

Most information about Cleon comes from the written work of his contemporary, the Athenian historian THUCYDIDES (1). The normally objective Thucydides viewed Cleon with distaste and underestimated his importance. Similarly, Cleon was despised by the Athenian comic playwright ARISTOPHANES, who mocked him in the *Knights* (424 B.C.) and other comedies as a crowd-pleasing opportunist. Yet despite the disapproval of such intellectuals, Cleon probably was widely viewed as Pericles' legitimate successor. Although Cleon came to prominence by attacking the aging Pericles (431 B.C.), he also imitated Pericles in his obsessive loyalty to the Athenian common people (*dēmos*), who were his power base. That is why, in the *Knights,* Aristophanes uses the name Philodemos (lover of the people) for his character who is a caricature of Cleon.

The son of a rich tanner of hides, Cleon (Greek: Kleon) was an accomplished orator who could whip up public opinion in the Athenian ASSEMBLY; he is said to have introduced a more vulgar and demonstrative mode of public speaking. He reached his peak of power in 425 B.C., after Athens had gained the advantage in the fighting against the Spartans at PYLOS. Accusing the Athenian generals of incompetence, Cleon won command of the entire Pylos campaign by acclamation of the assembly. He journeyed to Pylos, where—helped by the Athenian general DEMOSTHENES (2)—he won a total victory over the supposedly invincible Spartans.

Then preeminent in Athenian politics, Cleon presumably is the one who prompted the notorious "Thoudippos Decree" (425 B.C.), which authorized a reassessment of the annual tribute to be paid to Athens by its DELIAN LEAGUE allies. The decree resulted in a doubling or tripling of the amounts due from individual allied states. Around the same time, Cleon sponsored a law increasing jury pay, to the advantage of lower-income citizens.

Elected as a general for 422 B.C., he led an Athenian army to the north Aegean coast, to recapture the area from the Spartan commander BRASIDAS. But at the Battle of AMPHIPOLIS, Cleon was defeated and killed. Thucydides mentions that he was running away when an enemy skirmisher cut him down.

(See also DEMOCRACY; LAWS AND LAW COURTS; MYTILENE.)

Cleopatra   Dynastic female name of the Macedonian royal family in the 300s B.C., later used by the Macedonian-descended Ptolemies of EGYPT. The name Kleopatra means "glory of her father" in Greek. The famous Cleopatra—Cleopatra VII, daughter of Ptolemy XII—was the last Ptolemaic ruler of Egypt and also the last Hellenistic ruler outside Roman control. Upon her death in 30 B.C., Egypt was annexed by ROME.

(See also HELLENISTIC AGE; PTOLEMY (1).)

clothing   The ancient Greeks had no fashion industry; most clothing, typically made of wool or linen, was woven at home. Greek female servants and wives might spend much of their day indoors, spinning yarn and weaving on the loom. Clothing was simple and loose-fitting, with only a few basic forms and much similarity between garments for men and WOMEN.

Information about Greek clothing comes from written sources and from scenes in extant artwork, particularly vase paintings. Males and females wore the tunic, which looked like a sleeveless nightgown or dress. The woman's tunic, called a *peplos*, would typically fall to the feet, with extra material pinned around the shoulders—it could be worn with or without a belt. In addition, there might be an undergarment and a cloak around the shoulders.

Equipped for the gentlemanly pastime of hunting, a youth wears a woolen riding cloak and leather boots, with his broad-rimmed Greek traveler's hat slung back. This red-figure scene was painted on the inside bottom of an Athenian cup, circa 475 B.C.

The man's tunic was the *chiton*. Simpler and lighter than the Roman toga, the Greek *chiton* might fall to the feet (in the Ionian fashion) or merely to the knees or above (in the Dorian fashion). The shorter style was favored by workmen, farmers, and soldiers, who wore tunics underneath their body armor. Like women, men might wear a cloak (*himation*). For horseback riding, younger men often wore a distinctive wide cloak (the *chlamus*, or chlamys).

Travelers, workmen, and sailors might wear a conical cap known as a *pilos*; travelers, hunters, and others sometimes wore the low, broad-rimmed hat (*petasos*), to protect against the hot Greek sun. The footwear of choice for heavy walking was sandals or leather boots; otherwise clogs or slippers were worn.

(See also POTTERY).

Clytaemnestra   In MYTH, the wife and murderer of King AGAMEMNON of MYCENAE. Clytaemnestra was the daughter of the Spartan queen Leda. According to different versions of the tale, Clytaemnestra's father was either the god ZEUS or Leda's husband, the Spartan king Tyndareus. Clytaemnestra had the famous HELEN OF TROY for a twin sister and CASTOR AND POLYDEUCES for her brothers. Her name, Klutaimnēstra, probably means "famous wooing" or "famous intent."

As Agamemnon's wife, Clytaemnestra bore a son, ORESTES, and two daughters, ELECTRA and IPHIGENIA. But she grew to hate her husband when he chose to sacrifice Iphigenia to appease the goddess ARTEMIS, who was sending contrary winds to block the Greeks' sailing fleet at the start of the TROJAN WAR. During Agamemnon's 10-year absence at TROY, Clytaemnestra became the lover of Agamemnon's cousin Aegisthus, and the two plotted to kill the king on his return. In the act, they also killed the Trojan princess CASSANDRA, whom Agamemnon had brought home as his war prize.

Afterward, Clytaemnestra and Aegisthus ruled as queen and king at Mycenae. They were eventually killed in vengeance by Orestes, with Electra assisting.

Clytaemnestra's character shows a growth in strength and evil during the centuries of Greek literature. Where she is first mentioned in HOMER's epic poem the *Odyssey* (written down circa 750 B.C.), she is overshadowed by the vigorous Aegisthus, who seduces her and plots the murder. But in AESCHYLUS' tragedy *Agamemnon* (performed 458 B.C.), Clytaemnestra is the proud and malevolent prime mover, and Aegisthus is just her effete, subordinate lover. In the play, she persuades the newly arrived Agamemnon to tread atop a priceless tapestry; he thereby unwittingly calls down heaven's anger on himself. Then she leads him to his bath, where she murders him and Cassandra.

Agamemnon is the first play of Aeschylus' Oresteian Trilogy. In the following play, the *Choēphoroi* (or *Libation Bearers*), Clytaemnestra and Aegisthus are slain by Orestes. As she dies, she calls down the avenging FURIES upon her son. A hateful Clytaemnestra is portrayed also in SOPHOCLES' tragedy *Electra* and EURIPIDES' tragedy *Electra* (both circa 417 B.C.). In vase painting, Clytaemnestra sometimes is shown as wielding a double ax against Agamemnon or Cassandra or (unsuccessfully) against Orestes.

(See also HUBRIS; THEATER.)

Cnidus Prosperous Greek city of the southwestern coast of ASIA MINOR. Founded circa 900 B.C. by DORIAN GREEKS from mainland Greece, Cnidus and its neighbor HALICAR-NASSUS were the two important Dorian cities of Asia Minor, and were part of a larger eastern Mediterranean Dorian federation including the islands of Cos and RHODES.

Cnidus (Greek: Knidos) stood on the side of a lofty promontory jutting into the sea, and it thrived as a seaport and maritime power. In search of raw metals such as tin, the Cnidians founded trade depots on the Lipari Islands and elsewhere in the western Mediterranean. When the Persians attacked Asia Minor under King CYRUS (1) in 546 B.C., the Cnidians tried to convert their city into an inshore island by digging a canal across the peninsula. Finding the work slow and injurious, they consulted the Oracle of DELPHI and were told to abandon resistance and make submission.

After the liberation of Greek Asia Minor in 479 B.C., Cnidus became a tribute-paying member of the DELIAN LEAGUE, under Athenian domination. In 413 B.C., with ATHENS losing ground in the PELOPONNESIAN WAR, Cnidus joined the general Delian revolt and became a Spartan ally. In 394 B.C., during the CORINTHIAN WAR, the Athenian admiral CONON destroyed a Spartan fleet in a battle off Cnidus.

Returned to Persian overlordship by the terms of the KING'S PEACE (386 B.C.), Cnidus was reliberated in 334 B.C. by the Macedonian king ALEXANDER THE GREAT. Circa 330 B.C. the city's public and commercial buildings were rebuilt near the tip of its peninsula to take advantage of the superior harbor there. By then the city had reached its height of prosperity, being renowned for its exported WINE and its school of MEDICINE. Cnidus housed a statue that was considered to be the most beautiful in the world: the naked APHRODITE carved in marble by PRAXITILES circa 364 B.C. According to one ancient writer, people would voyage to Cnidus expressly to view this work.

During the HELLENISTIC AGE, Cnidus became subject to Ptolemaic EGYPT (200s B.C.). By the later 100s B.C. the city was part of the empire of ROME.

(See also BRONZE; PERSIAN WARS.)

Cnossus Chief city of the island of CRETE for most of the 2,000 years before Christ. Located in the north-central part of the island, about three miles inland, Cnossus had a good harbor—the site of the modern seaport of Heraklion—and also guarded a major land route southward across the middle of Crete. Cnossus was the capital city of the MINOAN CIVILIZATION, which thrived on Crete circa 2200–1450 B.C. and controlled a naval empire in the AEGEAN SEA. Although the Minoans were not themselves Greek, they stand at the threshold of Greek history insofar as they deeply influenced the emerging Greek MYCENAEAN CIVILIZATION (circa 1600–1200 B.C.). The name Knossos is in origin a pre-Greek word, probably from the lost Minoan language.

Cnossus today is one of the world's most important archaeological sites, containing remnants of the largest Minoan palace, the seat of the Minoan rulers. First erected in around 1950 B.C. and then rebuilt and enlarged after earthquakes in around 1700 and 1570 B.C., the palace was first revealed to modern eyes by the British archaeologist

Sir Arthur Evans in A.D. 1900. The building and environs, excavated almost continuously since then, have yielded such well-known Minoan artwork as the Bull's Head Rhyton and the Toreador Fresco, now in the Heraklion archaeological museum.

Built mainly of large blocks of Cretan limestone, the palace survives today mostly as a network of foundations and wall remnants covering five and a half acres. Around a central, square courtyard measuring 82 by 180 feet, the building contained pillared hallways, staircases, and hundreds of rooms and storage chambers in a mazelike configuration. There were two or even three upper floors, now partly reconstructed. Among the palace's splendors was running water, carried in clay pipes. The building's size and complexity—unequaled in 1700 B.C. outside the urban centers of EGYPT and Mesopotamia—probably inspired the later Greek legend of the Cretan LABYRINTH.

Remarkably, the palace had no enclosing wall; the Minoans evidently trusted in their navy for defense. Nevertheless, the palace was completely destroyed by fire in around 1400 B.C. or soon after, and was never rebuilt. As shown by ARCHAEOLOGY, every other known Minoan site on Crete also was destroyed at this time. The cause for such widespread ruin may have been an invasion of Crete by warlike Mycenaeans from the Greek mainland. Intriguingly, it seems that the Cnossus palace already had been occupied by certain Mycenaeans prior to its destruction. This conclusion is reached because the palace debris of this era has yielded up nearly 4,000 clay tablets, inscribed with inventory notes written in the Greek LINEAR B script, identical to the script later used at Mycenaean sites on the mainland. But whoever it was who destroyed the palace, evidently Cnossus and all of Crete were abandoned thereafter by the Mycenaeans.

In around 1000 B.C. Crete was occupied by new conquerors—the DORIAN GREEKS, invading from the PELOPONNESE. Cnossus, with its superior location, became Dorian Crete's foremost city-state. Like the other Cretan cities, it was governed as a military ARISTOCRACY, with social and political institutions similar to those at SPARTA. Dorian-ethnic nobles ruled over a rural population of non-Dorian serfs.

Cnossus shared in Crete's general decline after the 600s B.C. By the late 200s B.C. it had fallen into a debilitating conflict with its Cretan rival city, GORTYN. When the Romans annexed Crete in 67 B.C., they chose Gortyn over Cnossus as their provincial capital.

For the classical Greeks, Cnossus kept its associations with a dimly remembered, fictionalized Minoan past. The myths of DAEDALUS, MINOS, and THESEUS describe Cnossus as a city of grandeurs and horrors.

(See also GREEK LANGUAGE; HELOTS.)

coinage The first coins came into use in the 600s B.C. But long before then the ancient Greeks traded (by barter) and understood the concepts of value and profit. Among the Greeks, the forerunners of the coin were certain implements used for representing high value. One such was the bar of SILVER, usually called an ingot. Several ingots might comprise the monetary unit known as the TALENT (Greek *talanton*, "weight"), equivalent to just under 58 pounds of silver. Another precious metal of those days was IRON.

A silver Athenian tetradrachm, or four-drachma piece, minted circa 440 B.C. One side shows the city's patron goddess, Athena, garlanded with olive leaves; the other side shows Athena's bird, the owl. The Greek lettering reads: *ATHE.* This drawing presents the coin at three times its actual size.

The Greeks developed a high-level currency based on the iron rods (*oboloi*), traded by the handful (*drachmē*). These rods remained in circulation down through the 500s B.C. and even later in the reclusive city of SPARTA.

The invention of coins—easily stored, transported, and counted—marked an improvement over ingots or rods. The first nation on earth to mint coins was most likely the kingdom of LYDIA, in ASIA MINOR, circa 635 B.C. The Lydians were not Greek, but the Greeks seem to have imported and studied this new Lydian invention. Modern archaeologists have uncovered Lydian coins composed of electrum (an alloy of silver and GOLD) at the ancient Greek city of EPHESUS, in Asia Minor. Stamped with a lion figure "seal of approval" as a royal guarantee of weight and purity, these Lydian coins may have been given to pay large groups of artisans or mercenary soldiers, who surely included Greeks. Before long, Greeks were minting their own coins, copied from the Lydian ones.

According to ancient writers, the first Greek minting state was AEGINA (probably circa 595 B.C.). The Aeginetan coins were silver, in three sizes that cleverly employed the denominations already existing for iron rods. The smallest coin was called the obol, the next the drachm, and the largest the didrachm (two drachmas), or statēr. The Aeginetan statēr showed a sea turtle, the city symbol. The other two early Greek coining states were ATHENS (circa 575 B.C.) and CORINTH (circa 570 B.C.)—both, like Aegina, trading and maritime powers.

By the 400s B.C. every important Greek state was minting its own coins, as a sign of independence and an aid to TRADE. There was not yet a uniform system of denominations; rather, each city tended to follow one of two available systems. Silver remained the prime coining metal (gold being a scarce resource for the Greeks). But coinages of BRONZE, to cover lower denominations, began in the mid-400s B.C. And by the mid-300s B.C. gold coins were being minted by certain states such as MACEDON, which had supplies of gold ore.

Unlike some modern currency, a Greek coin was intended to contain an unadulterated amount of precious metal equal to the face value: The stamp on the coin was meant to guarantee this. The earliest Greek coins were stamped on only one side. To prepare such a coin, the smith would place a blank, heated disk of metal on an anvil atop a shallow die bearing the engraved shape of the intended imprint. The disk was then punched into the die by a rod (Greek: *charaktēr*), hammered at one end. The resulting coin would bear a relief created by the die on one side (the "obverse") and a mere indentation on the other (the "reverse"). By about 530 B.C. the Greeks had learned to make two-sided coins by using a rod whose lower end also bore an engraved die.

To judge from the hundreds of specimens surviving today, Greek coins were intended as objects of beauty and as means of civic propaganda. Extant coins bear such charming or stirring emblems as the Athenian owl, the Corinthian winged horse Pegasus, and the man-faced, bull-bodied river god of GELA. Coins also became a medium for accurate profile portraiture; it is from coins that we know what certain ancient personages looked like. In the late 300s B.C., for instance, the successors of ALEXANDER THE GREAT paid homage to his memory—and laid claim to his empire—by issuing coins showing his portrait.

Greek coinage changed at this time, in the aftermath of Alexander's conquest of the Persian Empire. Under Hellenistic kings ruling vast territories in an enlarged Greek world, there arose uniform coinages used over large areas and not necessarily differing from city to city. Important coining states of the 200s and 100s B.C. included Macedon, the SELEUCID EMPIRE, Hellenistic EGYPT, PERGAMUM, and the Greek leagues of ACHAEA and AETOLIA. Also, the Greco-Macedonian kings of BACTRIA commemorated themselves in a series of remarkably vivid personal portraits on coins. Of the older Greek states, only Athens and Rhodes continued minting.

Most Greek coinage ceased during the Roman conquests in the two centuries before Jesus. Henceforth the Greeks relied mainly on coins minted by the imperial city of ROME.

(See also ATHENA; BELLEROPHON; DIADOCHI; HELLENISTIC AGE; HIMERA.)

colonization   Even prior to the conquests of ALEXANDER THE GREAT (circa 334–323 B.C.), the ancient Greek world stretched from Libya and southern France to CYPRUS, ASIA MINOR, and the Crimean peninsula. This Greek proliferation around the Mediterranean and BLACK SEA took place during the great colonizing era of the 700s through 500s B.C., when Greek cities extended their TRADE routes (and alleviated domestic food shortages and other population problems) by sending out shipborne expeditions of young male colonists. Sailing along sea routes already scouted by Greek traders, these colonists might travel considerable distances to descend on a land typically occupied by a vulnerable, non-Greek people (such as in eastern SICILY). But coasts defended by powerful kingdoms such as EGYPT or Assyria were never colonized by early Greeks.

The colonists' new city would retain the laws, traditions, and religious cults of the mother city, or *mētropolis.* Metropolis and colony would typically enjoy cordial relations and trade agreements; for example, SYRACUSE, in Sicily, was surely bound to export surplus grain to its hungry mother city, CORINTH.

The earliest Greek colonizing took place during the MYCENAEAN CIVILIZATION, circa 1600–1200 B.C. The Mycenaean Greeks founded settlements on Cyprus and on the west coast of Asia Minor But the great age of colonization began in the mid-700s B.C., after trade and improved seamanship had begun the expansion of the Greek world. Parts of HOMER's epic poem the *Odyssey* (written down circa 750 B.C.) seem colored by a contemporary interest in trade and exploration around Sicily and the Adriatic Sea. Most modern knowledge of this period comes from archaeological evidence—building sites, POTTERY types, occasional inscriptions—and from literary sources such as the fifth-century-B.C. historians HERODOTUS and THUCYDIDES (1) and the Roman geographer Strabo.

The earliest datable colony was established circa 775 B.C. by Greeks from the commercial cities of CHALCIS and ERETRIA, in central Greece. It was a trading station on the island of PITHECUSAE, six miles off the Bay of Naples, on the central west coast of ITALY. The location reveals a purely mercantile motive; the settlement was intended as a safe haven for trade with the ETRUSCANS of mainland Italy. Later the Pithecusans crossed to the mainland, to found CUMAE.

In the 730s B.C. expeditions from mainland Greece ventured to the fertile east coast of Sicily; NAXOS (2) and ZANCLĒ were founded by Chalcis, and Syracuse by Corinth. By then the colonists were setting sail primarily for farmland. The later 700s B.C. saw colonies planted in southern coastal Italy: RHEGIUM (from Chalcis), TARAS (from SPARTA), and SYBARIS and CROTON (from ACHAEA). The colonists' hunger for Italian grainfields is symbolized in the ear-of-wheat emblem on coins minted by the Achaean colony of Metapontum, on the Italian "instep." In time, the entire southern Italian coastline, from "heel" to "toe," became dotted with Greek cities.

The north Aegean coast of THRACE received colonists by the late 700s B.C. Ousting the native Thracians, Greeks mainly from Chalcis occupied the region subsequently called the Chalcidian land—CHALCIDICĒ. Not far away, the island of THASOS was occupied by Greeks from the island of Paros. Later colonies on the Thracian coast included ABDERA, AENUS, and AMPHIPOLIS. The region offered farmland and valuable resources for export: grain, TIMBER, SLAVES, SILVER, and GOLD.

Farther east, the Black Sea and its approaches were colonized almost single-handedly by MILETUS. Of perhaps two dozen Milesian colonies here, the most important included SINOPE (founded circa 700 B.C.), CYZICUS (circa 675 B.C.), and PANTICAPAEUM (late 600s B.C.). But the city with the grandest destiny was BYZANTIUM, founded circa 667 B.C. by colonists from MEGARA (1). Among the assets of the Black Sea region were the boundless wheatfields of Ukraine and the metals trade of Asia Minor.

Circa 730 B.C. the Corinthians established CORCYRA (modern Corfu) on the northwestern coast of GREECE, 80 miles across the Adriatic from the "heel" of Italy. Later the Corinthians compensated for a Corcyrean rebellion by creating new northwestern colonies, including AMBRACIA, APOLLONIA, and Leucas (630–600 B.C.).

The North African Greek city of CYRENE (1), destined for commercial greatness, was founded by colonists from the humble island of THERA, circa 630 B.C.. To the northwest, Greeks from PHOCAEA endured Carthaginian hostility in order to establish MASSALIA (modern Marseille, in southern France) and other far-western Greek colonies, circa 600 B.C..

Like other great endeavors in the ancient world, colonization was a mixture of the utilitarian and the religious. The mother city would appoint an expedition leader, or "oikist" (*oikistēs*), who would organize the departure, lead the conquest of new land, and rule the new city as king or governor. Before departure, the oikist would seek approval for the project from the god APOLLO's oracle at DELPHI. Apollo was the patron of colonists—one of his titles was Archagetēs, "leader of expeditions"—and several colonies were named for him, including Apollonia on the Adriatic and Apollonia on the Black Sea. He was the only god who could sanction a colonizing expedition, and it was probably by careful politicking that the priesthood at Delphi was able to make its oracle of Apollo more important than any other. In the late 500s B.C. a Spartan prince Dorieus set out to found a colony without gaining Delphi's approval; eventually he and his followers were massacred by non-Greeks in western Sicily.

By the 500s B.C. colonizing had become regulated as a tool of imperialism, with great powers planting garrison colonies in militarily desirable areas. Athenian designs on the HELLESPONT in the late 500s B.C. brought Athenian colonists to Sigeum, in northwest Asia Minor, and to the Thracian CHERSONESE. The imperial ATHENS of the 400s B.C. punished its rebellious subject allies by establishing cleruchies (*klērouchiai*), which were land-grabbing Athenian colonies that acted as garrisons. Among the states to receive these onerous colonies were Chalcis, AEGINA, and LESBOS.

The use of military colonies was developed in the 330s–320s B.C. by Alexander the Great. The many cities that he established in the wake of his conquests, including several named ALEXANDRIA (1 and 2), were intended to settle veterans while also guarding lines of supply. These far-flung Greco-Macedonian settlements—such as the ancient city represented by Greek-style ruins at Aï Kanoum, in northern Afghanistan—played a crucial role in hellenizing the East during the HELLENISTIC AGE (300–150 B.C.).

Alexander's successors in EGYPT and the SELEUCID EMPIRE continued his practice of founding garrison settlements, either within the kingdom or along a frontier. The most successful of such foundations was the Seleucid city of ANTIOCH (330 B.C.). A major purpose of Hellenistic rulers' colonization was to allow the valuable Greco-Macedonian soldier class to breed and create a new generation to become heavy infantry.

(See also BOSPORUS; BRONZE; ILLYRIS; MARMARA, SEA OF; SHIPS AND SEAFARING.)

comedy   See THEATER.

commerce   See TRADE.

Conon   Athenian admiral active from 414–392 B.C. Born circa 444 B.C. into a noble family at ATHENS, Conon (Greek: Konon) commanded fleets in the final years of the PELOPONNESIAN WAR. At the disastrous Athenian naval defeat at AEGOSPOTAMI (405 B.C.), Conon alone of all the commanders got his squadron safely away from the Spartan ambush.

In the CORINTHIAN WAR (395–386 B.C.) he was active in developing the navy of Athens' ally PERSIA. Leading an Athenian squadron fighting alongside the Persians, Conon destroyed a Spartan fleet at the Battle of CNIDUS (394 B.C.). With funds from the Persian king Artaxerxes II, Conon oversaw the rebuilding of Athens' LONG WALLS. But his dreams of re-creating the Athenian empire died when the Persians switched sides in the war (392 B.C.). Conon died soon thereafter.

Corcyra   Major Greek city of the Adriatic coast, on the lush and attractive inshore island now known as Corfu. The city was situated on a peninsula on the island's east coast, opposite the Greek mainland region called EPIRUS. Corcyra (Greek: Kerkura) was one of the earliest Greek colonies, founded circa 734 B.C. by settlers from CORINTH.

Located only 80 miles across the Adriatic from the Italian "heel," Corcyra provided a vital anchorage on the coastal TRADE route from Greece to ITALY and SICILY. Corcyra also enjoyed local trade with the Illyrians, a non-Greek people who supplied SILVER ore, TIMBER, SLAVES, tin (for BRONZE-making), and wildflowers (for perfume-making). Agriculturally, the island was (and is) known for dense growths of olive trees.

Unlike most Greek colonies, Corcyra rebelled violently against its mother city. In 664 B.C., as mentioned by the Athenian historian THUCYDIDES (1), Corcyra and Corinth fought the first sea battle on record; Thucydides neglects to state who won. Circa 610 B.C. the Corinthian tyrant PERIANDER brought Corcyra temporarily to heel. At some point the two cities cooperated in founding the Adriatic colony of EPIDAMNUS, but Corinth continued to establish its own colonies in the area, partly to guard against Corcyrean hostility.

It was at prosperous Corcyra circa 580 B.C. that the first large, all-stone Greek building was erected—a temple of ARTEMIS, designed in the newly emerging Doric style. This building has been called the Gorgon temple, on account of its pedimental sculptures showing the Gorgon MEDUSA flanked by beasts. Today the temple survives only in its west pediment, preserved in the Corfu Museum.

Despite having one of the most powerful navies in Greece, Corcyra remained neutral in the PERSIAN WARS. Later its bitter relations with Corinth played a role in igniting the PELOPONNESIAN WAR (431–404 B.C.). These events began in 435 B.C., when Corcyra was drawn into conflict with Corinth over relations with Epidamnus. A Corcyrean fleet of 80 ships defeated 75 invading Corinthian ships at the Battle of Leukimme, off Corcyra's southeast coast. To defend against retaliation, the Corcyreans allied with the powerful city of ATHENS. The next episode saw 10 Athenian warships ranged alongside 110 Corcyrean ships against a Corinthian fleet of 150. This was the important Battle of Sybota (433 B.C.), fought off the mainland near Corcyra and ending in a Corinthian victory. As a consequence of this battle, Corinth urged SPARTA to declare war against Athens.

Corcyra fought in the Peloponnesian War and suffered greatly. The city was being governed as a pro-Athenian DEMOCRACY when a group of Corcyrean right-wingers launched a coup, hoping to swing Corcyra over to the Peloponnesian side. The coup failed, bringing on a gruesome civil war (427–425 B.C.). Thucydides' sympathetic but objective description of the Corcyrean *stasis* (civil strife) is one of the great set pieces in his history of the Peloponnesian War (book 3).

Later in the war, Corcyra was a staging base for Athens' disastrous invasion of SYRACUSE (415 B.C.). In 410 B.C. Corcyra ended its alliance with Athens. But in 375 B.C. Corcyra joined the SECOND ATHENIAN LEAGUE as protection against Spartan domination.

With its wealth and strategic position, Corcyra became a bone of contention among the rival dynasts after the death of the Macedonian king ALEXANDER THE GREAT (323 B.C.). The city was occupied variously by Macedonians, Syracusans, Epirotes, and Illyrians, before passing to the empire of ROME (229 B.C.). It served for many years as a Roman naval base.

(See also AGATHOCLES; ARCHITECTURE; COLONIZATION; ILLYRIS; WARFARE, NAVAL.)

Corinth   Major city of the northeastern PELOPONNESE, known for its manufacturing and seaborne TRADE. Located on the narrow isthmus that connects southern and central Greece, Corinth became great through its geography: It guarded the landroute along the isthmus, and it controlled harbors on both shores, eastward on the Saronic Gulf and westward on the aptly named Corinthian Gulf. Also, the city's lofty ACROPOLIS—the "Acrocorinth," atop a limestone mountain standing outside the lower town—gave Corinth a nearly impregnable citadel.

Corinth's heyday came in the 600s and early 500s B.C., when its shipping network dwarfed that of the other mainland Greek cities. Although it eventually lost this preeminence to ATHENS, Corinth remained a center for commerce and luxury throughout ancient history. Among its most lucrative tourist attractions were the sacred PROSTITUTES at the temple of APHRODITE.

The name Korinthos is not Greek, containing as it does the *nth* sound that identifies certain words surviving from the language of the pre-Greek people of Greece. The invading Greek-speaking tribesmen of circa 2100 B.C. took over an existing, pre-Greek settlement and kept the non-Greek name. After the fall of MYCENAEAN CIVILIZATION the region was overrun by the invading DORIAN GREEKS, circa 1100–1000 B.C. Later MYTHS connect the Dorian conquest of Corinth with that of ARGOS, farther south. The Dorian city eventually became governed as an ARISTOCRACY, dominated by an endogamous clan called the Bacchiads. By the 700s B.C. Corinth was the foremost Greek port and manufacturing center, known to HOMER and other poets by the epithet *aphneios*, "wealthy." Corinthian shipbuilding was renowned. Imports included textiles, worked metal, and carved ivory from the non-Greek kingdoms of western Asia. Exports included POTTERY in the beautiful painted styles now known as Protocorinthian and Corinthian. This pottery dominated all markets from about 700 to 550 B.C., until it was superceded by Athenian black-figure ware.

Corinth's exports traveled beyond the Greek world. One avid market was the powerful, non-Greek people called the ETRUSCANS, in northern and central ITALY. Archaeological excavations have revealed immense troves of Corinthian pottery at Etruscan sites; such remnants surely indicate other export items, now vanished, such as perfumes, textiles, and metalwork.

To provide anchorages and local depots along the western trade route, Corinth (circa 734 B.C.) founded two colonies destined to become great cities in their own right: SYRACUSE, on the southeast coast of SICILY, and CORCYRA, on an Adriatic island. But Corcyra rebelled against its mother city, and Corinthian-Corcyrean hostilities would later be an important cause of the PELOPONNESIAN WAR (431–404 B.C.).

Meanwhile, prosperity brought violent political change to Corinth, as the middle class chafed under the Bacchiads' monopoly of power. Circa 657 B.C. a revolution toppled the aristocrats and installed a popular leader, CYPSELUS, as dictator (*turannos*). Cypselus usually is considered to be the earliest of the Greek TYRANTS; soon this pattern of revolution was sweeping the other major cities of Greece.

Under Cypselus and his son PERIANDER (reigned circa 625–585 B.C.), Corinth reached new commercial heights. New northwestern colonies—AMBRACIA, APOLLONIA, and others—were founded to develop the western trade route and guard the approaches to the Corinthian Gulf. With Periander's paving of a five-mile-long dragway across the isthmus' narrowest section, merchant ships could be trundled on trolleys between the eastern and western seas, thus eliminating the voyage around the Peloponnese and bringing to Corinth a rich revenue in tolls from non-Corinthian shipping. In artwork, Corinth became the birthplace of the monumental ARCHITECTURE that we know as the Doric order. (The more ornate Corinthian order would emerge later.) The influential ISTHMIAN GAMES were instituted around this time.

After Periander's death, his successor was quickly deposed in favor of a constitutional OLIGARCHY that remained Corinth's typical form of government down to Roman times. During the late 500s B.C. Athens arose as Corinth's trade rival. However, the two cities remained friendly, and 40 Corinthian warships fought alongside the Athenian fleet against the invasion of the Persian King XERXES (480 B.C.).

By the mid-400s B.C., however, Corinth—along with its ally SPARTA—was feeling the threat of an expansionist, democratic Athens. Alarmed by an Athenian alliance with Corcyra (433 B.C.), Corinth urged Sparta and the other Peloponnesian states to declare war on Athens. The resulting Peloponnesian War enveloped the Greek world for nearly 30 years and saw Corinthian war fleets and troops in many battles. The fighting ended in defeat for Athens and exhaustion for Corinth.

Rebelling from the onerous rule then imposed by Sparta, Corinth fought against its former ally (and alongside Athens, Argos, and other states) in the CORINTHIAN WAR of 395–386 B.C.. In these troubled years the city also underwent a brief democratic coup. In 338 B.C. Corinth shared in the failed defense of Greece against King PHILIP II of MACEDON. Corinth received a Macedonian garrison and remained a Macedonian holding until 243 B.C., when it was liberated by the statesman Aratus for the Achaean League. But in 222 B.C. Corinth returned to Macedonian control.

When the Romans freed Greece from Macedonian rule in 196 B.C., Corinth again became the foremost city of the Achaean League. But the Greeks' resistance to Roman interference led to the disastrous Achaean War of 146 B.C., in which Corinth was captured and sacked by Roman troops. The Roman senate decreed that the city should be burned down and its art treasures either be sold or carried off to Rome. This pillaged art is said to have increased the Greek influence on the emerging Roman imperial culture.

Historians usually consider the destruction of Corinth in 146 B.C.—and the associated annexing of ACHAEA to become part of a Roman province—as the end of the ancient Greek world. Although other Greek cities thrived under Roman rule and Corinth itself eventually revived, mainland Greece as a political entity had ceased to exist. Greece had become part of ROME.

(See also BELLEROPHON; COINAGE; COLONIZATION; GREECE, GEOGRAPHY OF; HOPLITE; LELANTINE WAR.)

Corinthian order   See ARCHITECTURE.

Corinthian War   Name given by modern historians to the conflict of 395–386 B.C., fought between SPARTA (with its allies) and an alliance of CORINTH, ATHENS, BOEOTIA, ARGOS, EUBOEA, and the kingdom of PERSIA. The grand alliance was remarkable for combining traditional enemies in a united campaign against Spartan supremacy. This anti-Spartan axis introduces the politics of the next generation, when the Boeotian city of THEBES would emerge to challenge and finally defeat Sparta (371 B.C.).

The background of the Corinthian War is Sparta's victory over Athens in the huge PELOPONNESIAN WAR (404 B.C.), which marked the beginning of Sparta's oppressive rule over all the Greek states, former friend and foe alike. Claiming also to protect and rule the Greek cities of ASIA MINOR, Sparta came into conflict with the Persian king Artaxerxes II (399–395 B.C.). As a result, Persian funds became available for the anti-Spartan alliance in Greece.

The course of the war is described in the account titled *Hellenica*, by the Athenian historian XENOPHON (who was present at some of the events). The Spartan general LYSANDER invaded Boeotia at the head of a Spartan-allied army, but was defeated and killed by the Thebans at the Battle of Haliartus (395 B.C.). The next summer the Spartans defeated an allied army in battle outside Corinth, but this was counterbalanced when a Spartan fleet was destroyed by the Athenian admiral CONON, leading a Persian-Athenian fleet at the Battle of CNIDUS, off the coast of Asia Minor (394 B.C.).

Meanwhile, the Spartan king AGESILAUS, summoned home from campaigning against Persian land forces in Asia Minor, led his army along the north Aegean coastline into northeastern Greece. Descending southward, he invaded Boeotia. At the desperate Battle of Coronea (394 B.C.), Agesilaus narrowly defeated an allied army but then withdrew southward toward Sparta without attacking any Boeotian cities.

Thereafter the war became bogged down with maneuverings around Corinth and Argos. In around 392 B.C. Corinth, traditionally an OLIGARCHY, underwent a short-lived democratic coup. But the most important event of the war was its ending: The fighting stopped in 386 B.C., when Persia withdrew its support after King Artaxerxes II had negotiated a separate peace with Sparta. According to this treaty, known as the KING'S PEACE, Sparta ceded the Greek cities of Asia Minor and CYPRUS back to Persian control. This notorious treaty unmasked Sparta once and for all as an oppressive power, bent on dominating mainland Greece even at the cost of selling out the eastern Greek cities. The rise of Thebes in the following years was buoyed partly by widespread anger at this treaty.

(See also EPAMINONDAS; IONIA.)

council   Evidence in HOMER's epic poems and in the LINEAR B tablets indicates that a council (*boulē*) of king's advisers was an important facet of government in primitive Greek societies (circa 1600–1000 B.C.). As the age of kings gave way to the age of ARISTOCRACY (circa 1000–600 B.C.), a Greek city-state's council more or less became the government, combining legislative, executive, and judiciary powers. In this era ATHENS was governed by an aristocratic council called the AREOPAGUS, whose several hundred members, probably serving for life, were drawn exclusively from the city's narrow circle of noble families.

The democratic reforms of CLEISTHENES (1) (circa 508 B.C.) removed the Areopagus from the heart of government in Athens and created instead a council of 500 members selected annually from upper- and middle-income citizens. (By the late 400s B.C., lower-income citizens apparently were admitted.) Under the Athenian DEMOCRACY of the 400s and 300s B.C., the council had important legislative and executive duties but was always subordinate to the sovereign ASSEMBLY of citizens.

The most important job of the Athenian council was to prepare the agenda for the 40 assembly meetings each year. Specifically, the council drafted the proposals to be debated at the next assembly—apparently the assembly could vote only on proposals prepared beforehand by the council. Council meetings might include debate and voting, the hearing of citizens' petitions, the summoning of witnesses, and other information-gathering, for which the council had high authority. Like the assembly, the council had judicial duties. The councillors could act as judge and jury in trying cases of certain state offenses, such as misconduct by officials.

The council also served as an executive body, responsible for the enactment and enforcement of the assembly's decisions and for much of the day-to-day running of the state. The council received foreign ambassadors, had responsibility for the care of public buildings, and oversaw the construction of new warships and the maintenance of the fleets and dockyards for Athens' all-important navy. The council seems to have been especially important in administering finances: Among other duties, it audited the books of all outgoing officials who had handled public funds.

Yet the citizens who served on the council were not career politicians or public servants, but amateurs fulfilling a public duty not so different from our modern jury duty. The 500 council members for the year were selected by lot, in procedures at the 139 local city wards, or DEMES (*dēmoi*). Only male citizens over the age of 30 were eligible—there, as everywhere else in the Athenian government, WOMEN were excluded. By the late 400s B.C. councillors were receiving state pay for their service. (This important provision, enabling less-wealthy citizens to serve, probably began circa 457 B.C. amid the left-wing reforms of EPHIALTES and PERICLES.)

Each new council began its term in midsummer, at the start of the Athenian year. Aside from festivals and days of ill omen, the members met daily, usually in the council chamber in the AGORA. By nature of its selection, the council always consisted of 10 50-man contingents from the 10 Athenian tribes. Each of these 50-man groups took one turn, through the year, as the council's presiding committee, or *prutaneis*.

(See also LAW AND LAW COURTS; POLIS.)

courtesans   See PROSTITUTES.

Cratinus   One of the three great comic playwrights of classical ATHENS, alongside ARISTOPHANES and EUPOLIS. Cratinus (Greek: Kratinos) was Aristophanes' older contemporary and rival, and greatly influenced him. Apparently Cratinus' plays relied even more on obscene farce and personal derision of public figures than those of Aristophanes.

Cratinus' comedies, of which 27 titles and some 460 fragments survive, were presented in the mid-400s down to 423 B.C. We know he won first prize nine times in competitions at the two major Athenian drama festivals, the City Dionysia (in early spring) and the Lenaea (in midwinter). His titles, often styled as plural nouns, include *The Thracian Women, The Soft Fellows, The Dionysuses,* and *The Odysseuses* (which apparently used the chorus as ODYSSEUS' crew and included a large model of his ship).

No complete play by Cratinus survives, but there exists a synopsis of his *Dionysalexandros* ("Dionysus-Paris"), performed circa 430 B.C. There the god DIONYSUS substitutes for the Trojan prince PARIS in judging the famous beauty contest of the three goddesses. Deciding in Aphrodite's favor, the god acquires the beautiful HELEN OF TROY as his reward but is terrified by the approach of Paris himself; farcical action follows, including the start of the TROJAN WAR. The play—clearly a burlesque on the recent outbreak of the very real and serious PELOPONNESIAN WAR—contained much indirect ridicule of the Athenian statesman PERICLES, who was cast as the meddling Dionysus, while his common-law wife, ASPASIA, doubtlessly received a few hits as Helen.

Cratinus' final success came in 423 B.C., with his comedy *The Bottle*. The year before, Aristophanes' *Knights* had publicly mocked Cratinus as a drunken has-been; this year Cratinus responded with a comic self-portrait featuring: a character named Cratinus; his estranged wife, Komoidia (comedy); his sluttish girlfriend, Methē (drunkenness); and the tempting pretty-boy Oiniskos (little wine). The play contained the proverb that an artist who drinks only water can never create anything worthwhile. *The Bottle* won first place at the City Dionysia, well over Aristophanes' *Clouds*, which took third. Cratinus died shortly thereafter.

(See also THEATER.)

cremation   See FUNERAL CUSTOMS.

Crete Largest and southernmost island of the AEGEAN SEA. Crete is long and thin in shape—about 160 miles long and between circa 30–40 miles wide—and on a map it extends horizontally east-west. The island's western shore lies only about 65 miles southeast of the mainland Greek PELOPONNESE and about 200 miles northeast of the Libyan coast. Crete's eastern shore is 130 miles from the coast of ASIA MINOR. Due partly to this dominant position on the sea routes linking the Aegean with the Egyptian and Near Eastern worlds, Crete in the late third millennium B.C. gave birth to a brilliant BRONZE AGE culture, the MINOAN CIVILIZATION. The Minoans were not Greeks, but they are considered as marking the start of Greek prehistory, since they deeply influenced the emerging Greek MYCENAEAN CIVILIZATION of the mainland.

The traditional Greek name Krētē is not a genuine Greek word and may reflect the vanished language of the Minoans. Crete's terrain rises in mountainous humps, peaking at 8,000 feet midisland at Mt. Ida and in the west at the White Mountains. Limestone formations include caves, some of which housed important religious cults in antiquity. Arable land is found in small lowland pockets, where olives, grapes, and grain were farmed, and the many upland plateaus offered grazing for livestock. Mountain TIMBER provided shipbuilding material and a prized export.

Ancient populations tended to favor the warmer and drier eastern half of the island, especially the flatter north coast. ARCHAEOLOGY reveals that the humans first came to Crete in the Neolithic era, around 5000 B.C. These seaborne pioneers, coming perhaps from the Levant, brought the island's first pigs, sheep, and cattle. Newcomers arrived around 2900 B.C., possibly from Asia Minor, bringing BRONZE weapons to Crete and intermarrying with the existing people. From this fusion there arose, circa 2200 B.C., the Minoan civilization, the earliest great nation on European soil. The seafaring Minoans traded with EGYPT and the Levant, and dominated the Aegean.

The Minoan kings' capital was the north-central city of CNOSSUS, inland of the modern seaport of Heraklion. At Cnossus in A.D. 1900 the British archaeologist Sir Arthur Evans discovered the remnants of an elaborate palace complex, begun in around 1950 B.C. and reaching its existing form in around 1700 B.C. Other surviving Minoan monuments on Crete include the palace at Phaestus (mid south coast, across the island from Cnossus), the villas at Hagia Triada (Phaestus' harbor town), the palace at Mallia (eastern north coast), and the remnants of a Minoan town at Gournia (eastern north coast). Current scant knowledge of the Minoans comes largely from the archaeology of these sites. Minoan artworks found in excavation are collected in the Heraklion archaeological museum.

The Minoan sites on Crete tell a tale of vigorous construction after 1950 B.C. and of fiery ruin in around 1400 B.C. or soon after. The cause of this simultaneous destruction was probably an invasion of Crete by warlike Mycenaean Greeks from the mainland. Oddly, the Mycenaeans seem to have abandoned Crete after the palaces' destruction.

In around 1000 B.C. a new people occupied the island. These were the DORIAN GREEKS, who had previously invaded southward through mainland Greece, overrunning the Peloponnese and continuing their conquests by sea.

For the rest of antiquity, Crete remained a Dorian-Greek island, with governmental and social institutions that resembled those at SPARTA.

Dorian Crete was divided into city-states governed as military aristocracies. The chief of these were Cnossus, GORTYN (in the south-central island), and, later, Cydonia (modern Khania, on the western north coast). As was the case at Sparta, Dorian-Greek nobles ruled over a population of rural serfs—probably the descendants of the subjugated non-Dorians.

The island was active in the seaborne expansion of the Greek world in the later 700s and 600s B.C. Cretan colonists helped to found the city of GELA, in southeastern SICILY, and Cretan workshops exported an admired Geometric-style POTTERY and contributed to the style of statuary now known as Daedalic. But gradually the Cretan cities withdrew into isolation, and Crete declined amid internal conflicts, mainly between Cnossus and Gortyn. By the late 200s B.C. the island had become notorious as a haunt of pirates. Order was restored by the Romans, who annexed Crete in 67 B.C. and made it part of a Roman province.

The Cretans were the best archers in the Greek world (where archery was generally not practiced), and many Greek armies from the 400s B.C. onward employed Cretan bowmen as mercenaries. Cretans also had the reputation of being liars.

The RELIGION of Dorian Crete was distinguished by certain cults and beliefs that probably contained pre-Greek, Minoan elements. It was said that the great god ZEUS, as a baby, had been hidden in a cave on Crete's Mt. Dicte to save him from his malevolent father, CRONUS. More amazing to classical Greeks was the Cretans' claim that the immortal Zeus was born and died annually on Crete and that his tomb could be seen at Cnossus. This "Zeus" may have been the surviving form of a mythical son or consort of the prehistoric Minoan mother goddess.

(See also ARISTOCRACY; ARTEMIS; ATLANTIS; COLONIZATION; GREEK LANGUAGE; HELOTS; ROME; SCULPTURE; SHIPS AND SEAFARING.)

Critias Athenian oligarch who lived circa 460–403 B.C. As leader of the THIRTY TYRANTS, who ruled ATHENS by terror in 404–403 B.C., Critias was one of the true villains of Athenian history.

Born into an aristocratic clan, Critias (Greek: Kritias) was pupil of certain SOPHISTS and of the philosopher SOCRATES. Critias was an elder kinsman of the philosopher PLATO (specifically, cousin to Plato's mother) and was also the uncle and guardian of Plato's uncle Charmides. Both Critias and Charmides appear as glamorous, youthful figures in several of Plato's (fictional) dialogues, written in the first quarter of the 300s B.C.

As a suspected enemy of the DEMOCRACY, Critias was arrested but then released after the incident of the Mutilation of the Herms (415 B.C.), during the PELOPONNESIAN WAR. Later Critias proposed to the Athenian ASSEMBLY the decree recalling the exiled Alcibiades (probably 411 B.C.), but when the Athenians turned against Alcibiades again (406 B.C.), Critias apparently suffered incidental blame and was banished. He went in exile to THESSALY.

Like other exiles, Critias was recalled as part of the peace terms imposed on Athens by the victorious Spartans at the end of the Peloponnesian War, in 404 B.C. He was then elected to the dictatorial, pro-Spartan government commonly known as the Thirty Tyrants. The Athenian historian XENOPHON, who lived through these events, portrays Critias as leader of the Thirty's extremist faction, against the more moderate THERAMENES. Critias directed the Thirty's reign of terror, executing anyone who was likely to organize resistance or whose personal wealth was attractive. He eventually denounced his colleague Theramenes and had him executed. Critias' crowning outrage was to arrange the mass execution of 300 men (probably the entire male citizen population) of the nearby town of Eleusis.

In early 403 B.C. the Thirty were toppled. Critias was killed, with Charmides and others, in street-fighting at PIRAEUS. The hatred of Critias' memory played a role in the prosecution of his former teacher Socrates under the restored democracy (399 B.C.).

A man of intelligence and talent, Critias wrote LYRIC POETRY, tragedies, and prose. His prose style was admired, and one of his works, now lost, was titled "Conversations" (Homilia). It is possible that this was a model for Plato's literary dialogues. As a thinker, Plato seems to have inherited some of his uncle's authoritarian nature.

Critius   See SCULPTURE.

Croesus   Last king of LYDIA, a powerful non-Greek nation of west-central ASIA MINOR. Croesus (Greek: Kroisos) inherited the throne at age 35 from his father, Alyattes, and reigned circa 560–546 B.C., until his country was conquered by the Persian king CYRUS (1).

Croesus' wealth was proverbial. Friendly toward the Greek world, he was a patron of the god APOLLO's shrine at DELPHI and was the first foreign ruler to form an alliance with a mainland Greek state, SPARTA. Closer to home, he subdued the Greek cities of western Asia Minor, but dealt benevolently with them as subjects.

On his eastern frontier he met disaster. Seeking to conquer east-central Asia Minor from the Persians, Croesus led an army across the River Halys, the border between Lydia and the Persian domain. After an inconsequential battle against King Cyrus, Croesus returned to Lydia, where Cyrus, following quickly, defeated and captured him. Croesus' subsequent fate is unknown. One legend says he was carried off by his divine protector Apollo to safety in the magical land of the Hyperboreans.

Like other Eastern despots, Croesus inspired the Greek imagination. The tales told about him by the historian HERODOTUS (circa 435 B.C.) are a fascinating mix of fact and storytelling. With his grand style and sudden fall, Croesus represented for the Greeks a real-life example of HUBRIS— excessive pride that leads to a divinely prompted blunder in judgment, which leads to disaster.

One legend claims that, at the height of Croesus' reign, he was visited by the Athenian sage SOLON. Croesus asked Solon to name the happiest man he had ever seen, expecting to hear himself named, but Solon explained to Croesus that no man may be called "happy" until he is dead; before then, he is merely lucky. This Greek proverb

later reappears at the end of SOPHOCLES' tragedy *Oedipus the King*.

The best-known story tells how, before his campaign against PERSIA, Croesus consulted the Delphic Oracle. He was advised that if he crossed the Halys River he would destroy a mighty empire. Heartened by this prophecy, he decided to march. Unfortunately, the mighty empire turned out to be his own.

(See also MIDAS; PROPHECY AND DIVINATION.)

Cronus   In MYTH, the primeval king of the TITANS and father of ZEUS and other gods. According to HESIOD's epic poem the *Theogony*, Cronus was born to GAEA (Mother Earth) and Uranus (Ouranos, "Sky"). On his mother's advice, Cronus castrated his father with a sickle and ruled in his place.

Cronus married his own sister, Rhea, who bore him the gods HESTIA, DEMETER, HERA, HADES, POSEIDON, and, last, Zeus. But Cronus had been warned that his offspring would subdue him, and so he swallowed each newborn child. Finally, at Zeus' birth, Rhea tricked her husband— presenting him with a stone wrapped in swaddling clothes—and spirited the infant off to CRETE. Eventually Cronus was made to vomit up all his swallowed children, who (still alive) followed Zeus in revolt against their father. A different vein of legend, at odds with this grim picture, described Cronus as supervising a time of innocence and blessing—if not in heaven, at least on earth. Cronus' reign was said to have marked the Golden Age of human history, when people lived without greed, violence, toil, or need for laws.

The name Cronus (Greek: Kronos) seems to have no meaning in the Greek language. Like other elements of the Greek Creation myths, the Cronus story may have derived from non-Greek, Near Eastern sources. Specifically, it resembles the tale of the Mesopotamian god Kumarbi, which was current in the second millennium B.C. Modern scholars believe that the Cronus myth may have come to Greece via the Phoenicians, with whom the Greeks had extensive trading contacts in 900–700 B.C.

At classical ATHENS there was a feast of Cronus, the Kronia, celebrated in midsummer, just after the Greek New Year. The Kronia was probably a harvest festival, and Cronus was often portrayed in art as carrying a sickle, the harvester's tool. (The sickle also was the weapon he used to castrate his father.)

The primitive figure of Cronus was the object of attempted rationalization during the Athenian Enlightenment of the 400s–300s B.C. A theory claimed that his name was not really Kronos but rather Chronos, "time," and that his myth of impious violence to father and children was simply an allegory for the ravages of time. This confused interpretation created an image that, surviving 2,500 years, can be seen every New Year's—old Father Time, holding his emblematic sickle.

(See also PHOENICIA; RELIGION.)

Croton   Important Greek city on the southern rim of the Gulf of Taranto, on the "sole" of south ITALY. Located high above a small double harbor, near fertile farmland, Croton (Greek: Kroton) was founded by colonists from ACHAEA, probably around 700 B.C. The city carved out a sizable domain at the expense of the local Italian inhabitants, the Brutii.

Circa 530 B.C. the Samian-born philosopher PYTHAGORAS founded his mystical school of study at Croton and apparently helped to run the city government, as an OLIGARCHY. By the late 500s B.C., prosperous Croton had a famous school of MEDICINE, producing, among others, the philosopher-physician Alcmaeon. Another distinguished citizen of the day was Milon the Strongman, a champion in WRESTLING at the OLYMPIC and PYTHIAN GAMES.

The city's zenith came in 510 B.C., when it destroyed its archrival, the Italian Greek city SYBARIS. But Croton soon was weakened by conflicts with two other Italian Greek cities, RHEGIUM and LOCRI, and with the Brutii. Croton was captured and plundered in 379 B.C. by the Syracusan ruler DIONYSIUS (1). Exhausted by the wars that accompanied ROME's expansion through Italy in the 300s and 200s B.C., Croton eventually became a Roman subject state.

Cumae   Ancient Greek city of Campania, on the west coast of ITALY, located just north of the Bay of Naples, 10 miles west of modern-day Naples.

Cumae (Greek: Kumē) was one of the earliest datable Greek colonies, established by Euboean Greeks who moved ashore from their nearby island holding of PITHECUSAE circa 750 B.C. One story claims that the new city included eastern Greek settlers who named it for their native CYMĒ, in ASIA MINOR.

The founding of Italian Cumae marks an early milestone in Greek COLONIZATION, namely the decision by a band of Greeks to make a first landing on the Italian coast. Possibly they went ashore at the invitation of the ETRUSCANS, a powerful Italian people who were avid consumers of Greek goods and who had a stronghold at nearby Capua.

Cumae thrived, supplying the Etruscans with Corinthian painted POTTERY, Euboean worked BRONZE, and other wares. It sent out colonists of its own, founding ZANCLĒ (modern Messina, in SICILY, circa 725 B.C.) and Neapolis ("new city," modern Naples, circa 600 B.C.), among other settlements. As a northern outpost of Greek culture in Italy, Cumae played a crucial role in the hellenization of the Etruscans.

But Cumae's relations with the Etruscans eventually worsened, and in the late 500s B.C. the Cumaean leader Aristodemus twice defeated Etruscan armies (and then made himself tyrant of the city). In 474 B.C., in alliance with the Syracusan tyrant HIERON (1), Cumae won a great sea battle against the Etruscans and crushed their power. But in 421 B.C. the city fell to another Italian people, the Samnites, and later passed to the Romans. Throughout antiquity Cumae was known for its priestess called the Sibyl, who was a Greek oracle of the god APOLLO similar to that at DELPHI.

(See also PROPHECY AND DIVINATION; ROME; TYRANTS.)

Cyclades   Group of islands in the AEGEAN SEA roughly forming a circle, *kuklos,* around the holy isle of DELOS. Aside from Delos, the major Cyclades were Naxos (1), Paros, Andros, Ceos, THERA, and MELOS. Paros was famous for its marble; Naxos, the largest and most fertile of the

Cyclades, was known for its WINE and its associated worship of the god DIONYSUS.

The Cyclades enjoyed a flourishing civilization in the third and second millennia B.C., well before the Greeks arrived. Archaeological evidence such as surviving POTTERY gives a picture of two-way TRADE with Minoan CRETE, including the export of obsidian (volcanic glass, mined on Melos and used as a cutting edge for axes, adzes, and the like, circa 2000 B.C.). By 1600 B.C. these pre-Greek Cyclades had come under direct control of Crete. After 1400 B.C. the Cyclades seem to have been ruled by Mycenaean Greeks from the mainland. Before 1000 B.C. most of the Cyclades were occupied by migrating IONIAN GREEKS. For the main centuries of Greek history, the Cyclades were inhabited by ethnic Ionian Greeks; of the principal islands, only Melos and Thera were settled by DORIAN GREEKS.

The Cyclades fell to the invading Persians in 490 B.C.; Naxos, resisting, was ravaged. At the end of the PERSIAN WARS, most of the islands joined the DELIAN LEAGUE, headquartered at Delos but led by ATHENS (478 B.C.). The league died with Athens' defeat in the PELOPONNESIAN WAR (404 B.C.), but by 377 B.C. most of the islands had joined the SECOND ATHENIAN LEAGUE. With the rest of Greece, they passed into the hands of the Macedonian king PHILIP II in 338 B.C.. During the HELLENISTIC AGE (300–150 B.C.), the Cyclades were a bone of contention mainly between the Greek dynasties of MACEDON and EGYPT. In the mid-100s B.C. they passed to the domain of ROME.

Cyclops (plural: Cyclopes)   A type of mythical, gigantic, semihuman monster, first described in HOMER's epic poem the *Odyssey* (written down circa 750 B.C.). The name Kuklops, "round eye," refers to the one large eye that such creatures had in midforehead. Descended from the earth goddess GAEA and her husband, Uranus (Ouranos, "Sky"), the Cyclopes dwelt in a distant land (sometimes identified as eastern SICILY), with no cities or laws. The *Odyssey* (book 9) describes the hero ODYSSEUS' violent encounter with the Cyclops POLYPHEMUS.

A slightly different tradition, presented in HESIOD's epic poem the *Theogony* (circa 700 B.C.), made the Cyclopes a guild of supernatural, one-eyed blacksmiths, who forged thunderbolts for the great god ZEUS. These Cyclopes were associated with the smith god, HEPHAESTUS. The classical Greeks ascribed to the Cyclopes the building of certain ancient walls made of huge blocks without mortar, such as the walls at TIRYNS. In reality, these had been built by Mycenaean Greeks circa 1300 B.C., but to later generations they looked like the work of giants. The term cyclopean was used to describe such masonry.

(See MYCENAEAN CIVILIZATION.)

Cylon   Athenian aristocrat who attempted to seize supreme power at ATHENS, circa 632 B.C., at a time when the city was still governed as an ARISTOCRACY. Cylon (Greek: Kulon) and his followers captured the Athenian ACROPOLIS; yet the common people did not rise in support, and government forces besieged the conspirators. Cylon escaped but his men were massacred, despite having claimed sanctuary at religious altars. This mishap was the origin of the "Alcmaeonid curse"—the taint of pollution considered to lie perpetually on the entire clan of the ALCMAEONIDS, because one of the clan, Megacles, had overseen the massacre.

(See also FURIES; TYRANTS.)

Cymē Southernmost and main city of AEOLIS, a Greek region on the northwestern coast of ASIA MINOR. Like other cities of Aeolis, Cymē was settled circa 900 B.C. by AEOLIAN GREEKS who had migrated eastward, via LESBOS, from mainland Greece. As indicated by the name Kumē (wave or sea), the city was a port, advantageously located alongside the mouth of the Hermus River (which allowed trading contact with interior Asia Minor).

Cymē's fortunes followed those of the Aeolis region. Captured by the Persians circa 545 B.C., Cymē took part in the failed IONIAN REVOLT in 499–493 B.C. Liberated by the Greeks at the end of the PERSIAN WARS (479 B.C.), Cymē became part of the Athenian-controlled DELIAN LEAGUE. After ATHENS' defeat in the PELOPONNESIAN WAR (404 B.C.), Cymē reverted to Persian control by the terms of the KING'S PEACE (386 B.C.). By about 377 B.C. Cymē had joined the SECOND ATHENIAN LEAGUE. After ALEXANDER THE GREAT'S death (323 B.C.), Cymē passed through the SELEUCID EMPIRE and the kingdom of PERGAMUM, before becoming part of the Roman Empire in the 100s B.C.

Cymē's best-known citizen was the historian Ephorus (circa 400–330 B.C.), who wrote a world history as well as a history of Cymē, neither of which has survived. An inferior scholar, Ephorus was notorious for including in his world history such comments as "In this year the citizens of Cymē were at peace."

(See also CUMAE.)

Cynics The English words *cynic* and *cynicism* describe an informal, embittered frame of mind. But the original Cynics comprised a major Greek philosophical movement, which arose in the early 300s B.C. The name Kunikoi, "doglike," derived from one of the movement's pioneers, DIOGENES of SINOPE (400–325 B.C.), whose austere and immodest way of life won him the nickname the Dog (Kuon). Unlike other philosophies, Cynicism was never organized around a formal place of study. Although overshadowed in the 200s B.C. by two new and partly derivative schools of thought, STOICISM and EPICUREANISM, Cynicism nevertheless continued to attract a following in response to the spiritual crisis in the HELLENISTIC ERA (300–150 B.C.). In the first century A.D. the cities of the Roman Empire teemed with traveling Cynic beggars.

The Cynics taught a radical doctrine of moral self-sufficiency. They renounced wealth and social convention, preferring to go homeless, do no work, wear simple clothes or rags, and avoid such niceties as finding privacy before relieving themselves. They sought knowledge and harmony through a liberation from materialism. But, far from withdrawing to live as hermits, they chose to dwell in cities and (often) to travel from city to city, preaching. They would sermonize and hold philosophical discussions on streetcorners and were notorious for their outspokenness. Their lampoons against vice and pride were often directed personally against passersby.

The movement's roots lay with the Athenian philosopher SOCRATES (469–399 B.C.). Although not himself a Cynic, Socrates was known for his austerity and his habit of questioning people on the street. After Socrates' death, one of his followers, Antisthenes, an Athenian, lived in exaggerated imitation of Socrates' plain living. In a modified Socratic belief, Antisthenes taught that happiness comes from personal virtue (*aretē*), not from pleasure, and that the best virtue comes from triumph over hardship.

Antisthenes was the first Cynic, but the movement's most famous master was Diogenes, who began as Antisthenes' pupil. Other important Cynics included Bion of Borysthenes and Menippus of Gadara (early 200s B.C.); Menippus adapted the Cynics' haranguing speaking style to a written form that was a precursor of the literary satire later produced by the Romans.

With their doctrine of self-improvement through painful effort, the Cynics revered the mythical hero HERACLES, whose twelve Labors were seen as an ideal example of moral victory and self-liberation.

(See also PHILOSOPHY; POLIS.)

Cyprus Large eastern Mediterranean island, 140 miles long, which was an eastern frontier of the Greek world. Located 60 miles off the coast of northern Syria and 50 miles south of ASIA MINOR's southern coast, Cyprus played a vital role in TRADE and warfare between East and West. The island's Oriental contacts and remoteness from mainland Greece gave rise to a distinctive, sometimes peculiar, Greek culture.

As shown by ARCHAEOLOGY, the island was host to a flourishing non-Greek civilization, derived from Asia Minor, during the first half of the second millennium B.C.. After about 1400 B.C. Cyprus was intensively colonized by Mycenaean Greeks from mainland Greece. What lured them to Cyprus was copper—the major component of the alloy BRONZE, upon which the Mycenaeans depended for war and FARMING. Cyprus had the richest copper deposits in the eastern Mediterranean; the English word *copper* comes from the Latin term *Cyprium aes*, "the Cypriot metal." A copper ingot eventually became the island's emblem on COINAGE.

Greek Cyprus was largely undisturbed by the collapse of MYCENAEAN CIVILIZATION in mainland Greece (circa 1200–1000 B.C.). The island's spoken Greek dialect, unaffected by any change or immigration, retained certain characteristics of old Mycenaean Greek. Other Mycenaean survivals included the Cypriot Syllabary (as it is now called), a primitive form of writing using pictograms, employed on Cyprus circa 700–200 B.C.

In the 800s B.C. the seafaring Phoenicians, seeking copper and shipping stations, established a stronghold in southeast Cyprus. Kart Hadasht, "new city," called Kition (Citium) by the Greeks and Kittim in the Bible. The Phoenicians, in steady conflict with the Greeks, remained a powerful presence and later served as puppets of the Persian overlords. Meanwhile Cyprus became a place where Greeks could observe and imitate Phoenician shipbuilding, trade techniques, and religious beliefs. The Phoenician cult of ADONIS may have reached Greece by way of Cyprus, as probably did a more important religious borrowing from the Near East—the cult of the goddess APHRODITE.

The Cypriot Greeks became expert seafarers. By 700 B.C. their population was centered in eight cities, roughly ringing the island's east-south-west perimeter. Each city had its own king; foremost of these Greek cities was Salamis (often called Cypriot Salamis, to distinguish it from the island near ATHENS). Located on a hospitable bay on Cyprus' east coast, site of modern Famagusta, Salamis commanded the shipping run to north Syria. The ninth city of Cyprus was Phoenician Citium; in later centuries it became partially Greek.

In 525 B.C. Cyprus submitted to the conquering Persians. As Persian subjects, the Cypriots—both Greeks and Phoenicians—supplied warships and crews for their overlords' campaigns. The Cypriot Greeks joined the IONIAN REVOLT against Persian rule but were defeated (circa 497 B.C.). Modern archaeology at the southwest city of Paphos has uncovered the lower levels of an ancient Persian siege mound, littered with hundreds of bronze arrowheads—the remnants of Greek defensive arrow volleys from the city's walls.

In the mid-400s B.C. Cyprus was a bone of contention between the Persians and imperial Athens. The Athenian commander CIMON had begun a large-scale attempt to liberate Cyprus when he died there (450 B.C.), and the island relapsed into Persian-Phoenician control, despite the hellenic cultural program of the dynamic king Evagoras of Salamis (circa 411 B.C.). By the terms of the KING'S PEACE (386 B.C.), the mainland Greeks recognized Persian mastery of Cyprus.

In 332 B.C., after the Macedonian king ALEXANDER THE GREAT had invaded the Persian Empire, Greek Cyprus dramatically joined his side and contributed 120 warships for the conqueror's massive siege of Tyre. After Alexander's death, PTOLEMY (1), the Macedonian-born ruler of EGYPT, captured Cyprus despite suffering a naval defeat by his enemy DEMETRIUS POLIORCETES off Salamis (306 B.C.). Ptolemy suppressed Cyprus' traditional nine kingships, replaced them with democratic forms, and established an Egyptian overlordship that lasted until 58 B.C., when the island was taken over by the Romans.

(See also GREEK LANGUAGE; PHOENICIA; SHIPS AND SEAFARING; WARFARE, NAVAL.)

Cypselus Corinthian dictator who reigned circa 657–625 B.C., after seizing the city from the oppressive, aristocratic Bacchiad clan. CORINTH was at that time the foremost commercial power in Greece, and Cypselus gained control by leading a revolution of the affluent middle class that had previously been denied political power. Cypselus (Greek: Kupselos) reigned mildly and is said to have kept no bodyguard. But as usurper and dictator, he usually is counted as one of the first Greek TYRANTS, who began arising in the mid-600s B.C. to wrest power violently from the aristocratic ruling class throughout the Greek world.

According to a folktale recorded by the Greek historian HERODOTUS (circa 435 B.C.), Cypselus was born to a Bacchiad mother and a non-Bacchiad father. Members of the Bacchiad clan, alerted by a prophecy that the baby was

destined to destroy them, arrived to kill him. But Cypselus' mother hid him in a wooden chest (*kupselē*) and outwitted the assassins.

This concept of the blessed but hunted infant is a Near Eastern mythological theme that recurs in the stories of Moses, Sargon the Assyrian, CYRUS (1) the Persian, and Jesus. The Greeks—having learned this type of legend from the Phoenicians, circa 900–700 B.C.—applied it to certain Greek mythical heroes, such as OEDIPUS. Herodotus' tale evidently derives from propaganda that Cypselus himself issued during his reign; a cedarwood chest, supposedly the one used to hide the infant Cypselus, was eventually kept on display in the Temple of HERA at OLYMPIA.

Cypselus and his son and successor, PERIANDER, increased Corinth's power through TRADE and manufacturing. Export markets were developed in Etruscan ITALY and other western locales, and Corinthian vase painting blossomed into the perfection of style that modern scholars call Early Corinthian.

(See also ETRUSCANS; POTTERY; PROPHECY AND DIVINATION.)

Cyrene (1) Major Greek city of North Africa, near modern-day Benghazi in eastern Libya, founded by DORIAN GREEKS from the island of THERA circa 630 B.C. Located inland, on a hill surrounded by fertile plains, Cyrene (Greek: Kurēnē) thrived in TRADE with mainland Greece, which lay 300 miles due north across the Mediterranean. (CRETE was 200 miles northeast.) Through its harbor town of Apollonia, Cyrene exported grain, woolens, oxhides, and silphium—a local plant, prized as a laxative and digestive. Far surpassing Thera in wealth and power, Cyrene established local colonies of its own and was an important early outpost of the Greek world.

The circumstances of Cyrene's foundation are well known, thanks to an account by the historian HERODOTUS (circa 435 B.C.) and a surviving inscription, dating from the 300s B.C., claiming to record the Therans' decision to send out ships of colonists 300 years earlier. The expedition was organized to relieve overpopulation and water shortage on Thera. Although volunteers were welcome, one son from each family was required to join, the penalty for default being death. The sea route to the intended landfall had already been explored by Greek traders from Crete. The Theran colonists, landing on the then-fertile Libyan coast, were at first welcomed by the native Libyans.

Cyrene's foundation offers one of the clearest examples of the role played by APOLLO, patron god of colonists, and by Apollo's oracle at DELPHI, in central Greece. The Theran expedition and its leader were approved beforehand by Delphic Apollo, and the new city was named for the god. (The name Kurēnē is related to Kouros, "young man," a cult title of Apollo.)

Early Cyrene was governed by kings of a family named the Battiads, or "sons of Battus." (Battos, "stammerer," was supposedly the name of the original expedition's leader.) The dynasty customarily used the royal names Battus and Arcesilaus (meaning "leader of the people"). A prominent king was Battus II, surnamed the Lucky, under whom the city attracted a new influx of Greek settlers and fought off a Libyan-Egyptian attack, circa 570 B.C. In this era Cyrene founded its own nearby colonies: Barca and Euhesperides (modern Benghazi). The territory of these Greek cities, in the "hump" of eastern Libya, was named Cyrenaica, as it is still called today.

Cyrene submitted to the Persians in around 525 B.C., but the Battiads remained in power, amid some dynastic violence, until about 440 B.C., when Arcesilaus IV was deposed in favor of an Athenian-style DEMOCRACY. Remote from the political centers of the Greek world, Cyrene was unaffected by the PELOPONNESIAN WAR (431–404 B.C.) but was absorbed into the domain of ALEXANDER THE GREAT after he reached EGYPT in his invasion of the Persian empire (332 B.C.). On Alexander's death in 323 B.C. the city passed to PTOLEMY (1), the Macedonian-born ruler of Egypt. Ptolemy removed the city's democracy and installed a liberal OLIGARCHY, which he could better control.

Under lenient Egyptian rule, the city reached a peak of prosperity in the late 300s and 200s B.C., with a public building program and such cultural ornaments as a native school of PHILOSOPHY—the Cyrenaics, founded by Aristippus, a follower of SOCRATES. In the mid-200s B.C. the Cyrenaic cities banded into a federation, which remained part of Egypt until the 100s B.C., when the Romans began to interfere in Egyptian administration. In 74 B.C. Cyrenaica became a province of the Roman domain.

(See also COLONIZATION; CYRENE (2); ROME.)

Cyrene (2)   In MYTH, a nymph who was beloved by the god APOLLO. Cyrene (Greek: Kurēnē) lived in THESSALY, where she delighted in the woodlands and in hunting wild beasts.

Apollo spied Cyrene one day as she wrestled with a lion on Mt. Pelion. He immediately fell in love with her for her beauty and "manly" strength. The god carried her off in his golden chariot to Libya in North Africa. There, on a hill surrounded by fertile plains, Apollo founded the Greek city that he named CYRENE (1), for her to rule. She bore him a hero son, Aristaeus, who introduced to humankind such civilizing arts as bee-keeping and cheese-making.

The legend of Cyrene reveals at least two layers. The earlier layer—describing Apollo and the nymph in Thessaly—appears in a fragment by the epic poet HESIOD, who wrote circa 700 B.C. (before the Greeks founded the city of Cyrene, in circa 630 B.C.). In the original version, Apollo probably did not carry his beloved off to North Africa—a detail not needed for the story. But at some point, perhaps circa 600 B.C., the older tale was developed into a political "foundation myth," explaining the origin of the city of Cyrene. This later legend is told in the poet PINDAR's ninth Pythian ode, written circa 474 B.C. for an athlete of Cyrene.

(See also NYMPHS.)

Cyrus (1)   Persian king and conqueror who ruled from 559–530 B.C. and built PERSIA into a vast empire. Cyrus (Greek: Kuros) also brought Persia to its first, hostile contact with the Greek world. Despite this, Cyrus was viewed by later Greek thinkers as a model of the wise and righteous ruler; the historians HERODOTUS (circa 435 B.C.) and XENOPHON (circa 380 B.C.) wrote about his life in legendary terms.

Cyrus—sometimes called Cyrus the Great or Cyrus II—was the grandson of a prior King Cyrus and son of King Cambyses. He ruled after the death of his father. The Persians at that time were a simple, seminomadic people of the southwestern Iranian plateau; they and their king were subordinate to a kindred people, the Medes. Cyrus revolted against the Medes, captured their capital city of Ecbatana, and made himself supreme king. Henceforth the Persians were the dominant people. The Medes became their inferiors, and there arose a new imperial dynasty—Cyrus' family, called the Achaemenids (descendants of Achaemenes).

The domain that Cyrus had seized was one of the three great powers of western Asia; the others were the kingdoms of LYDIA and Babylonia. Over his 20-year reign, Cyrus eliminated these two rival kingdoms and carved out an empire stretching from the AEGEAN SEA to Afghanistan.

First, provoked by the (undoubtedly welcome) aggression of the Lydian king CROESUS, Cyrus marched to ASIA MINOR in 546 B.C. and conquered Lydia. It was then that he encountered the Greek cities of IONIA, in western Asia Minor, which had been privileged subject states under Croesus. After some resistance, the Greeks of Asia Minor submitted to the Persians (circa 545 B.C.). These events could be described as the starting point of the PERSIAN WARS.

Later Cyrus seized the city of Babylon and its empire—in effect avenging the Babylonian subjugation of the JEWS—a triumph for which he is praised in the Old Testament book of Isaiah. He seems to have governed benevolently, allowing nations to keep their laws and religious customs once they had offered submission. He died in battle on his northeastern frontier (perhaps modern-day Uzbekistan) and was succeeded by his son Cambyses (530 B.C.).

Cyrus (2)   See XENOPHON.

Cyzicus   Greek seaport of northwestern ASIA MINOR, on the south coast of the SEA OF MARMARA, about 60 miles east of the HELLESPONT. Lying in the territory of the non-Greek Mysians, Cyzicus (Greek: Kuzikos) was founded by Greeks from MILETUS, circa 675 B.C. According to legend, the city was named for an ancient native King Cyzicus, who had been killed in a mishap involving the Greek hero JASON (1) and his Argonauts.

Cyzicus was located on the southern tip of an inshore island called Arctonnessus ("bear island," now a peninsula of the Turkish mainland). The site commanded a double harbor, formed by the narrow channel between island and shore; this superior anchorage became an important station along the Greek shipping route to the BLACK SEA. Cyzicus thrived from TRADE by sea and by the land routes from interior Asia Minor; it also enjoyed rich local fisheries.

From the late 500s until the late 300s B.C., Cyzicus minted coins of electrum (an alloy of GOLD and SILVER) in the high denomination known as the statēr. Stamped with the city's emblem, a tuna, Cyzicene statērs were renowned for their beauty and reliable measure.

By about 493 B.C. the city had submitted to the conquering Persian king DARIUS (1). Liberated by the Greek counteroffensive after 479 B.C., Cyzicus joined the Athenian-led

DELIAN LEAGUE and (a sign of its prosperity) contributed a sizable annual tribute of nine silver TALENTS.

Revolting from Athenian rule in the Delian uprising of 411 B.C., during the PELOPONNESIAN WAR, Cyzicus welcomed a Spartan-Peloponnesian fleet under the Spartan commander Mindarus. The following spring, 410 B.C., saw one of the war's great sea battles, off Cyzicus. The Athenian commander ALCIBIADES, arriving with 86 warships, surprised the 60 Spartan ships at their naval exercises and cut them off from Cyzicus harbor. The Spartans fled inshore and moored. When Alcibiades brought some of his ships ashore, the Spartan commander, Mindarus, also led some of his men ashore, but was killed in the fighting.

The Athenians captured the entire enemy fleet with the exception of one squadron, set afire by its fleeing crew. The victorious Alcibiades extorted large sums of money from Cyzicus to pay his crews, but sailed off without doing other damage to the recaptured rebel city.

After passing into the empire of ALEXANDER THE GREAT (334 B.C.), Cyzicus was absorbed into the east Greek SELEUCID EMPIRE circa 300 B.C. The city continued to prosper, enjoying good trade relations with the Seleucids' rivals, the kings of nearby PERGAMUM. Like other portions of western Seleucid territory, Cyzicus came under Roman control circa 188 B.C.

(See also COINAGE.)

D

Daedalus Mythical Athenian inventor, regarded as a patron hero of craftsmen. According to legend, Daedalus (Greek: Daidalos) invented carpentry and woodworking, among other skills. But he fled from ATHENS after murdering his nephew-apprentice, who showed signs of surpassing him in talent. Traveling to CRETE, Daedalus constructed a number of fabulous works, including the mechanical cow in which Queen Pasiphaë was able to quench her unnatural lust for a bull. Imprisoned by the enraged king MINOS on account of the Pasiphaë episode, Daedalus and his son, Icarus, escaped by flying away on mechanical wings attached to their arms. But Icarus, despite his father's warning, soared too close to the sun, which melted his wings' adhesive wax, and plummeted to his death in the AEGEAN SEA. Icarus' fatal flight has often been interpreted as a metaphor for HUBRIS and overreaching ambition.

Landing in SICILY, Daedalus was protected by the native king Cocalus. The mighty Minos, arriving in pursuit, was murdered at Cocalus' order. Daedalus stayed in Sicily and built a number of works.

In real life, the classical Greeks—especially the Sicilian Greeks—ascribed to Daedalus many existing ancient monuments whose origin they could not otherwise explain. Supposedly he was the first sculptor to free the statue's arms from its sides and show the eyes open.

The Athenians commemorated Daedalus in a DEME (city ward) named Daidalidai, "the descendants of Daedalus." The Athenian philosopher SOCRATES (469–399 B.C.), a sculptor or stonecutter by profession, claimed personal descent from Daedalus—perhaps jokingly or symbolically.

(See also LABYRINTH; SCULPTURE.)

Damocles Syracusan courtier during the reign of the tyrant DIONYSIUS (1), in the early 300s B.C. Damocles praised the luxury and power of a ruler's life, until one day Dionysius ordered Damocles to be feasted at a banquet, underneath a downward-pointing sword, suspended by a single hair. The object lesson was that a ruler's life, for all its splendors, is fraught with worry and fear.

Danaids See DANAUS.

Danaus In Greek MYTH, Danaus and Aegyptus were brothers who lived in EGYPT and had 50 children each; Aegyptus had all boys, Danaus, all girls (the Danaidai, "daughters of Danaus.") When the children reached maturity, Aegyptus insisted that his sons marry their cousins, the Danaids. Danaus refused and fled with his daughters

to the Greek city of ARGOS, where they were received as suppliants. When the sons of Aegyptus arrived in pursuit, Danaus—to spare the Argives harm—consented to the 50-fold marriage. But he secretly instructed his daughters to murder their husbands on their wedding night. All obeyed except for Hypermnestra (whose name is translatable as "excessive wooing" or "special intent"); she spared her husband, Lynceus, and helped him to escape.

Danaus was enraged to learn of Hypermnestra's disobedience, but she was acquitted by an Argive law court following a plea by the love goddess APHRODITE. Lynceus later returned, killed Danaus, ruled Argos with Hypermnestra, and founded a dynasty of Argive kings. The other Danaids remarried among the Argives; their descendants were known as the Danaans (Danai), a name that in the epic poems of HOMER simply means "Greeks." The tale of the Danaids was the subject of a trilogy by the Athenian tragedian AESCHYLUS; one play from this trilogy survives, the *Suppliants* (463 B.C.).

According to one story, the 49 guilty Danaids were punished after death for their outrage to the MARRIAGE bed. In the Underworld, they are forced forever to fetch water in leaky jars or sieves.

The odd myth of Danaus possibly presents a distorted reflection of some contact between Egypt and the Mycenaean Greeks, circa 1600–1200 B.C.

(See also AFTERLIFE; MYCENAEAN CIVILIZATION.)

Dardanelles See HELLESPONT.

Darius (1) King of PERSIA from 522 to 486 B.C., known for his soldiering and administrative abilities. His reign saw hostilities intensify between the Persian Empire and its relatively weak western neighbors, the Greeks.

Although not the son of a king, Darius was of Persian royal blood. Coming to the throne at around age 30, following the death of the childless king Cambyses, Darius soon advanced the empire's boundaries. On the northwestern frontier, he subdued several eastern Greek states, including SAMOS, CHIOS, LESBOS, and BYZANTIUM. He was the first Persian king to cross into Europe, bridging the BOSPORUS and the Danube and leading an expedition against the nomads of western Scythia (circa 512 B.C.). This expedition failed, but Darius did gain the submission of THRACE and MACEDON, which brought his domain right up to the northeastern border of mainland Greece. The Persian Empire had reached its greatest extent, stretching (in modern terms) from Pakistan to Bulgaria and southern EGYPT. It was the largest empire the world had yet seen.

Darius ruled strictly but wisely. He was the first Persian ruler to mint coins, and he reorganized the empire into 20 provinces, or "satrapies," each governed by a satrap, answerable to the king. (In a future century, this apparatus would be taken over en bloc by the Macedonian conqueror ALEXANDER THE GREAT.) Darius built a road system with relay stations for mounted messengers: This Persian "pony express" became a marvel of the ancient world. He aggrandized the city of Susa as his capital and began work on a summer capital at Persepolis. Darius practiced the Zoroastrian faith, but he enforced Persian tolerance toward the religions of subject peoples, such as JEWS and Greeks. One ancient Greek inscription records Darius' show of respect for the god APOLLO.

Darius employed Greek subjects as soldiers and craftsmen; his personal physician was a Greek, Democedes of CROTON. But in 499 B.C. the empire's Greek cities erupted in rebellion. This IONIAN REVOLT was finally crushed by Darius (in 493 B.C.), but meanwhile it had drawn in two free cities of mainland Greece to fight against Persia: ATHENS and ERETRIA. Angry at these two cities, Darius sent a seaborne expedition to capture them. At the ensuing Battle of MARATHON (summer 490 B.C.), the Persians were unexpectedly defeated by the Athenians.

This distant defeat must have mattered little to the mighty Darius. He died in 486 B.C. It was his son and successor, XERXES, who mobilized the full strength of Persia against mainland Greece.

(See also PERSIAN WARS.)

Darius (2) III See ALEXANDER THE GREAT.

Dark Age Term sometimes used by modern historians to describe the approximately 200 years of barbarism that descended on mainland Greece after about 1100 B.C., when the invasion of the DORIAN GREEKS finally eradicated the remnants of MYCENAEAN CIVILIZATION. The beginning of the Dark Age corresponds to the start of the Iron Age in Greece.

This era is "dark" because of modern ignorance of the events of these years and because of its grimness—archaeological evidence gives a picture of widespread destruction and impoverishment. The Greek Dark Age was named in imitation of the Dark Ages of medieval Europe (circa A.D. 476–1000), which similarly saw chaos after the fall of a dominant civilization, the Roman Empire.

(See also IRON; GREEK LANGUAGE; LEFKANDI.)

death See AFTERLIFE; FUNERAL CUSTOMS; HADES; PHILOSOPHY; RELIGION.

Delian League Modern name for the Athenian-controlled alliance of Greek states, mostly in and around the AEGEAN SEA, that arose at the end of the PERSIAN WARS (circa 478 B.C.) and lasted, with much erosion, until ATHENS' defeat in the PELOPONNESIAN WAR (404 B.C.). The league—based for its first 25 years at the sacred island of DELOS—was formed as a mutual-defense pact against PERSIA, but eventually became the basis for an Athenian naval empire in the Aegean. The number of league member states swelled to about 200 by the mid-400s B.C. In exchange

for Athenian protection, these member states paid an annual tribute (although a few powerful allies, such as SAMOS, CHIOS, and LESBOS, chose to supply warships instead). The allies' tribute, paid in TALENTS of SILVER, was originally used to finance league naval operations, but later came to be used by the Athenians to aggrandize and fortify their own city. By the start of the Peloponnesian War (431 B.C.), the Delian League had become an Athenian weapon against not Persia but SPARTA.

The history of the league is one of Athens' increasing arrogance and authoritarianism toward its subject allies. The milestones in this process are: (1) the removal of the league treasury from Delos to Athens (454 B.C.); (2) the Peace of CALLIAS, which formally ended hostilities with Persia but also ended the league's logical reason for existence (449 B.C.); (3) the revolt of Samos, which, although not the first rebellion within the league, came close to succeeding (440 B.C.); and (4) the reassessment of 425 B.C., by which league members had their annual dues doubled or trebled, as Athens strove to raise funds for the Peloponnesian War. After the Athenian disaster at SYRACUSE (413 B.C.), many league members revolted and went over to the Spartan side in the war; among these rebellious states were Chios, MILETUS, BYZANTIUM, MYTILENE, EPHESUS, THASOS, and the cities of EUBOEA. But after the war, Spartan domination proved so loathsome that many former allies returned to Athens to form a SECOND ATHENIAN LEAGUE.

Partial lists exist of the Delian League members and their annual tributes for certain years of the mid-400s B.C. These lists were preserved as inscriptions cut into marble and set up on the Athenian ACROPOLIS. The state that paid by far the most tribute was Athens' old enemy AEGINA—a crushing 30 talents a year. For other states, the tribute may have been demanding but not punitive: ABDERA and Byzantium paid 15 talents each in 457 B.C. (more later, after the reassessment); Paros was paying 16 talents by the mid-400s; AENUS, CYMĒ, and Lampsacus each paid 12 talents; Miletus and Perinthus, 10. League membership offered many attractions—and not just access to the cultural glories of Athens. The league was based partly on the notion that Athenian-style DEMOCRACY was available to the member states, and lower- and middle-class citizens usually supported league membership. (Sparta, on the other hand, always appealed to the upper class; "liberation" by Sparta meant local rule by an OLIGARCHY.)

(See also ARISTIDES; CIMON; CLEON; EGYPT; THUCYDIDES [2].)

Delium See PELOPONNESIAN WAR; WARFARE, LAND.

Delos Island in the AEGEAN SEA, in the center of the CYCLADES group. Inhabited by pre-Greek peoples in the third millennium B.C., Delos was occupied circa 1050 B.C. by IONIAN GREEKS from the mainland. As the mythical birthplace of the divine APOLLO and ARTEMIS, Delos eventually became the second-greatest sanctuary of Apollo, after DELPHI. By the 700s B.C. Delos was the scene of a yearly Aegean festival in the god's honor.

The island's scant two-square-mile area contained temples and monuments, including a famous artificial lake with swans and geese sacred to Apollo. Much of ancient

Delos can be seen today, thanks to more than a century of French ARCHAEOLOGY on the site. Among the preserved monuments is the famous Lion Terrace, with its five surviving marble lions from the 600s B.C.

Delos' sanctity made it politically attractive to various Greek rulers. Both the Athenian tyrant PISISTRATUS (circa 543 B.C.) and the Samian tyrant POLYCRATES (circa 525 B.C.) held public ceremonies there. In 478 or 477 B.C. Delos became the headquarters and treasury of the DELIAN LEAGUE, the Aegean-Greek alliance organized by ATHENS against PERSIA. But in 454 B.C., amid increased authoritarianism, the Athenians removed the league treasury from Delos to Athens.

However, Athenian stewardship of Delos continued. In 426 B.C., during the PELOPONNESIAN WAR, the Athenian general NICIAS conducted ceremonies to resanctify the island in gratitude for Apollo's ending of the plague at Athens. The Athenians built a new temple to the god and inaugurated a new festival, called the Delia, to be celebrated every four years.

After Athens' defeat in the war (404 B.C.) and a generation of hated Spartan rule, Delos in 387 B.C. became the capital of a new Athenian-led alliance, the so-called SECOND ATHENIAN LEAGUE. In the late 300s B.C. Delos became the center of another Aegean alliance, the League of Islanders, most likely established by the Macedonian commander ANTIGONUS (1). In the 200s B.C. Macedonian kings were patrons of the island; one of their gifts was the Stoa of PHILIP V, a colonnade that still is partly standing today. This friendship with MACEDON brought Delos into hostility with ROME. After their victory in the Third Macedonian War (167 B.C.), the Romans handed over Delos to their allies the Athenians, who colonized the island.

Under Roman-Athenian control, Delos became a thriving free port. In the 100s B.C. it was the notorious center of the Greek slave trade. Later it dwindled in importance and was abandoned.

(See also SLAVES.)

Delphi   Sanctuary of the god APOLLO in central Greece. Delphi was the most influential of all ancient Greek shrines and contained the most famous of the Greek world's oracles, or priestly soothsayers. The Delphic oracle was a priestess, the Pythia, who would go into a trance or seizure to speak Apollo's answers to suppliants' questions. During Delphi's busy heyday, in the 500s B.C., as many as three Pythias held the office at once.

Located about 2,000 feet above sea level, Delphi sits on a southern spur of Mt. Parnassus, north of the central Corinthian Gulf, in the region once known as PHOCIS. The name Delphi may commemorate Apollo's cult title *Delphinios* (meaning dolphin or porpoise). The site, terraced into the mountainside, was thought to be the center of the world, and one of Delphi's relics was a carved "navel stone" (*omphalos*) symbolizing this geographic position. Delphi served as a meeting place for the AMPHICTYONIC LEAGUE, a powerful coalition of central Greek states. Because of its oracle and its sports competition held every four years, the PYTHIAN GAMES, Delphi attracted religious pilgrims and other visitors from all over the Greek world.

Delphi's buildings were ruined by an earthquake and scavengers in late antiquity but have been excavated and partly reconstructed by French archaeologists since the end of the 19th century A.D. They now comprise the single most spectacular collection of surviving Greek monuments.

Long before the first Greek invaders arrived circa 2100 B.C., Delphi was a holy place of the pre-Greek inhabitants. Modern ARCHAEOLOGY at Delphi has uncovered traces of these people's religious sacrifices but do not reveal what kind of deity was worshipped. Perhaps in those early days Delphi was the seat of a non-Greek oracular priestess. According to Greek tradition, the shrine's original name was Pytho. Greek MYTH tells how the young Apollo took over Pytho after slaying its protector, the serpent Python. In the Greek historical era (700s B.C. and later), a sacred serpent was part of Apollo's cult there. Also, a second god, DIONYSUS, was said to inhabit Delphi during the winter months, when Apollo was absent.

It is not known when the earliest temple to Apollo was built at Delphi but it is known that the building was replaced twice during historical times. A stone temple, dating from the 600s B.C., burned down in 548 B.C. and was replaced by an elaborate Doric-style building, completed circa 510 B.C. with the help of the powerful Alcmaeonid clan of ATHENS. That structure collapsed in an earthquake in 373 B.C. and was replaced by the Doric-style, limestone temple that partly survives today.

Amid a clutter of smaller buildings, the grand temple stood atop its terraced platform in the center of a walled, rectangular, hillside enclosure. The site's secondary structures eventually included colonnades, meeting halls, a theater where the Pythian Games' musical and dramatic contests were held, and a dozen or so "treasuries" (small, elegant stone buildings erected by various Greek states to hold statuary, relics, and other precious offerings to the god).

Today the Doric-style Treasury of the Athenians is the only treasury standing, reconstructed by modern archaeologists to look as it did in 490 B.C., when the Athenians built it to commemorate their victory over the Persians at MARATHON. Another important treasury was built circa 525 B.C. by the island of Siphnos; financed by the island's GOLD mines, this treasury was meant to surpass all others in size and beauty. The Delphi Museum now holds part of the Siphnian treasury's frieze; its marble carvings, showing the mythical combat between gods and GIANTS, supply one of the best surviving examples of early Greek architectural SCULPTURE.

Within the temple was the sanctum where the Pythia gave Apollo's prophecies. After a ritual purification, a suppliant (males only) could enter the Pythia's presence and hand over his written question for the god. Some suppliants might seek guidance on personal matters—MARRIAGE, business, and the like—while others would be representing city governments on questions of public importance. The Pythia would go into a trance or fit (despite a common belief, it is not certain that she inhaled some sort of narcotic vapor) and would then deliver the god's answer in sometimes-unintelligible exclamations, which an attending priest would render into hexameter verse.

The facts behind this soothsaying cannot be fully explained. Clearly some pious fraud was involved. Like the medieval Vatican, Delphi was a rich, opportunistic organization, with widespread eyes and ears. The suppliants tended to be wealthy men, whose dealings and affiliations might be well known. The priesthood could learn about upcoming questions while individual suppliants or their messengers made the long and public pilgrimage to Delphi. Nor were the god's answers often clear: Of the 75 Delphic responses that are reliably recorded by ancient historians or inscriptions, most are either vague, commonsensical, or nonsensical.

The most notorious answers, as reported by the historian HERODOTUS, were gloriously ambiguous. When the Lydian king CROESUS inquired circa 546 B.C. if he should invade Persian territory, the oracle replied that if he did so a mighty empire would be destroyed. So Croesus invaded—but it was his own empire that was destroyed.

Delphi reached its peak of power early in Greek history. The shrine became important amid the great movement of overseas Greek COLONIZATION, beginning in the mid-700s B.C. Apollo was the god of colonists, and by skillful politicking, the priests at Delphi were able to position "their" Apollo as the official sanction for all Greek colonizing expeditions. Delphi's prestige was further enhanced circa 582 B.C., when a reorganization of the Pythian Games made them into a major event of the Greek world.

By endorsing TYRANTS such as the Corinthian CYPSELUS (mid-600s B.C.), the Delphic oracle attracted gifts and support from this new class of Greek rulers. Delphi also won the patronage of non-Greek kings in ASIA MINOR—including Croesus and the Phrygian MIDAS—who sought to establish contacts and allies in mainland Greece.

But Delphi's Eastern contacts brought about its undoing, for when the Persians prepared to invade Greece shortly before 480 B.C. the Delphic oracle advised the Greeks to surrender. The Delphi priesthood may have hoped to see their shrine become the capital of Greece under Persian occupation. Several major Delphic prophecies in these years warned (with only slight equivocation) that Greek resistance would be futile. But in fact the Greeks triumphed over the invaders in the PERSIAN WARS of 490–479 B.C. The Delphic priesthood was henceforth stigmatized for its defeatism as well as for its reputed susceptibility to bribery.

Nevertheless, Delphi remained politically influential through the 300s B.C. and remained a central religious shrine for more than 600 years after that, down to the late Roman Empire. The oracle was shut down circa A.D. 391 by order of the Christian Roman emperor Theodosius I, in his campaign to eliminate pagan rites throughout his domain.

(See also ALCMAEONIDS; CELTS; PHILIP II; PROPHECY AND DIVINATION; RELIGION.)

deme (*dēmos*) Village or city ward constituting part of a larger territory. The term usually is used to describe the political wards of ATTICA (the 1,000-square-mile territory of ATHENS), as organized by the democratic reformer CLEISTHENES (1) in 508 B.C. The Attic demes numbered 139 and ranged in type from city neighborhoods to townships to patches of rural area.

The demes were the foundation blocks of the Athenian DEMOCRACY: for example, the 500-man Athenian COUNCIL drew its members from each deme, in proportion to population. The demes' headquarters maintained local census figures, with each male citizen formally enrolling on his 19th birthday. There were kept deeds of property and other legal documents and there "town meetings" were held.

Demeter Greek goddess of grain and fertility. Unlike many other major Greek goddesses, Demeter seems to have been purely Greek in origin. Her name is Greek: *dēmētēr* probably means "spelt mother." ('Spelt' is a form of grain.) In MYTH, Demeter and ZEUS had a daughter, Kore ("virgin"). However, at an early date Kore seems to have been assimilated into a more complex, pre-Greek diety, PERSEPHONE, who was goddess of the dead.

Demeter's main cult was at the town of Eleusis, located 15 miles northwest of ATHENS in the fertile Thriasian plain. There the prestigious and stately ELEUSINIAN MYSTERIES were held in honor of Demeter and her daughter. This cult, celebrating the goddess' gift of grain to mankind, surely arose from Eleusis' function as a barley and wheat-growing center.

According to myth, Kore-Persephone was carried to the Underworld by the amorous HADES, god of death. Frantically seeking her daughter, Demeter neglected her duties and let the earth go barren and the grain wither. Her search eventually brought her to Eleusis, where, disguised as an old woman, she was hospitably received at the home of the local king. Later Zeus decreed that Kore might return to the upper world. But because Kore had eaten several pomegranate seeds while in Hades' realm, she was partly obligated to him, and Zeus decided that she would henceforth spend four months of every year belowground as Hades' wife and eight months on the earth with her mother. The myth offers an explanation or allegory for the soil's unproductivity in the fierce Greek summer, while at the same time "explaining" why Eleusis is Demeter's cult center.

In some versions of the myth, Demeter's search is localized in SICILY—for instance, to light her way by night she lit two torches at volcanic Mt. Etna. Such details evidently emerged from the important cult of Persephone observed by the Sicilian Greeks.

(See also FARMING; ORPHISM.)

Demetrius Poliorcetes Macedonian-born soldier and ruler who lived 336–283 B.C. Brilliant but unstable, he received the surname Poliorkētēs (the besieger) on account of his spectacular yet unsuccessful siege of the city of RHODES in 305 B.C.

Demetrius' father, ANTIGONUS (1), served as a general under the Macedonian king ALEXANDER THE GREAT and was his governor in ASIA MINOR. After Alexander's death (323 B.C.), Antigonus sought to maintain Alexander's empire against the secessionist claims of the other DIADOCHI (the successors to Alexander), including CASSANDER, PTOLEMY (1), LYSIMACHUS and SELEUCUS (1). Demetrius was positioned for power at age 15, when he married Phila, the daughter of the Macedonian regent ANTIPATER. By age 25, Demetrius had become his father's field commander and admiral, in this doomed cause of reuniting the empire.

From Antigonus' base in central Asia Minor, Demetrius led his fleets to and fro across the eastern Mediterranean. In 307 B.C. he captured ATHENS, ejected Cassander's governor, and proclaimed that Athens was free. After nearly 17 years of Cassander's overlordship, the Athenians welcomed the conquering Demetrius with adulation.

Demetrius' most famous victory came the following spring, 306 B.C., in the sea battle off the Cyprian city of Salamis. With 108 warships, he totally defeated Ptolemy's fleet of 140 (albeit smaller) warships. Ptolemy lost 120 ships and thousands of shipboard mercenaries; he also lost CYPRUS and command of the sea for the next 20 years. On the basis of this victory, Antigonus proclaimed himself and Demetrius to be joint kings of Alexander's empire. However, in the following year (spring 304–spring 303 B.C.) Demetrius failed in his efforts to capture Rhodes. Rhodes was an important trading city and potential naval base for Ptolemy, but Demetrius' willful decision to waste a year on the siege when he had already captured the more important island of CYPRUS demonstrates his flaws as commander.

Meanwhile Demetrius' enemy Cassander had recaptured central Greece and was besieging Athens. With a fleet of 330 warships and transports, Demetrius sailed from Rhodes and rescued Athens a second time, then defeated Cassander's army at THERMOPYLAE (304 B.C.). Demetrius spent that winter at Athens, carousing with his courtesans, whom he installed in the PARTHENON. The following year he liberated central and southern Greece from Cassander's troops. Although he still had Phila as his wife, he also married Deidameia, sister of the Epirote king PYRRHUS. These years mark Demetrius and his father's peak of power.

Soon, however, their enemies had allied against them. At the huge Battle of Ipsus, in central Asia Minor (301 B.C.), Antigonus and Demetrius were defeated by the combined forces of Seleucus and Lysimachus. Demetrius, leading 10,000 CAVALRY, pressed his attacks too far forward and was cut off by the enemy's elephant brigade, containing 480 beasts. Meanwhile Antigonus was surrounded and killed. Surviving, Demetrius fled to EPHESUS and rallied a fleet, but the disastrous defeat had left him a mere pirate, without a kingdom.

Cassander's death (297 B.C.) and the subsequent turmoil in MACEDON provided an opportunity to acquire that country's throne (to which Demetrius had a claim through his marriage with Phila). By 294 B.C. he was king of Macedon and by 289 had reestablished his old control over Greece. Yet the following year he lost this kingdom also, when his foolhardy scheme to attack Seleucus in Asia Minor resulted in his army's desertion. In 285 B.C. the 51-year-old Demetrius was captured in Asia Minor by Seleucus. Comfortably imprisoned, Demetrius idly drank himself to death with WINE (283 B.C.). Antigonus II, who was Demetrius' son by Phila, eventually left a stable dynasty on the Macedonian throne.

(See also WARFARE, NAVAL; WARFARE, SIEGE.)

democracy The form of government that we call democracy (Greek: *dēmokratia*, "power by the people") was invented at ATHENS in the late 500s and early 400s B.C. "It is called a democracy because it is directed, not by a privileged few, but by the populace," explained the Athenian statesman PERICLES in his Funeral Oration of 431 B.C. (as recounted by the historian THUCYDIDES (1)). The Athenian democracy was a marvel and inspiration to the Greek world, as it remains today; one reason for Athens' successful imperialism in the 400s B.C. was the city's appeal to the underprivileged classes in Greek cities governed as old-fashioned oligarchies. It was not the Athenian army and navy that SPARTA feared so much as the menace of Athenian-sponsored democracies taking over the rest of Greece.

Current knowledge of the Athenian democracy comes partly from literary sources, such as the political speeches of DEMOSTHENES (1) (mid-300s B.C.) and other orators and the comedies of ARISTOPHANES (late 400s B.C.). The most important extant literary source is a treatise preserved among the works of ARISTOTLE (mid-300s B.C.) titled the *Constitution of Athens* (*Athēnaion Politeia*), which briefly describes the different branches of Athenian government. Filling out this meager picture is the archaeological evidence, such as several dozen surviving decrees of the Athenians of this era, preserved as inscriptions in stone.

Democracy at Athens was forged by the political reforms of SOLON (circa 594 B.C.) and CLEISTHENES (1) (508 B.C.). The immediate purpose was to assuage the Athenian middle class, who supplied the backbone of the HOPLITE army and whose discontent was creating the threat of civil war and of usurpation by TYRANTS. Similarly, lower-class Athenians benefited politically when Athens' need to maintain a large navy made the urban poor important as naval oarsmen (400s B.C.). The losers in these reforms were members of the traditional Athenian ARISTOCRACY, who had previously monopolized political office and decision making. Yet by the early 400s B.C. individual aristocrats such as THEMISTOCLES and Pericles had adapted to the new reality and were holding power as left-wing champions of the common people.

The sovereign governing body of the Athenian democracy was the citizens' ASSEMBLY (*ekklēsia*). This was open to all 30,000 to 40,000 adult male Athenian citizens but was usually attended by only about 5,000. (Although individual WOMEN were classed as citizens or noncitizens, they had no political voice either way.) The assembly convened 40 times a year, normally in a natural hillside auditorium called the Pnyx. There, by public debate and vote, the people directed foreign policy, revised the laws, approved or condemned the conduct of public officials, and made many other state decisions. The assembly's agenda was prepared by the 500-member COUNCIL (*boulē*), which also had important executive duties in enacting the assembly's decrees. Councillors were ordinary Athenian citizens of the upper or middle classes, chosen by lot to serve for one year.

It was essential to the Athenian democracy that its public officials not have much individual power. There was no such office as president of Athens. Pericles enjoyed 20 years of nearly unrivaled influence because he was the leader of a political party (the left wing) and because he was able to win the people's trust. But, in terms of elected office, Pericles was always just a *stratēgos*—a military general, one of 10 such elected annually at Athens. Having endured the tyrannies of PISISTRATUS and HIPPIAS (1) (late 500s B.C.), the Athenians feared that other politicians might try to take over the government, and the odd procedure known as OSTRACISM existed as a safeguard against anyone even suspected of thirsting for supreme power.

Aside from the generalships, Athenian state offices tended to be narrowly defined. The top civilian jobs were the nine archonships, which by the mid-400s B.C. were filled by lot, annually, from candidates among the upper and middle classes. An ARCHON might supervise various judicial or religious procedures; the most prestigious post was the *archon eponumos*, where the officeholder's personal name was used to identify the calendar year. Beneath the archonships were the 400-odd lesser executive jobs for the day-to-day running of the Athenian state, such as the commissioners of weights and measures and the commissioners of highway repair. These posts were filled by Athenian citizens, normally chosen by lot to serve for one year with pay. The prominent use of lottery was part of a radical-democratic theory of government which held that an honest lottery is more democratic than an election, because lotteries cannot be unduly influenced by a candidate's wealth or personality. However, elections were used to award certain posts, such as naval architects, army officers, and liturgists.

A liturgy (*leitourgia*, "public duty") was a prestigious service that a rich Athenian might undertake at his own expense. The most prominent liturgy was the *triērarchia*, whereby a citizen would finance, out of pocket, the maintenance of a naval warship for a year. In the mid-300s B.C. 1,200 citizens were recognized as rich enough to be nominated as trierarchs.

Jury duty was a vital aspect of the democracy. Athenian jury panels had considerable courtroom authority and discretion (more akin to modern judges than modern juries), and jurymen were paid reasonably well (although less than an able-bodied man could earn in a day). Consequently, jury duty was known as a resort of old men wishing to pass the time profitably. This social pattern is mocked by Aristophanes in his comedy *Wasps* (422 B.C.). Juries were filled by volunteers—male citizens over age 30—who were enrolled at the start of the Athenian year.

Jury pay, like the salaries for other government jobs, presented an important political card for Athenian statesmen in the 400s and 300s B.C. By increasing such payments, left-wing politicians could please the crowd and genuinely broaden the democracy's base by making such jobs more accessible to lower-income citizens. Pericles introduced jury pay (circa 457 B.C.) and his imitator CLEON increased it (circa 423 B.C.).

Democracy at Athens was an expensive proposition. Classical Athens was an imperial power, enjoying monetary tribute from its DELIAN LEAGUE subject cities as well as a publicly owned SILVER mine. Such revenues financed the democracy's programs and helped prevent power from being monopolized by the wealthiest citizens.

(See also DEME; LAWS AND LAW COURTS; OLIGARCHY; POLIS.)

Democritus   Philosopher of the Greek city of ABDERA, circa 460–390 B.C. Democritus shares with his teacher LEUCIPPUS the credit for having developed the concept of material PHILOSOPHY that is now called the atomic theory. In a remarkable anticipation of 20th-century physics, the atomists decided that the basic components of matter are tiny particles, which they called *atomoi*, "indivisible." These indivisible particles, infinite in shape and number, move in the void and combine variously; their movements and changes produce the compounds of the visible world.

Modern scholars are unsure how to apportion credit between Leucippus and Democritus for the atomic theory. Democritus' contribution probably lay in blending the idea into a theory of ethics. He believed, for example, that moderation and knowledge can produce happiness because they protect the soul's atoms from turmoil.

Democritus was a prolific author, said to have written 70 treatises on subjects such as MATHEMATICS and MUSIC as well as physics and ethics. His atomist theory was presented in a book called the *Little World-system*, probably written to complement Leucippus' *Big World-system*. (Alternatively, both works may have been by Democritus.) None of Democritus' books survives, and, although there are many fragments quoted in works by later authors, these come mostly from the ethical works, not from the atomist writings.

Within a century of Democritus' death, his ideas greatly influenced the philosopher Epicurus (circa 300 B.C.), founder of EPICUREANISM. In later centuries Democritus was sometimes remembered as the "laughing philosopher," possibly because of his ethical emphasis on happiness or cheerfulness (*euthumiē*).

(See also SCIENCE.)

Demosthenes (1)   Greatest of the Athenian orators, best known for opposing the Macedonian king PHILIP II's ambitions in Greece in 351–338 B.C. Although Demosthenes' rallying of his countrymen against Philip brought defeat for ATHENS and could not save Greece from subjugation, it also produced the finest surviving political speeches of the ancient Greek world. Demosthenes was not a great statesman; his defiance of Philip led him to urge foolhardy extremes, and he was badly distracted by Athenian political infighting. But he was a true patriot, for which, under Macedonian rule, he eventually paid with his life.

Demosthenes lived 384–322 B.C. He was born into the well-off middle class—his name means "strength of the people"—but his father, who owned an arms-manufacturing business, died when Demosthenes was seven, and the boy's brothers dissipated the estate. The young Demosthenes' first public speech was directed against his brother Aphobus and an associate, in a lawsuit over Demosthenes' withheld inheritance. Although skinny, awkward, and dour, Demosthenes soon gained prominence as a paid attorney in private cases, and then began serving as an assistant prosecutor in public trials. He also began speaking in the Athenian political ASSEMBLY on questions of public importance.

Alarmed by Philip's aggressions in the northeast, Demosthenes in 351 B.C. delivered his *First Philippic*, urging the Athenians to recapture their old colony of AMPHIPOLIS from the Macedonians. Demosthenes' military advice was not heeded. When Philip besieged the Greek city of OLYN-THUS, in the CHALCIDICE region (349 B.C.), Demosthenes, in his three speeches called the *Olynthiacs*, again urged an Athenian military expedition to save the town; again the Athenians voted down such an action.

Meanwhile, Demosthenes was embroiled in partisan conflicts with his Athenian enemies, notably Eubulus and the orator AESCHINES. Demosthenes and Aeschines had been amicable partners on an embassy to MACEDON to make peace with Philip in 346 B.C. But after Philip made a mockery of the peace by immediately marching into central Greece, occupying THERMOPYLAE and taking control of DELPHI, Demosthenes began his long and bitter feud with Aeschines, denouncing him as Philip's paid lackey.

In 340 B.C. Demosthenes engineered an Athenian alliance with the vital northeastern city of BYZANTIUM; this spurred Philip to declare war on Athens and besiege Byzantium (unsuccessfully). As Philip led his army south into Greece in 338 B.C., Demosthenes proposed and established an alliance with THEBES, resulting in an Athenian-Theban army that confronted the Macedonian advance at CHAERO-NEA, in northern BOEOTIA. The Battle of Chaeronea, fought in the summer of 338 B.C., was a disastrous Greek defeat. Demosthenes fought on the field as an Athenian HOPLITE and joined the Athenian retreat; according to one story, when the fleeing Demosthenes' cloak got tangled in a bush, he shouted, "Don't kill me! I'm Demosthenes!"

After the battle, however, he became the leader of the moment, organizing Athens' defense and arranging for grain imports. Demosthenes was not persecuted by the Macedonians when they came to terms with Athens, and he was chosen by the city to deliver the funeral oration for the Athenians slain at Chaeronea. The Athenians later awarded him an honorific crown or garland for his state services, and when Aeschines accused him of improper conduct in this (330 B.C.), Demosthenes won such a resounding acquittal with his extant defense speech *On the Crown* that Aeschines emigrated from Athens in humiliation. Later, however, Demosthenes was condemned for embezzlement and was exiled from the city.

Meanwhile, Philip's son and successor ALEXANDER THE GREAT had died at Babylon after conquering the Persian Empire (323 B.C.), and the time looked ripe for a Greek rebellion against Macedonian rule. Recalled to Athens, Demosthenes helped organize this revolt, which was crushed by the Macedonian governor ANTIPATER. Demosthenes fled from Athens and committed suicide as Antipater's men were closing in. He is said to have died by drinking the poison that he always carried in a pen (322 B.C.).

(See also FUNERAL CUSTOMS; LAWS AND LAW COURTS; RHETORIC.)

Demosthenes (2)   Accomplished Athenian general of the PELOPONNESIAN WAR, active 426–413 B.C. By developing the use of light-armed javelin men in hilly terrain, Demosthenes made a lasting contribution not only to the Athenian war effort but to the progress of Greek military science. He was the first commander to compensate for the limited mobility of the heavy-infantry HOPLITE.

Defeated by light-armed skirmishers in the hills of AE-TOLIA (426 B.C.), Demosthenes took the lesson to heart in his next campaign that same season, against the northwestern Greek city of AMBRACIA. With a force of Athenian hoplites and light-armed local allies, Demosthenes destroyed nearly the entire Ambracian army.

In 425 B.C. came his greatest triumph: the Battle of PYLOS and the capture of nearly 200 Spartan hoplites on the inshore island of Sphacteria. Archers and javelin men played a crucial role in the final assault. The operation was commanded by the Athenian politician CLEON who undoubtedly used Demosthenes' troops and battle plan. By then Demosthenes was acting as Cleon's unofficial military adviser; after Cleon's death (422 B.C.), Demosthenes seems to have fallen into disfavor. He was not elected to another generalship until 413 B.C., when he was sent to reinforce the Athenian general NICIAS at the disastrously stalled Athenian siege of SYRACUSE.

There Demosthenes commanded the rear guard in the calamitous Athenian retreat. Surrounded, he eventually surrendered, and was later put to death by the Syracusans.

(See also WARFARE, LAND.)

Diadochi   The "successors" (Greek: diadochoi) to the Macedonian king ALEXANDER THE GREAT. The term applies to those of his generals who emerged after his death (323 B.C.) to lay claim to—and fight over—parts of Alexander's vast empire, which stretched from Greece to the Indus River. The main Diadochi were: ANTIGONUS (1) and his son DEMETRIUS POLIORCETES (who, based in ASIA MINOR, sought to preserve and rule the empire); PTOLEMY (1) (who seized EGYPT and founded his dynasty there); SELEUCUS (1) (who did likewise in the Near East and other parts of the old Persian domain); CASSANDER (who claimed MACEDON and Greece); and LYSIMACHUS (who took THRACE). The Macedonian regent ANTIPATER was active in the early years, as the overlord to Antigonus. In addition, an able commander named Eumenes posed an early threat but was driven eastward out of Asia Minor by Antigonus, then was killed.

The chaotic campaigns and maneuverings of the Diadochi lasted for over 25 years. Antigonus' death at the Battle of Ipsus (301 B.C.), in Asia Minor, destroyed the possibility that Alexander's domain could be reknit. The boundaries of the Hellenistic kingdoms were more or less settled by circa 280 B.C.

(See also HELLENISTIC AGE.)

dialects   See GREEK LANGUAGE.

Diodorus Siculus   Greek historian born at Agyrium, in central SICILY. Diodorus the Sicilian (as his surname means) lived in the first century B.C. and wrote a world history, from earliest times to the end of Julius Caesar's Gallic Wars (54 B.C.). Much of the work is lost, but books 11–20 survive fully and provide much information (and some misinformation) about events in Greek history of the 400s and 300s B.C. While Diodorus sometimes relies on inferior source material, he provides the best available account for many events of the 300s, such as the wars of the DIADOCHI.

Diogenes   Best known of the Cynic philosphers (circa 400–325 B.C.). As an extreme devotee of Cynic simplicity and rejection of social convention, Diogenes voluntarily lived in a brutish and immodest manner that supposedly won him the nickname "the Dog" (Kuon). From this, his followers became known as Kunikoi, or CYNICS. Diogenes did not, however, start the Cynic movement; it had been founded by an Athenian, Antisthenes.

Diogenes was born in the Greek city of SINOPE, on the southern coast of the BLACK SEA. He learned the Cynic's creed upon moving to ATHENS in middle age. According to one story, he was taught by Antisthenes himself, after pursuing him relentlessly for instruction.

Living homeless and impoverished, sleeping in public colonnades or in an overturned clay storage jar (not exactly the "bathtub" of legend), Diogenes traveled to CORINTH and probably to other cities, preaching the Cynic doctrine of spiritual self-sufficiency. Despite his avowed apathy to social matters, he seems to have been a skilled exhibitionist, attracting the attention of passersby while preaching his sermons. He is said to have walked the streets with a lit lamp in daylight, remarking that he was searching for an honest man. Another story claims that he threw away his only possession, a cup, after watching a boy scoop up cistern water with his hands. Supposedly Diogenes also had the scandalous habit of masturbating in the public places where he lived—a practice he defended by saying he wished he could satisfy hunger as easily, by just rubbing his stomach.

According to legend, when the young Macedonian king ALEXANDER THE GREAT visited Corinth in 335 B.C. he found Diogenes at some public haunt and asked if he could do anything for Diogenes. "Yes," replied the sage. "Move a little, out of my sunlight." Later the king declared, "If I were not Alexander, I would be Diogenes." (That is, If I did not have my conquests to pursue, I would emulate Diogenes' asceticism.)

Diomedes Mythical Greek hero of ARGOS who played a prominent role in the TROJAN WAR. The son of the Calydonian hero Tydeus and the Argive princess Deipyle, Diomedes as a young man avenged his father's death at THEBES by helping to capture the city in the expedition of the Epigoni (Descendants).

Diomedes appears in HOMER's epic poem the *Iliad* as a superb fighter and good councillor, somewhat resembling ACHILLES in prowess but without the latter's complexity. Helped by the goddess ATHENA, Diomedes has the odd distinction of wounding the goddess APHRODITE and the war god ARES himself in two separate combats (book 5). Later he and ODYSSEUS make a night raid on the Trojan allies' camp and kill the Thracian champion Rhesus (book 10).

In tales told by later writers, Diomedes was sometimes paired with Odysseus in bringing the wounded hero PHILOCTETES from the island of Lemnos and in stealing the sacred image of Athena from inside Troy, thus fulfilling one of the fated preconditions for the city's capture.

Diomedes survived the war and returned to Argos. According to one version of the tale, he found that his wife, Aegialeia, had been unfaithful, and so departed again, this time for ITALY.

(See also SEVEN AGAINST THEBES.)

Dionysius (1) Ruthless and dynamic dictator of the Sicilian Greek city of SYRACUSE (reigned 405–367 B.C.). Like other Sicilian TYRANTS, Dionysius was able to seize supreme power largely due to the external threat of Carthaginian domination. A brilliant battlefield commander— he introduced the first Greek use of siege artillery, in the form of arrow-shooting giant crossbows—Dionysius confined the expansionist Carthaginians to the western third of SICILY. Ruling also over Greek southern ITALY, he was, for a time, master of the Greek West. He is best remembered for briefly hosting the Athenian philosopher PLATO at his court (387 B.C.).

Born circa 430 B.C., Dionysius became a promising young soldier-politician in the democratic Syracuse of the late 400s, and he married the daughter of the statesman Hermocrates. Amid renewed Carthaginian attacks on the Sicilian Greeks, Dionysius was elected to the Syracusan board of generals (406 B.C.). Supplanting his colleagues, he easily convinced the Syracusan people to vote him supreme powers, for they were seeking a military savior.

Over the next 15 years Dionysius stymied the Carthaginian advance in Sicily, while quelling uprisings at home and subduing many Sicilian Greeks and native Sicels. He destroyed the Sicilian Greek city of NAXOS (2) and captured and sacked the Carthaginian stronghold of Moyta, at Sicily's western tip, after a famous siege (circa 398 B.C.). Twice he beat back the Carthaginians from the walls of Syracuse. By 390 B.C. peace had been made with the island's two domains—Carthaginian (west) and Syracusan (east)—now officially recognized.

Dionysius next sought conquest over southern Italy. Allied with the Italian-Greek city of LOCRIS and the native Lucanii, he destroyed the Italian-Greek city of RHEGIUM (circa 387 B.C.). But a renewed Carthaginian war in Sicily brought battlefield defeat and loss of territory.

Dionysius' cruelty and greed were notorious: He constantly needed money to finance his campaigns. Yet he was also a cultured man who wrote tragedies and owned relics (including a desk and writing tablets) that had belonged to the great Athenian playwrights AESCHYLUS and EURIPIDES. Dionysius' death, at about age 64 in 367 B.C., supposedly came from the effects of his carousing after receiving the news that his play *Hector's Ransom* had won first prize at an Athenian tragedy competition.

He was succeeded by his son Dionysius II, a far less capable figure.

(See also CARTHAGE; THEATER; WARFARE, SIEGE.)

Dionysius (2) II See SYRACUSE.

Dionysus Greek god of WINE, vegetation, and religious possession. Like the goddess DEMETER, Dionysus was an agrarian deity whose cult was more popular among the Greek common people than among the aristocrats. He had probably entered Greek RELIGION by about 1200 B.C., since his name evidently appears on LINEAR B tablets from Mycenaean-era PYLOS.

The distinguishing feature of Dionysus was that he was a god with whom humans could commune, either through intoxication or through spiritual ecstasy. Worshippers achieved a divinely inspired frenzy or "ecstasy" (*ekstasis*,

The god Dionysus, pictured as a youth garlanded with fruit and flowers, in a mosaic from the Syrian-Greek city of Antioch, circa A.D. 175. Originally worshipped in the second millennium B.C. as a rustic deity of wine and vegetation, Dionysus had, by the later Greek era, become a favorite god of urban mystery cults. In this role he was associated with rebirth and the promise of a happy afterlife.

"standing outside oneself"), in which the human personality briefly vanished, supposedly replaced by the identity of the god.

In MYTH, Dionysus was the son of ZEUS and the Theban princess Semele. Semele was pregnant with Zeus' child when Zeus' jealous wife, HERA, approached her in disguise and convinced her to ask Zeus this favor: that he should visit her in his true shape. When Semele made this request, Zeus came to her as a thunderbolt, which killed Semele but made her child immortal. Zeus wrapped the unborn baby in his thigh until it was born. Hera persecuted the child by sending monsters, but the boy evaded or survived their torments, and was at last welcomed by the other deities as the 12th god on MT. OLYMPUS.

Some ancient Greeks believed that the worship of Dionysus had been introduced to Greece from the uncivilized, non-Greek land of THRACE, northeast of Greece. Other evidence points to origins in the non-Greek region of Phrygia, in central ASIA MINOR. (The Thracians and Phrygians might have been kindred peoples.) The name Dionusos may mean "son of Zeus." Alternatively it may mean "god of Nysa" (referring to Mt. Nysa in Phrygia). It is probable that by the 400s B.C. the Greek Dionysus had come to include religious elements from both lands—the drunken frenzies of the Thracians and the vegetation cult and child-god tradition of Asia Minor.

The Greeks sometimes called him Bacchos (the name later adopted as Bacchus when the Romans borrowed the god for their religion). Greek legend told of Dionysus' human female followers called Bacchae or MAENADS, who would roam the mountains in frenzied bands, dancing and singing the god's honor. EURIPIDES' tragedy The Bacchae (405 B.C.) recounts how the god, on returning to his mother's city of THEBES to claim divine worship, discovered that his followers had been persecuted and his worship prohibited by the young Theban king Pentheus (lamenting), who was also his uncle. In retaliation, Dionysus inspired the Theban women to wander the countryside as Bacchae; then, in human disguise, he convinced Pentheus to spy on them. Outraged at this intrusion, the WOMEN hunted down their king—whom, in their divine frenzy, they did not recognize—and tore him limb from limb. Pentheus' mother, Agavë, led these horrible proceedings.

But in actual Greek ritual, Dionysian worship and possession took less grotesque forms. No doubt Dionysus' worshippers got agreeably drunk at his festivals, as people in more recent centuries have done at county fairs and on St. Patrick's Day. There was also symbolic possession, in the wearing of masks. Dionysus had several annual festivals at ATHENS, the most important one being the City Dionysia or Greater Dionysia, held in early spring. At this festival in primitive times, masked worshippers would impersonate the god, speaking words in his character. By the late 500s B.C. these rites had developed into the beginnings of Athenian stage comedy.

Athens, BOEOTIA, and the Aegean island of Naxos were the main sites of Dionysus' worship in Greece; all were important vine-growing regions. As a vegetation god, Dionysus was associated with all fruit-bearing trees and with the pine and plane trees. His fertility aspect was suggested in the unquenchable lust of his attendant creatures, the SATYRS and Silenoi. Sexual relations did not play a major role in his myths (that was the province of the goddess APHRODITE), but Dionysus did have one well-known lover, the Cretan princess Ariadne, whom he carried off from Naxos after she had been abandoned by the Athenian hero THESEUS.

As a favorite subject of vase painting, Dionysus was at first (500s and 400s B.C.) always portrayed as a bearded man. Later representations tended to show him as a beardless youth or child.

For the classical Greeks, Dionysus represented the irrational aspect of the human soul. The frenzies wrought by Dionysus were the natural complement to the virtues of reason and restraint embodied in the god APOLLO. Symbolically, Dionysus was said to inhabit Apollo's sanctuary at DELPHI during the latter's annual winter absence. Later, amid the hunger for personal religion in the HELLENISTIC AGE (300–150 B.C.), Dionysus was one of the few Greek deities whose worship produced a mystery cult, offering the hope of a happy AFTERLIFE to its initiates.

(See also LYRIC POETRY; MUSIC; NYMPHS; ORPHISM; THEATER; PRAXITELES.)

Dioscuri   See CASTOR AND POLYDEUCES.

dithyramb   See LYRIC POETRY; THEATER.

divination   See PROPHECY AND DIVINATION.

divorce   See MARRIAGE.

Dodona Famous sanctuary and oracle of the god ZEUS, in a region of northwest Greece called EPIRUS. Although purely Greek in origin, the sanctuary was very ancient, and it retained primitive aspects in historical times. It lay mainly out in the open, and its central feature was an ancient oak tree, sacred to Zeus. In response to an applicant's questions, the god spoke in the oak leaves' rustlings, which were then interpreted by the priests; a sacred dove may have been part of the cult. HOMER's epic poem the *Iliad* (written down circa 750 B.C.) describes Zeus' priests at Dodona "sleeping on the ground, with unwashed feet." By the time of the historian HERODOTUS (circa 435 B.C.), three priestesses had somehow replaced the male priests. These priestesses called themselves "doves" (*peleiades*).

Although never as influential as the oracle of the god APOLLO at DELPHI, Dodona was the religious-political center of northwest Greece. The Epirote king PYRRHUS made it the religious capital of his domain and beautified it with a building program (circa 290 B.C.). Later Dodona was destroyed by the Aetolians but rebuilt by the Macedonian king PHILIP V (late 200s B.C.). However, during the Third War, Dodona was wrecked again, this time by the Romans (167 B.C.).

Excavations at the site since the 1950s A.D. have restored the beautiful amphitheater, originally constructed under Pyrrhus. There are also remnants of the temple of Zeus and the council house, both built or enlarged by Pyrrhus.

(See also AETOLIA; PROPHECY AND DIVINATION.)

Dorian Greeks One of the three main ethnic branches of the ancient Greek people; the other two were the IONIAN and AEOLIAN GREEKS. Archaeological evidence, combined with a cautious reading of Greek MYTH, indicates that Dorian invaders overran mainland GREECE circa 1100–1000 B.C., in the last wave of violent, prehistoric Greek immigration. Emerging (probably) from the northwestern Greek region called EPIRUS, the Dorians descended southward, battling their fellow Greeks for possession of desired sites. They bypassed central Greece but occupied much of the PELOPONNESE and the isthmus and Megarid. Taking to ships, the Dorians then conquered eastward across the southern AEGEAN SEA and won a small area of southwestern ASIA MINOR. The Dorian invasion obviously was associated with the collapse of MYCENAEAN CIVILIZATION, but recent scholarship considers the invasion to be an effect, rather than a cause, of the Mycenaeans' downfall. Similarly, some historians have believed that the Dorians' success was due to their possession of IRON weapons—superior to the defenders' BRONZE—but it seems equally likely that all Greeks acquired iron-forging only after the Dorian conquest.

The word Dorian (Greek: *Dorieus*) may be related to the Greek word *doru*, "spear." Ancient legend also connected the name to the hero Dorus, son of HELLĒN. A small Dorian region called Doris, in the mountains of central Greece, was erroneously thought to be the people's original homeland.

By the classical era (400s B.C.), the important Dorian states included the Peloponnesian cities of CORINTH and ARGOS, the Aegean islands of CRETE and RHODES, and the Asian Greek cities of HALICARNASSUS and CNIDUS. Farther afield, prosperous Dorian colonies existed in SICILY (particularly SYRACUSE), in southern ITALY, and in Libya, at CYRENE (1). But the most important Dorian site, and the one that other Dorians looked to as their protector, was the militaristic city of SPARTA, in the southeastern Peloponnese.

Dorian states were distinguished by their dialect (called Doric) and by their peculiar social institutions, including a tripartite tribal division and the brutal practice—at Sparta, Crete, Syracuse and elsewhere—of maintaining an underclass of serfs, or HELOTS. Due largely to the superior armies of Sparta, the Dorians were considered the best soldiers in Greece, until the early 300s B.C. saw the emergence of non-Dorian BOEOTIA.

Although Dorian cities such as Corinth were at the forefront of Greek TRADE and culture in the 700s and 600s B.C., by the following centuries the Dorians had acquired the reputation for being crude and violent (at least in the eyes of the Athenians and other Ionian Greeks). Ethnic tensions between Dorians and Ionians in mainland Greece and Sicily reached a bloody crisis in the PELOPONNESIAN WAR (431–404 B.C.). During the HELLENISTIC AGE (300–150 B.C.), Syracuse, Rhodes, and Halicarnassus were among the Dorian states important in commerce and art.

(See also ACRAGAS; AEGINA; CORCYRA; DARK AGE; GELA; GREEK LANGUAGE; LOCRI; MEGARA (1); MELOS; MESSENIA; SICYON; TARAS.)

Doric dialect See GREEK LANGUAGE.

Doric order See ARCHITECTURE.

Doris See DORIAN GREEKS.

Draco Athenian statesman who supposedly gave the city its first written code of law, circa 621 B.C. Draco's laws were aristocratically biased and egregiously harsh, involving wide use of the death penalty. One later thinker remarked that the laws had been written in blood, not ink. Draco's severity is commemorated in the English word "Draconian," used to describe excessively harsh law or administration. Within 30 years, Draco's code was replaced by that of the great lawgiver SOLON (circa 594 B.C.).

(See also ARISTOCRACY; LAWS AND LAW COURTS.)

drama See THEATER.

E

education Literacy became widespread at a surprisingly early date in the ancient Greek world. Surviving public inscriptions and historical anecdotes suggest that, in the more advanced Greek states, a majority of at least the male citizens could read and write by circa 600 B.C.—barely 175 years after the Greeks had first adapted the Phoenician ALPHABET. The impetus for this learning was probably not love of literature but the necessity of TRADE—a need that included the middle and lower-middle classes.

As today, literacy and numeracy were taught to boys at school. The earliest surviving reference to a school in the Western world occurs in the history of HERODOTUS (circa 435 B.C.), in reference to the year 494 B.C. on the Greek island of CHIOS. Similarly, school scenes first appear on Athenian vase paintings soon after 500 B.C. Schools were private, fee-paid institutions: There were no state-funded schools at this time and no laws requiring children to receive education. There were separate schools for girls (coeducation did not exist), but girls' schooling was generally not as widespread or thorough as boys'.

In classical ATHENS (400s–300s B.C.), a boy's schooling usually began at age seven, and many of the lower-income students probably left after the three or four years needed to learn the basic skills. For the rest, there might be as much as 10 years' elementary school, under three types of teachers. The *grammatistēs* gave lessons in reading, WRITING, arithmetic, and literature. Literary studies emphasized the rote memorization of passages from revered poets, particularly HOMER and (in later centuries) the Athenian tragic playwrights of the 400s B.C. SPORT comprised the second branch of Greek education, under a coach (*paidotribēs*). WRESTLING and gymnastics were among the preferred disciplines. Militaristic states such as SPARTA greatly emphasized sports as a preparation for soldiering; the rugged art of BOXING was considered a typically Spartan boy's sport. Sparta was unusual in encouraging gymnastics training for girls.

The third teacher, the *kitharistēs,* gave instruction in MUSIC—specifically, in singing and playing the lyre for the recitation of LYRIC POETRY. This branch of Athenian-style education may have been less esteemed outside of Athens. Supposedly, the Macedonian king PHILIP II once rebuked his young son Alexander after the boy's musical performance at a banquet. "Are you not ashamed, my son, to play the lyre so well?" Philip asked the future king ALEXANDER THE GREAT (340s B.C.).

At age 18 an Athenian male became known as an *ephebos* (youth) and began two years of military training; similar programs existed at other Greek states. That a rich young man might then resume his studies was a practice that evolved at Athens in the mid- and late 400s B.C. The pioneers in this practice were the SOPHISTS and teachers of RHETORIC who came flocking to Athens. Charging high fees, tutors such as PROTAGORAS of ABDERA and GORGIAS of Leontini gave lessons in disputation and public speaking to young men planning to enter public life. The Athenian philosopher SOCRATES (469–399 B.C.), while not himself a sophist, occupies an important place in this evolution, as does the Athenian orator ISOCRATES (436–338 B.C.). Such

This image from an Athenian red-figure cup, circa 480 B.C., may represent a *paidotribēs,* or a boys' sports instructor. His power to punish is embodied in the stick he carries. In classical Athens, sports provided a major facet of boys' primary education, along with reading, writing, arithmetic, and music.

tutors answered a growing need at Athens for higher education.

Socrates and the sophists paved the way for the Western world's first university—the ACADEMY, established by the Athenian philosopher PLATO in parkland buildings just outside the city wall, circa 385 B.C. The Academy was known as a school of PHILOSOPHY, but offered lectures and advanced study in many areas that might not be associated with philosophy, such as MATHEMATICS. An even broader range of study was offered at the LYCEUM, founded at Athens by ARISTOTLE (circa 335 B.C.). Two other major philosophical schools, of EPICUREANISM and STOICISM, were established at Athens by about 300 B.C. During the HELLE-NISTIC AGE (300–150 B.C.), a new center of higher learning arose at the royal court of ALEXANDRIA (1).

(See also ASTRONOMY; HOMOSEXUALITY; SCIENCE; WOMEN.)

Egypt Located in northeast Africa, roughly 600 miles southeast of mainland Greece, Egypt was (and is) a non-Greek land lying about 700 miles along the lower Nile River, with coastlines along the Mediterranean and the Red seas. At the beginning of the Greek era (in the second millennium B.C.), Egypt was a magnificent kingdom that awed the humble Greeks. By 300 B.C. the conquests of ALEXANDER THE GREAT had brought Egypt into the Greek world as a land ruled by a Macedonian-Greek court, where some of the finest Greek poetry of the ancient world was being written.

The Egyptian Middle and New Kingdoms probably influenced the emerging MYCENAEAN CIVILIZATION of mainland Greece (circa 1600 B.C.). The royal tombs at MYCENAE may have been inspired by the pharaohs' pyramids and graves. The Greek MYTH of DANAUS and Aegyptus—among other tales—seems to commemorate some early Greek-Egyptian contact. The Mycenaeans would have visited Egypt for TRADE, for service as hired mercenaries, or for pirate raids. Almost certainly the "Sea Peoples" who ravaged Egypt's Mediterranean coast around 1100 B.C. included groups of displaced Mycenaeans, fleeing from social collapse in Greece.

For several centuries in the first millennium B.C., the pharaohs banned Greek merchants from Egypt. (As a result, Egypt never influenced the ripening Greek culture of the 700s B.C. as strongly as did another Near Eastern civilization, PHOENICIA). But in around 650 B.C. Greek traders were allowed to set up an emporium in the Nile delta. This was NAUCRATIS, where the Greeks offered SILVER ore and SLAVES in exchange for Egyptian grain and luxury goods, such as carved ivory. The Greek poet BACCHYLIDES (circa 470 B.C.) mentions grain ships bringing a fat profit home from Egypt. It was the Naucratis trade that brought Egyptian artwork in quantity to Greece, to be imitated by Greek artists: The famous Greek *kouroi* statues of the early and mid-500s B.C. preserve the postures of Egyptian statuary.

Greek soldiers were more welcome than traders. By 600 B.C. pharaohs were hiring and bringing to Egypt Greek HOPLITE mercenaries to serve in their wars. Among the oldest surviving Greek inscription is a Greek soldier's graffito, scratched onto a colossal statue at Abu Simbel, 700 miles up the Nile (591 B.C.).

Egypt was conquered by the Persian king Cambyses in 525 B.C. As a Persian subject state, Egypt provided warships and crews in the PERSIAN WARS against the Greeks. In 460 B.C. a Greek invasion force—120 ships of the Athenian-led DELIAN LEAGUE—sailed into the Nile to attack the Persian-garrisoned city of Memphis. The invasion was destroyed by the Persians in 455 B.C., and Egypt remained securely within the Persian Empire for another 120 years. But in 332 B.C. the Macedonian king Alexander the Great captured Egypt, in his conquest of the Persian Empire. On Egypt's Mediterranean coast Alexander founded a city destined to be one of the greatest of the ancient world, ALEXANDRIA (1).

At Alexander's death, Egypt fell into the hands of a Macedonian general, PTOLEMY (1), who founded a dynasty. With its brilliant capital at Alexandria, Ptolemaic Egypt became the wealthiest and most important kingdom in the HELLENISTIC AGE (300–150 B.C.). The Ptolemies took over the apparatus of the pharaohs and modernized it, creating an immense, efficient civil service for drawing taxes from the Egyptian peasantry who worked the fertile Nile valley.

In foreign affairs, the Syrian-based SELEUCID EMPIRE soon emerged as the enemy of Ptolemaic Egypt. Between 274 and 168 B.C., the two kingdoms fought the six Syrian Wars, disputing their common boundary in the Levant. The Ptolemies ruled Egypt until the Roman conquest of 30 B.C. The last Ptolemaic ruler was the famous Cleopatra VII.

(See also BLACK PEOPLES; GOLD; HERODOTUS; PTOLEMY (2) II; SCULPTURE; WARFARE, LAND; WARFARE, NAVAL.)

ekklesia See ASSEMBLY.

Elea See PARMENIDES.

Electra In MYTH, a daughter of King AGAMEMNON of MYCENAE and his queen, CLYTAEMNESTRA. Not mentioned in HOMER, Electra made her first known literary appearance in STESICHORUS' poem the *Oresteia* (circa 590 B.C.). In Athenian tragedy, she appears as a main character in the story—handled by all three of the great tragedians—of how her brother ORESTES avenged Agamemnon's murder by slaying Clytaemnestra and her lover, Aegisthus.

In AESCHYLUS' play the *Libation Bearers* (458 B.C.), Electra welcomes Orestes and supports his scheme to kill her hated mother and Aegisthus. In SOPHOCLES' *Electra* (circa 418–410 B.C.) she acts similarly, and is the focus of the play. But in EURIPIDES' *Electra* (circa 417 B.C.) she appears obsessively hateful and jealous of her mother, who has denied Electra the chance to marry, thereby punning on her name: *alektron* ("without marriage"). In this play, Electra wields an ax and actually helps Orestes to kill Clytaemnestra (offstage), then goes wild with guilt. Euripides' treatment of Electra provides one of the best examples of that playwright's innovative interest in psychology and the plight of WOMEN in Greek society.

elegy See LYRIC POETRY.

Eleusinian Mysteries Important Athenian religious cult in honor of the grain goddess DEMETER, observed at the town of Eleusis (which lies 15 miles northwest of ATHENS, in the region's main wheat- and barley-growing plain). The cult was given the title "Mysteries" (*mustēriai*, from *mustēs*, "an initiate") on account of its secretive nature. Only those who had been formally initiated could participate, and details of the rites (which seem to have been harmless enough) were forbidden to be revealed publicly. The Eleusinian Mysteries were a rare form of worship in classical Greece (mid-400s B.C.), where city-states emphasized public cults; later, however, in the HELLENISTIC AGE (300–150 B.C.), mystery religions began to proliferate.

The cult was run by the Athenian state and was officiated by two noble families of Eleusis: the Eumolpidae and Kerykes. Despite the emphasis on secrecy, the requirements for initiation were lenient: Anyone of Greek speech and without blood guilt was eligible to join. This inclusion of SLAVES and WOMEN is remarkable. The initiate's oath of secrecy was taken seriously; no knowledgeable ancient writer has left us a description of the rites, and in the 400s B.C. such prominent men as the playwright AESCHYLUS and the politician ALCIBIADES were investigated or prosecuted for supposedly revealing the mysteries. Clearly the initiates' conduct was thought to affect the goddess Demeter's goodwill and the all-important fertility of the grainfields.

The "bible" of the mysteries was the central myth of Demeter. According to legend, the death god HADES stole away Demeter's daughter Korē (also called PERSEPHONE). Demeter searched the world for her, letting the fields go barren in her grief; and the god ZEUS restored order by allowing Korē-Persephone to remain with her mother for eight months out of every year.

The mysteries probably reenacted this story every spring, as a kind of pageant, with dance and incantation. At the climactic, secret, nocturnal ceremony in Demeter's temple, the priest would hold up an ear of grain amid reverent silence. The "doctrine" of the mysteries was probably very simple: thanksgiving for Demeter's gift to the living and the hope that she and her daughter Persephone would take further care of the initiates' souls in the Underworld. This hope of a happy AFTERLIFE became a cornerstone of later mystery cults.

(See also DEMETER; ORPHISM.)

Eleusis See ATTICA; ELEUSINIAN MYSTERIES.

Elis Plain in the western PELOPONNESE. In about 471 B.C., the inhabitants established a city, also called Elis, as their political center. The Eleans had charge of the highly important OLYMPIC GAMES, the sports-and-religious festival held every four years in honor of the god ZEUS. The actual site of the games was the sanctuary and sports complex known as OLYMPIA. Since Olympia lay closer to the city of Pisa than to the city of Elis, there was intermittent strife between Elis and Pisa for control.

Formidable soldiers, the Eleans remained staunch allies of SPARTA until 420 B.C., when events led them to make alliances with Sparta's enemies ATHENS and ARGOS, in the PELOPONNESIAN WAR. Later, still an enemy of Sparta, Elis made an alliance with ARCADIA (369 B.C.). In the 200s B.C. it was an enemy of Arcadia and a member of the Aetolian League.

(See also AETOLIA; PHEIDON.)

Empedocles Influential early philosopher who lived circa 495–430 B.C. Empedocles was born to an aristocratic family of the Sicilian Greek city of ACRAGAS. As a thinker, poet, statesman, and physician Empedocles became a semi-legendary figure among his contemporaries. He is plausibly said to have helped establish DEMOCRACY at Acragas after the expulsion of the reigning tyrant, circa 472 B.C., and he supposedly declined a public offer of kingship. He is said to have later been exiled from Acragas. He was an admired orator, who reportedly tutored the greatest Greek orator of the next generation, GORGIAS of Leontini.

His philosophy, partly inspired by the Italian-based Greek philosophical schools of PARMENIDES and PYTHAGORAS, was presented in two epic poems in hexameter verse, *On Nature* and *Purifications*; he is said to have recited the latter at the OLYMPIC GAMES. About 450 verses of these poems (approximately one-tenth of their combined total) survive today as quotations in works by later writers. The poems' ideas had a profound effect on subsequent thinkers, including ARISTOTLE.

On Nature introduced the concept, later fundamental to Aristotle's physics, that all matter derives from four elements: air, water, fire, and earth. These elements are eternal and unchanging; apparent creation and destruction in the world merely indicates the ceaseless reorganizations of these four elements into new ratios. Love (Philia) and Strife (Neikos) are cosmic forces seeking to unify and divide, respectively. Empedocles' theory of elements has been interpreted as a correction of Parmenides' belief that ultimate reality is unified and immobile. Here Empedocles probably helped inspire the elemental theories of the early "atomists," DEMOCRITUS and LEUCIPPUS.

The *Purifications* was concerned with humankind's Original Sin and restoration—ideas that had already been developed in the mystic ORPHISM of Acragantine aristocratic circles. Empedocles apparently identified the primal sin as the first shedding of blood and eating of meat. Tainted by this ancestral pollution, the individual human soul must be purified through a series of incarnations, bringing the soul through the round of elements to a renewed state of bliss. In the *Purifications'* most famous verse, Empedocles declares, "Already I have been a boy and a girl, a bush and a bird, and speechless fish in the sea." The Orphic-derived notion of the soul's transmigration was also a feature of Pythagorean belief, taught at certain Greek cities of nearby southern ITALY. While not a Pythagorean himself, Empedocles was clearly influenced by such teachings.

(See also AFTERLIFE; MEDICINE; SCIENCE.)

Epaminondas Brilliant Theban statesman and general who lived circa 410–362 B.C. Epaminondas (Greek: Epameinondas) engineered the rise of THEBES as the foremost Greek city, in defiance of SPARTA. He destroyed the legend of Spartan military invincibility and ended Sparta's domination of Greece that had lasted for 35 years since Sparta's victory in the PELOPONNESIAN WAR.

Thebes and Sparta were already at war when Epaminondas first came to prominence, in 371 B.C. As an elected commander for that year, he came to quarrel with the Spartan king AGESILAUS at a peace conference. But the resulting Spartan invasion of Theban territory ended in a Theban triumph, when Epaminondas destroyed a Spartan army at the Battle of LEUCTRA.

After the battle, Epaminondas simply dismantled the Spartan empire. Marching into the PELOPONNESE in winter 370–369 B.C., he liberated ARCADIA from Spartan overlordship and (then or later) established his "big city," Megalopolis, to be the center of an Arcadian league. Soon afterward Epaminondas entered the Spartan-ruled region called MESSENIA, where he founded another city, Messene, to be a political center against Sparta. Epaminondas' liberation of Messenia had a devastating affect on Sparta, which had traditionally relied on Messenian grain, grown by the Messenian serfs known as HELOTS.

Epaminondas' later exploits included further invasions of the Peloponnese and a naval expedition against the Athenians. In 362 B.C. he again led an army into the Peloponnese, to oppose a Spartan threat against Arcadia. Although the Battle of MANTINEA was another Theban victory, Epaminondas died there from wounds. He was the greatest leader to emerge in the tumultuous half century between the end of the Peloponnesian War (404 B.C.) and the rise of MACEDON (350s B.C.).

(See also WARFARE, LAND.)

Ephesus   Greek city of IONIA, on the central west coast of ASIA MINOR, known for its TRADE and its elaborate cult of the goddess ARTEMIS. Founded circa 1050 B.C. by IONIAN GREEKS from mainland Greece, Ephesus lay at the mouth of the Cayster River, at a site that commanded the coastal farming plain, the riverine route inland, and the sea passage to the nearby Greek island of SAMOS.

Ephesus was one of the Greek world's foremost cities during the Ionian heyday of the 600s and 500s B.C. Although never a great seagoing power like its neighbor and trade rival MILETUS, Ephesus thrived as a terminus for caravans from the Asian interior and as an artisan center; its ivory carving was famous. In the mid-600s B.C. Ephesus withstood attack by a nomadic people, the Cimmerians, who had swept westward through Asia Minor. Patriotic resistance was urged in verses by the Ephesian poet CALLINUS (whose surviving fragments are among the earliest extant Greek LYRIC POETRY). But Ephesus' most famous resident was the early Greek philosopher HERACLITUS (circa 500 B.C.).

Around 600 B.C. the city's oligarchic government gave way to a line of TYRANTS. One of these rulers, in the mid-500s B.C., began construction of a magnificent temple of Artemis, later reckoned as one of the SEVEN WONDERS OF THE WORLD. This temple, known as the Artemisium, was the largest Greek building of its day, measuring 358 feet in length and 171 feet in width. Apparently not completed until about 430 B.C., it burned down in 356 B.C. at the hands of an arsonist who wanted his deed to be remembered forever.

Like the rest of Ionia, Ephesus fell to the Lydian king CROESUS in the mid-500s B.C. and soon thereafter to the

Persian king CYRUS (1). The city fared better than other Ionian cities under the Persians. Although it joined in the ill-fated IONIAN REVOLT of 499 B.C., it apparently made a timely surrender and avoided the worst retaliations, while the Persians' sack of Miletus in 493 B.C. removed Ephesus' main rival. In 479 B.C. Ephesus was liberated, along with the rest of Ionia, by the mainland Greeks.

Ephesus then became part of the Athenian-controlled DELIAN LEAGUE (circa 478 B.C.), but joined the general Delian revolt against ATHENS toward the end of the PELOPONNESIAN WAR (in 411 B.C.). As an important Spartan naval base, Ephesus served the commander LYSANDER in his defeat of an Athenian fleet at the nearby Battle of Notium (406 B.C.), and after the war Ephesus continued as a Spartan base for sea operations against PERSIA. But, with the KING's PEACE of 386 B.C., Ephesus and all other Asian Greek cities passed back to Persian rule, until they were again liberated in 334 B.C., by ALEXANDER THE GREAT.

The city then embarked on its second era of greatness. Rebuilt at a new site by the Macedonian dynast LYSIMACHUS around 294 B.C., Ephesus became an emporium of the HELLENISTIC AGE, rivaled only by ALEXANDRIA (1) and ANTIOCH. Ephesus passed into the influence of the Seleucid kings in the mid-200s B.C., then to the kingdom of PERGAMUM and, finally, in 133 B.C., to ROME. In Roman times it continued to be a great city of the East.

Ephialtes   Left-wing Athenian statesman and mentor of PERICLES. Born circa 500 B.C. into a humble family, Ephialtes arose in the 460s B.C. as the democratic leader against the conservative party of CIMON; in this, he was the political heir of THEMISTOCLES.

In 462 B.C., taking advantage of Cimon's recent disgrace, Ephialtes and Pericles proposed stripping the powers and jurisdictions from the conservative law court known as the AREOPAGUS. The proposals were passed, but within a year Ephialtes was dead—probably murdered by political reactionaries. The mantle of leadership of the left wing passed to Pericles.

(See also DEMOCRACY.)

ephor   Title of an annually elected chief official at SPARTA and other Dorian Greek states; the name suggests "one who watches over." The Spartan ephors, who numbered five by the 400s B.C., served as an important counterweight to the two Spartan kings. The ephors oversaw the kings' administration and personal conduct; they could summon the kings to their presence or prosecute them. Two ephors always accompanied a king on campaign (a sign of the Spartan fear of the corrupting outside world). Every month ephors and kings exchanged oaths to observe each other's authority.

(See also CHILON; LYCURGUS (1).)

epic poetry   The earliest and greatest works of extant Greek literature are the two long narrative poems titled the *Iliad* and *Odyssey*, ascribed to the poet HOMER. Employing dactylic hexameter verse and a distinctive, elevated vocabulary, the *Iliad* and *Odyssey* typify the Greek literary genre called *epikē* (from *epos*, "word").

Today most scholars recognize that the *Iliad* and *Odyssey*—written down circa 750 B.C., soon after the invention of the Greek ALPHABET—represent the final stage in a prior traditon of unwritten verse composition, stretching back some 500 years to the second millennium B.C. This unwritten poetry-making is today known as oral composition. The foremost geographic region for this poetic tradition was the eastern Greek area called IONIA.

In preliterate cultures, poetry serves a mnemonic purpose: The rhyme and rhythm of a poem or song make the words easier to remember. Many preliterate societies have used poetry (in unwritten forms) for the memorization and recital of legends and folktales. In the early Greek world, oral poetry typically recounted tales from Greek MYTH—tales of olden-day heroes and their interractions with the gods.

These stories were preserved and retold by a professional class of bards or minstrels known as *aoidoi* or *rhapsoidoi* (rhapsodes, "song-stitchers"). The skill of these bards lay in their knowledge of the vast mythological material and in their ability to select and shape episodes for public recitation. This oral poetry was sung or recited in the flowing rhythm of dactylic hexameter. (Greek poetry did not employ rhyme: The GREEK LANGUAGE had too many natural rhymes for this to be considered beautiful.) An idea of the bard's function is communicated in book 8 of the *Odyssey*, where the blind minstrel Demodocus recites to his own accompaniment on the lyre at a royal feast. The technique by which a bard might draw on familiar subject matter while composing individual lines spontaneously from a mental trove of formulaic expressions has been illuminated in modern times by Milman Parry's studies of oral composition in Serbia and Croatia in the 1930s A.D.

The second well-known Greek epic poet is HESIOD (circa 700 B.C.). The rural, middle-class Hesiod was an individualist in the art: In his *Works and Days* he fitted the epic verse form to a most unusual content, a moralizing farming calendar.

But the main epic tradition is exemplified by Homer's poems of aristocratic war and voyaging. We know that, by about 550 B.C., there existed about 10 other epic poems—written down after the *Iliad* and *Odyssey*, shorter than they, and probably inspired by them. Known collectively as the epic cycle (*epikos kuklos*), these poems taken together recounted a loose mythical world history from the Creation to the aftermath of the TROJAN WAR. Among the non-Homeric epics were the *Oedipodia*, the *Thebaïd*, and the *Epigoni*, recounting the tragic history of the ruling house of the city of THEBES (including the tales of OEDIPUS and of the SEVEN AGAINST THEBES). But most of the epic cycle described episodes of the Trojan War not recounted in Homer; these poems included the *Cypria*, *Little Iliad*, *Destruction of Troy*, and *Homecomings*.

Today the non-Homeric epics exist only in fragments quoted by later writers. But many of the legends that they described have been preserved for us—in Athenian stage tragedy (400s B.C.), in the prose works of ancient scholars, and in such later epics as the Roman Ovid's *Metamorphoses*.

By the mid-500s B.C., epic composition had died out in favor of newer forms, such as LYRIC POETRY and then THEATER. Epic was revived in a more self-conscious, literary form in the mid-200s B.C. by the Alexandrian poet APOLLONIUS. The Alexandrian epic tradition strongly affected Roman literature, culminating in the Roman poet Vergil's patriotic masterpiece, the *Aeneid* (circa 20 B.C.).

(See also ACHILLES; JASON (1); MUSIC; ODYSSEUS.)

Epicureanism Influential Greek philosophical school of the HELLENISTIC AGE (300–150 B.C.) and after, founded by Epicurus. Born at SAMOS to an Athenian father circa 341 B.C., Epicurus (Greek: Epikouros) resided at ATHENS from the late 300s B.C. until his death in 270 B.C. There he and his followers lived in privacy and simplicity on his property (a house and garden), where he taught pupils. The fact that these pupils included SLAVES and WOMEN is a sign of Epicurus' innovative and liberal outlook, by ancient Greek standards.

His doctrine of Epicureanism was a daring intellectual breakthrough. For the Epicureans, the purpose of life was pleasure (*hēdonē*), as derived from a simple, even ascetic, mode of existence. Pursuits that brought pain, ill health, frustration, anxiety, or unending desire were not considered appropriate pleasures. Since the chief cause of pain is unsatisfied desire, Epicureans were taught to limit their desires rather than seeking to satisfy each one. The ideal state of the soul is freedom from agitation (*ataraxia*); this can be achieved through temperance and study. Teaching his followers to renounce political ambition, with its cares and corruptions, Epicurus went boldly against the traditional grain of the Greek city-state and anticipated the more personal, individualistic values of Hellenistic society.

On the metaphysical side, Epicureanism relied on the atomist theory of DEMOCRITUS and LEUCIPPUS. Epicurus concluded that, because the human soul is composed of atoms like the body, these atoms must disperse at the person's death. In other words, the soul dies with the body. And thus there is no such thing as an AFTERLIFE. It was this revolutionary idea that led to much criticism of Epicureanism by religious circles in the ancient world.

Also offensive to religious thinkers was the Epicurean idea that the gods, although they exist, are completely detached from human events. Like good Epicureans themselves, the gods live in contentment and self-restraint. Humans should revere them, but not hope for favors or fear their anger.

Although it remained overshadowed by the rival school of STOICISM, Epicureanism did influence later thinkers, such as the Roman poets Lucretius and Horace (who lived more than 200 years after Epicurus). Ironically, because Epicurus' own voluminous writings have been lost to us, scholars have relied largely on Lucretius' philosophical epic poem *De Rerum Natura* (*On the Nature of Things*) in order to reconstruct the tenets of Epicureanism.

Epicureanism suffered from "bad press" through the centuries, insofar as its beliefs flatly contradicted both ARISTOTLE and Christianity. The Epicurean doctrine of pleasure has been misunderstood as vulgar hedonism, and this is reflected in our modern English word *epicure*, meaning someone with well developed tastes in food, wine, and the like.

Epicurus See EPICUREANISM.

Epidamnus A Greek city located on the eastern Adriatic shore, at the site of modern-day Durazzo in Albania. Founded in the late 600s B.C. by colonists from CORCYRA and CORINTH, Epidamnus occupied an isthmus beside a harbor in the non-Greek region known as ILLYRIS. The city was ideally located as an anchorage on the coastal route to ITALY and as a depot for TRADE with the Illyrians. Prosperity eventually brought class warfare, however, as Epidamnus' middle class rose up against their aristocratic rulers.

By 435 B.C. the citizens had established a DEMOCRACY and expelled the aristocrats, who in turn besieged the city. The democrats appealed to Corinth for help. But nearby Corcyra sent out its powerful navy, which captured Epidamnus for the aristocrats and also defeated the Corinthian fleet at the sea battle of Leukimme (435 B.C.), fought off of Corcyra island. This conflict between Corinth and Corcyra was an important cause in igniting the PELOPONNESIAN WAR (431–404 B.C.).

Epidamnus itself remained remote from the great events of the 400s and 300s B.C. Eventually known by a new name, Dyrrhachium, the city passed to King PYRRHUS of EPIRUS (circa 280 B.C.) and thereafter into the expanding empire of ROME.

(See also ARISTOCRACY.)

Epidaurus Region of the northeastern PELOPONNESE, facing the Saronic Gulf, known principally for its sanctuary of the physician hero god ASCLEPIUS. A great temple of Asclepius, built in the 300s B.C., was the center of a large complex, devoted to healing and worship. The site included a GYMNASIUM, baths, hostels, lesser shrines, and a THEATER for dramatic presentations. The temple boasted a huge GOLD-and-ivory statue of Asclepius, shown seated with two of his emblems: a staff in one hand and a serpent under the other. Excavated since the 1880s A.D., the site is noteworthy today for its beautifully restored theater.

As the focus of pilgrimages by invalids seeking cures from the hero god, Epidaurus combined aspects of a modern spa with those of medieval healing shrines. Suppliants would spend the night in a dormitory associated with the temple, and there (supposedly) they would be visited by the god in a dream. This process, known as incubation, is attested to in many surviving inscriptions of the ancient Greek world. The next morning or so, Asclepius' priests would give the worshipper specific medical advice, including regimens to be followed in the nearby facilities.

(See also MEDICINE; PELOPONNESIAN WAR.)

Epirus Northwest region of mainland Greece, bordered on the west by the Adriatic Sea and on the east by the Pindus mountain range. Epirus (Greek: *epeiros*, "the mainland") was a humid and forested region, inhabited by 14 tribes or clans, some of Dorian-Greek descent and others of non-Greek, Illyrian blood. The ruling clan, the Molossians, claimed to be descended from the hero NEOPTOLEMUS.

Epirus contained two primitive but important religious sanctuaries: the ancient oracle of ZEUS at DODONA; and an oracle of the dead, situated along the River Acheron, where an entrance to the Underworld was believed to be.

A political backwater for most of Greek history, Epirus came into prominence briefly under its dynamic Molossian king PYRRHUS (319–272 B.C.), who made AMBRACIA his capital. Later Epirus sided with MACEDON against the encroaching Romans. After the Roman victory in the Third Macedonian War (167 B.C.), Epirus passed to Roman rule.

(See also AFTERLIFE; DORIAN GREEKS; ROME.)

Eratosthenes See MATHEMATICS.

Erectheum See ACROPOLIS; ARCHITECTURE; ATHENA.

Eretria City of the large island of EUBOEA, in east-central Greece. Located midway along the island's west coast, Eretria was established circa 800 B.C., apparently by Ionian-Greek refugees from the nearby site now called LEFKANDI. Eretria allied itself with its important neighbor, CHALCIS, and together these cities were among the most prominent in the Greek world during the early era of TRADE and COLONIZATION (circa mid-800s to mid-600s B.C.). The Eretrians and Chalcidians set up trading depots on the coasts of Syria and ITALY, and founded the first Greek colonies in Italy and SICILY. Later these two cities warred over the fertile Lelantine plain, which lay between them; Eretria seems to have fared somewhat the worse in this LELANTINE WAR (circa 720–680 B.C.), and soon both Euboean cities had been surpassed by CORINTH and ATHENS.

In 499 B.C. the Eretrians sent five warships to aid the Greek IONIAN REVOLT against Persian rule in ASIA MINOR. This tiny expedition bore disastrous fruit in 490 B.C., when a Persian seaborne army captured the city and burned it in retaliation. After the PERSIAN WARS (490–479 B.C.), Eretria was forced to join the Athenian-run DELIAN LEAGUE. With the rest of Euboea, Eretria revolted from Athens unsuccessfully in 446 B.C. and successfully in 411 B.C. Chafing under Spartan domination, Eretria joined the SECOND ATHENIAN LEAGUE (377 B.C.) but again revolted (349 B.C.). Along with the rest of Euboea, Eretria came under control of the Macedonian king PHILIP II in 338 B.C.. With the rest of Greece, Eretria passed to Roman control in the mid-100s B.C.

(See also AL MINA; CATANA; CHALCIDICĒ; CUMAE; IONIAN GREEKS; MARATHON; NAXOS (2); PITHECUSAE; ZANCLĒ.)

Erinna Female poet of the Greek island of Telos, near southwestern ASIA MINOR. Despite one story that makes her a contemporary of SAPPHO (circa 590 B.C.), Erinna probably lived in the 300s B.C. She was known for her 300-line poem, *The Distaff*, composed in memory of a young woman or girl who had died unwed. The poem's surviving fragments, written in Erinna's native Doric dialect, present a touching picture of the dead girl's sweet personality and unfulfilled life.

(See also GREEK LANGUAGE; WOMEN.)

Erinyes See FURIES.

Eros Greek god of love, often described as the son of the love goddess APHRODITE. While Aphrodite personified a universal sexual principle, Eros represented more the romantic feelings that one has for a specific person.

Eros was a relative latecomer to Greek religion. In the earliest Greek literature—the epic poems of HOMER (written down circa 750 B.C.)—the word *eros* is a common noun denoting sexual desire. Later HESIOD's epic poem the *Theogony* mentions a personified Eros as an attendant, not son, of Aphrodite (circa 700 B.C.). Lyric poets such as ANACREON (circa 520 B.C.) imagined him as the cruel, mischievous boy who is familiar to us as Cupid; his bow and arrow were first mentioned, as far as we know, by the Athenian playwright EURIPIDES (circa 430 B.C.). As a god of male beauty or of fertility, Eros had cults in BOEOTIA and at ATHENS. The love story of Eros and Psyche (soul) was a philosophical allegory that arose in the 300s B.C.

Borrowed by the Romans, Eros became the Roman god Cupid (Latin *cupido*, meaning "desire").

Eteocles   See SEVEN AGAINST THEBES.

Ethiopia   See BLACK PEOPLES.

Etruscans   Powerful non-Greek people who occupied the region of northwest ITALY now known as Tuscany. By the 700s B.C. they controlled a domain extending south to Campania, on the Bay of Naples. When the first Greek traders began arriving at the Campanian coast after 775 B.C., it was probably the Etruscans, as overlords of the region, who invited the newcomers to make a permanent colony at CUMAE.

The Etruscans' significance for Greek history is twofold: (1) as avid consumers of Greek goods, they provided an important overseas market for the Greeks in the 700s–500s B.C.; and (2) having imbibed Greek material culture and RELIGION, they then transmitted aspects of this to their non-Etruscan subject cities, including the Latin town of ROME. The Etruscans were a crucial early link between the Greek and Roman worlds.

The Greeks called the Etruscans Tursenoi and believed, perhaps rightly, that they had emigrated from ASIA MINOR. The Etruscans were able seafarers, with a reputation for piracy. Their craving for Greek goods has been proven by ARCHAEOLOGY: Excavations in Tuscany since the early 1800s A.D. have unearthed vast troves of Corinthian POTTERY. This surviving pottery is a clear sign of a much-larger TRADE in goods that have not survived, such as textiles, metalwork, and WINE. The importance of this foreign market for CORINTH can be seen in the systematic founding of Corinthian western colonies—CORCYRA, AMBRACIA, and others (mid-700s to 600 B.C.)—to serve as anchorages on the coastal route to Italy. Later (500s B.C.) the Athenians dominated this market—as evidenced from archaeological finds of Athenian black- and red-figure pottery in Italy. What the Etruscans may have supplied in exchange was raw metal: tin (for BRONZE-making), lead, and SILVER.

Eventually the Etruscans came into conflict with their proliferating Greek guests. In alliance with the Carthaginians, the Etruscans defeated the Phocaean Greeks in a naval campaign near Corsica (circa 545 B.C.). Soon, however, they suffered defeats on land from the Greek leader Aristodemus of Cumae (c. 524–505 B.C.). In 474 B.C. the Etruscans lost their claim to Campania forever, when they were defeated in a sea battle off Cumae, at the hands of the Syracusan tyrant HIERON (1). The Etruscans continued as a power in their northern home region for another 200 years but were finally absorbed by their former subjects, the Romans.

(See also CARTHAGE.)

Euboea   Large inshore Greek island, nearly 100 miles long, running parallel to the east coast of central Greece, alongside the regions of LOCRIS, BOEOTIA, and ATTICA. Euboea lies closest to the mainland at a narrow channel called the Euripus. There lay the most important Euboean city, CHALCIS. Close to Chalcis in locale and importance was ERETRIA; the other significant town was Carystus, on the island's southern coast.

The island's name means something like "rich in cattle." It emerged from the DARK AGE circa 900 B.C. as an Ionian-Greek region. Chalcis and Eretria soon became the two foremost cities of early Greece, both in TRADE and in COLONIZATION. Eventually, however, the two cities fought for possession of the fertile Lelantine plain, which stretched between them; this LELANTINE WAR (circa 720–680 B.C.) was remembered as the first major conflict in Greek history. Later the island was a target of Athenian expansionism, as ATHENS and Chalcis became enemies. The Athenians defeated the Chalcidians and seized part of the Lelantine plain for Athenian colonists (506 B.C.).

During the PERSIAN WARS, the Persians landed an expedition on Euboea and destroyed Eretria (490 B.C.); in 480 B.C. the Euboeans supplied crews and warships against the invaders, and the major sea battle of ARTEMISIUM was fought off the northwestern tip of Euboea. After the war the Euboean cities were coerced into joining the Athenian-controlled DELIAN LEAGUE, from which the whole island unsuccessfully revolted in 446 B.C. The Athenian reconquest of Euboea was personally led by PERICLES, who installed Athenian garrison colonies. However, a successful revolt followed amid Athens' decline during the PELOPONNESIAN WAR (411 B.C.).

In about 377 B.C., after chafing under Spartan domination, the Euboean cities joined the SECOND ATHENIAN LEAGUE, but revolted again, in 349 B.C. After 338 B.C. the island was under control of the Macedonian king PHILIP II, who garrisoned Chalcis as one of his strategic holds on the Greek mainland. Thereafter Euboea remained in Macedonian hands until 196 B.C. Eventually it became part of the Roman province of Macedonia (146 B.C.)

(See also GREECE, GEOGRAPHY OF.)

Eubulus   See AESCHINES.

Euclid (Eukleides)   See MATHEMATICS.

Eumenes (1)   See DIADOCHI.

Eumenes (2)   See PERGAMUM.

Eumenides   See EURIPIDES; FURIES.

Euphorion   Poet and scholar of the HELLENISTIC AGE, born circa 260 B.C. at CHALCIS, in CENTRAL GREECE. After enriching himself by marrying a wealthy widow, Euphorion was appointed head of the library at ANTIOCH by the Seleucid king Antiochus II (223–187 B.C.). His poems—

typically short epics on mythological subjects—were influential in the Greco-Roman world but have not survived, and now exist only as a few fragments quoted by later writers. His work apparently provided models for Roman poets such as Catullus and his circle (circa 60 B.C.) and Vergil (circa 30 B.C.).

(See also EPIC POETRY.)

Eupolis One of the three masters of classical Athenian comedy, along with ARISTOPHANES and CRATINUS. Titles of 19 plays by Eupolis are known. None of these has survived, but many fragments of his work exist, quoted by later writers. In his relatively short career (429–411 B.C.), Eupolis won first prize in annual Athenian drama-competitions at least four times—three times at the midwinter festival known as the Lenaea and once at the City Dionysia, a grand event held in early spring. Eupolis died circa 411 B.C. in the HELLESPONT region, on duty in one of the Athenian naval campaigns of the later PELOPONNESIAN WAR.

In the tradition of comedy under the Athenian DEMOCRACY, Eupolis' plays seem to have been political, obscene, and insulting to various public figures. The Golden Age (424 B.C.) ridiculed the powerful left-wing politician CLEON. The Demes (412 B.C.) showed great Athenians of bygone years arising from the dead to counsel a city in turmoil.

(See also THEATER.)

Euripides Youngest and most controversial of the three great Athenian tragedians of the 400s B.C. Euripides lived approximately 485–406 B.C. His place in literature alongside AESCHYLUS and SOPHOCLES is due to his insight into human psychology (especially abnormal psychology, such as madness or obsessive love), his frequent and sympathetic use of female protagonists (unusual for a classical Greek male), and his bold questioning of the traditional religious ideas in the Greek MYTHS. His most well-known plays include Medea (431 B.C.), Hippolytus (428 B.C.), Trojan Women (415 B.C.), and Bacchae and Iphigenia in Aulis (both presented posthumously, perhaps in 405 B.C.). These and other works show protagonists (often female) caught in the grip of obsession or disaster, in tales that combine suspense and human detail with brooding questions about the nature of the universe and of the supposed gods.

On the other hand, as critics ancient and modern have observed, Euripides' distortion of certain myths can approach mere caricature, with certain gods shown as repulsive (e.g., HERA in the Heracles Insane and APOLLO in the Ion). One of Euripides' faults is the intrusion of his love of ideas. This has the effect of turning his characters into mere mouthpieces for clever arguments that are unnecessary to the action. Euripides' contemporaries clearly found his religious irreverence to be disturbing: Although he competed 22 times at Athenian festival drama competitions, he was awarded first place only five times (as compared with Aeschylus' 13 and Sophocles' 24 in their lifetimes). Yet he was always considered thought-provoking enough to be allowed a hearing. The Athenian officials never rejected his application to compete. The ambivalent Athenian attitude toward Euripides is shown in ARISTOPHANES' comedy Frogs (405 B.C.), presented soon after Euripides' death. In this

play, Euripides and Aeschylus hold a contest in the Underworld for the privilege of returning to ATHENS, and Euripides loses.

Euripides was said to have written 92 plays, of which 80 titles are known. His large number of surviving works make him better represented than any other Athenian playwright: 19 of his tragedies have come down complete, as opposed to only six or seven by Aeschylus and seven by Sophocles. This generous legacy has perhaps hurt Euripides' reputation among modern thinkers, since, unlike the other two tragedians, some of the plays that he is represented by include work that is not his best.

Little is known about his life. He came from a family of Phyle outside Athens that might have been wealthy. Tradition holds (probably falsely) that he was born on the same day as the Greek naval victory over the Persians at SALAMIS (1) (480 B.C.). Unlike Sophocles, Euripides was not politically active, but he did compose an epitaph for the Athenians slain in the disastrous expedition to SYRACUSE during the PELOPONNESIAN WAR (415–413 B.C.).

He was associated with the intellectual movement of the SOPHISTS, who often presented disturbing ideas to their contemporaries. It was supposedly at Euripides' home that the sophist PROTAGORAS recited a treatise that cast doubt on the existence of the gods. Euripides also was said to be friends with the philosophers ANAXAGORAS and SOCRATES as well as with the politician and general ALCIBIADES. Twice married, Euripides was supposedly surly and reclusive; he is said to have done his writing in a cave on the island of Salamis. Like many intellectuals, he was thought to be hostile to the radical Athenian DEMOCRACY.

Medea, a play about the mythical queen who eventually kills her children out of obsessive hatred for her husband, is now considered one of the greatest Greek tragedies. But at the City Dionysia drama competition in 431 B.C. the Athenian judges awarded Medea's three-play group only third prize. However, in 428 B.C. they voted first prize to Euripides' three-play group, which included Hippolytus, an insightful play that features a psychological portrait of the mythical queen Phaedra and her hopeless love for her stepson, HIPPOLYTUS.

Trojan Women—one of a trilogy of plays about the TROJAN WAR—was performed in 415 B.C., at the height of the Peloponnesian War. Opening after TROY's capture by the Greeks, the play catalogues the woes that befall the royal Trojan female captives (HECUBA, ANDROMACHE, and CASSANDRA) at the hands of the bullying conquerors—who are themselves unknowingly doomed to meet disaster on their voyage home. The play is a clear protest against Athenian imperialism, including the Athenians' contemporary expedition against Syracuse and their destruction of the resistant, helpless Aegean island of MELOS. The Athenians voted the trilogy second prize.

In 408 B.C. Euripides, then nearly 80 years old, departed Athens, having accepted an invitation from the Macedonian king Archelaus, an enthusiastic literary patron. The reason why Euripides decided to leave home remains a mystery. Possibly his right-wing views were making him unpopular in the increasingly desperate atmosphere at Athens, after the Sicilian disaster and the aborted right-wing coup of the FOUR HUNDRED. At any rate, Euripides died in MACEDON, probably in 406 B.C. It is said that Sophocles, at the next Dionysia, dressed his chorus in mourning for his dead rival.

The *Bacchae,* produced after Euripides' death, presents the story of the god DIONYSUS' destruction of his kinsman, the Theban king Pentheus. The play is admired as a study of human delusion and a disturbing inquiry into the cruelty of the gods.

(See also IPHIGENIA; MAENADS; MEDEA.)

Europa   In Greek MYTH, Europa (Greek Europē, "wide eyes") was a Phoenician princess of the city of Tyre. Seeing her by the Mediterranean shore, the great god ZEUS, became inflamed with desire. He changed himself into a handsome bull and enticed her to climb atop his back, then swam quickly out to sea to the island of CRETE. There Europa bore the god two sons, the Cretan princes MINOS and Rhadamanthys. (Some versions add the hero Sarpedon.) Meanwhile, Europa's brother CADMUS began a futile search for her, during which he crossed to Greece and eventually founded the city of THEBES.

The myth may reflect in some dark way Mycenaean-Greek relations with the Near East and Crete circa 1400–1200 B.C. The modern English word Europe, meaning the continent, seems to derive from this mythical character's name.

(See also EUROPE AND ASIA; MYCENAEAN CIVILIZATION; PHOENICIA.)

Europe and Asia   The English words *Europe* and *Asia* come from the ancient Greeks. By the 700s B.C. the Greeks had developed the notion that these were two different continents, separated by the AEGEAN SEA. The Greek word Europē seems to have been derived from the name of the mythical princess EUROPA. As used as a place-name, the word originally referred to central Greece. *Asia* originally denoted interior ASIA MINOR, east of the Greek-settled region called IONIA.

As Greek TRADE and COLONIZATION opened up the Mediterranean and other waterways (800–500 B.C.), the name *Europe* was applied to the coastlines of SICILY, ITALY, France, Spain, and the western and northern BLACK SEA. Similarly, the region indicated by the name *Asia* grew with time. After the Eastern conquests of ALEXANDER THE GREAT (334–323 B.C.), Asia came to include the Near East, PERSIA, and other lands, east to the Indus and Ganges river valleys. But EGYPT was usually considered to be outside both Asia and Europe.

In Greek MYTH, a character named Asia is a nymph, sometimes described as the wife of PROMETHEUS. In fact, the Greeks may have taken that name circa 1200 B.C. from the Hittites, whose word *Assuiuva* denoted western Asia Minor.

(See also HECATEAUS; HERODOTUS; NYMPHS.)

Eurydice   See ORPHEUS.

Eurypontid clan   The Eurypontids (eurupontidai) were the junior royal family at SPARTA, a city that had an unusual government insofar as it was ruled simultaneously by two kings. The Eurypontids traced their ancestry back to a legendary King Eurypontis, one of the sons of HERACLES.

Eurypontid kings took second place in protocol to their partners, the Agiad kings, but they tended to share power equally. Among the best-known Eurypontids was the King ARCHIDAMUS who reigned circa 469–426 B.C.

(See also AGIAD CLAN; DORIAN GREEKS.)

Euxine   See BLACK SEA.

family   See KINSHIP.

farming   Mainland Greece is a mountainous country, and ancient Greek society was shaped by the scarcity of farmland. Individuals owning land in the plains tended to be much richer and more elevated socially than those who farmed the foothills. Hilly terrain dictated cultivation of olive trees, grape vines, and other fruit-bearing plants that thrive on rough ground.

MYCENAEAN CIVILIZATION (1600–1200 B.C.) was a feudal society based on sheep- and cattle-ranching, which involved baronial estates worked by serfs. Cattle rustling and meat feasts are two favorite activities of the aristocrats in HOMER's *Iliad* and *Odyssey* (written circa 750 B.C. but reflecting the Mycenaen world of some 500 years prior). The classical Greek religious custom of sacrificing cattle and sheep to the gods is clearly a Mycenaean vestige. Preoccupation with grazing is reflected in such regional names as EUBOEA and BOEOTIA, containing the Greek root *boes*, "cattle."

The social upheavals of the DARK AGE and years following (circa 1100–700 B.C.) saw the emergence of smaller holdings, owned by nobles, yeomen, or poor subsistence farmers. Developments in metallurgy brought an improved plowshare, tipped with IRON rather than BRONZE (circa 1050 B.C.). By the start of the historical era (750 B.C.), Mycenaean-style ranches survived mainly on the plains of THESSALY; elsewhere, a more efficient use of the land arose in the raising of crops.

Information on Greek farming in this epoch comes from the Boeotian poet HESIOD's verse calendar *Works and Days* (circa 700 B.C.) and from agricultural writers of later years. Details are added by archaeological evidence, ranging from farming scenes on vase paintings to recovered ancient pollen spores. The primary Greek farm crops were grain, olives, grapes (mainly for WINE-making); other fruits such as apples, pears, figs, and pomegranates; and beans and other greens. Barley was the most common grain grown in mainland Greece, but by the 400s B.C. imports of Ukrainian and Sicilian wheat were displacing barley on the market at many cities. Millet was grown for fodder. Flax was grown for weaving into linen. The ancient Greeks knew about cotton, which was cultivated in EGYPT but could not be grown easily on Greek terrain. However, North American–type corn (maize) was unknown to the Greeks, as were tomatoes and potatoes.

Crucial to the ancient Greek economy was olive cultivation, which in the Aegean dates back at least to the Minoan era (circa 2000 B.C.). Eventually the Greeks had more than 25 varieties of olive; they used olive oil for cooking, washing, lamp fuel, religious devotions, and as a treatment for athletes. Olive oil was a principal export of the city of ATHENS, where the olive tree was honored in MYTH as the goddess ATHENA's gift to the city.

Early Greek farmers had to let a field lie fallow every other year (or sometimes two years for each one cultivated),

Harvesters gather the olive crop, in this black-figure painting on an Athenian amphora of the late 500s B.C. Olives were a staple of the Athenian economy, supplying the city's principal export, olive oil, which the Greeks used in cooking, washing, and religious ceremonies.

so the soil could replenish its nutrients. But by circa 400 B.C. the Greeks had discovered the much more productive method of raising different crops in annual rotation on the same land. The Greeks did their plowing and grain-sowing in October, at the start of the rainy season. In order to plow a field, a farmer would guide a wooden rig behind a pair of yoked oxen. (Ancient Greek horse breeds were too small for draft, aside from pulling CHARIOTS.) Plowing was hard work: Unlike the much-improved plowshare of medieval northern Europe, the ancient Greek tool did not turn the soil but only scratched the surface, and the plowman had to keep pushing the blade into the earth as he proceeded.

Grain grew through the relatively mild Greek winter and was harvested in May. During the parching Greek summer the crop was winnowed and stored. September brought a second harvest—of grapes, olives, and other fruit.

(See also ASTRONOMY; ELEUSINIAN MYSTERIES; GREECE, GEOGRAPHY OF; MINOAN CIVILIZATION; SPORT.)

fate   A supernatural power imagined as preordaining certain or all human events. In Greek MYTH and RELIGION, a belief in fate paradoxically existed alongside the belief in the divine guidance and decision making of ZEUS and his subordinate gods.

The main words for fate were *moira* and *aisa*, also translatable as "lot" or "share"—a person's fate is what has been apportioned to him or her. Obviously the final and most dramatic item of human fate is death. Greek notions of fate are best understood as elaborating on the simple knowledge that every person will die and that the gods are unwilling or unable to prevent this.

The god Zeus was imagined as working in harmony with fate or somehow causing fate. One of his titles was Moiragetēs, "leader of fate." HOMER's epic poem the *Iliad* (written down circa 750 B.C.) repeatedly shows Zeus holding a pair of golden scales and weighing the respective dooms (*kēres*) of two human antagonists on the battlefield; the warrior indicated by the heavier pan is doomed. Zeus will not avert a doomed warrior's fate—even his beloved human son Sarpedon is fated to die, slain by the Greek warrior PATROCLUS (book 16). Conversely, the angry god POSEIDON in the *Odyssey* cannot completely destroy the hero ODYSSEUS, because Odysseus is fated to survive his voyage and return home (book five). But the hero ACHILLES in the *Iliad* is aware of a choice in his fate: He can either stay and die gloriously, fighting at TROY, or can return home and live to a safe, undistinguished old age (book 9).

The personification of fate as three goddesses, the Moirai, is first clearly described in HESIOD's epic poem the *Theogony* (circa 700 B.C.). Hesiod presents the Moirai as the daughters of Zeus and the goddess Themis. They are imagined as working at the womanly task of spinning—drawing out a thread of yarn that determines or represents each person's life. Into the thread may be woven sorrow, wealth, travel, and the like. Hesiod names the three fates Clotho (spinner), Lachesis (disposer of lots), and Atropos (unavoidable). Later writers distinguished the goddesses' duties, with Clotho spinning the thread, Lachesis measuring it out, and Atropos snipping it. Either the cutting produced the person's death or, in another version, the

thread was entirely spun out and cut at the baby's birth, to contain the person's future.

The pretty conceit of divine spinners was probably more important to poets than to the Greek religious public. But the Moirai were widely worshipped as goddesses of childbirth and as promoters of good harvest. Athenian brides, for instance, brought cuttings of their hair as offerings to the fates.

(See also PROPHECY AND DIVINATION.)

Four Hundred, The   Oligarchic committee that briefly seized power at ATHENS in 411 B.C., during the PELOPONNESIAN WAR. The Four Hundred were led by the politician Pisander and by the orator ANTIPHON. Taking advantage of the absence from Athens of large numbers of working-class, pro-democratic citizens (who were manning the large fleet in operation at SAMOS), the conspirators began intimidating the populace in the spring of 411 B.C. with a series of political murders and demonstrations. The coup d'etat was performed in June in the Athenian ASSEMBLY. Led by Pisander, the plotters pushed through a number of revolutionary decrees, amounting to a dismantling of the DEMOCRACY; all existing executive posts were abolished and a new COUNCIL, of 400 men (replacing the democratic council of 500), was appointed.

The conspirators ruled Athens for the duration of the summer. But the Athenian troops on distant Samos remained staunchly pro-democratic, perpetuating the Athenian democracy by holding their own assemblies and elections. After a home-defense war fleet dispatched by the Four Hundred was defeated by the Spartans in the Straits of EUBOEA, the oligarchs were discredited and overthrown (in September 411 B.C.). Pisander fled to SPARTA; Antiphon, disdaining to flee, was tried and executed under the restored democracy.

(See also OLIGARCHY.)

funeral customs   Despite the cremation of slain heroes described in HOMER's epic poems, the Greeks outside of the DARK AGE (circa 1100–900 B.C.) generally buried their dead. The elaborate tombs of Mycenaen kings have supplied archaeologists with most of their information about Greek prehistory for the era 1600–1200 B.C. The Greeks of historical times, after about 750 B.C., had their own burial customs. Their need to cover a corpse with earth was not simply a matter of hygiene or decorum; it was believed that the sight of a dead body would offend the Olympian gods, and that the dead person's ghost could not enter the Underworld until the body had been covered. This helps explain the insistence of SOPHOCLES' tragic heroine ANTIGONE on sprinkling dirt over her slain brother's corpse, although forbidden by a ruler's decree from doing so. As Antigone's action suggests, such a "burial" could be merely ceremonial, performed with a few handfuls of dirt.

For a regular funeral (Greek: *taphē*), the body was bathed and clothed. At the home, it was mourned over by relatives and household—but excessive lamentation actually was forbidden by law at ATHENS; there seems to have been a deep-seated fear that WOMEN's lamenting might bring the dead back to life. The body would then be carried on a stretcher to the place of burial, where it would be placed

might be left—to "refresh" the dead in the grave or for the journey to the Underworld.

After the burial, the grave would receive some kind of marker. Again, for the wealthy, there was marble—specifically, the type of monument known as a *stēlē*, with

An Athenian marble gravestone, or *stēlē*, circa 535 B.C. Standing nearly 14 feet tall, the monument has a carved bas-relief of the dead person and is topped with a statuette of a guardian sphinx. The sphinx—a mythical winged monster, with a woman's head and lion's body—was adapted by the Greeks from a Near Eastern design originating in Egypt. The palmette pattern, appearing below the sphinx, was a familiar Greek funerary motif, originally inspired by the Tree of Life of Near Eastern art.

in a coffin or—for the rich of a certain era—a stone sarcophagus ("flesh-eater"). Certain marble sarcophagi, carved with beautiful reliefs showing scenes of hunting and war, are among the finest Greek SCULPTURE of the late 300s–200s B.C.. At the graveside, offerings of food and drink

This broken marble gravestone dates from about 510 B.C. and commemorates an Athenian named Aristion. (The name was carved into the stone's base.) The life-size bas-relief shows Aristion in soldier's armor: The top parts of his spear and helmet have broken off, as has the extension of his beard. Gravestone carvings conventionally portrayed mature men as bearded soldiers and younger men as clean-shaven athletes. However, it is possible that Aristion actually died in battle, living up to the aristocratic creed expressed in his name, "one of the noblest."

an idealized portrait of the dead. At Athens the Ceramicus district, outside the northwest city wall, contained monumental graveyards owned by aristocratic families.

For public funerals, such as the mass observances by which the classical Athenians honored their war dead, a prominent citizen might be chosen to deliver a speech (or, alternatively, compose a poem) honoring the departed. This kind of funerary speech was known by the adjective *epitaphios,* from which comes our word "epitaph." The most famous funeral oration of the ancient world was delivered by the Athenian statesman PERICLES in the first year of the PELOPONNESIAN WAR (431 B.C.). As recounted by the historian THUCYDIDES (1), Pericles' speech presents a glorification of the Athenian DEMOCRACY, for which the men had died.

(See also AFTERLIFE; MYCENAEAN CIVILIZATION.)

Furies   In Greek RELIGION and MYTH, the Furies (Greek: Erinues) were horrible female spirits of divine retribution. Tormenting their victims by nonphysical means—inciting fear and madness—they especially punished the crime of murdering a family member. But they might pursue oathbreakers or anyone else who had broken a bond of society. Their best-known appearance in literature is in AESCHYLUS' tragedy *Eumenides* (458 B.C.), where they constitute the play's 12-member chorus. In the story, they torment the hero ORESTES, who has slain his mother.

In HESIOD's Creation poem, the *Theogony* (circa 700 B.C.), they are described as being the daughters of GAEA (Mother Earth), born from the spattered blood of the castration wound that CRONUS inflicted on his father, Uranus (Ouranos, "Sky").

The Furies were usually worshipped under some euphemistic name; Aeschylus' title *Eumenides* means "kindly ones." An altar to them as the Dreaded Goddesses, at the foot of the Athenian ACROPOLIS, became associated with the curse of the Alcmaeonid family.

(See also ALCMAEON (1); ALCMAEONIDS; CYLON; ELECTRA.)

G

Gaea Greek earth goddess. Unlike the grain goddess DEMETER, Gaea (Greek: Gaia) was not a central deity of the Greek RELIGION. Rather she was a personification of the element of land (as opposed to sky or sea). Her name reflects the Greek common noun for "land," *gē* or *gā*. Gaea had a cult at several locales, particularly in Greek SICILY.

According to the creation myth in HESIOD's epic poem *Theogony* (circa 700 B.C.), Gaea emerged from primeval Chaos, then gave birth to Uranus (*Ouranos*, "Sky"), whom she married. Their monstrous children included the TITANS, the Cyclopes, and the "Hundred-handed Ones" (Hekatoncheires). When their son CRONUS castrated his father, fertile Gaea was impregnated by the spattered blood and gave birth to the FURIES and the GIANTS. Later she produced the monster TYPHON. In turn, the Giants and Typhon impiously attacked the immortal gods atop Mt. OLYMPUS.

(See also CYCLOPS; ZEUS.)

Galatea See POLYPHEMUS; PYGMALION.

Galatia See ASIA MINOR; CELTS.

Games See ISTHMIAN GAMES; NEMEAN GAMES; OLYMPIC GAMES; PANATHENAEA; PYTHIAN GAMES; SPORT.

Ganymede In Greek MYTH, Ganymede was a handsome Trojan prince, son of King Tros. The earliest surviving mention of him, in HOMER's epic poem the *Iliad* (written down circa 750 B.C.) says that Ganymede was abducted by the gods to be cupbearer for the great god ZEUS on Mt. OLYMPUS; in exchange, Ganymede's father received a herd of wondrous horses.

Later versions add that the boy was stolen by Zeus himself in the shape of an eagle, or that the eagle was sent by Zeus. Unlike Homer, poets such as THEOGNIS (circa 542 B.C.) portrayed the abduction as a rape, assuming that Zeus desired Ganymede sexually. Modern scholars believe that this sexual nuance is not intended in the original tale told by Homer, the added homosexual coloration would seem to reflect new upper-class values that arose after Homer's time, perhaps in the late 600s B.C. The version adopted by the ETRUSCANS of ITALY included the sexual aspect. The Etruscan rendition of the boy's name was Catamitus, a word that eventually went into Latin and subsequently into our own language as the pejorative noun *catamite*, meaning "a male who receives sexual penetration."

In Greek vase painting of the 500s and 400s B.C., Ganymede is portrayed as an idealized youth or boy with long hair. Sometimes he holds a playing hoop (suggesting boyhood) and a rooster (Zeus' courting gift).

(See also HOMOSEXUALITY.)

Gaugmela, battle of See ALEXANDER THE GREAT.

Gela Greek city on the southeastern coast of SICILY, near the mouth of the River Gelas. Founded circa 688 B.C. by DORIAN GREEKS from CRETE and RHODES, Gela was a small city on a fertile plain that enjoyed prosperity. In around 580 B.C. it established its important daughter city, ACRAGAS, farther west on the south coast. Gela was ruled by a horse-breeding ARISTOCRACY until the late 500s B.C., when (like other cities of the Greek world) it passed into the hands of TYRANTS.

Gela became the most powerful Sicilian city circa 490 B.C., after the Geloan tyrant Hippocrates conquered much of eastern Sicily. But Gela's preeminence ended when Hippocrates' successor, GELON, captured the great city of SYRACUSE in 485 B.C. and made it his capital, going so far as to transplant the richer half of Gela's population to Syracuse.

By the mid-400s B.C. the tyrants had fallen from power, but Dorian Gela remained an ally of Dorian Syracuse against the region's Ionian-Greek cities. Gela assisted Syracuse's triumphant defense against the Athenian invasion of 415–413 B.C. In the 300s B.C., with Sicily a battleground between the Greeks and the Carthaginians, Gela suffered from the exploits of Greek tyrants such as AGATHOCLES, who executed 4,000 Geloans for suspected treason. In 311 B.C. Gela's population was entirely transplanted to a new city by the tyrant Phintias of Acragas.

Gelon Dictator or tyrant (*turannos*) of the Greek cities GELA and SYRACUSE, in SICILY. Gelon lived circa 540–478 B.C. An able military commander, he is remembered for his defeat of the Carthaginians at the Battle of HIMERA (480 B.C.)—an event that made him the most powerful individual in the Greek world.

As his name suggests, Gelon was descended from the first Greek colonists of Gela. He was an aristocrat, and before seizing power he served as a leader of CAVALRY for the Geloan tyrant Hippocrates (who carved out a small empire in eastern Sicily). After Hippocrates' death, Gelon dispossessed the tyrant's sons and assumed full power, at about age 50 (circa 490 B.C.).

In 485 B.C. Gelon captured Syracuse, the foremost city of Sicily. Making Syracuse his new capital, Gelon grandiosely transferred the richer half of Gela's population there, as well as the richer citizens of other captured Greek towns. (Other Sicilian tyrants soon copied this ruthless new practice of transplantation.) Gelon installed his brother HIERON (1) as tyrant of Gela and allied himself with Theron, tyrant of ACRAGAS, taking Theron's daughter Demareta as one of his wives.

Meanwhile, the Greek world was being threatened by two foreign empires, the Persians in the East and the Carthaginians in the West. Around 481 B.C. a delegation of mainland Greeks went to Syracuse to appeal for Gelon's aid against the coming invasion of Greece by the Persian king XERXES. Gelon offered to contribute a large force on the condition that he himself receive chief command of either the Greek army or navy. When these two options were rejected, Gelon sent the ambassadors away, remarking that they seemed better equipped with generals than with troops.

In 480 B.C.—coinciding with the Persian invasion of Greece—the Carthaginian leader Hamilcar sailed from North Africa with an army and landed on Sicily's north coast. But a Greek army under Gelon destroyed Hamilcar and his force at the Battle of Himera.

After making peace with CARTHAGE and imposing on them a huge indemnity of 1,000 TALENTS, Gelon began a program of propagandistic cultural display. He dedicated lavish offerings at the sanctuaries of DELPHI and OLYMPIA, in Greece; he enlarged and adorned Syracuse with public building; and he minted a celebrated victory-issue coin, called the Demareteion (after his wife). Gelon died in 478 B.C., and was succeeded by his brother Hieron, who proved to be a less popular ruler.

(See also COINAGE; PERSIAN WARS; TYRANTS.)

Geometric pottery   See POTTERY.

geometry   See MATHEMATICS.

Geryon   See HERACLES.

Giants   In MYTH, the Gigantes were a primeval race of monsters who unsuccessfully rebelled against ZEUS and the other gods, piling Mt. Ossa atop Mt. Pelion in order to assault Mt. OLYMPUS. In the Creation myth in HESIOD's epic poem *Theogony* (circa 700 B.C.), the Giants are described as children of Mother Earth, GAEA. (Her name is reflected in theirs.) She gave birth to them after being impregnated by the blood of the god Uranus (Ouranos, "Sky"), which fell to earth when Uranus was castrated by his son CRONUS. The Giants were sometimes portrayed in art as large, snake-legged humanoids.

The Gigantomachy (battle with the giants) was one of the most popular mythological subjects in Greek art and poetry, symbolizing the victory of civilization over savagery. On grand artistic vistas, such as the architectural sculptures of the PARTHENON, the battle might be shown in conjunction with the fight between CENTAURS and Lapiths or the battle between Greeks and AMAZONS. Later writers embellished the tale, adding that the gods enlisted the hero HERACLES after being warned that they must include a mortal in order to win.

(See also ATHENA; THESSALY; ZEUS.)

gold   Ancient Greeks prized gold for the casting of precious SCULPTURE and other artifacts. However, gold as a mineral deposit was scarce in the Aegean region. The source for the gold used for the royal tomb offerings at MYCENAE circa 1550 B.C. is unknown. The ore may have come from EGYPT or ASIA MINOR, traveling by way of TRADE or plunder of war.

By the 600s B.C. Greek pioneers were prospecting for gold at Mt. Pangaeus, on the Aegean coast of THRACE. Despite the hostility of the native Thracians, the Greeks, based in the nearby island of THASOS, panned the streams of Pangaeus and perhaps dug mines; SILVER seems to have been more abundant there than gold. Eventually Pangaeus was seized by imperial ATHENS (mid-400s B.C.) and then by the Macedonian king PHILIP II (mid-300s B.C.). The nearby Athenian colony at AMPHIPOLIS was strategic to these interests. Another Aegean gold source, closer to mainland Greece, was the Greek island of Siphnos, in the western CYCLADES. The Siphnian mines financed the construction of an elegant treasury building at DELPHI, circa 525 B.C.; later the mines were ruined by natural flooding.

Most gold probably reached early Greece through trade with non-Greek nations beyond the Aegean basin. Trading partners in the 600s and 500s B.C. included the Asia Minor kingdoms of Phrygia and LYDIA, where gold could be panned from certain rivers, and where such kings as MIDAS and CROESUS, fabled for their wealth, ruled. In Lydia, a gold-silver alloy called electrum—panned from the rivers where it formed naturally—supplied the metal for the world's first coins, circa 635 B.C. The Greeks, however, rarely used gold for their COINAGE; since gold was so difficult for them to acquire, they minted with silver and, eventually, with BRONZE.

In the mid-500s B.C. the gold fields of Asia Minor and Mesopotamia passed into the hands of the conquering Persians, who continued the gold trade. Like other precious goods, gold became more plentiful for the Greeks of the HELLENISTIC AGE (circa 300–150 B.C.), after the conquests of the Macedonian king ALEXANDER THE GREAT had opened up the mines and treasure troves of the Persian empire.

(See also PHIDIAS.)

Gordian Knot   See ALEXANDER THE GREAT.

Gorgias   Greek orator of the east-coast Sicilian Greek city of Leontini (circa 483–376 B.C.). Visiting ATHENS on a political embassy in 427 B.C., he created a cultural sensation with his highly wrought style of public speaking. His display pieces, using rhyme, alliteration, and rhythmical parallel clauses, were soon widely imitated at Athens; his visit marked a revolution in ancient Greek RHETORIC. Gorgias periodically returned to Athens to teach; his greatest pupil was the Athenian orator ISOCRATES. Gorgias' influence has been noted in the works of the historian THUCYDIDES (1) and the playwright AGATHON.

Because of his love of the ingenious and shameless argument, Gorgias was associated with the intellectual movement of the SOPHISTS. One of his surviving speeches, the *Encomium of Helen*, is a defense of the mythical HELEN OF TROY and her adulterous, disastrous elopement with the Trojan prince PARIS. The speech shows Gorgias' soothing, jingling style, which apparently seeks to charm the listener by incantation.

A dignified, amiable Gorgias appears as a character in PLATO's fictional dialogue *Gorgias* (written circa 380 B.C.).

Gorgons   See MEDUSA.

Gortyn   City of central CRETE, settled by the DORIAN GREEKS after about 1000 B.C. By 500 B.C. it was a flourishing city, the largest on the island. In the first century B.C. it became the capital of the Roman province of Crete and Cyrenaica.

Archaeological excavations of the ancient town in the 1880s uncovered the now-famous marble inscription called the Law Code of Gortyn, carved circa 500 B.C. The code, written in the Doric dialect, addresses such civil-law issues as land tenure, mortgages, and the status of SLAVES. Although the surviving inscription contains no sections on criminal law, the Gortyn code remains the most important, single, extant source for Greek law prior to 300 B.C.

(See also GREEK LANGUAGE; LAWS AND LAW COURTS; WRITING.)

grain supply   See BLACK SEA; EGYPT; FARMING; HELLESPONT; SICILY; THRACE.

Greece, geography of   The key to Greece's history lies in its geography. The mountainous terrain compartmentalized the country into separate population centers, with distinctive dialects, cultures, and politics. This is the background of the Greek "city-state," or POLIS. The rough terrain also placed great economic importance on the few rich FARMING plains. The earliest Greek culture, the MYCENAEAN CIVILIZATION (circa 1600–1200 B.C.) was centered mainly on the two major farmlands of southern and central Greece: the Argive plain, containing the cities of MYCENAE, ARGOS, and TIRYNS; and the twin Boeotian plains, containing THEBES and ORCHOMENUS.

Threatened by famine, Greek cities fought desperate wars over farmland. The first fully remembered conflict in Greek history was the LELANTINE WAR, fought for control of the plain lying between the central Greek cities of CHALCIS and ERETRIA (circa 720–680 B.C.). In the south, the rising state of SPARTA waged a series of wars to annex the plain of MESSENIA (mid-700s–600 B.C.).

Cities unable to retain or capture farmland might take to shipping—for Greece comprises a large, ragged peninsula that juts into the northeastern Mediterranean, and many Greek cities lie near the sea. After acquiring seafaring skills from the prehellenic inhabitants of the land (second millennium B.C.), and after copying the technologies and trade routes of the brilliant Phoenicians (circa 900–800 B.C.), the Greeks emerged as a great seagoing people. The vast enlargement of the Greek world through overseas TRADE and COLONIZATION (circa 800–500 B.C.) was in part due to

individual states using seafaring to solve their problems of lack of food supply and employment. The tiny Greek state of AEGINA, perched on a rocky island, became rich as a middleman in overseas trade (500s–early 400s B.C.). The city of ATHENS became a superpower through its strong navy (400s–300s B.C.).

Cities could prosper by controlling critical points on a trade route—a sea channel, an anchorage, or a mountain road. The best example is CORINTH, superbly located on the narrow isthmus stretching northeastward from the PELOPONNESE. By land, Corinth commanded the route north to central Greece. By sea, Corinth possessed two harbors, facing east and west across the midpoint of Greece, which enabled the city to develop trade routes in both directions, to the Near East and to ITALY and SICILY.

Of strategic importance were the mountains of north-central Greece. Any invading army marching southward from the northeast was forced to face a defensible bottleneck at the mountain pass of THERMOPYLAE, in southern THESSALY. Themopylae played a repeated role in Greek military history, most famously as the site of a failed Greek defense in the PERSIAN WARS (480 B.C.), but also in the machinations of the Macedonian king PHILIP II (in 346–338 B.C.).

The Macedonian kings who kept Greece subjugated in the 200s B.C. recognized four "fetters" or "keys" of Greece—four critical geographic points, possession of which were vital for control. The fetters were Corinth, Chalcis (guarding the narrows of the Euboean Straits), the Athenian port city of PIRAEUS, and the coastal stronghold of Demetrias, beside Thessaly's Gulf of Pagasae (near modern Volos).

(See also ACARNANIA; AEGEAN SEA; AETOLIA; ATTICA; BOEOTIA; CHALCIDICĒ; EPIRUS; EUROPE AND ASIA; EUBOEA; IONIAN SEA; LOCRIS; MACEDON; PHOCIS; SHIPS AND SEAFARING; THRACE.)

Greece, history of   See ALEXANDER THE GREAT; ATHENS; COLONIZATION; CORINTH; DARK AGE; DIADOCHI; HELLENISTIC AGE; MACEDON; MINOAN CIVILIZATION; MYCENAEAN CIVILIZATION; PELOPONNESIAN WAR; PERSIAN WARS; ROME; SPARTA; THEBES; TRADE; TYRANTS.

Greek language   The ancient Greek language belonged to the Indo-European family of languages that now includes English, German, Russian, Persian, and such Latin-derived tongues as French and Spanish. These languages share certain resemblances in grammar and vocabulary (e.g., English "father," ancient Greek *patēr*, ancient Latin *pater*). According to modern linguistic theory, the prototype of all these languages was spoken by a people living in the Caucasus region (now in southern Russia) in the third millennium B.C. At some later date, this people—or, at least, their language—began "radiating" outward, presumably by migration and conquest.

The decipherment in A.D. 1952 of LINEAR B inscriptions from the MYCENAEAN CIVILIZATION confirmed that the Mycenaeans of 1400–1200 B.C. spoke an early form of Greek. It seems that probably in about 2100 B.C. the developing Greek language entered the land of Greece with invaders from the Danube basin. These invaders—who can be called the first Greeks—overran the land, subduing the prior inhabitants by war and assimilation. In later centuries the Greek language contained many words of non-Greek etymology, presumably derived from the pre-Greek inhabitants' language. Often distinguished by the endings -*nthos*, -*sos*, or -*ēnē*, these words included names of local plants, certain gods' names, and most of the place-names in mainland Greece. Examples are CORINTH (Korinthos), HYACINTHUS (Huakinthos), acanthus (akanthos), NARCISSUS (Narkissos), and ATHENA (Athēnē)—also, words such as *thalassa*, "sea," and *nēsos*, "island."

The final forging of the Greek language came with the end of the Mycenaeans, soon after 1200 B.C. As Mycenaean society toppled, Greece became subject to a new immigration of Greeks—the DORIAN GREEKS, speaking their own dialect. The story of what happened in the centuries following has been pieced together by ARCHAEOLOGY, philology, MYTH, and a few precious references by later Greek writers.

Entering central Greece from the northwest (circa 1100 B.C.), the Dorians failed to capture the territory of ATHENS. But farther south they overran almost all of the PELOPONNESE (although mountainous ARCADIA held out), and they continued conquering by sea across a band of the southern AEGEAN SEA, to CRETE and southwestern ASIA MINOR. In historical times, this swath of territory was distinctive for the Dorian culture and Doric dialect shared by its various inhabitants. The best-known Dorian city was SPARTA. Modern linguists tend to group the Doric dialect into a larger category known as West Greek, which includes the language of the ancient Greeks around the western Corinthian Gulf.

Meanwhile (circa 1000 B.C.), other migrations from mainland Greece were taking place. The AEOLIAN GREEKS of BOEOTIA and THESSALY, buffeted by the invading Dorians, sent refugees fleeing eastward across the Aegean to the island of LESBOS and beyond, to northwestern Asia Minor. These disparate areas became known by their shared Aeolic dialect.

But the most fateful migration was of those Ionian-ethnic Greeks whom the Dorians had chased from the Peloponnese. These Ionians emigrated across the Aegean to the central west coast of Asia Minor, where they eventually flourished as the rich and advanced society of IONIA. Athens and the CYCLADES islands remained Ionian territory, all distinguished by an Ionic dialect. The Athenian language developed as a subcategory of Ionic, called Attic (from the Athenian home territory of ATTICA).

Such were the three main divisions of Greek language and culture, although other categories existed. The highlanders of Arcadia spoke a very old form of Greek that retained aspects of ancient Mycenaean speech and that resembled the speech of another, but very distant, Greek enclave, the island of CYPRUS. Modern scholars call this shared dialect Arcado-Cyprian.

(See also ALPHABET; EPIC POETRY; IONIAN GREEKS; LABYRINTH; LYRIC POETRY; MYCENAE; RELIGION; SHIPS AND SEAFARING; TIRYNS; WRITING.)

gymnasium   Sports complex. The Greek word *gumnasion* comes from the verb *gumnazo*, "exercise" (from the adjective *gumnos*, "naked" or "loinclothed," which was how Greek athletes usually trained and competed). Typically located outside a city's walls, the gymnasium featured a running track, a WRESTLING court, and fields for throwing the javelin and discus; also, rooms for changing, oiling down, and so on. A more elaborate type might also include parklands, colonnaded walks, and a horse-riding track.

Gymnasiums first appeared in the 500s B.C. They were usually state-run institutions open to men and boys of the citizen classes. Within this group, the majority of regular customers would be aristocrats and other leisured rich, who did not need to work for a living. The gymnasium played a central role in the Greek city-state, fostering male competition and camaraderie. Schoolboys would receive training in SPORT, and men would pass their time in exercise and conversation. The gymnasium was also central to the male-homosexual climate of the 500s–300s B.C., being the place where men could observe, and try to meet, boys and youths.

With its gathering of educated people, the gymnasium was a natural scene for philosophical discussion—at least in ATHENS during its age of intellect (400s and 300s B.C.). The Athenian philosopher SOCRATES often could be found in one or another of the city's gymnasiums, conversing with his following of aristocratic men. Two Athenian gymnasiums, the ACADEMY and the LYCEUM, gave their names to nearby philosophical schools, set up by PLATO and ARISTOTLE, respectively (300s B.C.). The intellectual and social-sexual energy of the Athenian gymnasium is conveyed in certain of Plato's fictional dialogues, such as the *Charmides*.

(See also ARISTOCRACY; EDUCATION; HOMOSEXUALITY; POLIS.)

H

Hades In MYTH, the god of the Underworld, and brother of ZEUS and POSEIDON. The name Hades ("the unseen") properly refers to the god and not his kingdom. Unlike the Judeo-Christian Satan, Hades is not evil; as king of the dead, he rules a domain in nature that complements the happier realm of his brother Zeus. Hades is, however, rather colorless. He has no MYTH, except for his abduction of PERSEPHONE. By Zeus' decree, she lives with Hades as his queen for four months of every year.

Like other gods of death or ill omen, Hades often was worshipped under euphemistic titles. One of the most common of these was Pluton, "the Rich One," probably referring to the rich metal ore in the ground. The early Romans, in adapting Greek RELIGION to their own use, adapted this title as the name for their god of the dead, Pluto.

(See also AFTERLIFE.)

Halicarnassus Greek seaport of southwestern ASIA MINOR, in the non-Greek territory known as Caria. Founded circa 900 B.C. by DORIAN GREEKS from Troezen (in the eastern PELOPONNESE), Halicarnassus lay at the northern shore of what is now called the Bay of Gökova, in Turkey. As a gateway to and from the southeastern AEGEAN SEA, the city had a lively commercial culture, combining Carian and Dorian-Greek elements. Halicarnassus was part of the local Dorian federation, centered at nearby CNIDUS.

Like other east Greek cities, Halicarnassus flourished in the 600s and 500s B.C., was captured by the Persians circa 545 B.C., and endured a series of Persian-run Greek TYRANTS. Remarkably, one such tyrant was a woman, named Artemisia, who accompanied the Persian king XERXES on his invasion of Greece and led a naval squadron against the mainland Greeks at the Battle of SALAMIS (1) (480 B.C.).

Halicarnassus' most famous native—the first writer of history, HERODOTUS—fled the city circa 460 B.C. after taking part in a failed coup against another tyrant, Lygdamis. By 450 B.C., however, Halicarnassus was a DEMOCRACY and a member of the Athenian-led DELIAN LEAGUE. In 412 B.C., during the PELOPONNESIAN WAR, the city became a major Athenian naval base, after other sites had been lost to widespread revolt by the Delian allies. Later Halicarnassus reverted to Persian control, by the terms of the KING's PEACE (386 B.C.).

Under Persian rule, Halicarnassus became one of the most beautiful and dynamic cities of the Greek world. The ruler Mausolus—Carian by birth but reigning under Persian suzerainty—glorified the city as his capital, build-ing a circuit wall, public monuments, dockyards, and a citadel (circa 370 B.C.). The crown of the building program was his own monumental tomb, the famous Mausoleum, erected after his death by his adoring widow (who was also his sister, Artemisia). Now vanished, but described by ancient writers, the Mausoleum was a squared, pyramidlike structure of white marble, adorned with a colonnade at its base and ascending in layers to a sculpted chariot group at the top. Numerous exterior sculptures (some now housed in the British Museum) showed a battle between Greeks and AMAZONS and other mythological scenes. Because of its tremendous size and splendor, the Mausoleum was counted as one of the SEVEN WONDERS OF THE WORLD.

Defended by a Persian garrison, Halicarnassus was besieged and captured by the Macedonian king ALEXANDER THE GREAT in 334 B.C., and passed into his empire. His successors warred over it, with the Ptolemies of EGYPT eventually winning possession (200s B.C.). The city came under Roman rule in the 100s B.C.

Harmodius and Aristogiton Known as the tyrannicides (tyrant slayers), these two young male Athenian aristocrats became semilegendary figures after they died while assassinating Hipparchus, younger brother of the Athenian dictator HIPPIAS (1), in 514 B.C. Far from ending Hippias' reign at ATHENS, the assassination brought on repression from the ruler; but Harmodius and Aristogiton's bravery and sacrifice—and the fact that the two men were linked by romantic love—struck a sentimental chord in their fellow Athenians.

Harmodius and Aristogiton were kinsmen in an ancient noble clan. In accordance with the usual pattern of upper-class Greek homosexual pairings, Aristogiton was the protective older lover, perhaps in his late 20s; Harmodius was probably in his late teens. When Harmodius ignored the unwelcome advances of Hipparchus, the thwarted Hipparchus insulted Harmodius' sister in public.

In revenge, Aristogiton plotted with Harmodius and a few sympathizers to murder the dictator Hippias and overthrow the regime. But the plot went awry. At the summer festival of the PANATHENAEA, Harmodius and Aristogiton, attacking with daggers, had the chance to kill only Hipparchus. The young Harmodius was slain by bodyguards. Aristogiton, escaping into the crowd, was later captured and tortured to death.

After Hippias was expelled from Athens by other forces in 510 B.C., the dead tyrannicides came to be seen as forerunners of the newly installed DEMOCRACY and were commemorated with yearly religious sacrifices and a famous public statue. At the same time, they were viewed by the upper class as models of aristocratic conduct. One symposiastic song praised them in mythical terms, including the stanza "Dearest Harmodius, they say surely you are not dead but live forever in the Islands of the Blessed, with swift-footed Achilles and Diomedes."

The Athenian historian THUCYDIDES (1), in his history of the PELOPONNESIAN WAR, devotes an unusual digression to the subject of the tyrannicides, trying to correct the exaggerated, unhistorical stories about them.

(See also ACHILLES; AFTERLIFE; ARISTOCRACY; DIOMEDES; HOMOSEXUALITY; SYMPOSIUM; TYRANTS.)

harpies In MYTH, the harpies (Greek: harpuiai) were winged female demons who would fly down to steal food, people, and so on; their name means "snatchers-away." They are mentioned in HOMER's epic poem the *Odyssey* (written down circa 750 B.C.) as carrying off the daughters of the hero Pandareus. HESIOD's *Theogony* (circa 700 B.C.) describes them as three in number, named Celaeno ("dark"), Ocypete ("swift-wing"), and Aello ("storm"). The harpies are most familiar from APOLLONIUS' epic poem, the *Argonautica* (circa 245 B.C.). There they are said to torment the Thracian king Phineus on a regular basis by flying down, snatching away his food, and departing, leaving their feces on everything.

Possibly the harpies originated as spirits or personifications of the wind. In their general role as winged, malevolent females, they resemble the FURIES and the SIRENS.

Hecataeus Early geographer and "logographer" (travel writer) of the Greek city of MILETUS, in ASIA MINOR. He lived circa 550–490 B.C. On the basis of travels in EGYPT, Scythia, the Persian interior, and elsewhere, Hecataeus wrote a prose treatise called the *Periodos Gēs*, or "Trip Around the World" (which today survives only in fragments quoted by later writers). The book accompanied a map Hecataeus had made—perhaps painted onto textile or incised on a copper plate—showing the world as he had encountered it; although this was not the world's first map, the map and book together were revolutionary for Greek learning. We know that the book gave accounts of local histories, customs, and so on. There were two volumes: *Europe* and *Asia*. Hecataeus is an important forerunner of the world's first historian, HERODOTUS (born circa 485 B.C.).

We know almost nothing about Hecataeus' life. His father was said to have been a landowner at Miletus, and Hecataeus must have been wealthy to undertake his travels. He surely had contacts among Miletus' merchant community, for his journeys included sites along the Milesian shipping route northeastward to the BLACK SEA. Herodotus mentions Hecataeus amid events of the IONIAN REVOLT against Persian rule (499–493 B.C.): Hecataeus was present at the first Milesian war council and advised against the revolt. Herodotus tells us no more about Hecataeus; perhaps he was killed in the Persian capture of Miletus in 493 B.C.

In addition to his travel book, Hecataeus wrote a treatise called *Geneologies*, about the legendary pedigrees of noble Greek families and mythical heroes. The few surviving fragments of this work suggest a strong rationalizing purpose: For example, DANAUS could not have had 50 daughters as the MYTH claims, but perhaps 20. The book's opening words announce the writer's logical approach: "I write what I believe to be the truth. For the stories of the Greeks are many and laughable."

(See also EUROPE AND ASIA; IONIA.)

Hecatē Mysterious and sinister goddess, associated with night, witchcraft, ghosts, the moon, and the supernatural danger of the crossroads. Hecatē was very much a chthonian deity, whom the Greeks attempted to propitiate by leaving out monthly "Hecatē's suppers." She had shrines at crossroads, apparently intended to keep her away. To our knowledge, she had no MYTH.

Her name means "One Hundred" in Greek and may have originated as a euphemism for some unspoken name. Hecatē was probably a survival of a pre-Greek goddess of black magic.

(See also RELIGION.)

Hector In myth, a Trojan prince, eldest son of King PRIAM and Queen HECUBA, and commander of TROY's forces in the TROJAN WAR. His lasting portrait occurs in HOMER's epic poem the *Iliad*, which reaches its climax in Hector's death at the hands of the Greek hero ACHILLES.

Although Achilles is the *Iliad*'s protagonist, Hector is by far the poem's most sympathetic character—brave, generous, a devoted husband, father, and son. His poetic epithets include *hippodamos*, "tamer of horses." He is a civilized figure, remarkably unselfish as compared with his Greek counterparts. Also unlike them, he is shown as having a domestic role: In the *Iliad* (book 6) he visits his wife, ANDROMACHE, and their child, Astyanax, for what will be the last time. This poignant scene reveals his certainty that doom will overtake him and his family.

Hector's deeds in the story include his single combat with the Greek hero AJAX (1) (who gets somewhat the upper hand before it ends in a draw) and his attack with his men against the Greeks' camp and the beached Greek ships (which he almost succeeds in burning up). In the course of this action, Hector slays the Greek warrior PATROCLUS, who has entered the fray dressed in the armor of his friend Achilles. This fateful act sets the scene for Hector's single combat with the enraged Achilles the next day.

In the *Iliad*'s climactic scene (book 22), Hector waits for Achilles on the plain in front of Troy, despite the appeals of his parents from the city walls. But he turns and flees as Achilles approaches. After a long chase on foot, the heroes duel. Achilles kills Hector, ties the corpse to his chariot, and drags it back to camp. Later relenting, he allows Priam to ransom the body, and the *Iliad* ends with Hector's funeral.

Unlike many of Homer's Trojans, Hector has a Greek name ("warder-off"). We know that this name was used by at least one Greek prince in ASIA MINOR in the 700s B.C.; Hector's name and portrayal might possibly be based on some Greek leader living in the era when the *Iliad* was written down (circa 750 B.C.).

Hecuba In MYTH, the wife and queen of the Trojan king PRIAM. She was the mother of the princes HECTOR and PARIS and 18 of Priam's other sons. Later writers also assign to her a daughter, Polyxena.

In HOMER's epic poem the *Iliad* (written down circa 750 B.C.), Hecuba (Greek: Hekabē) is a secondary character, regal and gracious. Later writers, describing her relentless sorrows and decline after TROY's fall, treat her as a symbol of ruined happiness. She is portrayed as a Greek captive in two of EURIPIDES' surviving tragedies, *Trojan Women* (415 B.C.) and *Hecuba* (424 B.C.). *Hecuba* presents her vengeance on the Greek champion Polymnestor, who had killed Polyxena as a sacrifice to ACHILLES' ghost. Lured into Hecuba's tent, Polymnestor is blinded, and his two young sons murdered, by her waiting women. Later authors, such as the Roman Ovid, describe Hecuba's death; forgiven for her violence against Polymnestor, she was handed over as a prize to ODYSSEUS. But her hatred of him was such that she was supernaturally transformed into a snarling, barking dog. In this shape, she leapt into the sea. Her grave became a landmark, Cynos Sema (dog's tomb), along the HELLESPONT.

Helen of Troy In MYTH, a Spartan princess of great physical beauty, daughter of the god ZEUS and the Spartan queen LEDA.

Helen was married to the Spartan king MENELAUS. But at the prompting of the love-goddess APHRODITE, Helen eloped with the handsome Trojan prince PARIS. This infatuation was the cause of the disastrous TROJAN WAR, which was to end, after a 10-year siege, in Troy's destruction and the death of Paris and many others, Trojan and Greek. HOMER's epic poem the *Iliad* shows Helen installed at Troy, protected and admired by the people to whom she has brought so much trouble. She is portrayed as a glamorous and gracious lady, well aware of her reprehensible position. In one famous scene (book 5), the Trojan elders, admiring her beauty, agree once again that she is worth fighting for. In Homer's *Odyssey*, Helen is shown living contentedly again with Menelaus back in Sparta, after the war.

Later writers elaborated on Helen's story. In one version, Menelaus intends to kill her after the Greeks take Troy, but, on seeing her, forgives her. The most famous reworking of Helen's story was the *Palinodia* of the Sicilian Greek poet STESICHORUS (circa 590 B.C.), which claimed that Helen had never left Sparta at all; rather, the gods had sent a phantom-Helen with Paris to Troy, so that Troy's doom might be fulfilled.

At SPARTA Helen was worshipped as a goddess associated with TREES and nature. This divine Helen was probably a survival of a pre-Greek goddess—one of many who infiltrated Greek RELIGION in various guises.

(See also EURIPIDES; GORGIAS.)

Helios In MYTH, a god personifying the sun. Helios was not important in Greek RELIGION, except for his nationalistic cult on the island of RHODES. Elsewhere he was more of a poetic fancy—a charioteer who drives his horses across the sky each day and returns by night, sailing in a giant cup around the stream of ocean, to start again next morn-

ing. His best-known myth told how he had a human son, Phaëthon, who won Helios' permission to drive the solar chariot in Helios' place for one day. But Phaëthon, unable to control the reins, careened too close to the earth, until the god ZEUS was forced to kill him with a thunderbolt, to save the world from fire.

As the god who sees everything from above, Helios was sometimes invoked as the guarantor of oaths. Some myths give him the minor function of bringing news to the gods of certain events that he has witnessed.

In the philosophical climate of the 400s B.C., there arose a theory identifying Helios with the major god APOLLO. Later writers of the ancient world sometimes referred to Apollo as a sun god, and this idea persists in popular belief today; but in Greek myth the sun generally had its own god.

As the patron deity of Rhodes, Helios was honored with a grand annual festival. This cult was clearly shaped by non-Greek, Oriental beliefs. The famous Colossus of Rhodes, built circa 275 B.C. outside the harbor of Rhodes city, was a giant statue of the sun god.

(See also OCEANUS.)

Hellas See Hellēn

Hellēn In MYTH, the father of the Greek people. Hellēn—who should not be confused with the princess HELEN OF TROY—had three sons: Dorus, Aeolus, and Xuthus. From these came the main ancient Greek ethnic branches—the DORIAN GREEKS, the AEOLIAN GREEKS, the IONIAN GREEKS, and the Greeks of ACHAEA (the latter two categories are named for Xuthus' sons, Ion and Achaeus). According to the myth, this is why the Greek people are known collectively as the Hellēnes, "the sons of Hellēn."

The legend's purpose was simply to explain the origins of these various ethnic groups. In true fact the name *Hellēnes* seems to be derived from the word *Hellas*, which was the Greeks' name for mainland Greece.

Hellenistic Age Term used by scholars to describe the era of the enlarged, cosmopolitan Greek world of 300–150 B.C. Unlike the word *Hellenic*, which refers straightforwardly to the Greeks, the word *Hellenistic* comes from a verb *Hellazein*, "to speak Greek or identify with the Greeks," and refers to the Greek-influenced societies that arose in the wake of ALEXANDER THE GREAT's conquests (334–323 B.C.). This Hellenistic world extended from southern France to northern Afghanistan. Its characteristic nature was a mingling of Greek and Eastern cultures, particularly in the Near East and in ASIA MINOR. The political units of this world were the rich and large kingdoms of Alexander's successors—MACEDON, Ptolemaic EGYPT, the SELEUCID EMPIRE, and, eventually, PERGAMUM—and the Syracusan monarchy. Gone was the society built around the traditional Greek POLIS, or city-state, where citizens debated public policy in political assemblies and served as soldiers in time of war. In the Hellenistic world, kings did the governing, war was the business of professionals, and citizens turned to more individualistic pursuits: mystery religions and new, more personal philosophies.

Corinthian-style columns and other Greek architectural remnants at Palmyra, in the Syrian desert. Palmyra, an oasis town on the caravan route between Damascus and Mesopotamia, flourished in the Hellenistic world that arose in the wake of Alexander's conquests. From circa 300 B.C. to 64 B.C. Palmyra owed allegiance to the Seleucid kings; thereafter, it was a half-Greek, half-Syrian frontier city of the Roman Empire. These columns were part of a grandiose sanctuary of the local god Bel, built in A.D. 32.

Mainland Greece lay under Macedonian rule for much of this era. ATHENS, still a revered "university town," was no longer the cultural center of the Greek world. That honor had passed to Egyptian ALEXANDRIA (1) and secondarily, to ANTIOCH, Pergamum, and SYRACUSE. At these places, rich kings sponsored courts full of scientists and poets.

The Hellenistic world was absorbed by ROME in several stages. Syracuse fell to Roman siege in 211 B.C. The Romans dismantled the Macedonian kingdom in 167 B.C., after the Third Macedonian War. Mainland Greece was occupied by the Romans in 146 B.C., after the Achaean War. In 133 B.C. the Greek cities of Asia Minor were bequeathed to the Romans by the last king of Pergamum (effective 129 B.C.), and the remnants of the Seleucid kingdom and Ptolemaic Egypt were annexed by Rome in the first century B.C.

(See also AFTERLIFE; APOLLONIUS; ARCHIMEDES; ASTRONOMY; BACTRIA; CALLIMACHUS; DIONYSUS; EPICUREANISM; MATHEMATICS; MEDICINE; PHALANX; RELIGION; RHODES; SCIENCE; SCULPTURE; SKEPTICISM; STOICISM; THEOCRITUS; WARFARE, LAND; WARFARE, NAVAL; WARFARE, SIEGE.)

Hellespont   Thirty-three-mile-long sea strait that separates the Gallipoli peninsula from the northwestern coast of ASIA MINOR. Through this channel, which ranges between one and five miles wide, a strong current flows southwestward from the SEA OF MARMARA to the AEGEAN SEA. Also known as the Dardanelles, the Hellespont is the more western of two bottlenecks—the other being the BOSPORUS—along the shipping route to the BLACK SEA. Like the Bosporus, the Hellespont traditionally has been considered a boundary between the continents of EUROPE AND ASIA.

The ancient Greek name Hellēspontos, "Hellē's Sea," was said to commemorate the young daughter of Athamas, a mythical king of EUBOEA. According to legend, Hellē fell to her death in the strait when she slipped off the back of the flying ram that was carrying her and her brother to safety from their stepmother. (This was the first episode in the story of JASON (1) and the Golden Fleece.)

As a bottleneck where shipping could be attacked or tolled systematically, the Hellespont was a critical link in the eastern TRADE route. The opportunities of this locale, combined with the channel's excellent commercial fishing, raised several local cities to wealth and prominence. The earliest and most important of these was TROY, situated on the Asian side, just outside the strait's western mouth. Archaeological evidence suggests that a wealthy Troy, inhabited by non-Greeks, was destroyed abruptly around 1220 B.C.—probably by Mycenaean Greeks driven to remove Troy's disruption of metal imports to Greece.

As the Black Sea region began supplying grain for the cities of mainland Greece, control of the Hellespont became crucial to the ambitious, food-importing city of ATHENS. By 600 B.C. Athenian colonists were warring with settlers from LESBOS over possession of Sigeum, near the old site of Troy. By the mid-400s B.C. Athens had a naval base at the Hellespontine fortress of SESTOS, on the European shore. There all westbound, non-Athenian, merchant grain ships were subject to a 10 percent tax, which would be reimbursed if the ship brought its cargo to Athens' port.

During the later PELOPONNESIAN WAR, Athenian and Spartan navies fought no less than three battles in the Hellespont (411 and 405 B.C.), as the Spartans sought to destroy Athens' lifeline of imported grain. The third such battle, the Spartan victory at AEGOSPOTAMI, won the war for SPARTA.

Besides Sestos, prominent Greek cities of the Hellespont included Abydos and Lampsacus, both on the Asian shore. The fact that Abydos faced Sestos across the channel's narrowest part (one mile wide) helped to inspire the charming legend of Hero and Leander. This tale described how a man of Abydos (Leander) swam the Hellespont every night to visit his mistress in Sestos.

(See also ALCAEUS; CHERSONESE; PERSIAN WARS.)

helots   Publicly owned serfs, or non-citizens, who farmed the land in virtual captivity, providing food for the citizen population of a given state. Unlike SLAVES, these serfs kept their own language, customs, and communities on the land (which of course they did not own). They were typically the descendants of a once-free people, either Greek or non-Greek, who had been conquered in a prior era.

The public use of serfs may have been a tradition specifically of the DORIAN GREEKS, because most of the attested locales were Dorian (including CRETE and SYRACUSE). The serfs were known by various names: At ARGOS, for instance, they were called *gumnētes,* or "naked ones." But the most notorious use of such people was at SPARTA, where they were called *helotai,* or helots. This name supposedly came from the town of Helos ("marsh"), annexed and subjugated by Sparta in the late 700s B.C. By 600 B.C. further Spartan conquests had created helots in two large geographic areas: LACONIA (the territory around Sparta) and MESSENIA (the large plain west of Laconia's mountains). These people were Dorian Greeks, just like their conquerors, the Spartans.

Although helot farm labor freed Sparta's citizens to concentrate on war, this subjugated population had a warping affect on the Spartan mentality. Between Messenia and Laconia, the helots outnumbered their Spartan masters, and the fear of a helot revolt—such as that of 464 B.C.— kept the Spartan army close to home and drove Sparta to repressive measures. The Krypteia ("secret society") was an official Spartan group dedicated to eliminating subversive helots.

Helots might accompany Spartan armies to war, serving as soldiers' servants or as skirmishers. But such loyalty did not win Spartan trust. In 424 B.C., during the PELOPONNESIAN WAR, the Spartans decreed that they would honor those helots who claimed to have done the best battlefield service for Sparta. Two thousand helots came forward in the belief that they would be made Spartan citizens. But the treacherous Spartans, having thus identified the most spirited of the helots, eventually murdered them.

(See also PYLOS.)

Hephaestus Lame smith god, patron of craftsmen, worshipped mainly at ATHENS and other manufacturing centers. Hephaestus was also the god of fire and volcanoes, and this more primitive aspect was probably his original one. He had a cult on the volcanic Greek island of Lemnos, and he was associated with volcanic Mt. Etna, in SICILY. To the imaginative Greeks, these volcanoes must have suggested a smithy furnace.

Hephaestus' MYTHS are few but picturesque. According to the poet HOMER, Hepaestus was the son of ZEUS and HERA. When he sided with his mother in a quarrel, Zeus threw him off of Mt. OLYMPUS. He fell for nine days and nights and hit the island of Lemnos. His subsequent return to heaven was a favorite subject in art.

Hephaestus' wife was the love-goddess APHRODITE. Tired of her adulteries, he fashioned a marvelous chain-link net, with which he captured his wife and the war god ARES together in bed. Then he hauled them, netted, before the assembled gods. Hephaestus also had a minor role in many other tales, providing such marvelous handiwork as the invincible armor of ACHILLES. The Romans adopted Hephaestus' myth and cult, attaching these to their fire god Vulcan (*Volcanus*).

(See also ATHENA; SEVEN AGAINST THEBES.)

Hera One of the most important Olympian deities, both wife and sister of the great god ZEUS, and patron of WOMEN and MARRIAGE. Hera had major cult centers at the city of ARGOS (a very ancient cult) and on the island of SAMOS, but

This head of the goddess Hera, carved in limestone 20 inches high, is all that remains of the colossal statue that stood in her temple at Olympia, circa 600 B.C. As Zeus' jealous wife, Hera often plays malevolent roles in Greek myth; but in daily religious life she was honored as a goddess of marriage and childbearing, and the guardian deity of Argos, Samos, and other Greek states.

she was worshipped throughout the Greek world. Her name means "lady" in Greek.

In MYTH she cuts a strong figure—an independent wife, but jealous of Zeus' many extramarital amours. In one famous scene in HOMER's epic poem the *Iliad,* she seduces her husband as part of a scheme to distract Zeus from observing the TROJAN WAR and aiding the Trojans (book 14). Other stories show her as oppressively cruel toward her rivals—that is, toward the female humans and demigods who involuntarily attracted Zeus' lust. Among such persecuted rivals were Leto (who gave birth to Zeus' children APOLLO and ARTEMIS) and IO. But the most important example is Hera's enmity toward the hero HERACLES, son of Zeus and the mortal woman Alcmene. Hera is Heracles' constant antagonist and is reconciled with him only at the end of his labors, at Zeus' command.

Her children by Zeus are ARES, HEPHAESTUS, Eileithyia (goddess of birth), and Hebe (goddess of youth). In art, she appears as a mature, physically attractive woman. She has a definite sexual nuance and is sometimes paired with APHRODITE. There was reportedly an ancient statue of her at SPARTA called Hera Aphrodite. The Romans identified Hera with their goddess Juno.

Despite her Greek name and her place in Greek RELIGION, Hera was probably not Greek in origin. It has been plausibly suggested that she is a vestige of the mother goddess who was the chief deity of the non-Greek occupants of Greece, before the first Greeks arrived circa 2100 B.C. The immigrating Greeks conquered the land and assimilated this goddess' cult into their own religion, to a position subordinate to the Greek father god, Zeus. Whether this was done as a political expedient or because it was religiously attractive to the early Greeks we will never know, nor can we know this goddess' original name. (See also CRONUS.)

Heracles   The most popular of all Greek mythical heroes, famous for his strength, courage, and generosity of spirit. By virtue of his 12 Labors performed for the good of mankind, Heracles (Greek: Herakles) was worshipped as both god and man throughout antiquity. Philosophical schools such as STOICISM saw him as an ideal of human fortitude. The early Christians called him a forerunner of Christ. Better known today by his Roman name, Hercules,

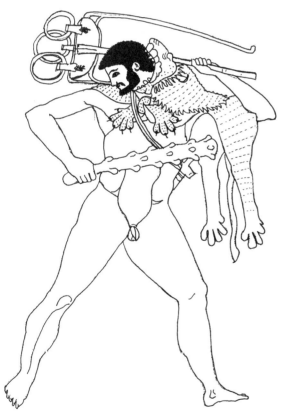

An angry Heracles carries off the holy tripod from the god Apollo's sanctuary at Delphi, after the god has refused to grant advice. From an Athenian red-figure vase, circa 480 B.C. The hero wears the invincibility-bestowing skin of the Nemean Lion, his opponent in his First Labor.

the hero continues to have a life of his own, although in debased form, in such media as comic books, films, and advertising. Heracles is one of our single most vital legacies from ancient Greece.

His name means "glory of HERA." In the legends that have come down to us, the goddess Hera is his implacable enemy. But, given the hero's name, it seems plausible that at some early stage of Greek mythology (circa 1200 B.C.), Hera was his divine patron and he her servant, performing his helpful labors at her command. Possibly the Greek Heracles derived from a pre-Greek god or hero—a servant or consort of the mother goddess who was worshipped on the Argive plain long before the first Greeks arrived, circa 2100 B.C.

In MYTH, Heracles was associated with both of the two centers of Mycenaean Greece—the Argive plain and the Theban plain. Born at THEBES, he was the son of Alcmēnē, a princess of MYCENAE or TIRYNS. Alcmēnē was married to Amphitryon, but Heracles' true father was the great god ZEUS, who had visited Alcmēnē disguised as her husband. (Heracles had a mortal twin brother, Iphicles, begotten by Amphitryon.)

The goddess Hera, chronically jealous of her husband's infidelities, was Heracles' enemy from the first. She sent two snakes to kill the twins in their cradle, but the baby Heracles strangled them. Hera continued to plague him throughout his life, and was reconciled with him only after his death and transformation into a god.

As a child at Thebes, Heracles showed strength but wildness. When his MUSIC teacher tried to beat him for misbehavior, Heracles brained the man with a lyre. Later his weapons were the club and the archer's bow. He defended Thebes from an attack from the city of ORCHOMENUS and married the Theban princess Megara. But when Hera blighted him with a fit of madness, he killed Megara and their children. (This episode is described in EURIPIDES' surviving tragedy *Heracles*, circa 417 B.C.) Seeking expiation at the god APOLLO's shrine at DELPHI, Heracles was instructed by the priestess to return to his parents' home region in the PELOPONNESE and place himself in servitude for 12 years to his kinsman Eurystheus, king of Tiryns.

The tasks set by Eurystheus comprise the famous 12 Labors (*athloi* or *ponoi*), which are the heart of the Heracles myth. In each case, Heracles had either to destroy a noxious monster or to retrieve a prize. The Labors' objectives begin with the elimination of certain local monsters in the Peloponnese, but gradually the goals become more distant and fabular until, by the last two Labors—capturing the monstrous dog CERBERUS from the Underworld and fetching apples from the supernatural sisters called the Hesperides—Heracles was symbolically conquering death.

The 12 Labors were: (1) kill the lion of Nemea, (2) kill the hydra (water snake) of Lerna, (3) capture alive the boar of Erymanthus, (4) capture the hind (female deer) of Ceryneia, (5) destroy the birds of Stymphalia, (6) cleanse the stables of King Augeas of ELIS, (7) capture the bull of CRETE, (8) capture the horses of the Thracian king Diomedes, (9) fetch the belt ("girdle") of the queen of the AMAZONS, (10) steal the cattle of the monster Geryon, in the far West, (11) fetch Cerberus from the realm of HADES, and (12) bring back some of the golden apples from the

A beardless, soldierly Heracles, as portrayed in a marble sculpture from the east pediment of the goddess Aphaea's temple at Aegina, circa 480 B.C. Wearing his lion skin, Heracles bends his bow (since lost from the sculpture)—this and the club were his favorite weapons. The figure was part of a scene showing the "first" Trojan War, in which Heracles led his fellow Greeks in capturing the city of Troy.

Hesperides' garden, in the far West. The hero accomplished these tasks, albeit with the goddess ATHENA's occasional help, and so he won purification for his crime.

Besides the Labors, Heracles had many mythical exploits, in part because so many Greek cities wanted to claim an association with him. In a dispute with the Delphic oracle, he tried to steal Apollo's holy tripod from the sanctuary. He sailed with the Thessalian hero JASON (1) in the quest for the Golden Fleece. He vanquished the wrestler Antaeus, a Giant who was son of POSEIDON. And, after a quarrel with the Trojan king Laomedon, Heracles raised an army and captured TROY, in the generation before the TROJAN WAR.

When Nessus the centaur tried to rape Heracles' second wife, Deianira, the hero killed him with arrows dipped in venom of the Lernean hydra. But the dying centaur gave Deianira his bloody shirt, convincing her that it could be used as a love charm on Heracles, if needed. Later, seeking to retain the love of her unfaithful husband, Deianira laid the shirt on his shoulders. Heracles died in rage and excruciating pain from the venom-soaked blood (as described in SOPHOCLES' tragedy *The Women of Trachis*, circa 429–420 B.C.). But on the funeral pyre Heracles' mortal part was burned away, and he ascended as a god to Mt. OLYMPUS. There he was welcomed by his divine father, reconciled with Hera, and married to Zeus and Hera's daughter, the goddess Hebe.

In a politically angled legend, the DORIAN GREEKS claimed descent from Heracles. Supposedly the Heraclidae (the "sons of Heracles"), reclaiming their lost birthright, had led the Dorians in their invasion of central and southern Greece, circa 1100–1000 B.C.

(See also AFTERLIFE; AGIAD CLAN; CENTAURS; CYNICS; EURYPONTID CLAN; GIANTS.)

Heraclitus   Early philosopher, of the Greek city of EPHESUS, in western ASIA MINOR. Almost nothing is known of his life, but he apparently he lived circa 500 B.C. He is said to have been of high aristocratic lineage and of an arrogant and reclusive nature. Some of the writings ascribed to him are derisive of the democratic politics at Ephesus.

Heraclitus (Greek: Herakleitos) was the last of the great Ionian thinkers who, in the 500s B.C., pioneered the study that we call PHILOSOPHY. His writings consisted of a collection of prose proverbs, fashioned in an oracular style. A number of individual proverbs have come down to us in quotations by later writers. Although often obscure in wording, these aphorisms seem to show remarkable originality in their search for universal order amid worldly flux.

Where his Ionian predecessors—THALES, ANAXIMANDER, and ANAXIMENES—had looked for cosmic unity in some elemental substance such as water or mist, Heraclitus sought in the universe's defining arrangement (Greek: *logos*). He saw everything in the world as part of single, continuous process of change—"All things flow" and "You cannot step into the same river twice" are two of his more famous sayings. This change, he said, is regulated by a balance or measure typically involving the conflict of opposing forces. Heraclitus found deep significance in the opposing tensions employed in the stringing of the musician's lyre and the archer's bow (both of which were inventions associated with the god APOLLO, lord of harmony and order). Heraclitus evidently saw the lyre and bow's "backward-stretched unity" (Greek: *palintonos harmoniē*) as a key to understanding the cosmos.

Similarly, many of Heraclitus' proverbs seek to show that opposites such as hot and cold are actually related or connected. "The road up and the road down are one and the same," he wrote, apparently referring to a footpath that leads both ways (so to speak), up and down a mountain. Other surviving proverbs suggest an innovative belief in one God, reflecting this notion of cosmic unity—for example, "The god is day, night, winter, summer, war, peace, satiety, hunger."

The cosmic order was somehow maintained by fire, according to Heraclitus. He believed that a person's soul was a kind of fire, which could be harmfully "dampened" by bad behavior such as sexual excess or drunkenness. Spiritually healthy souls remained dry; after death they would be able to reach higher places in the heavens.

A brilliant but eccentric thinker, Heraclitus did not inspire an immediate following. However, in the 200s B.C. the philosophical movement called STOICISM honored his memory and adapted some of his ideas.

(See also IONIA.)

Hercules   See HERACLES.

Hermes   In MYTH, Hermes was the messenger of the gods, and son of the great god ZEUS and the demigoddess Maia (daughter of ATLAS). In human society, Hermes was the patron of land travel, heralds, commerce, weights and

The affable god Hermes holds a ram, in a bronze figurine of the late 500s B.C. As the patron deity of travel, Hermes wears his familiar winged shoes; his peaked cap and short, Dorian-style tunic are both of a type favored by travelers, workmen, and shepherds. Like his half brother Apollo and son Pan, Hermes was worshiped as a guardian of shepherds and flocks.

measures, RHETORIC, guile, thieves, WRESTLING, and other SPORT. Often portrayed as a young man in traveler's or herald's garb, Hermes was an attractive and picturesque deity, somewhat resembling his half brother, the god APOLLO. As the mythical inventor of the lyre, Hermes was a minor patron of poetry, which was normally Apollo's province.

In origin he may have been a protector of wayfarers, commemorated at roadside stone piles or carved images. Hermes' name most probably comes from the Greek word *herma* (plural: *hermai*), meaning "pile of marker stones." In an era when travel was uncomfortable and dangerous, Hermes safeguarded travelers.

The legend of his birth is told in the charming *Homeric Hymn to Hermes*, written circa 675 B.C. Hermes was conceived when his mother was ravished by Zeus. At dawn he was born on Mt. Cyllene in ARCADIA; by noon he was playing the lyre (which he had invented, using a tortoise shell as a sounding board); and that evening he ventured out and stole a herd of cattle from Apollo. The story shows the mixture of creativity and dishonesty that characterized the mythical Hermes—and the Greeks themselves. Hermes was believed to guide the spirts of the dead to the Underworld. Other legends name him as a lover of APHRODITE, who bore him a child, an androgynous creature named Hermaphroditus.

By the 400s B.C., cities such as ATHENS contained stylized *hermai*, erected at streetcorners and in the AGORA. These were bronze or marble pillars sacred to the god, with sculpting showing only the god's face and genitals. Shortly before the Athenian sea expedition against SYRACUSE during the PELOPONNESIAN WAR (415 B.C.), the hermai throughout the city were mutilated overnight—probably by gangs of defeatist right-wingers, seeking to cast bad omens over the expedition by doing outrage to the god of travel.

(See also AFTERLIFE; ALCIBIADES; ANDOCIDES; MUSIC.)

Herodas (or Herondas)   Writer of "mimes" (Greek: *mimiamboi*, "satirical sketches") of the 200s B.C. We are unsure when and where he lived, but an ancient papyrus discovered in the 1800s A.D. has left us with seven of his detailed urban scenes in verse. The best of these give delightful portraits of matrons, pimps, and vendors.

Herodotus   Greek historian from HALICARNASSUS in southwest ASIA MINOR. He lived circa 485–420 B.C. and wrote a detailed, surviving account of the PERSIAN WARS, which had culminated when he was a child. Herodotus' lengthy history describes how the Persian expansion westward after the mid-500s B.C. was eventually defeated by the Greeks' defense of their homeland in 480–479 B.C. Herodotus is considered the world's first historian, the first writer ever to make systematic factual inquiries into the past. He has been called the father of history.

Prior to him, there had been only "logographers"—writers of travelogue, recounting local sights and local histories. Although Herodotus himself traveled widely to acquire local lore, his major accomplishment was that he arranged his voluminous material around a central theme and that he was the first to try to explain historical cause and effect. This approach is summed up in his opening words: "Here is the account of the inquiry (Greek: *historiē*) of Herodotus of Halicarnassus, in order that the deeds of men not be erased by time, and that the great and miraculous works—both of the Greeks and the foreigners—not go unrecorded, and, not least, in order to show what caused them to fight one another."

Herodotus was inspired by a predecessor. Forty or 50 years before his time a Milesian Greek logographer named HECATAEUS had written a travel account of EGYPT, Scythia, and other locales. Herodotus mentions Hecataeus' work with disdain, while apparently borrowing from it liberally. Herodotus began by imitating Hecataeus, visiting Egypt and the Scythian BLACK SEA coast early on. He probably intended to write Hecataean-style travelogue. But at some point Herodotus warmed to a second inspiration—the mythical TROJAN WAR, as described in HOMER's *Iliad* and other Greek EPIC POETRY. If the Trojan War was seen as the original clash between East and West, then the Persian Wars could be explained in the same light, as part of an ongoing, destructive pattern.

Another idea of Herodotus', that pride goeth before a fall, was perhaps borrowed from contemporary Athenian stage tragedy. In Herodotus, the grandeur of monarchs often leads to foolhardy decisions resulting in disaster. This is conveyed clearly in his literary portrait of the Persian king XERXES, whose vanity and arrogance resulted in the Persians' failed invasion of Greece and the deaths of so many good men on both sides. Herodotus himself never observed Xerxes, and his treatment of the king probably owes much to literary imagination. Herodotus' lecherous, violent, cowardly but aesthetic-minded and occasionally gracious Xerxes is one of the most enjoyable villains in Western literature.

We know little of Herodotus' life. He was born in Halicarnassus, a Greek city of international commerce that at the time was still ruled by Persian overlords and included a second non-Greek people, called Carians. Herodotus' father had a Carian name, Lyxes; the family was probably an affluent merchant clan of Greek-Carian blood.

Perhaps around age 25, Herodotus fled into exile after his involvement in a failed coup against the city's reigning Greek tyrant. By 454 B.C. the tyrant had fallen and Halicarnassus was part of the Athenian-controlled DELIAN LEAGUE. Despite this, Herodotus never returned home, but rather spent the next decade traveling and writing. Beside Egypt and Scythia, he evidently visited mainland Greece and the Levantine seaboard. His travels were probably helped by a Persian-Greek peace treaty that ended hostilities at that time (circa 449 B.C.).

Sometime in the 440s–420s B.C. Herodotus became known in the Greek world for giving paid readings aloud of his work-in-progress. He is said to have sought quick notoriety by reading at OLYMPIA during the Games. The Athenians supposedly voted to pay him the astounding sum of 10 TALENTS out of gratitude for his favorable portrayal of their city. He certainly had ties to ATHENS (which by then had become the cultural center of Greece). Supposedly, the Athenian playwright SOPHOCLES wrote verses to

Herodotus, and the noble Athenian clan of the ALCMAEONIDS seems to have been a major source of information for him. Although Herodotus' history is generally respectful of Athens' rival, SPARTA, he does in one passage credit Athenian naval resistance as the single factor that saved Greece in the Persian Wars (book 7).

In 443 B.C. Herodotus joined an Athenian-sponsored project to colonize a city, Thurii, in southern ITALY. He died there in around 420 B.C. These last 20 years probably saw him traveling, giving readings, and revising his work. His history was being published in (or near) its present form by 425 B.C., when the Athenian comic playwright ARISTOPHANES parodied its opening passages in his play *Acharnians*.

Herodotus' native tongue was probably the Doric Greek dialect of Halicarnassus, but he wrote his history in Ionic—the dialect generally used for prose explication—and used a clear, pleasant, storytelling style. On its completion, this history was the longest Greek prose work ever written. Later editors divided it into nine "books." Not only is it far and away our major written source for the Persian Wars and prior events in Greece and PERSIA in the 700s–500s B.C., but it also makes for delightful reading. In telling his story, Herodotus shows himself interested in war, politics, and the gods, also in personality, gossip, and sex. Unusual for a classical Greek writer, Herodotus is fascinated by WOMEN and their influence in a man's world both East and West.

Remarkably, a large part of his story is told from the Persian viewpoint. In this Herodotus was imitating such Athenian stage tragedy as AESCHYLUS' play *The Persians*, which describes the Battle of SALAMIS (1) from the Persian side. Some of Herodotus' Persian scenes were surely fabricated by the author; yet it is equally clear that he conducted original research, interviewing individual Persians as well as Greeks. Despite the fact that Persia was the Greeks' enemy, Herodotus portrays many Persians as brave and noble, and he shows a deep respect for their culture. The later Greek writer PLUTARCH accused Herodotus of being *philobarbaros*, "overfond of foreigners."

Literary pioneer though he was, Herodotus shows certain endearing flaws. He often strays from his main narrative with digressions. Although dedicated to finding out historical causes, he sometimes fastens on trivial or fairytale causes. For example, he claims (in book 3) that the attack of the great Persian king DARIUS (1) on Greece was prompted by the bedroom persuasion of his wife. Further, Herodotus is not above telling the occasional tall tale—claiming, for instance, that he visited Babylon, even though his work lacks any description of that majestic Mesopotamian city. Besides being called the father of history, Herodotus has been called the father of lies.

Nevertheless, his history was a monumental achievement: the first rational inquiry into the past. In this, he paved the way for his greater successor, the Athenian historian THUCYDIDES (1).

(See also CALLIAS; EUROPE AND ASIA; GREEK LANGUAGE; HUBRIS.)

heroes   See MYTH.

Herondas See HERODAS.

Hesiod Greek epic poet, one of the earliest whose verses have survived. Hesiod lived circa 700 B.C., perhaps 50 years after HOMER. Together with Homer, he is often considered a pioneer of early Greek literature. Two major works by him are extant: the *Theogony*, or *Birth of the Gods*, which describes the world's creation and the origins of the Olympian gods and lesser deities; and *Works and Days*, a kind of farmer's almanac laced with advice on how to live a good life through honest work. For modern readers, the *Theogony* is a treasury of information for Greek MYTH, while the *Works and Days* supplies a unique picture of early Greek rural society.

The two poems give some autobiographical details. Hesiod lived in the central Greek region of BOEOTIA, in a town called Ascra ("bad in winter, worse in summer, not good anytime," as he describes it in *Works and Days*.). His father, having abandoned a seafaring life, had come from CYMĒ, in ASIA MINOR. According to the *Theogony*, Hesiod was tending sheep on Mt. Helicon as a boy when the MUSES appeared and gave him the gift of song. Later he won a prize at nearby CHALCIS, in a song contest at certain funeral games. Hesiod quarreled with his brother Perses, who had apparently stolen part of Hesiod's inheritance, and the *Works and Days* was written partly as an instructional rebuke to Perses. The poet's personality, as conveyed in the poems, is surly, practical, and conservative—an old-fashioned Greek yeoman farmer, who happened to have the poetic gift.

In addition to providing facts and genealogies about the gods, the *Theogony* supplies evidence of Near Eastern influence on the formative Greek culture of the 700s and 600s B.C., for a number of Hesiod's myths closely resemble certain older legends from Mesopotamia. This influence came from Greek TRADE with the Near East, via Phoenician middlemen.

(See also CRONUS; EPIC POETRY; PHOENICIA.)

Hesperides See HERACLES.

Hestia Goddess of the hearth and of domestic fire. The least important of the 12 Olympian deities, Hestia ("hearth") was the sister of ZEUS. Little MYTH was attached to her name; having refused to marry, she remained a virgin and lived as a kind of respected spinster aunt on Mt. OLYMPUS.

Her cult, however, was important. In an era before manufactured matches, the hearth was the crucial place where cooking fire was maintained perpetually, winter and summer. The hearth helped to preserve order and civilization, and many governmental buildings had public hearths that symbolized the public good. Accordingly, Hestia was the patron goddess of town halls and similar; one of her epithets was *boulaia*, "she of the council house."

(See also COUNCIL.)

hetairai See PROSTITUTES.

Hieron (1) Dictator of the Greek cities GELA and SYRACUSE in SICILY, and the most powerful individual in the Greek world circa 470 B.C. Hieron ("holy one") came to power under his brother GELON, who ruled in Syracuse and appointed him as his governor in Gela. On Gelon's death, Hieron succeeded as lord (*turannos*, "tyrant") of Syracuse, the foremost city of the Greek West (478 B.C.). Although less popular than his brother, Hieron ruled in grand style. He formed an alliance with the other great Sicilian-Greek tyrant, Theron of ACRAGAS. When the Greeks of CUMAE, in western ITALY, appealed for help against the encroaching ETRUSCANS, Hieron achieved his greatest triumph—his sea victory at Cumae, in the Bay of Naples, which broke the Etruscans' sea power forever and removed them as a threat to the Italian Greeks (474 B.C.).

At home he consolidated his power through social engineering and cultural display. He continued the Sicilian rulers' ruthless practice of transplantation, removing 10,000 citizens of CATANA in order to reestablish the site as a new, Dorian-Greek city, Aetna. The "founding" of Aetna was commemorated in the tragedy *Women of Aetna* by the Athenian playwright AESCHYLUS, who visited Hieron's court at the ruler's invitation around 470 B.C.

Other luminaries of Hieron's court were the great Theban choral poet PINDAR and the poets SIMONIDES and BACCHYLIDES of Ceos. Pindar and Bacchylides were commissioned to write poems celebrating Hieron's prestigious victories in horse- and chariot-racing at the OLYMPIC and PYTHIAN GAMES (476–468 B.C.). Hieron is the addressee of Pindar's famous First Olympian ode and First Pythian ode.

Hieron died, probably of cancer, in 467 B.C. He was succeeded by his son Deinomenes, but by 466 B.C. Syracuse had overthrown the tyrant and installed a DEMOCRACY in its place.

(See also CHARIOTS; TYRANTS.)

Hieron (2) II See SYRACUSE.

Himera Greek city located midway along the northern coast of SICILY, founded circa 649 B.C. by colonists from ZANCLĒ in northeastern Sicily. Himera's most famous citizen was the poet STESICHORUS (circa 590 B.C.). Himera was a Greek frontier town, close to the Carthaginian-controlled western part of Sicily. In the late summer of 480 B.C., the vicinity of Himera was the site of a great battle in which a Greek army totally defeated an invading force from CARTHAGE.

In the years prior to the battle, the town was ruled by a Greek tyrant, Terillus, who eventually was ejected by Theron, tyrant of ACRAGAS. Terillus appealed to his ally, the Carthaginian leader Hamilcar, and in 480 B.C. Hamilcar sailed from North Africa with a large army to reinstate Terillus and conquer Greek Sicily. Landing in Sicily, the Carthaginians marched on Himera, but outside the town Hamilcar and his army were destroyed by an allied Greek force under GELON, the tyrant of SYRACUSE. According to legend, the battle was fought on the very same day as another great victory of liberation, the sea battle of SALAMIS (1), against the invading Persians in mainland Greece.

To commemorate the victory at Himera, Gelon minted what is perhaps the most beautiful coin of the 400s B.C.—the SILVER Syracusan decadrachm known as the Demareteion.

The Carthaginians' defeat stymied their ambitions in Sicily for three generations. But in 409 B.C. they captured Himera and razed it in vengeance.

(See also COINAGE; TYRANTS.)

Hipparchus   See HIPPIAS (1).

Hippias (1)   Athenian dictator who reigned 527–510 B.C., the son and successor of PISISTRATUS. Succeeding his father as ruler at about age 40, Hippias aggrandized ATHENS with public works, ambitious diplomacy, and economic projects. Under him, the city continued its emergence as the future cultural capital of Greece. Hippias' younger brother Hipparchus brought to Athens two of the greatest poets of the era: ANACREON and SIMONIDES. But the days of Greek TYRANTS like Hippias were numbered by the late 500s B.C., and Hippias eventually was ousted by Athenian opposition and Spartan intervention.

In 510 B.C. the Spartan king CLEOMENES led an army to Athens, against Hippias. The Spartans had been urged to do so by the oracle at DELPHI, but Cleomenes himself surely wanted to stop Hippias' diplomatic overtures to the Persian king DARIUS (1). Cleomenes probably feared that Hippias was planning to submit to Darius in order to retain personal power.

Aided by Athenians who were hostile to the tyranny, the Spartans surrounded Hippias and his followers on the ACROPOLIS. Hippias abdicated in exchange for a safe-conduct out. His departure brought to an end more than 35 years of Pisistratid rule at Athens, setting the stage for the political reforms of CLEISTHENES (1) and the full-fledged Athenian DEMOCRACY.

Traveling eastward to PERSIA, Hippias became an adviser at Darius' court. In 490 B.C., when the Persians launched their seaborne expedition against Athens, Hippias (by now nearly 80) accompanied the Persian army. Apparently he was intended as the puppet ruler.

He guided the Persian fleet to the sheltered bay at MARATHON, about 26 miles from Athens. It was there, more than 50 years before, that Hippias had helped his father, Pisistratus, bring a different invading army ashore. But this time fortune favored the defenders, and the Persian force was totally defeated by the Athenians at the famous Battle of Marathon. Hippias withdrew with the Persian fleet and, according to one story, died on the return voyage.

(See also ALCMAEONIDS; HARMODIUS AND ARISTOGITON; PERSIAN WARS; POTTERY; THEATER.)

Hippias (2)   See SOPHISIS.

Hippocrates (1)   Greek physician and medical writer, usually considered to be the founder of scientific medical practice. Hippocrates lived circa 460–390 B.C. and was a native of the Dorian-Greek island of Cos, near southwestern ASIA MINOR.

At Cos, Hippocrates established a school of MEDICINE that became renowned in the ancient world. While not the first Greek doctor, Hippocrates was apparently the first to systematize the existing knowledge and procedures and to ground the medical practice in solid observation rather than theory. The later writer Celsus (circa A.D. 30) remarked that Hippocrates separated medicine from PHILOSOPHY.

Of the 60 medical treatises that have survived from the Hippocratic school, possibly none was written by Hippocrates himself. But certain shared traits of these writings, such as their emphasis on observation and diagnosis, convey the spirit of the school. The treatises include *Airs, Waters, and Places*, which describes the effects of different climates on health and psychology, and *The Sacred Disease*, a discussion of epilepsy (concluding that there is nothing sacred about it).

The "Hippocratic Oath" taken by graduates of that school is still administered to new doctors today, in modified form, 2,400 years later. In the ancient oath, the swearer promised to honor the brotherhood of the school, never to treat a patient with any purpose other than healing, never to give poison or induce abortion, and never as a doctor to enter a house with any ulterior motive, such as seduction of SLAVES.

Hippocrates (2)   See GELA; GELON.

Hippodamus   Town planner of the mid-400s B.C., born at MILETUS but active in the service of Periclean ATHENS. Circa 450 B.C. he designed the grid pattern for the Athenian port city of PIRAEUS (his design is still in use there today), and he probably did likewise for the Athenian-sponsored colony of Thurii, in southern ITALY. He was one of the colonists who emigrated to Thurii circa 443 B.C. ARISTOTLE'S *Politics* (circa 340 B.C.) mentions Hippodamus' affected physical appearance—long hair and adorned robes in the Ionian manner.

(See also IONIAN GREEKS.)

Hippolyta   See AMAZONS; HERACLES; THESEUS.

Hippolytus   In MYTH, the son of the Athenian king THESEUS and the Amazon queen Hippolyta. After his mother's death, Hippolytus grew to manhood at ATHENS as a hunter and male virgin, devoted to the goddess ARTEMIS. The love goddess APHRODITE, irked by Hippolytus' celibacy, caused Theseus' young wife, the Cretan princess Phaedra, to fall in love with Hippolytus, her stepson. Rebuffed by him, she hanged herself, but left behind a letter accusing him of rape. Theseus, not believing his son's declarations of innocence, banished him and then cursed him. The curse was effective (as being one of three wishes that Theseus had been granted by his guardian, the god POSEIDON), and a monstrous bull emerged from the sea while Hippolytus was driving his chariot on the road. Hippolytus' terrified horses threw him from the chariot, and so his death was fulfilled in the manner suggested by his name: "loosed horse," or stampede. Theseus learned the truth from Artemis after it was too late.

Our main source for the legend is the admirable, surviving tragedy *Hippolytus* (431 B.C.) by the Athenian playwright EURIPIDES. In the play, Hippolytus appears as priggish and lacking in compassion, while Phaedra is convincingly imagined as an unhappy woman in the unwelcome grip of an obsession.

A later legend claimed that Hippolytus was restored to life by the physician-hero ASCLEPIUS. But then the god ZEUS, fearing a disruption of natural order, killed both men with a thunderbolt.

(See also AMAZONS.)

Hipponax   Greek lyric poet of EPHESUS who lived in the mid-500s B.C. Banished by one of the city's Persian-controlled TYRANTS around 540 B.C., he supposedly lived as a beggar in nearby Clazomenae. His wrote satirical poems in various meters, with the flavor of the gutter. He was said to have been the inventor of parody; one of his surviving fragments is a mock-Homeric description of a glutton.

Hipponax is credited with inventing the *skazon,* or "lame" iambic meter—which, to the Greek ear, had a halting, comic affect, appropriate to satire.

(See also IONIA; LYRIC POETRY.)

Homer   According to tradition, Homer was the earliest and greatest Greek poet. Two epic poems were ascribed to him: the *Iliad* and *Odyssey,* which present certain events of the mythical TROJAN WAR and its aftermath. These two works, totaling about 27,800 lines in dactylic hexameter verse, supplied the "bible" of ancient Greece. Greeks of subsequent centuries looked to them for insight into the

"Blind is the man, and he lives in rocky Chios." This portrait of Homer comes from a marble bust of the Roman era, probably copied from a Greek original from circa 150 B.C. Although plausible-looking, the likeness is imaginary: Homer himself—if he was an individual person—lived during or before the mid-700s B.C., and later generations had no authentic portrait of him.

gods' nature, for answers to moral questions, and for inspiration for new literature. The Athenian playwright AESCHYLUS (circa 460 B.C.) described his own tragedies as "morsels from the banquet of Homer." It is a token of the Greeks' reverence for the *Iliad* and *Odyssey* that both these long poems survived antiquity. Each poem's division into 24 "books," still used in modern editions, was made long after Homer's time, by ancient editors at ALEXANDRIA (1) in the early 100s B.C.

Despite a few legends, nothing is known about the life of Homer (Greek: Homeros, possibly meaning "hostage"). It is not even known that "he" was a man, except that the Greek world's social structure makes it likely. Similarly, it is not impossible that the *Iliad* and *Odyssey* were each composed by a different person. The two poems differ in tone and narrative style: The *Odyssey,* which relies far more than the *Iliad* on fable and folktale, may have been produced much later than the *Iliad.* Furthermore, given the collaborative nature of preliterate Greek EPIC POETRY, either poem could have been created by a group of poets rather than by one alone.

If there was a single Homer, he may have lived sometime between 850 and 750 B.C. The *Iliad* and *Odyssey* were probably first written down around 750 B.C., after the invention of the Greek ALPHABET, but evidently both poems were fully composed before that date. Apparently they were created by the oral techniques of preliterate Greek epic poetry—that is, by a centuries-old method of using memorized verses, stock phrases, and spontaneous elaboration, without WRITING. It is not known if Homer wrote the poems down (or dictated them to scribes) in the mid-700s B.C., or whether Homer was long dead when others wrote down his verses that had been preserved by oral retelling.

The *Iliad* and *Odyssey* reveal no autobiographical information. A single supposed autobiographical item is found in the *Hymn to Delian Apollo,* one of 33 choral songs that the ancient Greeks ascribed to Homer. In the hymn, the unnamed poet describes himself with these words: "If anyone should ask you whose song is sweetest, say: 'Blind is the man, and he lives in rocky Chios.'" Many ancient Greeks believed this to be a true description of the mysterious Homer, although modern scholars are wary of accepting it.

Homer could have been a bard who performed at the court of some Greek baron or king—much like the character Demodocus in book 8 of the *Odyssey,* who earns his livelihood singing traditional tales to entertain noblemen and ladies. Homer may have lived on the east Greek island of CHIOS, as the hymn claims, or elsewhere in the Greek region called IONIA, on the west coast of ASIA MINOR. That Homer was Ionian is suggested by the mainly Ionic dialect of the poems and by the fact that Ionia was at that time the most culturally advanced part of the Greek world. In later centuries Chios was home to a guild of bards who called themselves the Homeridae, the sons of Homer. But other Ionian locales, such as Smyrna, also claimed to have been the poet's home.

More important than the poet's identity are the values and traditions that his poetry is based on. Homer and other bards of his day sang about an idealized ancestral society that was 500 years in the past. Homer's audience imagined this bygone era as an Age of Heroes, when men of superior strength, courage, and wealth lived in communion with the gods. Homer's aristocratic protagonists—ACHILLES in the *Iliad* and ODYSSEUS in the *Odyssey*—live by a code of honor that shapes all their actions. For them, disgrace was the worst thing of all—far worse than death. If a man's honor was slighted, then the man was obliged to seek extreme or violent redress.

Greek MYTH contains hundreds of stories from the Age of Heroes. Homer's genius lay in selecting certain tales and imposing order on the material, to fashion (in each poem) a cohesive, suspenseful tale, with vivid character portraits. Contrary to some popular belief, the *Iliad* does not describe the entire Trojan War and fall of TROY; rather, it presents a tightly wrapped narrative, focusing on certain episodes from war's 10th and last year, involving the Greek champion Achilles. The poem tells of the "anger of Achilles"—that is, his quarrel with the Greek commander AGAMEMNON, after Agamemnon has needlessly slighted Achilles' honor. Achilles' withdrawal from the battlefield brings reversals for the Greeks, culminating in the death of Achilles' friend PATROCLUS at the hands of the Trojan prince HECTOR. At the story's climax (book 22), Achilles slays Hector in single combat, even though he knows that this act is ordained by FATE to seal his own doom. The *Iliad* ends not with Achilles' death or Troy's fall—those are still in the future—but with Hector's funeral, after Achilles has magnanimously allowed the Trojans to ransom back the corpse.

The *Odyssey*, although it stands on its own merits, presents a loose sequel to the *Iliad*. There the war is over, Troy having fallen to the Greeks. The wily and resourceful Greek hero Odysseus, king of ITHACA, is making his way home to his kingdom amid supernatural adventures, both violent and sexual. Like the *Iliad*, the *Odyssey* displays narrative skill in maintaining suspense. Daringly not introducing the hero until book 4, the poem opens with scenes at the disrupted kingdom of Ithaca, where more than 100 arrogant suitors (assuming Odysseus to be dead) have taken over the palace and are individually wooing his intelligent and gracious wife, PENELOPE, while threatening his adolescent son, TELEMACHUS. The reader or listener thus observes the consequences of Odysseus' absence and shares in the longing for his return. We then meet Odysseus, who is nearing the end of his journey. Aided by the goddess ATHENA, he returns to Ithaca in disguise (book 14) and scouts out the dangerous situation at the palace, then reveals his identity, slays the suitors, and reclaims his wife and kingdom (books 22–23). The suspense that precedes this violent climax is remarkably modern in tone.

(See also GREEK LANGUAGE; MYCENAEAN CIVILIZATION; WARFARE, LAND.)

homosexuality   Ancient Greek literature and art clearly show that certain types of homosexual relationships were considered natural and even admirable in many Greek cities during the epoch between about 600 B.C. and the spread of Christianity. Especially, male homosexuality was encouraged in some (not all) forms. Love between males was seen as harmonious with other Greek social values,

The hero Achilles, at right, bandages a wound for his friend Patroclus, in a red-figure scene from an Athenian cup, circa 500 B.C. The painting conveys Patroclus' distress and Achilles' sympathetic concentration; the sexuality of the two men is suggested by the gratuitous peek at Patroclus' genitals. Although the *Iliad* never portrays Achilles and Patroclus as lovers, the Greeks after Homer came to view the pair as models for aristocratic, military, male homosexuality.

such as athletic skill, military courage, and the idealization of male youth and beauty (reflected also in surviving Greek SCULPTURE). Such relationships provided males with a romance not usually found in MARRIAGE, since Greek society viewed WOMEN as morally and intellectually inferior.

Relatedly, female homosexuality was an approved practice in some locales, at least in the 600s–500s B.C. Extant verses by the poets SAPPHO and ALCMAN document sexual feelings and acts between aristocratic young women on the Aegean island of LESBOS and at SPARTA, both circa 600 B.C. Also, a single sentence in the work of the later writer PLUTARCH suggests that at Sparta it was usual for mature women to have affairs with unmarried girls. But little other information survives regarding love between women. The silence is due partly to scarcity of extant writings by Greek women and partly to the fact that female homosexuality was not encouraged as widely as its male counterpart. Relations between females may even have been forbidden in certain cities that had male-homosexual traditions, such as ATHENS in the 400s B.C.

The ancient literary sources for information on Greek homosexuality include LYRIC POETRY composed between about 600 and 100 B.C., Athenian stage comedy of the 400s B.C., the works of the philosopher PLATO and the historian XENOPHON (both of them Athenians writing in the early 300s B.C.), and Athenian courtroom speeches of the 300s B.C. The visual evidence consists mostly of vase paintings from the 500s and 400s B.C., some showing courtship or sex between males. As is usual for any aspect of ancient

Greek society, much of the extant source-material is from Athens. But other Greek states—including Sparta, ELIS, CHALCIS, and especially THEBES—had important male-homosexual cultures, linked to the training and esprit of citizen armies.

Homosexuality as a social norm evidently arose in Greece at a specific time, the late 600s B.C. Modern scholars have found no homosexual content in the poetry of HOMER (circa 750 B.C.), HESIOD (circa 700 B.C.), or ARCHILOCHUS (circa 660 B.C.). Expressions of homosexual desire first appear in the extant verses of Sappho (circa 600 B.C.) and SOLON (circa 590 B.C.).

This new social custom probably derived in part from the military reorganizations that swept Greek cities after the arrival of HOPLITE tactics in the 600s B.C. Other, related social changes at this time included the glorification of masculinity and (at Sparta) the elimination of family life by the mass military training of boys. The Greeks tended to associate homosexuality with manliness and soldiering. Significantly, the IONIAN GREEKS of ASIA MINOR were reputed to be the softest, the least military, and the least interested in homosexual pursuits, of all Greek peoples.

The ancient Greeks did not classify a person as strictly homosexual or heterosexual, as modern society tends to do. The Greeks assumed that an attractive, young individual of either gender could inspire sexual desire in either gender. Adult male citizens—the one class of people who had sexual freedom—often led private lives that were bisexual. (Yet not always: The Greeks did recognize that some men preferred one or the other gender exclusively.)

Male citizens were expected to marry female citizens and beget children, but evidently most men were not in love with their wives, as the society did not encourage this. Instead, a husband was legally and morally free to seek partners outside of marriage. (Wives enjoyed no such privilege.) Possible partners for a married or unmarried man included male or female PROSTITUTES and SLAVES, who were of the lower social ranks and who received payment or sustinence in exchange for giving sexual favors. However, if a male citizen wished for romance with someone who was his social equal—that is, if he wished to conduct courtship and seduction, with the possibility of mutual love and admiration—then his choices were limited. In most cities, the wives and daughters of citizens were often kept away from public places, and their chastity was protected by severe laws. There was only one kind of publicly approved romance available for people of the citizen classes—namely, the romance that might arise between a mature man and younger male.

This pairing—older male citizen/younger male citizen— was the classic pattern of ancient Greek homosexual love, as idealized in legend and art. This was the love pursued especially by wealthier and aristocratic citizens. Perhaps the best-known couple in this tradition were the Athenian tyrannicides of 514 B.C., HARMODIUS AND ARISTOGITON.

The younger male was typically a well-bred boy between about 12 and 20 years old—that is, between early puberty and full maturity. Youths around ages 16 and 17 were considered especially desirable as being in the prime of beauty. The young man or boy would be the passive partner, the recipient of the older man's courtship and gifts. The most handsome and accomplished youths became glamorous social figures, over whom men would conduct fierce rivalries. The teenage aristocrat ALCIBIADES was one such figure, and Plato's dialogue *Charmides* includes a vivid scene where the teenage Charmides enters a GYMNASIUM followed by a boisterous crowd of quarreling admirers. But only citizen males were allowed to woo such love objects; any male slave who pursued a citizen boy in this way was liable to dire punishment.

Among the qualities the classical Greeks admired in their boys were masculinity and bodily strength. Such attributes are clearly indicated in several hundred surviving Greek vase paintings showing images of boys or young men, often labeled with the inscribed word *kalos*, "beautiful." (These are the famous kalos vases, the homosexual "pin-ups" of ancient Greece.) Boys with more feminine bodies or mannerisms were apparently not much sought after in the 500s and 400s B.C., although they seem to have come into vogue by the late 300s.

Painted scenes of Greek homosexual couples nearly always show the older male as bearded, indicating adulthood. He might be in his 20s, 30s, or possibly 40s— anywhere from about five to 25 years older than his partner. The younger male always appears as beardless. Written evidence reveals that—in fifth-century B.C. Athens, but not always elsewhere—young men were considered no longer desirable once they began sprouting facial hair. Probably at around age 20 a young Athenian would feel social pressure to relinquish his junior sex role. He might maintain a close friendship with his former lover(s), but he would now be ready to take on the adult role, as the active pursuer of a younger male. This change by him was part of his larger transition to adulthood and to his full identity of a citizen.

Men could meet boys and youths at public places and upper-class venues such as gymnasiums, riding tracks, religious sacrifices and processions, and city streets where boys traveled to and from school. The sons of wealthy homes went out accompanied by a *paidagogos*, a slave whose duties included keeping would-be suitors away. Part of the pursuer's challenge might lie in intimidating or evading the paidagogos, in order to make the boy's acquaintance.

Once a suitor had won the approval of the boy's father, the courtship progressed through stages that included the suitor giving gifts; one gift often appearing on vase paintings is a live rooster. Together the two males would partake of upper-class recreations such as SPORT, hunting, and the drinking party known as the SYMPOSIUM, where politics or intellectual topics might be discussed.

In a society that did not foster close ties between father and son, the suitor served as a role model. He played a vital part in the boy's EDUCATION, helping to improve the boy's athletic skills, military aptitude, and general readiness for manhood. At Sparta, for example, legend claimed that after a boy once cried out in pain during a fistfight, the boy's lover was punished for failing to teach manliness.

Beyond mere instruction, a lover might provide a boy with financial help and career contacts that supplemented, perhaps vastly, what the boy's family could provide. At Thebes the lover customarily supplied the younger man's first suit of armor (no small expense). At Athens many a politician, lawyer, and poet seems to have gotten his career-start as a handsome boy, meeting older men who would become his benefactors and allies.

The relationship between man and boy was thought to be mutually inspiring: The man strove to be admirable in his public conduct; the boy strove to be worthy of the man. In Elis and Thebes, where love relationships often continued after the younger male reached adulthood, it was customary to station lovers side-by-side in battle, on the theory that each would fight more fiercely if observed by his partner. At Thebes this theory led to the creation, in around 378 B.C., of an elite, 300-soldier unit called the Sacred Band, comprised entirely of paired lovers.

Exactly what sexual activity was involved in such relationships is not clear to modern scholars; sexual customs evidently varied from region to region. In general the Greeks valued sexual restraint, much as they valued the ability to endure hunger or fatigue. Apparently one school of thought believed that lovers should practice abstinence. Plato, in his dialogue *The Symposium,* glorifies male homosexual love as a search for beauty and truth, yet he argues that love in its most exalted form involves no sexual contact—the famous "Platonic love." Similarly Xenophon, while describing homosexual pairings at Sparta, makes the surprising statement that Spartan law severely punished any man who had sexual relations with a boy. On the other hand, extant vase paintings (mostly from Athens) show more than one form of genital activity between males.

The question is: Was the younger male typically subjected to sexual penetration by the older? The answer seems to be that at Thebes and certain other Greek cities this was socially permitted, while at Athens and at many other cities it was officially discouraged but it sometimes occurred anyway. At Athens the "better sort" of older partner did not try to seduce his beloved, as revealed by an anecdote in Xenophon's memoirs where the Athenian philosopher SOCRATES rebukes the young man CRITIAS over his unseemly lust for the boy Euthydemus. Socrates says that Critias wants "to rub himself against Eurthydemus the way itchy pigs want to rub against stones." For sexual outlet, Greek men had recourse to their wives, concubines, and male and female prostitutes and slaves. Citizen boys— at Athens and Sparta, at least—were supposed to be kept pure (although that rule might be disobeyed).

This complicated outlook was part of the Greeks' attitude toward sex in general. Sex was seen as a form of power: One partner was considered dominant and one subordinate in any relationship. Typically the dominant partner was the male whose penis entered a bodily orifice of the other person. The recipient's submission was proof of inferior status. Although there was an awareness that women could enjoy sex—as suggested in the legend of the seer TIRESIAS—the Greeks were uncomfortable with the idea that any subordinate partner could feel pleasure. Sex was for the dominant person's benefit.

In all sexual relations, an adult male citizen was expected to dominate. Males who willingly received sexual penetration were supposed to be either slaves or prostitutes— noncitizens, unlucky in their servitude or poverty. Any male citizen who wanted to be penetrated sexually was considered bizarre and morally debased. A citizen who gave his body for money was deemed a prostitute and was liable to lose most of his citizenship rights. This was the background of the speech *Against Timarchus* (346 B.C.), in which the Athenian orator AESCHINES convinced an Athenian court that his enemy Timarchus had prostituted himself in his younger days.

The contradiction in Greek homosexual love was that it placed young male citizens in danger of being sexually subordinated and thus dishonored. Any boy might receive expensive gifts from an admirer; many a boy probably succumbed to a lover's seduction. What distinguished this behavior from a prostitute's? The answer lay partly in monogamy. A boy who gave sexual favors might avoid disrepute by not being promiscuous and by choosing a worthy, discreet lover. A second way to avoid dishonor may have been by limiting sexual contact to an activity known today as intercrural intercourse (shown on vase paintings). This involved the two males standing or lying face to face, with the older man moving his penis between the younger's clamped thighs. Because the younger male was not actually being penetrated, this submission was probably thought of as being less degrading.

Modern scholars believe that the homosexual themes in Greek MYTH all represent a relatively late layer, added after 600 B.C. In other words, legends about friendships between males had existed without homosexual nuance for centuries prior; these included the tales of GANYMEDE and the god ZEUS, of PELOPS and the god POSEIDON, and of the heroes ACHILLES and PATROCLUS. Eventually these myths received a sexual coloring, reflecting real-life social norms of the 500s B.C. and later. Legend claimed that Greek homosexual practices had been initiated by the Theban king Laius (father of OEDIPUS), when he carried off the boy Chrysippus.

(See also ANACREON; CALLIMACHUS; CHAERONEA; HYACINTHUS; IBYCUS; PINDAR; POTTERY; THEOGNIS.)

hoplite   Heavy infantryman of the Greek world, from about 700–300 B.C. The famous land campaigns of the 400s B.C.—in the PERSIAN WARS and the PELOPONNESIAN WAR— were fought by hoplite armies. In the late 300s B.C., hoplite, tactics were superceded by the tactics of the Macedonian PHALANX.

The early hoplite was named for his innovative shield, the *hoplon,* which was round, wide (three feet in diameter), heavy (about 16 pounds), and deeply concave on the inside; it was made of wood reinforced with BRONZE, often with a bronze facing. The soldier held the shield by passing his left forearm through a loop on the inside center and then gripping a handle at the far inside edge. This arrangement helped with the necessary task of keeping the shield rigidly away from the man's chest. The shield was notoriously difficult to hold up for a long period of time; a hoplite fleeing from battle always threw away his cumbersome shield, and even victorious soldiers could lose their shields in the melee. In militaristic societies such as SPARTA, keeping your shield meant keeping your honor, as indicated by the Spartan mother's proverbial command to her son: "Return with your shield or upon it."

The standard hoplite helmet was the "Corinthian" type, developed in the early 600s B.C. and modified in the 400s B.C. to the shape shown here; the higher crown of the new design better protected the top of the head. For display and further protection, a horsehair crest might be attached to the helmet's top. Beaten skillfully from a single sheet of bronze, the Corinthian helmet had no ear-holes—which must have made the wearer practically deaf. Away from combat, the helmet could be pushed up to rest above the face.

The rest of the hoplite's armor, or panoply, included a helmet—typically beaten from a single sheet of bronze and topped with a crest of bronze or horsehair—and a bronze breastplate and greaves (metal shin guards); under the breastplate the man would wear a cloth tunic. The offensive weapons were a six- to eight-foot-long spear for thrusting (not throwing) and a sword of forged IRON, carried in a scabbard at the waist. By various modern estimates, the whole panoply weighed 50–70 pounds, and it seems that, on the march and up until the last moments before battle, much of a hoplite's equipment was carried for him by a servant or slave.

A hoplite did not normally fight alone; he was trained and equipped to stand, charge, and fight side by side with his comrades, in an orderly, multiranked formation. The hoplite relied foremost on his spear, thrusting overhand at the enemy while trying to shield himself from their spear-points. The sword was used if the spear was broken or lost.

The armor's weight, plus the need to keep in formation, meant that hoplites could not charge at full speed for any distance. Two hundred yards would seem to be the farthest that hoplites actually could run and still be in a condition to fight.

Yet this heavy armor did not make the hoplite invulnerable. It was not practical for armor to cover a man's neck, groin, or thighs, and these were left exposed. References in ancient poetry and art make it clear that deadly wounds to the neck and groin were common, as were fatal blows to the head (possibly received from an inward denting of the helmet). Sometimes the bronze breastplate could be pierced—as demonstrated by evidence that includes the recently recovered remains of a Spartan hoplite, buried at a battle-site with the fatal, iron spear-point lodged inside his chest.

Hoplites could fight effectively only on level ground; hilly terrain scattered their formation and left the individual soldiers open to attacks from lighter-armed skirmishers. Similarly, hoplites who broke ranks and became isolated—in retreat, for example—were easy prey for enemy CAVALRY.

On warships, hoplites served as "marines." There they were armed mainly with javelins (for throwing) and were employed in grapple-and-board tactics. Soldiers unlucky enough to fall overboard would be dragged to the bottom by their heavy armor.

Hoplite armies began their history as citizen armies. In most Greek cities, each man up through middle age who could afford the cost of a panoply was required to serve as a hoplite if his city went to war. (Alternatively, those rich enough to maintain horses might serve in the cavalry.) In states governed as oligarchies, a man had to be of hoplite status or better in order to be admitted as a citizen. What distinguished a DEMOCRACY such as ATHENS was that the Athenian citizenry included men whose income level was below the hoplite level.

There also existed professional hoplites, recruited for service in the pay of some other power, whether Greek or foreign. The best-known mercenary from Greek history is the Athenian XENOPHON who, with 10,000 Greek hoplites, marched deep into the Persian Empire in 401 B.C., in the service of a rebel Persian prince.

(See also OLIGARCHY; PHEIDON; ARCHILOCHUS; WARFARE, LAND; WARFARE, NAVAL.)

hubris (sometimes written as *hybris*)   Human arrogance or excessive pride, which usually leads to disaster. Implicit in much of Greek MYTH, the concept of hubris received its full expression in Greek tragedy. A prime example of hubris is AGAMEMNON's decision to tread on the purple tapestry in AESCHYLUS' tragedy *Agamemnon*—a wanton desecration of expensive finery that called down upon Agamemnon the wrath of the gods. Extreme examples of hubris include mythical villains such as IXION or SISYPHUS, who betrayed the friendship of the gods.

In Athenian legal parlance, hubris had a second meaning: assault against an Athenian citizen. The term was used in the sense of statutory rape or any kind of violence. As in the primary definition of hubris, the concept involved an unacceptable flouting of boundaries.

(See also AJAX (2); TANTALUS; THEATER; XERXES.)

Hyacinthus   In Greek MYTH, Hyacinthus (Greek: Huakinthos) was a handsome Spartan youth loved by the god APOLLO. While Apollo was teaching him how to throw the discus one day, the jealous West Wind god, Zephyrus, sent the discus flying back into the young man's skull. Hyacinthus lay dying, and from his blood there sprang the type of scarlet flower that the Greeks called the hyacinth (perhaps our iris or anemone, but not what is called the hyacinth now).

Hyacinthus was honored in a three-day early-summer festival throughout the Spartan countryside. His tomb was displayed at Apollo's shrine at Amyclae, near SPARTA. One ancient writer noted that Hyacinthus' statue at Amyclae showed a bearded, mature man, not a youth.

The name Hyacinthus is pre-Greek in origin, as indicated by its distinctive *nth* sound. Modern scholars believe that Hyacinthus' cult dates back to pre-Greek times and that he was originally a local non-Greek god, associated with a local flower but not imagined as a young man and not yet associated with the Greek god Apollo. Sometime in the second millennium B.C., Hyacinthus was adapted to the RELIGION of the conquering Greeks and was made into a human follower of Apollo. The element of romantic love between them may have been added later, after 600 B.C.

(See also GREEK LANGUAGE; HOMOSEXUALITY.)

I

Ibycus Lyric poet of circa 535 B.C., known particularly for his love poetry. Coming from the Greek city of RHEGIUM, located in the "toe" of ITALY, he supposedly refused an offered dictatorship and traveled instead to the east Greek island of SAMOS, where he flourished at the wealthy court of the tyrant POLYCRATES.

Only a few fragments of Ibycus' verses survive, either quoted by later ancient writers or discovered recently in ancient papyri from EGYPT. It is known that Ibycus' work featured two very different genres of Greek LYRIC POETRY: mythological storytelling, as developed previously by the poet STESICHORUS, another western Greek; and short, personal love poems.

The love-poem tradition comes from the eastern Greeks, a product of the sophisticated cities of IONIA and LESBOS. In keeping with the upper-class tastes of the time, the feeling expressed in these poems was homosexual. Such poems usually were written by a man of aristocratic blood to proclaim his infatuation for some teenager or young man of equal social status. Ibycus was considered one of the great poets of this genre, and he had the personal reputation of being crazy for the love of boys.

Ibycus' verses included choral poetry—poems to be sung or chanted by choruses at religious festivals or other great occasions. Recently discovered fragments suggest that Ibycus pioneered the choral form known as the victory ode (*epinikion*), years in advance of the poets SIMONIDES and PINDAR.

Ibycus is perhaps best known for the dubious story of his death. He was supposedly attacked by robbers in a deserted place and died saying that his murder would be avenged by the cranes that were flying overhead. Later, in the city, one of the murderers, seeing some cranes, declared, "Look! The avengers of Ibycus." The statement drew an inquiring crowd, and the killers were apprehended. Appropriately, Ibycus' extant verses show a love of the natural world, especially of birdlife.

(See also HOMOSEXUALITY.)

Icarus See DAEDALUS.

Iliad See ACHILLES; HOMER; TROJAN WAR.

Ilium See TROY.

Illyris Non-Greek territory of the Adriatic coast, northwest of Greece, corresponding roughly to modern Albania. Organized into warlike tribes that were hungry for Greek goods, the Illyrians played a role in the development of northern Greece. The Corinthian colonies EPIDAMNUS (founded circa 625 B.C.) and APOLLONIA (founded circa 600 B.C.) conducted TRADE with the Illyrians, acquiring TIMBER, SLAVES, raw metals, and wildflowers (for perfume-making).

In the 300s and early 200s B.C., the Illyrians were enemies of the kings of MACEDON and EPIRUS. The Illyrians raided these kingdoms and, in turn, suffered annexation of their own territories. By the late 200s B.C. the Illyrians were fighting against Roman armies, until both Illyris and Macedon were defeated and occupied by the Romans in the Third Macedonian War (171–167 B.C.). Illyrian territory supplied part of the Roman province of Illyricum.

(See also PHILIP II; PYRRHUS; ROME.)

Io In MYTH, a woman of the city of ARGOS. The great god ZEUS loved her, but to conceal her from his jealous wife, HERA, he changed Io into a young cow. After several misadventures she was restored by Zeus to human shape in EGYPT, and there bore him a son, whose descendants were the DANAIDS.

This odd myth might possibly reflect Mycenaean-Greek attempts to connect the Egyptian cow-goddess Hathor with the Argive worship of Hera in the shape of a cow.

(See also DANAUS; MYCENAEAN CIVILIZATION; RELIGION.)

Ion (1) Mythical ancestor of the IONIAN GREEKS. According to legend, Creusa, daughter of the Athenian king Erechtheus, was seduced by the god APOLLO and bore Ion in secret. Apollo took Ion away. Later Ion discovered the secret of his birth and subsequently became king of ATHENS. The legend was the subject of an extant tragedy by EURIPIDES (circa 410 B.C.).

(See also HELLĒN.)

Ion (2) Tragic playwright and social figure of the island of CHIOS, circa 490–421 B.C. A wealthy aristocrat, Ion wrote tragedies (all now lost) on mythological subjects for competition in the theater festivals at ATHENS. After winning first prize in two categories (tragedy and dithyramb) at the major annual festival known as the City Dionysia, he made a gift of Chian WINE to every Athenian citizen.

Ion is better remembered for his lively memoirs, which survive as fragments quoted by later writers. Equally at home in Athens or Chios, he hobnobbed with some of the greatest Athenians of the mid-400s B.C., including the statesman CIMON (whose affability Ion contrasts with the coldness of PERICLES) and the tragedian SOPHOCLES (whose charm and wit Ion conveys).

Ion embodied the spirit of the Athenian empire, which saw cultured and talented people flocking to Athens from all over the Greek world.

(See also LYRIC POETRY; THEATER.)

Ionia   Greek-occupied central part of the west coast of ASIA MINOR. The area was named for Greeks of the Ionian ethnic group who invaded circa 1050–950 B.C., displacing prior, non-Greek inhabitants. In later centuries the Asian IONIAN GREEKS retained links with the most important Ionian-Greek city of old Greece, ATHENS.

By the 700s B.C. an Ionian League had been formed from 12 states of the Asia Minor coast. These were: the islands of CHIOS and SAMOS, and the mainland cities of PHOCAEA, Clazomenae, Erythrae, Teos, Colophon, Lebedus, EPHESUS, Priēnē, Myus, and MILETUS. At least one other local city, Smyrna, could claim Ionian kinship but was not a league member. The league held meetings at the Panionium, a sanctuary of the god POSEIDON at Cape MYCALĒ. There were internal rivalries and even wars, especially between the two preeminent powers, Miletus and Samos.

In TRADE, naval power, and culture, Ionia was at the forefront of the early Greek world. The poet HOMER lived and composed in Ionia, possibly in Chios (circa 750 B.C.). In the 600s and 500s B.C., Miletus and Phocaea planted colonies from the BLACK SEA to southern Spain, and traded with EGYPT and other non-Greek empires. The JEWS of the Levant knew Ionia as "Javan"—mentioned in the biblical book of Ezekiel (early 500s B.C.) for its exports of SLAVES and worked BRONZE. Woolen textiles were another prized Ionian export.

The term *Ionian Enlightenment* sometimes is used to describe the intellectual explosion that occurred, chiefly at Miletus, in the 500s B.C. There Western SCIENCE and PHILOSOPHY were born together, when THALES, ANAXIMANDER, and ANAXIMENES first tried to explain the world in rational, nonreligious terms. In Ionia there arose the grandest Greek temples of the 500s B.C., at Ephesus, Samos, and Didyma (near Miletus). The decorative schemes developed for such buildings are still employed today, in the Ionic order of ARCHITECTURE.

But this confident culture existed precariously alongside the restless Asiatic empires of the interior. The non-Greek kingdom of LYDIA warred constantly against the Ionians and finally conquered them under King CROESUS (mid-500s B.C.). Croesus dealt favorably with Ionia, but in 546 B.C. the Persian king CYRUS (1) rode out of the East to defeat Croesus and seize his kingdom.

Ionia, after a brief resistance, became a tribute-paying part of the Persian Empire. Many Ionians left home; the populations of Phocaea and Teos sailed away en masse. Throughout the cities, the Persians installed unpopular Greek puppet rulers. After the doomed IONIAN REVOLT (499–493 B.C.), Persian rule was harshly reaffirmed.

In the Persian invasions of mainland Greece (490 and 480 B.C.), Ionian troops and ships' crews were made to fight as Persian levies against their fellow Greeks. In 479 B.C. a seaborne force of mainland Greeks landed in Ionia, beat a Persian army at the Battle of Mycale, and liberated Ionia.

The leadership of an exhausted Ionia now passed to Athens, which established the DELIAN LEAGUE as an Ionian kinship–based mutual alliance against PERSIA (478 B.C.). Eventually, however, the onus of tribute and the fading of the Persian threat served to disenchant the allies. Samos revolted spectacularly (but unsuccessfully) against Athens in 440 B.C., and once the tide had turned against Athens in the PELOPONNESIAN WAR (after 413 B.C.), Chios, Miletus, Ephesus, and other Ionian states went over to Athens' enemy, SPARTA.

After Athens' defeat by Sparta (404 B.C.), Ionian freedom was short-lived. Spartan overlordship was worse than Athenian, and in 386 B.C. Sparta cynically handed Ionia back to the Persians, by the terms of the KING'S PEACE. Ionia was liberated again in 334 B.C., by ALEXANDER THE GREAT's invasion of the Persian Empire. Under Alexander, the Ionian cities enjoyed DEMOCRACY and freedom from paying tribute.

Several Ionian cities, notably Ephesus and Smyrna, went on to thrive in the HELLENISTIC AGE (300–150 B.C.) and Roman eras. But Ionia as a distinctive culture was finished.

(See also ANACREON; ANAXAGORAS; CALLIAS; HECATAEUS; HERACLITUS; PERSIAN WARS; PYTHAGORAS; XENOPHANES.)

Ionian Greeks   Greek cultural and linguistic group, distinct from other ethnic groups, such as the DORIAN GREEKS and AEOLIAN GREEKS. The adjective *Ionic* usually refers to dialect of the Ionians or to the distinctive architectural style—the Ionic order—that was developed in Ionia for monumental buildings of stone.

After the collapse of MYCENAEAN CIVILIZATION and the subsequent Greek migrations (circa 1150–950 B.C.), the Ionians were left occupying various sites in and around the AEGEAN SEA—namely, ATHENS, EUBOEA, most of the CYCLADES islands, and IONIA (as it came to be called), on the west coast of ASIA MINOR. Starting in the mid-700s B.C., Ionian-Greek seafarers colonized parts of ITALY, SICILY, the BLACK SEA coasts, and the northwestern Aegean region known as CHALCIDICĒ, among other regions.

Claiming descent from a common ancestor, ION (1), the far-flung Ionian Greeks retained a sense of kinship. In Sicily and southern Italy, Ionian cities banded together for protection against hostile Dorian settlements. During the 400s B.C., imperial Athens made the propagandistic claim to be the protector of all the Ionian Greeks.

In contrast to the stolid Dorians, the Ionians had the reputation for being intellectual, artistic, unsoldierly, elaborate in dress, and luxury-loving. Intriguingly, Ionian societies—other than Athens—were thought to be the least conducive to HOMOSEXUALITY.

(See also ARCHITECTURE; DELIAN LEAGUE; GREEK LANGUAGE.)

Ionian Revolt   Failed rebellion of the Greek cities of ASIA MINOR against the Persian king DARIUS (1), marking the beginning of the PERSIAN WARS. Emanating from the prosperous Greek region called IONIA, the revolt lasted more than five years (499–493 B.C.) and might have succeeded but for internal rifts and weak leadership. The war demonstrated to the Persians that, in order to secure their western frontier, they would have to invade and subjugate mainland Greece itself.

In the mid-500s B.C. the Greeks of Asia Minor and the eastern Aegean islands had been engulfed by the Persian Empire. Persian rule was moderate (in the absence of resistance), but the Greeks had to pay tribute and contribute ships, soldiers, and craftsmen to Persian wars and other projects. Seagoing states such as MILETUS, which had previously built up networks of TRADE, found commerce dampened by the Persians (who at this stage in their history were antimercantile). Greek discontent was rife—particularly against the Greek TYRANTS whom the Persians had set up as their puppet rulers in the cities.

Information about the revolt comes from the Greek historian HERODOTUS (circa 435 B.C.). The rebellion began in an Ionian-Greek fleet that was returning home from naval duty for the Persians. The ships' crews and officers rose up and arrested those tyrants who were serving aboard as squadron commanders. The ringleader of this mutiny was Aristogoras of Miletus, himself one of the tyrants. Advised by his father-in-law, Histiaeus, Aristagoras became leader of the revolt.

The home cities followed. At SAMOS, CHIOS, LESBOS, and EPHESUS, tyrants were deposed in favor of DEMOCRACY. Two cities of mainland Greece, ATHENS and ERETRIA, sent warships as aid—an anti-Persian act that would later have dire consequences for both Greek cities.

The Athenians and Eretrians sailed home again after an allied land raid against Sardis, the Persians' main base in Asia Minor (498 B.C.). Meanwhile the revolt spread to other Greek regions under Persian rule: BYZANTIUM, the HELLESPONT, and the Greek cities of CYPRUS.

There followed the methodical Persian counteroffensive. With a navy supplied by their subject state PHOENICIA, the Persians landed in Cyprus and besieged the rebel cities. As Persian armies campaigned through western Asia Minor, the erratic Aristagoras found himself unpopular with his fellow Greeks. He relinquished command and sailed to the north Aegean coast to prepare a refuge in case of defeat, but was killed by native Thracians.

The climactic battle came in 494 B.C. Seeking to destroy the Persians at sea, the Greeks assembled a large fleet (353 warships) from the nine major states still combatant. But the Greek side was divided by jealousies and mistrust, while the Persians offered preferential treatment for quick surrender. When the Greek fleet rowed out to fight the Battle of Lade, off Samos, 49 Samian warships hoisted sail and fled. Most of the other Greek ships followed, leaving only the Chians and Milesians to fight and lose.

The Persians took fierce vengeance on the defeated Greeks. Samos was spared, but Miletus was besieged, sacked, and depopulated, its people transported to interior PERSIA or sold as SLAVES. Returning eventually to their more usual leniency, the Persians reduced the cities' tribute and replaced the old systems of tyrant puppets with democratic governments. But Ionia—the birthplace of Western SCIENCE and PHILOSOPHY—had ceased to exist as a culture or a mercantile power.

(See also MARATHON; PHRYNICHUS; WARFARE, NAVAL.)

Ionian Sea The name, both modern and traditional, for the southward extension of the Adriatic Sea, which separates western Greece from southern ITALY and eastern SICILY. Principal islands in this sea are ITHACA and Corfu (ancient CORCYRA).

Confusingly, the Ionian Sea is nowhere near the ancient Greek territory of IONIA (located some 300 miles to the east, on the ASIA MINOR coast). Nor was the Ionian Sea region inhabited by Greeks of the Ionian ethnic group. The name probably derives from the Greek term *Ionian Gulf* (Ionios Kolpos), used by ancient writers to denote the Adriatic. That term possibly dates back to the 800s–700s B.C., when the Adriatic was being explored by Ionian-ethnic Greek seafarers from EUBOEA.

(See also COLONIZATION; IONIAN GREEKS.)

Ionic dialect See GREEK LANGUAGE.

Ionic order See ARCHITECTURE.

Iphigenia In MYTH, the daughter of CLYTAEMNESTRA and AGAMEMNON, king of MYCENAE and grand marshal of the Greek army in the TROJAN WAR. At the war's outset the Greek fleet assembled at Aulis—a port in BOEOTIA, in the Euripus channel—but departure for TROY was perpetually delayed by contrary winds, sent by the hostile goddess ARTEMIS. Agamemnon, learning through a seer the divine cause of his troubles, agreed to sacrifice his daughter Iphigenia to propitiate the goddess' anger. Iphigenia was summoned to Aulis on the pretense that she was to marry the Greek champion ACHILLES; on arrival, she was either killed or (in some versions) carried away by the goddess Artemis to safety among the distant Tauroi, a tribe on the Crimean peninsula of the northern BLACK SEA. The Athenian playwright EURIPIDES follows the latter version in his tragedy *Iphigenia at Tauris* (circa 413 B.C.). In any case, this affair was the cause of Clytaemnestra's hatred toward her husband, and she then schemed to murder him after his return from Troy.

iron Cheaper and easier to acquire than BRONZE, iron began replacing bronze in mainland Greece circa 1050 B.C. as the metal of choice for swords, spear-points, ax heads, hammerheads, and other cutting or striking tools.

As produced by ancient foundries, iron and bronze were about equal in their toughness; iron's advantage lay in the fact that it was far more plentiful than bronze, both for the Greeks and for other ancient peoples. Bronze, on the other hand, is an alloy of copper and tin, and tin is very scarce in the eastern Mediterranean. Ancient Greek bronze production depended on long-range routes of TRADE, to provide tin. But iron ore—which needs only refining, not mixing—could be found in parts of mainland Greece and ASIA MINOR, among other Mediterranean locales.

Ancient iron forging involved repeated heating and hammering of the metal in order to refine it, weld it into workable quantities, and finally shape it. This process—far different from the casting of molten bronze—apparently was invented circa 1500 B.C. by non-Greek peoples in the region now known as Armenia. At first the technology was kept secret and monopolized by the Hittite overlords of Armenia and Asia Minor. But after the Hittite Empire's collapse circa 1200 B.C., ironworking quickly spread through eastern Mediterranean regions, both Greek and non-Greek. This was the era of social upheaval and migration that historians refer to as the early Iron Age. One reason why ironworking spread amid violence was that iron democratized warfare: A warrior no longer needed to be rich, or a rich man's follower, in order to have a superior weapon.

The arrival of ironworking in Greece can be connected to the final disappearance of MYCENAEAN CIVILIZATION and the invasion of the DORIAN GREEKS, circa 1100–1000 B.C. Either the Dorians used iron weapons in conquering Greece or (more likely) they arrived with bronze weapons, but, having destroyed the old Mycenaean trade routes, found themselves without bronze supplies and immediately embraced the new metal. The Dorians possibly learned iron forging via maritime contact with the eastern Mediterranean island of CYPRUS, which was a meeting place of East and West.

The foremost early Greek ironworking cities included ATHENS, CORINTH, CHALCIS, and ERETRIA. Iron's importance in this economy can be seen in the Greeks' use of iron rods as a primitive form of currency. Only gradually were these replaced by the use of coins, in the 500s B.C.

By the 600s B.C. the Greeks had developed seaborne trade routes to major iron sources outside of Greece, in the western Mediterranean. These locales included western ITALY (where the ETRUSCANS traded with iron ore mined on the island of Elba) and southern Spain.

Ancient foundries never developed the technique, mastered during the European Middle Ages, of casting iron—that is, of heating iron hot enough to pour into a mold. For this application, bronze remained the premier metal. Throughout antiquity, bronze continued to supply such items as military breastplates, helmets, decorative tripods, and SCULPTURE, where casting or intricate shaping was required.

(See also COINAGE; HEPHAESTUS; PITHECUSAE; WARFARE, LAND.)

Iron Age See IRON.

Isaeus Greek orator, active at ATHENS, who lived circa 420–350 B.C. He may have been an Athenian. He is said to have been a pupil of the orator ISOCRATES and a teacher of the great DEMOSTHENES (1). Of Isaeus' speeches, 11 survive: They are all courtroom speeches, dealing with disputed inheritance and other civil matters. Isaeus provides us with much of our information about Athenian laws of inheritance in the 300s B.C.

(See also LAWS AND LAW COURTS; RHETORIC.)

Ischia See PITHECUSAE.

Isocrates Influential Athenian orator, educator, and pamphleteer who lived 436–338 B.C. Isocrates' importance for Greek history is in his attempts to make the Greeks unite in a military crusade against the Persian empire. His most significant written work was his *Philippus*, or *Address to Philip* (346 B.C.). This work, which survives today, was an "open letter" addressed to King PHILIP II of MACEDON, calling on the king to lead such a campaign. The letter surely came as a propaganda blessing to the opportunistic Philip, who was preparing to subdue Greece. Perhaps it

was Isocrates who first inspired Philip's further ambition to conquer PERSIA (an ambition eventually fulfilled by Philip's son ALEXANDER THE GREAT).

Born into a wealthy family, Isocrates studied RHETORIC under the famous GORGIAS. Like certain other Greek orators, Isocrates wrote speeches for his clients to deliver themselves. He rarely, if ever, argued in court or spoke in the Athenian political ASSEMBLY. But his indirect influence was great. His students of rhetoric included the future historian Androtion and the future orator ISAEUS. At some point Isocrates had a school on the island of CHIOS.

It was the news of the humiliating terms of the KING'S PEACE (386 B.C.) that fired Isocrates' vision of the Greeks uniting to liberate the Greek cities of ASIA MINOR. Isocrates' first published pamphlet on the subject was the *Panegyricus* (380 B.C.), an idealistic tract that pictured ATHENS and SPARTA leading the crusade. The *Panegyricus* strongly anticipates the letter to Philip, written 24 years later. In the intervening years Isocrates somewhat shamelessly addressed similar pleas to other rulers of the Greek world, including the Spartan king AGESILAUS and the Syracusan tyrant DIONYSIUS (1).

But Isocrates' idealism could not stem Philip's ambition of conquering Greece. After the failure of a final plea following the Battle of CHAERONEA (338 B.C.), the 98-year-old Isocrates starved himself to death.

Ancient writers knew of 60 works by him; we possess 21. Six of these are court speeches; the rest are political pamphlets.

(See also EDUCATION; LAWS AND LAW COURTS.)

Isthmian Games One of the four Greek-international sports-and-religious festivals; the other three were the OLYMPIC, PYTHIAN, and NEMEAN GAMES. The Isthmian Games, or Isthmia, took place every two years at CORINTH (located on the isthmus of central Greece). The festival honored the god POSEIDON, and the ritual prize for the victors was a garland of wild celery. The games were first organized during the early 500s B.C.

isthmus See CORINTH; PELOPONNESE.

Italy Like SICILY, Italy contained a number of powerful Greek cities in ancient times. Two separate regions of the Italian peninsula saw intensive COLONIZATION by the land- and commerce-hungry Greeks, circa 750–550 B.C. One region is now called Campania, on the Bay of Naples on the Italian west coast. There the Euboean settlement of CUMAE became the first Greek landfall in Italy and one of the very earliest Greek colonies anywhere (circa 750 B.C.). The attraction was TRADE with the powerful ETRUSCANS.

The other major focus of COLONIZATION was in the south, along the south coast of the Italian "toe" and "instep." There the Spartan colony of TARAS (founded circa 700 B.C.) occupied the best harbor in Italy, on what is now called the Gulf of Taranto. Other Greek cities of south Italy included SYBARIS, CROTON, RHEGIUM, LOCRI, Metapontum, and Siris. The main attraction at these sites was farmland, which the Greeks seized from the native Brutii and Lucanii.

The Greek name Italia—applying originally only to the south coast of the Italian "toe"—was probably a Greek rendering of a local Italian place-name: Vitelia, "calf land."

The "heel" of Italy originally had a different Greek name, Iapygia. Later the name Italia, passing into the Latin language of the conquering Romans, came to be applied to the entire peninsula, north to the Alps.

To the Greeks of southern Italy, coming from mountainous and overpopulated Greece, the land of Italy seemed to extend forever. The Greeks gave the region a nickname—Great Greece, Megalē Hellas—or (as it has been more traditionally known, in its Latin name) Magna Graecia.

By the 400s B.C. the Italian Greeks were subject to influence and control by the successive rulers of the Sicilian-Greek city of SYRACUSE. In the 200s B.C., after centuries of war with each other and with their Italian neighbors, the Greek cities of Italy became absorbed by the expansionist power of ROME.

(See also AGATHOCLES; DIONYSIUS (1); HIERON (1); PARMENIDES; PITHECUSAE; POSEIDONIA; PYTHAGORAS.)

Ithaca   Small (44 square miles) island of the northwest coast of Greece, located outside the Gulf of Patras. Beautiful but unfertile, its coastline fretted with inlets of sea, Ithaca was inhabited throughout ancient times yet played almost no role in Greek history. It is best remembered as the domain of the Greek king ODYSSEUS. Archaeological excavations have uncovered POTTERY and house foundations from the Mycenaean era, confirming the island's importance circa 1200 B.C., when Odysseus would have lived.

(See also IONIAN SEA; MYCENAEAN CIVILIZATION.)

Ixion   Villain of Greek MYTH. Ixion was a prince of the Lapith tribe of THESSALY who murdered his father-in-law so as to avoid paying the bride price for the MARRIAGE. Although pardoned by the great god ZEUS, Ixion next schemed to seduce Zeus' wife, the goddess HERA. But Zeus, aware of Ixion's plan, deceived Ixion with a facsimile of Hera, shaped from a cloud. (Supposedly Ixion's semen impregnated the cloud-Hera, which gave birth to the race of CENTAURS.)

At Zeus' order, Ixion was whipped until he repeated the words "Benefactors deserve honor." Then he was tied to a fiery wheel and sent spinning through the sky—or through the Underworld—for eternity. Ixion was one of several great sinners of Greek legend—others include SISYPHUS and TANTALUS—whose crime involved betraying the friendship of the gods.

(See also AFTERLIFE; HUBRIS.)

J

Jason (1) In MYTH, a Thessalian hero who led the Argonauts (sailors of the ship *Argo*) to the distant land of Colchis, to acquire the fabulous Golden Fleece. The tale of the Argonauts is mentioned in HOMER's *Odyssey* (written down circa 750 B.C.) and elaborated in PINDAR's fourth Pythian ode (462 B.C.), but the main source is APOLLONIUS' clever Alexandrian epic, the *Argonautica* (circa 245 B.C.).

The Argonaut tale seems to combine two different layers: (1) a very ancient legend going back to Mycenaean times (second millennium B.C.), of significance for Mycenaean centers in THESSALY and BOEOTIA; and (2) later traders' tales of the Sea of MARMARA and the BLACK SEA, developed during the Greek exploration of that region in the 700s and 600s B.C. In the earlier version (now lost), the Argonauts may have sailed to a fabled land called Aea, somewhere at the edge of the world. But the surviving version has the Argonauts voyaging to Colchis, a real (although distant), non-Greek region on the eastern Black Sea. (Colchis was an emporium for caravans from north-central Asia, and by the 500s B.C. the Milesian Greeks had a TRADE depot there.)

In the myth, Jason (Greek: Iason, "healer") was the son of Aeson and heir to the kingship of the Thessalian city of Iolcus (modern Volos, the region's only seaport). As a child, he was smuggled away by his mother after Aeson's stepbrother Pelias had seized the throne. Raised in the Thessalian wilds by the wise Chiron—the centaur who regularly tutors mythical young heroes—Jason returned as a young man to Iolcus, to claim his birthright. He entered the city with one sandal missing, having lost it crossing a river. Pelias—knowing by that foretold sign to beware of this man—immediately persuaded the newcomer to go out in search of the Golden Fleece.

This fleece was the skin of a winged, golden-fleeced ram, which in prior times the gods had supplied to carry the young Phrixus and Hellē (the children of the Boeotian hero Athamas) away from their evil stepmother. Carried eastward through the sky, Hellē had lost her grip and fallen off, drowning in the waterway thenceforth called the HELLESPONT (in her honor). Her brother had safely reached the far-off land of Colchis, where he sacrificed the ram to ZEUS the Savior.

Jason, aided by his divine patron, HERA, then assembled an expedition consisting of the noblest heroes in Greece. The roster varies, but the most familiar names include: the Calydonian hero MELEAGER; the female warrior ATALANTA; the brothers PELEUS (father of ACHILLES) and Telamon (father of AJAX [1]); the Thracian musician ORPHEUS; the Spartan twins CASTOR AND POLYDEUCES; the twins Calais and Zetes (sons of the North Wind); and the greatest of heroes, HERACLES (who soon gets "written out" of the story, so as not to monopolize the adventures).

Their ship was the *Argo*, built by a shipwright named Argos, who went along on the expedition. The Argonauts were sometimes called by the name MINYANS (*Minuai*), which was also the name of the ruling family of the Boeotian city of ORCHOMENUS. These Boeotian Minyans may have figured in the early (lost) version of the myth.

Sailing northeastward from Greece to the Black Sea, the heroes had several adventures. They dawdled for a year on the Aegean island of Lemnos, busily impregnating the man-hungry Lemnian WOMEN, who had all murdered their husbands out of resentment of the latter's Thracian slave girls. Finally continuing to the Sea of Marmara, the Argonauts were welcomed by the native king Cyzicus, but he was killed by them in a mishap. Soon Heracles was separated from the expedition, having gone ashore to search for his page, Hylas.

Still in the Marmara, the Argonauts rescued the old, blind Thracian king Phineus who, for some offense, was living in eternal torment. The HARPIES, hideous winged female demons, would relentlessly fly down to snatch away his food and leave behind their feces. The Argonauts Calais and Zetes, who could fly, chased away the harpies forever. In gratitude, Phineus gave Jason advice on how to slip through the Symplegades, the Clashing Rocks (which are a mythical rendering of the narrow BOSPORUS, channel, leading into the Black Sea).

At the eastward end of the Black Sea, the adventurers reached Colchis, where the evil king Aeëtes set his conditions for surrendering the fleece. One of the Argonauts must plow a field with a pair of fire-breathing BRONZE bulls and sow the magical dragon's teeth (remnants of the hero CADMUS' adventure at THEBES), which Aeëtes had in his possession. From the seeds, there would arise armed men, who must be conquered.

Aeëtes was sure that these conditions could never be met. But his sorceress daughter MEDEA, having fallen in love with Jason (at APHRODITE's hand, from Hera's bidding), provided the hero with a magic ointment to make him invulnerable for a day. Thus Jason was able to fulfill Aeëtes' terms. Then the Argonauts fled Colchis with the fleece and Medea (who had stolen the fleece for them after charming to sleep the dragon that guarded it).

Aeëtes led his ships in pursuit. But Medea, who had brought her young brother Apsyrtus aboard the *Argo*, now murdered the child and cut him up, throwing the body sections into the sea. Aeëtes and his followers halted, collecting the royal corpse for burial.

The Argonauts returned to Thessaly, either the way they had come or via a fantastical route up the Danube and into the Mediterranean. Apollonius' *Argonautica* ends with the return to Iolcus. Other writers describe how Jason and Medea took vengeance on Pelias by fatally tricking him into climbing into a cauldron of boiling water that was supposed to rejuvenate him.

Driven from Iolcus by Pelias' son, Jason and Medea hung up the Golden Fleece in the temple of Zeus at Orchomenus. They settled at CORINTH, where the final chapter of Jason's drama was played out, as described in EURIPIDES' tragedy *Medea* (431 B.C.). Jason divorced Medea, intending to marry Glauce, daughter of the Corinthian king Creon. Medea, insane with rage, avenged herself by killing Glauce, Creon, and her own two children by Jason. She then fled to ATHENS. Jason, meanwhile, had set up the *Argo* on land and dedicated it to the god POSEIDON. As he slept beneath the ship's stern one day, a section fell off and killed him.

(See also CENTAURS; CYZICUS; EPIC POETRY; SHIPS AND SEA-FARING.)

Jason (2) Tyrant of Pherae in THESSALY, reigning circa 385–370 B.C. In a period of political turmoil throughout Greece, he united Thessaly under himself and tried to forge it into a major power. An ally of THEBES, he negotiated a treaty between Thebes and SPARTA after the Spartan defeat at LEUCTRA (371 B.C.) but was assassinated the following year. In history he stands as a precursor to the Macedonian king PHILIP II (reigned 359–336 B.C.), who may have modeled himself on Jason to some extent. In warfare, Jason developed the use of primitive siege artillery—a military science later taken up by Philip. (See also TYRANTS; WARFARE, SIEGE.)

Jews The Jews and the Greeks, despite their respective importance in ancient history, had little to do with each other prior to the 300s B.C. An independent Jewish kingdom, with its capital at Jerusalem, ceased to exist in 586 B.C., when the Babylonians captured Jerusalem and removed the population to Babylon. This Babylonian Exile ended in 539 B.C., when the Persian king CYRUS (1) conquered much of the Near East and permitted his new Jewish subjects to return to their homeland in the Levant. (Not all did so, however.)

It was now that the Jews came into contact with another subject-people of the Persians—Greeks from IONIA, in western ASIA MINOR. The biblical prophet Ezekiel (late 500s B.C.) wrote disdainfully of the profit-minded Greek traders of "Javan" (Ionia), trading in SLAVES and worked BRONZE. The Greek historian HERODOTUS (circa 435 B.C.) knew of the Jews—he called them "Palestinian Syrians"—and listed them among the naval levies serving in the Persian king XERXES' invasion of Greece in 480 B.C.

The destruction of the Persian Empire by the Macedonian king ALEXANDER THE GREAT between 334 and 323 B.C. left Macedonian and Greek governors over the various Jewish pockets of the Near East. By about 300 B.C. Alexander's domain had fragmented into the large Greco-Macedonian kingdoms of the HELLENISTIC AGE. Ptolemaic EGYPT seized Jerusalem and the southern Levant, while the SELEUCID EMPIRE ruled Babylon and other Jewish-inhabited regions. Consequently Jewish immigrants flooded to such newly founded Hellenistic cities as Egyptian ALEXANDRIA (1) and Seleucid ANTIOCH. Alexandria in particular developed an important Jewish minority that occasionally endured ethnic violence from the Greek population.

Jewish monotheism was not deeply affected by the polytheistic RELIGION of the Greeks. However, the glamorous Greek style of life attracted many of the wealthier Jews, creating an assimilated, pro-Greek class. This process occurred not only in the Hellenistic cities but also in Jerusalem itself (where at least one Greek-style GYMNASIUM and THEATER were each built in the 100s B.C.). Greek nomenclature infiltrated Judaism: The word synagogue, for example, is Greek ("assembly place"). Among surviving customs, Greek influence can be seen in the ceremonial Jewish Passover meal: The ritual drinking of cups of WINE and the prayerbook references to dining in a reclining position are best understood as elements borrowed from the Greek drinking party known as the SYMPOSIUM.

With Greek the language of commerce, administration, and secular law in the Hellenistic kingdoms, the emigrant Jewish communities began to forget the Hebrew tongue. In Alexandria this process had taken hold by around 260 B.C., when certain books of the Jewish Bible began appearing in Greek translation. The complete Greek translation of the Jewish Bible—a work supposedly ordered by the Macedonian-Egyptian king PTOLEMY (2) II and conducted by 70 scholars—became known as the Septuagint (from the Latin *septuaginta*, "seventy"). In the Greco-Roman world of later centuries, the Septuagint contributed greatly to the survival of Judaism and the spread of Christianity.

In 198 B.C. the Seleucid king ANTIOCHUS (2) III conquered much of the Levant, including the Jewish heartland. There the next generation saw the best-known, tragic encounter between Jews and Greeks—the Maccabean Revolt of 167–164 B.C., which is commemorated in the Jewish festival of Hanukkah. The biblical First Book of Maccabees describes how certain rural Jews rebelled after the Seleucid king Antiochus IV tried to impose Greek religious customs and convert the temple at Jerusalem into a temple of the Greek god ZEUS. The spreading revolt was led by Judas Maccabee ("the hammer"), of the priestly Hasmonaean family. Judas defeated Seleucid armies in battle and recaptured the Jerusalem temple, but the rebellion decayed into a Jewish civil war of anti-Greek versus pro-Greek factions. Finally, in 142 B.C., the rebels ejected the Seleucid garrison from the citadel at Jerusalem. For the next 80 years the Jews of the Levant comprised a sovereign nation ruled by a Hasmonaean dynasty. But in 63 B.C. the country fell to the Roman legions of Pompey the Great.

Jocasta See OEDIPUS.

K

King's Peace The treaty drawn up in 386 or 387 B.C. between SPARTA and the Persian king Artaxerxes II, sometimes known as the Peace of Antalcidas (from the name of a Spartan ambassador). This treaty ended recent Spartan-Persian hostilities in the CORINTHIAN WAR and severed PERSIA's alliance with Sparta's enemies, ATHENS, CORINTH, BOEOTIA, and ARGOS. But the notorious aspect of the treaty was Sparta's renunciation of its former claim to protect the Greek cities of IONIA and of other parts of ASIA MINOR. The King's Peace ceded the Greek cities of Asia Minor and CYPRUS back to the Persian king, even though these cities had been liberated by the Greeks after the PERSIAN WARS.

For the Persians, the King's Peace marked a high point in their designs against Greece, a return to the western conquests of DARIUS (1) (circa 500 B.C.). For the Greeks, the peace unmasked the "real" Sparta from its pretense of being a liberator. Amid the resulting anti-Spartan anger, Athens was able to attract allies for its new SECOND ATHENIAN LEAGUE (circa 377 B.C.), and the city of THEBES began to emerge as a rival to Sparta. It was then (380 B.C.) that the Athenian orator ISOCRATES began to publish pamphlets urging the Greeks to unite and liberate Ionia by invading the Persian Empire—a plea that would later bear fruit in the conquests of the Macedonian king ALEXANDER THE GREAT (334–323 B.C.).

kinship From earliest times, Greek society was organized along multiple levels of kinship. The largest and simplest divisions were the different Greek ethnic groups, chiefly the IONIAN, AEOLIAN, and DORIAN GREEKS. All Dorian and many Ionian settlements were originally subdivided into citizens' groupings called *phulai* (or phylae, usually translated as "tribes"). Dorian cities such as SPARTA or SYRACUSE had three phylae. Ionian cities such as ATHENS or MILETUS might have had four or more. Undoubtedly the phylae predate the Greek cities and reflect the tribal organizations of a nomadic era in the BRONZE AGE.

Appropriate to this primitive origin, the phylae were religious-military societies with inherited membership, centered on aristocratic families. Phylae were themselves divided into groups called *phratriai* (brotherhoods), whose members were *phrateres* (brothers). This Greek word—connected in origin to other Indo-European words such as Latin *frater* and English *brother*—described men who were not literally brothers but who fought together in the retinue of aristocratic war leaders. In HOMER's epic poem the *Iliad* (written down circa 750 B.C.), the Greek leader AGAMEMNON is advised to marshal the army into battalions consisting of men from the same tribe and phratry. Early Sparta (circa 700 B.C.) had 27 phratries, probably nine from each tribe.

Like other aspects of Greek citizenship and military life, the phratry was mainly the province of adult, citizen males. During the era of Greek aristocratic rule (circa 1000–600 B.C.), a man did not need to be of noble blood to belong to a phratry, but he did have to be associated with one of the aristocratic families—for example, as a spear-carrier in war. For the individual citizen, the phratry provided aristocratic patronage and an extended family, giving assurance of support in legal proceedings, blood feuds, and similar events.

At the head of each phratry was a *genos* or (plural) *genē*. The *genos* was an aristocratic clan—a group of kinsmen claiming a single noble ancestor through male descent. A *genos* typically had a name formed with a Greek suffix meaning "the sons of"—for example, the Athenian Alcmaeonidae (sons of the ancestor Alcmaeon) and the Corinthian Bacchiadae (sons of Bacchis). As a center of political power, religious authority, and military might, the *genos* dominated the (larger and less elite) phratry, but presumably a phratry might be headed by more than one *genos*. We know the names of about 60 Athenian *genē*; they were also called by the blanket term *Eupatridai*, "sons of noble fathers."

With the arising middle-class challenge to aristocratic rule in the 600s–400s B.C., the old-fashioned, aristocratic-based phyle and phratry in many Greek cities were completely reorganized by political decree. At Sparta this occurred probably under the reforms of LYCURGUS (1), circa 650 B.C. At Athens such revamping was at the heart of the democratic reforms of CLEISTHENES (1) (circa 594 B.C.). Abolishing the four traditional Athenian phylae, Cleisthenes created 10 new phylae and reconstituted the phratries so as to include newly enfranchised, lower-income citizens.

In the democratic Athens of the 400s and 300s B.C., the phratry remained a vital social-political entity, connecting the individual citizen with the political life of the state. As a young child and again as a teenager, the young male citizen was presented by his father and near kinsmen to his *phrateres* at the altar of ZEUS Phratrios, the Zeus of the

Phratry. The adolescent presentation—at which the youth dedicated his newly shorn childhood hair to the god—signified the young man's entrance into the community. Later in the man's life, his *phrateres* witnessed his betrothal ceremony and feasted at his MARRIAGE. Less elaborately, it was at the local phratry office that a female Athenian's name would be enrolled, thus assuring her of the rights (regarding marriage, public assistance, etc.) available to citizen WOMEN.

(See also ARISTOCRACY; DEMOCRACY; POLIS.)

Knossus   See CNOSSUS.

Korē   See DEMETER; PERSEPHONE.

Labyrinth In MYTH, the Labyrinth was the mazelike palace designed by the Athenian craftsman DAEDALUS at CNOSSUS, in CRETE, to house the monstrous Minotaur. The Athenian hero THESEUS, making his way through the Labyrinth's corridors with the help of the Cretan princess Ariadne, slew the Minotaur. The classical Greeks described any kind of architectural maze as a labyrinth (*laburinthos*)—much as we use the word today.

Like other myths, this one contains a kernel of fact: The name *Labyrinth* was probably applied to the Minoan palace at Cnossus, sometime in the second millennium B.C. *Laburinthos* was not originally a Greek word, as shown by its distinctive *nth* sound (which distinguishes such other pre-Greek names as CORINTH and HYANCINTHUS). It was probably a Minoan word, meaning "house of the double ax"—the two-headed ax (*labrus*) being a Minoan royal symbol.

(See also GREEK LANGUAGE; MINOAN CIVILIZATION; MINOS.)

Laconia Local territory of SPARTA, in the southeastern PELOPONNESE. The word apparently was a shortened form of the region's alternate name, Lacedaemon.

Of the Peloponnese's three southern peninsulas, Laconia included the eastern (Cape Malea) and middle one (Cape Taenarum). The two capes and much of the interior consist of limestone mountains; two ranges—Mt. Parnon in the east and Mt. Taygetus in the west—run north to south. Between these mountain ranges lay the fertile Eurotas River valley, which widens southward to the Laconian Gulf. In the north, Laconia shared a mountainous (and often-disputed) border with ARCADIA and the territory of ARGOS. To the west, beyond the Taygetus range, lay the region of MESSENIA.

In the second millennium B.C. Laconia was the site of a thriving Mycenaean-Greek kingdom; the semimythical king MENELAUS would have ruled there. Overrun by DORIAN GREEKS circa 1100–1000 B.C., Laconia eventually produced a number of Dorian settlements, including Sparta, in the upper Eurotas valley. By about 700 B.C. Sparta had conquered the Eurotas down to the sea. The town of Gytheum, on the western Laconian Gulf, became Sparta's port. The Eurotas farmland became the home of the Spartan elite, the "true" Spartans (Spartiatai). Other parts of Laconia were inhabited by Spartan citizens of lesser social rank—the PERIOECI (Greek: *peroikoi*, "dwellers about"). Together these two groups comprised the Spartan free population, the Lacedaemonians (*Lakedaimonioi*).

The name *Laconia* has provided the modern English word *laconic*, referring originally to the Spartan brevity of speech. (See also HELOTS.)

Lampsacus See HELLESPONT.

Laocoön Trojan priest of APOLLO, in the MYTH of the TROJAN WAR. Laocoön was the brother of Anchises and uncle of the hero AENEAS. After the Greeks had apparently abandoned the siege of TROY, leaving behind the wooden Trojan Horse, Laocoön objected vehemently to the Trojans' plan to bring the horse within the city's walls. (In fact, the horse was full of Greek soldiers.) To stifle Laocoön's objections, and thus fulfill the ordained doom of Troy, the goddess ATHENA sent two huge serpents from the sea.

The horrible death of Laocoön and his two sons is shown in an original marble statue group, variously dated between about 150 B.C. and A.D. 30 and ascribed to three sculptors of Rhodes. Notice the serpent's head at center, biting Laocoön's hip. Now in the Vatican Museum, this ambitious work adorned the Roman emperor Tiberius' grotto at Sperlonga, south of Rome. circa A.D. 30.

These enwrapped Laocoön and his two small sons and crushed them to death.

lapiths   See CENTAURS.

laws and law courts   By the 700s B.C.—and probably long before—Greek states had developed official and public procedures for administering justice. No information is available on laws or law courts during the Mycenaean era (circa 1600–1200 B.C.), but HOMER's epic poem the *Iliad* (written down circa 750 B.C.) mentions a public trial as one of the scenes embossed on the shield of ACHILLES (book 18). In the scene, elders seated in a city's AGORA arbitrate a dispute between two men over payment of blood money for a murder done by one of the two. A crowd stands around, and heralds call for order.

The judges at such court cases would have been the individuals who ran the city government—that is, the aristocratic COUNCIL or a committee thereof. The ancient Greeks never distinguished between the judiciary and the legislative or executive branches, as modern American society does; there was no class of professional judges. Rather, in early Greek history (circa 900–500 B.C.), the judges might be the same men who decreed the laws, commanded the army, oversaw the state RELIGION, and owned most of the land. Such law courts obviously were biased in favor of aristocratic plaintiffs and defendants, and this unfairness contributed to the popular anger that produced the Greek TYRANTS (600s B.C.) and, later, the Athenian DEMOCRACY (500s B.C.).

Systems of law differed from one city-state to another. Before the invention of the Greek ALPHABET, the law would have been handed down by oral tradition, with officials and their underlings memorizing whole legal codes. But in the 600s B.C., with the spread of WRITING in the Greek world, laws came to be written down for permanence and easy reference. (By contrast, written law codes had existed in the Near East since at least 1800 B.C.)

The writing-down of Greek legal codes came in response to the tense political climate of the 600s B.C., as middle-class citizens demanded fair, permanent, and publicly accessible laws. Naturally this was also an occasion for legal reforms and revisions. The earliest written Greek law code was supposedly composed by a certain Zaleucus at LOCRI, in Greek southern ITALY, circa 662 B.C. At ATHENS, new laws were drafted and written down under DRACO (circa 625 B.C.) and SOLON (circa 594 B.C.). Solon's laws, carved into wooden blocks, were displayed for centuries afterward in the Athenian agora. Today the law code of the city of GORTYN partly survives in a lengthy inscription, carved in stone circa 450 B.C.

Law codes covered civil cases such as disputes over inheritance and land boundaries, as well as criminal cases such as homicide and forgery. A comparison with American laws shows some surprising differences. For instance, in Athens in the 400s–300s B.C., raping a nonslave woman was merely a finable offense, but a man who seduced such a woman could be punished much more severely. (The legal theory here was that rape was a spontaneous crime while seduction was not only premeditated but corruptive to the woman's morals and to the Athenian household.)

The most serious crime at Athens was homicide; conviction brought the death penalty for an intentional killing or exile for an unintentional one (aside from an excusable accident or self-defense). Penalties for other crimes included loss of citizenship or confiscation of property.

Most information on the day-to-day workings of Greek law courts comes from the democratic Athens of the 400s–300s B.C. Sources include inscriptions, courtroom speeches, and factual references in the writings of PLATO, ARISTOTLE, and other thinkers. Cases were heard by large groups of jurors, often numbering 501 but otherwise ranging between about 201 and 2,501. Odd numbers were employed to avoid a tie jury vote—unlike modern American juries, ancient Greek juries did not need to reach a unanimous verdict.

The jurors were ordinary Athenian citizens, chosen by lottery. But their responsibilities far surpassed those of modern American jurors. Although an Athenian courtroom had an officiating magistrate to maintain procedure, there was no learned judge to interpret the law, enforce the rules of evidence, or pass sentence. These decisions were made by the jury itself, on the basis of the speeches and examination of witnesses by prosecutor and defendant (or, in a civil case, by the two disputants).

Similarly, there was no state-employed district attorney, whose job was to prosecute in court. State prosecutions were usually brought by volunteers; any adult male citizen could do so. A private individual might decide to prosecute out of civic duty or for public attention toward a political career. In case of conviction, the prosecutor might be entitled to a portion of the defendant's paid fine or confiscated property. Frivolous prosecution was discouraged by a law requiring the prosecutor to pay a fine himself if his case won less than one-fifth of the jury vote. Nevertheless, the courts undoubtedly became the scene of personal and political vendettas, and it is no coincidence that the Athenians were known to be a litigious people.

(See also AESCHINES; ANDOCIDES; ANTIPHON; AREOPAGUS; ARISTOCRACY; ARISTOPHANES; CATANA; CLEON; DEMOSTHENES (1); HOMOSEXUALITY; ISAEUS; ISOCRATES; LYCURGUS (1); LYCURGUS (2); LYSIAS; MARRIAGE; PERICLES; PITTACUS; PROSTITUTES; PROTAGORAS; RHETORIC; SLAVES; SOCRATES; WOMEN; ZEUS.)

Leda   In MYTH, the beautiful wife of the Spartan king Tyndareus. The god ZEUS became infatuated with her and raped her, having approached her in the shape of a swan. Leda bore two sets of twins, all of whom had important destinies: HELEN OF TROY and CLYTAEMNESTRA, and CASTOR AND POLYDEUCES. According to a familiar pattern of Greek storytelling, it was sometimes claimed that only one member of each pair of twins was Zeus' child, the other being Tyndareus'. Helen and Polydeuces were Zeus' children, and hence eligible for immortality. In some versions, the two pairs of twins were hatched from two giant bird eggs.

Lefkandi   Modern village and archaeological site on the Lelantine plain, on the west coast of the island of EUBOEA. In the 1960s A.D. British excavations there found traces of an ancient settlement whose earliest level predated the Greeks' arrival (circa 2100 B.C.). As a Greek town, the site apparently prospered during the Mycenaean era and later, down to about 825 B.C., before being abandoned circa 700 B.C.

Lefkandi has shed rare light on Greek life during the DARK AGE (circa 1100–900 B.C.). The pride of Lefkandi's archaeological yieldings is the so-called Hero's Tomb, a surprisingly rich grave of an unknown baron who died circa 900 B.C. and was buried amid his finery, including ornaments of GOLD, imported from the East. The tomb's evidence of wealth and TRADE has forced historians to revise their otherwise grim picture of Dark Age Greece.

Lefkandi's apparent abrupt decline after 825 B.C. seems related to the emergence of the nearby ancient city of ERETRIA. ARCHAEOLOGY suggests that Eretria arose abruptly, in prosperity, around 825 B.C., and modern historians have guessed that Lefkandi was the original city of the Eretrians. Lefkandi sits halfway along the Lelantine plain between Eretria (southeast) and CHALCIS (northwest). Probably under pressure from nearby Chalcis, Lefkandi was abandoned and a new settlement, Eretria, was founded farther away from Chalcis.

(See also LELANTINE WAR.)

Lelantine War   Earliest Greek conflict for which any reliable historical record exists. The war was fought circa 720–680 B.C. between the neighboring cities of CHALCIS and ERETRIA, on the west coast of the large island of EUBOEA, in central Greece. Chalcis and Eretria were the most powerful Greek cities of the day; they had previously cooperated in overseas TRADE and COLONIZATION ventures. But now they fought over possession of the fertile plain of Lelanton, which stretched between them.

According to the Athenian historian THUCYDIDES (1) (circa 410 B.C.), the Lelantine War marked the first time that the Greek world divided itself into alliances on one side or the other. It seems to have been a primitive world war, in which the most powerful Greeks states squared off with each other according to traditional local enmities: MILETUS (Eretria's ally) versus its old rival and neighbor SAMOS (Chalcis' ally); CHIOS (Eretria's side) versus its mainland neighbor Erythrae (Chalcis' side); and SPARTA (Chalcis') against its bitter enemy, the neighboring region of MESSENIA (Eretria's).

The fighting between Chalcis and Eretria on the Lelantine plain may have been an old-fashioned, gentlemen's affair. One later writer reports seeing an old inscription recording the belligerents' agreement not to use "long-distance missiles"—that is, arrows, javelins, and sling-stones. Another inscription mentions CHARIOTS, a very old-fashioned military device. These battles were probably fought by dueling aristocrats rather than by the massed concentrations of HOPLITE citizen-soldiers who would come to define warfare in the mid-600s B.C.

The war ended circa 680 B.C., apparently with Chalcis as the marginal winner. In any case, both cities soon were overtaken as commercial and military powers by Corinth, Sparta, and ATHENS. But the war's alliances had lasting effects. With the help of Corinth and Samos, Sparta later conquered Messenia. And seafaring Corinth, shut out of the BLACK SEA by its "Lelantine" enemy Miletus, instead enlarged its grain supplies and foreign markets in SICILY and ITALY.

(See also WARFARE, LAND.)

Leonidas   See THERMOPYLAE.

Leontini   See CATANA; SICILY.

lesbianism   See HOMOSEXUALITY; SAPPHO.

Lesbos   Largest island (630 square miles) of the eastern AEGEAN SEA, close to the northwestern coast of ASIA MINOR. The first inhabitants of Lesbos may have been descendants of the civilization of TROY. In around the 900s B.C., Lesbos was conquered by AEOLIAN GREEKS who had migrated east from the Greek-mainland regions of THESSALY and BOEOTIA. In the following centuries, Lesbos was the departure point for further Aeolian expeditions that colonized the northwest Asia Minor coast.

By the 600s B.C. Lesbos was the homeland of a thriving Aeolian culture, with MYTILENE its foremost city. The island prospered by seaborne TRADE, with mainland Greece and with the Eastern kingdoms of LYDIA and EGYPT. Lesbos' tradition of poetry-making found its culmination in the verses of SAPPHO (circa 600 B.C.). Lesbos' heyday also saw the political reforms of the Mytilenian statesman PITTACUS (circa 600 B.C.) and the short-lived appearance of Aeloic-style temple architecture at Mytilene and Nape (early 500s B.C.). But the golden age had ended by the time the Persians captured the island in 527 B.C.

(See also PERSIAN WARS.)

Leto   See APOLLO; ARTEMIS.

Leucippus   Greek philosopher of the mid-400s B.C., usually credited—alongside his follower DEMOCRITUS—as the inventor of the "atomic" theory of natural philosophy. This theory held that the basic components of matter and reality are tiny particles, which Leucippus called *atomoi*, an adjective meaning "indivisible". All creation, destruction, and change is accomplished by the perpetual reorganization of these atoms into new combinations.

Basic facts of Leucippus' life and works are unknown. He was probably older than Democritus (born 460 B.C.) and was probably his teacher. Leucippus may have been a native of ABDERA (Democritus' home) or MILETUS or Elea, in Greek southern ITALY. No written works survive under Leucippus' name, but two treatises preserved under Democritus' name—*The Great World-system* and *On Mind*—may in fact have been written by Leucippus.

Leuctra   Ancient village in northern BOEOTIA, site of one of the most eventful battles in Greek history. There, in the summer of 371 B.C., the legend of Spartan invincibility was destroyed when an army of Spartans and allies under King Cleombrotus met defeat by a force of Thebans and allies commanded by the Theban leader EPAMINONDAS. In the battle's aftermath, Epaminondas simply removed SPARTA as a first-class power, mainly by liberating the Spartan-ruled HELOTS of MESSENIA (362 B.C.). Sparta, previously master of Greece, never recovered its former power, and the mantle of Greek leadership passed (briefly) to THEBES.

At the heart of the Theban victory was Epaminondas' decision to deepen his battle line's left wing to 50 rows, against the Spartans' more usual 12-man depth. Epaminondas' intent was to destroy the Spartans along their strongest front—their right wing, where the elite "Spartiates" (the Spartan upper class) were arrayed and where the king commanded personally. Traditionally, Greek armies had won their battles on their right wings. The better troops customarily were stationed there, and, due to the battle rows' natural drift rightward, the advancing right wing tended to overlap (advantageously) the enemy left—for both armies. Victory, prior to Leuctra, lay in winning on the right while withstanding the enemy's advantage on its right; traditionally, the left wing performed more poorly. Epaminondas' tactic was to make his left wing the better-performing, by deepening it.

The success was devastating. The Spartan right was pushed back and crushed by the heavy Theban left, and the Spartan left wing scattered in retreat. Nearly 1,000 from the Spartan-led army were killed, including King Cleombrotus and 400 other Spartiates. The Theban side lost 47 men.

Epaminondas' innovation—striking at the enemy's strongest point—changed the nature of Greek warfare. Within a few decades, the technique had been elaborated by the Macedonian king PHILIP II.

(See also CHAERONEA; WARFARE, LAND.)

Linear B   Modern name for a pre-alphabetic form of WRITING used by the Mycenaean Greeks, circa 1400–1200 B.C. This was a syllabary script: It basically employed about 90 symbols, each representing a vowel-consonant combination, with pictograms sometimes added to help identify certain words. Linear B was revealed to modern eyes in 1900 A.D. by archaeologist Sir Arthur Evans in his excavations at Mycenaean-era CNOSSUS, on the island of CRETE. The writing, incised into clay tablets, had been incidentally preserved when the tablets were fired during the violent burning of the palace, circa 1400 B.C. Evans named the then-undeciphered script Linear B to distinguish it from an earlier, Minoan script found at Cnossus, called Linear A.

Soon similar tablets were found at PYLOS, THEBES, and MYCENAE, at archaeological levels corresponding to about 1200 B.C. In each case the inscriptions had been preserved by unintended firing of the clay. To date, over 5,000 tablets have been discovered.

Linear B was finally deciphered in 1952 by British architect Michael Ventris. Ventris' breakthrough showed that the writing's language was an early form of Greek—that is, when the symbols are correctly sounded out, they yield words that are Greek. This discovery confirmed the assumption (not previously proven) that the Mycenaeans had spoken Greek. The deciphered tablets were revealed to be palace records—inventories, lists of employees and administrative notes—that have shed valuable light on the organization and material culture of late Mycenaean society.

Evidently the Mycenaeans acquired Linear B writing by adapting Minoan Crete's Linear A script to the Greek language. Linear A—which records a vanished, non-Greek language—remains largely undeciphered to this day.

(See also ALPHABET; MINOAN CIVILIZATION; MYCENAEAN CIVILIZATION.)

literacy   See WRITING.

literature   See EPIC POETRY; LYRIC POETRY; THEATER; WRITING.

Locri   City on the east coast of the "toe" of ITALY, founded circa 700 B.C. by Dorian-Greek colonists from LOCRIS, in central Greece. The city's official name was Lokroi Epizephurioi, "West Wind Locrians." After ejecting the native Sicels from the area, the Greek settlers established a well-run OLIGARCHY, called the Hundred Houses. Locri boasted the Greek world's earliest written law code, attributed to the statesman Zaleucus (circa 622 B.C.).

A sprawling community defended by a wall more than four miles long, Locri feuded with neighboring Italian peoples and with CROTON and RHEGIUM, two nearby Greek cities inhabited by non-Dorians. In around 500 B.C. the Locrians—supposedly aided by the divine twins CASTOR AND POLYDEUCES—won a famous victory over the Crotonians at the Battle of the Sagras River.

Locri's allies included the powerful Dorian-Greek city of SYRACUSE, in eastern SICILY. Circa 387 B.C. Locri helped the Syracusan tyrant DIONYSIUS (1) to destroy Rhegium. But Locri was later weakened by the wars that accompanied the expansion of ROME through the Italian peninsula, and the city surrendered to the Romans in 205 B.C. It remained an important town of Roman Italy.

(See also DORIAN GREEKS; LAWS AND LAW COURTS.)

Locris   Bipartite region in the mountains of central Greece, divided by the states of PHOCIS and Doris. West Locris—or Ozolian Locris, named for a local tribe—bordered the northern Corinthian Gulf from NAUPACTUS eastward to Crisa, the harbor of DELPHI. The heart of West Locris was the fertile coastal valley of Amphissa. East Locris—or Opuntian Locris, named for its center at Opus—lay along the Euboean Straits on the mainland's east coast, from THERMOPYLAE southward to a border with BOEOTIA.

East Locris, governed as a 1,000-man OLIGARCHY, was the more advanced of the two regions. It sent colonists to found LOCRI, in southern ITALY, circa 700 B.C., and was minting coins in the 300s B.C. The Locrians were DORIAN GREEKS, but their dialect (called Northwest Greek by modern scholars) was one shared by many of the peoples dwelling around the western Corinthian Gulf.

(See also GREEK LANGUAGE.)

Long Walls, the   Walls built between 461 and 456 B.C. at the urging of the Athenian statesman PERICLES, to connect ATHENS with its port city of PIRAEUS, four miles away. The completed Long Walls consisted of two parallel walls, about 200 yards apart. The result was to make Athens and Piraeus into a single, linked fortress, suppliable by sea and easily in contact with its navy. By building the Long Walls, Periclean Athens became the Greek naval power par excellence.

Greek poetry was originally meant to be sung to the music of a lyre or flute. The singer here accompanies himself on a cithara, an elaborate form of lyre, in a scene from an Athenian red-figure vase, circa 500 B.C. The cithara was played with a plectrum, which this singer holds in his right hand. He wears a long, Ionian-style tunic and a short cloak over his shoulder.

But the walls affected civilian concerns as well. The city was henceforth connected with the "party of the Piraeus"—the pro-democratic, lower-income citizens who supplied the bulk of the navy's crews. These people began exercising more power in the Athenian ASSEMBLY, resulting in the left-leaning Periclean legislation of these years, such as the introduction of jury pay (457 B.C.). This political association was so odious to certain Athenian right-wingers that in 457 B.C. a band of Athenian extremists hatched a treasonous plot to deliver the Long Walls to the Spartans. The scheme was discovered and averted.

After the outbreak of the PELOPONNESIAN WAR (431 B.C.), the Long Walls permitted Pericles to employ his tortoiselike land strategy of abandoning the countryside to Spartan invasion and collecting the rural Athenian populace within the city's fortifications. The area between the Long Walls became crowded with refugees, resulting in the disastrous plague of 430–427 B.C.

After Athens' defeat in the war, the Long Walls were pulled down by Spartan order, to the MUSIC of flutes (404 B.C.). The Athenian leader CONON rebuilt the walls in 393 B.C.; but after 322 B.C., under Macedonian overlordship, they gradually fell into disuse. Hardly any trace of them remains today.

(See also DEMOCRACY; OLIGARCHY; WARFARE, NAVAL; WARFARE, SIEGE.)

Lotus Eaters   See ODYSSEUS.

love   See APHRODITE; EROS; HOMOSEXUALITY; LYRIC POETRY; MARRIAGE.

Lyceum   Grove and GYMNASIUM outside ATHENS, sacred to the god APOLLO under his title *Lukeios*, "wolf god." It was at the Lukeion or Lyceum that ARISTOTLE opened his philosophical school, in 335 B.C. The Lyceum operated as a rival to the ACADEMY, which was the Athenian philosophical school founded by PLATO.

In around 286 B.C., after the death of Aristotle's successor, THEOPHRASTUS, the Aristotelian school relocated to new buildings at Athens, donated by Theophrastus in his will. According to one version, the new site included a colonnaded walk (Greek: *peripatos*), which gave the institution its famous name, the Peripatetic School. Theophrastus' successor, Straton of Lampsacus, was the last great thinker to preside over the school (circa 286–269 B.C.).

The Peripatetics suffered a decline in influence in the later 200s B.C. Whereas Aristotle and Theophrastus had overseen inquiries into every known branch of SCIENCE and PHILOSOPHY, later scholars focused mainly on literary criticism and biography writing; the movement acquired a reputation for pedantry. The decline may have resulted partly from the gradual disappearance of many of Aristotle's original writings, and when these were rediscovered and published in the first century B.C., the school did enjoy a partial revival. But by then the Peripatetics were being permanently overshadowed by other Greek philosophical movements, primarily STOICISM and EPICUREANISM, which were flourishing among the Romans.

Lycia   See ASIA MINOR.

Lycurgus (1)   Semilegendary, early Spartan lawgiver who founded the government and social organization of classical SPARTA. The Spartans revered the memory of Lycurgus (Greek: Lukourgos), yet today little is known of his life or even when he lived.

By the most plausible modern theory, Lycurgus arose as a political savior circa 665 B.C., after Sparta had been disastrously defeated in a war with ARGOS. In the decades following this defeat, Sparta completely reorganized itself as a militaristic state, devoted to the HOPLITE style of warfare and governed as a moderate OLIGARCHY built around the hoplite class of citizens. The name given to this new form of government was *eunomia*: "good law" or "good discipline." It is reasonable to see this swift, comprehensive change as the work of individual political genius.

In later centuries the Spartans preserved the text of a brief "commandment" (*rhētra*), supposedly written by Lycurgus as the basis for his reforms.

Lycurgus (2)   Athenian orator and statesman of the mid-300s B.C. Known for his fierce public prosecutions of various enemies, Lycurgus was an able administrator, who received a special commission to oversee the city's finances. He was active in opposition to the Macedonian king PHILIP II, before Philip's conquest of Greece (338 B.C.). One speech by Lycurgus survives, *Against Leocrates* (331 B.C.).

(See also LAWS AND LAW COURTS.)

Lydia   Wealthy and advanced non-Greek kingdom of western ASIA MINOR, centered at the city of Sardis, on the Hermus River. As a military and trading power—with riverborne GOLD and SILVER deposits, and access to eastern caravan routes—Lydia dominated Asia Minor in the 600s–500s B.C., before falling to the Persian conqueror CYRUS (1), in 546 B.C. Lydia's significance for Greek history lies in its relations, both hostile and friendly, with the Greeks of IONIA, on the coast of Asia Minor.

Lydia was the first non-Greek nation to take an active part in Greek affairs. King Gyges (circa 670 B.C.) sent gifts to the god APOLLO's shrine at DELPHI, in mainland Greece. King CROESUS, another patron of Delphi, also made a treaty of friendship with SPARTA (circa 550 B.C.). Yet in that same era the Lydian kings repeatedly attacked the Ionian cities, particularly MILETUS, coveting them as outlets to the sea. Finally submitting to Croesus, these Greek cities became privileged subject states under Lydian rule.

Lydia was probably the first nation on earth to mint coins (circa 635 B.C.). This invention was quickly copied by certain Greek cities.

Like certain other Asian peoples, the Lydians had a formidable CAVALRY; they also pioneered early techniques of siege warfare. But after Croesus succumbed to the Persian blitzkrieg, Lydia became a western province of the Persian Empire.

Although not independent thereafter, Lydia retained a cultural identity. After the conquests and death of ALEXANDER THE GREAT (334–323 B.C.), Lydia became a province of the Hellenistic SELEUCID EMPIRE. In the 100s B.C. Lydia passed briefly into the kingdom of PERGAMUM, before being absorbed into the empire of ROME.

(See also COINAGE; PERSIA; WARFARE, SIEGE.)

lyric poetry   Like Greek EPIC POETRY, lyric had its origins in MUSIC. *Lurika melē* (lyric verse) meant a solo song in which the singer accompanied him- or herself on the stringed instrument known as the lyre. These brief songs were distinct from epic verse, which told traditional tales of the deeds of heroes, using an on-flowing rhythm (the hexameter). Lyric used other meters, to convey more personal or immediate messages. Of the earliest lyric poets whose verses have survived, SAPPHO (circa 600 B.C.) is the art's greatest practitioner.

Early on, the term *lyric* was enlarged to include different forms of brief song. One such was the elegy, which had its own distinctive meter and was sung to the music of a flute (*elegos*); obviously, for this type of song, the singer used an accompanist. One natural setting for the elegy was the aristocratic drinking party known as the SYMPOSIUM, where female SLAVES would provide flute music as well as other pleasures. The Ephesan poet CALLINUS (circa

640 B.C.) produced what are probably our earliest surviving elegiac verses, urging his countrymen to defend themselves against the marauding Cimmerians. The Spartan TYRTAEUS (circa 630 B.C.) wrote elegies in a similar vein. The elegies of ARCHILOCHUS (circa 640 B.C.) are more angry and personal, and those of ANACREON (circa 520 B.C.) reflect a life that was fun-loving and decadent. One subcategory of elegy was the epigram, which was typically a brief poem, composed for inscription in stone; the epitaph, or gravestone inscription, was one type of epigram.

Another specialized lyric meter was the *iambos*, used by Archilochus, HIPPONAX (circa 540 B.C.), and others for conveying satire and derision. Eventually iambic meter was adopted by Athenian playwrights as sounding natural for individual speaking parts in stage comedy and tragedy.

The term *lyric* also encompassed the category of choral poetry. These verses, in various meters, were written for public performance by a chorus—of men, boys, or girls—usually at a religious festival. Typically accompanied by lyre music, the chorus (usually 30 in number) would dance and present interpretive movements.

The many categories of choral lyric include the *paian*, (religious hymn of praise), the maiden song (*parthenaion*), the dirge (*thrēnos*), and the victory ode (*epinikion*). The greatest Greek choral poet, PINDAR (circa 470 B.C.), is best remembered for his victory odes, which celebrated various patrons' triumphs at such panhellenic festivals as the OLYMPIC GAMES. Another form of choral was the dithyramb, which was a song narrating a mythological story. At ATHENS, dithyrambs were performed at festivals of the god DIONYSUS and included the wearing of masks and the impersonation of characters in the story. By the mid-500s B.C., this practice had given birth to a crude form of stage tragedy.

(See also ALCMAN; BACCHYLIDES; CALLIMACHUS; SIMONIDES; STESICHORUS; THEATER.)

Lysander   Leading Spartan commander of the later PELOPONNESIAN WAR and aftermath. He lived circa 445–395 B.C. First appointed as an admiral in 408 B.C., he pursued a strategy to capture the HELLESPONT waterway from the Athenians, and it was in the Hellespont that he won the sea battle of AEGOSPOTAMI (405 B.C.), which virtually won the war for SPARTA. After besieging ATHENS, Lysander received the Athenian surrender, occupied the city, and installed the puppet government of the THIRTY TYRANTS (404 B.C.). Similarly, he set up oligarchic governments in former Athenian ally cities.

However, the Spartan king Pausanias reversed Lysander's policies, abandoning the Thirty and permitting the restoration of DEMOCRACY at Athens and elsewhere (403 B.C.). Lysander became shut out of power by Pausanias and his colleague AGESILAUS. As a field commander at the outbreak of the CORINTHIAN WAR (395 B.C.), Lysander invaded BOEOTIA but was killed in battle against the Thebans.

Lysias   Athenian orator, circa 459–380 B.C.. Of his reportedly 200 speeches, 32 survive today. These provide an important source for our knowledge of the Athenian law courts.

Like other orators, Lysias wrote speeches for clients but

did not personally plead in court. (He was forbidden to do so, since he was a resident alien, or metic). His father, Cephalus, a Syracusan by birth, had a lucrative shield manufactory in PIRAEUS. (It is this Cephalus who, with Lysias' brother Polemarchus, is featured in the opening episode of PLATO's fictional dialogue *The Republic*.) Evidently the family knew SOCRATES and moved in intellectual circles.

Under the THIRTY TYRANTS (404 B.C.), Polemarchus was put to death and the family's wealth confiscated. Lysias escaped to MEGARA (1), returning under the restored DEMOCRACY of 403 B.C. His major speeches, such as his *Against Eratosthenes*—in which Lysias prosecuted a surviving member of the Thirty—were delivered in the period after this return.

(See also LAWS AND LAW COURTS; METICS; RHETORIC.)

Lysimachus   Macedonian general, and one of the DIADOCHI (successors) who carved up the empire of ALEXANDER THE GREAT. Born circa 360 B.C., Lysimachus was a friend and bodyguard of Alexander's. After Alexander's conquest of the Persian Empire and sudden death (323 B.C.), Lysimachus claimed a domain encompassing THRACE and northwest ASIA MINOR; his main enemy was ANTIGONUS (1), who sought to reconquer Alexander's empire from a base in Asia Minor. At the Battle of Ipsus (301 B.C.), in Asia Minor, Lysimachus and his ally SELEUCUS (1) destroyed Antigonus and divided his kingdom between themselves. By then Lysimachus was calling himself king and had built a royal capital, named Lysimacheia, on the west coast of the CHERSONESE.

In 285 B.C. he briefly captured MACEDON and THESSALY from Antigonus' son, DEMETRIUS POLIORCETES. But in 281 B.C. Lysimachus was defeated and killed by his former ally Seleucus at the Battle of Corupedium, in Asia Minor. Lysimachus' patchwork kingdom did not survive him, but was divided between the Seleucids and the Antigonids of Macedon.

Lysippus   See SCULPTURE.

M

Macedon Outlying Greek kingdom north of THESSALY, inland from the Thermaic Gulf, on the northwest Aegean coast. In modern reference, the name *Macedon* usually refers to the political entity, as opposed to the general territory called Macedonia. Macedon's heartland was the wide Thermaic plain, west of the modern Greek city of Thessaloniki, where the rivers Haliacmon and Axius flowed close together to the sea. The widely separated upper valleys of these rivers supplied two more regions of political and economic importance. Elsewhere the country was mountainous and forested. Its name came from an ancient Greek word meaning highlanders.

Macedon was inhabited by various peoples of Dorian-Greek, Illyrian, and Thracian descent, who spoke a Greek dialect and worshipped Greek gods. Prior to the mid-400s B.C. Macedon was a mere backwater, beleaguered by hostile Illyrians to the west and Thracians to the east, and significant mainly as an exporter of TIMBER and SILVER to the main Greek world.

Unification and modernization came gradually, at the hands of kings of Dorian descent. Alexander I "the Philhellene" (reigned circa 485–440 B.C.) began a hellenizing cultural program and minted Macedon's first coins, of native silver. The ruthless Archelaus I (413–399 B.C.) built forts and roads, improved military organization, chose PELLA as his capital city, and glorified his court by hosting the Athenian tragedians EURIPIDES and AGATHON (both of whom died in Macedon).

Macedon emerged as a major power in the next century. The brilliant Macedonian king PHILIP II (359–336 B.C.) created the best army in the Greek world and annexed territory in THRACE, ILLYRIS, and Greek CHALCIDICĒ, then subjugated Greece itself (338 B.C.). His son and successor, ALEXANDER THE GREAT (336–323 B.C.), conquered the Persian Empire and made Macedon, briefly, the largest kingdom on earth.

In the turmoil after Alexander's death, Macedon was seized by a series of rulers until the admirable king Antigonus II anchored a new, stable dynasty there (circa 272 B.C.). This century saw Macedon as one of the three great Hellenistic powers, alongside Ptolemaic EGYPT and the SELEUCID EMPIRE. Macedonian kings controlled Greece, with garrisons at CORINTH, at the Athenian port of PIRAEUS, and elsewhere. In 222 B.C. the Macedonian king Antigonus III captured the once-indomitable city of SPARTA.

To counter Macedonian domination, there arose two new Greek federal states, the Achaean and Aetolian leagues (mid-200s B.C.). The Macedonian king PHILIP V (221–179 B.C.) punished the Aetolians but came to grief against a new European power—the Italian city of ROME. Philip's two wars against Roman-Aetolian armies in Greece—the First and Second Macedonian wars (214–205 and 200–197 B.C.)—ended with Macedon's defeat and the Roman liberation of Greece (196 B.C.).

Macedon's last king was Philip's son Perseus (179–167 B.C.). After defeating Perseus in the Third Macedonian War (171–167 B.C.), the Romans imprisoned him and dismantled his kingdom. In 146 B.C. the region was annexed as a Roman province, called Macedonia.

(See also ACHAEA; AETOLIA; CASSANDER; DORIAN GREEKS; HELLENISTIC AGE; PHALANX; PYRRHUS.)

maenads In MYTH, the maenads (Greek: *mainadai*, "madwomen") were the frenzied female devotees of the god DIONYSUS. Usually imagined as Thracian WOMEN, the maenads symbolized the obliteration of personal identity and the liberation from conventional life that came with Dionysus' ecstatic worship. Clothed in fawn- or panther-skins, crowned with garlands of ivy, the maenads would rove across mountains and woods, to worship the god with

A figure of divine madness, this dancing maenad appears on an Athenian cup, painted in white-ground technique, circa 490 B.C. She grasps a leopard cub and the type of ivy-bound staff known as a thyrsus. Her headband is a live serpent.

dancing and song. In their abandon, they would capture wild animals and tear them limb from limb, even eating the beasts' raw flesh. Also known as the Bacchae, the maenads were female counterparts of the male SATYRS, but, unlike the satyrs, they were never comical figures. The maenads' rites are unforgettably portrayed in the Athenian tragedian EURIPIDES' masterpiece, *The Bacchae* (405 B.C.).

Although certain women's religious groups of central Greece did practice a midwinter ritual of "mountain dancing" (Greek: *oreibasia*) in Dionysus' honor, the maenads as presented in art and literature were not real. Rather, they were mythical projections of the self-abandonment found in Dionysus' conventional cult. Perhaps the idea of the maenads originated in savage, real-life Dionysian festivals in the non-Greek land of THRACE.

Magna Graecia   See ITALY.

Mantinea   Important city of ARCADIA. Located in the central Arcadian plain, Mantinea emerged circa 500 B.C. from an amalgamation of villages: the name *Mantineia*, suggesting holiness, may refer to a religious dedication at the city's founding. Mantinea was the implacable rival of its 10-mile-distant neighbor, TEGEA. The two cities fought over their boundary and the routing of the destructive water courses through the plain. Also, Mantinea tended to be the enemy of the mighty Spartans, who coveted Arcadia.

Mantinea became a moderate DEMOCRACY circa 470 B.C.—probably due to Athenian involvement—and in 420 B.C., during the PELOPONNESIAN WAR, Mantinea joined an anti-Spartan alliance of ATHENS, ARGOS, and ELIS. This led to a Spartan invasion and a Mantinean defeat at the first Battle of Mantinea (418 B.C.). In 385 B.C. the Spartan king AGESI-LAUS captured the city and pulled down its walls; but after the Spartans' defeat at LEUCTRA (371 B.C.), the Mantineans built the majestic fortifications whose remnants still stand today. In 362 B.C. Mantinean troops fought on the Spartan side and shared in the Spartan defeat at the second Battle of Mantinea, where the Theban commander EPAMINONDAS was killed in his hour of victory. This battle marked the final Theban invasion of the Peloponnese.

The city was captured and destroyed by the Macedonian king Antigonus III in 223 B.C., during his campaign that captured SPARTA. Mantinea was later reestablished under the name Antigoneia.

Marathon   Town in the Athenian territory of ATTICA, three miles from the sea and about 26 miles northeast of ATHENS, along a main road. The coastal plain at Marathon saw one of history's most famous battles, when an Athenian army defeated a seaborne invasion force sent by the Persian king DARIUS (1) (summer 490 B.C.). The Persians, masters of western Asia, were thought to be invincible. The victory at Marathon saved Athens from subjugation and came to be viewed as a nearly mythical event—the gods were said to have smiled on the city and its fledgling DEMOCRACY. Among many later commemorations of the battle was a famous wall PAINTING in Athens' AGORA.

The name *Marathon* may have referred to wild fennel (Greek: *marathon*) in the area. More than 50 years before

the battle, Marathon town played a role in the rise to power of the Athenian tyrant PISISTRATUS. Like other towns of eastern Attica, Marathon held traditional allegiance to Pisistratus' family, and it was at Marathon's hospitable coast that Pisistratus landed an army by sea, to capture Athens (546 B.C.). His son HIPPIAS (1) rode with the army that day. Hippias later succeeded his father as tyrant of Athens, but was ousted in 510 B.C. Making his way to PERSIA, he became one of King Darius' advisers. Then, in 490 B.C., Hippias returned with a Persian invasion fleet, which he guided to the shore near Marathon.

Darius had sent the Persian force to punish two mainland Greek cities, ERETRIA and Athens, for their role in the recent IONIAN REVOLT against Persia. Hippias, then nearly 80 years old, was intended as the Persians' puppet ruler in Athens. Apparently he had been in secret contact with partisans inside Athens who had promised to hand the city over to the invaders.

The ancient Greek historian HERODOTUS, who is the main extant information source for the Marathon campaign, says that the Persian fleet numbered 600 ships. A more accurate figure may have been 200. The fleet carried a land army of perhaps 20,000: armored spearmen, archers, and the formidable Persian CAVALRY, well suited to fighting on the Marathon plain.

After destroying Eretria, the Persian troops disembarked at Marathon to attack Athens. Against them came marching a HOPLITE army of about 9,000 Athenians, plus perhaps 600 from Athens' faithful ally PLATAEA. The Spartans too had promised to send aid, but their troops were delayed at home by certain religious obligations—a typical case of excessive Spartan piety. By the time they arrived, the fight was over.

The opposing armies faced each other for several days, retiring to their respective camps at night. The Greeks, who had no horsemen or archers, were unwilling to attack: They were outnumbered, probably two to one, and they feared the Persian cavalry. The Greeks' advantage was their BRONZE armor (heavier and more extensive than the Persians') and their organized hoplite tactics; man for man, they were to prove the better foot soldiers.

The Athenian command, at this point in history, consisted of 10 generals overseen by a *polemarchos*, or "war leader." Five of the generals wanted to march back to defend the walls of Athens; but the other five, led by the brilliant MILTIADES, convinced the polemarch, Callimachus, to attack. Apparently the timing involved a chance to catch the Persians without their cavalry; the Persian horsemen may have been reembarking to sail elsewhere, when the Athenian army charged.

Advancing quickly across the mile that separated the armies, the Greeks crashed into the Persian infantry ranks and sent both wings fleeing. In the center, the Persian spearmen stood firm but were destroyed when the two Greek wings—Athenians on the right and Plataeans on the left—wheeled inward in an unusual pincer movement.

The retreating Persians were slaughtered as they ran for their ships waiting inshore. The Greeks pursued them into the sea, right up to the ships. There Callimachus was killed. All but seven Persian ships got away, leaving behind 6,400 dead soldiers. The Athenians had lost 192. Later the

Athenian and Plataean dead were buried on the battlefield, under a mound still visible today.

A runner was sent to Athens to report the victory. (Twenty-five centuries later this run would be commemorated in the marathon footrace, first organized for the A.D. 1900 Paris Olympics.) Meanwhile, on distant Mt. Pentelicus, behind the battlefield, a shield was seen flashing in the morning sun—probably a heliographic signal to the Persian fleet. Presumably Hippias' Athenian partisans were reporting themselves ready to launch their coup d'etat. But no coup was ever attempted: The traitors were frightened off by news of the Athenian victory.

The Persian fleet sailed south and west around Cape Sunium, intending to land closer to Athens. But when they found the Athenian army waiting there, having marched from the battlefield, the Persians set sail for Asia. For the Persian command, the battle had demonstrated that future military action against mainland Greece would require a large army of occupation; 10 years later they would return with one.

The victory was a source of Greek religious awe. Legend claimed that the mythical Athenian hero THESEUS had been seen fighting alongside the Greeks and that an Athenian long-distance messenger had met the god PAN while running through the Arcadian wilds en route to SPARTA. For centuries afterward the battlefield was said to be haunted at night by the noise of combat.

Marathon inspired the confident outlook of a young generation of Athenians, who would defeat the Persians again (480–479 B.C.) and go on to forge an Athenian Empire. When the Athenian playwright AESCHYLUS died in 456 B.C., after a life full of honors, he recorded only one achievement in his epitaph: that he had fought at Marathon.

(See also OSTRACISM; PERSIAN WARS.)

marble   See ARCHITECTURE; SCULPTURE.

Marmara, Sea of   Modern name for the roughly diamond-shape saltwater body, 140 miles long and 40 miles wide at most, that connects the BOSPORUS and HELLESPONT seaways, along the northwestern coast of ASIA MINOR. The Greeks called this sea the Propontis—the "foresea" (i.e., in front of the BLACK SEA). The Propontis supplied a link in the crucial Greek TRADE route that brought metals and grain westward from the Black Sea.

Although not originally part of the Greek world, the Propontis had begun attracting Greek COLONIZATION by the early 600s B.C. Greek exploration is reflected (distortedly) in certain episodes in the legend of JASON (1) and the Argonauts.

The major Greek cities on the shores of the Propontis were CYZICUS and BYZANTIUM. The sea's abundant fish runs were commemorated in Cyzicus' COINAGE, which used a tuna as the city's emblem.

marriage   Ancient Greeks were monogamous; only the Macedonian royal house and certain other marginal traditions allowed for multiple wives. Brides could be as young as 14 in certain eras and locales, but more likely 18. The groom might be as much as 20 years older than the bride.

The earliest form of marriage was a purchase: The groom acquired the bride for a price, paid to her father or male guardian. The bride's consent was not necessary. At ATHENS in the 400s–300s B.C. (the one ancient Greek society about which there exists considerable information), the exchange of money was usually a dowry, paid to the groom, from the bride's family. The marriage was considered complete upon the groom's ritualized acceptance of the dowry or promise thereof.

The goddess of marriage was HERA, but the wedding did not require any clergy. The principal ceremony, for families with means, was a wedding feast, typically held at the bride's father's house. Afterward the veiled bride left her father's home and accompanied her husband to his house. A procession of revelers followed, and when bride and groom entered the wedding chamber the well-wishers stood outside the closed door and sang the epithalamion (outside-the-bedroom song).

The purpose of marriage was to make children. In the Athenian marriage ceremony the bride's guardian announced, "I give this woman for the begetting of legitimate offspring." The question of legitimacy bore on citizenship: By laws prompted by the statesman PERICLES in 451 B.C., an Athenian citizen could legally marry only another citizen, and citizenship for children was confined to the legal offspring of such marriages.

The exclusive emphasis on procreation rather than love, in a society that otherwise devalued WOMEN, tended to make Greek marriages unromantic. Husbands might find adventure outside marriage—with SLAVES, PROSTITUTES, or in the homosexual pursuits of the GYMNASIUM and other male gathering places. The husband's businesslike view of marriage is conveyed in the words of a male Athenian courtroom speaker of the mid-300s B.C.: "Prostitutes we have for our pleasure, concubines for our daily refreshment, but wives to give us legitimate children and be faithful guardians of our homes" (*Against Neaera*, 122; ascribed to DEMOSTHENES (1)).

At Athens, a husband's extramarital liaisons were not punishable as adultery unless they happened to involve another man's wife. Adultery was defined as the liaison of a wife with a man not her husband—the offense was that it defied the husband's authority and created the possibility of illegitimate children. In cases of adultery, both the erring wife and her male lover could be severely punished. (Due to a lack of evidence, it is not known what the classical Athenians' attitude might have been toward wives taking female lovers, but it too was probably very disapproving. In any case, a wife's secluded, housebound life offered few chances to find lovers of any type.)

Greek divorce was simple. A husband could just dismiss his wife from the house, or the wife could decide to walk away. But to petition for return of her dowry, a woman had to present herself in a court of law, which was biased in favor of her husband. For example, when Hipparete, the estranged wife of the Athenian statesman ALCIBIADES (circa 420 B.C.), arrived at court for this purpose, Alcibiades appeared, lifted her up, and carried her home unchallenged.

(See also ADONIS; ASPASIA; HOMOSEXUALITY; LAWS AND LAW COURTS.)

Massalia Greek seaport in southern France, located just east of the mouth of the Rhone River; in modern times the major French city of Marseille. Massalia was established circa 600 B.C. by long-range Greek seafarers from PHOCAEA, in ASIA MINOR; the founding was associated with a sea battle in which the Phocaeans defeated rival Carthaginians in the area.

The Ligurian tribes of the region apparently welcomed the Greeks. Massalia prospered through TRADE with the Ligurians as well as with the CELTS of interior Gaul and the Celtic kingdom of Tartessus in southern Spain. The Massaliote Greeks soon established their own Mediterranean colonies, including Nicaea (modern Nice) and Emporion (meaning "seaport"—modern Ampurias, in southern Spain). These contacts supplied the raw metals—SILVER, IRON, tin, and lead—that the Massaliotes craved for manufacturing or lucrative export to Greece. In exchange the Greeks offered luxury goods, such as worked BRONZE. Greek goods made their way into the continent: Modern ARCHAEOLOGY has discovered Greek bronzes of the 500s B.C. (cauldrons, a helmet, vasehandles) in southern Spain, southern France, and at a site 100 miles southeast of Paris.

Another important Greek export was WINE, the key that unlocked the wealth of native peoples. Like the French fur traders of the 1600s A.D. who took brandy into the Canadian wilderness to sell to Indians for pelts, so did the ancient Greeks take Greek wine into interior Gaul, introducing it among the Celtic tribes. A later Greek writer (circa 20 B.C.) described how cheaply the Celts sold their SLAVES for wine, "trading a servant for a drink." In time, the peoples of southern France learned how to cultivate their own grapes. The creation of the French wine industry is not the least cultural legacy of the ancient Greeks.

This infusion of Greek influences up the Rhone in the 500s B.C. played a vital role in shaping the Celtic "La Tène" culture that was to emerge in Gaul in the next century. From the Greeks, the Gauls learned improved methods of FARMING, fortification, and local administration. They copied the Greek ALPHABET, which Julius Caesar would find still in use throughout Gaul in 59 B.C. Aspects of the Gauls' religious beliefs may have been shaped by images of the Greek gods. One ancient writer observed that it seemed as if Gaul had become part of Greece.

Circa 310–306 B.C. a Massaliote seafarer named Pytheas sailed through the Straits of Gibraltar and around the British Isles, perhaps reaching as far as Norway, in search of the sources of traded tin and other goods. Later ancient writers plausibly describe his exploration.

Massalia was known for the stability of its aristocratic government. Remote from the agitations of mainland Greece, the city thrived without social conflict, while keeping contact with the Greek homeland through such means as a Massaliote treasury house at DELPHI. For centuries, Massalia's only principal enemy was CARTHAGE, and Massalia finally allied itself with the Italian city of ROME against Carthage in the Second Punic War (218–201 B.C.). In 125 B.C. hostility from local tribes compelled Massalia to appeal to Rome, resulting in the Roman occupation of the region. The Romans called this territory "the province," Provincia—modern Provence.

(See also ARISTOCRACY; SHIPS AND SEAFARING.)

mathematics The study of mathematics represents the most permanent achievement of ancient Greek thought. Many aspects of modern mathematics, particularly the rules and nomenclature of geometry, derive from the Greeks.

The Greek term *mathematikē* simply means "learning." From the 500s B.C. the Greeks saw mathematics as an ideal study and exercise of pure intellect, relevant to PHILOSOPHY. The mystic philosopher PYTHAGORAS (circa 530 B.C.) sought the secrets of the universe in numbers, while PLATO (427–347 B.C.) undoubtedly found inspiration for his theory of Forms in the analogy of perfect mathematical concepts. The Greeks were not the only ancient mathematicians— the Babylonians (especially) and Egyptians were also masters in the field—but the Greeks' abiding contribution was their practice of devising rigorous proofs for their theorems.

Like modern peoples, the Greeks counted by 10s, but their numerical symbols were awkward. (Arabic numerals had not been invented yet.) By the 400s B.C. Greek numbers were represented mainly by modified letters of the Greek ALPHABET in accumulative combinations. For example 6,000 was written as ⴼX; 6,852 was ⴼXⴼHHHⴼII. While arithmetic calculations could be difficult, plane and solid geometry came more naturally to the Greeks, partly from the age-old inspiration of FARMING patterns and boundary demarcation—the Greek word *geometria* means "land survey." The study of geometry was at the heart of early Greek ASTRONOMY, as brilliant mathematicians such as Eudoxus of CNIDUS (circa 350 B.C.) and Apollonius of Pergē (circa 200 B.C.) devised geometric models to explain the heavenly bodies' movements.

As for the accumulation of mathematical knowledge, a brief sketch must suffice here. By about 500 B.C. Pythagoras had discovered the geometric theorem that still bears his name, which states that the squared value of the hypotenuse of a right triangle is equal to the sums of the squares of the two adjacent sides. The very concept of square numbers was a Pythagorean discovery; the category was used for numbers that could be shown as dots forming a square, such as:

```
              •   •   •

•    •        •   •   •

•    • (4)  or   •   •   • (9)
```

These and other principles probably had been uncovered by the Babylonians centuries before, but the Greeks most likely made independent discoveries rather than somehow copying Babylonian technique.

Most likely, the earliest Greek mathematical textbook was the now-lost *Elements of Geometry* by Hippocrates of CHIOS, circa 430 B.C., (He is not be confused with his contemporary, the physician HIPPOCRATES (1) of Cos.) Mathematics were emphasized at Plato's Athenian school of higher learning, the ACADEMY (founded circa 385 B.C.). The most important mathematician of the day was Plato's pupil Eudoxus, who lived circa 390–340 B.C. None of his writing survives, but he apparently developed the general laws of geometric proportion that now comprise Euclid's book 5. Eudoxus is probably the one who discovered that

...covered by

...ANDRIA (1),
...useum, had
...;. Among the
...), who wrote a
...survives today.
...s forth the total
...clid was not an
...tematic statement
...ar and methodical
...became canonical,
...ie *Elements'* first six
...were used in barely
...an and North Ameri-
...ury.

Greek mathematics in
...EDES of SYRACUSE (circa
...Pergē (active circa 200
...today as an inventor and
...ndbreaking mathematical
...e part of *On the Sphere and
the Cylinder,* ... ...roids, and the *Sand Reckoner*
(in which he invented a ... ...m for denoting very large
numbers). Of all his life's achievements, he is said to have
been most proud of a certain geometric proof, namely, that
a cylinder circumscribing a sphere will always have an area
in ratio 3–2 to the sphere.

Apollonius was born at a Greek city of southern ASIA
MINOR and studied mathematics at Alexandria with the
followers of Euclid. Later he sought the patronage of King
Attalus I of PERGAMUM. Apollonius' major treatise, *Conics,*
has survived in most part and provides a milestone in
post-Euclidean solid geometry. From Apollonius, for example, come the modern names by which the three types
of conic sections are known: ellipse, parabola, and hy-
perbola.

The most famous practical application of mathematics in
the ancient world was that of Eratosthenes of CYRENE (1),
who was head of the Alexandrian Library circa 245–194
B.C. and who used simple geometric principles to calculate
the earth's polar circumference. Eratosthenes discovered
that an upright stick would cast no shadow at noon on the
summer solstice at Syene (modern Aswan, in southern
EGYPT), while at the same moment a stick at Alexandria
would cast a small shadow at a 7.2-degree angle. Believing
Alexandria to be due north of Syene at a distance of 5,000
stades, Eratosthenes multiplied 5,000 by 50, in ratio to the
calculation $50 \times 7.2 = 360$. To the resultant figure of
250,000 stades he added 2,000 more, to offset possible
error. Assuming Eratosthenes' stade measure to equal 200
yards, then his figure for the earth's north-south circumference equals about 28,636 miles; assuming a stade measure
of 175 yards (as seems more likely, from the Alexandria–
Syene figure), then Eratosthenes' figure equals about
25,057 miles. This is remarkably close to the modern measurement of 24,805 miles.

(See also SCIENCE.)

Mausolus See HALICARNASSUS.

Medea In MYTH, the daughter of King Aeëtes of Colchis
and the niece of the witch CIRCE. Medea herself was a
sorceress; her name, Medeia, means "cunning." In the
story of JASON (1) and the Argonauts, as told by the epic
poet APOLLONIUS (circa 245 B.C.), the young Medea fell in
love with the handsome hero when he arrived at Colchis
in search of the Golden Fleece. Against her father's interest,
she helped Jason with magic ointments and instructions,
and escaped with him and the fleece aboard the ship *Argo.*

Later, on arriving at the city of Ioclus, in THESSALY,
Medea helped Jason avenge himself on his enemy, King
Pelias. First, she boiled a cauldron of water and magic
herbs for Jason's old father, Aeson. After submerging himself in the boiling water, Aeson emerged as a young man.
Medea then suggested that Pelias' daughters do the same
for him. But this time she supplied useless herbs, and
when the king entered his daughters' bath he was boiled
to death.

Ousted from Ioclus by Pelias' son, Jason and Medea
settled at CORINTH, where they had a son and daughter.
What followed is the subject of EURIPIDES' tragedy *Medea*
(431 B.C.). Learning that Jason planned to desert her and
marry Glauce—daughter of the Corinthian king—Medea
went insane with anger. She sent Glauce a robe and tiara
smeared in poison, resulting in the death of both the bride
and her father. Next, to avenge herself fully on Jason,
Medea stabbed both of their young children to death, then
flew off in a magic chariot, taking refuge with the Athenian
king Aegeus (father of THESEUS). Euripides' *Medea* provides
an almost modern study of pathological jealousy and hatred, emanating from a woman wronged.

Medes See PERSIA.

medicine Today knowledge of Greek medicine comes
largely from the surviving works of medical writers of
antiquity, from references in the works of nonmedical
writers, and from artwork depicting medical scenes. The
greatest Greek medical writer was Galen of PERGAMUM,
who lived in the 100s A.D. In the centuries before Galen,
existing medical knowledge was organized and written
down by HIPPOCRATES (1) of Cos and his followers (late
400s B.C. and after) and by various physicians based at
ALEXANDRIA (1).

To a surprising degree, the Greeks distinguished medicine from RELIGION or superstition. Although APOLLO, AS-
CLEPIUS, and other gods were believed to have healing
powers—and although crude healing magic existed—such
beliefs did not prevent the development of scientific methods. Since the Greeks lacked such modern marvels as
antibiotics and anesthesia, surgery was a drastic and dangerous recourse. There was also no knowledge of microor-
ganisms as the cause of disease. But a knowledge of
dietetics, healing herbs, primitive orthopedics, and techniques of bandaging provided the beginnings of Greek
medicine in the centuries prior to 400 B.C.

There was no medical licensing in ancient Greece. Physicians were considered to be on par with skilled craftsmen
such as poets or architects. The historian HERODOTUS mentions a famous Greek doctor, Democedes of CROTON, who
in the late 500s B.C. became the court physician to the

tyrant POLYCRATES of SAMOS and then to the Persian king DARIUS (1). But it is Hippocrates (circa 460–377 B.C.) who provides the first milestone.

On his native island of Cos, Hippocrates in circa 430 B.C. established a school to create standards of medical and ethical procedure: The modern "Hippocratic Oath" is one legacy of this school. The Hippocratics emphasized careful observation and diagnosis. Among the writings known as the Hippocratic Collection (produced by Hippocrates' followers in the late 400s and early 300s B.C.), the two books entitled *Epidemics*—presenting 42 case histories of severely ill patients—are unequaled in clarity by any extant European medical writing prior to the 16th century A.D. Modern readers of the *Epidemics* are able to identify cases of diphtheria and typhoid fever from the symptoms·described. It is a testament to the medical ignorance of the day, and to the honesty of the writer, that about 60 percent of the *Epidemics'* cases end with the patient's death.

Another Hippocratic writing is a treatise whose title is traditionally translated as *On the Nature of Man*. Written circa 400 B.C., this work presents the famous (but incorrect) theory of the Four Humors, destined to dominate medical thought for the next 2,000 years. According to the theory, the human body consists of four elementary fluids—blood, phlegm (*pituita*), yellow bile (*cholē*), and black bile (*melancholia*)—whose correct proportion maintains health and whose imbalance causes illness. One crude procedure of the day was to apply heated metal cups to a patient's skin, in an attempt to draw off any excessive humors; gravestones and other surviving artwork sometimes show the physician with two metal cups, as a badge of profession. The practice of bleeding a patient, to purge "excessive" blood, was another misguided procedure inspired by the Four Humors belief.

The 300s B.C. saw a growing interest in anatomy, due partly to the biological studies of ARISTOTLE and his school, the LYCEUM. Anatomical knowledge was greatly advanced by two Alexandrian physicians of the middle and late 200s B.C.—Herophilus of Chalcedon and Eristratus of Ceos, whose respective writings survive only in fragments but whose work is described by the Roman writer Celsus (first century A.D.). Working separately, Herophilus and Eristratus were among the first to perform dissection on the human body—and, according to rumor, they also practiced human vivisection in the name of medical knowledge, using condemned criminals handed over by royal permission. These doctors and their colleagues added greatly to the knowledge of human circulation and respiration, and several of the anatomical terms coined by them survive in use today.

(See also SCIENCE.)

Medusa   In MYTH, a winged female monster with hair of snakes and a face that caused any humans who looked at it to turn to stone. Medusa ("cunning") was mortal but had two immortal sisters, Sthenno ("strong") and Euryalē ("wide jumping"). Known collectively as the Gorgons ("grim ones"), they lived together in the far West. With the aid of the goddess ATHENA, the Greek hero PERSEUS cut off Medusa's head and put it in a bag. The head—with its abiding ability to petrify an onlooker—aided Perseus in

his subsequent adventures. The head was later given to Athena, who set it in the center of her cloak known as the aegis.

Clearly, in early Greek or pre-Greek RELIGION, Medusa and her sisters had an apotropaic function; that is, they were worshipped or represented as protective demons who could scare away evil from the community. The protective head of Medusa was said to be buried under the AGORA at Perseus' city, ARGOS. By the 600s B.C., Medusa (or an unspecified Gorgon) had became a favorite subject in PAINTING and SCULPTURE, particularly at CORINTH and at Corinthian colonies such as CORCYRA. Portrayed as a winged running demon grimacing at the viewer, the monster would be shown in vivid colors. Probably the best-known surviving example is the Gorgon pediment sculpture from the temple of ARTEMIS at Corcyra (circa 600–580 B.C.).

Megara (1)   City of south-central Greece, located in the widening, northeastern isthmus region known as the Megarid. Lying in a fertile valley near the Saronic Gulf and the island of SALAMIS (1), Megara is surrounded on three sides by mountains, which separate the city from the regions of ATHENS (to the north east), CORINTH (to the southwest), and THEBES (to the north). In particular, the southwestern mountain range, the Geranea, formed a natural barrier between central Greece and the PELOPONNESE, and was of strategic importance in Greek history.

After a promising start, the city slipped into a largely unhappy pattern of resistance to its powerful neighbors. Megara was founded by DORIAN GREEKS who had invaded the Peloponnese (circa 1100 B.C.). Unlike older Greek cities founded by pre-Greek inhabitants, Megara has a name that actually means something in Greek: "the great hall." In the age of TRADE and COLONIZATION (circa 800–550 B.C.), Megara was a foremost power, exporting its prized woolens and establishing the colonies Megara Hyblaea, on the east coast of SICILY (circa 750 B.C.), and Heraclea Pontica, on the south shore of the BLACK SEA (circa 560 B.C.). In the LELANTINE WAR (circa 720–680 B.C.), Megara sided with ERETRIA, the enemy of Megara's neighbor and rival, Corinth.

Like other commercial cities of this era, Megara came under the sway of TYRANTS. A certain Theagenes (circa 630 B.C.) seized power after leading the common people in slaughtering the nobles' cattle. Theagenes was the father-in-law of the Athenian aristocrat CYLON and seems to have played a role in Cylon's failed coup at Athens (circa 625 B.C.). Later the tyrant fell.

Engulfed by class war between nobles and commoners, the city declined, losing border land to Corinth and the coveted island of Salamis to Athens (mid-500s B.C.). The poems of the Megarian aristocrat THEOGNIS (circa 540 B.C.) are filled with hatred toward the common people, signifying the discord that drained Megarian power in these years.

As part of the Spartan alliance, the Megarians fought on sea and land against the Persian king XERXES' invasion of Greece (480–79 B.C.). Later, after seeking help against Corinth in a border dispute, Megara allied itself with Athens (460 B.C.). The Athenians occupied the region and helped set up a DEMOCRACY at Megara. They also built "long walls," extending the mile's distance between Megara and its port of Nisaea, on the Saronic Gulf. The walls turned Megara and Nisaea into a linked fortress, suppliable directly by sea and impregnable by land.

Ironically, Megara's defenses came into use against Athens. In the 430s B.C. the Megarians withdrew from the Athenian alliance, encroached on Athenian territory, and murdered an Athenian herald. The Athenian statesman PERICLES responded with the notorious Megarian Decree, which attempted to starve the Megarians into submission by placing embargoes on their food imports and their export trade. This hostile act alarmed the Spartans and other Greeks, and played a role in causing the PELOPONNESIAN WAR (431–404 B.C.).

As a Spartan ally near Athenian territory in the war, Megara was a constant target for the Athenians, who invaded the Megarid with a huge force in 431 B.C. and kept invading—without capturing the city—every year until 421 B.C. In 424 B.C. a faction within Megara attempted to betray the city to the Athenian general DEMOSTHENES (2); he seized Nisaea and the Long Walls, but Megara itself was saved by the Spartan general BRASIDAS.

A brief phase of prosperity came in the 300s B.C., when the city was host to a school of SCULPTURE and to the Megarian School of PHILOSOPHY (founded by Eukleides, a disciple of the Athenian SOCRATES). Thereafter, although still inhabited, Megara fades from history.

Megara (2)   See HERACLES.

Meleager   See CALYDONIAN BOAR HUNT.

Melian Dialogue   See THUCYDIDES (1).

Melos   Small island of the western AEGEAN SEA, in the island group known as the CYCLADES. ARCHAEOLOGY reveals that in the pre-Greek "Cycladic" culture of the third millennium B.C. Melos was the exclusive source of obsidian—a volcanic glass that when quarried and honed, supplied axblades, plowshares, and the like, in the days before general use of metals. By the 1600s B.C. Melos was an ally or subject of Minoan CRETE and by 1400 B.C. was part of the Aegean empire of the Mycenaean Greeks.

Circa 1000 B.C. Melos was occupied by DORIAN GREEKS from LACONIA. With its capital city, also called Melos, in the north of the island, Melos existed as a Dorian state amid the predominantly Ionian-Greek Cyclades. By about 475 B.C. the Cyclades were the heart of the Athenian-dominated DELIAN LEAGUE, of which Melos was not a member.

Melos remained neutral at the outbreak of the PELOPONNESIAN WAR between ATHENS and SPARTA (431 B.C.). The Athenians attacked Melos in 426 B.C., and in 416 B.C. they again landed there, demanding that Melos join the Delian League. The Melians refused, preferring to look for help from their kinsmen the Spartans. This "Melian Dialogue" provides one of the set pieces of THUCYDIDES' (1) history of the Peloponnesian War (book 5). Although the dialogue often has been interpreted as an argument between Might and Right, it seems clear that Thucydides' heart is with the Athenians, who deliver their argument in terms of expedience and common sense. In any case, Melos city was besieged and captured by the Athenians, who enslaved and deported the islanders and planted an Athenian garrison colony there.

The celebrated statue called the Venus de Milo, now in the Louvre, is a marble APHRODITE discovered at Melos in A.D. 1820. ("Milo" being the Italian form of Melos.) Dated to the 100s B.C., it is probably a copy of a lost original of the 300s B.C..

(See also BRONZE AGE; MINOAN CIVILIZATION; MYCENAEAN CIVILIZATION.)

Memnon   In Greek MYTH, Memnon was an Ethiopian king, son of the dawn goddess Eos and the mortal man Tithonus. Memnon, whose name means "resolute," led a contingent of his countrymen to TROY, to help defend the city against the Greeks in the TROJAN WAR. In battle Memnon slew NESTOR's son Antilochus, but was himself killed by the Greek champion, ACHILLES. The dawn goddess carried away her son's corpse, and the great god ZEUS revived him as an immortal in heaven. The story of Memnon was told in a now-lost epic poem, the *Aithiopis*.

Memnon was a favorite subject of Greek vase painting in the 500s and 400s B.C. Like other mythological figures from Ethiopia, he was sometimes shown with distinctly negroid facial features. During the HELLENISTIC AGE (300–150 B.C.), the Greeks in EGYPT associated Memnon with certain preexisting monuments of the ancient pharaohs, including the so-called Colossi of Memnon—two huge sandstone statues of Pharaoh Amenophis III, seen at Luxor today.

(See also BLACK PEOPLES.)

Menander   Athenian comic playwright of the late 300s–early 200s B.C. Menander (Greek: Menandros) is the last great Athenian literary artist whose writings have survived from antiquity. He wrote over 100 plays, yet only one complete work exists today: *The Misanthrope* (Greek: *Duskolos*). Portions of other plays are known from quotations by later ancient authors and by modern archaeological discoveries of papyrus remnants in EGYPT, where Menander was apparently a favorite author of the Greco-Roman educated classes during the Roman Empire.

Little is known of his life. Born in 342 or 341 B.C., he grew up in an ATHENS that was well past its imperial prime and was dominated (like all of Greece) by the powerful kingdom of MACEDON. Menander apparently moved in the highest circles of Athenian society and politics. He studied under the Aristotelian philosopher THEOPHRASTUS and was a friend of Demetrius of Phalerum, an Athenian who served as governor for the Macedonian king CASSANDER. Demetrius' overthrow in 307 B.C. is said to have put Menander in temporary danger.

In 321 B.C., at about age 20, Menander won his first drama-victory, when his comedy *Anger* (not extant today) took first prize at an Athenian festival. His surviving masterpiece, *The Misanthrope*, won first prize in 316 B.C., at the midwinter festival called the Lenaea. Among his plays that survive in part today are *The Woman from Samos*, *The Hated Lover*, and *The Girl with the Short Haircut*.

Menander died in around 291 B.C., having won first prize eight times—a respectable but not dazzling record. However, his reputation grew soon after his death, and he came to be considered one of the classic Athenian authors. His plays served as models for the work of the Roman comic playwrights Plautus (circa 200 B.C.) and Terence (circa 150 B.C.).

For modern readers, *The Misanthrope* was discovered on an ancient papyrus only in A.D. 1958. (The French comic playwright Molière may have known the title but did not have the play as a model for his own *Misanthrope*, performed in A.D. 1666.) Set in the Athenian countryside, Menander's fanciful tale involves an old farmer, Knemon, who loathes humanity and lives, secluded, with his daughter. A rich young man, falling in love with the daughter, poses as a rustic laborer in order to win her hand in MARRIAGE. He succeeds after pulling Knemon out of a well where the old man has fallen.

Ancient and modern scholars have seen Menander's work as the high point of the "New Comedy" (circa 321–264 B.C.), which marks the last phase of evolution for Athenian stage comedy. "Old Comedy," as developed by ARISTOPHANES and others in the 400s B.C., was the product of the powerful Athenian city-state; Menander and the New Comedy are products of the more cosmopolitan and uncertain HELLENISTIC AGE, where most citizens lived cut off from major political events. Whereas Old Comedy presented fantasy, political satire, and obscene farce, New Comedy offered realistic settings and domestic plots, often "boy meets girl." In keeping with other conventions of New Comedy, Menander's plays show a great reduction in the onstage role of the comic chorus, which is used only for song-and-dance interludes.

(See also THEATER.)

Menelaus In MYTH, king of Lacedaemon and younger brother of King AGAMEMNON of MYCENAE. Menelaus was married to the Spartan princess Helen, later known as HELEN OF TROY. At the prompting of the love goddess APHRODITE, Helen abandoned Menelaus to elope with the Trojan prince PARIS. It was to punish this outrage that Agamemnon organized the Greek expedition against TROY, in the TROJAN WAR.

In the *Iliad* (book 3) Menelaus agrees to settle the entire war by single combat with Paris. Menelaus overwhelms his rival, but is deprived, by Aphrodite, of the chance to kill him. In the *Odyssey* Menelaus is shown briefly, back home with Helen and reconciled with her.

Messana See ZANCLE.

Messenia Southwest region of the PELOPONNESE. Messenia's eastern frontier is separated from the Spartan region of LACONIA by the lofty Mt. Taygetus range; on the west and south, Messenia is bounded by the sea; and in the north, it borders ELIS and ARCADIA. Largely mountainous, Messenia includes the westernmost of the Peloponnese's three southern peninsulas, Cape Acritas.

The heart of the region is the fertile Messenian plain, opening southward around the River Pamisus to the Mes-

senian Gulf. On the west coast, a second, narrower plain was home to a thriving kingdom in Mycenaean times, circa 1400–1200 B.C. Later Greeks remembered this kingdom by the name PYLOS and associated it with the mythical king NESTOR. This domain vanished prior to or during the invasion of the DORIAN GREEKS, circa 1100–1000 B.C., and consequently, Messenia became a Dorian region.

Messenia had a tragic history, being the most complete victim of Spartan domination. In the 700s B.C. the Spartans, crossing the Taygetus range, began their long campaign of conquest. The First and Second Messenian wars (circa 730–710 B.C. and circa 650–620 B.C.) were bitter conflicts; the Messenian leaders Aristodemus and Aristomenes were later remembered for their failed, heroic defense. By 620 B.C. the Messenian plain was in Spartan hands, and those Messenians who had not fled were virtually enslaved as Spartan-owned HELOTS.

Under the helot system, the Messenians were serfs, owned in common by the Spartan state. They were not deported to Sparta, but were left on the Messenian land (which they no longer owned), to farm it and produce food for their overlords. Half of all their produce went to Sparta.

The Messenians were allowed to maintain their local cults, customs, and family structures, but they were brutalized and terrorized. The Spartan poet TYRTAEUS writes of a Messenian's hopeless drudgery and his dutiful mourning when his Spartan master dies. Discipline was maintained by Spartan garrisons and by the Krypteia—the Spartan "secret society" whose job was to identify and do away with subversive helots. The Spartans' ferocity toward the Messenians—who were, after all, their fellow Dorian Greeks—comprised the single most warped aspect of the Spartan mentality.

The Third Messenian War was a rebellion sparked by news of a devastating earthquake at Sparta (464 B.C.). The revolt died with the surrender of the Messenian hilltop fortress of Ithome ("the step"), circa 460 B.C. At least some of the Messenian defenders were permitted to depart under safe-conduct, and the Athenians later relocated them to NAUPACTUS, a city on the northwest shore of the Corinthian Gulf.

During the PELOPONNESIAN WAR (431–404 B.C.) Messenian helots served their Spartan masters loyally while, on the other side, refugee Messenians fought as valuable Athenian allies. After the Athenian victory at the site called Pylos, on Navarino Bay (425 B.C.), the Athenians built a fortified naval base there. But the hoped-for Messenian revolt against Sparta never materialized.

Messenia was finally liberated in 369 B.C. by the Theban statesman and general EPAMINONDAS, after his destruction of a Spartan army in 371 B.C. Under Epaminondas' guidance, the Messenians founded a city, Messene (modern Messini), to be the capital of the new, free territory. Messene and Messenia thrived for a century, but suffered in the 200s and 100s B.C. from the intervention of MACEDON and the Achaean League, before passing into the hands of ROME after 146 B.C.

(See also ACHAEA; DEMOSTHENES (2); ZANCLE.)

meter See EPIC POETRY; LYRIC POETRY.

metics   Resident aliens of legal status. A metic (Greek: *metoikos*, "dweller among") was usually a Greek who had immigrated to a Greek city other than his birthplace. Metics abounded in the wealthier and more populous Greek cities, but their existence is best attested at ATHENS.

The rules for acquiring metic status and the legal restrictions applying to metics somewhat resembled those surrounding resident aliens in the United States today. The applicant had to be sponsored by a citizen, had to register in an Athenian DEME (city ward), and had to pay a special annual tax. Metics owed the state certain public duties and military service, usually as crewmen in the Athenian navy. They could not set foot inside (much less vote at) the Athenian political ASSEMBLY, usually could not own land, and could not marry an Athenian citizen. In exchange, metics enjoyed the courts' protection, the right to engage in business, and a recognized position in the community. At Athens, much of the import-export and manufacturing was in the hands of metics, some of whom became very rich. One example is the Syracusan-born Cephalus, father of the orator LYSIAS. The most famous person who was a metic at Athens was ARISTOTLE.

(See also POLIS.)

Midas   Last king of the wealthy, non-Greek nation of Phrygia, in ASIA MINOR. Midas reigned through the late 700s B.C. and was said to be the first non-Greek to send gifts to the god APOLLO's shrine at DELPHI, that is, the first foreign ruler to open diplomatic relations with mainland Greece. He also was said to have married the daughter of the king of the east Greek city of CYMĒ, in Asia Minor. Midas died when his kingdom was overrun by the nomadic Cimmerians, circa 696 B.C.

On account of his fabulous wealth, Midas—like the later king CROESUS of LYDIA—became a figure in Greek legend. Best known is the tale of the Midas Touch. Offered any wish by the god DIONYSUS, Midas asked that whatever he touched might turn to GOLD. But, finding that this ruined the food that he touched, he prayed to lose the gift. In another version, it was his daughter whom he accidentally turned to gold.

Miletus   Greek city on the central west coast of ASIA MINOR, preeminent in TRADE, COLONIZATION, and cultural achievements in the 600s–500s B.C. Situated at the mouth of the River Maeander, Miletus enjoyed communication seaward and inland. According to archaeological evidence, this advantageous site was occupied in the second millennium B.C. first by Minoans, then by Mycenaean Greeks, and last by non-Greek Carians. Around 1000 B.C. IONIAN GREEKS arrived and founded the historical Miletus, which became the southernmost city of the Greek region known as IONIA. The city's patron god was APOLLO.

Expert seafarers, the Milesians led the way in the expansion of the Greek world in the 600s B.C. They exported prized woolens and metalwork, and founded a remarkable string of colonies along the trade route to the BLACK SEA, as far as distant Crimea.

By the late 600s B.C. Miletus was ruled by TYRANTS. In the mid-500s B.C. Miletus and the rest of Ionia were conquered by King CROESUS of LYDIA, only to be conquered

shortly thereafter by the Persian king CYRUS (1). From about 546 to 499 B.C. Miletus enjoyed privileged status under the Persians, who maintained control through a series of Greek puppet rulers.

In the 500s B.C. the wealthy city witnessed the twin birth of PHILOSOPHY and SCIENCE, as the Milesian School of natural philosophers—THALES, ANAXIMANDER, and ANAXIMENES—took the first, revolutionary steps toward explaining the universe in nonreligious terms. Another innovative Milesian thinker of the day was the geographer HECATEAUS.

But the city's heyday was ending. After leading the doomed IONIAN REVOLT against Persian overlordship, Miletus was captured, sacked, and depopulated by the vengeful Persians (probably in 493 B.C.). The survivors were resettled inside PERSIA. Miletus recovered, but not as a world power. After Ionia was liberated by the Greeks in 479 B.C., Miletus joined the Athenian-dominated DELIAN LEAGUE. Then governed as a DEMOCRACY, the city was an Athenian ally for much of the PELOPONNESIAN WAR. But in 412 B.C., Miletus revolted from Athens and became a naval base for the Spartan side. In 386 B.C. the Spartans returned Miletus and all Ionia to Persian rule, by the terms of the KING'S PEACE.

In 334 B.C. Ionia was again freed of Persian rule, this time by the Macedonian king ALEXANDER THE GREAT, who stormed Miletus to capture it from a Persian garrison. In the HELLENISTIC AGE (circa 300–150 B.C.), Miletus enjoyed self-rule, prosperity, and an admirable building program, but the gradual silting up of the harbor brought economic decline. In Roman times Miletus was eclipsed by its neighbors EPHESUS and Smyrna.

(See also CYZICUS; MINOAN CIVILIZATION; MYCENAEAN CIVILIZATION; PANTICAPAEUM; PHRYNICHUS; SINOPE.)

Miltiades   Athenian general and politician who lived circa 550–489 B.C. Miltiades masterminded the Athenian victory over the invading Persians at the Battle of MARATHON (490 B.C.) and afterward enjoyed a brief preeminence at ATHENS before succumbing to political enemies. He was the first of a series of dynamic Athenian leaders in the 400s B.C.

Born into the rich and aristocratic Philaïd family, he began his career under the Athenian tyrant HIPPIAS (1). In around 522 B.C. Miltiades left Athens for the Thracian CHERSONESE—the 50-mile-long peninsula that forms the European side of the HELLESPONT—to rule the region, inherited from his maternal uncle, the elder Miltiades.

There the young Miltiades reigned as *turannos* (dictator) over native Thracians and Athenian colonists, but served as a vassal of the Persian king DARIUS (1). Miltiades married a Thracian king's daughter, who bore his son CIMON. Like other eastern Greek rulers, Miltiades took part in Darius' expedition across the Danube into Scythia (circa 513 B.C.). However, after participating in the doomed IONIAN REVOLT against Darius, Miltiades fled back to Athens (493 B.C.).

Athens, by then a full-fledged DEMOCRACY, was entirely different from the place that Miltiades had left 30 years before. In the turbulent political climate, Miltiades had enemies who resented his prior dictatorship in the Chersonese and his association with Hippias. But before long

Miltiades moved to the political fore, being elected as one of Athens' generals for the year 490 B.C.

That summer, when a seaborne Persian army landed at Marathon with the aim of capturing Athens, it was Miltiades who convinced the Athenian commander-in-chief to attack, rather than just defend the city walls. The Battle of Marathon—a complete victory by an outnumbered force over a supposedly invincible foe—was one of the crucial moments in Greek history. The unique battle plan, involving an enveloping tactic by the army's wings, probably came from Miltiades.

His glory lasted barely a year. Ambitious, he led a 70-ship Athenian fleet to seize Paros, a wealthy Greek island that had submitted to Darius. But the attack failed, and the 60-year-old Miltiades, with a badly injured knee, returned to face public anger at Athens. The left-wing leader XANTHIPPUS accused Miltiades of deceiving the Athenian people. The hero of Marathon was tried and convicted in the ASSEMBLY and fined a ruinous 50 TALENTS. Soon Miltiades died from his gangrenous injury, and the fine was paid by the young Cimon (himself destined to become the foremost Athenian soldier and statesman of his day).

Among the ancient artifacts now displayed at the OLYMPIA museum is a Greek HOPLITE helmet discovered by archaeologists in A.D. 1961 and inscribed with the words in Greek, "Miltiades dedicated this to Zeus." Presumably it is Miltiades' own helmet, worn at the Battle of Marathon and afterward given as an offering to the king of the gods and the lord of victory.

(See also PERSIAN WARS; ZEUS.)

Mimnermus   Early Greek lyric poet of Colophon, in western ASIA MINOR (latter 600s B.C.). His work survives only in fragments. He was a writer of the elegy—a form meant to be sung to flute accompaniment—and many of his verses were love poems addressed to a flute girl named Nanno. Mimnermus was a forerunner of the later love elegists of ALEXANDRIA (1) and imperial ROME. His best-known fragment deals with a topic destined to become a favorite of Greek and Latin poets: the transience of youth and the implacable approach of old age and death.

(See also LYRIC POETRY.)

Minoan Civilization   A name invented in A.D. 1900 by the British archaeologist Sir Arthur Evans, to describe the civilization of ancient CRETE, of roughly 2200–1400 B.C. Evans was the first to discover remnants of this accomplished society, the earliest imperial power in Europe. Evans' adjective "Minoan" refers to a hero in Greek mythology, the powerful Cretan king MINOS.

The Minoans were not Greeks, and their language, RELIGION, and social structures were not Greek. Most of what is known or can be guessed about the Minoans comes from modern ARCHAEOLOGY on Crete. (The little island of THERA also has yielded an important Minoan site.) Evidence suggests that the Minoans emerged from a fusion between existing Cretan inhabitants and invaders from ASIA MINOR during the era 2900–2200 B.C. These people became master seafarers and built a society inspired partly by contact with the Egyptian Old Kingdom (circa 2650–2250 B.C.). By about 1900 B.C. the Minoans were acquiring an AEGEAN SEA em-

The famous Toreador Fresco from the palace at Cnossus in Crete, circa 1500 B.C. The scene shows the mysterious Minoan practice of bull leaping: A male dancer, painted as red-skinned, vaults over the bull's back, with two female dancers nearby. The speed of the bull's charge is denoted by the elongated body and outstretched legs. This sport may have been a religious rite, intended to capture the strength and sexual power of the bull.

pire and were constructing palaces on Crete—at CNOSSUS, Phaestus, Mallia, and Khania—that were bigger and more elaborate than any buildings outside the Near East. So confident were the Minoans in their naval power that they declined to encircle their palaces with defensive walls.

Wealth came from Cretan FARMING and fishing, from taxes paid by subject peoples in the CYCLADES and other Aegean locales, and from long-distance TRADE. Minoan objects discovered by archaeologists outside Crete indicate two-way commerce with EGYPT, Asia Minor, and the Levant as well as with western ITALY (a region that offered raw tin and copper, the components of BRONZE). But much Minoan trade, especially after 1600 B.C., was with the northwestern Aegean mainland now called Greece, where Greek-speaking tribes had been settling since about 2100 B.C.

The Minoans' importance for Greek history is that they supplied the model for the Greeks' MYCENAEAN CIVILIZATION, which arose on the mainland circa 1600 B.C. The Mycenaean fortress palaces at MYCENAE, TIRYNS, and elsewhere were warlike imitations of Minoan palaces on Crete. Mycenaean skills in metalworking, POTTERY-making, and other handicrafts were improved by copying Cretan models. The Mycenaean form of WRITING—a syllabary script that modern scholars call LINEAR B, invented soon before 1400 B.C.—was copied from the Minoan system (a yet-undeciphered script called Linear A). Eventually the Mycenaeans were ready to challenge Minoan supremacy in the Aegean.

Daily scenes of the Minoans' life are preserved on some of their beautiful art objects, which include cut gems, worked GOLD, terra-cotta figurines, vase paintings, and frescoes. Sensuous and modern-seeming in design, Minoan pictorial art favors sea animals and other subjects from nature. Religious scenes often show a goddess (or priestess) with a subordinate male figure or with wild beasts, such as lions, in tame postures. Evidence of this kind leads many scholars to conclude that Minoan religion was centered on a mother goddess or a group of goddesses overseeing nature and bounty. Aspects of Minoan worship apparently infiltrated Greek religion in the cult of certain goddesses, such as ARTEMIS and HERA.

The Minoans ascribed religious or magical power to dancing and to the remarkable athletic performance now known as bull leaping. Minoan reverence for the bull is probably reflected in Greek MYTHS of later days, such as the interrelated tales of Minos and of THESEUS and the Minotaur, or the tale of HERACLES and the Cretan bull.

Minoan high society probably revolved around a priest-king or priest-queen whose capital city was Cnossus and whose royal emblem was the *labrus*, a double-headed ax. Scenes in art suggest a confident, vivacious life at court. Upper-class WOMEN—portrayed as wearing flounced skirts and open-breasted tunics—apparently played prominent roles in court life (as opposed to the secluded existence of women in Greece in later centuries).

The material level enjoyed by the Minoan ruling class was probably unsurpassed anywhere before the late 19th century A.D. The Cnossus palace, reaching three stories in parts, boasted clay-piped plumbing and a clever system of air wells to bring light and ventilation to interior rooms. COINAGE had not yet been invented, but Minoan wealth was measured in luxury items and in farm surplus such as sheep, pigs, and olive oil (great quantities of which were stored at Cnossus).

The Minoan golden age on Crete, circa 1900–1450 B.C., was a time of peace but was troubled by natural disasters. Archaeology at Cnossus shows that the palace was destroyed twice by earthquake, circa 1730 and 1570 B.C. Circa 1480 B.C. Cretan coastal regions suffered damage and depopulation, possibly caused by tidal waves from the volcanic explosion of Thera, 70 miles away.

The Cnossus palace, on high ground, survived, but new archaeological signs of distress in the mid-1400s B.C. include proliferation of war equipment and the first appearance on Crete of the horse (presumably imported as a tool of war). Overseas, Minoan pottery from this time is absent from certain sites—a sign of disrupted trade routes. Presumably a foreign enemy or number of enemies, taking advantage of Cretan natural disaster, had begun to cut into the Minoan Empire. These enemies surely included groups of Mycenaean Greeks.

In about 1400 B.C. or soon after, all the Cretan palaces were destroyed by fire, presumably in war. The most obvious explanation for this simultaneous destruction is a Mycenaean invasion of Crete. Intriguingly, archaeological evidence suggests that, prior to this invasion, Mycenaean Greeks had already taken over the Cnossus palace and that it was they who were destroyed in the palace's ruin. There may have been rival Mycenaean armies, battling each other for control of Crete.

Although the Mycenaean victors seem to have abandoned Crete soon after 1400 B.C., the Minoan culture was finished.

(See also ATLANTIS; BRONZE AGE; DAEDALUS; LABYRINTH; SHIPS AND SEAFARING.)

Minos   According to Greek MYTH, Minos was a Cretan king who ruled the AEGEAN SEA with fleets of warships in olden times. A son of the god ZEUS and the Phoenician princess EUROPA, Minos was born in CRETE with his two brothers, Rhadamanthys and Sarpedon. As a young man at the royal city of CNOSSUS, Minos married Pasiphaë, daughter of the sun god, HELIOS. During a dispute over who should become the next king of Crete, Minos prayed to the god POSEIDON to send a bull from the sea as a sign of divine favor. The bull emerged, thus assuring Minos of the kingship; but the pure-white animal was so beautiful that Minos neglected to sacrifice it to Poseidon, as he had promised to do.

In retaliation, the god inspired Pasiphaë with an unnatural lust for the animal, and she acquired—from the immigrant Athenian craftsman DAEDALUS—a wooden device that disguised her as a cow. In this costume she approached the bull and was mounted by it. She conceived its child, which proved to be a grotesque creature, half human, half bull—the Minotaur (Greek: Minotauros, "the bull of Minos").

To hide the Minotaur, Minos angrily ordered the meddling Daedalus to build the palace known as the LABYRINTH. Then Minos imprisoned Daedalus and his son, Icarus, inside a tower. But Daedalus escaped from Crete on mechanical wings. (Icarus fell to his death en route.)

By ship, Minos pursued Daedalus to SICILY, where he was treacherously murdered in his bath by King Cocalus' daughters, who did not want to relinquish the miraculous inventor Daedalus. Zeus then installed Minos as one of the judges of the dead in the Underworld.

The Minos legend probably represents the Greeks' distorted memory of the great days of Cretan wealth and naval power, circa 1950–1450 B.C. For this reason, in A.D. 1900 the pioneering British archaeologist Sir Arthur Evans coined the adjective "Minoan" to describe that real-life civilization on Crete. The name Minos is not Greek in origin and may possibly have been a hereditary royal title of the Minoan rulers.

(See also AFTERLIFE; MINOAN CIVILIZATION.)

Minotaur   See LABYRINTH; MINOS; THESEUS.

Minyans   In MYTH, the Minyans (Greek: Minuai) were a powerful Greek clan that had controlled parts of BOEOTIA and THESSALY in the old days. This legend probably commemorates an actual northern Greek dynasty of the Mycenaean era, circa 1200 B.C. Relatedly, in the Thessalian-based legend of JASON (1) and the Argonauts, the Argonauts traditionally are referred to as Minyans.

The modern term *Minyan Ware* was coined by archaeologist Heinrich Schliemann in A.D. 1880 to describe a kind of POTTERY he had discovered at the Boeotian city of ORCHOMENUS. The pottery, now dated to circa 1900 B.C., usually is considered to have been made by early Greeks—that is, by early descendants of the Greek-speaking invaders who occupied mainland Greece after about 2100 B.C.

(See also MYCENAEAN CIVILIZATION.)

Mitylene   See MYTILENE.

Muses   Greek goddesses of poetry, MUSIC, dance, and the arts in general. The word *Muse* (Greek: Mousa) is related to *mousikē*, "music." In MYTH, they were the daughters of ZEUS and Mnemosyne—that is, the god of universal order and the goddess Memory—and this is surely a metaphor for the reliance on verse rhythm and the singer's memory in the traditional technique of oral composition, prior to the spread of literacy.

The Muses, together or individually, were imagined as inspiring human song and poetry. HOMER'S *Odyssey* (written circa 750 B.C.) opens with an appeal to an unspecified Muse to help the poet sing about his subject. In his epic poem *Theogony* (circa 700 B.C.), HESIOD describes how the Muses approached him on Mt. Helicon, in BOEOTIA, and breathed the gift of song into him. Hesiod named nine goddesses, but it was only a later elaboration that assigned to each Muse a separate function. The nine were Calliope, Clio, Euterpe, Terpsichore, Erato, Melpomene, Thalia, Polyhymnia, and Urania.

(See also APOLLO; EPIC POETRY; WRITING.)

music Greek music—*mousikē*, "the art of the MUSE"—was closely related to the recitation of Greek poetry. Greek poetic meter was a form of rhythm, and verses were sung or chanted to instrument accompaniment. The two principal instruments were the lyre (*lura*), a stringed instrument played by plucking, and the *aulos*, a wind instrument often described as a flute but really more akin to our clarinet or oboe. The lyre's sound was considered dignified and soothing, while flute music was more exciting.

The lyre was associated with the god APOLLO, lord of order and harmony. The ennobling and civilizing power of music was emphasized in legends of the great lyre musicians, such as ORPHEUS, who could charm wild beasts with his song, or Amphion, whose music brought stones trooping of their own accord to build the perimeter wall of THEBES. By contrast, the flute was associated with the riotous god DIONYSUS.

Different forms of poetic verse were considered appropriate to each instrument. The lyre had very ancient associations with the singing or chanting of EPIC POETRY. LYRIC POETRY (*lurikē melē*) too was developed primarily for lyre accompaniment, but by the mid-600s B.C. lyric had come to include verse forms such as the elegy, intended for flute music. Early surviving verses of elegy—such as those by the poets CALLINUS (mid-600s B.C.) and TYRTAEUS (circa 630 B.C.)—convey military-patriotic themes, intended to rouse and encourage an audience. Other forms of flute poetry included the dithyramb, which was a choral song sacred to Dionysus. Descended from the dithyramb (by the late 500s B.C.) was the choral ode of Athenian stage tragedy, also accompanied by flutes.

Flute and lyre had important functions in other walks of life. Instructions in lyre-playing formed an important part in the EDUCATION of upper- and middle-class boys at ATHENS. Flute-playing was more the resort of professional musicians, including SLAVES and PROSTITUTES. Flutes supplied lively dance music, also background music for SPORT competitions and for the drinking party known as the SYMPOSIUM. From about the mid-600s B.C. onward, Spartan armies always marched into battle with flute players, to keep the soldiers in step and rouse their courage. Stately flute music was used as background at sacrifices and other religious ceremonies.

Greek MYTH ascribed the lyre's invention to the god HERMES. In fact, the Greeks probably adopted the instrument in the second millennium B.C. from the Cretan MINOAN CIVILIZATION. The simplest form of lyre had a sound box of tortoiseshell (or wooden facsimile), with strings of gut stretched down from a crossbar between two extended horns. Seven strings was the conventional number, although archaeological evidence suggests some lyres had as many as 12. Unlike modern harp strings, lyre strings were uniform in length, but a skilled musician might vary the sound by stopping a string partway. A bigger, more elaborate form of lyre was the cithara (*kithara*), used mostly for public performance. With the instrument held in place by a strap, the cithara player typically used both hands—the bare fingers of his left hand and an ivory plectrum in his right.

The flute was made of wood, ivory, or bone, with a double reed in the mouthpiece. Artwork often shows a player blowing a pair of flutes, sometimes strapped around his or her head.

The question of Greek musical notation is obscure. Surviving artwork never shows musicians reading musical notes, but it is believed that some form of written musical notation did exist by the late 400s B.C.

Being a form of measurement susceptible to mathematical laws, yet with an emotional appeal, music was studied reverently by certain philosophers. PYTHAGORAS (circa 530 B.C.) sought in music the secrets of the universe. Similarly, PLATO (427–347 B.C.) saw music as a powerful force for either good or ill, with the ability to mold human character permanently.

The best-known musical theorist of ancient Greece was Aristoxenus (active circa 330 B.C.), who was born at TARAS and studied under ARISTOTLE at the LYCEUM. Of his works there currently exists, in part, *Principles and Elements of Harmonics* and *Elements of Rhythm*.

(See also APOLLO; PYTHIAN GAMES.)

Mycalē Mountain peninsula on the central west coast of ASIA MINOR, opposite the island of SAMOS, in the Greek-inhabited region known as IONIA. On Mycalē's north side was a sanctuary area called the Panionium, where delegates from the 12 Ionian cities met and where an annual Ionian festival was held. The site was sacred to POSEIDON.

In late summer of 479 B.C., at the end of the PERSIAN WARS, Cape Mycalē was the scene of a small but significant land battle, resulting in the liberation of Ionia after about 75 years of Persian domination. This battle supposedly occurred on the same day as the decisive Battle of PLATAEA, in mainland Greece.

At the Battle of Mycalē, a Greek force of about 4,400 HOPLITES landed from ships and destroyed a Persian army twice as large. More significantly, the Greeks then were able to burn the Persians' beached warships—numbering perhaps 100—which had comprised the last remnant of the Persian navy. (The rest had been destroyed at the Greek sea victory at SALAMIS the year before.) Without a navy, PERSIA became temporarily helpless to defend its other east Greek possessions, such as the HELLESPONT district or the island of CYPRUS, and these regions fell to the Greek counteroffensive in the following months.

The Greek commander-in-chief at Mycale was the Spartan king Leotychides, at the head of a Spartan contingent. But—according to the version told by the historian HERODOTUS—the brunt of the fighting was borne by the Athenian contingent, under command of the soldier-politician XANTHIPPUS.

In the battle's aftermath, Xanthippus and other Athenian commanders enrolled the nearby Aegean island states in a common alliance against Persia. This union led quickly to the creation of the DELIAN LEAGUE, the power base for the Athenian Empire during the next 75 years.

Mycenae   Greek city in the northeast PELOPONNESE, of great significance in early Greek history. Situated in the hills at the northeastern edge of the Argive plain, Mycenae was the capital of a rich and accomplished early Greek culture (circa 1600–1200 B.C.). The name MYCENAEAN CIVILIZATION was coined by the pioneering German archaeologist Heinrich Schliemann on the basis of his excavations at Mycenae in A.D. 1876. The ARCHAEOLOGY of the site has provided the single most important source of information about the Mycenaean Greeks, who left behind no written history.

Mycenae was one of the first places occupied by the invading Greek tribesmen of about 2100 B.C., but it predates their arrival. Archaeology shows that the site—commanding the fertile plain to the south and the land route northward to the isthmus—was first inhabited circa 3000 B.C. by Neolithic settlers. The Greek takeover of the region may be indicated in the destruction of a pre-Greek palace (often called the House of the Tiles) at Lerna, at the opposite edge of the Argive plain, circa 2100 B.C. Greek presence is almost certainly indicated in changes in style of POTTERY found at Mycenae, datable to about 1900 B.C. The Greek name Mukēnai has no apparent meaning in the GREEK LANGUAGE, and surely preserves a pre-Greek name.

Greek Mycenae's preeminence by the mid-millennium is clearly shown by the 31 lavish royal tombs now called Grave Circle A and Grave Circle B and dated to about 1550 B.C. and 1650 B.C., respectively. Circle A, located atop Mycenae's ACROPOLIS, was discovered by Schliemann; the tombs' treasure of GOLD and SILVER gave the first archaeological proof of the existence of an early-Greek high civilization.

Mycenae's heyday came in 1400–1200 B.C., when the huge limestone walls and hilltop citadel were built. Circa 1260 B.C. the city received its most distinctive surviving feature: the Lion Gate, surmounted by rampant carved-limestone lions (now headless).

To this era belongs the supreme Mycenae later recalled in the MYTHS of the classical Greeks—the city "rich in gold" (as the poet HOMER called it), with a high king who was overlord of many lesser Greek rulers. The legendary AGAMEMNON, king of Mycenae, raises an army against TROY, by summoning his various vassal kings. This is probably an accurate reflection of Mycenae's feudal dominance in the Mycenaean age.

Archaeology also tells the tale of the city's decline in the 1200s B.C. A series of burnings culminated circa 1200 B.C. in major destruction, which probably indicates internal strife or several defeats at the hands of other Mycenaean-

The monumental Lion Gate at Mycenae, built circa 1250 B.C., when Mycenae was the greatest city in Greece. Seen from outside the wall, the 10-foot-tall, carved-limestone slab shows two lions (now minus their heads) flanking a pillar. The lions' heraldic stance may derive from the adoring postures of animals in certain Minoan religious art. Architecturally, the slab relieves the weight on the massive lintel, which stretches over a 10.5-foot-high gateway.

Greek cities. There followed perhaps three generations of depopulation, culminating in Mycenae's final ruin, possibly at the hands of the invading DORIAN GREEKS (circa 1120 B.C.).

Later Mycenae existed as a Dorian town whose inhabitants probably lived amid the ruins of vanished grandeur. Men of Mycenae fought as allies of SPARTA against the Persians at THERMOPYLAE (480 B.C.) and PLATAEA (479 B.C.). This Mycenae was destroyed by its powerful neighbor ARGOS circa 468 B.C., but reemerged in the 200s B.C.

(See also ATREUS; TROJAN WAR.)

Mycenaean Civilization   The term used by modern scholars to describe the earliest flowering of mainland Greek culture, circa 1600–1200 B.C. The Mycenaeans were Greeks whose warlike society rose and fell long before the era of classical Greece. The classical Greeks of circa 400 B.C. half remembered their Mycenaean forebears as a race of heroes, celebrated in MYTH and EPIC POETRY.

In world prehistory, the Mycenaeans comprised the last of several great civilizations to emerge in the eastern Mediterranean during the BRONZE AGE. The Mycenaeans' urban building, military organization, and TRADE seem to have been partly copied from a few preexisting, non-Greek, Bronze Age cultures—namely, the Middle and New Kingdoms of EGYPT, the Hittite kingdom of ASIA MINOR, and especially, the MINOAN CIVILIZATION of CRETE.

The adjective "Mycenaean" was coined in A.D. 1876 by the pioneering German archaeologist Heinrich Schliemann, on the basis of his spectacular discoveries at the site of MYCENAE, in the northeastern PELOPONNESE, in southern Greece. The Mycenaeans lived before the era of history-writing, and thus most details of their story—such as their rulers' names or the reasons why their entire society collapsed in fiery ruin around 1200 B.C.—remain unknown. Modern knowledge relies mostly on artifacts uncovered by ARCHAEOLOGY at a few sites, such as Mycenae, TIRYNS, and PYLOS (in the Peloponnese) and THEBES, ORCHOMENUS, and ATHENS (in central Greece). The artifacts include POTTERY, stone carvings, jewelry, and armor—most of it found in the tombs of rulers—as well as the remnants of Mycenaean stone palaces and defenses. Particularly, the sites of Mycenae and Tiryns still show huge fortifications built by Mycenaean inhabitants in the 1300s and 1200s B.C.

In addition, a few sites have yielded primitive Mycenaean written records, inscribed on clay tablets that seem

The face of early Western civilization. This beaten-gold mask, probably the best-known artifact from Mycenaean times, was among the treasures discovered at Mycenae in A.D. 1876 by German archaeologist Heinrich Schliemann. The mask had been placed over the face of a male corpse, presumably a king, who had lived circa 1550 B.C. His name is unknown to us, but he sometimes is misidentified as the mythical king Agamemnon (who belonged to a later century). The mask—shaped by being hammered over a hard form, such as carved wood—is probably the man's portrait, made during his lifetime.

to date from about 1400 B.C. or 1200 B.C., depending on the site. Written in a script that modern scholars call LINEAR B, the records have been deciphered mainly as lists of inventory—produce, livestock, military equipment—and accounts of goods-distribution, religious rites, and similar daily events. The tablets provide precious information on the social structure, economy, and RELIGION of the Mycenaeans, as well as on the early-stage GREEK LANGUAGE that they spoke.

Aside from archaeology, some insight into the Mycenaeans has been gained from a cautious reading of HOMER's epic poems, the *Illiad* and *Odyssey*. Although written circa 750 B.C., more than 400 years after the Mycenaeans' disappearance, these poems derive from oral tradition that stretches back to the Mycenaeans. It is believed that the poems faithfully record certain aspects of Mycenaean upper-class life—such as the warrior code and the network of local kings—amid distortions and overlays.

The first Greek-speaking tribes arrived in mainland Greece circa 2100 B.C., from the Danube region. But 500 years went by before the emergence of the culture that we call Mycenaean: The remarkable social and technological changes of these intervening centuries can only be guessed at. No doubt the Greeks were deeply influenced by the non-Greek people they had conquered, and from them the Greeks probably learned skills such as stone masonry, shipbuilding, navigation, the cultivation of the olive and certain other crops, and the worship of certain female deities (with associated, new spiritual concepts). Similarly, the Greeks were inspired by the palace society of Minoan Crete.

The Mycenaean era began around 1600 B.C., as archaeology reveals. Several sites in Greece came under control of powerful rulers who were buried in elaborate tombs, unlike the simple graves of prior centuries. And within a few generations the tomb designs altered again, suggesting further dynastic changes and evolving organization. The six treasure-filled tombs at Mycenae known as Grave Circle A—built in the era 1550–1500 B.C. and discovered intact by Schliemann—provide clear proof of the rulers' wealth and overseas contacts. For example, the tombs contain items of GOLD that were shaped by Greek smiths, but the raw metal probably came from Asia Minor or Egypt. The warlike nature of these leaders is suggested by the many weapons left as offerings in the tombs.

In Greece's terrain, where mountain ranges separate the flatlands, the Mycenaeans apparently emerged as four or so major kingdoms, each based at a large farming plain. Two of these domains were in the Peloponnese: the plain of ARGOS (with its capital at Mycenae) and the plain of MESSENIA (capital at Pylos). One was in central Greece: the plain of BOEOTIA (with the cities Thebes and Orchomenus vying for supremacy). And one was in the north, on the great plain of THESSALY (capital at Iolcus). Lesser kingdoms probably existed as well. But the greatest domain was Mycenae, as indicated by its signs of superior wealth and by the testimony of Greek myth. In Homer's *Illiad*, the Mycenaean king AGAMEMNON is the supreme commander, to whom all other kings, such as ODYSSEUS and NESTOR, owe obedience.

One event of the Mycenaean era that modern scholars are sure of is that by around 1450 B.C. Mycenaeans had

A lion hunt scene, inlaid on a Mycenaean dagger found at Mycenae. The dagger was deposited as an offering in a royal tomb circa 1575 B.C., not long after the dawn of Greek civilization. Two of the hunters carry the distinctively Mycenaean, hourglass-shape, ox-hide shields. In later centuries, wild lions did not inhabit mainland Greece: Either they were exterminated in the Mycenaean era, or this scene is imaginary, based on lion hunts shown in Near Eastern art.

taken over the Cretan palace at CNOSSUS—probably as the result of a Mycenaean naval invasion of Crete. Mysteriously, the Mycenaeans seem to have abandoned Crete soon thereafter, circa 1400 B.C. But the years of occupation there taught Mycenaean rulers certain organizational skills—such as improved architectural techniques and the use of Cretan WRITING (adapted at this time, as the Linear B script)—that ushered in 200 years of the Mycenaean heyday in mainland Greece, circa 1400–1200 B.C.

It was now that the Mycenaeans built their own palaces, adapted from the Minoan palaces on Crete. Mycenae and Tiryns were turned into elaborate, high-walled castles; other palaces, such as at Pylos, arose without huge defenses. The social and economic structure of these centers is partly revealed by the Linear B tablets. The palace was the seat of the king (*wanax* in Mycenaean Greek); beyond the capital city, a network of outlying villages paid taxes, obeyed the king's laws, and relied on him for defense against other rulers. Tha palace was also a center of industry, where metalworkers, weavers, perfumers, and many other crafts people turned out finished goods, to enrich the king or to be distributed by him. Raw materials came from local taxes (sheep's wool, for example) and from overseas trade.

The premier metal for war and industry was BRONZE (the use of IRON being introduced to the Greek world only later). The search for bronze's two components—copper and tin—led Mycenaean sea traders far and wide. Large remains of Mycenaean pottery in CYPRUS show that parts of that copper-rich island were colonized by Mycenaeans. On the western Asia Minor coast, the site of MILETUS probably became a Mycenaean trading colony, mainly for the acquisition of raw metals. Toward the other end of the Mediterranean, extant pottery suggests a Mycenaean presence in western ITALY, where tin could be found.

The Mycenaean rulers commanded armies of heavy infantry. The soldiers' standardized equipment, including bronze breastplates and helmets, is recorded on Linear B tablets. Various evidence paints a picture of Mycenaean kings or princes leading Viking-like raids overseas, of which the biggest were the (presumed) invasions of Crete and Cyprus. On certain Linear B tablets, SLAVES are mentioned by names that suggest they came from Asia Minor; probably they were captured in Mycenaean raids there. The Greek myth of JASON (1) and the Argonauts may distortedly commemorate such an overseas expedition. But the Mycenaean kingdoms fought also against each other: the legend of the SEVEN AGAINST THEBES seems clearly based on actual warfare between Mycenae and Thebes.

By about 1250 B.C. the Mycenaean world had come under pressure, due partly to upheavals in the Near East. The decline of the Hittite kingdom in Asia Minor probably brought a gradual closing of the Mycenaeans' eastern trade routes. Deprived of raw metals for industry and conquest, Mycenaean society began to whither. The Greek legend of the TROJAN WAR may recall the Mycenaeans' attempt to keep trade routes open by removing the interfering, non-Greek, Hellespontine city TROY, circa 1220 B.C.

Finally, it seems, the Mycenaean kingdoms turned against each other and destroyed each other, in a desperate bid for survival. Archaeology clearly reveals the fiery ruin of Thebes, Mycenae, and other centers in the 50 years leading down to 1200 B.C. At Pylos, the final days are dramatically indicated in emergency troop movements and religious sacrifices recorded on Linear B tablets.

Modern historians used to believe that this wholesale destruction was the work of outsiders—specifically, DORIAN GREEKS invading from the northwest. But more recent scholarship concludes that the Dorian invasion, circa 1100 B.C., was merely opportunistic: The Mycenaeans had already exhausted themselves through internal war.

In the villages outside of the wrecked palaces, Mycenaean society survived on an improverished scale during the 1100s B.C. Social change in these rural areas can be glimpsed in the development of a certain Greek word: The official title *quasireu*, which during the Mycenaean heyday had indicated a local sheriff (a relatively low position), gradually changed to *basileus* and took on a new meaning, "king." These men became the new local rulers within the disintegrated Mycenaean kingdoms.

(See also ACHAEA; ACHAEANS; ARCADIA; ATREUS; CHARIOTS; DARK AGE; FUNERAL CUSTOMS; PERSEUS (1); SHIPS AND SEAFARING; WARFARE, LAND.)

mystery cults See AFTERLIFE; DIONYSUS; ELEUSINIAN MYSTERIES; ORPHISM; SAMOTHRACE.

myth The Greek word *muthos* means simply "a tale." In modern use, that word has come to mean a popular tale, elaborated by generations of storytelling, that may contain a kernel of historical fact and that is significant for understanding a people's mass mentality.

Greek myths may reflect events in the distant past or popular unfulfilled aspirations. Some myths have a moral, such as the need to be hospitable to strangers. Other myths are "aetiological"; that is, they attempt to explain local geographical features, religious rites, or other phenomena not fully understood by other means. Related to this type is the propagandistic "charter myth," which seeks to sanctify a custom or institution—examples include the myth connecting the DORIAN GREEKS with the prestigious sons of HERACLES, or the myth claiming that the city of CYRENE (1) was founded by the god APOLLO for his mistress, named CYRENE (2).

Modern scholarship has shown that the most important Greek myths tend to present distorted memories of the Greek MYCENAEAN CIVILIZATION (circa 1600–1200 B.C.), which later generations of Greeks remembered as an Age of Heroes. Among many examples of such historical myths are the SEVEN AGAINST THEBES and the TROJAN WAR. Because the Mycenaeans kept no written histories, certain real-life events were commemorated by heroic songs, handed down through the years and elaborated in a tradition of oral EPIC POETRY.

A remarkable number of Greek myths have survived antiquity. Their quantity and diversity are due partly to the fact that Greek society passed from a preliterate stage to a literate one in (probably) a single generation, circa 775–750 B.C., after the invention of the Greek ALPHABET. Many legends previously maintained by oral versifying were written down then or soon thereafter. HOMER's *Iliad* and *Odyssey* are the earliest and most important of these writings with mythological content. Among the many other ancient authors whose work recounts Greek myth are: the Boeotian epic poet HESIOD; the Theban choral poet PINDAR; the Athenian tragedians AESCHYLUS, SOPHOCLES, and EURIPIDES; the Alexandrian poets CALLIMACHUS and APOLLONIUS; and the Roman poet Ovid.

(See also CALYDONIAN BOAR HUNT; JASON (1); ODYSSEUS; OEDIPUS; ORESTES; PERSEUS; THESEUS; ZEUS.)

Mytilene The principal city of the eastern Greek island of LESBOS, in ancient times and still today (under the name Mitilini). Located on the island's southeastern shore, 12 miles from the northern west coast of ASIA MINOR, Mytilene was a prosperous Greek seaport, connecting East and West.

Archaeological study of the ancient site has been hampered by the modern city, but we know that this advantageous locale was occupied before the arrival of the first Greeks. We also know that the name Mytilene—sometimes rendered as Mitylene—is not Greek, for the ending *-ene* is similar to the endings of other pre-Greek place-names. Mycenaean-Greek POTTERY from about 1200 B.C. has been discovered on Lesbos; very possibly the seafaring Mycenaeans captured Mytilene at this time. Later, circa 1000 B.C., the city became a refuge for eastward-migrating AEOLIAN GREEKS. During 1000–900 B.C., Mytilene was an important departure point for further Aeolian colonizing, along the northwest Asia Minor coast.

By 625 B.C. Mytilene was a leading city of the eastern Greek world. Lesbos' traditions of LYRIC POETRY reached their zenith with the Mytileneans SAPPHO (circa 600 B.C.) and ALCAEUS (circa 590 B.C.). In this era the city was governed as an ARISTOCRACY. The chief clan was the Penthilidae, who had the oppressive habit of arbitrarily beating people with clubs in the street. Class tensions were enflamed by an overseas military failure—Mytilene's loss of the Hellespontine colony of Sigeum to Athenian settlers (circa 600 B.C.).

TYRANTS arose in Mytilene to lead the common people against the nobles. But civil war was averted by the statesman PITTACUS, who served as an elected 10-year dictator (circa 590–580 B.C.) and was later enshrined as one of the SEVEN SAGES of Greece. The turmoil of this era is conveyed in the poems of Pittacus' enemy Alcaeus.

Circa 522 B.C. Mytilene and the rest of the island fell to the advancing Persians under King DARIUS (1). The Mytileneans joined the doomed IONIAN REVOLT against Persian rule and distinguished themselves by their cowardice at the sea battle of Lade (494 B.C.). Liberated by the Greek counteroffensive at the end of the PERSIAN WARS (479 B.C.), Mytilene became a leading member of the Athenian-controlled DELIAN LEAGUE. For the next 50 years, Mytilene was one of the few league states to pay its annual obligation in the form of warships and crews rather than in SILVER.

During the PELOPONNESIAN WAR (431–404 B.C.), Mytilene twice revolted unsuccessfully against Athenian rule. The first revolt (428–427 B.C.) ended with Athenian troops occupying the island. Afterward, there occurred a famous debate in the ASSEMBLY at ATHENS, where a decision to destroy Mytilene and execute the adult male population was rescinded by a revote. This Mytilenean Debate forms a set piece in book 3 of the war history written by THUCYDIDES (1). After the second revolt was crushed (412 B.C.), the Mytileneans lost their fleet, their city walls, and much of their farmland to the vengeful Athenians. With the defeat of Athens in 404 B.C., a reduced Mytilene came under Spartan control.

After a generation of Spartan oppression, Mytilene joined the SECOND ATHENIAN LEAGUE, circa 377 B.C. In 333 B.C. the city fell briefly to the Persian navy but was liberated by the conquering Macedonian king ALEXANDER THE GREAT. After Alexander's death (323 B.C.), Mytilene and Lesbos passed to various Hellenistic rulers. Acquired by the kings of nearby PERGAMUM in 188 B.C., Mytilene was part of the domain bequeathed to the Romans by the Pergamene king Attalus III in 133 B.C. The city soon became part of the Roman province of Asia.

(See also GREEK LANGUAGE.)

N

names Unlike modern Americans, ancient Greek males and females typically carried only one personal name—for example, Socrates. In formal address, a man or boy might be specified by a patronymic (his father's name): "Themistocles, son of Neocles." However, at some Greek cities, specifically ATHENS, the use of the patronymic was discouraged due to social-leveling legislation aimed at removing distinctions and stigmas of lineage. Hence "Themistocles of the DEME of Phrearrus" was the preferred form. The masculine or feminine ending of a name clearly distinguished the person's gender—Diotima and Elpinice are female; Pericles and Diodorus, male.

Greek names, like those in German and certain other Indo-European tongues, usually contained common words in compound form. The Greek female name Cleopatra means "glory of her father." One of the elements might typically be a deity's name, as in Herodotus, "given by HERA." Two male names popular after the 500s B.C. were Demetrius and Dionysius, which were adjectival forms of the names of well-loved agrarian gods, DEMETER and DIONYSUS.

Because the keeping of horses was a sign of wealth, many aristocratic names included the proud element *hippo*—: Philip (Philippos), "horse-lover," Hippocrates, "horse power," Xanthippe, "yellow horse." For some reason, an aristocratic boy usually was not named after his father, but often after a grandfather—for example, CLEISTHENES (1) and (2), and THUCYDIDES (1) and (2). Collectively, members of a noble clan might be known by a family name—such as the ALCMAEONIDS (descendants of Alcmaeon).

Not only bluebloods had identifying names. Children of left-wing families might receive names with such politically charged elements as Demo—("the people") or Iso—("equality")—for instance, Demosthenes, "the people's strength," or Isodice, "equal justice."

Acquired nicknames came into use, mainly for royalty, starting in the late 300s B.C. The Macedonian soldier-prince Demetrius was honored with the surname Poliorketēs, "the city-besieger"; his father, ANTIGONUS (1), was Monophthalmos, "the one-eyed." And the conquering Macedonian king Alexander was surnamed Megas, "the Great."

(See ALEXANDER THE GREAT; DEMETRIUS POLIORCETES.)

Narcissus In MYTH, a handsome Boeotian youth, son of the river god Cephisus and the nymph Liriopē, who fell in love with his own reflection in a pond. In one version, he pined away and died of hopeless longing, in another, he stabbed himself with a dagger in frustration. From his body or blood there arose the white flower that the ancient Greeks called the *narkissos* (possibly a type of iris or lily, but not the same as our modern narcissus flower). This tale has produced the English words *narcissism* and *narcissistic*.

Narcissus' connection with a local flower, along with the pre-Greek *issos* ending of his name, suggest that he was originally a god or demigod of the pre-Greek peoples, absorbed into Greek mythology during the second millennium B.C.

(See also GREEK LANGUAGE; HYACINTHUS; NYMPHS; RELIGION.)

Naucratis Ancient port city of EGYPT, about 50 miles inland, on the westernmost branch of the Nile River. In the later 600s B.C. the pharaohs assigned Naucratis as the one emporium for all Greek TRADE in Egypt. The city then became the site of Greek temples and offices where various Greek states were represented. As listed by the historian HERODOTUS, these states included the great seagoing powers of the day: AEGINA, SAMOS, CHIOS, MILETUS, PHOCAEA, MYTILENE, and RHODES. The name *Naukratis* seems to be Greek, meaning "ship power"—that is, shipping place.

Archaeological excavations at Naucratis, combined with written references, give one idea of the commerce between Greece and Egypt in the 600s–500s B.C. Much of this trade apparently consisted of Greek SILVER ore and SLAVES (both acquired in the northern Aegean) exchanged for Egyptian grain, which was shipped by Greek merchants at a large profit to the hungry cities of the Greek world. Egyptian luxury goods, such as carved ivory, were also exported.

Like other port cities throughout history, Naucratis offered its share of men's entertainment. Herodotus describes Naucratis as "a place for lovely courtesans" (*hetairai*). Certain verses by the Greek poet SAPPHO (circa 600 B.C.) lament the predicament of Sappho's brother, ensnared at Naucratis by a fascinating *hetaira* on whom he has squandered his fortune.

Naucratis' fortunes declined after 525 B.C., when the Persian occupation of Egypt disrupted the Greek trade. After ALEXANDER THE GREAT's conquest of Egypt (332 B.C.), Naucratis was completely eclipsed by the founding of nearby ALEXANDRIA (1).

(See also PROSTITUTES; THRACE.)

Naupactus Seaport of West LOCRIS, situated at the mouth of the Corinthian Gulf. Naupactus' position controlling the gulf's narrow outlet made the town a natural naval base—its name in Greek means "shipbuilding." In the mid-400s B.C. Naupactus was captured by ATHENS and repopulated with fugitives from MESSENIA who had unsuccessfully revolted from Spartan rule (464–460 B.C.). During the PELOPONNESIAN WAR (431–404 B.C.), Naupactus was the main Athenian naval base in western Greece; it was off Naupactus that the Athenian admiral Phormion won his two brilliant sea victories over Peloponnesian fleets in 429 B.C.

After Athens' defeat in the war, Naupactus passed to the state of ACHAEA. In 338 B.C. the Macedonian king PHILIP II gave Naupactus to his ally, the state of AETOLIA. Naupactus had lost its importance by the 100s B.C., when the Aetolian League was defeated by ROME.

Nausicaa   Princess of the virtuous Phaeacians in HOMER's *Odyssey*. In one of the poem's most charming episodes (book 6), she leads her waiting women to wash clothes at a stream and there encounters the shipwrecked hero ODYSSEUS. Approaching naked and shielded only by a leafy branch, Odysseus unintentionally scares away the servants, but not Nausicaa. Inspired by the goddess ATHENA, she supplies food and clothing to the hero, then shows him the way to her father's palace, where he is suitably received.

navies   See WARFARE, NAVAL.

navigation   See SHIPS AND SEAFARING.

Naxos (1)   See CYCLADES.

Naxos (2)   First Greek colony in SICILY, and one of the earliest Greek colonies anywhere. Situated on a promontory on the island's east coast, at the foot of Mt. Etna, Naxos was a natural landfall for westbound ships rounding the "toe" of ITALY from the northeast. Naxos was founded circa 734 B.C. by Greeks from CHALCIS under a leader named Thucles. Supposedly, the expedition included Greeks from the Aegean island of Naxos, who gave the new city its name.

Naxos itself seems to have been intended only as a Greek foothold in Sicily: Six years after its founding, Thucles and his followers drove the native Sicels from the fertile plain of Catania and founded the cities of CATANA and Leontini. These cities and others, such as nearby SYRACUSE, soon exceeded Naxos in importance.

By the early 400s B.C. Naxos was ruled by Syracusan TYRANTS. As an Ionian-Greek city in a realm dominated by DORIAN GREEKS, Naxos became a target of ruthless social engineering when the Syracusan tyrant HIERON (1) depopulated it and moved the people to Leontini (476 B.C.).

Reconstituted, Naxos made an alliance with ATHENS against Syracuse in 415 B.C., during the PELOPONNESIAN WAR, and served as an Athenian base for the disastrous expedition against Syracuse. In 403 B.C. Naxos was captured and razed by the Syracusan tyrant DIONYSIUS (1).

(See also COLONIZATION.)

Nemean Games   One of the four great sports-and-religious festivals of ancient Greece, along with the OLYMPIC, PYTHIAN, and ISTHMIAN GAMES. Sacred to the god ZEUS,

the Nemean festival was held every other year at the valley and sanctuary called Nemea in the northeastern PELOPONNESE, in the region of ARGOS but close to the town of Cleonae. There, according to myth, the hero HERACLES instituted the games after slaying the Nemean Lion—the first of his 12 Labors. In fact, the Nemean festival first became important in 573 B.C., when Argos took over its administration from Cleonae and enlarged it on the model of the Olympic Games. The prize for victors at Nemea was a garland of wild celery (as at the Isthmian Games).

The ruins of a Doric-style temple of Zeus, built circa 340–320 B.C., have been excavated in Nemea. The temple was destroyed by earthquakes in late antiquity.

Neoptolemus   Greek mythical hero of the island of Scyros, the son of the Thessalian hero ACHILLES and the princess Deidameia. Neoptolemus ("new warrior") was begotten while Achilles was hiding among the WOMEN of Scyros in an attempt to avoid serving in the TROJAN WAR.

HOMER's epic poem the *Odyssey* mentions that Neoptolemus himself went to TROY after his father's death. He was summoned by the Greeks, who had learned in a prophecy that Neoptolemus' presence was a fated precondition of the city's fall. Although Neoptolemus would have been only about 10 years old at that time, this detail was overlooked in the legend, and he was said to have fought fiercely at Troy, winning the nickname Pyrrhus ("fiery" or "red").

Neoptolemus was one of the select Greek commandoes who hid inside the Trojan Horse. During the capture of the city, he slew the Trojan king PRIAM—despite the fact that Priam had taken sanctuary at the altar of the great god ZEUS. This brutal act brought the hatred of the Trojans' patron god APOLLO against Neoptolemus.

According to one version, Neoptolemus was killed after the war in a dispute at Apollo's shrine at DELPHI. Another version says he sailed to EPIRUS, in northwestern Greece, where he fathered the ruling clan, the Molossians. In historical times the Molossians used the hero's nickname, Pyrrhus, as a given name. The most famous such person was the Epirote king PYRRHUS (reigned 297–272 B.C.).

(See also ANDROMACHE.)

Nereids   See NEREUS.

Nereus   In MYTH, Nereus was a minor sea god, a kind of old man of the sea. He and his wife, Doris (the daughter of OCEANUS), had 50 daughters, known as the Nereids (Greek: Nereidai "daughters of Nereus"). These sea-dwelling young goddesses, often imagined as fish tailed, have been favorite subjects of art and poetry since ancient times. The best known of the Nereids were Amphitritē, who married the Olympian sea god POSEIDON, and Thetis, who married the mortal PELEUS and gave birth to the hero ACHILLES.

The name Amphitritē is not Greek, and surely derives from the language of the prehistoric people who occupied the land of Greece before the first Greek-speaking tribes arrived, circa 2100 B.C. The Nereids are probably survivals of the pre-Greek people's RELIGION.

(See also ARTEMIS; NYMPHS.)

The Nereids, elusive sea goddesses, were among several types of Greek female deities embodying the spirit of wilderness places. This figure, sometimes identified as a Nereid, appears on a marble carving of about 500 B.C. from a temple of Hera near the ancient Greek city of Poseidonia, in southeastern Italy.

Nestor In MYTH, the king of PYLOS, in the southwestern PELOPONNESE, and the most elderly of the Greek commanders in the TROJAN WAR. Nestor—the son and successor of King Neleus—was probably imagined as being over the age of 50 when the war began and over the age of 60 at its conclusion. HOMER's *Iliad* and *Odyssey* give a charming portrait of an admirable but garrulous old man, often ineffectual in combat and councils of war. In both poems he delivers meandering but lively speeches recalling his youthful achievements.

The *Iliad* presents Nestor's fond relationship with his soldier-son Antilochus but omits the tale of Antilochus' death. We know from other ancient sources that Antilochus was killed while defending his father from the Ethiopian champion MEMNON. In the *Odyssey*, Nestor is shown safely back in Pylos, where he welcomes the prince TELEMACHUS in the latter's search for his father, ODYSSEUS.

Nicias Athenian general and politician of the PELOPONNESIAN WAR, who lived circa 470–413 B.C. Rich and devoutly religious, Nicias served his city loyally. But his hesitancy and befuddlement in the Athenian campaign against SYRACUSE (415–413 B.C.) produced an epic disaster that destroyed an Athenian force of perhaps 50,000 men, including Nicias himself.

Nicias (Greek: Nikias, "victorious") was the son of Niceratus, of a distinguished Athenian family whose income came from the leasing of large numbers of SLAVES to work the Athenian SILVER mines at Laurium. Upon the death of PERICLES (429 B.C.), the soldierly Nicias became the heir to Pericles' defensive strategy in the Peloponnesian War.

As a politician, Nicias headed the conservative peace party, composed of the upper class and the smallholding farmers. Nicias' opponent and personal enemy was the pro-war radical democrat CLEON. After Cleon's death, Nicias arranged the short-lived peace with SPARTA that bears his name—the Peace of Nicias (421 B.C.).

In 415 B.C. Nicias was appointed alongside the generals ALCIBIADES and Lamachus to command a 134-ship armada to besiege and capture Syracuse, in SICILY. Unfortunately, the 55-year-old Nicias disapproved of the ambitious venture and, after Alcibiades was recalled, Nicias proved to be a dangerously indecisive leader. The death of Lamachus, combined with Nicias' kidney ailment, contributed to the deteriorating situation, despite Nicias' field victory at the River Anapus (late 415 B.C.). By summer of 413 B.C. the Athenians—although reinforced by fresh troops—were surrounded by the enemy on land and sea, after Nicias had hesitated too long to abandon the siege and sail away. Leading a hopeless attempt to escape overland, Nicias was captured by the Syracusans amid the slaughter of his men at the River Assinarus. He was later executed by the Syracusans.

(See also DELOS; DEMOSTHENES [2].)

Nikē Goddess of victory, in war or SPORT. Like many other minor deities, Nikē was more a symbol than an important character in Greek MYTH. The name Nikē was sometimes reduced to an epithet of the goddess ATHENA—Athena Nikē, the patron of victory through strategy.

From the 500s B.C. onward, Nikē was picturesquely shown in art as having two feathery wings. She became a favorite subject after the Greek triumph in the PERSIAN WARS, and was often associated with the god ZEUS—most famously in the colossal statue of Zeus sculpted by PHIDIAS for the temple at OLYMPIA. In this monument (completed circa 430 B.C.; now lost, but represented on coins), Nikē appeared standing on the god's upturned palm.

The best-known surviving Nikē in art is the marble statue called the Winged Victory of Samothrace, sculpted circa 190 B.C. and now in the Louvre. In the Greco-Roman world, Nikē often was shown on coins and medallions, sometimes elevated, garlanding a victorious general's head.

(See also PARTHENON; SAMOTHRACE.)

Niobē In MYTH, the wife of the Theban hero Amphion. As the mother of six youths and six maidens, Niobē boasted arrogantly that she was superior to the demigoddess Leto, who had borne only two children—the deities APOLLO and ARTEMIS. Angered at this affront to their mother, Apollo and Artemis hunted down, with bow and arrow, all 12 of Niobē's children. Niobē wept ceaselessly until, on the 10th day of her lamenting, the god ZEUS turned her to stone. This tale is first told in HOMER's *Iliad*, as background to the grief of the parents of the slain Trojan hero HECTOR. As a symbol of maternal grief, Niobē became a popular subject in Greco-Roman art and poetry.

(See also HUBRIS.)

numbers See MATHEMATICS.

nymphs The numphai were mythical female spirits of the wilderness, representing the beauty and fertility of nature. They were daughters of ZEUS or of other gods, but they themselves were not usually immortal. Rather, they were like leprechauns, living for centuries in the wild and avoiding contact with humans.

Usually imagined as young and amorous, nymphs were associated with the god DIONYSUS and his coterie of lusty male SATYRS. (This association is behind the pseudopsychiatric term *nymphomaniac*, meaning a woman with obsessive sexual desire.) Individual nymphs of MYTH include CALYPSO, lover of the hero ODYSSEUS, and CYRENE (2), lover of the god APOLLO. In the ancient GREEK LANGUAGE, *numphē* could also mean a young marriageable woman.

Eventually these pretty wilderness creatures became the subject of poets' elaborations, especially in the Hellenistic and Roman eras, after 300 B.C. There we find specialized categories of nymphs, such as the Naiads (stream nymphs) and the Dryads or Hamadryads (tree nymphs).

Like the NEREIDS and other demigoddesses, the nymphs may date back to the RELIGION of the pre-Greek people who inhabited the land of Greece before 2100 B.C.

O

Oceanids See OCEANUS.

Oceanus In MYTH, Okeanos was a river that encircles the world and serves as the underground source for all earthly rivers. The poet HESIOD described the river god Oceanus as one of the primeval offspring of Uranus (Greek: Ouranos, "Sky") and GAEA (Mother Earth). Oceanus and his wife, Tethys, produced the 3,000 Oceanids, the "daughters of Oceanus." These Oceanids were NYMPHS inhabiting bodies of water and other wilderness sites. In HOMER's *Iliad* and *Odyssey*, Oceanus was associated with the far West; there he flowed past shores inhabited by such fabulous creatures as MEDUSA, Geryon, and the Hesperides.

The notion of an encircling world stream is common to many mythologies. The Greeks may have borrowed it from the Near East, since the word Okeanos does not seem to be Greek. But the Greeks soon added their own layer, when their concept of *Okeanos* became colored by rumors of the Atlantic sea, lying west of the Mediterranean. The Greeks chose the word Okeanos to identify the Atlantic, once they began to venture beyond the straits of Gibraltar in the wake of the pioneering Phoenicians (600s B.C.). The English word *ocean* of course derives from Okeanos.

(See also ATLANTIS; ATLAS; HERACLES; PHOENICIA.)

Odysseus In MYTH, the wily king of ITHACA (a small island on the northwest coast of Greece) and a captain of the Greeks in the TROJAN WAR. Odysseus' 10-year-long journey home from TROY, and his strategy to rid his kingdom of troubles brewed by his absence, constitute the story of the 12,000-line epic poem the *Odyssey*. Written down circa 750 B.C. and ascribed in ancient times to the poet HOMER, the *Odyssey*—with its associated poem, the *Iliad*—stands at the beginning of Western literature, as one of the greatest works of Western literature.

The name Odusseus means "angry." The Romans, in retelling the myth, latinized the name to Ulixes, from which we get the form Ulysses. In some versions, Ulysses or Odysseus was said to be secretly the son of the cunning hero SISYPHUS, begotten on Anticleia, wife of the Ithacan king Laertes. In any case, Odysseus was raised as Laertes' son and succeeded him as king after Laertes abdicated in old age. Soon, however, Odysseus was summoned, along with other Greek vassal kings, to bring troops and ships to the expedition against Troy organized by King AGAMEMNON of MYCENAE. Odysseus left behind a dedicated and highly intelligent wife, PENELOPE, and their infant son, TELEMACHUS. The Trojan War itself was to last for 10 years.

In the *Iliad*, which describes events of the war's 10th year, Odysseus appears as one of the foremost Greek commanders, valiant in combat and wise in counsel. He often is associated with the Greek hero DIOMEDES. Together they make a night raid against the Trojan allies (book 10) and later, amid fierce fighting, they stop a Greek retreat (book 11). Being the swiftest-running Greek aside from ACHILLES, Odysseus wins the footrace at the Funeral Games of PATROCLUS (book 23). He also wrestles the hero AJAX (1) to a draw, using skill to offset his opponent's greater strength. Later Greek writers, such as SOPHOCLES (400s B.C.), enlarged on the rivalry between these two heroes, contrasting the cleverness or deviousness of Odysseus with the simplicity or honesty of Ajax.

The chronological sequence of Odysseus' homeward progress—not presented in this simple order in the *Odyssey*—is as follows: Leaving the ruins of Troy, he and his 12 ships raid the coast of THRACE but are beaten off by the warlike Cicones (book 9). Thereafter the voyage enters the realm of fable and is no longer geographically recognizable. (However, certain of its supernatural landmarks seem to be associated with the shores of southern ITALY and eastern SICILY, which real-life Greek mariners were exploring in the 800s and 700s B.C.)

Lashed to the mast, Odysseus endures the Sirens' hypnotic song while his men row on, their ears plugged with beeswax. This famous incident from Homer's *Odyssey* is shown in a red-figure scene from an Athenian vase, circa 480 B.C. The Sirens, although never precisely described by Homer, were pictured by Greek artists as being part woman, part bird.

156

of several prominent people, including his own mother and such former comrades as Achilles and Ajax.

After lingering with Circe for a year, Odysseus reembarks, having received Circe's directions for reaching home. His ship bypasses the SIRENS, survives the channel of SCYLLA and the whirlpool Charybdis, and reaches the island where the cattle of the sun god, HELIOS, graze. There, despite his warnings, his men slaughter the cattle for food. Consequently, the ship is destroyed at sea by the thunderbolt of the great god ZEUS. Everyone aboard perishes except Odysseus, who drifts to the isle of the amorous CALYPSO (book 12).

Seven years later, at Zeus' command, Calypso allows Odysseus to depart in a boat of his own construction (book 5). But he is shipwrecked again, this time by Poseidon, in vengeance for Polyphemus' distress. With the help of the goddess ATHENA, Odysseus reaches the land of the virtuous Phaeacians and encounters the princess NAUSICAA, who directs him to the palace of her father, King Alcinous (book 6). There the hero, welcomed royally (books 7–8), tells the tale of his wanderings since Troy (books 9–12).

By then nearly 10 years have passed since Troy's destruction and Odysseus' departure for home and nearly 20 years have gone by since he first left Ithaca. Unknown to Odysseus, Ithaca has meanwhile fallen prey to more than 100 visiting lords and petty kings, who crowd the palace, competing to marry the presumably widowed Penelope; she remains elusive, in the hope that Odysseus might yet return. The prince Telemachus, now a young man, has gone abroad in search of his father, hoping to free his home from the loathsome suitors.

The *Odyssey*'s entire second half (books 13–24) describes Odysseus' return to Ithaca, his espionage there in disguise as a beggar, and how—with the help of Athena, Telemachus, and two trusted retainers—he destroys the suitors, reclaims his wife and throne, and restores harmony to the island.

The story of Odysseus' death, not told in the *Odyssey*, was described in a later epic poem, now lost, called the *Telegonia*. Tiresias in the Underworld had predicted that Odysseus' death would come from the sea, but Odysseus reigned for many happy years on Ithaca. Meanwhile his three illegitimate sons by Circe grew to manhood. The youngest, Telegonus ("distant born"), set out to meet his father and somehow encountered Odysseus en route, not knowing who he was. A fight ensued, and Telegonus slew Odysseus. (This episode bears comparison with the similar tale of OEDIPUS.) The weapon that Telegonus used was a sharp fishbone, thereby fulfilling the terms of Tiresias' prophecy.

Odysseus is the best-known example of the "trickster" type of Greek mythical figure. Other tricksters from Greek myth include the god HERMES, the demigod PROMETHEUS, and Odysseus' putative father, Sisyphus.

(See also AFTERLIFE; EPIC POETRY; PROPHECY AND DIVINATION.)

Odyssey See HOMER; ODYSSEUS.

Oedipus In MYTH, a Theban king who could not escape his FATE. Oedipus married a woman who, unbeknownst

The weathered, wily face of Odysseus, as imagined by an unknown sculptor, probably from the early first century A.D. This carving, discovered in 1957, was part of a marble statue group in the Roman emperor Tiberius' grotto at Sperlonga, south of Rome.

The voyagers' next landfall is among the friendly Lotuseaters, who are perpetually narcotized by their magical *lotos*-fruit food. Fleeing from this seductive danger, the squadron puts ashore in the territory of the one-eyed monsters known as Cyclopes (book 9). Odysseus is captured by one of them, named POLYPHEMUS, but escapes after blinding the creature. Polyphemus prays to his father, the god POSEIDON, for revenge.

Next Odysseus and his ships reach the island of the hospitable wind king, Aeolus (book 10). Aeolus gives Odysseus a tied-up bag containing all the winds except the favorable one needed for Odysseus' voyage home. But out at sea, while Odysseus sleeps, his men greedily open the mysterious bag: The released winds blow the ships back to the isle of Aeolus, who refuses to help again. Later, Odysseus loses all ships and crews except his own to the cannabalistic Laestrygonians.

The hero's ship arrives at the island of the beautiful witch CIRCE (book 10). After saving his men from Circe's evil magic, Odysseus becomes her lover. She tells him that in order to reach home he must journey down to the Underworld and consult the ghost of the seer TIRESIAS. In the Underworld (book 11) Odysseus observes the ghosts to him, was his own mother, Jocasta (Iocastē). The story is mentioned in HOMER's *Odyssey*, but the classic telling of the Oedipus tale is the Athenian playwright SOPHOCLES' extant tragedy *Oedipus the King* (presented circa 429–420 B.C.).

Oedipus was the son of Laius, king of THEBES, and Jocasta, his wife. Warned by prophecy that his son would kill him, Laius abandoned the infant on Mt. Cithaeron, after first running a spike through the baby's feet—from which the child later got his name, Oidipous, "swollen foot." As in all such folktales, the infant did not die but was rescued, in this case by a Corinthian shepherd, servant of the Corinthian king. This king and his wife, being childless, were happy to adopt the boy and pass him off as their own.

Nevertheless, the young Oedipus was taunted by others for being adopted, and eventually he went to DELPHI to ask the god APOLLO who his real parents might be. The oracle withheld this information but told Oedipus that he would kill his father and marry his mother. Disgusted, Oedipus decided never to return to CORINTH. Journeying by chance toward Thebes, he fell into a dispute at a cross-roads with a stranger. Not knowing that this was Laius, his own father, Oedipus killed him. Then he reached Thebes, which was at that time being terrorized by a supernatural female monster, the Sphinx.

When the Sphinx encountered people, it would ask them a riddle, and eat them when they failed to guess the answer. The riddle asked: "What goes on four legs at morning, two at noon, and three at evening?" Oedipus deduced the correct answer: a human being. (The "legs" represent, respectively, the baby's hands and knees, the adult's upright legs, and the elderly person's legs and cane.) At this point the Sphinx killed itself or was killed by Oedipus. Acclaimed by the Thebans, Oedipus now married the newly widowed queen, Jocasta, whom he did not know to be his mother. In most versions they had four children: the girls ANTIGONE and Ismenē and the boys Eteocles and Polynices. These children were also doomed to unhappy ends.

In Sophocles' play, these events are revealed through Oedipus' own careful investigations (prompted by a plague and famine in Thebes that can be resolved only by dis-covering the murderer of Laius). Jocasta hanged herself in grief, and Oedipus blinded himself and abdicated his throne, going into exile with Antigone. In Sophocles' play *Oedipus at Colonus* (performed 401 B.C.), the aged hero is shown as having wandered to Colonus, an outlying Athenian village (and Sophocles' own home). There Oedi-pus disappeared from earth, having been taken up by the gods.

The subject of Oedipus and the Sphinx was a popular one of vase painting in the 400s B.C.

(See also PROPHECY AND DIVINATION; SEVEN AGAINST THEBES.)

oligarchy   "Government by the few." In ancient Greece, an oligarchy was a city-state in which only a small minority of citizens could be admitted to political power. While the mass of citizenry might enjoy certain protections, they lacked any important say in government.

ARISTOTLE and other political thinkers recognized the distinction between an oligarchy and an ARISTOCRACY (where familial lineage was the sole means of deciding who could hold power). In oligarchies, the exclusive ruling circle consisted of rich men, not only men of noble birth. Of course, there was some overlap between these two groups, and oligarchy usually represented a development from aristocracy, due to urbanization and commercializa-tion in the 700s–400s B.C. The inroads made by wealth against privileges of birth are well documented in the indignant verses of aristocratic poets such as THEOGNIS (circa 550 B.C.).

Oligarchy and DEMOCRACY were the two opposing gov-ernment forms of classical Greece (400s–300s B.C.). The champion of oligarchies everywhere was SPARTA, and its enemy was ATHENS, the beacon of democracy (whose citi-zens, nevertheless, included an angry pro-oligarchic minor-ity). The PELOPONNESIAN WAR (431–404 B.C.) was in part a conflict between these two forms of government.

Prominent oligarchies of the 400s B.C. included CORINTH, THEBES, and LOCRI (in Greek ITALY).

(See also HOPLITE; POLIS.)

olives   See FARMING.

Olympia   Sanctuary and sports complex, sacred to the great god ZEUS, in the region known as ELIS, in the western PELOPONNESE. This was the site of the most important panhellenic festival of ancient Greece, the OLYMPIC GAMES. The name Olympia refers to Olympian Zeus—that is, Zeus, king of the gods on MT. OLYMPUS. (However, Mt. Olympus itself stands in THESSALY, in northeastern Greece, hundreds of miles from Olympia.)

The elaborate complex, which has been partly restored by archaeologists since 1829, lay in a pleasant valley, near the confluence of the rivers Alphaeus and Cladeus. AR-CHAEOLOGY has revealed traces of pre-Greek settlement, and it may be that Olympia—like DELPHI and certain other Greek sanctuaries—was a holy place for the inhabitants of the land long before the first Greek invaders arrived circa 2100 B.C. The site was inhabited by Greeks of the Mycen-aean era (circa 1600–1200 B.C.), but Olympia truly emerged after 776 B.C., the traditional date for the first Olympic Games.

In its heyday, Olympia contained hostels, restaurants, a meeting hall, and many other amenities, but it was never a city in the political sense, for it had neither citizens nor a government. The heart of Olympia was the sacred precinct, or Altis—a walled enclosure whose name appar-ently comes from *alsos*, "grove." From early times the Altis contained a temple of the goddess HERA and a shrine to the hero PELOPS (mythical founder of the Games). In 457 B.C. the magnificent Doric-style temple of Zeus was com-pleted inside the Altis. This building was wrecked by an earthquake at the end of antiquity, but the foundations and platform are visible today, as are the temple's huge, collapsed column drums (made of a limestone visibly com-prised of fossilized shellfish). The temple's pedimental sculptures, now partly preserved in the Olympia Museum, showed two mythical scenes: the battle between Lapiths and CENTAURS at King Pirithous' wedding, and the chariot race of Pelops and Oenomaus. The temple housed a colossal cult statue of Zeus, fashioned by the Athenian sculptor PHIDIAS (circa 430 B.C.) and reckoned as one of the SEVEN WONDERS OF THE WORLD for its size and solemn majesty.

The statue, about 40 feet high, showed the god seated, enthroned. One ancient viewer objected that Zeus' head was so close to the roofbeams that he could not have stood up without taking off the roof, but in the temple's darkened interior this disproportion was probably not obvious. The god's flesh was made of ivory; his cloak, sandals, and accoutrements were GOLD. A human-size figure of the goddess NIKĒ, in ivory and gold, stood atop his right-hand palm, and his left hand held a scepter of various precious metals, tipped with a golden eagle. His cloak was inlaid with images of animals and lilies, and on his head was a golden wreath of facsimile olive leaves.

This statue had the power to awe those who stood before it. The Roman orator Quintilian (circa A.D. 70) stated that it added something to human religion. The great work survived through the Roman era until the 400s A.D. when, having been removed to the eastern Roman capital at Constantinople, it was accidentally destroyed in a fire. Our scanty knowledge of the statue's appearance comes from its image on ancient Elean coins and its description by the travel writer PAUSANIAS (2) (circa A.D. 150).

Modern archaeological excavations at the site of Phidias' workshop at Olympia have uncovered traces of ivory and gold, and terra-cotta molds (apparently for the casting of Zeus' golden cloak). Also, rather spectacularly, a red-figure ceramic jug has been found, inscribed with Phidias' name—his "office coffee mug."

Other ancient splendors of Olympia included many statues of prior victors and a row of 12 treasury houses, built between about 600 and 480 B.C. by various rich states of the Greek world, to hold offerings to the god. Of these, the Treasury of the Sicyonians has been reconstructed by modern archaeologists. Along the valley were the structures for the sporting events: a huge GYMNASIUM; a hippodrome for horse and chariot races; and a stadium (now fully restored) for footraces, where 40,000 spectators could be seated on grass embankments that had no need of benches.

(See also ARCHITECTURE; MILTIADES; SCULPTURE.)

Olympic Games   Oldest and most important of the ancient Greek sports-and-religious festivals. Open to all male, free-born Greeks, the Olympic Games were held every four years in honor of the god ZEUS, at OLYMPIA, in the western PELOPONNESE. Traditionally the games were said to have been established by the hero HERACLES, or alternatively by the hero PELOPS, but in practical terms the Greeks recognized 776 B.C. as the inaugural date, the date at which a record of victors was first begun.

The games were administered by the people of ELIS (the general region of Olympia). However, after King PHEIDON of ARGOS marched his troops into Olympia and took over the games in (probably) 668 B.C., he handed Olympia over to be run by the people of the nearby town of Pisa. The Pisans held Olympia for about 90 years, until the Eleans, with Spartan support, won it back (circa 580 B.C.).

In the earliest years, the contests took place all on one day and consisted of only two events: WRESTLING and the footrace (one lap of the stadium). Later, perhaps after King Pheidon's intervention, the games were enlarged to include races for saddle horses and for horse- and mule-drawn CHARIOTS. By 471 B.C. the games spanned five days—involving competitions, religious sacrifices, and feasting—and included most of the famous sports events of classical Greece: BOXING; PANKRATION; the PENTATHLON; boys' categories in footrace, · wrestling, and boxing; and, the final event of the sequence, the footrace for men in armor. A single event for girls, a footrace, also may have been part of the games. For every contest, the prize for victory was nothing more than a garland of olive leaves.

The games were of immense political and social importance. To Olympia every four years crowded the most influential people (almost exclusively men) of the Greek world, as spectators and competitors. Statesmen such as the Syracusan tyrant HIERON (1) (circa 468 B.C.) and the Athenian ALCIBIADES (circa 416 B.C.) spent fortunes developing chariot teams to enroll at the games. Famous writers such as HERODOTUS and EMPEDOCLES gave readings at Olympia, probably at privately organized side events. Drinking parties of the rich and powerful took place. The spirit of the Olympic Games—religious fervor and aristocratic pride—can be found in the victory odes of the Theban poet PINDAR (circa 470 B.C.).

The four-year cycle between Olympic festivals was known as an Olympiad and was used as a chronological device in the ancient world. For instance, "the 67th Olympiad" signified the period that we would call 512–508 B.C., which began 264 years (66 by 4 years) after the first Olympiad (776 B.C.). Sometimes the ancients remembered a specific year by noting that that was the year when so-and-so won the footrace at Olympia.

The most striking aspect of the games was the Olympic Truce, which was announced by heralds in all major cities of mainland Greece months before the start of each Olympic festival. Whatever wars might be in progress elsewhere, the region of Elis and the site of Olympia were sacrosanct for the truce. During the PELOPONNESIAN WAR, for example, visitors from enemy cities coexisted peaceably at Olympia during the games. In 420 B.C. the Spartans, having attacked Elean territory after the truce was declared, were barred from competing that year. To enforce the ban, several thousand troops from Elis, ARGOS, and MANTINEA (all enemies of Sparta) guarded Olympia during the competition. A more notorious truce-breaking occurred in 364 B.C., when the Pisans and Arcadians invaded Olympia and fought a battle against the Eleans that raged within the sanctuary itself.

The games remained prestigious—although less central—in the Roman era (after about 150 B.C.), and survived nearly to the end of antiquity. In about A.D. 391 they were abolished by an edict of the Christian Roman emperor Theodosius I that prohibited all pagan festivals.

(See also SPORT.)

Olympias   See ALEXANDER THE GREAT.

Olympus, Mt.   Tallest mountain in mainland Greece and, in MYTH, the celestial home of ZEUS and most of the other important gods. The Olympus massif, whose height reaches 9,570 feet, rises in the region of THESSALY, in northeastern Greece.

The religious awe that Mt. Olympus inspired probably had to do with the mystery of its summit, often cloaked in stormclouds appropriate to the weather god Zeus. The massif also served as a barrier to any invasion force moving southward from MACEDON, and it may have represented an important milestone for the first immigrating Greeks of circa 2100 B.C.

Throughout Greek literature, Mt. Olympus is identified as the royal court of Zeus—the "Olympian"—and of his foremost subordinate gods. These 12 Olympian gods, aside from Zeus, were: HERA, POSEIDON, APOLLO, ARTEMIS, ATHENA, APHRODITE, ARES, DEMETER, DIONYSUS, HERMES, and HESTIA. They comprised the important deities for most spheres of life, with the exception of the Underworld.

(See also AFTERLIFE; HADES; RELIGION.)

Olynthus   Major Greek city of the northwestern Aegean region known as CHALCIDICĒ. Located on the coastal plain of the Chalcidic mainland, at the head of the Gulf of Torone, Olynthus was originally a settlement of the non-Greek, native Bottiaeans. It was occupied by local Chalcidic Greeks after the non-Greek settlement was destroyed by the army of the Persian king XERXES, in 479 B.C.

With its southern neighbor POTIDAEA, Olynthus became one of the two premier cities of Chalcidice. After Potidaea revolted from the Athenian-controlled DELIAN LEAGUE (432 B.C.), Olynthus served as a regional fortress against the retaliatory Athenian invasion. Soon thereafter, Olynthus became the capital of the newly formed local federation known as the Chalcidic League.

In 349 B.C. war broke out between the Chalcidic League and the aggressive Macedonian king PHILIP II. Philip besieged Olynthus. Despite the efforts at ATHENS of the statesman DEMOSTHENES (1) to organize military aid for Olynthus (in his three extant speeches called the *Olynthiacs*), Philip captured the city with the help of traitors within (348 B.C.). He razed Olynthus to the ground and sold the inhabitants as SLAVES. Reports of the pitiful condition of these captives provided Demosthenes with material for more of his speeches, the famous *Philippics*. Demosthenes' *Third Philippic* (341 B.C.) contains the comment that a visitor to the Olynthus site would never know that a city had stood there.

Olynthus was excavated by American archaeologists in A.D. 1928–1934. The site, free from any later buildings, has provided one of the clearest pictures of the floor plans of ordinary ancient Greek houses. The city was laid out on a grid pattern, an admirable example of the Greek town planning that developed in the mid-400s B.C.

(See also ARCHAEOLOGY.)

orators   See RHETORIC.

Orchomenus   Name of three ancient Greek cities, the most important being "Minyan" Orchomenus in BOEOTIA, in central Greece. The other two cities called Orchomenus were in ARCADIA and THESSALY. The name seems to be Greek, meaning "place of the strong battle rank."

The site of Boeotian Orchomenus was first excavated by archaeologist Heinrich Schliemann in A.D. 1880. Buildings uncovered from the Mycenaean era (1600–1200 B.C.) include a palace and an elaborate tomb. Such remnants—along with certain hints in extant Greek MYTH—indicate that Orchomenus was one of the wealthiest Mycenaean-Greek cities, surpassing its neighbor and enemy, THEBES.

This Mycenaean Orchomenus was the seat of a rich and powerful clan named the MINYANS (Minuai), who may originally have come from the Thessalian Orchomenus. The Boeotian city thrived from its location—controlling the land route through central Greece—and from its fertile farmland, claimed by the engineered draining of nearby Lake Copaïs.

But by the main centuries of ancient Greek history, Orchomenus had declined greatly, due to Thebes' dominance and the refilling of Lake Copaïs. Orchomenus fought as a Theban ally against ATHENS in the PELOPONNESIAN WAR (431–404 B.C.) but sided with SPARTA against Thebes during the CORINTHIAN WAR (395–386 B.C.). After Thebes had replaced Sparta as the foremost Greek power (371 B.C.), revenge was swift. Orchomenus was destroyed by the Theban-led Boeotian League in 364 B.C. It was rebuilt, then again destroyed in 349 B.C.

(See also ARCHAEOLOGY; MYCENAEAN CIVILIZATION; POTTERY.)

Orestes   In MYTH, the son of King AGAMEMNON and CLYTAEMNESTRA, of the city of MYCENAE (alternatively, of the city of ARGOS). In the best-known version of the tale, told by the Athenian playwright AESCHYLUS in his Oresteian Trilogy (presented 458 B.C.), Orestes murders his mother and her lover, Aegisthus, in vengeance for their murder of his father. But, having broken the bonds of nature by committing matricide, Orestes is driven mad by the demonic FURIES, the agents of divine punishment. Orestes flees to DELPHI—and then, in Aeschylus' version, to ATHENS—and is eventually cleansed of his sin. The Greeks were intrigued by the horror and legalism of Orestes' dilemma—compelled by filial duty to avenge his father (even against his mother), but doomed to be punished for doing so. A similar myth developed around the Argive hero ALCMAEON (1).

The earliest surviving version of the story is a mention in HOMER's epic poem the *Odyssey* (written down circa 750 B.C.). There Orestes has killed Aegisthus, who (in this version) is the principal culprit in Agamemnon's murder. It is not stated specifically whether Orestes has also killed Clytaemnestra, but it is implied. Homer says nothing of the Furies.

The Furies may have been introduced into the story by STESICHORUS (circa 580 B.C.), the sophisticated Sicilian-Greek poet whose work had a strong influence on Aeschylus and other later writers. Stesichorus wrote a narrative poem called the *Oresteia*, which survives only in fragments. In this version the Furies pursued Orestes and Apollo gave him a special bow, designed to ward them off.

The Orestes story also is told in surviving plays by SOPHOCLES and EURIPIDES. A side-by-side comparison of the three great Athenian tragedians' versions sheds light on differing values and messages. Aeschylus is concerned (primarily) with settling Orestes' controversial position in the world order and (secondarily) with glorifying the playwright's beloved Athens. Orestes is introduced in the second play of Aeschylus' trilogy, the *Libation Bearers* (*Choëphoroi*), as having been ordered by Apollo to take vengeance on Clytaemnestra and Aegisthus. Assisted by his friend Pylades and sister ELECTRA, Orestes can hardly bring himself to kill his mother but, having done so, he is immediately assailed by the Furies. The trilogy's third play, the *Eumenides* (kindly ones), features Orestes' legal acquittal at the hands of the Athenian homicide court, the AREOPAGUS, with the help of Apollo and ATHENA.

The version presented in Sophocles' *Electra* (circa 418–410 B.C.) is closer to the simple Homeric story. Orestes shows only a little natural reluctance to do the deed, and afterward there are no Furies. Euripides in his *Orestes* (408 B.C.) and *Electra* (probably 417 B.C.), seeks to bring out the myth's most disturbing implications. His Orestes emerges, not as a heroic figure, but as an enthusiastic killer who has sexual feelings for his own sister. After the crime, the Furies (not shown onstage) are made to be simply phantoms of Orestes' troubled mind. In Euripides' *Iphigenia in Tauris* (circa 413 B.C.), Orestes must expiate his guilt by journeying to the Crimean peninsula, at the edge of the known world.

Orestes' slaying of Aegisthus was a popular subject of vase painting and SCULPTURE in the 500s and 400s B.C.

Orion   In MYTH, a hunter of enormous size, skilled with bow and arrow. He is variously described as the son of the earth goddess GAEA or as the son of the god POSEIDON and Euryalē the Gorgon. Orion was killed by the goddess ARTEMIS. His offense may have been his arrogant challenge of Artemis to a discus-throwing contest or his attempted rape of one of her attendants. Or his great hunting prowess may have proved to be an affront to the jealous goddess of the hunt. In any case, his huge corpse was set in the sky as the constellation Orion.

Orpheus   In Greek MYTH, Orpheus was a Thracian lyre-player and singer of supernatural ability. Although THRACE was a savage, non-Greek land, Orpheus was a civilizing influence; his song could charm not only humans and beasts, but trees and stones as well. He served as one of the Argonauts who sailed with the Thessalian hero JASON (1) to win the Golden Fleece. But the best-known story about Orpheus tells how when his wife, Eurydicē, died from snakebite, he ventured down into the Underworld to seek the god HADES' permission to bring her up from the dead. Permission was granted, on condition that Orpheus not look back as Eurydicē followed, until they should reach the upper world. But as they approached the upper world Orpheus, not hearing her footsteps behind him, did look back, and with a cry Eurydicē disappeared forever.

Despondent, Orpheus neglected all other WOMEN, thereby infuriating the Thracian women—or, more specifically in some versions, those female followers of the god DIONYSUS known as MAENADS. These women tore Orpheus limb from limb in the course of a Dionysian frenzy and pitched his head into the Thracian River Hebrus. The head floated, singing, out to sea, to the Aegean island of LESBOS.

The background to these legends is uncertain. Orpheus may have been an actual poet and musician, perhaps of royal blood, in Thrace circa 700 B.C. He was said to be the founder of the mystic religious cult known as ORPHISM, which arose in the Greek world in the 600s B.C. and revered certain religious poems supposedly written by him. He also was said to have introduced male HOMOSEXUALITY among the Thracians, in consequence of his later aversion to women. Alternatively, he was said to have lived celebate after Eurydicē's death.

For the classical Greeks, Orpheus symbolized the civilizing or soothing power of MUSIC. One well-known Athenian vase painting of circa 500 B.C. shows him playing his lyre and singing to a group of charmed (but fierce-looking) Thracian warriors. The Athenian playwright AESCHYLUS wrote a tragic trilogy (now lost) about Orpheus.

(See also LYRIC POETRY.)

Orphism   Religious cult, arising probably in the 600s B.C., with followers eventually at ATHENS and the Greek cities of SICILY and southern ITALY. Orphism's beliefs were set down in religious poems supposedly composed by the Thracian musician ORPHEUS. These poems, now lost, are known from mentions by later writers.

Orphism emphasized a belief in the transmigration of souls. This concept, later adapted by the Greek philosophers PYTHAGORAS (circa 530 B.C.) and EMPEDOCLES (circa 450 B.C.), claimed that a dead person's soul generally on to inhabit another life form, whether human, animal, or vegetable. Like the ELEUSINIAN MYSTERIES and other mystery cults, Orphism promised its followers a happy existence in the AFTERLIFE.

The Orphic MYTH centered on a holy infant named Zagreus, who was seen as an alter ego of the god DIONYSUS. In this peculiar tale, perhaps derived from Thracian legend, the great god ZEUS seduced or raped his own daughter, the goddess PERSEPHONE. She bore the baby Zagreus, whom Zeus intended to make supreme among the gods. However, the jealous TITANS, after luring the child to their midst, tore him limb from limb and ate him. Zeus angrily blasted the Titans with a thunderbolt, incinerating them. From their ashes emerged the first humans. Zagreus' living heart, saved from the butchery, was now swallowed by Zeus, who passed it on supernaturally in begetting his next divine son, Dionysus.

In Orphic belief, Zagreus' ghoulish murder was a kind of Original Sin, in which all humans shared. Consequently, atonement had to be made to Zagreus' bereaved mother, Persephone, who, as queen of the Underworld, judges people after death. Apparently Orphism viewed the cycle of transmigration as a kind of purgatory: Only by living successive lives (on earth and also in the Underworld) could a person's soul be cleansed of its Original Sin. Reincarnation might mean reward or punishment, depending on Persephone's judgment of one's conduct in a prior life. The soul might descend to inhabit beasts or paupers, or ascend to statesmen and heroes. The Orphic devotee hoped eventually for release from this round of reincarnations. "I have escaped from the wheel of pain," one Orphic verse announces, referring to the achievement of bliss in the other world. The golden leaves discovered by archaeologists in Greek tombs of southern Italy from circa 400 B.C., containing precise instructions for the soul's procedure on reaching the Underworld, are thought to be Orphic documents.

Related to this spiritual preparation, Orphism also involved strict behavioral taboos. Orphics were notorious for abstaining from hunting and meat-eating, and even from wearing wool. They also were known for sexual abstinence—or at least for discouraging heterosexual intercourse—in order to thwart pregnancy; pregnancy was lamentable because it imprisoned another soul in a human body. The Orphics said that the body (*soma*) was the tomb (*sēma*) of the soul. The higher life was the purified soul's existence in Persephone's realm.

Orphism's otherworldliness and contempt for bodily existence recommended it to the Athenian philosopher PLATO (circa 370 B.C.). But its strict code of behavior struck many Greeks as crankish and kept Orphism on the mystic fringe.

ostracism   Political practice unique to Athenian DEMOCRACY in the 400s B.C., whereby the people could vote to banish any citizen for 10 years. Created in reaction to the tyrannies of PISISTRATUS and HIPPIAS (1), ostracism was intended for use against wealthy politicians who, while not

Votes for banishment: four *ostraka* (potsherds), incised with the names of four Athenian politicians of the 400s B.C., found in archaeological excavations of the Athenian agora. The ballots read, clockwise from top left: "Aristides, son of Lysimachus," "Themistocles, son of Neocles, of the deme Phrearrus," "Pericles, son of Xanthippus," and "Cimon, son of Miltiades." Each of these prominent men earned suspicion that he was aiming to make himself dictator, and of the four only Pericles avoided being voted into ostracism.

guilty of wrongdoing, might still be suspected of hoping to seize supreme power.

Once a year, at an appointed time in winter, the citizens in ASSEMBLY voted on whether an ostracism should be held that spring—no candidates were named. If the majority voted yes, then the ostracism vote itself took place a few months later. There each citizen had the chance to write down the name of one person for exile. Because clay potsherds were the ancient world's equivalent of scrap paper, each voter used a sherd (Greek: *ostrakon*, plural: *ostraka*), on which to scratch the intended victim's name. The potsherds gave this unique practice its name, *ostrakismos*. The vote was secret, with officials making sure no one handed in more than one ballot. If a quorum of 6,000 votes was reached, then the man with the most votes had to remove himself from the city within 10 days.

Unlike more punitive forms of banishment, ostracism allowed the victim to retain his Athenian citizenship and property while absent and to return after the allotted 10 years. During the state emergency of the PERSIAN WARS, two Athenians under ostracism, ARISTIDES and XANTHIPPUS, were allowed to return immediately (480 B.C.).

According to ARISTOTLE's treatise the *Constitution of Athens*, the ostracism law was created by the reformer CLEISTHENES (1) circa 508 B.C., soon after the expulsion of Hippias. Clearly, the law was aimed against Hippias' friends who might dream of reinstating a dictator. But what puzzles modern scholars is that the people did not vote their first ostracism until 487 B.C. (The victim was Hippias' kinsman Hipparchus.) This 20-year delay has led some historians to suggest that the ostracism law really was created soon after the Battle of MARATHON (490 B.C.), but was later falsely ascribed to Cleisthenes.

After Hipparchus, four more men were soon ostracized amid the political turmoil of the 480s B.C., and it is thought that about eight others fell victim during the rest of the 400s B.C. These included the left-wing statesman-soldier THEMISTOCLES (circa 471 B.C.) and the conservative statesman-soldier CIMON (462 B.C.). This clearly shows that ostracism had quickly become a tool by which the two political parties could attack each other. Many other Athenians were named as ostracism candidates but did not receive majority votes—as indicated by the 64 names compiled from the several thousand *ostraka* discovered in modern archaeological excavations of the Athenaian AGORA and other sites.

The last successful ostracism was of the demogogue Hyperbolus (417 B.C.), after which the law fell out of use. (See also THUCYDIDES [2].)

P

paean See LYRIC POETRY.

Paestum See POSEIDONIA.

painting For the painting of scenes and portraits, the Greeks used various surface materials, including POTTERY, wooden panels, stone walls, leather, and textiles. Of these, only pottery has preserved Greek painting in any quantity, due to the ceramic's durability and the paint being baked into the clay during firing. Secondarily, there exist some examples of tomb paintings—from walls of graves or the insides of coffins—that were preserved underground. But most other Greek paintings have vanished over time, as their surfaces crumbled to dust.

The paintings on pottery can reveal only a certain amount about general Greek painting, because pottery was a miniaturist discipline, with colors limited to those that would survive firing. Modern scholars must therefore rely partly on indirect evidence, such as ancient writers' descriptions of specific paintings and techniques and certain surviving mosaics and wall paintings of the Roman era, believed to be copies of earlier Greek paintings.

Aegean painting traditions predate the Greeks. By the third millennium B.C. the Minoan peoples were making pigments by processing and grinding down various vegetation, and were painting lively murals at their palaces in CRETE. Among several existing examples is the famous Toreador Fresco (circa 1500 B.C.). Minoan whorl designs, sea-life subjects, and human figures helped inspire Mycenaean-Greek paintings on walls and pottery, from the 1500s B.C. onward.

Examples of Greek painting in the centuries after the Mycenaeans' fall are represented now mainly by works on pottery: the whorls and other designs of the Protogeometric style (circa 1050–900 B.C.), the stick-figure human and animal silhouettes of the Geometric style (circa 900–700 B.C.), and the colors, detail, and primitive depth perception of the ripe Corinthian style (circa 625–550 B.C.).

CORINTH was a center for painting in the 600s B.C., and one rare surviving example of nonvase painting of this era is a wooden plaque of circa 500 B.C., found at a site near Corinth. The painting shows a sacrificial procession, in a style reminiscent of the Corinthian vase painting that had peaked a century before. With its vivid red, blue, and flesh tones, the work suggests the color range available to the ancient Greek painter—well beyond the restricted colors of the vase painter. The painting's background is white, which would remain the chosen background color for decades to come.

ATHENS arose to replace Corinth as the artistic center of Greece in the mid-500s B.C. By about 460 B.C. the splendors of the Athenian AGORA included a Painted Colonnade (Stoa Poikilē) where large wall paintings on mythological and patriotic subjects were displayed. This era produced the first Old Master of Greek painting—the artist Polygnotus, born at THASOS but active at Athens in the 470s–450s B.C. He is best remembered for two mythological wall paintings, neither of which survives: a scene of the fall of TROY, at the Painted Colonnade, and a scene of the Underworld, painted at the Meeting House at DELPHI. Polygnotus apparently used no foreshortening but did innovatively convey depth by showing his human figures standing at different levels—a device that subsequently appears in Athenian vase painting. He also pioneered the technique called encaustic, which used heated wax for applying colors. Micon of Athens is another painter remembered for public wall paintings in these years.

Use of perspective is said to have developed at Athens in the mid-400s B.C. partly through the production of painted backdrops for Athenian stage performances. The second half of the 400s B.C.—the Athenian cultural heyday—saw greater use of shading to indicate depth: The great name of the day was Apollodorus of Athens, surnamed *skiagraphos*, "shade painter." His younger contemporary and imitator Zeuxis—from Greek ITALY but active at Athens circa 430–400 B.C.—was known for his illusionary realism: Supposedly Zeuxis' outdoor paintings of grapes attracted hungry birds. Apollodorus, Zeuxis, and the painter-sculptor Parrhasius (active at Athens in these years) were all known for their mythological subjects. But scenes from everyday life—a woman spinning, young WOMEN playing at dice—are indicated by later Roman copies of lost originals.

With Athens' decline after the PELOPONNESIAN WAR (431–404 B.C.), the Peloponnesian city of SICYON emerged briefly as a painting center. But it was the Macedonian king ALEXANDER THE GREAT (reigned 336–323 B.C.) who inspired a revival of Greek painting, at his wealthy court. The best-known surviving painting of this school comes from the Macedonian city of Aegae (modern Vergina, in northern Greece), from a wall of the royal tombs excavated in A.D. 1977. The scene shows HADES, the god of death, abducting the maiden goddess PERSEPHONE. Factual subjects are indicated by the admirable Roman mosaic from the "House of the Faun" at Pompeii (first century A.D.), showing the Persian king Darius III fleeing from Alexander at the Battle of the Issus; this is believed to be a copy of a Greek painting of the late 300s B.C., presumably commissioned by Alexander or one of his followers. The crowded battle scene shows intricate use of detail and foreshortening.

The HELLENISTIC AGE (300–150 B.C.) saw changes that anticipate the surviving examples of Roman painting (first centuries B.C. and A.D., mainly). These include development of landscape and other backgrounds to the extent of dwarfing the foreground figures and a new value placed on *trompe l'oeil* affects, such as mural-painted false windows or corridors, opening to realistic background scenes. Subjects became more whimsical while expert techniques were forgotten, and by about A.D. 50 the Roman writer Pliny the Elder could describe painting as a dying art.

(See also ARCHITECTURE.)

Palladium See ATHENA.

Pallas See ATHENA.

Pan Minor but picturesque Greek god of flocks, herds, and mountain pasturage, worshipped mainly in the rural area of ARCADIA. Pan's name probably meant "feeder" or "pasturer." He was described as a son of HERMES and was pictured as having a human face, torso, and arms, with a goat's legs, hooves, ears, and horns. He played tunes on a reed pipe, traditionally called a panpipe. As a god of animal fertility, he was thought of as highly sexed.

At ATHENS, Pan had a shrine on the ACROPOLIS and yearly festivities involving torch races. The Athenians had adopted his worship after an incident associated with the Battle of MARATHON (490 B.C.), in which the god supposedly appeared to an Athenian dispatch runner in Arcadia.

Panathenaea Athenian festival celebrated annually in midsummer, and especially elaborately every fourth year. Although its roots were in prehistory, the Panathenaea ("all-Athens") was instituted by the Athenian tyrant PISISTRATUS in the mid-500s B.C., to serve as a nationalist-religious holiday. Considered to be the birthday of the city's patron goddess, ATHENA, the festival included sacrifices, sports competitions, and a procession of citizens (illustrated on the famous PARTHENON frieze). At the fourth-yearly celebration—called the Great Panathenaea—the procession would carry a new *pelops*, or lady's gown, up to the Athenian ACROPOLIS. There the *pelops* would be presented to the ancient olivewood statue of Athena Polias ("of the city") that was housed, after about 410 B.C., in the Erectheum.

Pandora See PROMETHEUS.

pankration One-on-one combative SPORT combining BOXING and WRESTLING. The rules allowed for punching, kicking, strangleholds, and twisting of arms and fingers; only biting and gouging were forbidden. Opponents fought naked, sometimes with light boxing thongs to protect their hands. Victory occurred when a contestant either signaled surrender or was unable to continue. The bout was overseen by a referee, but pankration ("total strength" or "complete victory") was a brutal sport: Contestants sometimes died from injuries.

Pankration was an important event at the OLYMPIC GAMES and other major athletic festivals. Successful pankratiasts were celebrities throughout the Greek world. Ancient vase paintings and stone carvings show pankration scenes, and further details are given by ancient writers and athletes' tombstone inscriptions.

Pankration was a relative latecomer to Greek sport. It is not mentioned in HOMER's poems or in any writing before the 400s B.C.

Panticapaeum Important Greek colony on the northern BLACK SEA coast, founded circa 625 B.C. by settlers from MILETUS. Panticapaeum (Pantikapaion, "ditch town") guarded the Straits of Kerch in the eastern Crimean Peninsula, in what is now southern Ukraine. With access to the interior steppes along the River Don, the city thrived from the export of Ukrainian grain to the distant cities of the central Greek world. In the era circa 438–404 B.C., under the powerful Thracian-Greek dynasty of the Spartocids, Panticapaeum became the premier supplier of grain to imperial ATHENS. Threatened in later centuries by local Scythian and Sarmatian peoples, Panticapaeum passed into the hands of King Mithridates VI of Pontus, who made it his capital (110 B.C.). After Mithridates' defeat by the Romans, the city came under control of ROME (63 B.C.).

papyrus See WRITING.

Paris In MYTH, a handsome Trojan prince, son of King PRIAM and Queen HECUBA. The name Paris (which has nothing to do with the capital city of France) means "wallet" in Greek. It may have been a nickname, since Paris had another name, Alexander (Greek: Alexandros, "defender").

With the help of the goddess APHRODITE, Paris seduced Helen, wife of King MENELAUS of Lacedaemon, and stole her away to TROY. This provoked the TROJAN WAR, in which the Greeks besieged Troy for 10 years to get Helen back. At the war's end, Paris was dead, Troy destroyed, and Helen was contentedly reunited with Menelaus.

In HOMER's *Iliad*, which presents events of the war's 10th year, Paris is portrayed as affable but irresponsible, in contrast to his elder brother, the champion HECTOR. In the *Iliad* (book 3) Paris challenges Menelaus to single combat but is nearly killed, and is saved only by Aphrodite's intervention. The goddess carries him back to his bedchamber within the walls of Troy and summons Helen to join him there.

The other tales of Paris' life were told in various post-Homeric works, including two epic poems now lost, the *Cypria* ("Tales of Cyprus") and *Little Iliad*. The narrative is as follows. Hecuba, while pregnant with Paris, dreamed that she gave birth to a flaming torch (a reference to the fated destruction of Troy). On advice of soothsayers the infant Paris was handed over to be killed, but—as in all similar Greek legends, such as that of OEDIPUS—the entrusted servant merely abandoned the baby in the wild. Rescued by shepherds, Paris grew to manhood and reclaimed his royal title after an incident of recognition at Troy.

The Judgment of Paris, the hero's most famous adventure, was recounted in the *Cypria* and was a favorite subject in Greek vase painting and other art from the 600s B.C. onward. After the goddess Eris ("strife") had set off a female rivalry in heaven (by offering a golden apple inscribed "For the fairest"), the goddesses HERA, ATHENA, and Aphrodite invited Paris to judge a beauty contest among them. They presented themselves naked to the young man. He chose the love goddess Aphrodite, whose bribe had been to promise him the world's most beautiful woman. Paris thus won Helen and the favor of Aphrodite. But henceforth he and all the Trojans suffered the hatred of Hera and Athena.

In the war's 10th year, sometime after the Greek champion ACHILLES had slain Hector, it was Paris, with the god APOLLO's help, who killed Achilles. Paris shot an arrow that struck Achilles in his only vulnerable spot, his right heel, and the wound proved fatal. Later Paris was slain by the Greek hero PHILOCTETES. Helen was briefly married to Paris' brother or half brother Deiphobus, before rejoining with Menelaus after the war.

(See also EPIC POETRY; HELEN OF TROY.)

Parmenides The most important Greek philosopher before SOCRATES. Parmenides lived circa 515–440 B.C. in the Greek city of Elea, in southwest ITALY. A member of a rich and influential family, he supposedly served Elea as a statesman and lawgiver. Supposedly one of his teachers was the immigrant philosopher XENOPHANES. Parmenides founded a school of philosophy at Elea, the Eleatic School. He is said to have visited ATHENS at least once, circa 448 B.C.; this occasion is the setting for the Athenian philosopher PLATO's fictional dialogue *Parmenides*.

Parmenides' importance to PHILOSOPHY lies in his breakthrough idea that the material world as we observe it is not real. Prior to Parmenides, the foremost philosophers sought out essential reality by searching for the material world's fundamental ingredient (hence the use of the name *material philosophers* to describe such thinkers). THALES (circa 570 B.C.) decided that the basic element is water; ANAXIMENES (circa 546 B.C.) called it *aer*, or mist. For Parmenides, however, the real world is not what we see and feel around us; rather, it can be understood only by mental contemplation. Reality is an ideal world, a timeless unity, free of change, variation, generation, or destruction. Parmenides' notion of an ideal world, inherited in part from the Pythagoreans, would later contribute significantly to Plato's Theory of Forms (mid-300s B.C.).

Parmenides' best-known written work was a didactic poem in hexameters, couched in the oracular language of religious revelation and perhaps titled *On Nature*. The poem was comprised of two parts, "The Way of Truth" and "The Way of Seeming." Of these, the former seems to have been the more important part, and, luckily, we possess about 150 lines of it. "The Way of Truth" describes how an unnamed goddess instructs the poet that only the statement "It is"—or "It exists"—can be valid. Nothing, the goddess says, does not exist.

Parnassus, Mt. See DELPHI.

Parthenon Temple of the goddess ATHENA the Virgin (*Parthenos*), built atop the Athenian ACROPOLIS in 447–432 B.C. Still partly standing and currently being reconstructed, the Parthenon is considered the most glorious building from the ancient world—the epitome of the Doric order of ARCHITECTURE and the embodiment of the classical Greek values of harmony and proportion. The Parthenon crowned a rich, powerful ATHENS that was the cultural capital of Greece. The temple was a focus of international tourism in ancient times, as it still is today; its survival for nearly 2,500 years is due to its superior design and workmanship. In fact, it would be in far better shape today had it not been blown half apart in A.D. 1687 amid fighting between Turks and Venetians, when a Venetian cannonball ignited a Turkish powder magazine inside the building.

The Parthenon was constructed in the statesman PERICLES' building program, overseen by the sculptor PHIDIAS and meant to celebrate the conclusion of hostilities with PERSIA. Designed by the architects Ictinus and Callicrates, the temple was intended as the building program's masterpiece. The Parthenon stood close to the site of a prior temple of Athena, which had been burned down by the occupying Persians of 480 B.C..

Intriguingly, the Parthenon never housed the ancient, olivewood statue of Athena Polias (which was eventually placed in the nearby Erectheum). The Parthenon was devoted to a grander, more modern vision of goddess and city. The Parthenon's cult statue was a 35-foot-high, GOLD-and-ivory figure of Athena, sculpted by Phidias. Although this statue is lost, marble copies and descriptions by ancient writers give some idea of its appearance. The goddess wore a warrior's helmet, sleeveless robe, and biblike aegis. On the palm of her right hand stood a human-size statue of the goddess NIKĒ (Victory). Athena's left hand grasped the top rim of an upright shield, which stood grounded by her left leg; a giant snake coiled within the shield, and a long spear stood upright in the crook of her left arm. The

The Parthenon's western facade, circa 430 B.C. The steps held dedicatory plaques and larger-than-life statues commemorating various citizens. On the building's western pediment, the sculpture group showed the mythical contest between Athena and Poseidon for possession of Athens.

The northwestern view of the Parthenon today. Many of the decaying sculptures of the upper structure were purchased and removed in 1800–1812 by the British ambassador to Greece, Thomas Bruce, Lord Elgin. These Elgin Marbles, as they are called, remain today in London's British Museum.

flesh of Athena and Nikē was sculpted in ivory; the rest was gold.

The temple, measuring 228 feet by 101 feet at the top of its entrance stairs, is built almost entirely of marble quarried at Mt. Pentelicus, near Athens. It has 17 columns at each side and eight columns across the front and back, rather than the more usual six.

Like other elaborate ancient Greek temples, the Parthenon had its upper structures adorned by painted, marble SCULPTURE. There were carved figures at the two pediments (the triangular gables at front and back), at the metopes (plaques along the sides), and along the frieze (the continuous paneling that ran around the outside top of the inner block, or cella). The pedimental sculptures were carved entirely in the round. The east pediment showed the mythical birth of Athena from the head of ZEUS; the west showed the contest between Athena and POSEIDON for mastery of Athens.

The metopes' figures were carved nearly in the round. They showed various mythical combats, each symbolizing the triumph of civilization over barbarism or West over East—a victory that, to the classical Greek mind, had been actually reenacted in the recent PERSIAN WARS. The combats in sculpture were: on the east, gods versus GIANTS; on the south, Lapiths versus CENTAURS; on the west, Greeks versus AMAZONS; and on the north, the TROJAN WAR.

The frieze carvings were in bas-relief. They were unique in Greek temple sculpture for showing not a mythical scene but a scene from real-life Athens—namely, the procession at the festival of the PANATHENAEA. This daring glorification of contemporary Athens must have struck some ancient observers as crass or sacriligious.

Through decay and vandalism over the centuries, many of the sculptures fell or were torn from their high places. In A.D. 1800–1812, the British ambassador to Greece—Thomas Bruce, Lord Elgin—bought and removed many of the sculptures; these "Elgin Marbles" are displayed in the British Museum. At the Parthenon today, modern casts of the Panathenaic frieze replace those carted off by Lord Elgin.

(See also CAVALRY.)

Patroclus In HOMER's epic poem the *Iliad*, Patroclus is the close friend of the Greek hero ACHILLES in the TROJAN WAR. Patroclus is the older of the two. In the *Iliad* (book 22) he charges into battle wearing Achilles' armor (with Achilles' permission) to rally the retreating Greeks. Slain by the Trojan champion HECTOR, Patroclus is avenged ferociously by Achilles, who kills numerous Trojans, including Hector. Book 23 describes Patroclus' funeral games.

The Greeks of the 500s B.C. and later, judging Patroclus and Achilles by the social standards of those days, assumed that the two men were sexual partners, in the familiar aristocratic pattern of an older man educating and protecting a younger. But the *Iliad* never states this to be, and modern scholars believe that such socially sanctioned male couplings were not part of the poet Homer's world (circa 750 B.C.) nor part of the Mycenaean world (circa 1200 B.C.) that inspired the *Iliad*. The modern consensus is that Homer imagined Patroclus strictly as Achilles' comrade and confidant.

(See also HOMOSEXUALITY.)

Pausanias (1) See PERSIAN WARS; PLATAEA, BATTLE OF.

Pausanias (2) Greek travel writer, circa A.D. 150 said to have been a physician from ASIA MINOR. His surviving prose work, *A Description of Greece,* is a valuable source of information on the physical monuments and local histories of all the important mainland Greek cities and sanctuaries, including ATHENS, SPARTA, DELPHI, and OLYMPIA.

Pegasus See BELLEROPHON.

Peirithous See PIRITHOUS.

Peisistratus See PISISTRATUS.

Peleus Mythical hero, father of ACHILLES. Peleus' father was Aeacus, king of AEGINA and a son of the god ZEUS. As an adult, Peleus had various misadventures—including murdering his half brother and accidentally killing a man during the CALYDONIAN BOAR HUNT—before arriving in THESSALY. There he married the sea goddess Thetis, a daughter of NEREUS. The match was arranged by Zeus, who (knowing that Thetis' son was preordained to be greater than his father) was anxious that she marry a mortal, rather than a god. But in order to win the resentful Thetis' hand in MARRIAGE, Peleus had to defeat her in a WRESTLING bout, during which she took on various harmful shapes: fire, water, a lion, a serpent, and an ink-squirting cuttlefish.

Later, when Thetis abandoned him and the baby Achilles, Peleus took the boy to be raised by the centaur Chiron in the glens of Thessaly's Mt. Pelion. Eventually Peleus and Thetis were reconciled, and Peleus was made immortal in repayment for his hardships.

(See also CENTAURS.)

Pelias See JASON (1).

Pella Capital city of the kingdom of MACEDON, from about 410 B.C. until the Roman conquest of 167 B.C. Located in the Thermaic coastal plain, about 25 miles northwest of the modern Greek seaport of Thessaloniki, Pella was in existence by the mid-400s B.C. and was chosen by the Macedonian king Archelaus I as his capital. In this, Pella replaced the old royal capital at nearby Aegae (modern Vergina). Archelaus, who reigned 413–399 B.C., made Pella a showplace of Greek building and culture.

At Pella ruled such mighty Macedonian kings as PHILIP II, ALEXANDER THE GREAT, and PHILIP V, in the 300s and 200s B.C. But under Roman rule Pella was totally overshadowed by the development of Thessalonica (Thessaloniki).

Archaeological excavations at Pella since A.D. 1957 have turned up the remnants of grand homes containing superb mosaics of circa 300 B.C. These works include the famous Lion Hunt of Pella and a scene of the god DIONYSUS riding on a leopard's back.

Peloponnese (Peloponnēsos) "Island of PELOPS," the wide, jagged-shape, mountainous peninsula of southern Greece, measuring 132 miles north to south and 134 east to west (maximum) and connected with central Greece by the narrow (seven-mile-wide) Isthmus of CORINTH. Other major sites in the Peloponnese include MYCENAE, SICYON, EPIDAURUS, OLYMPIA, and SPARTA. In classical times the Peloponnese was the heartland of Dorian-Greek culture—the "other" Greece, in conflict with democratic, Ionian-Greek ATHENS.

Despite a coastline hundreds of miles long, the Peloponnese has few natural harbors; only Corinth and the Argos region became great from seaborne TRADE. Coastal geography includes four mountainous peninsulas jutting southward into the AEGEAN SEA; from west to east, these four capes were named Acritas, Taenarum, Malea, and (far to the northeast) Scyllaeum. Between these peninsulas, the sea forms three wide gulfs, whose shoreline typically features a fertile alluvial plain. Important events of Greek history centered on these three coastal flats named, from west to east, the plains of MESSENIA, LACONIA, and ARGOS.

It was on the plain of Argos that Greek civilization began, circa 1600 B.C. There stood the chief group of Mycenaean-Greek cities: Mycenae, Argos, and TIRYNS. After the MYCENAEAN CIVILIZATION's downfall, the Peloponnese was largely overrun by DORIAN GREEKS, circa 1100–1000 B.C. But one Mycenaean contingent fled inland to the mountains of the central Peloponnese, to reemerge in historical times as the hard-bitten "highlanders" of ARCADIA. Of the Dorian settlements, one in particular grew to power—Sparta ("the sown land"), located in interior Laconia. By 600 B.C. the Spartans had conquered Messenia as well as Laconia, thus controlling the entire southern Peloponnese.

Two other principal Peloponnesian regions were ELIS, in the west, and ACHAEA, in the northwest. The inhabitants of these two regions were not Dorians but had affinities in race and language with the Greeks of AETOLIA and other areas north of the Corinthian Gulf.

(See also FARMING; GREECE, GEOGRAPHY OF; GREEK LANGUAGE.)

Peloponnesian War The world war of ancient Greece, in which SPARTA and its allies defeated ATHENS and its allies after 27 years of intermittent fighting, 431–404 B.C. The defeat ended Athens' 75-year reign as the richest and most powerful Greek city, and left Sparta in control of an exhausted Greece.

The Greeks called this conflict "the war between the Peloponnesians and the Athenians." One side consisted of Sparta and its core allies throughout the PELOPONNESE, grouped into a Spartan-led alliance known as the Peloponnesian League. The Athenian side included most of the islands and cities of the AEGEAN SEA and western ASIA MINOR—perhaps 200 states in all—organized into the Athenian-controlled DELIAN LEAGUE. Most of the Delian League states were peopled by IONIAN GREEKS, while the Spartan side consisted largely of DORIAN GREEKS. With some important exceptions, the war was fought along these ethnic lines, Ionians versus Dorians.

The fighting ranged across the Greek world, from eastern SICILY to BYZANTIUM. Yet the war often was mired in stalemate: Sparta remained invincible on land and Athens supreme at sea. Against the mainly defensive Athenian strategy, the cautious Spartans frequently proved ineffectual.

Low military technology contributed to the stalemate: Greek armies of the 400s B.C. had not yet developed the tactics and machinery for storming fortified cities. Catapults and elaborate siege-towers were still unknown. Siege warfare was a slow and expensive game of encircling the enemy city and waiting for its defenders to succumb to starvation, fear, or betrayal. A fortified city suppliable by sea, such as Athens, was impossible to capture unless the besieger also could block the harbor.

Sparta finally gained the upper hand in the war after two critical changes occurred. First, the Athenian disaster at SYRACUSE (413 B.C.) inspired a widespread revolt of Athens' unhappy Delian League allies. Second, Sparta allied with the non-Greek empire of PERSIA (412 B.C.), which brought Persian funds to finance Spartan war fleets. Gradually Sparta was able to challenge Athenian naval supremacy, and the Spartan naval victory at AEGOSPOTAMI (405 B.C.) made Athens' surrender inevitable (404 B.C.). The victorious Spartans—over the objections of some of their allies—spared the defeated city from destruction.

Modern knowledge of the war comes partly from archaeological evidence (such as inscribed Athenian legislative decrees) but mostly from the works of ancient writers—principally the Athenian historian THUCYDIDES (1), who served briefly as a general in the war and who produced a highly reliable history of it. Thucydides' account, unfinished, breaks off in describing the events of 411 B.C. The war's final years, 411–404 B.C., are recorded in the first part of the Hellenica, by the Athenian XENOPHON. Xenophon, like Thucydides, witnessed some of the events he describes. A third contemporary source was the Athenian comic playwright ARISTOPHANES, who addressed war politics in such plays as Acharnians (performed 425 B.C.) and Peace (421 B.C.). Later sources include the biographer PLUTARCH (circa A.D. 100).

In a famous passage, Thucydides states that the ultimate cause of the war was Spartan fear of the growth of Athenian power. For decades prior to 431 B.C., Athens showed military aggression toward its Delian League allies and toward the supposedly sovereign states of central Greece. But, more than Athens' navy and army, Sparta feared Athens' magnetic cultural appeal and the appeal of Athenian DEMOCRACY. Thus, the Peloponnesian War was partly a conflict between two political ideologies—radical democracy, embodied by Athens and most of its allies, and the old-fashioned government of OLIGARCHY, championed by Sparta. Sparta's control of the Peloponnese depended on the oligarchic ruling class in the ally cities. The politically excluded underclass in these cities posed a tremendous potential threat, liable to be exploited by the agents of democratic Athens.

Similarly, in almost every democratic city allied with Athens, a few rich right-wingers secretly wished for oligarchy. Athens itself contained such people; they seized power briefly in 411 B.C. The defections and attempted defections of cities on each side in the war came partly from this internal struggle between rich and poor, one side naturally pro-Spartan, the other naturally pro-Athenian. The most devastating civil strife occurred at the northwestern Greek city of CORCYRA, which at the war's start was an important Athenian ally but which soon (427 B.C.) succumbed to riots between democrats and oligarchs.

An immediate cause of the Peloponnesian War was Athens' cavalier attitude toward the Thirty Years' Peace of 446 B.C., which had ended prior hostilities between Athens and Sparta. Although this religiously sanctioned treaty had guaranteed that Athens would not interfere with other mainland Greek cities, the treaty was flouted by the Athen-

ian statesman PERICLES, who apparently saw a future war as inevitable. The most provocative Athenian violations were domination of AEGINA and designs against MEGARA (1). The notorious Megarian Decree, passed at Athens circa 433 B.C., effectively prohibited the Megarians from conducting TRADE throughout the Athenian empire.

Next, Athens slipped into an undeclared war against CORINTH, an important Spartan ally. First, the Corinthian navy defeated a joint Corcyrean-Athenian fleet at Sybota, near Corcyra island (433 B.C.), then Corinthian and Athenian land troops fought outside POTIDAEA (432 B.C.). Incited by the Corinthians, the Peloponnesian League voted for war against Athens (432 B.C.). The Athenian ASSEMBLY, on Pericles' urging, rejected Spartan ultimatums (fall and winter 432–431 B.C.). Both sides prepared for war.

The Spartan bloc was joined by THEBES and other cities of BOEOTIA (a central Greek region traditionally hostile to Athens). Because Boeotia bordered Athenian territory to the northwest and the Peloponnese bordered it to the west, the peninsular Athenian home region of ATTICA now faced enemies along its entire land frontier.

But Athens was ready, with its navy of 200 warships, its impregnable fortifications (including the LONG WALLS, linking the city to its harbor at PIRAEUS), and its huge financial reserve, supplied by the tribute-paying Delian League allies. Foremost among the Delian states were the eastern Aegean islands of LESBOS and CHIOS, which contributed warships and crews to Athens' navy. Outside of the league, Athens had several allies on a non-tribute-paying basis, including Corcyra, the Boeotian city of PLATAEA (a traditional enemy of Thebes), and the northwestern regions known as ACARNANIA and Amphilochia.

The Athenian war strategy was innovative and odd. Faced with a numerically superior enemy land army that boasted the best soldiers in Greece (the Spartans, Thebans, Eleans, and Arcadians), Pericles planned to avoid land battles. Instead, Athens would rely on static defense by land and amphibious attacks by sea. If the Spartans attacked Athens, as expected, the Athenians would wait out the assault, relying on the city's fortifications and sea imports of food and supplies. Meanwhile, Athenian war fleets could sail from Piraeus even if a Spartan army was outside the walls. Carrying land troops aboard, Athenian fleets could attack enemy coastal sites. These attacks might be intended as either harassments or as wholesale attempts to capture enemy cities.

The drastic aspect of Pericles' strategy was that it would abandon the Athenian countryside to the Spartans. The Athenian rural population would be housed in camps within the Long Walls and the walls of the city and Piraeus—at least for the summer campaigns if not for the whole war. The farmers' livestock would be evacuated to the Athenian-controlled island of EUBOEA.

Pericles apparently believed that his one-sided strategy would not be needed for long. He seems to have expected the war to end in about three years, with Sparta's allies demoralized. But events were destined to take a far different turn.

The war's first military action was a failed Theban night attack against Plataea (spring 431 B.C.). Then, in midsummer, the Spartan king ARCHIDAMUS led a Peloponnesian army of 24,000 HOPLITE infantry into Athenian territory. Events followed much as Pericles had forseen: Archidamus devastated crops and farm buildings in the evacuated countryside but was powerless against Athens' walls. After perhaps a month the Peloponnesians withdrew. This pattern of ineffectual Spartan invasion would recur in several following summers. The war's first 10 years (431–421 B.C.) are sometimes known as the Archidamian War, after the Spartan king who led these initial attacks.

After Archidamus had marched away that first year, Pericles himself led 13,000 hoplites and 100 warships against nearby Megara. But, like so many assaults against fortified cities in the Peloponnesian War, this one failed— as did Pericles' similar attack on EPIDAURUS the following year.

In the summer of 430 B.C., Athens suffered its first catastrophe of the war. When the Spartan army invaded for the second time, and the Athenian rural population again gathered within the walls, a deadly plague broke out at Athens (the disease's identity is unknown to us.) The cramped, unsanitary conditions of the Athenian refugees provided a breeding ground for the contagion, which raged for the next year and a half, and recurred briefly two years after that (427 B.C.). Eventually one-fourth of the population, perhaps 50,000 people, had died.

The plague removed Athens' initial advantage in the war, creating problems in manpower and leadership. Pericles himself died of the sickness in 429 B.C., at about age 65. Most significantly, the plague encouraged the Spartans by seeming to show the will of the gods.

In 429 B.C. the Spartans began besieging the defiant little city of Plataea. Two years later, the starving inhabitants surrendered (after half the garrison had escaped in a nighttime breakout through the Spartan siege lines). To please their Theban allies, the Spartans executed the male prisoners—200 Plataeans and 25 Athenians—and sold the WOMEN as SLAVES. Later, the empty town was leveled. Many Greeks felt that Plataea's destruction was an impious act, because during the PERSIAN WARS Plataea had been the site of a famous oath sworn by the Spartans and other Greeks, promising forever to honor the city.

The Athenians, now deprived of Pericles, sought more aggressively to drive Sparta's allies out of the war. Based at the West Locrian seaport of NAUPACTUS in northwestern Greece, the Athenian admiral Phormion won two spectacular naval victories against larger, Corinthian-led fleets (429 B.C.). In 426 B.C. the Athenian general DEMOSTHENES (2) brought an army of light-armed Acarnanians and Amphilochians to victory against their traditional enemy, the Corinthian colony of AMBRACIA. Demosthenes failed to capture Ambracia, but his experiences in the hilly, wooded terrain taught him the possible advantage of javelin men and slingers over heavier-armed hoplites. The subsequent Athenian development of light-armed projectile troops was one of the few tactical advances of the Peloponnesian War.

Meanwhile the important Delian League city of MYTILENE, capital of Lesbos, revolted against Athens (428 B.C.) but fell to a besieging Athenian force (427 B.C.). Back in Athens, the citizens' assembly debated how to punish the captured Mytileneans. Rescinding a vote led by the Athenian politician CLEON for massacre of the entire adult male population and enslavement of the women and children, the assembly voted a lesser penalty—execution of the 1,000 Mytileneans judged responsible for the rebellion. Certain speeches of this Mytilenean Debate provide a famous scene in Thucydides' history (book 3). Later, amid the war's increasing brutality, the Athenians would begin treating rebellion more cruelly.

Cleon, now emerging as Pericles' political heir, was a leader who could have won the war for Athens. Although not a military man by training, he embodied an aggressive, can-do spirit that was at odds with the Pericles-derived passivity of much of the Athenian officer class. In partnership with Demosthenes, Cleon would soon give Athens the upper hand in the war.

This critical campaign began when Demosthenes established an Athenian naval base at PYLOS, in the southwestern Peloponnese, only about 50 miles west of Sparta (425 B.C.). Pylos had a superb harbor, sheltered by the forested, inshore island of Sphacteria ("wasp place"). The site was especially apt because it lay in the region of MESSENIA, whose subjugated population might be incited to rebel against their Spartan overlords.

The threat of an Athenian-inspired Messenian revolt brought Spartan naval and land forces rushing against Pylos. In the ensuing sea battle, the victorious Athenians trapped 420 Spartan hoplites on Sphacteria island. The loss of these soldiers—then confined by Athenian naval patrols around the island—was disastrous for Sparta; all of the young men belonged to the dwindling Spartan warrior class, and perhaps a third of their number were "Spartiates" (Spartiatai), members of the military elite.

At the summer's end, 425 B.C., Sphacteria was overrun by an Athenian force of 800 hoplites and several thousand light-armed troops, under Demosthenes. Of the Spartans, 292 surrendered and survived. The political impetus for this Athenian assault had come from Cleon, who was present at Pylos as an elected Athenian general.

Taken as prisoners to Athens, the 292 Spartans served as diplomatic pawns until 421 B.C., when they were returned home. That their government welcomed them back rather than punishing them for their surrender—as a prior generation of Spartan leaders might have done—is a sign of how valuable their bloodstock was thought to be, amid Sparta's long-term problem of falling birthrate.

Sparta then faced its low point in the war. Its supposedly invincibile army had been humiliated, while the Athenian fort at Pylos became a rallying point for rebellious Messenians. At Athens, the Pylos victory made Cleon politically supreme, ushering in a period of Athenian military boldness in pursuit of total victory (425–421 B.C.). Spartan peace overtures were rebuffed. An imperialistic tone is evident in the surviving Athenian inscription called the Thoudippos Decree, which effectively doubled the tribute owed to Athens by its Delian League subject allies (autumn 425 B.C.). But Cleon's aggressive policy brought some Athenian setbacks. Particularly, a foolhardy Athenian invasion of Boeotia was defeated at the land battle of Delium, fought near a temple of Delian Apollo alongside the Straits of Euboea (autumn 424 B.C.).

More bad news followed for Athens: The brilliant Spartan general BRASIDAS, having marched a small Peloponnesian army to the north Aegean coast, convinced several Delian League subject towns to defect to the Spartan side. Then, in a night attack, he captured the strategic Athenian colony of AMPHIPOLIS (December 424 B.C.). The city's loss caused an outrage at Athens: Without possessing a single ship, Brasidas had dealt a blow to Athens' northeastern shipping route and had opened the threat of a wider north Aegean revolt. The Athenian general inside Amphipolis apparently had been killed or captured, while the other Athenian general in the vicinity had arrived with a naval squadron too late to save the city. This general was Thucydides, the same man whose written history of the war is our major source. Blamed by his countrymen for the loss, Thucydides was banished from Athens.

However, Brasidas was not supported by a new Spartan king, Pleistoanax, who viewed these successes mainly as bargaining chips to end the war. Yet a year's truce for peace talks passed inconsequentially (spring 423–422 B.C.), while in the north, Brasidas—ignoring the truce—continued to bring local towns into revolt against Athens.

Promising to recapture Amphipolis and eliminate Brasidas, Cleon sailed from Athens in the summer of 422 B.C. with 30 warships and a small army. But for all his pugnacity, Cleon was not an experienced tactician; while scouting the terrain around Amphipolis, he and his force were surprised by a sortie from the city, led by Brasidas. In the fight, the Athenians retreated with 600 dead, including Cleon—but Brasidas too had been killed. The Battle of Amphipolis removed at once the two most warlike leaders of the day.

In March 421 B.C. the two sides agreed to peace, which was to last 50 years. (In fact, it lasted barely three.) Modern scholars call this treaty the Peace of NICIAS, named for the cautious soldier-politician who was then the leading Athenian. The peace's terms amounted to a triumph for Athens, which was left free to maintain its empire and to recapture rebellious subject cities. It was all that Pericles could have hoped for. The peace was followed quickly by an alliance between Athens and Sparta, designed to give them dual hegemony over the rest of Greece.

The losers in this process were the Spartan ally states, which had endured hardship only to see their interests ignored. Certain states then began looking for a new leader in the Peloponnese. This they found in the previously neutral, east Peloponnesian city of ARGOS.

By 420 B.C. an anti-Spartan axis had arisen, consisting of Argos, MANTINEA, ELIS, and—surprisingly—Athens, which flouted the Peace of Nicias. The driving force behind this Athenian policy was ALCIBIADES, a volatile, left-wing aristocrat, perhaps 30 years old, who had emerged as Nicias' political opponent. Alcibiades embodied the reckless mood of an Athenian citizenry that—far from being exhausted by 11 years of war—was overconfident from the advantageous peace.

Provoked by the four-city alliance, the Spartans marched. At the Battle of Mantinea, in the central Peloponnese, a Spartan-led army of 3,600 hoplites crushed a roughly equal force of Argive, Mantinean, Elean, and Athenian troops (418 B.C.). The alliance dissolved, bringing Elis and Mantinea back into the Spartan fold. Hostilities between Athens

and Sparta did not recommence outright, but the angry Spartans awaited their chance.

In 416 B.C., the Athenians—tightening their control over their Aegean sea routes—landed a force on the Cycladic island of MELOS. The Melians were Dorian Greeks, descended from Spartan colonists. They had shown prior hostility to Athens and were now commanded to submit to Athenian rule. Under truce, Melian leaders refused the Athenian demands: Political-philosophical arguments purporting to be the positions of both sides are presented in the famous Melian Dialogue in Thucydides' history (book 5). Besieged, the Melians were starved into surrender. The Athenians killed all adult male prisoners and sold the women and children into slavery. The island was later repopulated with Athenian colonists.

The year 415 B.C. brought the most fateful event of the war—the Athenian expedition against the city of Syracuse, in southeastern Sicily. A wealthy, seafaring, Dorian-Greek democracy, Syracuse was an ally of Sparta and the enemy of the Ionian Greeks of Sicily and southern Italy.

At Alcibiades' urging, the Athenian assembly voted to send out a major force. The intended capture of Syracuse would give Athens control of the wheatfields that supplied grain to Corinth and other Spartan-allied cities. Although Alcibiades was the natural choice to lead the expedition, the Athenians mistrusted him because of his flamboyant and licentious private life. So they split the command among three generals—Alcibiades, Nicias (who had opposed the whole idea of the venture), and the able Lamachus.

Just before the departure, an act of religious terrorism occurred: Under cover of darkness, a group (probably propeace, right-wing conspirators) smashed the carved faces and genitals of the stone effigies of the god HERMES, called herms (*hermai*) that stood in front of houses throughout Athens. This sacrilegious event is known as the Mutilation of the Herms. Undoubtedly intended to create a bad omen against the expedition, the act succeeded well, because the Athenian people irrationally turned their suspicion on the commander Alcibiades.

The armada sailed in late spring. It consisted of 134 warships, 130 supply ships, 5,100 hoplites, and 1,300 archers, javelin men, and slingers (mostly allies and mercenaries), plus about 20,000 crewmen. But Alcibiades was soon summoned back to Athens to face impiety charges. He instead fled to Sparta, where he gave strategic advice against his fellow Athenians. Among other things, he advised that a Spartan officer be sent to Syracuse to organize the city's defense.

The Athenian attack on Syracuse stalled under the indecisive, ailing, 55-year-old Nicias, who took nearly a year to settle down to a siege (the spring of 414 B.C.). Outside the city wall, Athenian troops began constructing a siege wall to cut off the city's landward side; on the seaward side, Athenian naval patrols kept the Syracusan navy (about 80 warships) bottled inside the harbor. When Lamachus was killed in a skirmish at the siege works, Nicias took sole command. Meanwhile, the pessimistic Syracusans were urged to resistance by their statesman-general Hermocrates.

The tide turned when a Spartan general, Gylippus, led a small army of Peloponnesians and Sicilian Greeks into Syracuse on the landward side, around the incomplete Athenian siege wall. Gylippus blocked completion of the Athenians' wall and captured their naval base at the mouth of the bay known as the Great Harbor. This loss forced the Athenians henceforth to beach their ships on an exposed shore at the head of the bay, where they could be bottled in by the Syracusan navy. As troops and supplies trickled into Syracuse by land and sea, the besiegers became the besieged.

In the spring of 413 B.C., in response to Nicias' appeal for help, a second Athenian armada sailed for Syracuse: 73 warships carrying 5,000 Athenian and allied hoplites and 3,000 light-armed troops. The force brought two generals, Eurymedon and (Athens' finest battlefield commander of the war) Demosthenes.

By then—with Nicias' warships having been defeated in a sea battle in the Great Harbor—the Athenian position at Syracuse was so vulnerable that the reinforcements were simply entering a death trap. Demosthenes and Eurymedon urged an evacuation by sea, but Nicias (still the senior general) hesitated, believing he could yet take the city. An unlucky eclipse of the moon (August 27, 413 B.C.) led the superstitious Nicias to delay further. Another sea battle in the Great Harbor brought a second Athenian defeat and the death of Eurymedon. When Nicias finally gave the order to evacuate by sea (September 413 B.C.), the Syracusan navy blocked the Athenians from leaving the harbor mouth. Driven back to shore, the Athenians abandoned their dead and wounded and marched inland, hoping to escape to the neutral territory of the native Sicels. The bedraggled refugees numbered perhaps 40,000, largely crewmen from the ships.

"No prior Greek army had ever endured such a reversal. They had come to enslave others, but were now fleeing in fear of slavery themselves." So writes Thucydides, whose solemn account of the Athenians' final destruction (book 7) is the most moving section in his history. On the seventh day, the Athenian rear column, under Demosthenes, was surrounded and captured. The Athenian main column, under Nicias, was surrounded the next day in a riverbed and massacred with arrows and javelins. Of the approximately 7,000 captured, most died in captivity or were sold as slaves. Nicias and Demosthenes were captured and put to death.

It was the worst disaster in Athenian history: Losses included perhaps 50,000 men, 173 warships, and immense expense. Yet such were Athens' financial and spiritual resources that the city fought on for nearly another nine years (413–404 B.C.). In mainland Greece, the war had recommenced. In the spring of 413 B.C., the Spartans had invaded Athenian territory for the first time since 425 B.C. However, they did not withdraw entirely at the summer's end, but fortified the site called Decelea, about 13 miles north of Athens, to be a permanent base in Athenian territory.

Under personal command of the Spartan king Agis II, Decelea served Sparta much as Pylos had served Athens—as a front-line fort for raids and for rallying of the enemy's disaffected underclass. Thucydides says that 20,000 skilled Athenian slaves escaped to Decelea during the remaining war years.

The Spartan presence at Decelea threw Athens finally onto the defensive: Overland communication outside the walls became a hardship. The Athenian CAVALRY was now obliged to make daily patrols against Spartan war parties in the Athenian countryside. Local resources, such as food and SILVER ore, became less available. The Athenians grew increasingly reliant on purchased supplies imported by ship.

The Peloponnesian War's final nine years are sometimes known as the Ionian War, because the major campaigns shifted to the eastern Aegean and the shorelines of Asia Minor (particularly to the Greek region of western Asia Minor called IONIA). There lay the most important Athenian allies and the sea routes bringing resources westward to Athens; the most essential of these imports was grain, brought by merchant ships from the ports of the BLACK SEA. The vulnerable links in the sea route were the narrow waterways of the HELLESPONT and BOSPORUS, which Athenian forces controlled out of the naval base at SESTOS. It was against these regions that the Spartans directed their operations, aiming first to dislodge the unhappy and heavily taxed Athenian allies, and then to block Athens' supply route and bring the city to starvation.

Sparta's new role as a naval power was made possible because Athens had lost nearly three-fourths of its navy at Syracuse, and because Sparta now found a source of funds for its own shipbuilding and crews' wages, in an alliance with the Persian king Darius II (412 B.C.). In exchange, Darius received the right to reclaim the Greek cities of Asia Minor after the war.

The year after the Sicilian disaster saw the Greek world turn against Athens. Warships from the Peloponnese and Dorian Sicily began to invade the eastern Aegean. The Delian League unraveled amid revolts. The first rebel was Chios, with its considerable navy, followed by MILETUS, EPHESUS, PHOCAEA, CYMĒ, RHODES, Mytilene, and others. Of Athens' greatest east Aegean possessions, only the island state of SAMOS remained loyal. The Athenians responded with new war fleets, built with emergency funds. Samos became Athens' eastern naval base, as amphibious operations began against the rebels. Miletus and Dorian-Greek CNIDUS became Sparta's eastern naval bases.

By winter of 412–411 B.C., the scene was set for Alcibiades' return. After earning the mistrust of his Spartan masters, Alcibiades had fled to Persian protection in western Asia Minor, and from there conducted secret intrigues with the Athenians at Samos to get himself recalled to Athens' service. His chance came when the oligarchic FOUR HUNDRED seized power at Athens, and the Athenian sailors and soldiers at Samos formed a democratic government-in-exile (June 411 B.C.). Alcibiades was brought to Samos and elected as a general.

At Athens, the government of the Four Hundred, using untrained emergency crews, suffered a naval defeat against Peloponnesian ships in the Straits of Euboea (summer 411 B.C.). With all of Euboea now in revolt against Athens, the disgraced Four Hundred soon fell from power.

The next four years marked the final Athenian high point of the war, under Alcibiades' leadership. The Spartans suffered a disastrous naval defeat at Alcibiades' hands at CYZICUS (410 B.C.) and soon offered peace on generous terms. The overconfident Athenians, however, rejected the offer as insufficient. In 408 B.C. Alcibiades captured the strategically vital, rebellious Delian city of Byzantium. In 407 B.C. Alcibiades was recalled to Athens to receive extraordinary powers of command.

But when Alcibiades returned to the east Aegean in the autumn of 407 B.C., he faced a ruthless new opponent—the Spartan LYSANDER, commanding a fleet at Ephesus. After Lysander defeated a lieutenant of Alcibiades in a sea battle (spring 406 B.C.), Alcibiades was blamed at Athens and was not reelected as general. Knowing that his life was in danger from his ungrateful fellow citizens, the greatest naval commander of the day retired to an estate beside the Hellespont.

Athens—foolishly trying to re-create its lost empire—was running out of resources. To man the newest fleet off the blocks, the Athenians resorted to enlisting slaves and resident aliens as oarsmen (a duty usually taken by lower-income Athenian citizens). In August of 406 B.C. these motley crewmen won the huge sea battle of Arginusae ("the white islands") off Mytilene. But the triumph was soured when the crews of the Athenian disabled vessels—about 5,000 men—perished in a storm immediately afterward. At Athens, hysteria reigned over the failure to rescue the crews: Six of the responsible naval commanders, including Pericles' son, were executed. Worse, on the urging of the demagogue Cleophon, the assembly again rejected Spartan peace proposals.

Now a weak and inexperienced Athenian naval command led an irreplaceable force of about 200 ships. In the summer of 405 B.C. the wily Lysander sailed from Ephesus with 150 ships and slipped into the Hellespont, where he captured Lampsacus. When an 180-ship Athenian fleet arrived in pursuit, Lysander ambushed and destroyed it at the sea battle of Aegospotami ("the goat's rivers"). The Athenian navy had ceased to exist.

Spartan forces converged on the fortress of Athens, which endured six months of siege, without food imports. At last, the starving inhabitants voted to accept Sparta's terms—peace in exchange for the destruction of certain city fortifications, the surrender of overseas holdings and of most of the remaining warships, the recall of political exiles, and a military alliance with Sparta. The city capitulated in April 404 B.C. Lysander's forces occupied Athens and Piraeus. The Long Walls were torn down to the MUSIC of flutes. It was the end of Athens as the dominant power in Greece.

(See also CONON; CORINTHIAN WAR; EURIPIDES; SOCRATES; SOPHOCLES; THERAMENES; THIRTY TYRANTS, THE; WARFARE, LAND; WARFARE, NAVAL; WARFARE, SIEGE.)

Pelops　In Greek MYTH, Pelops was a prince of a non-Greek kingdom in ASIA MINOR—either LYDIA or Paphlagonia. His father was TANTALUS, who was a son of the god ZEUS and who offended the gods in an infamous episode. Pelops eventually emigrated to southern Greece, where he supposedly founded the OLYMPIC GAMES and fathered the

line of kings at MYCENAE. He is commemorated in the name of the southern Greek peninsular region, the PELOPONNESE (Greek: Peloponnēsos, "island of Pelops"). The name Pelops (dark face) may refer to his Asian origin.

The best-known version of the Pelops story is told in the poet PINDAR's First Olympian ode, written in 476 B.C. As a youth in Asia Minor, Pelops became the favorite of POSEIDON (god of horses as well of the sea), who taught Pelops to be a great horseman and charioteer. Arriving in Greece, Pelops went to Pisa (the future site of OLYMPIA). There he asked for the hand in MARRIAGE of Hippodameia, the daughter of King Oenomaus.

Oenomaus secretly intended that his daughter never marry, either because he harbored an incestuous desire for her or because he knew a prophecy that his son-in-law would kill him. His terms of courtship were that anyone might carry Hippodameia off by chariot, but Oenomaus would follow and, upon overtaking, could spear the suitor. Twelve or 13 men had already died in this manner; their heads were nailed above the gates of Oenomaus' palace.

But Pelops cleverly bribed Oenomaus' groom, Myrtilus, to remove the linchpins from his master's chariot axle and replace them with wax. In the contest, Oenomaus' chariot collapsed and the evil king was dragged to death behind his horses. Pelops then married Hippodameia and became king of Pisa. Later he deceitfully killed Myrtilus, either to avoid acknowledging his help or to avoid sharing Hippodameia's favors with him, as promised. But the dying Myrtilus cursed Pelops and his family, and the curse proved effective. Pelops' son ATREUS and grandson AGAMEMNON ruled households riven by bloodshed.

The myth of Pelops and Oenomaus was in part aetiological—that is, it explained the origin of a custom, namely the Olympic chariot race. In historical times Pelops was worshipped as a hero at Olympia, where his purported tomb was located. At Olympia's Temple of Zeus, the sculptures on the east pediment showed Pelops and Oenomaus preparing for the fateful chariot race, with Zeus standing between them and looking toward his grandson Pelops.

(See also CHARIOTS.)

Penelope　In MYTH, the Spartan-born wife of the Ithacan king ODYSSEUS; their son was TELEMACHUS. Penelope faithfully awaited her husband's return during his 20-year absence—10 years fighting the TROJAN WAR and another 10 years for his homeward voyage.

In HOMER's epic poem the *Odyssey*, Penelope appears as a gracious and clever lady. Since about the seventh year of Odysseus' disappearance during his voyage from TROY, she has been pressured to assume him dead and to marry one of the 108 suitors—local nobles and nearby kings—who have flocked to the palace at ITHACA. She puts them off by claiming she cannot remarry until she finishes weaving a shroud for Odysseus' elderly (but still living) father, Laertes. Every night she secretly unravels what she has woven that day, so that the work never progresses. At length the deceit is discovered, and she is compelled to make known the day on which she will choose a new husband. Finally she announces that she will marry whoever can bend and string Odysseus' mighty bow, then shoot an arrow through the empty sockets of 12 axheads sunk in a line. In fact, it is Odysseus himself who performs this feat, having returned to Ithaca disguised as a beggar. Then he slaughters the suitors and reclaims his throne (*Odyssey* books 21–22).

Afterward, Penelope and Odysseus lived happily for years. After his death—according to one post-Homeric version—Penelope married Telegonus, who was Odysseus' son by CIRCE.

pentathlon The "fivefold contest," one of the most prestigious events at such Greek sports festivals as the OLYMPIC GAMES. Contestants competed in the footrace, long jump, throwing the discus, and throwing the javelin. The two men scoring highest in these events were selected for the final contest, a WRESTLING match. The winner of this was declared to be the pentathlete.

(See also SPORT.)

Penthesilea See AMAZONS.

Pentheus See DIONYSUS.

Pergamum One of the wealthiest and most important Greek cities of the later HELLENISTIC AGE (circa 250–133 B.C.). Located on the north-central west coast of ASIA MINOR, about 15 miles inland in the hills along the River Caïcus, Pergamum (Greek: Pergamon) thrived from local SILVER mines and exports of grain, textiles, and parchment (Greek: *pergamēnē*).

We first hear of Pergamum after about 400 B.C., when it was one of many Greek cities of the region called AEOLIS. Soon after 300 B.C. Pergamum was a subject city of the sprawling SELEUCID EMPIRE. But by 262 B.C. the Pergamenes, under their leaders Philetaerus and his adopted son Eumenes, had revolted from Seleucid rule. The royal dynasty of the Attalids—"the sons of Attalus" (Philetaerus' father)—brought the city to its zenith. Pergamum dominated Asia Minor and became a center of Greek culture, with a royal library that was second in size only to the one at Egyptian ALEXANDRIA (1).

Eumenes' successor was King Attalus I (reigned 269–197 B.C.). He defeated the invading CELTS, resisted the ambitions of the Macedonian king PHILIP V, and wisely sided with the Romans against Philip in the Second Macedonian War (200–197 B.C.). Attalus' friendship with ROME helped assure Pergamum's survival amid Roman conquest of the eastern Mediterranean. When Attalus III died in 133 B.C., he bequeathed his kingdom to the Romans.

The grandeur of ancient Pergamum is suggested in the Great Altar of ZEUS, erected by King Eumenes II (reigned 197–159 B.C.) and now housed in a Berlin museum. Carved with marble bas-reliefs showing the gods' mythical combat with the GIANTS, the altar is one of the most admired surviving Hellenistic artworks.

The site of Pergamum, terraced cleverly into high hills, has been excavated since the late 19th century A.D. The partly restored city is one of the most dramatic ancient Greek sites in Turkey. Particularly grand is the ancient THEATER, nestled into a hill near the ACROPOLIS.

(See also WRITING.)

Periander Dictator of CORINTH from about 625 to 585 B.C. The son and successor of CYPSELUS, Periander reigned energetically over a city that was the most prosperous in Greece. Combining total power with wise statesmanship, he was the most famous example of the breed of Greek rulers known as TYRANTS. Later generations counted him among the SEVEN SAGES of Greece.

Periander extended his power through the Greek world by war and diplomacy. He brought Corinth's rebellious colony CORCYRA to heel and captured the Peloponnesian city of EPIDAURUS. Looking to western ASIA MINOR, he forged ties with the Greek city of MILETUS and the non-Greek kingdom of LYDIA. Asked to arbitrate in a war between ATHENS and MYTILENE, he in effect judged in favor of Athens. This act inaugurated a period of Corinthian-Athenian friendship. (The two cities had a mutual trading rival, AEGINA.)

In TRADE, Periander brought Corinth to new heights. Responding to the great demand for Corinthian goods among the ETRUSCANS of western ITALY, Periander enlarged the westward shipping route, establishing Adriatic colonies such as APOLLONIA and EPIDAMNUS to serve as anchorages and local depots. In the distant northeastern region called CHALCIDICĒ, Periander founded the colony of POTIDAEA. Apparently he also pursued trade with EGYPT, as suggested by the Egyptian royal name Psammetichus that he gave to his son.

Exploiting Corinth's geography, Periander constructed a ships' dragway (Greek: *diolkos*) across the seven-mile-wide isthmus that separates the Saronic Gulf from the Corinthian Gulf. A stretch of this stone roadbed, with grooves for trolley wheels, still can be seen today. The *diolkos* provided Greek merchant ships with an east–west overland shortcut across central Greece—and provided Corinth with revenue from tolls.

Periander's city was the cultural capital of mainland Greece. Poets such as the famous ARION came to Periander's court. The tyrant's public-building program stimulated the development of the form of monumental ARCHITECTURE known as the Doric order. In painted POTTERY, Corinthian artists achieved the style that we call Corinthian and that monopolized the Mediterranean market in that day.

Periander could be ruthless. He used surveillance and intimidation against Corinthians who might pose a threat to his power, and he executed the most important of them. After one of Periander's sons was killed in Corcyra (probably as governor), Periander took 300 boys from Corcyra's foremost families and shipped them as a gift to the Lydians, to be turned into eunuchs. (As it happened, they were rescued.) Periander's passions were uncontrolled: Gossip claimed that he murdered his beloved wife, Melissa, in an irrational rage of jealousy and then, in remorse, had sexual intercourse with her corpse.

Dying at an old age in 585 B.C., Periander left his dynasty beleaguered. His son Psammetichus reigned for three years before being ousted in favor of a liberal OLIGARCHY.

(See also COLONIZATION.)

Pericles The greatest Athenian statesman, living circa 495–429 B.C. Despite his aristocratic blood, he entered politics as a left-wing radical and by the mid-440s B.C. was preeminent in the government, steering ATHENS through its heyday of power and cultural achievement. More than any other individual, Pericles shaped classical Athens as a radical DEMOCRACY and naval power, as a center of learning, and as a city of architectural splendors, ascending to the PARTHENON. Pericles' ambitious vision created this Athens that (to use his own phrase) was an EDUCATION to the rest of Greece. Yet he ended his days in disfavor, after his belligerence toward other Greek states had provoked the PELOPONNESIAN WAR and his defensive military strategy had brought plague and demoralization to his city.

Pericles never held any such post as "president" of Athens, since no such job existed under the democracy. His highest title was *stratēgos*, "military general," a post to which the Athenians elected 10 different men annually. Unlike most other generals, however, Pericles was elected at least 20 times; we know that he served without interruption from 443 to 430 B.C..

Pericles' source of power was the *dēmos*—the common people, the mass of lower- and middle-income citizens. He was a politician they trusted to protect them against the

Fleet commander, imperialist, left-wing politician: Pericles was the statesman who made Athens into the greatest city of its day. This likeness comes from a surviving Roman marble bust, which was probably copied from an Athenian bronze portrait statue (now lost) sculpted by Cresilas, a contemporary of Pericles.

rich and to guide the city. A rigorously intellectual man, Pericles was an accomplished orator, whose speeches in the public ASSEMBLY could sway his listeners to vote for his proposals.

Most of our knowledge of him comes from the Athenian historian THUCYDIDES (1), who wrote circa 430–400 B.C., and from the biographer PLUTARCH, who wrote circa A.D. 100. Thucydides is especially helpful because he knew Pericles personally and understood his politics. Some details are added by other writers and by inscriptions recording Periclean-inspired legislation.

Pericles' father was XANTHIPPUS, a distinguished Athenian soldier-politician. Pericles' mother was Agariste, a niece of the Athenian statesman CLEISTHENES (1) and a member of the noble clan of the ALCMAEONIDS. The family's wealth and influence no doubt helped Pericles enter politics, but he soon disassociated himself from the Alcmaeonids and from other right-wing connections.

At about age 23 he served as *chorēgos* (paying sponsor) for AESCHYLUS' stage drama *The Persians* (472 B.C.). Pericles' involvement in this politically charged play identifies him as a follower of the beleaguered left-wing Athenian statesman THEMISTOCLES. In the 480s B.C. Themistocles had pushed two interrelated programs—radical democracy and a buildup of the navy. The lower-income citizens who followed Themistocles were the same men who served as crews in the labor-intensive warships. Gradually Pericles emerged as Themistocles' political heir.

In 463 B.C., at about age 32, Pericles (unsuccessfully) prosecuted the conservative leader CIMON for bribery. The following year Pericles assisted the radical reformer EPHIALTES in proposing legislation that dismantled the power of the AREOPAGUS. Ephialtes' death and Cimon's OSTRACISM (both in 461 B.C.) left Pericles as the foremost Athenian politician. His influence can be seen in the next decade, in Athens' left-leaning domestic policies and in its bellicose stance toward SPARTA and certain other Greek states, such as AEGINA.

In 461 B.C. Pericles urged the creation of the LONG WALLS, which were to stretch four miles from Athens down to its harbor at PIRAEUS. Completed circa 457 B.C., the walls turned Athens into an impregnable naval fortress. They also brought Piraeus' laborers and citizen-sailors more directly into Athenian politics.

Circa 457 B.C. Pericles sponsored a bill creating jury pay. This important democratic measure effectively opened jury duty to lower-income citizens. It was probably also Pericles who, sometime in the mid-400s B.C., instituted public assistance for the poorest citizens.

By 460 B.C. Athens had slipped into an undeclared war against Sparta and its allies. Repeatedly elected as general, Pericles led a seaborne raid against the enemy city of SICYON (circa 454 B.C.) and led an Athenian fleet to the BLACK SEA to make alliance with Greek cities there that could supply precious grain to Athens (circa 452 B.C.).

Circa 449 B.C. Pericles convinced his fellow citizens to accept an offered peace with PERSIA, officially ending the PERSIAN WARS. To mark the event and to glorify the city, Pericles initiated a public building program, directed by the sculptor PHIDIAS. This program—which created most of the famous buildings still standing today on the Athenian

ACROPOLIS—amounted to a show of dominance over Athens' Greek ally states in the DELIAN LEAGUE. The league had been formed (circa 478 B.C.) as a mutual-defense alliance against Persia, but now Pericles was demonstrating that, rather than reduce or forgive the allies' war dues on account of the new peace, Athens would continue collecting dues and would use them as it pleased.

Pericles' imperialism is also evident in the use of Athenian garrison colonies (known as cleruchies) to punish and guard resistant Delian League states. Among the Greek regions that received these hated, land-grabbing, Athenian settler communities were Aegina, EUBOEA, and the Cycladic island of Naxos.

As reported by Thucydides, Pericles' grim imperialism is summarized in a speech to the Athenian assembly in 430 B.C., after the outbreak of the Peloponnesian War. "It is no longer possible for you to give up your empire," Pericles told the people. "You hold the empire as a tyrant holds power: you may have been wrong to take it, but you cannot safely let it go." He went on in the speech to glorify Athens as "the greatest name in history . . . the greatest power that has ever yet arisen, a power to be remembered forever."

In 446 B.C. the Spartans invaded Athenian territory. Although Pericles was able to appease them with bribery and diplomatic concessions, the resulting Thirty Years' Peace was unpopular at Athens. Pericles was attacked by an Athenian right-winger named THUCYDIDES (2)—not the historian, but his maternal grandfather. By 443 B.C. Pericles and his followers had rallied, convincing the Athenian people to ostracize Thucydides.

Having become preeminent, Pericles became inaccessible. The biographer Plutarch records a change in Pericles' personality at this point; no longer the straightforward man of the people, Pericles adopted a formal style that Plutach calls "aristocratic or even kingly." More than just indulging in arrogance, Pericles apparently was seeking to keep control of the people and to make himself impervious to bribery or undue influence. He became known for never accepting an invitation to dinner or to the drinking parties where rich men discussed politics. His cold, rational aloofness earned him the nickname "the Olympian" (as though he were a god of MT. OLYMPUS).

His supremacy was severely tested by the revolt of the Delian League allies SAMOS and BYZANTIUM (440 B.C.). The defeat of Samos required a huge Athenian naval effort, and Pericles' generalship seems to have come in for some criticism on the Athenian comic stage. In 440 or 439 B.C. Pericles sponsored a law suspending the performance of all comedy for three years.

He endured an indirect political attack in around 438 B.C., when his friends Phidias and ANAXAGORAS were charged with the crime of impiety. ASPASIA, Pericles' common-law wife, might have been a third defendant. Phidias and Anaxagoras each departed from Athens at this time.

In the late 430s B.C., when hostilities with Sparta and CORINTH loomed, Pericles apparently saw war as inevitable, and refused to appease. It was undoubtedly he who advised the Athenians to make their fateful defense pact with CORCYRA (433 B.C.), which Corinth found so alarming, and he was likewise the author of the bellicose Megarian Decree

(circa 432 B.C.), directed against the nearby city of MEGARA.

When the Peloponnesian War broke out (431 B.C.), Pericles advised defense by land and offensive strikes by sea. With his faith in Athens' immense resources and fortifications, he convinced the rural citizens to evacuate their homes and contain themselves within the city walls, while the invading Spartans ravaged the countryside. This strategy backfired, however, when plague broke out among the Athenian refugees in their unsanitary encampments and swept the city (430 B.C.). At the same time, large Athenian expeditions failed to capture either Megara or (in a siege directed by Pericles himself) EPIDAURUS.

The angry Athenians voted to depose the 65-year-old Pericles from office and fine him a crushing 10 TALENTS. Relenting, they elected him as general for the following year. But in that year, 429 B.C., he died, probably of the plague.

Pericles had two sons by an Athenian wife, whom he divorced for Aspasia circa 450 B.C. By a law of his own sponsoring, Pericles, being an Athenian citizen, could not legally marry Aspasia, who was an immigrant from MILETUS. Still, they lived together for 20 years until his death. Their son, named Pericles, was made an Athenian citizen by a special vote of the assembly, but he was one of the six Athenian generals executed by the people after the sea battle of Arginusae in 406 B.C.

(See also CALLIAS; CLEON; CRATINUS; FUNERAL CUSTOMS; LAWS AND LAW COURTS; MARRIAGE; PROTAGORAS; RHETORIC; SOPHOCLES; THEATER; WARFARE, NAVAL; WOMEN.)

perioeci   The Greek term *perioikoi* (dwellers around, often latinized to perioeci) describes certain second-class citizens in some Greek states. Perioeci were typically free-born and native; they had basic legal protections and obligations, such as military service, but were excluded by birth from the taking part in government. By occupation, many were smallholding farmers.

This citizen class existed at ARGOS, CRETE, THESSALY, and elsewhere. But the perioeci usually are spoken of in connection with SPARTA, where they were literally "dwellers around," inhabiting the foothills and secondary sites around the Eurotas River valley. The heart of this fertile plain was reserved for true Spartans—the Spartiatai. Together, Spartiates and perioeci constituted the united people known as Lakedaimonioi.

(See also LACONIA; POLIS.)

Peripatetic School   See LYCEUM.

Persephone   Greek goddess who was queen of the Underworld and wife of the god HADES. In MYTH, Persephone was identified with Korē, the daughter of the grain goddess, DEMETER. Modern writers, for the sake of thoroughness, sometimes refer to her as Korē-Persephone.

When the invading Greeks first entered the Greek mainland circa 2100 B.C., they probably encountered a pre-Greek, native goddess whom they called Persephone. This name, translatable as "destroyer" in Greek, presumably imitates the sound of some non-Greek name now lost to us. The pre-Greek goddess may have been a judge and ruler among the spirits of the dead. The Greeks amalgamated her into their own RELIGION, identifying her with their minor goddess Korē ("maiden").

The Persephone or Korē of Greek myth was the daughter of Demeter and the great god ZEUS. While gathering flowers one day, she was abducted by her uncle, the god Hades, to become his queen in the Underworld. After searching frantically for her, Demeter appealed to Zeus. He ruled that Persephone should spend four months of every year with her husband and eight months in the upper world with her mother. The classical Greeks interpreted the goddess' double name as a sign of her dual nature: Korē the Maiden aboveground and the sterner Queen Persephone below. (But neither Persephone nor Hades was thought of as evil; death was seen as a natural part of the world.)

By the 600s B.C. Persephone also had become part of the fringe cult called ORPHISM. Orphism involved a complicated belief in reincarnation after death: Only by living successive lives (on the earth and also in the Underworld) could a person's soul ascend to eternal bliss. Persephone, as the judge of the dead, directed each soul's sequence of transmigrations, according to how piously the person had lived each prior life.

For some reason, Orphism became quite popular among the Greeks of SICILY and southern ITALY. Consequently Persephone became a major goddess of the Sicilian Greeks, and her myth became localized in Sicily. Supposedly it was near the city of Henna (modern Enna) that Hades stole Persephone away, and supposedly volcanic Mt. Etna served as the hearth where Demeter lit two torches for night-searching. Obviously, such details represent a later layer of the story.

(See also AFTERLIFE; ELEUSINIAN MYSTERIES.)

Perseus (1)   In MYTH, a hero of ARGOS and TIRYNS, and the slayer of the monster MEDUSA. The story of Perseus' birth is one of the most picturesque Greek legends: King Acrisius of Argos had a beautiful daughter, Danaë, but he was warned by prophecy that he was destined to be killed by any son born to her. So he locked her in a tower or a bronze chamber, to keep anyone from approaching her. But the great god ZEUS came to her in the form of a shower of GOLD, and in due time she bore a son, whom she named Perseus (destroyer).

Acrisius, surprised to learn of these developments, put Danaë and Perseus to sea in a chest, which drifted south through the Aegean. Coming ashore at Seriphus, an island of the CYCLADES, mother and child were welcomed by the local king, Polydectes. There Perseus grew to manhood. Polydectes—intending to force Danaë to marry him, and wanting Perseus out of the way—sent the young man on a seemingly deadly mission: to go to the far West (or far South), find the three demon sisters known as the Gorgons, and bring back the head of the one called Medusa. The Gorgons were so hideous that merely looking at any one of them would cause a person to turn to stone. Nevertheless, Perseus set off, with sword and shield.

On advice of the goddess ATHENA, Perseus consulted the Graiae—three old sisters who had one eye and one tooth among them. Stealing their one eye until they would help him, Perseus received directions for finding the Gorgons' home. He also received from them a pair of winged flying shoes and a cap that would turn him invisible, as well as a pouch for carrying Medusa's severed head. Flying invisible to the land of the Gorgons, he sneaked up on Medusa with his face averted, guiding himself by watching her harmless reflection in his shield. Shearing off her head, he immediately hid it in his satchel, since the head itself could turn people to stone. Perseus flew off, still invisible, evading Medusa's two sisters.

Soaring over the sea toward Seriphus, he then saved the Ethiopian princess Andromeda from a sea monster. (Andromeda's parents had planned to sacrifice her, to save their kingdom from the god POSEIDON's wrath.) Perseus killed the monster, married Andromeda, and resumed his journey by ship with her. At Seriphus, Perseus rescued his mother, using Medusa's head to turn Polydectes and his followers to stone. Then, leaving the island in the hands of Polydectes' righteous brother Dictys, Perseus returned with Andromeda to his native Argos.

The prophecy that Perseus would kill his grandfather Acrisius was fulfilled when the hero, throwing the discus in competition, inadvertently struck and killed Acrisius, who was sitting among the spectators. Leaving the throne of Argos to a kinsman, Perseus became king of Tiryns and, according to one tradition, founded the nearby city of MYCENAE. Supposedly one of his sons, Perses, became the father of the Asian people known as the Persians.

The Perseus tale may distortedly recall the political unification of the Argive plain in early Mycenaean times (circa 1600 B.C.), as well as Mycenaean naval conquests in the Cyclades and beyond.

(See also MYCENAEAN CIVILIZATION.)

Perseus (2)   See MACEDON.

Persia   The vast, rich, non-Greek kingdom of Persia played a crucial role in Greek history—largely as an antagonist, but also as an employer, overlord, or ally for many Greeks, especially those in ASIA MINOR. At its height, circa 500 B.C., the Persian realm stretched westward from the Indus valley (modern-day Pakistan) to THRACE and MACEDON, on the northeastern border of Greece, with EGYPT included. Encompassing about 1 million square miles, unified by a network of roads, and ruled by an absolute monarch, Persia was the greatest empire the world had yet seen. Persian plans to conquer mainland Greece in 490 and 480 B.C. were miraculously defeated by the relatively puny Greek states. The empire's size eventually proved to be its undoing, as the delegation of power to local governors gradually weakened the king's authority. When the Macedonian king ALEXANDER THE GREAT invaded the Persian Empire with a mere 37,000 soldiers in 334 B.C., he found a disunified realm under a weak monarch, ripe for destruction. By the time of Alexander's death (323 B.C.), Persia was ruled as a Greek-Macedonian kingdom, eventually known as the SELEUCID EMPIRE. But the Iranian cultures of the central plateau continued to thrive, reclaiming power by the second century B.C.

The Persians enter recorded history circa 850 B.C. as a nomadic, pastoral people in the western Iranian plateau. They called themselves the Parsa; their territory (which shifted steadily in these years) was known as Parsua. By the 600s B.C. the Persians had settled in the southwest Iranian plateau, bounded on the west by the River Tigris and on the south by the Persian Gulf; this region would henceforth be their heartland. In these years the Persians were subjects of the kindred Medes, another Iranian people. As vassals of the Medes, the Persians kings reigned out of the provincial capital at Susa, near the head of the Persian Gulf.

In 549 B.C. the Persian king CYRUS (1) led a revolt against the Median overlords. The Persians captured the Median capital and imposed a new dynasty—a Persian one. Henceforth the Persians were the ruling class; the Medes became their subordinates, although still partners in the empire.

It was Cyrus' conquest of western Asia Minor (546 B.C.) that brought the Persians into contact with the Greeks, in the cities of IONIA.

(See also AGESILAUS; CALLIAS; CAVALRY; CYPRUS (1); DARIUS (1); DELIAN LEAGUE; HERODOTUS; KING'S PEACE; PERSIAN WARS; XENOPHON.)

Persian Wars   Although the Greeks and Persians were in intermittent conflict for over 200 years, the term *Persian Wars* refers mainly to the campaigns of 490 and 480–79 B.C., in which the Greeks successfully defended mainland Greece against two Persian invasions. These were the famous campaigns of MARATHON, THERMOPYLAE, and SALAMIS (1).

The Persian Wars were immensely important for Western civilization. The Greeks, a relatively small and disunified nation, unexpectedly defeated the greatest empire on earth. Afterward, this experience compelled the Greeks to identify themselves culturally. The world's first real historian, the Greek HERODOTUS, writing in the mid-400s B.C., chose the Persian Wars as his story to tell; it was the greatest understandable event in human memory, and it distinguished the Greek from the "barbarian." Similarly, the amazing Athenian cultural achievements of the 400s and 300s B.C.—in THEATER, PHILOSOPHY, SCULPTURE, ARCHITECTURE, and the development of DEMOCRACY—were products of a confidence or arrogance adopted because of the Persian Wars. Had the invading Persians won and had Greece become just another province of their empire, there would have been no brilliant Athenian century to serve as the foundation of modern culture.

The first stage of the conflict was the Persians' westward push into ASIA MINOR in the mid-500s B.C., when the Persian king CYRUS (1) conquered the east Greek region known as IONIA. Cyrus and his successors ruled moderately but demanded tribute, labor, and military service from their Greek subjects, governing them by means of Greek puppet rulers.

In 513 B.C. the Persian king DARIUS (1) led an army across the BOSPORUS and received the submission of THRACE and MACEDON. Southwest of Macedon, the land of Greece itself was still free, but for how long? It seemed obvious that the Persians would attack eventually, and equally obvious—to many—that Greece would fall. Certain Greeks began making friendly overtures to their expected overlords. A new verb appeared in the Greek language: Mēdizein, "to Medize," or to collaborate with the Medes (i.e., with the Persians). Among the most egregious Medizers were those

local Greek despots known as TYRANTS (*turannoi*), who hoped to retain power and become the Persians' puppets after the conquest. Another Medizing force was the priesthood of the god APOLLO at DELPHI. The Persian kings had traditionally sent gifts to Delphi, to develop contacts inside Greece; apparently the priesthood now decided that a Persian conquest would be to their god's advantage. Therefore, during the Persian Wars, the Delphic oracle consistently gave advice that was defeatist in tone.

The IONIAN REVOLT of 499–493 B.C. saw the Greek cities of Asia Minor rise up, ill-fatedly, against their Persian masters. Before being crushed, the revolt attracted help from two cities of mainland Greece: ATHENS and ERETRIA. This intervention backfired, convincing the Persians to subdue Greece immediately. Soon Persian heralds appeared in the cities and islands of Greece, demanding the tokens of earth and water that were the formal symbols of submission to the Persian king. Many frightened Greek states obeyed, but the Athenians, in a violation of diplomatic sacrosanctity, threw the Persian envoys into the condemned criminals' pit. At SPARTA the envoys were thrown down a well, where (they were told) there was plenty of earth and water. Thus did the militaristic state of Sparta, with the best army in Greece, signal its intention to stand alongside Athens, against Persia.

Darius had at his court an Athenian adviser, HIPPIAS (1), the former tyrant of Athens who had been expelled in 510 B.C. Darius resolved to capture Athens and install the aged Hippias as his puppet. In the summer of 490 B.C. a Persian seaborne expedition crossed the AEGEAN SEA, landed at Eretria, destroyed that city, and sailed south to the coastal town of Marathon, about 26 miles from Athens. There a Persian army of perhaps 20,000 troops disembarked; with them was Hippias. But at the Battle of Marathon the attackers were totally defeated by 9,000 Athenians and a few hundred Plataeans, in a plan devised by the general MILTIADES.

After Darius' death, his son and successor, XERXES, decided to invade Greece in full force. He gathered a massive army, perhaps 300,000 land troops, including subject peoples as well as Persian regulars. His navy, numbering perhaps 600 warships, was drawn from seafaring provinces such as PHOENICIA, EGYPT, and Greek Ionia. Other preparations included spanning of the HELLESPONT with twin bridges of boats, a marvel of Persian engineering skill.

Preparations were under way on the Greek side as well. At Athens the brilliant stateman and general THEMISTOCLES convinced the democratic ASSEMBLY to vote to build 100 new trireme warships, thereby giving Athens about 180 ships in all—the biggest navy of any Greek city. Themistocles foresaw that the defense of Greece would depend on fighting at sea. The Persians' land army was too vast to destroy; but cripple their navy, and the army would founder—from lack of transport, supply, and communication. With a large fleet, Athens could be protected or, if need be, evacuated.

The uneasy alliance of Greek states, dominated by the land power Sparta, mapped out a grand strategy. The terrain and shoreline of Greece naturally compel a southward-moving invader through a series of bottlenecks on land and sea, and the Greek plan was basically to fight at certain defensible bottlenecks—a mountain pass, a sea channel—where the invader's advantage of superior numbers would be canceled. On land, the Greeks would avoid battle in the open plains, where the mighty Persian CAVALRY would rule. Similarly, for a sea fight, a narrow channel would tend to offset the superior seamanship of the Persians' elite contingent, the Phoenicians.

One advantage for the Greeks, of which they were not yet fully aware, was that their HOPLITE heavy infantryman was better than his Persian counterpart—not in courage, but in equipment and training. The hoplite wore a BRONZE breastplate and helmet, and carried a bronze-plated shield and a thrusting spear up to eight feet long; the Persian trooper wore less armor and carried a shorter spear and a shield made only of wickerwork. In the crush of battle, the hoplites usually could push through. But hoplites were not invincible, and the Persians had the great advantage in numbers.

Led by Xerxes, the Persians crossed the Hellespont and descended through Thrace and Macedon (spring 480 B.C.). A Greek army marched to the mountain gorge of Tempe, in northern THESSALY, but then abandoned the site as being too far forward, in hostile territory. Thessaly submitted to the Persians, and the Greeks drew up a line of defense on Thessaly's southern frontier, at two interrelated sites: the mountain pass of Thermopylae and the six-mile-wide sea channel at ARTEMISIUM, on the northern shore of EUBOEA.

Simultaneous battles were fought on land and sea. The Battle of Thermopylae was a heroic Greek blunder; an army under the Spartan king Leonidas held the pass for three days but never received reinforcements, and was overrun. More creditable was the sea fight at Artemisium, where about 370 Greek warships met an enemy fleet that had been badly reduced—perhaps to 450 ships, from 600—by recent storms. The battle was a marginal Persian victory, but it showed the Greeks what they could do against the much-vaunted Phoenician crews, and it apparently encouraged the Greek admirals in their strategy of relying on narrow waterways to offset the enemy's advantages.

The defenders retreated south through central Greece. BOEOTIA submitted to the invaders and, like Thessaly, was forced to supply troops to fight against their fellow Greeks. In a dramatic decision, the Athenians voted to evacuate their city to the enemy: They would not stay and surrender. The noncombatants were transported to safe locales nearby, and the Athenian troops and warships remained on duty in the Greek forces. Athens was occupied and sacked by the Persians.

The summer was ending. Certain Greek commanders wanted to retreat farther south, to the naturally defensible Isthmus of CORINTH, but Themistocles and the Spartan commanding admiral, Eurybiades, pressed to offer battle at sea, in the one-mile-wide channel east of the island of Salamis, in the Saronic Gulf. There the Greek fleet stationed itself. Although Xerxes could have chosen to bypass, he overconfidently ordered his navy to attack the Greeks inside the channel, and the result was a complete Greek victory at the Battle of Salamis.

Suddenly the tables had turned. With his armada now in tatters, Xerxes was in danger of being trapped in Europe. Taking much of his army, he hurried back to the Hellespont before the Greek navy could arrive to sever the bridges there. Meanwhile, his able general Mardonius stayed in Greece with a force of perhaps 60,000.

Mardonius wintered in Thessaly and marched south again in the spring of 479 B.C.; his army was supplemented by collaborationist Greek troops from Thessaly and Boeotia. Athens, still evacuated, was reoccupied and burned. Mardonius reached the northeastern outskirts of MEGARA (1), the Persian high-water mark in Europe, but on news of an approaching Greek force he withdrew toward THEBES, the main Boeotian city, which was friendly to the Persians. The Greek army—nearly 39,000 Spartan, Peloponnesian, and Athenian hoplites, commanded by the Spartan general Pausanias—approached the town of PLATAEA in the late summer. Pausanias declined to attack, probably fearing what Mardonius' cavalry could do on the Boeotian plain. After almost two weeks of waiting—while both armies were plagued by a shortage of food and water—Mardonius launched a surprise attack. He was killed and his army destroyed at the BATTLE OF PLATAEA.

Historians debate whether it was Salamis or Plataea that saved Greece from Persian conquest. Probably the Persians' invasion was doomed once they had lost most of their fleet at Salamis. Greece, a mountainous country, does not lend itself to being conquered by a strictly land-bound army. Had the Persians won at Plataea, they would probably have lost the war anyway. The Greeks would have retreated south to the isthmus, to beat them there.

That same year, 479 B.C., saw the Greek counteroffensive begin. Supposedly on the same day as the Battle of Plataea, an amphibious Greek force under the Spartan king Leotychides landed at Cape MYCALE in western Asia Minor; the Greeks beat a Persian army and burned the remaining Persian fleet. Ionia had been liberated; over 90 years would pass before the Persians could reclaim it. By winter an Athenian fleet under the general XANTHIPPUS had captured the Hellespont after destroying the Persian garrison at SESTOS. In 478 B.C. the Spartan Pausanias took BYZANTIUM and the Bosporus. There the Spartans dropped out of the counteroffensive, but the Athenians—calculatedly building an empire—carried on their liberation of the east Greeks in Asia Minor and CYPRUS.

Around 449 B.C., Persia negotiated a peace treaty with Athens, and hostilities ceased. But the Persian kings continued to scheme for the recovery of their lost territory of Ionia. As the patriotic Greek alliances of 480 B.C. dissolved into the PELOPONNESIAN WAR (431–404 B.C.) and CORINTHIAN WAR (395–386 B.C.), Persia eventually began to help Sparta in exchange for a free hand in Ionia. It took ALEXANDER THE GREAT, with his dismantling of the Persian Empire in 334–323 B.C., finally to make peace between Persia and the Greeks.

(See also CALLIAS; CIMON; DELIAN LEAGUE; KING'S PEACE; WARFARE, LAND; WARFARE, NAVAL.)

Phaedra   See HIPPOLYTUS; THESEUS.

Phaethon   See HELIOS.

phalanx   Battle formation of heavy infantry. The noun *phalanx* is used by ancient Greek writers from HOMER (circa

750 B.C.) onward, but modern scholars usually reserve the word to describe the distinctive battle order of the Macedonian and Hellenistic heavy infantry (mid-300s to mid-100s B.C.). These soldiers employed equipment and tactics invented by the Macedonian king PHILIP II (circa 357 B.C.) and perfected by his son ALEXANDER THE GREAT. In several battles of the latter 300s B.C., the Macedonian phalanx proved itself superior to the classic HOPLITE armies of the Greek city-states.

Designed as an improvement on hoplite tactics, the Macedonian phalanx consisted of about 9,000 men arranged in orderly rows, one behind the other, up to 16 in number, with several hundred men in each row. Every man carried a 13- to 14-foot-long pike, called a *sarissa*. When the first five rows presented their sarissas forward, a hedge of metal pike-points was formed, extending in serried rows to about 10 feet ahead. As the phalanx moved forward, these points pushed toward the enemy with great force. Behind the first five rows, the soldiers kept their sarissas upright, waiting to move forward as their comrades in front fell.

Because hoplites and other heavy infantrymen of the day were armed only with six- to eight-foot-long jabbing spears, the phalanx enjoyed an advantage in reach and in density of offered weapons; the enemy formation could present its spears only from a depth of two or three rows. Also, the rows of the phalanx tended not to crush together as tightly as did rows of hoplites or other troops, and this made combat somewhat less exhausting for men in the phalanx.

Because the sarissa needed to be held with two hands, the man's shield was strapped to his left forearm or shoulder, without engaging the hand. This shield was necessarily smaller than the kind carried by Greek hoplites. In general, Macedonian soldiers seem to have worn less armor than their hoplite counterparts, using leather or cloth for helmets and corsets, in place of BRONZE. While this allowed the phalanx men greater maneuverability and endurance (and less expense for equipment), it also left them vulnerable to archers and javelin men, who might easily stay out of reach. Another weaknesses of the phalanx (one shared by the hoplite formation) was its unshielded right flank and rear.

The proper use of the phalanx involved coordination with CAVALRY and light-armed infantry to guard the flanks and chase away enemy projectile troops. In combat, the phalanx's natural function was defensive—to hold the enemy's charge and damage his formation—while the cavalry looked for a weak point to attack.

The Hellenistic kingdoms of the 200s and 100s B.C. continued the legacy of Macedonian-style warfare, but the phalanx became enlarged to such unwieldy sizes as 20,000 men. The wars of ROME against MACEDON and the SELEUCID EMPIRE saw the phalanx beaten repeatedly—at Cynocephalae (197 B.C.), at Magnesia (186 B.C.), and at Pydna (167 B.C.)—by the more maneuverable Roman legions.

(See also CHAERONEA; HELLENISTIC AGE; PHILIP V; WARFARE, LAND.)

Pheidias   See PHIDIAS.

Pheidon   Powerful king of ARGOS who probably reigned circa 675–655 B.C. Pheidon brought his city to a brief preeminence at the expense of its perennial enemy, SPARTA. With his army, Pheidon seized the sacred site of OLYMPIA and personally took over management of the OLYMPIC GAMES—"the most arrogant thing ever done by a Greek," according to the ancient Greek historian HERODOTUS. Probably after this coup, Pheidon introduced a uniform system of weights and measures throughout the PELOPONNESE (a step meant to extend Argive control over TRADE).

The philosopher ARISTOTLE, in his treatise *Politics*, written circa 340 B.C., states that Pheidon began as a king and ended as a tyrant (Greek: *turannos*). This means—not that Pheidon's rule grew more harsh—but that, after coming to the Argive throne by legal succession, he seized absolute power, probably at the expense of the city's aristocrats and with the support of the middle class. As such he anticipated the first wave of Greek TYRANTS, who began taking power violently at CORINTH, SICYON, and other cities in the mid-600s B.C.

It was almost certainly under Pheidon that the Argives reorganized their army for HOPLITE tactics and became the best soldiers in Greece. In 669 B.C. an Argive army soundly defeated a Spartan army at the Battle of Hysiae, in the eastern Peloponnese. According to the most plausible modern explanation, this battle marked the triumph of Argive hoplites over an enemy still using the older, disorganized tactics. It may have been in the following year that Pheidon marched his army across the Peloponnese to Olympia.

(See also WARFARE, LAND.)

Phidias   Athenian sculptor who lived circa 490–425 B.C. His masterpiece was the colossal GOLD-and-ivory cult statue of the god ZEUS, constructed circa 430 B.C. for Zeus' temple at OLYMPIA and counted as one of the SEVEN WONDERS OF THE WORLD for its size and solemn majesty. Today, however, Phidias is better remembered for his work on the Athenian PARTHENON.

Phidias (Greek: Pheidias) was the son of a man called Charmides (an Athenian aristocratic name that also crops up in the family of PLATO). The family was probably well off, which allowed the young Phidias to pursue his art. His genius encompassed not only SCULPTURE but also PAINTING, engraving, and metalworking. He eventually achieved great prestige as an associate of the Athenian statesman PERICLES.

One of Phidias' earlier works (circa 456 B.C.) was a 30-foot-high BRONZE statue of the armored Athena Promachos (the Defender), which stood among the outdoor statues atop the Athenian ACROPOLIS. The gleam from the point of the goddess' upright spear was said to be visible to ships as far as 15 miles away. Another early work was Phidias' bronze statue known as the Lemnian Athena, commissioned by inhabitants of the island of Lemnos (probably Athenian colonists who had settled there recently). This work's grace and dignity were much admired in ancient times.

Circa 448 B.C., Phidias was chosen as the artistic director of the public-building program organized by Pericles to commemorate peace with the Persians. It was in this job that Phidias oversaw the building of the Parthenon and the execution of the temple's famous architectural sculptures. We do not know whether Phidias himself carved any of these. But he did sculpt one central work, the 35-foot-high gold-and-ivory cult statue of the goddess ATHENA that stood inside the Parthenon.

The statue was completed by about 438 B.C., but soon Phidias had to pay for his success, for criminal charges were brought against him as part of a political scheme to discredit his friend Pericles. Phidias was accused of having stolen some of the gold entrusted to him for the statue's construction. This charge was disproved when the gold plates—which Phidias had constructed as detachable—were taken off the statue and weighed.

But a second accusation, of impiety, was more damaging. Phidias had incurred this charge by rashly including likenesses of himself and his patron Pericles amid the repoussé figures on the shield of Athena. There, in a battle scene of Greeks versus AMAZONS, Phidias had portrayed himself as a bald old man hurling a rock and Pericles as a warrior about to spear an Amazon.

Perhaps as a result of his legal troubles, Phidias left Athens soon after the Parthenon Athena was in place. (A later legend, claiming that he died in an Athenian prison, is untrue.) Around this time he won the prestigious commission to sculpt his second giant gold-and-ivory statue, at Olympia. The Olympian cult statue of Zeus was arguably the most important religious statue of the Greek world.

Philemon   See THEATER.

Philip II   Macedonian king who reigned 359–336 B.C. and fell to an assassin's knife at about age 46. A brilliant soldier and diplomat, Philip took his backward Greek kingdom of MACEDON and turned it into the mightiest nation in the Greek world. His creation of a new-style army and his subjugation of mainland Greece both proved essential for the subsequent career of his son, ALEXANDER THE GREAT. Although he did not live to see Alexander's conquest of the Persian Empire (334–323 B.C.), Philip made it possible.

In the absence of better surviving sources, our knowledge of Philip comes mostly from book 16 of the *World History* of DIODORUS SICULUS, a later Greek writer (circa 60–30 B.C.) prone to distortion. However, the following narrative seems plausible. Philip (Philippos, "horse lover") was the youngest son of the Macedonian king Amyntas, circa 382 B.C. As a hostage for three years at the powerful city of THEBES, in central Greece, the teenage Philip probably had contact with the great Theban leader EPAMINONDAS. Another model that may have inspired the young Philip was the dynasty of rulers at Pherae, in the northern Greek region called THESSALY. In 359 B.C. Philip's brother Perdiccas, king of Macedon, was killed in battle. Philip, then about 23, became king.

Soon he began his military reforms, which were destined to change ancient warfare. Previously, the Macedonian army had consisted of a capable, aristocratic CAVALRY alongside a ragamuffin light infantry of peasant levies. With training and new equipment, Philip created an expert heavy infantry, armed with 13- to 14-foot-long pikes, fight-

King Philip II of Macedon revolutionized military tactics, subdued mainland Greece, and became the most powerful man in the Greek world; he then bequeathed these advantages to his son Alexander. The shrewd, hard-drinking Philip is probably portrayed on the carved ivory head shown here. This damaged artifact, just over an inch tall, was discovered in 1977 in northern Greece, at excavations of royal tombs near the ancient Macedonian city of Aegae.

ing in the formation known as the PHALANX. Philip also pioneered new tactics of siege warfare, daring to storm fortified sites in direct attacks using siege-towers and arrow-shooting catapults. Among his other accomplishments, Philip was the most successful besieger of his day.

His early imperialism involved two strategies: the subjugation of Macedon's warlike, non-Greek neighbors, the Thracians and Illyrians; and the seizure of Greek cities of the north Aegean coast, to provide revenue and shipping outlets. Philip's rival for possession of this seacoast was the distant city of ATHENS, with its mighty navy.

In 357 B.C., the second year of his reign, Philip captured the north Aegean city of AMPHIPOLIS, a former Athenian colony located near the GOLD- and SILVER-mining region of Mt. Pangaeus. The Athenians declared war, but hostilities trailed off amid Athenian reluctance to commit land troops so far from home (a recurring factor that worked to Philip's advantage during the next two decades). Meanwhile the

Pangaeus mines provided Philip with an enormous yearly sum of 1,000 TALENTS.

Another foreign policy success of 357 B.C. was Philip's MARRIAGE to Olympias, a young noblewoman from the northwestern Greek region called EPIRUS. For 20 years Olympias was the foremost of Philip's multiple wives. (Eventually he had seven.) Although the royal marriage proved unhappy, it produced a son and a daughter; the boy, born in 356 B.C., was Alexander.

By involving himself in the Third Sacred War against the central Greek state of PHOCIS (355–346 B.C.), Philip began to influence affairs in Greece. Soon he dominated the leadership of Thessaly and made an alliance with formidable Thebes. Amid these events, Philip lost an eye when he was hit by an arrow during his siege of the rebellious Macedonian city of Methone (354 B.C.).

In 349 B.C. Philip moved to devour the Greek cities of the north Aegean region known as CHALCIDICE. He besieged the Chalcidic capital, OLYNTHUS, whose inhabitants appealed for help to Athens. The Athenians again declared war on Philip but again declined to send troops, despite the fiery oratory of the Athenian statesman DEMOSTHENES (1). Captured by Philip, Olynthus was leveled to the ground.

The year 346 B.C. saw Philip readying to conquer mainland Greece. As was typical of his style, he first made peace with Athens. When the Third Sacred War finally ended in Phocis' defeat, Philip marched his Macedonians unchallenged through THERMOPYLAE and into Phocis. At meetings of the influential AMPHICTYONIC LEAGUE, at DELPHI, Philip was admitted in place of the Phocian delegates and was personally awarded the two votes previously controlled by the Phocian people. Through influence, he also controlled the votes of the Thessalian delegates and others. King of Macedon, overlord of Thessaly, master of Phocis, and boss of Delphi—he was by now the most powerful man in Greece.

It was in this year that the Athenian orator ISOCRATES published his pamphlet *Philip,* urging the Macedonian king to liberate the Greek cities of ASIA MINOR from Persian rule. No doubt Philip welcomed the propaganda value of this romantic plea, but he also took the idea to heart. In his way, Philip was a lover of Greek culture. He may have sincerely wished to lead a united Greece against its traditional enemy, PERSIA.

The idea of conquest also held a strong financial appeal for Philip, who was running out of money, despite his Mt. Pangaeus revenues. His ceaseless military campaigning and frequent resort to bribery had taken a heavy financial toll. Only the booty of a rich conquest could save him from bankruptcy and downfall.

Meanwhile his Greek enemies organized against him, with funding from the alarmed Persian king, Artaxerxes III. Supported by the Athenian navy, the northeastern Greek colonies of BYZANTIUM and Perinthus held out against Philip's siege (340 B.C.). Then his erstwhile Greek ally Thebes turned against him, ejecting his garrison from Thermopylae (338 B.C.).

Philip invaded central Greece in the spring of 338 B.C. Bypassing the Theban garrison at Thermopylae, he marched through Phocis toward Thebes. In response, Athens and Thebes, although traditional enemies, patched together a hasty alliance and faced Philip's advancing army at the Battle of CHAERONEA, northwest of Thebes.

The battle was a complete Macedonian victory, and Thebes and Athens surrendered. Philip treated Athens leniently but Thebes harshly, staging executions and selling war prisoners as SLAVES. After 20 years of scheming, he had conquered Greece in one campaign.

Almost immediately, Philip began preparations for an invasion of Persian-held Asia Minor, for which his trusted general Parmenion secured a crossing of the HELLESPONT (337 B.C.). But in 336 B.C. Philip was assassinated at the old Macedonian royal city of Aegae (modern Vergina), on the morning of his daughter's wedding. The killer, an aggrieved Macedonian noble, probably acted at the instigation of Olympias (whom Philip had recently divorced) and the 20-year-old Alexander. Philip's new number-one wife had recently borne Philip a son, and no doubt Olympias feared this threat to Alexander's succession to the throne. The young wife and child were later murdered on Olympias' orders. Alexander, acclaimed as king, took up Philip's invasion plan and crossed to Asia Minor in 334 B.C.

In A.D. 1977–1980 archaeological excavations at Vergina uncovered two tombs dating from the 300s B.C. that were filled with treasure. The cremated remains in the tombs are thought to be those of Alexander's father and son (Alexander IV, who was murdered at age 13, in 310 B.C.). The skull believed to be Philip's apparently shows signs of an injured right eye socket—the wound from an arrow at the siege of Methone.

(See also ARCHAEOLOGY; ILLYRIS; THRACE; WARFARE, LAND; WARFARE, SIEGE.)

Philip V   Last great king of MACEDON (reigned 221–179 B.C.). Seeking to enlarge Macedon's traditional control over mainland Greece, Philip came to grief against a rival contender—the Italian city of ROME.

Philip ascended the Macedonian throne at age 17, on the death of his grandfather, Antigonus III. During the so-called Social War against the powerful Aetolian League in Greece, Philip led an army into the heart of enemy AETOLIA and sacked its capital, Thermon (218 B.C.). Faced with Roman domination of the nearby Illyrian coast, Philip in 215 B.C. made an anti-Roman alliance with the North African city of CARTHAGE (whose brilliant general Hannibal seemed on the verge of capturing Rome in the Second Punic War).

The Carthaginian alliance proved to be a disastrous decision. The Romans, despite their troubles with Hannibal, declared war on Philip and dispatched a fleet and land troops. This First Macedonian War (214–205 B.C.) saw Philip campaigning in Greece against an alliance of Romans and Aetolians. Hostilities ended in a treaty. But after defeating Carthage (201 B.C.), the Romans lent a ready ear to reports from their Greek allies PERGAMUM and RHODES, complaining of Philip's naval aggression in the eastern Mediterranean.

Again the Roman senate declared war on Philip. The Second Macedonian War (200–197 B.C.) culminated in Philip's defeat by a Roman-Aetolian army at the Battle of Cynocephalae ("dog heads," a hill in THESSALY). At the battle, the Roman general Titus Quinctius Flamininus managed to send his troops around the flank of the Macedonian PHALANX, to destroy it from behind. Cynocephalae marked the end of an independent Macedon; more significantly, it marked the end of the military era of the phalanx.

Philip was compelled to pay the Romans a huge cash penalty, hand over his son Demetrius as a hostage, and withdraw his troops forever from mainland Greece, which was declared by the Romans to be free of foreign taxation and interference. Philip became Rome's ally; his life's last decade was spent repairing Macedon's finances and warring against non-Greek peoples in the Balkans. Philip died on a military campaign and was succeeded by his son Perseus, Macedon's last king.

(See also ILLYRIS; WARFARE, LAND.)

Philoctetes   Mythical Greek hero of the TROJAN WAR. Philoctetes (his name means "lover of possessions") was an expert archer from central Greece who led five ships in the allied Greek expedition against TROY. En route he went ashore on Lemnos or another Aegean island and was bitten on the foot by a serpent. The wound was agonizing, foul-smelling, and incurable, and so the Greeks—on ODYSSEUS' advice—abandoned Philoctetes on Lemnos. There he languished, neither dying nor recovering. He lived by hunting, using the unerring bow and arrows that had once belonged to the hero HERACLES (and that had been bequeathed by Heracles to Philoctetes' father, Poeas).

Nearly 10 years went by. As the Greek siege of Troy became stalled, the Greeks learned of a prophecy that said the city could be captured only with the aid of Heracles' bow and arrows. Consequently two Greek leaders—in most versions, Odysseus and DIOMEDES—sailed to Lemnos and brought Philoctetes and the charmed weapons to the siege of Troy. There, at the Greek camp, Philoctetes was healed by the physician sons of ASCLEPIUS, Machaon and Podalirius. Taking to the field with Heracles' bow, Philoctetes killed the Trojan prince PARIS in an archery duel. After Troy's fall, Philoctetes survived the homeward voyage that claimed the lives of many other Greeks. He was said to have traveled to the West to establish Greek cities in eastern SICILY and southern ITALY.

The Athenian tragedian SOPHOCLES wrote a *Philoctetes* (performed in 409 B.C.), which survives today. In presenting the tale of the wounded hero on Lemnos, the play investigates the question of private wishes versus public duty. In Sophocles' version, the two arriving Greek captains are Odysseus and NEOPTOLEMUS (ACHILLES' son). Philoctetes loathes Odysseus as the one responsible for his being abandoned; but finally the honest, young Neoptolemus, with help from the gods, persuades Philoctetes to accompany them to the war to fulfill his destiny.

(See also FATE.)

philosophy   *Philosophia* is a Greek word, literally meaning "love of wisdom," but, in effect, translating to something like "love of arcane knowledge" or "a desire to find out the truth." The Greeks invented the concept of philosophy; for them, it meant a way of looking for reality and truth without strict reference to the traditional gods of RELIGION and mythology.

Philosophy began as a form of SCIENCE. The first philosophers, such as THALES of MILETUS (circa 560 B.C.), sought to discover the essential element in the material world and to explain the causes of physical change. The Italian-Greek philosopher PARMENIDES (circa 515–445 B.C.) revolutionized Western thought by theorizing that ultimate reality lies outside of the material world. Parmenides' younger contemporary SOCRATES of ATHENS (469–399 B.C.) redirected philosophy toward the pursuit of ethical truths and such moral questions as "What is virtue?" Both of these thinkers helped pave the way for PLATO (427–347 B.C.), who produced the first surviving philosophical system, in which questions about reality might shed light on ethical and epistomological questions. Plato's onetime pupil ARISTOTLE (384–322 B.C.) developed a system of logic and forever divorced science from philosophy by reorganizing them as separate disciplines. During the HELLENISTIC AGE (circa 300–150 B.C.) new Greek philosophies such as STOICISM and EPICUREANISM sought to assure people about their place in the universal order.

(See also ACADEMY; ANAXAGORAS; ANAXIMANDER; ANAXIMENES; CYNICS; DEMOCRITUS; DIOGENES; EMPEDOCLES; HERACLITUS; LEUCIPPUS; LYCEUM; PYTHAGORAS; SKEPTICISM; XENOPHANES.)

Phocaea   Greek city of IONIA, on the central west coast of ASIA MINOR. During the 600s and 500s B.C. Phocaea was at the forefront of long-range Greek TRADE and COLONIZATION, particularly in the western Mediterranean.

Located on the north shore of the entrance to the Bay of Smyrna, Phocaea (Greek: Phokaia) was established circa 1050 B.C. by IONIAN GREEKS who had emigrated from mainland Greece. The Phocaeans developed as brilliant seamen and began establishing anchorages and colonies to enlarge their shipping network. Probably one of their earliest colonies was Lampsacus, on the HELLESPONT (circa 650 B.C.).

Around 600 B.C., in a westward drive for raw tin, SILVER, IRON, and other resources, the Phocaeans founded their famous colony, MASSALIA (modern-day Marseille), at the mouth of the Rhone on the southern coast of France. This depot facilitated trade with the local Ligurians and CELTS. Farther west, the Phocaeans traded with the Celtic kingdom of Tartessus, in southern Spain. Such ventures brought Phocaean sailors into battle with the Carthaginians, a non-Greek people who had previously held a monopoly on maritime trade in the West.

The Greek historian HERODOTUS describes Phocaea's abrupt decline. Circa 545 B.C. the city was besieged by the invading Persians under King CYRUS (1). The Phocaeans, taking to their ships en masse, abandoned their home to the enemy. By way of an oath, they dropped an iron ingot into the sea and swore never to return until the metal should float up. (Nevertheless, half of them did decide to return.) The refugees sailed west. Rebuffed from Corsica by allied fleets of Carthaginians and ETRUSCANS, these Phocaeans eventually founded a new colony, Elea, on the southwestern coast of ITALY.

Phocaea, repopulated by the group that had returned, endured reduced fortunes under Persian rule. The city joined the doomed IONIAN REVOLT against the Persians

(499–493 B.C.). After Ionia was liberated at the end of the PERSIAN WARS (479 B.C.), Phocaea became part of the Athenian-controlled DELIAN LEAGUE.

Like the rest of Ionia, Phocaea passed to Spartan control at the end of the PELOPONNESIAN WAR (404 B.C.) and was handed back to the Persians by the terms of the KING'S PEACE (386 B.C.). Liberated by ALEXANDER THE GREAT'S conquest of the region in 334 B.C., Phocaea later passed to the Macedonian-Greek SELEUCID EMPIRE, then to the kingdom of PERGAMUM, and finally, in 129 B.C., to the domain of ROME.

(See also BRONZE; CARTHAGE; SHIPS AND SEAFARING.)

Phocis Small region in the mountains of central Greece. The Phocians' significance was their intermittent control of the important sanctuary of the god APOLLO at DELPHI, located within Phocian territory. Their designs on Delphi brought them into periodic conflict with Apollo's priests and administrators there, who sometimes went so far as to declare holy war against Phocis.

Settlement in Phocis centered on two separate valleys: in the west, the Crisaean valley, adjoining the northern Corinthian Gulf; in the east, the valley of the middle Cephissus River, bordering BOEOTIA. Between the two Phocian valleys stood the traversible southern spur of Mt. Parnassus, where Delphi was located.

Coveted for its envelopment of Delphi and for its communication routes through mountainous central Greece, Phocis was surrounded by hostile Greek neighbors: Boeotia (to the east), West LOCRIS and Doris (to the west), and East Locris (to the north). Farther north lay another occasional enemy, THESSALY. In response to these pressures, the Phocians had by 600 B.C. become a unified, warlike people. They extended their power north of their home territory, even walling up the distant pass of THERMOPYLAE against southward attacks by the Thessalians. The Phocians' major conflicts with their neighbors were the three "Sacred Wars," so named because each involved Delphi's declaration of war. The Sacred Wars were consequential in allowing opportunities for intervention to such powerful states as ATHENS, SPARTA, THEBES, and MACEDON.

In the First Sacred War (circa 590 B.C.), Phocis was overrun by an alliance of Sicyonians, Thessalians, Locrians, and Athenians. The Phocians were deprived of the fertile Crisaean plain (which was henceforth left as an uncultivated offering to Apollo), and control of Delphi was handed over to a league of neighboring states (including Phocis) known as the AMPHICTYONIC LEAGUE. At regular meetings of the League delegates, the Phocians had two of the 12 votes.

In 457 B.C. Delphi was recaptured by the Phocians, by now in alliance with the powerful city of Athens. There followed the bloodless Second Sacred War (448 B.C.), in which the Spartans marched into Phocis and restored Delphi to the Amphictyonic League. As soon as the Spartans had withdrawn, the Athenians—on PERICLES' direction—marched to Delphi and returned it to the Phocians. But sometime in the next decades, the Phocians lost Delphi again and ceased to be Athenian allies. In the PELOPONNESIAN WAR (431–404 B.C.) and years following, Phocis was allied with SPARTA against Athens.

The Third Sacred War (355–346 B.C.) involved most of mainland Greece and gave the Macedonian king PHILIP II a chance for serious involvement in Greek affairs. The war began as a struggle between Phocis and the powerful Boeotian city of Thebes. At Thebes' prompting, Delphi declared war against certain Phocians who were impiously growing food on the Crisaean plain. But the Phocians seized Delphi and used funds stolen from the sanctuary to hire a mercenary army. With this force the Phocians fought back a coalition of Boeotians, Locrians, and Thessalians. A Phocian army even invaded Thessaly, where the Phocian commander was killed in battle against Macedonian Philip, who had entered the war as a Theban-Thessalian ally (352 B.C.). But in 346 B.C. an exhausted Phocis, its stolen funds depleted, surrendered to Philip. He garrisoned the region, occupied Delphi, and personally took over Phocis' two votes on the Amphictyonic council. The Phocians were made to pay an indemnity against their theft of Apollo's treasure, and the Crisaean plain was once more left fallow for the god.

In the 200s B.C. Phocis ceased to be important in Greek politics, as new Greek powers, such as AETOLIA, arose to dominate Delphi.

(See also CLEISTHENES (2).)

Phoenicia Region corresponding roughly to modern-day Lebanon, located on the southern part of the east Mediterranean coast of ancient Syria. The Phoenicians were non-Greeks of Semitic race. They called themselves the Kinanu, and it is their ancestors who are known as Canaanites in the Bible. In the late second millennium B.C. these Canaanites were battered by foreign invaders, including the Jewish tribes led by Joshua (circa 1230 B.C.) and the Philistines (who may have been Mycenaean Greeks displaced by turmoil at home, circa 1190 B.C.). But by 1000 B.C. the Canaanites had compensated for lost territory by becoming the greatest seafarers of the ancient world.

Our word *Phoenician* comes from the Greeks, who called these people Phoinikes, "red men"—probably a reference to skin color (but not, apparently, to the purple murex dye, *porphura,* which was among the Phoenicians' most precious commodities). By about 900 B.C. Phoenician sea traders were visiting Greece as part of their middleman's network that stretched throughout the ancient Near East to the Red Sea and Persian Gulf, touching on EGYPT, Assyria, Babylonia, and the kingdoms of ASIA MINOR. Also by 900 B.C. (as ARCHAEOLOGY reveals) the Phoenicians had begun exploring the western Mediterranean, seeking out suppliers of SILVER, tin, and other coveted metals. To facilitate western TRADE, the Phoenicians founded colonies, notably CARTHAGE (Kart Hadasht, "new city,") in what is now Tunisia, and Gaddir ("walled place," modern Cadiz) in southern Spain.

At home, the three Phoenician seaports of BYBLOS, Sidon, and Tyre became wealthy commercial and manufacturing centers. It was probably at Tyre prior to 1000 B.C. that the Phoenicians invented their 22-character Semitic ALPHABET, a vast improvement over their prior, cuneiform script. When the Greeks learned to adapt this Phoenician alphabet to represent the Greek language (before 750 B.C.), Greek literature was born.

In other ways, the brilliant Phoenicians deeply affected the formative Greek culture of 900–700 B.C. Near Eastern textiles and bronzework, brought to Greece by Phoenician traders, helped to spark the Greek artistic revolution of the "Orientalizing period" (circa 730–630 B.C.). Certain oddities of Greek MYTH—such as the filial violence of both CRONUS and ZEUS, the flood of Deucalion, and the dying ADONIS—are best understood as being Near Eastern ideas that made their way to Greece via the Phoenicians (before 700 B.C.). Other Phoenician exports to Greece include the chicken (first domesticated in India) and the Semitic custom of reclining at meals, which the Greeks adapted to their drinking party known as the SYMPOSIUM.

The Greeks copied Phoenician shipbuilding techniques, circa 900–700 B.C. And it was surely in emulation of the Phoenicians that the Greeks embarked on their own sea-borne trade and COLONIZATION in the 800s–500s B.C. Inevitably the Greeks came into conflict with their former mentors, in competition for western trade privileges. Circa 600 B.C., related to the founding of a Phocaean-Greek colony at MASSALIA (in southern France), a first sea battle was fought between Greeks and Carthaginian Phoenicians. Many such conflicts were to follow, particularly between Greeks and Carthaginians in SICILY.

Phoenicia surrendered to the conquering Persian king CYRUS (1) circa 540 B.C., and henceforth the Phoenicians, like other subject peoples, supplied levies for the Persian armed forces. Phoenician ships and crews were the pride of the Persian navy. Phoenician squadrons fought fiercely against the Greeks in the PERSIAN WARS, in 499–480 B.C.

Phoenicia revolted unsuccessfully from Persian rule in the 300s B.C. When the Macedonian king ALEXANDER THE GREAT invaded the Persian Empire, the Phoenicians surrendered readily except for the Phoenician fortress of Tyre, which fell only after a monumental siege (332 B.C.).

In the HELLENISTIC AGE (300–150 B.C.), Phoenicia became a province of the SELEUCID EMPIRE, providing fleets and revenues. By the time of the Roman conquest (63 B.C.), Phoenicia had ceased to exist as a separate entity.

(See also AL MINA; CADMUS; CYPRUS; SHIPS AND SEAFARING; THALES; WARFARE, NAVAL.)

phratry   See KINSHIP.

Phrygia   See ASIA MINOR.

Phrynichus   Athenian tragic playwright of the late 500s and early 400s B.C. A pioneer of early Athenian tragedy, Phrynichus was reportedly the first to introduce female characters onstage. He exerted a strong influence on the younger tragedian AESCHYLUS, particularly with his innovative use of recent events from the PERSIAN WARS. Only a few fragments of Phrynichus' work survive.

Competing at the annual drama festival known as the City Dionysia, Phrynichus won his first victory in about 510 B.C. In around 492 B.C. he presented *The Capture of Miletus*, based on the recent ravaging of that Greek city by the Persians after the failed IONIAN REVOLT. The Athenian audience burst into tears at the rendition of their ally's fate, but Phrynichus was fined 1,000 drachmas for re-

minding the Athenians of their woes, and future performance of the play was banned.

In around 476 B.C. he presented another historical drama, *The Phoenician Women*, giving the tragic, Persian viewpoint of the recent Greek naval victory at SALAMIS (1). This play surely inspired Aeschylus' tragedy *The Persians* (472 B.C.).

(See also MILETUS; THEATER.)

phyle   See KINSHIP.

Pindar   Greatest choral poet of ancient Greece. Born near the central Greek city of THEBES but often traveling, Pindar (Pindaros) lived circa 518–438 B.C. He apparently claimed kinship with the noble Aegid clan, which had branches at SPARTA and other Greek cities, and much of his poetry beautifully conveys the old-fashioned values of the aristocratic class, whose power was waning throughout Greece during Pindar's own lifetime. Pindar wrote various types of LYRIC POETRY, most of it choral poetry—that is, intended for public performance by a chorus. He is best remembered for his victory odes (*epinikia,*) composed in honor of various patrons' triumphs at such important Greek sports festivals as the OLYMPIC GAMES. In ornate language that often attains magnificence, Pindar combines a sense of joyous occasion with a sublime religious piety and a sadness over human transience or human injustice.

Forty-five of Pindar's victory odes survive whole, having come down to us numbered and arranged by a later ancient editor into four categories—Olympians, Pythians, Nemeans, and Isthmians. These categories reflect the four major sports festivals that occasioned nearly all the poems. The odes' honorees include winners in WRESTLING, PANKRATION, footraces, and the four-horse chariot race.

In Pindar's day, international athletes were always rich and male, and were usually members of the traditional noble class, for whom the games were part of a distinctive, aristocratic identity. Pindar's patrons, from many Greek cities, included three rulers: King Arcesilas IV of CYRENE (1), the tyrant Theron of ACRAGAS, and the tyrant HIERON (1) of SYRACUSE, the most powerful individual in the Greek world. Pindar wrote four odes for Hieron; of these, two are usually considered the poet's masterpieces—Olympian 1 and Pythian 1.

Perhaps invented by the poet IBYCUS (circa 530 B.C.), the Greek victory ode was composed for a fee paid by the victor or his family, and was performed by a chorus of men or boys at the athlete's home city sometime after the sports event. Like most choral verse, Pindar's odes are written in a Doric Greek dialect (although Pindar himself would have spoken a different dialect, Aeolic). The meters and lengths vary; most of Pindar's odes run between about 45 and 120 lines.

Employing an associative flow of ideas and images, the typical Pindaric ode salutes the athlete's home region, praises the inherited superiority of the upper class, and broods over the precariousness of human happiness. Many odes recount one or another Greek MYTH in such a way as to compare the mythical hero with the poem's patron. Beyond flattery, these comparisons convey the message that victory—for hero or athlete—is proof of divine favor.

Pindar's frequent use of myth makes him one of our important sources for these stories; among many examples are Pythian 9's tale of APOLLO and the nymph CYRENE (2), and Nemean 10's tale of CASTOR AND POLYDEUCES. But the reverent Pindar always minimizes or bowdlerizes the gods' cruelty and injustice, in comparison with other extant versions of such myths.

We know little of Pindar's life. His parents' names are variously reported. As a boy he studied poetry at ATHENS when that city had recently emerged as the world's first DEMOCRACY (508 B.C.). Significantly, Pindar's Athenian contacts came from right-wing, aristocratic circles; these friends included Megacles of the noble Alcmaeonid clan and Melesias, a champion wrestler who was the future father of the conservative Athenian politician THUCYDIDES (2). Both Megacles and Melesias represented Athenian upper-class forces that were soon destined to come to grief against the radical policies of the democracy. Megacles was ostracized by the Athenians in 486 B.C., and Pindar's ode Pythian 7—written to celebrate Megacles' chariot victory at the PYTHIAN GAMES at DELPHI that same year—is partly a consolation for his friend's political misfortune.

Pindar's fateful connection with Greek SICILY was forged in 490 B.C., when he wrote ode Pythian 6 for Xenocrates, a nobleman of the Sicilian Greek city of Acragas. (Xenocrates' brother was Theron, who was destined to become dictator of Acragas and one of Pindar's patrons.) Xenocrates had won the chariot race, which was the most prestigious event and one of the few in which contestants did not have to compete personally: The drivers were usually professionals, and the official contestants were considered to be the chariots' owners.

Xenocrates had a teenage son named Thrasybulus. Pythian 6 is remarkable for its frank expression of Pindar's infatuation with Thrasybulus. Homosexual attachments were a prominent part of Greek aristocratic life in that era, and Thrasybulus was probably the sort of glamorous youth who created a sensation amid the games' intense social atmosphere. We know that Pindar also wrote a drinking song for Thrasybulus and a later ode, Isthmian 2, for a chariot victory by him (circa 470 B.C.). Pindar's tone in these verses—confident, personal, not at all subservient in addressing his eminent employers—is a sign of his high social status.

But Pindar's comfortable world was soon shaken, when Persian armies invaded mainland Greece in 490 and 480 B.C. The allied Greeks' victory over the Persians brought on changes that eventually swept away the aristocrats' traditional way of life. Pindar's Thebes fell into deep disgrace for having collaborated with the occupying Persian forces, and the two cities that had led the Greek defense—Sparta and Athens—emerged as rival leaders of Greece.

Meanwhile, in Sicily, the Greek city of Syracuse had become the foremost power of the western Mediterranean, having led the Sicilian Greeks in defeating a Carthaginian invasion (480 B.C.). And it was at Syracuse that Pindar would deliver his greatest poetry.

He visited in 476 B.C., probably at the invitation of the dictator Hieron, who had won the horse-and-rider race at that summer's Olympic Games. (Like the chariot race, the horse race was officially won by the owner, not the rider.) Pindar's victory ode for Hieron that year is perhaps the most famous lyric poem of antiquity, placed by ancient editors at the beginning of the Pindaric corpus, as Olympian 1:

> Best of things is water. And gold,
> Like a fire at night, outshines all other wealth.
> And if you wish to sing of glory in the Games,
> Look no further in the daytime sky for any star
> More warming than the sun,
> Nor any contest grander than at Olympia. (lines 1–8)

The 116-line ode celebrates Hieron's victory by telling the legend of PELOPS, who supposedly established the first Olympic Games. Just as Pelops was beloved by the god POSEIDON, so is Hieron blessed by some god.

While in Sicily, Pindar may have indulged in a feud with the poet SIMONIDES of Ceos and his poet-nephew BACCHYLIDES, who were likewise guests at Hieron's court. Pindar's Olympian 2 contains a mysterious reference to a pair of crows who "chatter vainly against the sacred eagle of ZEUS"—which is sometimes interpreted as the poet's rebuke to his rivals.

Pindar left Sicily in around 475 B.C. In 474 B.C. Hieron defeated an Etruscan invasion of Greek southern ITALY, at the sea battle of CUMAE. Soon thereafter Hieron founded a new Sicilian city, Aetna, near volcanic Mt. Etna. Then, in 470 B.C., Hieron won the chariot race at the Pythian Games and commissioned an ode from Pindar.

Pindar's resultant poem, Pythian 1, is probably his best. The 100-line ode successfully interweaves the above-mentioned events with a worldview of harmony versus discord, justice versus evil. The poem contains an unforgettable description of the mythical monster TYPHON, the god Zeus' defeated enemy, who now lies shackled beneath Mt. Etna and whose fire-breathing fury supposedly causes the volcano's eruptions. Cleverly linked to local geography, Pindar's Typhon serves as a cosmic symbol for the ETRUSCANS, Carthaginians, and other defeated enemies of Hieron and Greek civilization. Yet the poem ends with a bold warning to Hieron not to abuse his power, lest he too provoke the gods' anger.

In 468 B.C. Hieron, then dying, crowned his achievements with a chariot victory at the Olympic Games. But he hired Bacchylides, not Pindar, to commemorate this triumph. The ruler may have been offended by Pythian 1's presumptuous warning.

Pindar's last years saw the final erosion of his familiar world, with Greece divided by hostility between Sparta and the imperialist Athens of PERICLES. One prominent victim of Athenian aggression was the Greek island of AEGINA. The anti-Athenian anger of Pindar's friends is suggested in the anxious tone of Pindar's last surviving victory ode, Pythian 8, written in 446 B.C. for a boy wrestler of Aegina. The poem also contains (lines 95–97) a poignant expression of Pindar's aristocratic religious outlook, which saw victory in SPORT as a god-given gift providing a brief triumph over the doom that awaits all mortals:

> We are creatures of a day. What is someone? What is he not?
> A human being is a shadow in a dream.

But when a god grants a brightness,
Then humans have a radiant splendor and their life is sweet.

Pindar lived until age 80. Supposedly he had a wife and three children, but we hear also of another young male friend, Theoxenus of Tenedos, in whose arms the poet is said to have died at the city of ARGOS. Pindar's memory was revered for centuries. Supposedly the priests of APOLLO at Delphi would close the temple daily with the words "May Pindar join the gods at dinner." And when the Macedonian king ALEXANDER THE GREAT captured and destroyed Thebes in 335 B.C., he is said to have spared the house that had been Pindar's.

(See also ALCMAEONIDS; ARISTOCRACY; CATANA; CHARIOTS; FATE; GREEK LANGUAGE; HIMERA; HOMOSEXUALITY; ISTHMIAN GAMES; NEMEAN GAMES; PERSIAN WARS.)

Piraeus   Main port and naval base of ATHENS, located about four miles southwest of the city.

The westward-jutting peninsula known as the Piraeus (Greek: Peiraieus) was neglected in early Athenian times, when ships sheltered at the more southerly beachfront of Phalerum. In 510 B.C. the Athenian tyrant HIPPIAS (1) built a citadel on the Piraeus' hilltop, which was called Munychia. But it was the Athenian statesman THEMISTOCLES who, in 492 B.C., began developing the harbor for a growing Athenian war fleet.

By the mid-400s B.C. a walled town proper had arisen, laid out on a rectilinear grid by the city planner HIPPODAMUS. The naval base contained dockyards, arsenals, and ship sheds (covered drydocking for individual ships, the pride of Athenian naval technology). In addition, the port was a bustling commercial center, home to many of the METICS (resident aliens) who conducted Athens' import-export TRADE. It was also home to working-class Athenian citizens of left-wing loyalties, staunch supporters of such democratic politicians as PERICLES.

Piraeus had three harbors, whose entrances—flanked by half-immersed stone walls—could be sealed completely by the raising of massive chains. By 448 B.C. the town and harborfront were enclosed on north and south by the LONG WALLS, running up to Athens. The Long Walls made Piraeus and Athens into a single, linked fortress; even the Spartan land invasions in the PELOPONNESIAN WAR could not breach these defenses or obstruct Athens' communications with its naval base. The Long Walls were torn down after Athens' defeat in the war (404 B.C.), but were rebuilt by the Athenian general CONON (393 B.C.).

From 322 until 196 B.C. the citadel at Munychia held a Macedonian garrison—one of the Macedonians' four "fetters" of Greece. Today Piraeus remains vital as the harbor of modern Athens.

(See also GREECE, GEOGRAPHY OF; MACEDON; THIRTY TYRANTS, THE; WARFARE, NAVAL.)

Pirithous   See CENTAURS; THESEUS.

Pisistratus   Dictator or *turannos* who ruled ATHENS from 546 to 527 B.C. Like other Greek TYRANTS of that era, Pisistratus seized supreme power in his city with the common people's support, at the expense of the aristocrats.

His benevolent reign removed the nobles' grip on Athenian government and marked a step in the city's difficult progress from ARISTOCRACY to DEMOCRACY in the 500s B.C.

Pisistratus (Greek: Peisistratos, "adviser of the army") was himself born into an Athenian aristocratic family, circa 600 B.C. Before taking power, the dynamic and affable Pisistratus came to the political fore when he led an army against Athens' enemy, the city of MEGARA (1). He then set out to make himself dictator, by exploiting the volatile atmosphere of Athenian class tensions.

Despite the prior democratic reforms of the statesman SOLON (594 B.C.), Athenian politics and adjudication at this time were still dominated by the nobility. This dominance was resented by the middle class, which supplied the backbone of the army. When Pisistratus entered politics, the countryside held two opposing factions, divided along lines of region and class: the right-wing party of the plain, led by a certain Lycurgus; and the more democratic party of the coast, led by Megacles of the Alcmaeonid clan.

Pisistratus created a third, more left-wing party, by organizing a peasant following and styling himself as the champion of the common people. He then convinced the Athenian ASSEMBLY to vote him an escort of bodyguards. Legend claims that the aged Solon, who was Pisistratus' kinsman, warned the Athenians against the man's intentions, but Pisistratus, using his bodyguards, was able to seize the ACROPOLIS and become tyrant (circa 561 B.C.).

Soon pushed into exile by the combined effort of the two other factions, he was reinstated with the help of his former rival Megacles. But when this alliance broke down, Pisistratus fled once more (circa 556 B.C.). In around 546 B.C. he was back, leading a Greek mercenary army hired with a fortune he had made in SILVER-mining ventures in THRACE. Sailing from ERETRIA, the invaders landed near the town of MARATHON, where Pisistratus' family had its regional following. There Pisistratus was joined by other Athenians who wanted an end to aristocratic strife. On the road to Athens, Pisistratus defeated a government army at the Battle of Pallene, and the city was his again.

Pisistratus ruled shrewdly and moderately for 19 more years. He took aristocratic hostages but indulged in no vendettas or confiscations. He maintained Solon's laws and certain trappings of democratic government (although he also made sure that his own supporters held the top posts). He taxed reasonably—his tax on farm revenue, for instance, was 5 percent—and in return, he provided lavish building programs and public relief.

Like other dictators, Pisistratus aimed to make his city great. He assured Athens of a food supply by developing military outposts along the HELLESPONT, at Sigeum and in the Thracian CHERSONESE. These guarded the shipping lane for precious grain from the BLACK SEA. He elaborated Athens' national festivals, such as the PANATHENAEA, and encouraged industry and commerce. Under him, Athenian black-figure POTTERY reached its artistic peak and dominated the Mediterranean market. In SCULPTURE, ARCHITECTURE, and primitive THEATER, Pisistratus' Athens moved toward its amazing achievements in the next century. He fostered an Athenian patriotic culture that was partly intended to compete with cities such as CORINTH and partly intended to erase the old, local, aristocratic factionalism at home. His reign brought Athens forward in its progress from being a second-tier power in the 600s B.C. to being the capital of the Greek world in the 400s B.C.

Pisistratus died peacefully in 527 B.C. He was succeeded by his eldest son, HIPPIAS (1), whose reign was more troubled.

(See also ALCMAEONIDS.)

Pithecusae Greek trading colony located on a volcanic island now called Ischia, off the western coast of southern ITALY, near modern-day Naples. First occupied by Greeks from CHALCIS and ERETRIA circa 775 B.C., Pithecusae (Greek: Pithekoussai, "monkey island") was apparently the earliest substantial Greek settlement in the West. It was the first landfall in a wave of westward Greek COLONIZATION that swept across southern Italy and SICILY over the following two centuries.

Most knowledge of Pithecusae comes from modern AR-CHAEOLOGY on the site. The first Greeks found the island unoccupied. Their settlement site—atop a tall peninsula with two harbors, on the island's north shore—was chosen with an eye toward local seafaring. The island provided a safe base from which Greek merchant ships could sail the six miles to the Italian mainland, to conduct TRADE with the non-Greek peoples there. Foremost of these Italian trading partners were the ETRUSCANS, whose home region lay far to the north but who had an outpost at Capua, inland of the Bay of Naples.

What brought Greek traders from mainland Greece to western Italy was the lure of raw metals—IRON, SILVER, tin (for making BRONZE), and others—that would fetch high prices in the Greeks' home cities of Chalcis and Eretria. The Etruscans mined large amounts of iron ore on the island of Elba, off the western coast of northern Italy, and at least some of this valuable ore was then traded to the Greeks at Pithecusae. Archaeology at Pithecusae has yielded the remnants of ancient Greek foundries, probably indicating that the acquired iron was refined and forged into ingots by Greek smiths right there, before being shipped to Greece.

In exchange for Italian metals, the Pithecusae Greeks supplied WINE, painted POTTERY, worked metal, and other luxury goods. Modern discoveries at Pithecusae of ceramics and metalwork from ancient EGYPT and ASIA MINOR suggest that some of the Greeks' luxury items originated in the non-Greek Near East, traveling west via Greek trade networks.

By about 750 B.C. Pithecusae was crowded and prosperous. Affluence is suggested by the quantities of imported Near Eastern artifacts found in Greek tombs there. The most important archaeological item from Pithecusae is the so-called cup of Nestor, made between about 750 and 700 B.C. This is a Greek clay drinking cup, painted in Geometric style and inscribed with one of the earliest surviving examples of Greek alphabetic WRITING.

Pithecusae was largely abandoned in the late 700s B.C. One cause may have been the start of the LELANTINE WAR, which pitted Chalcidean Greeks against Eretrian Greeks as enemies. At least some of the Pithecusans—possibly the Chalcidean party—founded a new colony, CUMAE, on the Italian mainland opposite Pithecusae.

(See also ALPHABET.)

Pittacus Constitutional dictator of the city of MYTILENE, on the island of LESBOS circa 580 B.C. Among his enemies was the poet ALCAEUS, whose loathing of Pittacus has been immortalized in verse. Nevertheless, Pittacus seems to have governed well, calming the civil strife at Mytilene between the nobles and the middle class. His rule supplied an alternative to the brutal TYRANTS who in those years were arising throughout the Greek world to wrest power from the ARISTOCRACY. Pittacus later was listed among the SEVEN SAGES.

Born of noble blood, he was an illustrious soldier, having once killed an enemy champion in single combat during Mytilene's war against Athenian settlers at Sigeum, in northwestern ASIA MINOR, circa 600 B.C. Later Pittacus was elected as dictator for a term of 10 years. Like his contemporary, SOLON of ATHENS, he made new laws that loosened the aristocrats' monopoly on political power. By turning his back on the partisan interests of his own noble class, Pittacus earned the hatred of old-fashioned aristocrats such as Alcaeus.

Plataea Town of southern BOEOTIA, in central Greece. Plataea lies just north of Mt. Cithaeron, by the River Asopus. Due to fear of its powerful neighbor THEBES, Plataea formed an alliance with ATHENS circa 519 B.C. and remained a staunch ally during the PERSIAN WARS and PELOPONNESIAN WAR. Alone among the Greek states, Plataea sent soldiers to fight alongside the Athenians against the Persians at the Battle of MARATHON (490 B.C.). During the invasion of the Persian king XERXES, Plataea was occupied and sacked by the Persians (480 B.C.). Near the town in 479 B.C. the allied Greeks won the BATTLE OF PLATAEA, which destroyed the Persian threat in Greece.

At the outbreak of the Peloponnesian War in 431 B.C., Plataea was unsuccessfully attacked by Thebes. Plataea's civilians were soon evacuated to Athens. A garrison, left to defend Plataea, surrendered and was massacred after a grueling, two-year siege by the Spartans and Thebans (427 B.C.). Later the empty town was razed to the ground.

Rebuilt, Plataea was again destroyed by Thebes in 373 B.C. After conquering Greece in 338 B.C., the Macedonian king PHILIP II rebuilt Plataea in order to humiliate Thebes, and the town survived down to Roman times.

Plataea, battle of Climactic land battle in the Greeks' defense of their homeland in the PERSIAN WARS. This hard-fought Greek victory occurred in the late summer of 479 B.C., on the plain near the Boeotian town of PLATAEA. Coming about a year after the Greek naval triumph at SALAMIS (1), the Battle of Plataea destroyed the last remaining Persian force in Greece and ended the Persian king XERXES' dream of conquering Greece.

After his unexpected defeat at Salamis, Xerxes led most of his troops home in 480 B.C. To pursue the subjugation of Greece, he left behind his able general (and brother-in-law) Mardonius, with an army numbering perhaps 60,000. Mardonius' army included Greek soldiers from the mainland regions of THESSALY and BOEOTIA, whose cities were actively collaborating with the Persians.

After wintering in Thessaly, Mardonius and his army marched south in the spring of 479 B.C. On receiving news of a Greek allied army's approach from the south, Mardonius withdrew toward friendly THEBES, the chief city of Boeotia. About five miles south of Thebes, just north of Plataea, where the level terrain favored his CAVALRY, Mardonius and his army awaited the Greeks.

The Greek army, commanded by the Spartan general Pausanias, contained about 38,700 HOPLITES—armored infantry—with perhaps as many light-armed troops. The largest hoplite contingents came from SPARTA, ATHENS, and CORINTH. The town of Plataea fought on the Greek side, as a staunch ally of Athens and longtime enemy of Thebes.

The allied Greeks had the advantage of heavier armor and the high morale of a patriotic army. The Persians' advantage was their mighty cavalry, drawn from the Iranian plateau, from Scythia, and from Thessaly and Boeotia. In action against foot soldiers, these horsemen would ride up, send out arrows and javelins, then spur quickly out of reach, only to wheel and attack elsewhere. On flat land, they proved highly effective against the allied Greeks, who had no horse soldiers.

The battle was preceded by 12 days of waiting and skirmishing. The two main armies faced each other, separated by the Asopus River; they stood in battle array in the hot summer sun all day and retired to camps at night. Trying to provoke an attack, Mardonius repeatedly sent his horsemen to harass the Greeks and raid their arriving supply wagons. Both sides suffered from lack of food and fresh water. Pausanias was unwilling to risk an attack, yet each passing day made his army's position more difficult.

At dawn on the 13th day the Persians saw that the entire Greek force had withdrawn toward Plataea. The Greeks were marching in some disarray, having split into three different groups in the dark. Seizing his chance, Mardonius led a full-scale attack across the plain.

The Persian army rushed upon the two nearer Greek contingents. One of these numbered about 11,500 hoplites and contained the best soldiers in Greece, the Spartans, commanded by Pausanias. The other embattled Greek contingent was from Athens and (fittingly enough) Plataea; it numbered about 8,600 and was commanded by the Athenian general ARISTIDES. The Battle of Plataea consisted of two simultaneous actions, separated by perhaps a mile. Meanwhile the third Greek division, farthest away, began marching back toward the fighting.

In attacking so eagerly, Mardonius evidently underestimated the Greeks' discipline and defensive strength. Near a rural temple of DEMETER, the Spartans and their allies formed into battle order, while Mardonius, atop a white charger, brought on his elite Persian infantry. Equipped as archers, the Persians halted a distance from the Greeks and shot volleys of arrows. Greek hoplites, although armored, tended to be vulnerable at the neck, legs, and groin, and many were felled by the arrows before the command finally came to charge.

The hoplites pushed forward into the Persian ranks. The melee wore on until Mardonius was killed, hit in the head with a stone thrown by a Spartan. Seeing their general fall, the Persians broke ranks and fled. At the other end of the battlefield, the Athenians were locked in combat with Boeotian Greeks serving on the Persian side. But at the

sight of their Persian masters running away, the Boeotians retreated toward Thebes.

Many Persians ran to a large wooden palisade that Mardonius had built before the battle. This fort became a slaughterhouse, as the pursuing Greeks broke through and massacred the fugitives within. Although a sizable Persian contingent may have escaped back to Asia, the battle was a stunning Greek victory.

But Plataea marked a fleeting glory. Before the battle, the Greeks had sworn an oath of camaraderie—the famous Oath of Plataea—pledging, among other things, never to harm Athens, Sparta, or the town of Plataea. Yet within a few years hostilities had erupted between Athens and Sparta, and in the PELOPONNESIAN WAR Plataea itself was destroyed by the Spartans.

(See also WARFARE, LAND.)

Plato   Athenian philosopher who lived circa 427–347 B.C. and was one of the most influential thinkers in world history. Plato founded the Western world's first important

The authoritarianism in Plato's political philosophy is suggested in this stern portrait of the great thinker, from a marble bust of the Roman era. The likeness was probably copied from a Greek bronze statue of the 300s B.C.

institution of higher learning, the ACADEMY, which helped shape the course of PHILOSOPHY for the next 1,000 years. Among Plato's teachings, his theory of Forms provided a revolutionary concept of reality—a concept that he tied into corresponding theories of ethics and human knowledge, in a way that seemed to explain the universe.

Most prior Greek philosophers had searched for the universe's primal elements by examining the physical world. Plato, however, influenced by the earlier Greek philosopher PARMENIDES, theorized that true reality is not to be found in the visible, physical world but in an ideal world of eternal Forms. Our earthly phenomena are just imperfect copies of these Forms, Plato said. Such earthly copies include not only material items such as beds and tables, but human virtues such as justice and knowledge. Above all other Forms stands the Form of the Good, whose central and nutritive role in the universe is analogous to that of the sun in the visible world.

To later generations, Plato's concept of a supreme Form of the Good seemed to anticipate Christian monotheism, and so Plato's teachings enjoyed great prestige in the Christian-influenced Roman Empire, circa A.D. 100–400, when a movement called Neoplatonism arose. Probably because of his posthumous association with Christianity, Plato is almost unique among ancient Greek authors in that every major written work by him has been preserved.

For his philosophical writings, Plato chose a style that was unusual in his day—prose dialogue. We have about 30 of these. (A few, ascribed to Plato, are probably forgeries.) Each dialogue typically presents a philosophical discussion among several characters, many of whom are fictionalized versions of real-life personages of fifth-century-B.C. ATHENS. The characters debate a specific topic, such as the nature of courage. The beauty of Plato's technique is that it draws the reader directly into the inquiry. Of the dialogues, Plato's masterpiece is the *Republic* (Greek: Politeia, better translated as "form of government"), written circa 385–370 B.C. The *Republic* first addresses the question "What is justice?" and proceeds to sketch Plato's ideal government, run by a philosopher-king. Plato's theory of Forms receives its classic explanation in the lengthy *Republic*.

The scanty knowledge of Plato's life comes partly from information in the works of later ancient writers, such as the biographers Diogenes Laertius (A.D. 200s) and PLUTARCH (circa A.D. 100). Also preserved are a number of epistles supposedly written by Plato. Although these letters seem to be forgeries, many scholars today accept as accurate the autobiographical information in the famous "Seventh Letter."

Plato (Greek: Platon, "wide," perhaps a nickname) was born into a rich and aristocratic Athenian clan with strong political links; his mother's family claimed descent from the lawgiver SOLON. Plato grew up entirely during the epic PELOPONNESIAN WAR (431–404 B.C.). Like other wealthy Athenian youths, Plato probably did military service in the CAVALRY, perhaps on patrol in the countryside around Athens, circa 409–404 B.C.

Possibly through association with his slightly older kinsmen CRITIAS and Charmides, the young Plato joined the circle of the dynamic Athenian philosopher SOCRATES (circa 469–399 B.C.). Socrates' ethical-political inquiries proved to be the single greatest influence on Plato's thought. In most of his dialogues, written after Socrates' death, Plato immortalized his old mentor by making him the central speaker. Plato's choice of the dialogue form was undoubtedly an attempt to convey the mental excitement of Socrates' discussions.

The convulsive end of the Peloponnesian War changed Plato's life. After Athens' defeat (404 B.C.), Critias and Charmides became central figures in the dictatorship of the THIRTY TYRANTS. Invited to join them, Plato hesitated, and meanwhile the Thirty fell from power; Critias and Charmides were killed (403 B.C.). In 399 B.C., under the restored Athenian DEMOCRACY, Socrates was tried and executed—partly because of his association with Critias. As Socrates' disciple, Plato himself may have been in danger; in any case he seems to have been sickened by the bloody excesses of both right wing and left wing, and he rejected any plan of a political career, choosing instead a life of travel and reflection. But Socratic-type questions about politics and human nature remained foremost in Plato's mind, and he concluded (to use his later words) that there could be no end to human troubles until "either philosophers should become kings, or else those now ruling should become inspired to pursue philosophical wisdom" (*Republic* 473c).

Between about 399 and 387 B.C. Plato probably wrote many or all of the dialogues that modern scholars classify as "early." This group begins with the *Euthyphro, Apology,* and *Crito*—concerning Socrates' arrest, trial, and imprisonment—and culminates in the *Protagoras* and *Gorgias.* The early dialogues mainly explore ethical issues, of which the most important is the *Protagoras'* question, "Is moral virtue teachable?"

During these years Plato traveled to Greek southern ITALY, where he met followers of the early philosopher PYTHAGORAS. Aspects of Plato's views on death and the soul's immortality seem influenced by Pythagorean belief. Also, historical memories of a Pythagorean ruling class—which in prior centuries had existed in certain Italian-Greek cities—may have helped to shape Plato's goal to create a government of philosophers.

Circa 387 B.C., at about age 40, Plato made his fateful first voyage to SICILY, to the important Greek city of SYRACUSE, where the ruthless dictator DIONYSIUS (1) reigned. There Plato became both friend and teacher of a kinsman of the ruler—a handsome young nobleman named Dion. In keeping with prevalent Greek upper-class mores of the day, this male relationship was probably sexual: Plato's homosexual feelings are evident in surviving verses that he wrote for Dion. At the same time, the friendship may have suggested to Plato that he could win followers from among the Syracusan ruling circle and thus create his philosophers' government.

According to one story, the Sicilian visit became a fiasco when the cruel Dionysius, tiring of Plato's criticism, arranged for the philosopher to be sold into slavery; Plato's friends bought back his freedom. In any case, Plato soon returned to Athens and bought land and buildings in a park sacred to the mythical hero Academus, about a mile north of Athens' Dipylon Gate, circa 386 B.C. This holding became Plato's Academy, a university dedicated to philosophical inquiry and the preparation of future leaders of Athens and other Greek cities.

Plato devoted nearly the next 20 years to supervising the Academy and to writing the dialogues that modern scholars assign to his "middle" period. In addition to the *Republic*, these include the *Phaedo* (which combines an account of Socrates' last days in prison with Plato's introduction of his own theory of Forms) and the *Symposium* (on the nature of sexual love). The modern, popular notion of nonsexual, "Platonic" love is a distortion of Plato's views: Specifically addressing the aristocratic, male HOMOSEXUALITY of his own day, Plato believed that such feelings could ennoble and educate those partners who channeled their passion into a spiritual, not just a sexual, union. There is no evidence that Plato ever married, and from his writings he seems to have been of an abstemious homosexual nature.

Much of Plato's thought surely developed from life at the Academy—especially from his informal discussions and disputations with his colleagues (a procedure that derived from Socratic technique). This method of question-and-answer disputation was called dialectic (Greek: *dialektikē*, "discussion" or "dialogue"). In Plato's dialogues, Socrates employs dialectic to refute his opponents' preconceptions, by showing that certain conclusions logically drawn from those preconceptions are false. Plato saw dialectic as the premier philosophical technique, "the coping-stone set atop the other types of learning" (*Republic* 534e).

Only through dialectic can people hope to gain some knowledge of reality—that is, of the Forms. Otherwise we are in the dark. In the most famous allegory in all philosophical literature, the *Republic* compares nonphilosophical inquiry with the plight of prisoners trying to learn about reality by observing shadows in firelight on the wall of a cave.

In 367 B.C. Dionysius of Syracuse died and was succeeded by his son, Dionysius II. The 60-year-old Plato—at the invitation of his old friend Dion—again voyaged to Syracuse, in the hope of making a philosophical convert of the new ruler. But the younger Dionysius proved to be a weak and decadent leader, and was eventually ejected in a coup led by Dion himself (357 B.C.). Plato meanwhile returned to Athens (circa 361 B.C.), having despaired of ever creating an ideal state in Sicily.

The third and last stage of Plato's career covers the years circa 360 B.C. until his death, in 347 B.C. These years at the Academy saw the advancement of the brilliant "graduate student" ARISTOTLE, whom some considered to be Plato's likely successor as head of the school. Plato's dialogues of this period include the *Timaeus* (presenting Plato's picture of the physical cosmos) and the *Laws* (his longest and probably final work). Like the *Republic*, the *Laws* portray an ideal Platonic city-state, but in this later dialogue Plato's authoritarian bent is more pronounced—the laws of his utopian "Cretan city" include generous use of the death penalty—and the *Laws* can be read as evidence of an old man's embitterment. Plato died at age 80, pen in hand (according to legend). He was succeeded as head of the Academy by his nephew Speusippus.

(See also AFTERLIFE; ATLANTIS; EDUCATION; GORGIAS; MATHEMATICS; PROTAGORAS; SOPHISTS; SYMPOSIUM.)

Plutarch   Greek biographer and moral essayist who lived during the early Roman Empire, circa A.D. 50–125. Born in the central Greek region of BOEOTIA, Plutarch (Greek, Ploutarchos) lived in Greece but was also a Roman citizen, and may have held the local Roman post of procurator. He traveled, read, and wrote widely, and for the last 30 years of his life was a priest at the god APOLLO's shrine at DELPHI. Plutarch embodies the Greek-Roman assimilation under the Roman Empire.

Although he did not exactly write history, he happens to be a major source of information for events in the Greek world circa 600–200 B.C. This is due to one of his writings, known by the title *Parallel Lives of the Noble Greeks and Romans*, which in its surviving form consists of 22 paired short biographies ("Lives"), one of a Greek leader, one of a Roman. Most of these biographical subjects lived in the great centuries of classical Greece and the Roman Republic, prior to Plutarch's time. Among his more important Greek Lives are those of SOLON, PERICLES, ALCIBIADES, and ALEXANDER THE GREAT. Although often sloppy about chronology, the Lives are full of historical and personal detail.

polis   Ancient Greek city-state. The *polis* (from which word is derived the English word "politics") was the basic political unit of the classical Greeks. Between about 800 B.C. and 300 B.C., the map of Greece was a patchwork of autonomous city-states, some linked together by alliance or kinship, and some vying to dominate their neighbors, but each one capable of ruling itself as a self-contained political entity. Beginning as aristocracies, city-states developed as democracies or oligarchies in the 500s–400s B.C. The most important DEMOCRACY was ATHENS.

Two factors contributed to the city-state's emergence. One was the geography of Greece: mountains, islands, and small farming valleys naturally created discrete, small population centers, many with their own dialects and religious cults. The second reason, more peculiar to the 900s–800s B.C., has to do with the rejection of kingship in Greece during that era. A king may strive to unite various peoples under his single rule, because he is the government. But members of an aristocratic clan—who may rely for their power on local lands and on local religious cults, for which they supply the priesthood—might be prone to concentrate their rule in a smaller, more homogeneous area.

In population, the polis consisted of: full citizens (usually males over age 18, born of citizen parents); female and children citizens (protected by the law but without any voice in government); second-class citizens, such as PERIOECI; resident aliens or METICS; and SLAVES.

The age of the polis ended with the Macedonian conquest of Greece (338 B.C.), the campaigns of ALEXANDER THE GREAT (334–323 B.C.), and the subsequent rise of rich and powerful Greco-Macedonian kingdoms in the eastern Mediterranean and Near East. In the HELLENISTIC AGE (300–150 B.C.), individual Greek cities were not strong enough to survive independently.

(See also APOLLO; ARISTOCRACY; GREECE, GEOGRAPHY OF; HELOTS; HOPLITE; LAWS AND LAW COURTS; OLIGARCHY; TYRANTS; WOMEN.)

Polyclitus   Prominent sculptor of the mid- and late 400s B.C., known for his idealized view of the male body.

Polyclitus (Greek: Polukleitos) was born at ARGOS. Working mainly in BRONZE, he established his reputation with a number of commissioned statues of victorious Olympian athletes, displayed at OLYMPIA. Two famous nudes by Polyclitus have survived in the form of later marble copies—the Doryphorus (spear carrier, in the Naples Museum), representing a muscular athlete; and the more sensual Diadumenus (ribbon binder, in the Athens National Museum and elsewhere), showing a youth tying an athlete's ribbon around his head. The Doryphorus brought to perfection the "counterpoise" stance: The man is shown resting his weight on one leg, knee locked, with the other leg drawn back. This stance became a standard pose for statuary down through Renaissance times.

Polyclitus' masterpiece was considered to be the giant GOLD and ivory cult statue of the goddess HERA, sculpted for Hera's temple at Polyclitus' native Argos (circa 420 B.C.). The statue, now lost, showed the goddess seated, with a scepter in one hand and a pomegranate in the other. The statue was in ancient times compared with the colossal statue of Olympian ZEUS sculpted by Polyclitus' rival, PHIDIAS. The Roman geographer Strabo considered the Hera to be the more lovely in technique, although smaller and less magnificent than the Zeus.

(See also SCULPTURE.)

Polycrates Dynamic tyrant of the Greek island of SAMOS. Reigning circa 540–522 B.C., Polycrates was the last great Greek ruler in the eastern Aegean, in the path of the advancing Persians. Usurping power at Samos with the help of his two brothers, Polycrates soon ruled alone, executing one brother and banishing the other. He made an alliance with the Egyptian pharaoh Amasis and built a navy of 100 longboats, arming them with bowmen. Under him, Samos became the preeminent eastern Greek state—replacing Samos' nearby rival, MILETUS, now under Persian rule.

Polycrates was a visionary of naval power. The historian HERODOTUS (the main source for Polycrates' story) called him "the first Greek to plan an empire by sea," and the historian THUCYDIDES (1) saw his domain as a forerunner of the Athenian sea empire of the 400s B.C.

True to his name ("ruling much"), Polycrates led his fleet east and west across the Aegean, mainly against his fellow Greeks. Many of his ventures were pure piracy, but he probably hoped to drive the Persians from the ASIA MINOR coast and capture the Greek cities there for himself. He attacked the territory of Persian-controlled Miletus and defeated a fleet coming to Miletus' aid from the Greek island of LESBOS; he put the prisoners to work as SLAVES on Samos. Polycrates also took over the holy island of DELOS and enlarged the prestigious Delian Games, in the god APOLLO's honor. Like other dictators, Polycrates glorified his capital city (also named Samos), while providing employment and amenities for the common people. He completed Samos' grand temple of the goddess HERA, which was one of the largest existing Greek temples at that time. He developed Samos' harbor and built or completed a tunneled aqueduct, an engineering marvel of its day, bringing water to Samos city.

Polycrates kept the most magnificent court of the Greek world. With generous retaining fees, he attracted the dis-

tinguished physician Democedes of CROTON and the famous lyric poets IBYCUS of RHEGIUM and ANACREON of Teos. In keeping with the upper-class tastes of the era, Polycrates (although married and a father) was an enthusiastic lover of boys and young men. It was probably for Polycrates that Anacreon wrote many of his extant poems of homosexual content.

Eventually the shadow of disaster fell across this glamorous despot, as he became caught between (on one side) the unstoppable Persian advance and (on the other) the antityrant elements of the Greek world. Circa 525 B.C. the skippers of a Samian war fleet rebelled and attacked Polycrates on Samos. They were defeated, but the survivors sailed west to get help from SPARTA, the foremost antityrant state of mainland Greece. The Spartans sent out an overseas expedition, their first in recorded history. However, Polycrates held out against their six-week siege of Samos city, and they went home.

Polycrates did not survive for long. Circa 522 B.C. the Persian governor of western Asia Minor lured Polycrates in person to the mainland, then had him seized and killed. A few years later the Persian king DARIUS (1) conquered Samos and installed, as his vassal, Polycrates' surviving brother, Syloson ("preserver of booty"). Samos' sea holdings were lost, and henceforth Samos' warships served in the Persian navy.

Among the folktales that sprang up around Polycrates, one has been retold in variations over the centuries. According to Herodotus, Polycrates, at the height of success, was warned that—because the gods are jealous of human happiness—he should offset the danger by throwing away whatever he valued most in the world. He decided to discard his priceless signet ring, an engraved emerald set in GOLD. Aboard one of his ships, he threw the ring into the sea. But a few days later, as Polycrates sat down to dinner, his servants brought in that very ring; it had been found in the belly of a fine fish being prepared for the ruler's meal. The gods had rejected Polycrates' offering, and he was doomed to die a miserable death.

(See also FATE; HOMOSEXUALITY; TYRANTS; WARFARE, NAVAL.)

Polygnotus See PAINTING.

Polynices See SEVEN AGAINST THEBES.

Polyphemus In HOMER's epic poem the *Odyssey* (written down circa 750 B.C.) Polyphemus ("much fame") is a CYCLOPS—one of a race of gigantic, savage, one-eyed creatures who inhabit a legendary region in the West, vaguely associated with SICILY. Polyphemus is the son of the god POSEIDON and the nymph Thoösa. In what is probably the *Odyssey*'s best-known episode, Polyphemus captures the Greek hero ODYSSEUS (book 9).

Odysseus discovers the monster's cave after landing his ship in the Cyclopes' territory on his voyage home from the TROJAN WAR. With 12 of his men, Odysseus enters the deserted cave to steal supplies, then willfully remains inside the cave, hoping to have a look at the Cyclops. But when Polyphemus returns with his goats and sheep, he immediately traps the Greeks by sealing the cave mouth with a slab of rock, too large for humans to drag away.

Then, catching two of the Greeks in his hands, Polyphemus beats out their brains and eats them raw for dinner. Stretching out amid his sheep, he falls asleep. The Greeks do not attack him, realizing that they can never escape without Polyphemus to move that massive boulder.

The next morning Polyphemus eats two more men for breakfast, leaves the Greeks penned inside as he pastures his flock and herd for another day, and then eats two more men for supper. By then Odysseus has a plan: He makes Polyphemus drunk by giving him a goatskin-full of WINE. When the Cyclops falls into a drunken sleep, Odysseus and his men ram a sharpened post into the monster's one eyeball, blinding him forever. The other Cyclopes, hearing Polyphemus' cries, gather outside the cave and ask what's wrong; Polyphemus shouts out that "Nobody" is hurting him—Nobody (Outis) being the false name by which Odysseus had identified himself to the giant. The other Cyclopes wander off, assuming that Polyphemus' affliction must come from the gods. Then the blind Polyphemus drags away the door boulder and, squatting at the cave mouth, waits furiously for the Greeks to try to run out.

Again Odysseus has a scheme. He ties each of his six remaining men to the underbellies of three sheep abreast, and himself takes hold of the fleecy underbelly of a big ram. As the Cyclops' sheeps and goats move out of the cave for grazing, the Greeks ride concealed among them. The giant strokes each animal's back as it passes, but he misses the Greeks hiding underneath.

The Greeks escape back to their beached ship and shipmates. Once safely aboard and headed out to sea, Odysseus cannot resist the impulse to shout out taunts to Polyphemus and tell him his own true name and lineage. Guided by the voice, Polyphemus hurls a boulder that nearly smashes the departing ship, then he prays to his divine father, Poseidon, to curse Odysseus. Thereafter, in the *Odyssey*, Poseidon is Odysseus' enemy, working to disrupt the hero's voyage home.

Centuries later, in the HELLENISTIC AGE, Polyphemus became the subject of poetic elaboration. The Sicilian Greek poet THEOCRITUS (circa 275 B.C.) wrote two poems describing how, prior to the Odysseus episode, Polyphemus loved and wooed the sea nymph Galatea. The idea of turning a savage, ugly giant into a romantic hero is typical of the frivolous intellectual tastes of the Hellenistic era.

Unrelated to the Cyclops story, the name *Polyphemus* also belonged to one of the Argonauts who sailed with the Thessalian hero JASON (1) in search of the Golden Fleece.

Poseidon Greek god of the sea and all other bodies of water, as well as of earthquakes and horses. According to the Greek creation legend, Poseidon received the sea as his domain when he and his brothers, ZEUS and HADES, drew lots for their portions of the world, after deposing their royal father, CRONUS. Poseidon was variously described as younger or older than Zeus, but he was subordinate to Zeus in wisdom and moral significance.

A patron god of mariners and fishermen, Poseidon had important temples in certain Greek coastal regions in historical times. These sanctuaries included Cape MYCALĒ, on the central west coast of ASIA MINOR, and Cape Sunium, in the Athenian territory of ATTICA. The god was commemorated in the names of seaport cities such as POSEIDONIA

Poseidon aims his trident, on a silver coin known as a *statēr*, minted by the Greek city of Poseidonia (Paestum), in southern Italy, circa 540 B.C. The figure may represent a bronze statue of the god that stood in that prosperous city named after him. The Greek lettering reads POS.

and POTIDAEA. But his most famous shrine was at the Isthmus of CORINTH, in south-central Greece, where the biennial ISTHMIAN GAMES were held in his honor.

Poseidon was especially associated with storms at sea, which posed a deadly hazard to ancient shipping. In the god's sea-front temples, voyagers prayed for safe passage, and survivors of shipwrecks gave thanks for deliverance. When storms off the Thessalian coast in 480 B.C. destroyed part of the invading Persian fleet during the PERSIAN WARS, the Greeks paid thanks to Poseidon.

The name Poseidon clearly contains the Greek root *pos-*, "lord," but the rest of the meaning is lost to us. In Greek RELIGION, Poseidon (like Zeus) probably dates back to the earliest Greek-speaking tribesmen who arrived in Greece circa 2100 B.C. Poseidon's earliest form was probably not that of a sea god. (According to modern scholarship, the Greeks originally came from a landlocked region, the Danube basin, and at first lacked a word for "sea.") The prehistoric Poseidon may have been a deity of lakes, rivers, and mountain torrents. He became associated with earthquakes because they were thought to be caused by underground watercourses. In historical times, Poseidon's most common titles were "shaker of the earth" (Ennosigaios) and "holder of the earth" (Gaieochos).

Probably before or during the years of MYCENAEAN CIVILIZATION (circa 1600–1200 B.C.), Poseidon took on his familiar role as the sea god. This change surely occurred as the early Greeks learned shipbuilding and ventured out to sea for food supply, war, and TRADE. Poseidon is mentioned frequently in the surviving LINEAR B tablets from the late Mycenaean era, circa 1400–1200 B.C., but his precise roles in those years are unclear.

In taking over the sea, Poseidon's cult seems to have displaced the worship of certain pre-Greek sea deities.

Apparently some of these survived in Greek MYTH in the guise of lesser sea gods, such as NEREUS and his mermaid daughters, the Nereids. Poseidon was said to have married a Nereid named Amphitritē, after subduing her by pursuit and abduction. She bore him a son, Triton. The sound *trit*, which the names of mother and son share, is considered by scholars to be non-Greek and may represent a prehellenic word for "sea."

Poseidon's function as the horse god may date back to his earliest roots among prehistoric Greek-speaking tribes, who evidently arrived in mainland Greece with domesticated horses. In historical times there was a widespread cult of Poseidon Hippios (of the horse); images in some shrines showed the god as a horseman. According to one myth, the first horse had been born out of a rock where Poseidon's semen had fallen. Poseidon oversaw the horse- and chariot-racing at all Greek sports festivals, not just at his own Isthmian Games. He was said to have been the mentor of the hero PELOPS, founder of the OLYMPIC GAMES.

Mythologically, Poseidon embodied the raw power found in his elements—the sea, earthquakes, and horses. Legends portrayed him as strong, yet brutish and not clever, sometimes in contrast with the wise goddess ATHENA. Poseidon was an important god for the Athenians—he was associated with the hero THESEUS, and he had a shrine inside the patriotic-cult building known as the Erectheum, on the ACROPOLIS. But he was said to have lost a contest with Athena over who would become the chief Athenian deity. HOMER's *Odyssey* echoed this competition: Poseidon failed to destroy the wily hero ODYSSEUS, who was aided by Athena. Other legends described Athena as a civilizing influence over Poseidon's realm—she invented shipbuilding and the bridle, to bring humans to the sea and to tame the horse.

Poseidon's myths tended to associate him with monsters. He was the lover of the demon MEDUSA, and lover or father of the HARPIES. His beautiful mistress SCYLLA was transformed into a hideous sea monster by the jealous Amphitritē. His liaison with the earth goddess GAEA (who was technically his grandmother) produced the fierce giant Antaeus, later killed by HERACLES. With the nymph Thoösa, Poseidon was father of the brutal POLYPHEMUS. Less grotesquely, the Elean princess Tyro bore Poseidon twin sons, Neleus (later king of PYLOS and father of NESTOR) and Pelias (later king of Iolcus, in THESSALY, and enemy of JASON [1]).

In Greek art, Poseidon supplied a study in pure strength. He was often shown holding his trident—a three-pronged fish spear used by Greek fishermen. He resembled Zeus in his beard, physique, and mature age. A superb classical Greek statue found in the sea off Cape ARTEMISIUM in the A.D. 1920s, now identified as a likeness of Zeus, was for decades thought to represent Poseidon.

(See also CHARIOTS; GREEK LANGUAGE; SHIPS AND SEA-FARING.)

Poseidonia   Greek city on the southwestern coast of ITALY, on the Bay of Salerno. Located at the edge of a wide plain, Poseidonia was founded by colonists from the Italian Greek city of SYBARIS in the last quarter of the 600s B.C. and was named for the sea god POSEIDON. It was a sprawl-ing city, encircled by a wall nearly three miles long but without natural defenses, and it thrived from FARMING and seaborne TRADE. Captured circa 390 B.C. by neighboring Italian tribesmen, the Lucanii, the city passed in 273 B.C. into the hands of the Romans, who called it Paestum.

The site now boasts the standing remnants of three Doric-style temples, built between about 550 and 450 B.C., which are among the best-preserved examples of Greek monumental ARCHITECTURE. Of these, the famous "Temple of Neptune" (actually a temple of HERA) rivals the Athenian PARTHENON in magnificence. The site also contains tombs of the 400s and 300s B.C. that have provided some of the few surviving Greek wall paintings.

(See also PAINTING.)

Potidaea   Important Corinthian colony, founded circa 600 B.C. on the northern Aegean seacoast known as CHALCIDICĒ. Located on the narrow neck of the westernmost of Chalcidicē's three peninsulas, Potidaea had a fine harbor, facing west into the Thermaic Gulf and protected in later years by walls and by moles across the harbor mouth. Potidaea (Greek: *Poteidaia*, a form of the name of the god POSEIDON) was the only major Chalcidic city founded by Greeks who were not IONIAN GREEKS; it was also the only Corinthian colony located in the Aegean rather than in the Adriatic or farther west. Potidaea's location made it a gateway from Greece to the north Aegean. Exporting to Corinth, it was a source for TIMBER, SILVER, and SLAVES, available from nearby THRACE.

Potidaea became a foremost Chalcidic city, later surpassed only by its neighbor OLYNTHUS. With Thracian silver, Potidaea was minting coins by about 550 B.C. It led the local Greek resistance to the invading Persians of 480–479 B.C., its formidable defenses withstanding a Persian siege. After the Persian retreat, Potidaea joined the Athenian-led DELIAN LEAGUE. However, the city maintained close ties with Corinth—for instance, it received its chief political executives from Corinth every year.

As Athenian-Corinthian relations worsened in the mid-400s B.C., Potidaea became the object of increasing Athenian mistrust. In 434 B.C. the Athenians raised Potidaea's Delian annual tribute from six to 15 TALENTS. In resistance to Athenian demands, Potidaea rebelled, appealing to Corinth for help. Soon ATHENS and Corinth were in collision over Potidaea. At the Battle of Potidaea, fought outside the city (432 B.C.), an Athenian expeditionary force of 2,000 HOPLITES defeated a slightly smaller Corinthian-led army. This episode—like similar Athenian-Corinthian hostilities at the Adriatic city of CORCYRA—was a major cause in igniting the PELOPONNESIAN WAR.

Potidaea finally was captured by the Athenians in early 429 B.C., after an immense siege in which the Athenian army suffered from plague and the starving defenders were reduced to cannibalism. The Athenians allowed the Potidaeans to evacuate, and the city was repopulated with Athenian colonists. But after Athens' defeat in the Peloponnesian War (404 B.C.), the local Chalcidic Greeks took over the city.

As the second city (after Olynthus) of the powerful Chalcidic League, Potidaea again became a target of Athenian imperialism, in the early 300s B.C. It was captured by

Athenian troops in 363 B.C. The Athenians were expelled by the Macedonian king PHILIP II in 358 B.C., but Potidaea probably was destroyed by Philip in 348 B.C., in his war against Olynthus.

In around 316 B.C. the city was refounded as the capital of MACEDON under the ruler CASSANDER; the city's new name was Cassandreia. In the HELLENISTIC AGE (300–150 B.C.) it remained a major port of the north Aegean, and passed into the empire of ROME after the Romans dismantled the Macedonian kingdom in the mid-100s B.C.

(See also PERIANDER; PERSIAN WARS.)

pottery   The term *Greek pottery* refers mainly to ceramic vessels—storage jars, drinking cups, mixing bowls, plates, and the like, shaped from wet clay on a potter's wheel and fired to brittleness in a kiln heated to about 1,000 degrees Fahrenheit. In addition to hardening the pot, the baking permanently sets any glaze or paint, often with predictable changes of color.

Items of ceramic (Greek: *keramos,* "potter's clay") obviously played a large role in the TRADE and daily life of all ancient cultures. However, for modern archaeologists, pottery takes on a paramount importance well beyond its importance in ancient times, due to one simple fact: Pottery is nearly indestructible. A fired clay pot may shatter easily, but the sherds will last for 10,000 years once buried in the ground. Pottery is thus different from such perishable materials as textiles or wood, which also served major uses in ancient times but which have disappeared with barely a trace. Pottery provides the most available material link to the ancient world. Not every ancient site has a PAR-THENON to offer, but almost every site has a buried wealth of potsherds, full of data for the archaeologist.

For example, Greek pottery is the best-surviving medium for ancient Greek PAINTING. The painted scenes that once adorned walls, wood panels, and canvases in ancient Greece are lost, but the scenes on pottery, baked onto the clay, have survived. Such vase painting suggests the developing techniques of all Greek painting, and the rendered scenes also provide priceless information about life in ancient Greece—for RELIGION, FARMING, warfare, and the like. Many of the illustrations in this book depict scenes that were originally painted on pottery.

More generally, the geographic distribution of pottery remnants can reveal ancient trade routes and waves of migrations. Mycenaean potsherds found in southern CY-PRUS reveal that the early Greeks probably settled there circa 1300 B.C. Similarly, the huge troves of Corinthan and Athenian pottery found at sites in former Etruria (in northern ITALY, a region where the Greeks never settled) are a dramatic sign of the insatiable market for Greek goods that existed among the ETRUSCANS, circa 600–500 B.C.

The invention of pottery predates by thousands of years the dawn of Greek civilization, starting with pots shaped without a potter's wheel in Mesopotamia and eastern China, circa 5000 B.C. By 2500 B.C. pottery was being produced in the pre-Greek CYCLADES and by the Minoan people of CRETE. Technique was improved by introduction of the potter's wheel circa 2100 B.C.

Mainland Greece, with its soil rich in clay, was producing pottery before the Greeks arrived. The invading Greeks'

Athenian amphora of the mid-700s B.C., 16 inches tall, painted in the style known as Geometric. Geometric vase painting provides the first surviving sign of an awakened Greek artistic genius after the Dark Age (1100–900 B.C.). This impressive example shows how painters began to break up their abstract designs with renderings of live figures—in this case, deer (above), goats (middle), and geese (below). The repeated key pattern, sometimes called a meander, remained a familiar design on Greek textiles and other goods throughout antiquity.

conquest of Greece (circa 2100 B.C. and after) is probably signified by the disappearance of prior styles of pottery and the abrupt emergence (circa 1900 B.C.) of a new type, known to modern archaeologists as Minyan ware. Distinguished by its unadorned gray or gray-yellow glazing and

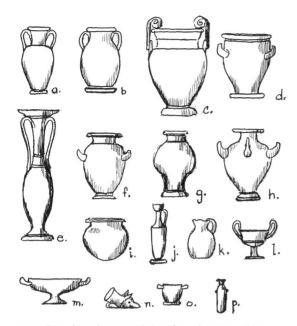

A sampling of Greek pottery designs from the 500s and 400s B.C. Several of these types had their specialized use at the upper-class drinking party known as the symposium. (a) Amphora, meaning "two handled"—the classic Greek wine-storage vessel; sealed with a lid or plug, the amphora was used for domestic storage and (in a modified shape) for seaborne export. (b) Pelike, another type of storage vessel. (c) Krater ("mixer"), used for mixing wine and water at a meal or symposium; this particular design is known as a volute (curl-handled) krater. (d) Bell Krater. (e) Loutrophoros, a ceremonial water vase, used at Athens for the special bath on the wedding day and for the funerary washing of a corpse. (f) Stamnos, a jar for storing wine or oil. (g) Psykter ("cooler"), used to cool undiluted wine prior to mixing and serving; the psykter's shape allowed it to fit partly inside a bowl of cold water. (h) Hydria, a water jug. (i) Lebes, a basin used like a krater, for mixing wine and water. (j) Lekythos, an oil flask. (k) Oinochoë, a "wine-pourer," for dispensing wine from the krater. (l) Kantharos, a type of wine cup. (m) Kylix, another type of wine cup: The shallow bowl was suited to a drinker reclining at a symposium. (n) Rhyton, a decorative form of wine cup, ending, at bottom, in an animal's head or other shape. (o) Skyphos, another wine cup. (p) Alabastron, a jar for perfumes and unguents; the jar acquired its name, in ancient times, because many specimens were carved from alabaster.

its shape that resembles vessels of beaten metal, Minyan ware was discovered and named in A.D. 1880 by the great archaeologist Heinrich Schliemann. This pottery has been found throughout Greece and is the earliest surviving vestige of those people whose descendants would create the MYCENAEAN CIVILIZATION (circa 1600–1200 B.C.).

More imaginative pottery shapes and painted designs emerge at the height of Mycenaean culture (circa 1400–1200 B.C.). Clearly influenced by Minoan pottery, Mycenaean ware included many shapes—such as the kylix (drinking bowl), pitcher (lekythos), and storage jar (amphora)—that would see use in later centuries in classical Greece.

Mycenaean artists typically painted brown on pale yellow. Designs include concentric bands and floral patterns, but a few discovered Mycenaean pots show animal figures such as birds and an octopus. One spectacular vase shows a column of soldiers.

The downfall of Mycenaean society (by 1100 B.C.) was followed by the gradual emergence of new pottery shapes and painted designs, recognizably derived from Mycenaean types. This new style, emerging specifically at ATHENS circa 1050 B.C., is today called Protogeometric—the forerunner to the Geometric style that developed circa 900 B.C. Protogeometric vase painting is distinguished by certain brown or black designs: concentric circles or half circles (drawn with a compass on the vase's side), triangles, cross-hatching, and the earliest appearance of the typically Greek right-angle pattern known as the meander.

The Geometric period (circa 900–700 B.C.) saw new methods of decoration, along with certain new pottery shapes. On a background of tan or light yellow, the best Geometric ware shows a density of design, including (after about 800 B.C.) silhouette stick figures representing animal life or human activity, at first confined to horizontal panels around the vase. One of the most characteristic Geometric human scenes (circa 750 B.C.) is on the Dipylon amphora, named because it was discovered near Athens' ancient Dipylon Gate. Amid bands of meanders and diamond shapes, a panel shows triangular-torsoed stick figures in postures of mourning around a skirted figure on a bier. Appropriately, the five-foot-tall vase was deposited as an offering in an aristocratic tomb. This vase's artist, named the Dipylon painter by scholars, is considered to be the first recognizably individual Greek artist.

Geometric style spread to workshops throughout Greece, but by about 730 B.C. artists at the mighty commercial center of CORINTH had abandoned Geometric in favor of new designs, strongly influenced by artwork imported from the Near East. The first stage of this development—part of a larger Orientalizing movement in all Greek art—is known as the Protocorinthian style (730–625 B.C.). Next came the ripe Corinthian style (circa 625–550 B.C.). Widely popular, Corinthian-made potteries monopolized the market, both inside the Greek world and beyond, for nearly 150 years.

Protocorinthian and Corinthian vase painting shows mainly human or animal scenes, with some intervening decorations (typically floral, copied from Near Eastern motifs). Gone are the dark stick figures of Geometric art; there is wide use of color and detail, with attempts at foreshortening. One of the most admired such works is the Chigi Vase (circa 650 B.C.), illustrated with a warfare scene. Under influence of the emerging Athenian black-figure technique, the full Corinthian style (circa 560 B.C.) combined color with solemnity in a packed, friezelike scene. New pottery shapes also came into use in this era.

In imitation of Corinthian technique, the region of SPARTA produced a school of pottery painting in the early 500s B.C.. A number of lively scenes survive on the inside bottoms of Spartan cups.

Meanwhile Athenian black-figure pottery, destined to oust Corinthian ware from the world market, was being produced by 600 B.C. Early black figure saw the vast reduction of decorative designs in favor of scenes from MYTH; later scenes from daily life—farming, seafaring—become more common. The name *black figure* refers to the fact that men's skin was painted dark and rendered into black by glazing and firing; in contrast, women's flesh was shown as white. Incisions helped create detail and fine lines. One early epitome of the style is the Athenian-made Francoise Vase (circa 570 B.C.), discovered in what used to be Etruscan territory and now in the Florence archaeological museum. The small vase (a volute krater, or form of mixing bowl) uses a light background to present lively mythological scenes in miniature. The black-figure technique reached its zenith in about 550–525 B.C., with the work of such Athenian artists as the Amasis Painter.

But by 520 B.C. a new Athenian style had emerged, now called red figure. Red figure reversed the black-figure technique: The human and animal figures were left open to the clay's red color, and it was now the background that was painted and fired black. This represented a breakthrough for creating realistic figures and (through incision) precise detail. The style reached perfection in the work of the artist now known as the Berlin Painter (circa 480 B.C.), who was able to show beautifully realistic musculature and detail.

Another popular Athenian style of the 400s B.C. was the white-ground technique, which rendered figures in delicate lines against a white background. This style was used particularly for *lekythoi* (or *lekuthoi*, pitchers) deposited as offerings in tombs.

The decline of Athenian red-figure style circa 400 B.C. marks the end of the great phases of Greek vase painting. But red-figure continued—the painted scenes become more crowded, the figures more florid—into the 300s B.C., especially in Greek south Italy and SICILY (where Athenian-influenced vase-painting movements arose in the 440s B.C.). By 300 B.C. the new trade routes of the Hellenistic world were making metal pots and vessels more accessible, thereby removing any rich market for vase painting. But the 200s B.C. saw a renaissance of sorts, in the polychrome ware from Greek Sicily.

(See also ARCHAEOLOGY; FUNERAL CUSTOMS; MINOAN CIVILIZATION; SYMPOSIUM.)

Praxiteles   The most important Greek sculptor of the 300s B.C. An Athenian, Praxiteles worked in the mid-century and was famous for his gorgeous, idealized nudes. He developed marble (as opposed to BRONZE) as a medium for free-standing statuary, and in keeping with the emerging tastes of the 300s B.C., he promoted the female nude as an object of artistic reverence, alongside the male.

Praxiteles' most celebrated work was his cult statue of APHRODITE for that goddess' temple at CNIDUS, in ASIA MINOR (circa 364 B.C.). Considered the most beautiful statue in the world, it showed the goddess standing naked, having disrobed for her bath, with one hand imperfectly covering her vulva. A later copy of this statue (not itself awe-inspiring) now stands in the Vatican Museum. Another well-known statue by Praxiteles, circa 340 B.C., showed the god HERMES holding the divine infant DIONYSUS; a statue of this type standing in the museum at OLYMPIA is now considered by modern scholars to be Praxiteles' original, rather than a later ancient copy.

(See also SCULPTURE.)

Priam   In MYTH, the last king of TROY, killed in the Greeks' capture of the city in the TROJAN WAR. Priam was the son and successor of King Laomedon, and the husband of HECUBA, by whom he had 17 sons, including HECTOR and PARIS. Between wife and concubines, Priam had 50 sons and 12 daughters in all.

In HOMER's epic poem the *Iliad*, which describes events of the 10th year of the war, Priam appears as an important secondary character, elderly and wise. He disapproves of Paris' abduction of the Spartan princess HELEN, which has caused the war, but he shows nobility in his courtesy to her and his determination not to give her back to the Greeks against her will. Near the poem's end, after Hector has been slain by the Greek hero ACHILLES, Priam journeys, with the supernatural aid of the gods ZEUS and HERMES, to the Greek camp. There he successfully pleads with Achilles for the privilege of ransoming back Hector's corpse. The old king's grief and suppliant posture clearly foreshadow the destruction of his city.

The story of Priam's death was originally told in a Greek epic poem titled *The Capture of Troy* (*Iliou Persis*), which has not survived, but whose general plot is known. During the Greeks' sack of the city, Priam took refuge at an altar of Zeus but was impiously slain there by Achilles' son, NEOPTOLEMUS. For the classical Greeks, Priam represented the extremes of good and bad fortune that can visit a man in his lifetime.

Priam's name is apparently not Greek, and he may represent a memory of a real-life Trojan king of the historical Trojan War, circa 1220 B.C..

(See also EPIC POETRY; HELEN OF TROY.)

Priapus   East Greek fertility god and guardian of orchards and gardens, often pictured as a puny or misshapen man with an enormous, erect penis. Priapus originated in the non-Greek regions of ASIA MINOR, and in classical times (400s B.C.) his worship among the Greeks was confined mainly to Lampsacus, on the east shore of the HELLESPONT. However, Priapus' cult spread during the HELLENISTIC AGE (circa 300–150 B.C.), becoming popular at ALEXANDRIA (1) and later at ROME. His worship involved the non-Greek custom of sacrificing donkeys. He seems to have had no MYTH, being described merely as the son of APHRODITE and DIONYSUS. His name is commemorated in the modern English adjective *priapic*.

Priapus' monstrous organ signified his guardian powers as well as his fertilizing aspect, for the Greeks had a notion that trespassers and thieves (male or female) are liable to rape by the rightful owners of a territory.

(See also HERMES.)

Procrustes   In MYTH, a sadistic brigand, son of the god POSEIDON who preyed upon travelers in ATTICA until slain by the Athenian hero THESEUS.

Meeting a wayfarer on the road, Procrustes ("hammerer-out") would deceptively offer him lodging for the night, then force the victim to lie down on one of two beds. Tall men he would place on the shorter bed, and saw off their lower legs, to fit; he placed short men on the longer bed and stretched them out (for the bed was a rack).

The modern English adjective *procrustean* describes an attempt to fit facts or individual examples into a preconceived, inappropriate theory or rule.

Prometheus   In MYTH, a benevolent Titan (demigod) who championed the cause of humankind against the gods. Although several characters in Greek myth defied or challenged the great god ZEUS, Prometheus is the only one who appears in a heroic light. Classical Greeks saw him as an example of the wily "trickster"—a type also represented by the god HERMES, the hero ODYSSEUS, and the real-life Athenian statesman THEMISTOCLES. Appropriately enough, *Promētheus* means "having forethought."

According to one version of the myth, it was Prometheus himself who created the first humans, shaping them out of clay while the goddess ATHENA breathed life into them. Zeus then called on Prometheus to decide the question of how humans should sacrifice to the gods—that is, which part of the sacrificed beast should be assigned as the gods' portion and which part should be eaten by mortals. In this arbitration, Prometheus chose to deceive and humiliate Zeus. As described in HESIOD's epic poem *Theogony* (circa 700 B.C.), Prometheus butchered an ox and disguised the bones in a wrapping of fat, but hid the ox's flesh and edible organs inside the stomach. He showed both items to Zeus, inviting him to choose between a bundle glistening with fat or a tripe. The king of the gods chose the inviting-looking bundle, and that is why (according to the legend) humans customarily keep the best sacrificial portions for themselves to eat, while burning only the animal's bones and hide for the gods.

Zeus retaliated by withholding the use of fire from humankind. But Prometheus stole fire from heaven inside a fennel stalk, to bestow on mortals.

Enraged at Prometheus' defiance, Zeus plotted revenge against him and his race of mortals (who up until then had included only one gender, the male). Zeus ordered the craftsman god HEPHAESTUS and other gods to create a new kind of human, lovely but treacherous: This was Pandora ("all gifts"), the first woman. She was sent to earth, where she married Prometheus' simple-minded brother, Epimetheus (having afterthought). Pandora brought with her, or otherwise acquired, a supernatural clay jar containing pain, toil, illness, and other evils not yet known in the world. When, out of curiosity, she opened the jar, the hateful contents flew out and propagated, leaving only hope inside the jar, to delude mortals.

For Prometheus himself, Zeus had a more terrible punishment. Hephaestus chained Prometheus to a lonely mountain crag, where every day an eagle would fly up and tear out the prisoner's liver, devouring it; but Prometheus never died, and every night his liver grew back, so that the torture could be repeated daily. Eventually the hero HERACLES released Prometheus, with Zeus' permission.

Prometheus' punishment is the subject of the stage tragedy *Prometheus Bound* (circa 455 B.C.), which traditionally has been ascribed to the Athenian playwright AESCHYLUS, but which lately is thought not to be his work.

(See also RELIGION; TITANS; WOMEN.)

prophecy and divination   Because the ancient Greeks believed that the gods had a hand in human events, they also believed that humans could interpret the gods' wishes. While prayer and sacrifice sought to win the gods' favor, the interpretation of divine will was the goal of certain other activities, which the Greeks called *manteia*, denoting prophecy and other forms of divination. Prophets and soothsayers abounded in Greek MYTH, but they also remained important among living Greeks right down to the end of the ancient world.

In its strictest English-language use, the word *prophecy* refers to a form of soothsaying in which the god speaks directly through the mouth of the human prophet (Greek: *prophētēs*). "Divination," a more general word, includes less inspirational forms of future-telling. The most famous ancient Greek example of inspirational prophecy was the Delphic oracle. The oracle was a priestess of APOLLO, at the god's most holy sanctuary at DELPHI in central Greece. In response to an inquirer's question, she would go into a trance and deliver frenzied utterings, which a male priest would interpret and write down in verse. Similar oracles of Apollo were found at CUMAE and elsewhere.

Apollo's father, ZEUS, was the other main god of prophecy. At Zeus' very ancient sanctuary at DODONA, in northwestern Greece, the priests gave answers after listening for Zeus' prompting in the rustle of leaves in the god's sacred oak tree.

Other modes of divination were practiced by a seer (*mantis*), whose methods might involve observation of animal life, such as the flights and cries of passing birds—a practice now called augury. But the most common of the seer's duties was extispicy—that is, examining the removed organs (particularly the liver) of a newly sacrificed animal: A healthy-looking liver meant that the gods approved of the inquirer's intended course of action; an unhealthy one meant disapproval.

Still other forms of divination sought to find messages in dreams, in random consultations of texts of HOMER's poems, or in events of everyday life. A sneeze, for instance, was considered a good omen, applicable to whatever was being discussed or thought of at the moment. One peculiar rite, known as *kledon*, was practiced at various shrines of the god HERMES. After whispering a question into the ear of the god's cult statue, the worshipper would immediately stop up his or her own ears and leave the temple; outside, beyond the town marketplace, the worshipper would unplug his or her ears and listen for the god's answer delivered in the chance conversations of passersby.

Despite the scorn of intellectuals such as the philosopher XENOPHANES (circa 520 B.C.) and the historian THUCYDIDES (1) (circa 410 B.C.), a belief in divination ran deep and wide in Greek society. City governments employed official seers, and in times of crisis populations sought guidance in oracles and published prophecies. A Greek army on the march brought along a detail of seers, to determine divine will for military purposes; they usually did this by examining the entrails of sacrificial birds. The poet SIMONIDES wrote an epitaph for a Spartan seer, Megistias, killed at the Battle of THERMOPYLAE (480 B.C.). Supposedly Megistias foresaw the Spartans' annihilation, but chose to remain beside his fighting king.

(See also CASSANDRA; RELIGION.)

Propontis See MARMARA, SEA OF.

Propylaea See ACROPOLIS.

prostitutes A society such as ancient Greece—with its slave population, discrimination against female employment, and lack of charitable relief for the poor—was bound to have many prostitutes of both genders, drawn from a needy underclass. There was also a strong demand for prostitutes because the unromantic nature of most ancient Greek marriages, combined with the enforced seclusion of citizen WOMEN, led many married men to seek sexual adventure outside the home. A market for teenage boys was fueled by the homosexual atmosphere of upper-class life in the 600s–300s B.C.

As with any aspect of ancient Greek society, much evidence for prostitution comes from ATHENS in the 400s–300s B.C. References to male or female prostitution occur in such Athenian writers as the comic playwright ARISTOPHANES (circa 410 B.C.) and the orator AESCHINES (circa 340 B.C.). The practice was legal at Athens, so long as the prostitute was not an Athenian citizen. If a male citizen was proved to have prostituted himself, he would basically lose his citizenship rights; a prostituted female citizen might suffer a similar penalty, while criminal charges could be brought against her male guardian. Prostitutes at Athens typically came from two social classes: METICS (resident aliens, meaning any Greeks not born of Athenian parents) and SLAVES. The slaves would be women or boys, sent out by their owners to earn money, which the owner then took.

No doubt many prostitutes lived the grim life of the streetwalker. But among females, the Greeks distinguished this lower-class type of prostitute, whom they called a *porne*, from the high-class *hetaira* (literally "companion," often translated as "courtesan"). The *hetairai* were women skilled in flute-playing, singing, dancing, or acrobatics, skilled also in flirtation and sexual techniques, artful in conversation, and better educated than most citizen women. A number of extant Athenian vase paintings of the 400s B.C. give an idea of the *hetaira*'s typical appearance and activities, while a later Greek writer, Athenaeus (circa A.D. 200), has preserved a collection of the sayings and exploits of famous Athenian *hetairai*.

Hetairai were often organized into "houses" run by managers, who would protect the women and supervise their schedules and fees. Such houses flourished at all commercial centers of the Greek world, including CORINTH and NAUCRATIS, in addition to Athens. Only SPARTA—austere, anticommercial, and with notoriously promiscuous citizen women—was said to have no prostitutes at all.

The natural setting for *hetairai* was the upper-class drinking party known as the SYMPOSIUM. Hired for the night, or perhaps owned as slaves of the host or guests, the *hetairai* might dance or provide flute music, but they were also obliged to give sexual favors to the guests, all of whom

would be men. Certain verses of the poet ANACREON convey his infatuation with one or another *hetaira* at a symposium.

Such women were the only ones permitted to socialize with men informally outside of their homes. In one speech, the Athenian orator DEMOSTHENES (1) maintains that a certain woman cannot be an Athenian citizen, for she has been observed dining and drinking in male company, "just as a *hetaira* would do."

The hazard of *hetairai*—from the established male viewpoint—was that they might captivate rich young men, who would squander entire fortunes on them. From the *hetaira*'s viewpoint, the best she could hope for was to win a rich man's heart, so that he would purchase her freedom (if she were a slave) and set her up as his wife or mistress. At Athens, where a *hetaira* could not legally marry a citizen, she might at least become a common-law wife, or *pallake*. Among the best-known *hetairai* were Thaïs, who was the mistress and mother of three children of PTOLEMY (1), and Phryne, who served as the sculptor PRAXITELES' model for his celebrated statue of APHRODITE.

Crude forms of birth control were no doubt an essential skill of the prostitute; unfortunately, little is known about this aspect. Ancient medical writers mention vaginal suppositories of woven fabric, used for contraception, and herbal potions thought to suppress fertility. But probably more significant are the several ancient references to abortion. A clause of the ancient Hippocratic Oath, for example, forbade physicians from inducing abortion, while the Roman poet Ovid (circa 20 B.C.) wrote a short poem lamenting his mistress' serious illness following a self-induced abortion.

(See also ASPASIA; HIPPOCRATES; HOMOSEXUALITY; MARRIAGE; MUSIC; SAPPHO.)

Protagoras The first and most famous of the SOPHISTS. Born at the Greek city of ABDERA, Protagoras lived circa 485–415 B.C. In his long and lucrative career, he traveled from city to city, instructing students in intellectual skills such as disputation and the arts of reasoning. Protagoras was the first thinker to acquire the title *sophistes*, "professor" or "disputer." One of Protagoras' doctrines—that any question could admit two contradicting but equally true answers—became the hallmark of later sophists, who were notorious for their ability to debate a controversy from either side.

Visiting ATHENS, Protagoras may have influenced the thinking of the young SOCRATES. Protagoras was also a friend of the Athenian statesman PERICLES, who once spent a whole day arguing with him over a famous criminal case, in which a boy at a GYMNASIUM had been accidentally killed by a thrown javelin: Was the javelin-thrower guilty in the death, or was the javelin itself guilty? In 443 B.C., when the Athenians organized a colonizing expedition to Thurii, in southern ITALY, Protagoras was chosen, no doubt on Pericles' influence, to draw up the law code for the departing colonists.

Protagoras taught an extreme form of moral relativism—that is, that there are no absolute truths, neither morally nor scientifically. Rather, he said, human convention and opinion determine completely what we can call "right" and "wrong" or "hot" and "cold." By Protagoras' teaching, perception *is* reality, for reality is determined by what we perceive. This was the background of Protagoras' best-known statement, which opened his treatise titled *Truth:* "Man is the measure of all things." Rather than extolling the beauty of the human spirit (as it is sometimes interpreted), the statement simply introduces the idea that there are no absolute truths outside of what humans agree upon.

Protagoras' writings survive only as quotations or references by later authors. He appears as a fictionalized character in PLATO's dialogue *Protagoras*, where he debates with Socrates the question, "Can moral virtue (*aretē*) be taught?"

(See also ANTIPHON; LAWS AND LAW COURTS.)

Psyche   See EROS.

Ptolemy (1)   Macedonian general and, eventually, founder of a ruling dynasty in EGYPT; he lived circa 367–283 B.C. Ptolemy (*Ptolemaios*, "warlike") was born the son of a Macedonian nobleman at the court of King PHILIP II; Ptolemy's mother, Arsinoë, was probably at some point the king's mistress. The young Ptolemy was a friend of Philip's son, later known as ALEXANDER THE GREAT; after Alexander became king (336 B.C.), Ptolemy was appointed to his bodyguard and general staff. He accompanied Alexander on the conquest of the Persian Empire (334–323 B.C.) and later published a campaign memoir that, although now lost, served as a major source for the surviving account written by Arrian.

At Alexander's death (323 B.C.), Ptolemy was serving as his governor of Egypt. In the ensuing turmoil, Ptolemy emerged as one of the DIADOCHI (Successors), who seized great chunks of Alexander's empire for themselves. Ptolemy's dangerous adversary in these years was the Macedonian general ANTIGONUS (1), who, from his base in ASIA MINOR, sought to reknit the old empire under his own rule. By 315 B.C. Ptolemy had joined the coalition of secessionist Diadochi—SELEUCUS (1), CASSANDER, and LYSIMACHUS—against Antigonus and his son, DEMETRIUS POLIORCETES.

At the sea battle of Cyprian Salamis (306 B.C.), Ptolemy suffered a major defeat at Demetrius' hands, thereby losing control of the AEGEAN SEA. But his Egyptian fleets remained strong in the southeastern Mediterranean. In 304 B.C. Ptolemy officially declared himself king of Egypt—modern scholars denote him henceforth as Ptolemy I. In 301 B.C. his army joined in the massive campaign that destroyed his enemy Antigonus. Ptolemy took the honorary title *Sotēr* (savior) to commemorate this victory. The next 15 years saw Ptolemy pushing to acquire or recapture territory in Antigonus' old empire, including CYPRUS, Asia Minor, and the Aegean.

Ruling from his capital at ALEXANDRIA (1), Ptolemy began organizing his Egyptian kingdom along lines that would last 700 years, down through the Roman Empire. He instituted such important "Ptolemaic" features as careful registration and taxation throughout the land, and established military colonies for the breeding of the vital Macedonian soldiering class.

In his private life, Ptolemy was devoted to his mistress, Thaïs, who bore him three children. More officially, his third wife, Berenice—who was also his half sister—bore

him two children: a girl, Arsinoë, and a boy, PTOLEMY (2) II (born 308 B.C.). In 285 B.C. the younger Ptolemy became joint ruler with his ailing father, who died in 283 or 282 B.C. Ptolemy's descendants would rule Egypt until 30 B.C.

(See also CLEOPATRA; COLONIZATION; WARFARE, NAVAL.)

Ptolemy (2) II   Macedonian-descended king of EGYPT who reigned circa 283–246 B.C., after succeeding his father, PTOLEMY (1). Under the younger Ptolemy's rule, the land of Egypt—already rich, powerful, and ancient—became home to a great Greek culture. Ptolemy turned his capital at ALEXANDRIA (1) into the cultural center of the Hellenistic world, a magnet for Greek thinkers, poets, and craftsmen, far surpassing contemporary ATHENS. It was Ptolemy II who built, at Alexandria, those famous institutions of learning and patronage, the Library and Museum, and who sponsored such "Alexandrian" poets as CALLIMACHUS and APOLLONIUS. It was also Ptolemy who built the lighthouse at Pharos, considered one of the SEVEN WONDERS OF THE WORLD.

Ptolemy developed his father's administrative system for the kingdom, creating an efficient bureaucracy to tax, govern, and police Egypt. Militarily, Ptolemy clashed with the SELEUCID EMPIRE, with which Egypt shared a shifting, uneasy border in the Levant. The resulting First Syrian War (circa 274–271 B.C.) ended with important Ptolemaic gains in Syria and ASIA MINOR. The Second Syrian War (266–253 B.C.), less conclusive, ended with the MARRIAGE of Ptolemy's daughter Berenice to the Seleucid ruler Antiochus II.

Ptolemy's first wife (circa 289 B.C.) was Arsinoë, daughter of LYSIMACHUS, the Macedonian-born king of THRACE. She bore Ptolemy three children but was eventually banished for plotting to kill him. Ptolemy's second wife (circa 276 B.C.) was his own full sister, also named Arsinoë. This Arsinoë died within a few years, but her influence was great and her reign marked the most brilliant years of the Alexandrian court. It was this marriage to his sister that earned Ptolemy the title—which he bore with pride—of Philadelphos (lover of his sibling). Brother-sister marriage among members of the royal family was an Egyptian tradition dating back to the pharaohs, and many subsequent Ptolemies embraced this custom so as to minimize the range for court intrigues and problems of succession.

Ptolemy died in 246 B.C. and was succeeded by Ptolemy III, his son by the first Arsinoë.

(See also HELLENISTIC AGE; JEWS; WOMEN.)

Ptolemy (3)   See ASTRONOMY.

Pygmalion   Mythical king of CYPRUS who sculpted an ivory statue of the goddess APHRODITE and then fell in love with it. The goddess herself, taking pity on him, breathed life into the statue, which became a living woman named Galatea. She and Pygmalion had a daughter, Paphos, after whom the Cypriot city was named.

Pylos   Coastal area of the southwest PELOPONNESE, encompassing the Bay of Navarino. In historical times, Pylos ("the gate") was part of the larger region known as MESSENIA.

Sheltered by the mile-and-a-half-long island of Sphacteria ("wasp place"), the bay provided an excellent harbor, one of the few of the entire Peloponnese. North and east of the harbor stretched the narrow but fertile coastal plain of western Messenia.

In Greek MYTH, Pylos was the home of King NESTOR, a Greek hero of the TROJAN WAR. Modern ARCHAEOLOGY confirms that the Pylos area was a western center of MYCENAEAN CIVILIZATION: Excavations in the foothills eight miles northeast of the bay have uncovered the foundations of an elaborate palace complex, built circa 1400 B.C. and second in size only to the Mycenaean citadels at MYCENAE and TIRYNS. Archaeologists have named this fortress the Palace of Nestor.

The palace consisted of three buildings, each two stories in height; their construction slightly resembled Tudor-style half-timbering. Their outer walls were made of limestone; interior elements included wooden columns and wainscoting. The complex was destroyed by fire circa 1200 B.C., probably amid the internecine wars that ended Mycenaean society.

Among the items recovered from the ruins by archaeologists are more than 1,200 clay tablets inscribed in LINEAR B script. A few of these tablets (datable to a spring season just before the palace's destruction) record the inhabitants' keeping of a coastal watch, presumably against enemy naval attack. It was probably just such an attack that demolished the palace.

Despite Pylos' rich natural resources and geographical features, the region remained unoccupied for centuries after the Mycenaean era (although it retained its name). In 425 B.C., during the PELOPONNESIAN WAR, the Athenian general DEMOSTHENES (2) fortified and garrisoned Pylos' harbor, which lay only 50 miles west of the enemy city of SPARTA. The ensuing fighting between Athenians and Spartans at Pylos, ending in an Athenian victory, was one of the most consequential events of the war.

After the battle, the Athenian fort at Pylos remained garrisoned until 409 B.C. Thereafter, the harbor front was uninhabited for the rest of antiquity. The general region is now home to the modern Greek city of Pylos, also called Navarino, located at the south end of Navarino Bay.

(See also CLEON.)

Pyrrhon   See SKEPTICISM.

Pyrrhus   King of the Molossian tribes in the northwestern Greek region called EPIRUS, reigning 297–272 B.C. With his magnetic but erratic personality, Pyrrhus brought his kingdom to a brief preeminence in Greek affairs. However, his ambition of conquering a western empire was destined to fail against the Romans' growing power in ITALY. Pyrrhus was the first Greek commander ever to fight the Romans, and is best remembered for his "Pyrrhic victory" at Ausculum, in southeastern Italy, where he lost so many men that he supposedly declared, "Another such victory and we are ruined."

Pyrrhus ("fiery") was born in 319 B.C., the son of the Molossian king Aiacides. The family was related by blood to the recently deceased Macedonian king ALEXANDER THE GREAT; they also claimed descent from the mythical hero NEOPTOLEMUS. When Aiacides was desposed and banished in 317 B.C., Pyrrhus began an exile that eventually involved him with some of the greatest personages of the day. As a teenager, Pyrrhus served as an officer for the Macedonian dynast DEMETRIUS POLIORCETES, who had married Pyrrhus' sister Deidameia. At about age 20, Pyrrhus married Antigone, the stepdaughter of King PTOLEMY (1) of EGYPT. With Ptolemy's support, Pyrrhus in 297 B.C. became a joint king of the Molossians. (He never officially called himself king of Epirus, although he is always referred to as such.) His partner-king was his kinsman Neoptolemus, whom he soon had murdered.

Discontented with the confines of humble Epirus, Pyrrhus spent much of his reign trying to conquer—or otherwise win the throne of—the nearby kingdom of MACEDON, the great realm to the northeast. In these years Macedon was ruled by Pyrrhus' former friend (now enemy) Demetrius, and later by Demetrius' son, Antigonus II.

At the same time, Pyrrhus sought to expand his domain westward toward the Adriatic and Italy. After his first wife died, Pyrrhus married Lanissa, the daughter of the Syracusan dictator AGATHOCLES (295 B.C.). Lanissa's dowry included the important Adriatic-Greek city of CORCYRA, to which Pyrrhus soon added other northwestern acquisitions, such as AMBRACIA, which he made into his capital. But when he polygamously took two more wives, Lanissa left him and married Demetrius (who soon claimed Corcyra).

In late 281 B.C. Pyrrhus received an appeal from the Greek city of TARAS, on the "heel" of Italy. The Tarentines had been contacting various Greek rulers, requesting military aid against the encroaching Romans. Lured by the hope of conquest, Pyrrhus sailed to Italy with 22,500 men and 20 Indian war elephants. In the spring of 280 B.C. the fighting began at Heraclea, on the Italian south-coast "instep," not far from Taras. The Romans—terrified by Pyrrhus' elephants (beasts they had never seen before)—retreated before the massed pikes of the Greek PHALANX. The Romans lost 7,000 men, with another 1,800 captured; but Pyrrhus lost 4,000.

Pyrrhus marched his army north to within 40 miles of ROME, but—discouraged by the lack of local Italian help—turned back south. The next year he experienced the costly victory at Ausculum that inspired his famous lament. After abruptly removing his forces to SICILY, to defend the Greek cities there against the Carthaginians, Pyrrhus returned to Italy to renew his Roman war. But he was defeated in battle near Capua, at Beneventum (where the Romans stampeded his elephants by shooting fire arrows), and he sailed back to Epirus, reportedly having lost two-thirds of his army (275 B.C.).

In a war against Antigonus II, Pyrrhus nearly conquered Macedon (274–273 B.C.). But he abruptly abandoned his advantage, marching far south to invade the territory of SPARTA. There the Spartans and Macedonians combined against him. Battling his way back northward, he encountered street-fighting in ARGOS and was killed—supposedly when an old woman threw a roof tile down onto his head.

A romantic figure and brilliant battlefield commander, Pyrrhus lacked the perseverance and long-range judgment to win an empire.

(See also DODONA; WARFARE, LAND.)

Pythagoras Greek philosopher, mathematician, and reputed miracle-worker, circa 570–500 B.C. No writings by Pythagoras exist, and his life and work are clouded in mystery; most information comes from statements by later writers.

Pythagoras apparently pioneered the study of MATHEMATICS in the Western world. Today he is best remembered for the discovery, made by him or one of his disciples, that the square of the length of the hypotenuse of a right triangle is equal to the sum of the squares of the two other sides' lengths—the famous Pythagorean theorem.

Born on the island of SAMOS, Pythagoras emigrated west in around 531 B.C., reportedly to escape the power of the Samian tyrant POLYCRATES. Settling at CROTON, the foremost Greek colony of south ITALY, Pythagoras founded a religious-philosophical society. He is said to have risen to great local influence. He wrote new laws for Croton and in effect governed the town with his followers, who numbered 300 and came from the Crotonian elite. This OLIGARCHY eventually provoked a people's revolution, and Pythagoras and his followers withdrew to the nearby Greek colony of Metapontum, where Pythagoras died and where his tomb stood in later days.

Two reported tenets of his teachings stand out. One is that the universe's secrets can be learned through the study of numbers. Pythagoras apparently drew great significance from his discovery that musical notes comprise an arithmetic progression; if a lyre string is stopped at its halfway point, the note produced by plucking the half-string is exactly one octave above the whole string's note. Since the Greeks associated MUSIC with the civilizing power of the god APOLLO, this discovery was thought to reveal part of the gods' scheme for the world. Similarly, Pythagoras saw the number 10 as a key to knowledge, mainly because 10 is the sum of the first four integers: $1 + 2 + 3 + 4$. The Pythagoreans were known to observe a mystic symbol of 10 dots arranged in rows forming an equilateral triangle:

.

. .

. . .

. . . .

The second major Pythagorean concept was the transmigration of souls, meaning that the individual soul does not descend to the Underworld at the body's death (as taught by Greek RELIGION) but passes into a new bodily form. In this, Pythagoras may have been influenced by the mystical cult of ORPHISM, which was popular in Greek southern Italy. Like the Orphics, the Pythagoreans viewed the human soul as a fallen divinity, imprisoned in the body and condemned to a series of reincarnations as human, animal, or even vegetable life, until the soul's impurities are cleansed away. As the soul becomes purified in successive lives, it is rewarded with higher forms of incarnation, such as statesmen or poets, until at last it wins some kind of release among the gods; more often, however, the soul might descend from human to beast. One tale records how Pythagoras saw a man beating a puppy and asked him to stop, because (said Pythagoras) he recognized in the puppy's howls the human voice of a deceased friend.

To purify the soul, Pythagoras developed elaborate rules of right conduct for his followers; several such rules are described by later writers. The eating of certain meats was prohibited, since an animal might house a human soul. (It is unclear, however, whether Pythagoras was a complete vegetarian.) The most famous Pythagorean taboo, forbidding the eating of beans probably involved a belief that beans contain little souls (whose attempts to escape are the cause of the bean-eater's flatulence).

The list of Pythagorean commandments strikes a modern reader as odd. The emphasis is not on ethical conduct but on what might be called superstition. Disciples were forbidden to wear rings, to stir a fire with IRON, or to speak of Pythagorean matters in the dark. On rising from bed, a Pythagorean was obliged to smooth away the body's impression in the bedclothes. These and other precepts apparently involved an attempt to avert the "evil eye" or similar bad luck.

Such superstitions reveal how primitive Pythagoras' society was, and how great were his achievements in mathematics and other areas. Pythagoras was said to admit WOMEN to his following on an equal footing with men—which, if true, represents a revolutionary notion in sixth-century-B.C. Greek society. The Pythagorean doctrine of transmigration influenced the Sicilian Greek philosopher EMPEDOCLES (mid-400s B.C.) and the Athenian philosopher PLATO (early 300s B.C.).

After Pythagoras' death (circa 500 B.C.), his followers split into two sects: Of these, the group known as the Mathematicians became a force in early Greek ASTRONOMY. It was these Pythagoreans who first concluded that the earth is spherical, not flat. They also originated the famous theory of the music of the spheres, which imagined that the earth, sun, moon, and planets all revolve around a central fire and create a harmonious sound by virtue of their synchronized speeds; the music is inaudible to us humans.

The political history of the Pythagoreans was unhappy. In the late 400s B.C. they were nearly exterminated in a civil war at Metapontum. The next century saw the school reorganize itself at the Italian-Greek city of TARAS, before dying out by 300 B.C.

(See also AFTERLIFE.)

Pythia See DELPHI.

Pythian Games The second most important of the great religious sports festivals of the ancient Greek world, after the OLYMPIC GAMES. The Pythian Games were held every four years in honor of the god APOLLO, at Apollo's holiest shrine, DELPHI. The name refers to Delphi's inner sanctum, known as Pytho.

An eight-yearly festival of Apollo at Delphi, featuring competitions of the lyre and choruses, was the ancient forerunner of these games. In 582 B.C., after an allied Greek coalition had broken the local power of PHOCIS during the First Sacred War, the Pythian Games were reorganized in their classic form and were placed under the administration of the AMPHICTYONIC LEAGUE. But the games never lost their original aspect—celebrating Apollo as the god of MUSIC.

Unlike other panhellenic fetes, these games included competitions in singing and drama. The footraces were held in a stadium on the slopes of Mt. Parnassus, near Delphi; the horse and chariot races took place far below, on the Crisaean plain. The prize for victors was a garland of laurel leaves. (The laurel tree was sacred to Apollo.)

The four-yearly Pythian Games fell halfway along the four-yearly Olympic cycle; that is, in the second spring after the last Olympics, and two years before the next one.

religion The ancient Greeks believed that their gods had a guiding hand in human affairs. Events as diverse as the annual sprouting of crops, disease epidemics, victory or defeat in war, and individual victories in sports events—which modern observers might assign to scientific causes—were seen by the Greeks as proof of the gods' involvement in human events great and small. Greek MYTH told of gods in "the old days" who had actually descended to earth to make love or war among mortals. Although the Greeks of 400 B.C. did not expect to meet a god in the street, they did expect their gods to be invisibly present—at least in major, public events.

This made the Greeks generally more pious than we are today, but also more legalistic and practical-minded in religious matters. Feeling close to their gods, the Greeks expected the gods to be influenced by prayers and sacrifices of animals or crops. The Greeks expected *results* from their faith. A farmer sowed his seeds in the field, then prayed to the gods to send the proper weather. To the ancient Greeks, both activities seemed equally practical.

Modern American society views religion as a purely private concern, legally separated from civic life. But the Greeks had the opposite view: Religion was a public matter. The goodwill of the gods toward the community was something to be carefully maintained (like the water supply or military defense). Therefore, Greek states kept certain priesthoods and temples at public expense, to oversee festivals, offer sacrifices, and generally safeguard the gods' benefaction. Relatedly, the crime of impiety (*asebeia*) was a serious one. When an Athenian jury condemned the philosopher SOCRATES to death on charges including impiety (399 B.C.), it was because some Athenians believed that Socrates' philosophical questioning had genuinely offended the gods and had threatened their care of ATHENS.

As is well known, Greek religion was polytheistic. This means that—unlike the JEWS, but like most other ancient peoples—the Greeks generally worshipped more than one god. Their gods were anthropomorphic, that is, they were pictured in human shape, male or female. The major gods were 12 in number; each was imagined as having power over one or more important aspects of human life. ATHENA was the goddess of handicraft and wisdom, but in "wisdom" she might overlap somewhat with APOLLO, whose province included reason and intellect, while in "handicraft" she might overlap with HEPHAESTUS, god of metallurgy. The king of the gods was ZEUS, sky-father, lord of justice and of universal order. Below him were HERA, POSEIDON, Athena, Apollo, ARTEMIS, APHRODITE, DIONYSUS, DEMETER, HERMES, Hephaestus, and ARES. Because they

A snake goddess or priestess of Minoan Crete, in an 11.6-inch-tall figurine made of a type of glazed earthenware known as faience, circa 1550 B.C., from Cnossus. The figure wears the Minoan aristocratic costume of a flounced skirt and open bodice that reveals the breasts. She holds two snakes, and atop her headdress sits a feline, perhaps a wildcat. The worship of a supreme nature goddess, or family of goddesses, was a central element of pre-Greek Aegean religion. The conquering Greek tribesmen of 2100 B.C. and later cautiously incorporated such elements into their own worship. Certain classical Greek female deities, such as Hera, Athena, and Artemis, are probably survivals of the ancient, non-Hellenic goddesses.

To the music of the flute and lyre, a lamb is brought to the altar for sacrifice, in this scene painted circa 500 B.C. on a wooden plaque found near Corinth. The priest carries on his head a tray with the utensils of sacrifice.

were imagined as dwelling in Zeus' palace in the sky atop MT. OLYMPUS, these 12 were known as the Olympian gods.

But the Greeks recognized a second important group of gods, called the chthonians (from the Greek word *chthon*, earth). These were deities of the earth and the Underworld, chief of whom were HADES and PERSEPHONE, the Underworld's king and queen. In SICILY and other parts of the western Greek world, Persephone became an important object of worship, as a guardian and judge of souls after death. The Greeks worshipped chthonian deities with rites different from those used for Olympian gods.

Aside from the Olympians and chthonians, there were lesser gods, demigods, and heroes, who might have shrines and cults confined to specific locales (such as the cult of HYACINTHUS in the region of SPARTA). Heroes were usually worshipped as the spirits of extraordinary, deceased mortal men. A few major heroes, such as HERACLES, were worshipped throughout the Greek world and were imagined as having turned into immortal gods after their death.

Worship of the gods involved the use of idols—manmade images, usually statues of wood, clay, stone, or BRONZE. With the advances in Greek marble carving in the 600s B.C. and the discovery of improved bronze-casting techniques in the 500s B.C., the representation of the gods became the highest calling of ancient Greek SCULPTURE. A god's idol might be miniature, life-size, or colossal (from the Greek *kolossos*, "a giant statue"). The god inhabited the idol, but not exclusively; a god could be everywhere at once, and many official statues of the same god might stand within a single city. All gods were portrayed as physically beautiful. They had been born but would never die; they lived forever in young adulthood or vigorous middle age. They were

omniscient regarding human affairs and were able to assume any shape. Every city probably kept a shrine to each of the major gods, but certain deities had special care of specific places: For instance, Athena was the guardian of Athens, Poseidon of CORINTH, and Hera of ARGOS and SAMOS.

The gods were imagined as concentrations of energy: The faces of their statues might be painted red, signifying life and power. But the gods were also capable of human flaws and emotions, such as anger, cruelty, and brutal sexual desire. In the latter 500s B.C. the philosopher XENOPHANES complained that conventional religion had ascribed to the gods "everything that is shameful and disgraceful among human beings—thieving and adultery and deceiving one another." One reason why Greek mythology has cast a spell over readers through the centuries is its vivid, endearing character portrayal of the gods, particularly in the poems of HOMER.

Modern scholars believe that the religious system presented by Homer (circa 750 B.C.) and HESIOD (circa 700 B.C.) arose gradually, starting with a fusion of two or three different cultures after 2100 B.C. But the facts are lost in prehistory, and scholars must rely on scant evidence from ARCHAEOLOGY in order to trace this process of religious fusion.

The Greeks were an Indo-European people, with a language and social patterns akin to other Indo-European peoples, such as the ancient Romans, Germans, and Persians. Almost certainly the Greek-speaking tribesmen who first invaded mainland Greece circa 2100 B.C. brought a patriarchal, warrior religion whose chief god was the sky-father, Zeus (a figure that scholars recognize under other names in other Indo-European mythologies). Over time, the Greek conquerors absorbed certain religious elements from the subjugated, pre-Greek inhabitants of the land (an agrarian, non-Indo-European folk with possible origins in ASIA MINOR). This people, like the non-Greeks of Asia Minor in later centuries, may have worshipped a central mother goddess or family of goddesses. Similarly, the non-Greek MINOAN CIVILIZATION of the Aegean islands, which strongly influenced the emerging Greek culture circa 2000–1400 B.C., evidently had important female deities. The prime result of these influences was the introduction into Greek religion of a few major goddesses not originally Greek; eventually they became known by the names Hera, Athena, Artemis, and Persephone.

By 1600 B.C. the mainland Greeks had organized themselves into the warlike and technologically advanced MYCENAEAN CIVILIZATION. It is this era that offers modern scholars the first clear glimpse at Greek religion, in the LINEAR B tablets excavated at Mycenaean CNOSSUS (circa 1400 B.C.) and PYLOS (circa 1200 B.C.). In their lists of religious ceremonies performed for various gods, the tablets reveal that the Mycenaean faith was surprisingly similar to the Greek religion of 700 or 1,000 years later. The tablets mention Zeus and Poseidon as important gods, as well as Hera, Athena, Dionysus, and other deities (some with names unfamiliar).

Of the 12 gods later to be known as the Olympians, only Apollo and Aphrodite definitely are not mentioned on the existing Linear B tablets. Scholars believe that these two latecomers entered Greek religion during the DARK AGE, after the collapse of Mycenaean society circa 1200 B.C. Both deities probably reached Greece from the Near East, via the mercantile island of CYPRUS. In general, Greek religion remained open to foreign deities, particularly goddesses; later in ancient times various Greek locales had important cults of the Egyptian goddess Isis, the Anatolian goddess Cybele, and the Thracian goddess Bendis.

By the 600s B.C., the principal gods and forms of worship were well established. Statues of the gods were housed in temples of simple design but elaborate craftsmanship. Probably descended from the design of Mycenaean palaces, the Greek temple was basically a glorified roof, suspended by pillars over a rectangular foundation, with a smaller area walled off within. There the idol of the god stood or sat. In the 600s B.C. wooden temples began to be replaced by buildings largely of stone, either limestone or marble. The famous Greek "orders" of ARCHITECTURE—the Doric, Ionic, and Corinthian—were invented as styles of temples.

A Greek temple was the sanctuary of a particular god; rarely would more than one god be worshipped in the same building. Unlike a modern church, a temple was not a place where congregations gathered. It had no rows of pews for multitudes of worshippers. Rather, the temple received individuals or small groups for prayer or sacrifice. The temple's priests or priestesses might be minor functionaries under the direction of a high priest who typically came from an aristocratic family associated with that specific sanctuary. At Athens, for example, a noble family named the Eteoboutadai traditionally supplied the priest and priestess for the two major cults on the ACROPOLIS. But Greek religion was noteworthy for the lack of power exercised by its priests (one important exception being

Apollo's priesthood at DELPHI). Technically, prayer and sacrifice could be conducted by worshippers without any priest.

The rite of sacrifice—practiced in various forms by many ancient religions—probably dates back to Stone Age hunters' rituals. The Greeks saw it as the essential way to win divine favor: "Gifts persuade the gods," a proverb ran. Although "bloodless" sacrifices of grain, cakes, or fruit might be offered, a more significant act involved the slaughter of a domestic animal. The noblest victim was a bull; the most common was a sheep. Goats, pigs, and chickens were also used. To the best modern knowledge, human sacrifice was extremely rare among the Greeks; one of the few such cases was the sacrifice of Persian prisoners during the national emergency of the PERSIAN WARS.

Greek sacrifice involved the notion that the god somehow fed upon the victim's blood—an essential rite was the splashing of the blood onto the altar (typically located outside the temple). But first the live animal would be led to the altar in a procession featuring the priest and the person who was providing the animal. The worshippers would be dressed in clean finery, their heads decked with garlands of leaves appropriate to the god: oak for Zeus, laurel for Apollo, and so on. A flute-player would provide stately background MUSIC.

Preliminary rituals included pelting the altar and the live animal with barley grains. Then the priest would cut the animal's throat. The carcass would be skinned and gutted. The inedible organs and bones would be burned at the altar for the god, the smoke ascending to the god's heavenly realm (for Olympian gods; for chthonian deities, the sacrifice emphasized the act of pouring blood into the ground). Then the edible flesh would be cooked as a meal for the celebrants. Large-scale animal sacrifices, sometimes at public expense, might provide community feasts for holidays.

The sacrifice thus benefited the human participants at least as much as it benefited the god. The god received blood, bones, and innards; the human participants received edible meat. Only in rare rituals would the meat be intentionally burned up or thrown away. The element of human self-interest in this rite was not lost upon certain thoughtful Greeks: In time there arose the explanatory myth of how the demigod PROMETHEUS had tricked Zeus into accepting the sacrifice's inferior portions for the gods.

Sacrifices, with their associated processions and feasts, defined the religious year. Although the religious calendar differed in its particulars from place to place, the calendar for any city or region told mainly which kind of offering was to go to which god or hero on which day of the year. At Athens, important holidays included the City Dionysia, an early spring festival of Dionysus, featuring the major annual stage-drama competition, and the PANATHENAEA, celebrating the goddess Athena's birthday in midsummer.

A society as intellectual as the Greeks' was bound to produce religious doubt. Independent thinkers such as the sophist PROTAGORAS (mid-400s B.C.) and the tragedian EURIPIDES (later 400s B.C.) were rumored to be atheists, disbelieving in the gods. Certain philosophers, such as Xenophanes, PLATO (early 300s B.C.), and ARISTOTLE (mid-300s B.C.), believed in a single, universal god. During the

HELLENISTIC AGE (circa 300–150 B.C.), the rise of giant Greco-Macedonian kingdoms created a new social order, and traditional religion—expressing as it did the public life of the old-fashioned Greek city-state—came in for questioning and modification. The philosophy STOICISM inclined toward a monotheism built around Zeus; the rival school of EPICUREANISM claimed that multiple gods existed but had no concern for humankind. Meanwhile there arose fringe "mystery" religions (Greek: *mustēria*, from *mustēs*, "an initiate"), offering to their followers a more personal faith and the promise of a happy life after death.

The great society of the Roman Empire saw further religious percolation, including the rise of Christianity among Greek communities of the eastern Mediterranean in the first century A.D. But many Greeks were still worshipping the old-fashioned gods in A.D. 391, when the Christian Roman emperor Theodosius I closed all pagan temples throughout his realm and decreed Christianity to be the only legal religion.

(See also ADONIS; AFTERLIFE; ASCLEPIUS; CASTOR AND PO-LYDEUCES; ELEUSINIAN MYSTERIES; FATE; FUNERAL CUSTOMS; FURIES; HECATĒ; HESTIA; NYMPHS; OLYMPIA; ORPHISM; PAN; PARTHENON; PHILOSOPHY; PHOENICIA; PINDAR; POLIS; PROPHECY AND DIVINATION; ROME; SAMOTHRACE; THEATER.)

Rhadamanthys   See AFTERLIFE; MINOS.

rhapsodes   See EPIC POETRY.

Rhegium   Greek seaport on the west coast of the "toe" of ITALY, commanding the Straits of Messina. Rhegium (Greek: *Rhēgion*) was founded in the late 700s B.C. by Ionian Greek colonists from CHALCIS; a second group founded a sister-city, ZANCLĒ, across the straits in SICILY. With its strategic position, Rhegium became one of the most important Ionian Greek cities of the West. Accordingly, it was an enemy of such powerful Dorian Greek cities as SYRACUSE, in eastern Sicily, and LOCRI, on the eastern Italian "toe."

Rhegium's most famous citizen was the lyric poet IBYCUS (circa 535 B.C.). The city reached a peak under its energetic tyrant Anaxilas (reigned 494–476 B.C.), who fortified the straits against Etruscan war fleets and enlarged the city population with refugees from the Spartan-dominated, Peloponnesian region of MESSENIA. In 433 B.C. Rhegium made an alliance with ATHENS for protection against Syracuse and Locri. In 415–413 B.C., during the PELOPONNESIAN WAR, Rhegium served as a naval base for the Athenians' campaign against Syracuse.

Circa 387 B.C. the Syracusan tyrant DIONYSIUS (1) captured Rhegium and destroyed it. Rebuilt, it eventually passed into the hands of ROME. The site is now the Italian seaport of Reggio.

(See DORIAN GREEKS; ETRUSCANS; IONIAN GREEKS.)

rhetoric   The art of public speaking. Although the word in modern English often implies empty or overblown verbiage, for the ancient Greeks the skill of *rhētorikē* meant nothing less than the ability to communicate in public. Rhetoric (also called oratory) was considered an essential skill for any active citizen in a DEMOCRACY because, in an

age before telecommunications, newspapers, or advertising, the one way for an individual citizen to help shape public policy was to stand up before the citizen ASSEMBLY and make a speech. Although speeches might also play decision-making roles in an OLIGARCHY such as SPARTA or CORINTH, it was at the democratic cities—and particularly at the greatest of these, ATHENS—that the best speakers emerged. Among the more famous Athenian orators were DEMOSTHENES (1) (circa 340 B.C.) and the statesman PER-ICLES (circa 440 B.C.). The philosopher ARISTOTLE (circa 340 B.C.) wrote an extant treatise on rhetoric, one of many produced in antiquity.

The roots of Greek rhetoric go back to the war councils of the Mycenaean princes (circa 1200 B.C.) and the civic councils of the early Greek aristocratic states (circa 800 B.C.). The poems of HOMER (written down circa 750 B.C.) show the assembled Greek heroes delivering speeches in turn at war council. There an artful speaker such as ODYS-SEUS is admired for his ability to persuade his fellow captains toward a certain course of action.

It was in the 400s B.C. that rhetoric emerged as an organized study, under the impetus of the developing Greek democracies. The strong poetic traditions of SICILY also may have played a role, because it was a Sicilian Greek who first brought advanced rhetoric to Athens—GORGIAS of Leontini who amazed the sophisticated Athenians with his spoken "display pieces" (427 B.C.).

Aside from the assembly, the other great arena for public speaking was the law courts, where citizens spoke as defendants or prosecutors in front of juries usually numbering several hundred. Some of the best-known surviving speeches are Athenian courtroom speeches from the 300s B.C., delivered by such powerful arguers as LYSIAS. Other men became rich as speechwriters, who did not usually deliver speeches personally but who would, for a fee, compose a courtroom speech for a client. Among the best known of these was ISOCRATES, who opened a school of rhetoric (the first one known) in around 390 B.C.

(See also AESCHINES; ANTIPHON; EDUCATION; ISAEUS; LAWS AND LAW COURTS; SOPHISTS.)

Rhetra   See LYCURGUS (1).

Rhodes   Large, diamond-shape Greek island, located off the southwest coast of ASIA MINOR. By 300 B.C. Rhodes had emerged as one of the foremost maritime powers of the Hellenistic world—wealthy from commerce and with a strong navy.

ARCHAEOLOGY has shown that the island engaged in Mycenaean-Greek TRADE and perhaps received settlers circa 1300 B.C., following an era of Minoan domination. But the main inhabitants at this time were most likely of non-Greek, Carian stock. Rhodes' recorded history begins circa 1000 B.C., with the arrival of DORIAN GREEKS, who sailed east from mainland Greece and founded three cities on the island—Ialysus, at the northern tip, Camirus (Kameiros), on the northwest coast, and Lindus (the largest of the three), in the east. These three cities formed part of a local Dorian federation that included the nearby island of Cos and the city of CNIDUS, on the Asia Minor coast. The Greek name *Rhodos* probably did not refer to the roses (*rhodai*) that still grow throughout the island, but rather came from some Carian name.

The Rhodian Greeks acquired certain non-Greek traditions from the East, chief of which was their national cult of the sun god, worshipped under his Greek name, HELIOS. Rhodes was unique among early Greek states in having a sun cult. According to one myth, Helios had chosen Rhodes as his own kingdom and had populated it with the descendants of his seven sons.

Rhodes' location made it a natural middleman between East and West, although early on it was overshadowed by other east Greek sea powers, such as MILETUS and SAMOS. The Rhodians took part in the trading and colonizing expansion in the 700s–500s B.C.: Rhodian Geometric POTTERY is among the main types found by archaeologists at the ancient Greek trade depot at AL MINA (on the Syrian coast), and it is known that Rhodians helped establish colonies in SICILY and south ITALY. By the 500s B.C. popular dictators known as TYRANTS had arisen in the Rhodian cities, as elsewhere in the Greek world. One such ruler, Cleobulus of Lindus, was later reckoned among the SEVEN SAGES of Greece.

After being conquered by the Persians in around 494 B.C., Rhodes was liberated circa 478 B.C. by the mainland Greeks, at the end of the PERSIAN WARS. Over the next 65 years the three Rhodian cities were members of the Athenian-dominated DELIAN LEAGUE. By then the Rhodian cities were governed as Athenian-inspired democracies—as they would remain, with one interruption, until the Roman conquest. But in 411–407 B.C., during the PELOPONNESIAN WAR, the Rhodian cities joined the widespread Delian revolt and won independence from ATHENS.

Then the three Rhodian cities agreed to combine their individual governments and form a union, with a new capital city, Rhodos. This Rhodes city—a seaport at the island's northern tip, near Ialysus—eventually became one of the most spectacular Greek cities, thriving from the shipping of grain and other essentials across the eastern Mediterranean.

Rhodes was recaptured by the Persians in 355 B.C. but regained independence and DEMOCRACY after the Macedonian king ALEXANDER THE GREAT invaded the Persian Empire (334 B.C.). Amid the turmoil following Alexander's death (323 B.C.), the island became a tempting target for the various DIADOCHI (Successors) who battled over Alexander's vast empire, and in 305–304 B.C. Rhodes city withstood a huge siege by the Macedonian prince DEMETRIUS POLIORCETES.

In the burst of self-confidence following this defense, the Rhodians erected a giant BRONZE statue of the sun god in around 290 B.C. that became known as the Colossus of Rhodes.

Designed by one Chares of Lindus, the 90-foot-tall Colossus (Greek: *Kolossos*, "giant statue") was counted as one of the SEVEN WONDERS OF THE WORLD. Although it collapsed in an earthquake after only about 65 years, its general appearance is known from ancient coins and an ancient writer's description. The Colossus stood alongside the city's harbor (but not bestriding the harbor entrance, legs apart, with ships passing between, as is sometimes claimed). The statue consisted of bronze plating over a frame with an interior staircase. The god, with a halo of sun rays, was shown holding up a torch, which workmen inside operated as a beacon fire to aid ships at sea. The design of the Colossus helped to inspire New York City's Statue of Liberty, erected in A.D. 1886.

The Rhodians were among the first east Greek allies of the emerging power of ROME; it was complaints from Rhodes and PERGAMUM that brought the Romans into the Second Macedonian War against the Macedonian king PHILIP V (200–197 B.C.). But Rhodes lost its prosperity when the Romans—seeking to punish Rhodes for its insufficient help in the Third Macedonian War (172–167 B.C.)—promoted the Aegean island of DELOS as the new center of east Mediterranean trade. Rhodes later became a Roman subject.

(See also COLONIZATION; SHIPS AND SEAFARING; WARFARE, NAVAL.)

Rome   Non-Greek city of west-central ITALY, located in Latium, about 16 miles from the Tyrrhenian coast. After being strongly influenced by the Greeks in such cultural rudiments as its ALPHABET and RELIGION, Rome emerged in the 300s B.C. as a dynamic military force, destined to conquer an empire that (by A.D. 117) stretched from Britain to Mesopotamia. The Romans subdued many peoples, but their conquest of the Greek world, accomplished between about 338 and 30 B.C., deeply affected their own civilization by introducing them to the material and literary splendors of the Greeks. As the Roman poet Horace wrote (circa 19 B.C.): "Captive Greece took mighty Rome captive, forcing culture onto rustic folk." Eventually Roman culture became largely Greek, even though the Romans spoke Latin, not Greek. As the Romans pushed their empire into Europe, they introduced Greek-originated ideas and customs to new places. It is because of the Romans that ancient Greek culture has colored European society, and hence American society.

The Romans belonged to the Latin ethnic group, but early on they were dominated by another Italian people, the ETRUSCANS. The name *Roma* may be of Etruscan origin; its meaning is unclear. Supposedly founded in 753 B.C. Rome surely partook of the pro-Greek atmosphere of Etruscan society in the 600s B.C. Greek goods and customs made their way north from Greek colonies of Campania, such as CUMAE and Neapolis (Naples). The Roman alphabet, used today for English as well as for most other European languages, was first adapted by the Romans (perhaps circa 600 B.C.) from an Etruscan model, itself based on the Greek alphabet. By the 400s B.C. the Romans were vigorously assimilating Greek gods, heroes, and MYTH into their own religion.

Rome supposedly expelled its last Etruscan king in 510 B.C. The next 150 years saw political strife between rich and poor: eventually Rome's government took shape as a republic, in which a wide citizen base was governed by a well-born elite, sitting on a legislative body called the senate.

These centuries also saw the spread of Roman control through Italy. First came the unification of Latium. By the mid-300s B.C. the Romans had reached Campania, where they entered into their first diplomatic relations with Italian-Greek cities. There followed an accelerated hellenization of Roman culture, including the first Roman copying of Greek ARCHITECTURE, COINAGE, and POTTERY.

After subduing the central-Italian people known as the Samnites, the Romans had by 290 B.C. won all of central Italy. In the extreme south, conflict with the Greek city of TARAS brought the Romans into their first war against a Greek army, led by the Epirote king PYRRHUS. The hard-won defeat of Pyrrhus (275 B.C.) left the Romans masters of all Italy south of the Po River. Rome had become a world power, comparable with the Hellenistic kingdoms of the eastern Mediterranean or—closer to home—the African-Phoenician city of CARTHAGE. By this era the formidable Roman army could draw on a manpower pool of several million men, due to Rome's policy of requiring military service from its Italian-ethnic subject peoples.

Rome now became drawn into conflict with other great Mediterranean powers—particularly Carthage and MACEDON—which led eventually to the Romans' subjugation of the Mediterranean Greek world. First came two bitter wars with Carthage. The First Punic (Carthaginian) War was fought from 264 to 241 B.C. It turned Rome into a naval power and left the victorious Romans in possession of SICILY, with the important Sicilian-Greek city of SYRACUSE as a Roman ally.

The Second Punic War (218–201 B.C.) saw Rome fighting for its life on Italian soil against the brilliant Carthaginian general Hannibal. Syracuse, siding this time with Carthage, was captured, plundered, and annexed by the vengeful Romans (211 B.C.). Another ally of Carthage was the dynamic Macedonian king PHILIP V, whose domain included most of mainland Greece. In a Punic War sideshow, the Romans invaded Philip's Greek territories—their first advance into Greece (214 B.C.). This First Macedonian War ended in a truce (205 B.C.), but Philip was by then a hated enemy of an increasingly eastward-looking Rome.

After the Second Punic War ended with Carthage's defeat, the Romans turned a receptive ear to complaints from their eastern Greek allies PERGAMUM and RHODES against Philip's adventuring. The Second Macedonian War (200–197 B.C.) saw the second Roman invasion of mainland Greece. With the help of Greek allies from AETOLIA, the Roman general Titus Quinctius Flamininus in 197 B.C. won a total victory against Philip's army at the Battle of Cynocephalae ("dog heads"), in THESSALY. The battle broke Macedon's imperial power forever and incidentally established the superiority of Roman battle tactics against the more cumbersome Macedonian PHALANX. But by the terms of a lenient treaty, Macedon was allowed to continue as an independent state.

It was at the ISTHMIAN GAMES of 196 B.C.—after Macedonian control of Greece had been removed—that Flamininus issued his famous proclamation declaring freedom for the mainland Greeks: Neither Macedon nor Rome would be overlord there. In 194 B.C. Roman troops evacuated Greece.

But even unwillingly, the Romans found themselves embroiled in Greek events. The Aetolians, disgruntled over Rome's light treatment of their defeated enemy Philip, invited the Seleucid king ANTIOCHUS (2) III to invade Greece as a new liberator. Reentering Greece in response, Roman forces defeated Antiochus at THERMOPYLAE (191 B.C.) and pursued him to ASIA MINOR—the Romans' first campaign in Asia—where they defeated him again, at the Battle of Magnesia (190 B.C.). This victory foreshadowed the future Roman conquest of the entire Greek East. By the treaty of Apamea (188 B.C.), Antiochus lost most of Asia Minor, which the Romans parceled to their allies Pergamum and Rhodes. In Greece, meanwhile, the Aetolians were defeated and their power curtailed.

The accession of Philip's ambitious son Perseus brought new Macedonian adventurism, and another Roman invasion. The Third Macedonian War (172–167 B.C.) ended with Perseus' complete defeat at the Battle of Pydna, in southern Macedon. Deposed, Perseus died in a Roman prison. His kingdom was dismantled and was later annexed as a Roman province called Macedonia. In Greece, the League of ACHAEA was punished for its pro-Macedonianism with the removal of 1,000 well-born hostages to Rome. (One of these, named Polybius, was destined to become the last great Greek historian; so impressed was he by Roman power that he chose to write, in Greek, about the rise of Rome.)

When the Achaean League resumed anti-Roman agitation in 148 B.C., Roman patience with Greece was at an end. Marching south from the province of Macedonia, a Roman army defeated the Achaeans in battle. CORINTH, the league's major city, was besieged and captured. By order of the Roman senate the city was leveled to the ground as a warning to the Greeks (146 B.C.).

Greece's freedom was at an end, and the country was then incorporated into the Roman province of Macedonia. In the following centuries the Greek East fell. Much of Asia Minor was legally bequeathed to the Romans by the last Pergamene king, Attalus III, in 133 B.C. In 64 B.C. the Roman general Pompey annexed Syria, once the Seleucid heartland. And in 30 B.C. the Romans captured the last remaining Hellenistic kingdom, EGYPT.

(See also AENEAS; CASTOR AND POLYDEUCES; CLEOPATRA; HELLENISTIC AGE; HERACLES; SELEUCID EMPIRE.)

Roxane   See ALEXANDER THE GREAT.

S

Sacred Wars See DELPHI; PHOCIS.

sacrifice See RELIGION.

Salamis (1) Inshore island in the northern Saronic Gulf, in central Greece. Salamis' eastern side is separated from the coast of ATTICA by a curved channel less than a mile wide in the narrows, and it was there that the crucial sea battle of the PERSIAN WARS was fought in late summer of 480 B.C., after the invading army of the Persian king XERXES had overrun northern and central Greece. The allied Greek victory at Salamis broke the Persian navy and stopped the invasion, opening the way for the Greeks' final land-victory, at PLATAEA, the following summer.

Well before the sea battle, Salamis was an important place, associated with the mythical hero AJAX (1). Salamis lay close offshore between the territories of ATHENS and MEGARA (1), and not far from the powerful island state of AEGINA. In the 600s B.C. the island was a bone of contention among those three warring states. By the mid-500s B.C. it was held by Athens.

In 480 B.C. the Persians and their allies overran a Spartan-led force at the Battle of THERMOPYLAE and swept southward into central Greece. The Persian navy sailed in escort. Reaching Athens, Xerxes' army found the city abandoned. The noncombatants had been evacuated, while most of Athens' fighting men were in the allied Greek navy, stationed inside Salamis' eastern channel.

Rounding the southern tip of Attica, the Persian navy sailed north into the Saronic Gulf. Not literally "Persian," this navy was manned largely by subject peoples—Phoenicians, Egyptians, and even IONIAN GREEKS—who were fighting for Xerxes. The Phoenician crews seem to have been superior seamen to any Greeks. Battered by prior fighting and storms, the Persians' warships by then probably numbered less than 400. Waiting at Salamis was a combined Greek fleet of perhaps 300 warships, with Athens supplying the largest contingent, almost 180 ships. The fleet's commander was Eurybiades, a Spartan.

The Greek plan to make a stand at Salamis probably originated with the brilliant Athenian soldier-statesman THEMISTOCLES, who foresaw that the way to offset the Persians' advantage in numbers and faster ships would be to lure them to battle inside the narrow straits. By vision and force of personality, he convinced Eurybiades and the other Greek sea commanders to stay together and risk a major fight, rather than dispersing to defend their homes.

According to two fifth-century-B.C. writers—the Athenian playwright AESCHYLUS (who may have fought at Sala-

mis) and the historian HERODOTUS—Themistocles tricked the Persian king by sending him an untruthful message, couched as a plea for personal favor, saying that the Greeks were ready to disband and flee. Supposedly Xerxes actually believed this report from an enemy commander. Whether this is true or not, we do know that Xerxes, overconfident and impatient, ordered his fleet to enter the Salamis channel at night and attack the Greeks at dawn. What followed was one of the most dramatic events in world history—the saving of Greece from foreign domination.

At dawn the Greeks sang their battle paean and launched their fleet in a concave crescent formation embracing the entire width of the channel. With the Persian ships rowing into this Greek "net," the two fleets collided.

As Themistocles had expected, the Persians' advantage in numbers and skill was lost in the crowded narrows. Whereas boarding tactics had been the rule at the recent sea battle at ARTEMISIUM, Salamis saw more use of Greek ramming techniques. The Persian ships—jammed together by the Greek enveloping tactic, and not as able to withstand ramming as the heavier ships of the Greeks—soon began to get the worst of it. Aeschylus gives a vivid description, presented from the Persian viewpoint, in his tragedy *The Persians* (472 B.C.): "The Greek ships, arrayed in a circle around us, bore in and rammed: our ships capsized, the sea was hidden in wrecks and corpses, and all the shores and reefs were heaped with dead . . ."

After most of the elite Phoenician squadron had been destroyed, the other Persian allies broke off and rowed away, pursued by the Greeks. At this point an amphibious landing of Athenian HOPLITES, under the general ARISTIDES, overran a contingent of Persian infantry on the nearby islet of Psytalleia.

The battle was over. The Greek side had lost 40 ships, the Persians (probably) several times that number. Among the Persian dead was the admiral Ariabignes, a brother of Xerxes.

Xerxes himself had watched the battle from a throne set up on the shore, and was so alarmed by his fleet's ruin that he soon started overland for home. Then vulnerable by sea, he was anxious to reach the HELLESPONT before the Greek navy could destroy his bridges there, to trap him inside Europe. Along with most of his huge invasion force, Xerxes crossed back into Asia, leaving behind a small army under his general Mardonius to continue the campaign on land. This army, in turn, was later destroyed by the Greeks at Plataea.

For the Athenians, who had abandoned their city yet still supplied the bulk of the Greek navy, the Battle of

Salamis was a patriotic triumph and a springboard to Athens' naval empire in the following decades. For the Persians, Salamis marked the turning point on their western frontier; no longer would they be purely the aggressors, as they had been for 70 years. With their naval power crippled for a decade, the Persians would subsequently go on the defensive—first against Athenian naval action in the eastern Mediterranean, and later, in the 300s B.C., against Spartan and Macedonian invasions of Asia. The process that would end with ALEXANDER THE GREAT's conquest of PERSIA (334–323 B.C.) began in the narrows at Salamis.

(See also WARFARE, NAVAL.)

Salamis (2)   See CYPRUS; DEMETRIUS POLIORCETES.

Samos   Fertile and mountainous Aegean island, 190 square miles in area, located two miles off the central west coast of ASIA MINOR. Samos was among the most prosperous and powerful Greek states of the 600s–400s B.C. The Samians were known for their seafaring, their domestic WINE, and their national cult of HERA, patron goddess of the island.

Occupied before 1200 B.C. by Greek colonists of the MYCENAEAN CIVILIZATION, Samos was resettled circa 1100–1000 B.C. by a new wave of immigrants—IONIAN GREEKS, fleeing from the Dorian invasion of mainland Greece. A capital city, also named Samos, arose in the southeast part of the island, opposite the Asia Minor coast.

Samos island became a foremost state of the eastern Greek region called IONIA, and played a major role in the Greek world's expansion through seaborne TRADE and COLONIZATION in the 800s–500s B.C. The principal Samian colony was at the north Aegean island of SAMOTHRACE (which, as the name suggests, served as an anchorage between Samos and THRACE). To buy luxury goods and raw metals, the Samians exported domestic products such as wine and woolens, along with Thracian SLAVES and SILVER acquired via Samothrace. Markets included both mainland Greece and Near Eastern kingdoms such as EGYPT. One Samian sea captain made a famously lucrative trading stop at the Celtic kingdom of Tartessus, in southern Spain, circa 650 B.C.

In this era Samos was governed as an ARISTOCRACY, with a ruling class known as *geomoroi,* "landholders." The island was home to famous craftsmen such as the architect Rhoecus, whose temple of Hera, begun circa 560 B.C., was the largest Greek building of its day (320 × 160 feet). All that survives of that proud structure today is a single Ionic column, standing at the site of ancient Samos city.

The island reached its zenith under POLYCRATES, who held supreme power circa 540–522 B.C. Polycrates carved out an Aegean sea empire and glorified Samos with engineering marvels such as an underground aqueduct and sea walls to defend the harbor entrance. His lavish court attracted poets, craftsmen, and other talents. But Samos' most important citizen, the philosopher and mathematician PYTHAGORAS, fled Polycrates' rule and emigrated to south ITALY.

After Polycrates was captured and murdered by the encroaching Persians under King DARIUS (1), Samos became a Persian holding, ruled by Greek puppet rulers. Joining the IONIAN REVOLT against the Persians, Samos contributed its entire navy, 60 ships. But at the revolt's climactic sea battle of Lade, fought near Samos, the Samian ships deserted for Persian offers of preferential treatment (494 B.C.). In 480 B.C., under Persian command, Samian crews fought against their fellow Greeks in King XERXES' invasion of Greece. The following year, Samos was liberated by the victorious Greek counteroffensive.

Then under the heavy influence of ATHENS, Samos became a DEMOCRACY and a foremost member of the Athenian-run DELIAN LEAGUE. Samos was one of the few Delian states to supply warships and crews in lieu of silver tribute. However, in 440 B.C. the island rebelled against Athens. The nine-month-long revolt amounted to an Athenian crisis: An attacking Athenian fleet was defeated by 70 ships under the Samian leader Melissus, but eventually Samos fell to an Athenian siege and blockade commanded by PERICLES himself. The island was purged of anti-Athenian elements and reduced to subject status, paying a yearly tribute as well as a huge war penalty of 1,400 TALENTS.

Samos remained a staunch Athenian ally—although no longer contributing warships—throughout the PELOPONNESIAN WAR (431–404 B.C.). After 413 B.C. the island was a major Athenian naval base. During the right-wing coup of the FOUR HUNDRED at Athens, the Samians supported the Athenian democratic government-in-exile, formed by the Athenian fleet and troops at Samos (411 B.C.). For their loyalty, the Samians received the unique honor of being made Athenian citizens (405 B.C.). But in the following year, at the war's end, Samos was captured by SPARTA.

In the next decades an independent Samos again fell into conflict with the Athenians, who captured the island and repopulated it with Athenian colonists (365 B.C.). Later the native population was allowed to return, by edict of the Macedonian conqueror ALEXANDER THE GREAT (effected posthumously, in 321 B.C.).

A bone of contention among the warring DIADOCHI (Successors) who divided up Alexander's empire after his death, Samos eventually passed to King PTOLEMY (2) II of Egypt (circa 281 B.C.). By then Samos was waning as an east Greek sea power, surpassed by the growing commercial might of RHODES. In 127 B.C. Samos was annexed by the Romans.

(See also BRONZE; PERSIAN WARS; SHIPS AND SEAFARING; TYRANTS.)

Samothrace   Small Greek island of the northeast AEGEAN SEA. Samothrace sits 25 miles south of the northern coast, which in antiquity belonged to the non-Greek land of THRACE. The oval island, only 68 square miles, consists of a single mountain, rising to 5,250 feet and heavily forested in ancient times. The pre-Greek inhabitants were probably of Thracian stock. Sometime between 700 and 550 B.C., Samothrace was conquered by seafaring Greeks, who sought it as a safe anchorage from which to make the trading run to the Thracian coast. (The mainland Thracians were a potentially hostile folk who nevertheless could offer such precious goods as SILVER and SLAVES.) As suggested by the name Samothrakē (Samos' Thrace), the island was probably occupied by Greeks from the island state of

SAMOS; possibly the Samians were preceded by Greeks from another (and nearer) Greek island state, LESBOS. Samothrace seems to have been a mixed settlement, where Greek and Thracian inhabitants lived in harmony; modern archaeological excavations have uncovered a cemetery that (as inscriptions reveal) was used by both peoples in the latter 500s B.C.

In classical times, Samothrace was known for its unique Greek religious cult, colored by the place's pre-Greek origins. This cult worshipped the Cabiri (Kabeiroi)—male deities, originally non-Greek, possibly from Thrace or Phrygia (in ASIA MINOR). The Cabiri varied between two and four in number and were patron gods of smiths and sailors as well as of fertility. Also called the Great Gods, they were sometimes identified with the Greek deities CASTOR AND POLYDEUCES. If the name Kabeiroi is Greek (which is uncertain), it probably means "the burners," in reference to the forge fire of an ancient smithy.

The Cabiri had cults at several shrines in the Greek world, but their main sanctuary was at Samothrace city, high in the island's hills. There were held the Mysteries of Samothrace—a secret cult, open only to initiates. These Mysteries (Greek: *mustēriai*, from *mustēs*, "an initiate") are often mentioned but rarely discussed by ancient writers, who feared to divulge secret details lest they provoke the Cabiri's wrath. The cult became popular in the HELLENISTIC AGE (300–150 B.C.): Men and WOMEN flocked to Samothrace for initiation and worship. King PTOLEMY (2) II of EGYPT (circa 270 B.C.) was an important patron of the sanctuary; remnants of the buildings that he financed can be seen today. Among the costly offerings that adorned the site was the wonderful second-century-B.C. marble statue known as the Winged Victory of Samothrace, excavated by French archaeologists in A.D. 1863 and now displayed at the Louvre.

Politically Samothrace became an ally of ATHENS, serving as a member of the Athenian-controlled DELIAN LEAGUE (478–404 B.C.) and the subsequent SECOND ATHENIAN LEAGUE (378–338 B.C.). Attractive as a naval base and propagandistic pawn, in Hellenistic times the island changed hands frequently, among the Macedonians, Ptolemaic Egyptians, and Seleucids.

(See also AFTERLIFE; SCULPTURE.)

Sappho   Lyric poet of MYTILENE on the island of LESBOS, born in about 630 B.C. Her verses, of which perhaps two short poems and some 150 fragments survive today, have been much admired since ancient times for their directness of expression and personal honesty. Most of Sappho's poems were composed for solo recitation to the accompaniment of the lyre. She wrote in the Aeolic dialect and vernacular of Lesbos, a place whose strong lyric tradition had already produced such poets as TERPANDER, ARION, and Sappho's contemporary ALCAEUS. Sappho is one of the few female poets whom we know of from ancient Greece.

The typical subject of Sappho's verse is her physical love for several of the young WOMEN who were her comembers in a local cult of the goddess APHRODITE. The clearly homosexual nature of Sappho's poetry (and the presumably homosexual atmosphere of her female circle on Lesbos) gave rise in the 19th century A.D. to the word *lesbian*,

meaning "a woman who has sexual feelings for other women."

The only reliable facts about Sappho's life are those that can be gleaned from her verses. She was born into an aristocratic family of Mytilene. Although her poetry does not deal with politics, she apparently shared in the privileges and hazards of upper-class life. She went into brief exile in SICILY during a period of civil unrest on Lesbos circa 600 B.C., and she writes of happier days when her brother Larichus served as cupbearer at aristocratic drinking parties in Mytilene. Sappho had another brother, Charaxus, who sailed as a trader to NAUCRATIS, in EGYPT, where he squandered a fortune on a courtesan named Doricha; in certain verses Sappho rails against Doricha and wishes Charaxus a return to sanity. Later writers say that Sappho was married—as most women of her social class were bound to be—and we know that she had a daughter, Cleïs; in one poem Sappho expresses joy at the beauty of her daughter's face. In later centuries there arose a ridiculous tale that Sappho had died by jumping off a cliff for hopeless love of a sturdy ferryman.

Modern writers often assume that Sappho was a music teacher or similar, but her poems show only that she led a group of younger women, probably teenagers, in an official worship of Aphrodite—specifically, in observing the goddess' religious calendar and in maintaining various shrines in and around Mytilene. Some of Sappho's loveliest verses show the women venturing into the countryside or plaiting wildflower garlands to adorn a cult statue or altar. Sappho's sexual involvements with her young colleagues would seem to grow out of this sincere devotion to the goddess of sex and nature. The one poem by Sappho that definitely survives in its complete form is a hymn to Aphrodite in which the goddess, appearing before Sappho, promises to help the poet woo her beloved.

Not that love always means happiness in Sappho's poetry. "O Atthis," she writes to a girlfriend, "you have come to hate me in your mind, and flee to Andromeda!" (Andromeda was a rival of Sappho's, possibly the leader of a rival cult.) There was also the melancholy fact that, no matter what liaisons might arise between the girls in Sappho's group, all of these aristocratic maidens were destined to be married off by their families. (In ancient Greece girls were usually married by age 18; often by 14 or even 12.) Several of Sappho's poems are wedding songs, while other verses show distress within the group as members depart for MARRIAGE. Sappho's most famous poem, which survives nearly complete, records her own unabated desire as she watches a girlfriend talk with a handsome young man—probably the girl's husband and evidently at their wedding feast. He looks calm and godlike, the poet writes, "but whenever *I* even glance at you, my voice is lost, my tongue is stopped, and a delicate fire has spread under my skin . . . ."

In another poem, which survives only as a mutilated fragment, Sappho recalls how she consoled a girlfriend who was departing from the group. " 'Honestly I want to die,' " the fragment begins, with the other woman talking. " 'Sappho, I swear it's against my will that I'm leaving you.' And I answered her thus: 'Go gladly and remember me, for you know how we cherished you. Or let me remind you, if you forget, what blissful days we enjoyed—how at my side you often put on garlands of violets and roses and crocuses . . . and on soft mattresses gently you satisfied desire. And there was . . . nothing sacred from which we kept away . . .' "

In the modern age of commercialized sex and sexual politics, it takes some effort to imagine the innocence of Sappho's world. Although Sappho has been appropriated as a feminist forerunner since the 1970s, the poems suggest a lady with an open and honest heart living in a land of private emotion, completely removed—as almost all women of those days were—from politics or grand social concerns. Such religious and homosexual involution may be typical of upper-class Greek females' lives in this era. Certain verses by the male Spartan poet ALCMAN (circa 630 B.C.) seem to commemorate similar emotional tides within a Spartan girls' chorus.

The private world of Sappho and her lovers represents the female response to an outside world created by men— a world of politics, war, and male HOMOSEXUALITY, which excluded women except as wives and mothers. One of Sappho's best-known poems involves a gentle rejection of male militarism: "Some say that a host of cavalry is the loveliest sight on earth, some say foot soldiers, some say warships. But I say it is the person you love."

What makes such verses great, despite their self-absorption, is their apparent honesty and unselfconsciousness. Sappho's eroticism is miles apart from the amused, detached male homosexuality in the poetry of IBYCUS or ANACREON (mid- and late 500s B.C.). Sappho's genius lies in her ability to convey her sincere feelings, in simple lyric meters and vocabulary. Her metaphors and similes are beautifully apt and often come from the natural world, as when she writes of a maiden who outshines other women as the moon outshines the stars. Among Sappho's admirers in later generations was the philosopher PLATO, who called her the tenth Muse. The Roman poet Catullus (circa 55 B.C.) imitated her verses in at least two of his poems.

(See also ARISTOCRACY; LYRIC POETRY; MUSES.)

satyrs   The *saturai* were mythical spirits of the countryside and wilderness, personifying fertility and sexual desire. Satyrs were semihuman in form, with the ears, tail, legs, and hooves of a goat (or, in some earlier versions, of a horse). They were favorite subjects in vase painting and other art, and were always shown naked, with beards and pug noses, often with bald heads, and usually with erect penises. Satyrs were typically shown getting drunk or pursuing sexual gratification with their female counterparts, the NYMPHS.

The satyrs were associated with DIONYSUS, the god of WINE and fertility. Processions honoring Dionysus and the satyrs were held in the Athenian countryside (among other places), and these bawdy ceremonies apparently supplied the origin for Athenian stage comedy. Classical Athens retained a form of stage farce, less elaborate than formal comedy, known as the satyr play (*saturikon*).

(See also THEATER.)

science   The ancient Greeks were the first Europeans to make inquiries into ASTRONOMY, physics, and biology, yet they were slow to recognize a separate discipline that might be called science. Greek scientific studies in the 500s and 400s B.C. were bound up in the concept of *philosophia* (love of arcane knowledge) and the search for philosophical truth. Such studies were conducted in imitation of MATHEMATICS, with emphasis on theory rather than on experiment and observation. It took the categorizing genius of ARISTOTLE (384–322 B.C.) to identify a separate discipline that he called *phusikē* (natural studies), in contrast to mathematics or PHILOSOPHY.

The origin of Western science is associated with the philosopher THALES of MILETUS (circa 585 B.C.). Thales was the first Greek to try to explain the universe without appeal to MYTH or RELIGION, but rather with reference to a primary physical substance (which he identified as water). Further crude theorizing in physics came from Thales' disciples ANAXIMANDER (circa 560 B.C.) and ANAXIMENES (circa 550 B.C.), and from such later philosophers as HERACLITUS (circa 500 B.C.), PARMENIDES (circa 490 B.C.), EMPEDOCLES (who originated the concept of four primal elements— earth, fire, water, and air, circa 450 B.C.), and the atomists LEUCIPPUS (circa 440 B.C.) and DEMOCRITUS (circa 430 B.C.). These thinkers all addressed, in highly original ways, the basic problem of physical change: How is it that matter apparently comes into being and grows out of nothing? (For instance, how is it that trees sprout leaves?)

But the single most important figure in ancient science was Aristotle, whose voluminous inquiries into all existing branches of knowledge served to create certain scientific categories still recognized today, such as physics and biology. Aristotle introduced the practice of studying by empirical observation, purely for the sake of scientific knowledge—a practice that became traditional at his Athenian school of higher learning, the LYCEUM (founded circa 335 B.C.).

In zoology specifically, Aristotle's inquiries were simply epoch-making. His zoological writings make reference to over 500 animal species, including about 120 kinds of fish and 60 kinds of insects, observed either in their natural habitat or in dissection. Although not the first Greek to practice animal dissection, he was the first to do so with a wide variety of species and to document his researches.

Aristotle tackled the problem of change with typical restraint and common sense, suggesting that a thing can come to be both what it already is and what it is not—in the sense that it fulfills an inborn potential, or *telos*. For example, the acorn "is" an oak tree, in terms of its *telos*. In physics, Aristotle pioneered the study of motion, which is now called dynamics.

Aristotle's work dominated Western science, for better or worse, for over 2,000 years, down to the 1600s A.D. His acceptance of Empedocles' notion of four elements guaranteed that that incorrect theory would remain for centuries the authoritative theory of chemistry. Even Aristotle's grosser errors became canonical: His treatise *On the Heavens* contains the notoriously inaccurate statement that a heavier object will fall at a proportionately faster speed than a lighter one. Although questioned in late antiquity, this false law of physics was taught in European schools until it was finally disproved by Galileo in around A.D. 1590.

Aristotle's successor at the Lyceum, THEOPHRASTUS (president circa 323–287 B.C.), carried on the master's studies in biology and physics, as did Theophrastus' successor, Straton (president circa 287–269 B.C.). Meanwhile, the Athenian philosophical movement of STOICISM popularized the Empedoclean-Aristotelian theory of four elements, while the rival school of EPICUREANISM adapted Leucippus' and Democritus' concept of atoms (*atomoi*, "indivisible particles"). But by the early 200s B.C. the center of scientific research was shifting from Athens to the wealthy court of the Ptolemies at ALEXANDRIA (1), where the Library and Museum attracted scholars from around the Greek world.

The main scientific advances at Alexandria were in the previously neglected field of mechanical engineering. From at least the 500s B.C. onward, the Greeks had possessed such simple mechanical devices as the lever, pulley, and winch, but in the 200s B.C. Alexandrian scientists explored new constructions and mechanical theories. Fueling this advance was the Ptolemies' eager financing of military technology, specifically the creation of bigger and better siege artillery, powered by torsion. The Alexandrian inventor Ctesibius (circa 270 B.C.) is credited with improvements in catapult design as well as with such peaceful inventions as the water pump and the water clock (which measured the passing hours through the controlled dripping of water). Ctesibius also pioneered the study of pneumatics (the action of air under pressure).

The century's greatest Greek scientist—and one of its greatest mathematicians—was ARCHIMEDES (active 260–212 B.C.), a lifelong citizen of the Sicilian-Greek city of SYRACUSE. Among his many accomplishments, Archimedes invented the branch of physics known today as hydrostatics (the study of properties of standing water). Archimedes added one important invention to Mediterranean technology—the Archimedes screw, still used today to draw water uphill continually, without suction.

One technological breakthrough of the late Greek world (circa 100 B.C.) was the simple expedient of powering a millstone by means of a donkey tethered to a pole, treading a circle. Further advances appeared under the Roman Empire, including the Alexandrian inventor Hero's famous experiment with steam power (circa A.D. 60). The slow advance of Greek technology can be explained partly by the availability of slave labor and by a lack of government funding for nonmilitary research.

(See also MEDICINE; SLAVES; WARFARE, SIEGE.)

Scopas   See SCULPTURE.

sculpture   The greatest artistic success of the ancient Greeks came in their shaping of marble (by carving) or metal (by casting) to represent the human body. By the mid-400s B.C. Greek sculptors, working mainly at the preeminent city of ATHENS, had achieved a realism in portraying human forms that went unequaled for nearly the next 2,000 years, until the Italian Renaissance. Modern art historians refer to the years 480–330 B.C. as the Greek "classical" era, meaning that that was when the Greeks established standards of excellence—in sculpture and in ARCHITECTURE—that helped to define those art forms for all time.

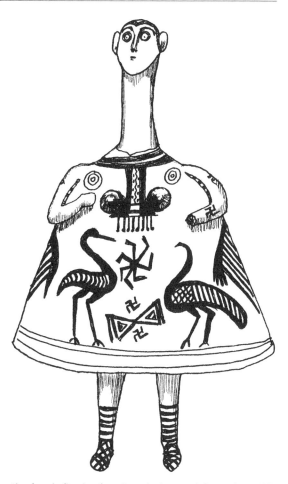

Clay female figurine from Boeotia, in central Greece, later 700s B.C. The bell-shape body was molded on a potter's wheel, then painted and baked in a kiln; the legs were made separately and fastened inside. The painted swastikas probably represent the good magic of rotating wheels or drills for making fire; it would be another 2,600 years before the Nazis appropriated that symbol as an emblem of hate.

Most Greek sculpture has not survived from ancient days. During late antiquity and the Middle Ages, priceless works were lost to neglect or plundered for their raw material. Today many ancient sculptures exist only as Roman copies of vanished Greek originals. Most of these Roman copies are marble, even if the Greek originals were BRONZE.

Classical Greek sculpture took several forms. A statue is by definition self-standing; Greek statues typically showed a human figure, male or female, representing a person or deity. Among the most important statues were idols of gods or goddesses set up in the deities' temples. Aside from statuary, there was architectural sculpture: Figures were carved in limestone or (usually) marble to be fastened to panels on the outside of temples and other public buildings. Typically showing scenes from MYTH, architectural

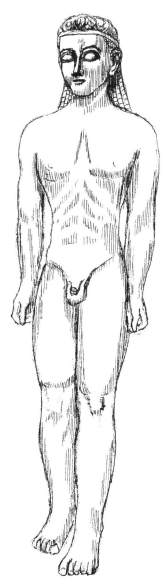

as bronze or GOLD, the earliest extant Greek sculpture is in stone—specifically, the soft limestone that lies plentifully in the mountains of mainland Greece. The best-known early item of carved limestone is the bas-relief slab at the gateway of MYCENAE (circa 1250 B.C.). No doubt such sculpture developed from primitive traditions of wood-carving—however, almost no wooden items have survived from the distant past, since wood is such a perishable material. The earliest Greeks surely used wood for carving their statues of the gods; even as late as the 400s B.C.

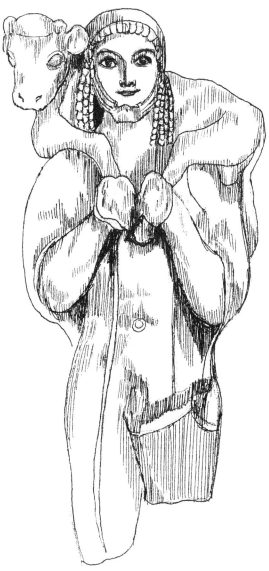

A marble *kouros* (male youth) from the temple of Poseidon at Cape Sunium, in Athenian territory, circa 585 B.C. This nearly 10-foot-tall statue has the typical *kouros* pose: face front, arms stiffly at sides, left leg advanced. The pose closely resembles that of earlier Egyptian statuary, and was probably originally copied by Greek artists who visited Egypt or who based their work on imported Egyptian figurines.

sculptures might be carved completely in the round (as though they were statues) or they might be left partly uncarved, where the figure would be fixed to the building. Another type of architectural sculpture was bas-relief, which was a panel of stone carved so that the figure (or, often, group of figures) would rise part-way out of the stone. Apart from buildings, bas-reliefs were also used for gravestones and public plaques.

Although classical sculptors could work in metals such

The Calf-bearer, an Athenian marble statue of about 560 B.C. Sculpted at just over life size, the man is bringing a bull calf to sacrifice. The artistic stylization of prior decades is still apparent, including the typical "Archaic smile" and *kouros*like leg positions, but the general pose is more daring, with a confident sense of motion. Here the Greeks have begun to make sculpture breathe life.

The celebrated Discobolus (Discus Thrower), a life-size marble statue of the Roman imperial age, copied from a bronze original (now lost) sculpted by Myron of Athens, circa 450 B.C. Intended to be seen only from this angle, the statue is unrealistically flattened in pose; nevertheless, the original work represented a landmark in the Greeks' quest to portray the human body in action.

wooden idols were still being worshipped at certain shrines.

After the collapse of MYCENAEAN CIVILIZATION, the grim DARK AGE (circa 1100–900 B.C.) saw artistic impoverishment throughout the Greek world. Sculpture may have been reduced largely to wood-carving and the shaping of clay. But sculpture in stone reemerged at the start of what scholars call the "archaic" era (circa 650–480 B.C.). Influenced by the monumental statuary carved in granite and porphyry that could be seen in EGYPT, Greek sculptors turned to the most suitable hard stone found in Greece— marble (a compacted form of limestone). Likewise, the Greeks copied the typical pose of Egyptian statuary—arms stiffly at sides, left leg advanced. A number of these early Greek statues survive, with the earliest dating from soon after 600 B.C. They are the figures known today as *kouroi* ("male youths"); typically they show a naked young man,

slightly larger than life size. The *kouroi* and their somewhat later female counterparts, the clothed figures known as *korai* ("maidens"), were works commissioned by wealthy families to stand at a young person's grave or as a dedicatory offering in a god's temple. Most extant *kouroi* and *korai* come from the region of Athens.

A comparison of individual *kouroi* reveals the advances made by Greek sculptors during the 500s B.C. Aided partly by a development in metal-carving tools, sculptors of the later part of the century were giving their figures more realistic musculature and facial expressions; Greek statues begin to show the famous "archaic smile"—intended to represent, not happiness necessarily, but the vividness of a living human face.

The defeat of the invading Persians in 480–479 B.C. opened a new phase in Greek art—the classical period—in which artistic confidence, religious piety, and prosperity all combined to produce one of the greatest cultural eras in world history. From about 450 to 404 B.C. the rich, imperial Athens—with its lavish public-building program begun by the statesman PERICLES—dominated the field. Greek sculptors abandoned the styles of prior generations and broke through to a new realism in showing the posture and proportions of the human form, particularly the male form; this breakthrough is embodied in the Athenian marble statue that modern scholars call the "Critius boy," carved circa 480 B.C. By the mid-400s B.C. the Argive sculptor POLYCLITUS had perfected the proportions of the standing male figure, with the statue known as the Doryphorus (spear carrier).

Meanwhile came an improved ability to show bodies in movement or in emotional poses. The best known surviving examples are the marble sculptures of gods and heroes that adorned the temple of ZEUS at OLYMPIA (circa 457 B.C.) and the Athenian PARTHENON (circa 440 B.C.).

The art was also revolutionized by improvements in metal casting: the early 400s B.C. saw the invention of a method of casting molten bronze around a wooden core, thus creating a hollow metal figure rather than (as in prior technology) a solid one. The new method allowed for

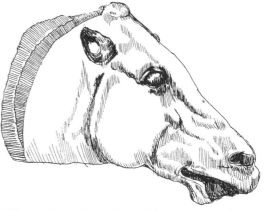

Vivid texture in marble: the head of the Moon goddess's chariot horse, from the east pediment of the Parthenon, circa 435 B.C. The sculpture is now among the Elgin Marbles in the British Museum in London.

The famous Winged Victory of Samothrace, now in the Louvre Museum in Paris. Carved in marble circa 190 B.C., the nearly eight-foot-tall statue is thought to commemorate a Rhodian naval victory over the Seleucids: The goddess Nike (Victory), now minus head and arms, is shown alighting on the prow of a ship. In ancient times the statue stood in an outdoor shrine on the holy island of Samothrace. The marble's gorgeous effects of movement and windswept drapery make this one of the most admired statues in the world.

greater realism in the rendering of musculature, clothing, and such fine details as beards and hair. Among the most famous Greek bronze statues surviving today are the Charioteer of DELPHI (circa 474 B.C.) and the Artemisium ZEUS (circa 455 B.C.). The new metal-casting method helped to create the century's two most famous statues—the colossal gold and ivory idols of ATHENA and Zeus, both sculpted by the Athenian PHIDIAS in the 430s B.C. but now lost.

Athens' defeat in the PELOPONNESIAN WAR (404 B.C.) saw the start of a less confident, less public-minded, but still innovative artistic era. In place of the former patriotism and piety, tastes in sculpture during the 300s B.C. turned to more personal subjects. Portraiture of living people became a growing field. In mythological subjects, the prior era's fascination with the male form was at last counterbalanced by an interest in the female form (usually shown clothed, sometimes nude). Relatedly, sculptors worked for

better realism in the rendering of flowing clothing fabric and facial expression. Marble carving became the foremost sculptural discipline at this time, ahead of metal casting. The spirit and values of the mid-300s B.C. were embodied in the work of the Athenian sculptor PRAXITELES.

The conquests of the Macedonian king ALEXANDER THE GREAT (334–323 B.C.) recreated the map of the Greek world, with new centers of Greek culture and patronage arising in the East. Although the classical era had passed, the subsequent HELLENISTIC AGE (circa 300–150 B.C.) saw some advanced realism in specific effects, such as in conveying emotion or movement through pose, facial gesture, and clothing. Among the most admired extant Hellenistic sculptures are the bas-reliefs carved on the Great Altar of Zeus from the eastern Greek city of PERGAMUM, circa 180 B.C. Now housed in a Berlin museum, the Pergamene carvings show a favorite mythological scene—the primeval battle between the gods and GIANTS, representing the triumph of civilization over savagery.

Whether marble or metal, most ancient Greek sculpture was painted: The figure's flesh, clothing, and other features were vividly colored so as to project from a distance. On buildings, architectural sculptures stood out against dark painted backgrounds of red or blue. Today the paint on most of the surviving Greek sculpture has faded away through time.

(See also AEGINA; FUNERAL CUSTOMS; LACOÖN; MELOS; RELIGION; RHODES; SAMOTHRACE; SEVEN WONDERS OF THE WORLD; WOMEN.)

Scylla   A mythical, female sea monster, semihuman in shape, described in HOMER's epic poem the *Odyssey* (book 12). Scylla lived in a narrow sea channel sometimes identified as the Straits of Messina, between SICILY and the "toe" of ITALY. Opposite her cave, the whirlpool Charybdis operated; ships moving through the channel had to risk encountering either Scylla at one side or Charybdis at the other. Scylla (Mangler) had six heads and 12 legs, and normally fed herself on fish; but she would attack any passing ship, grabbing men from shipboard and devouring them.

In the *Odyssey* the hero ODYSSEUS, having been forewarned by the witch CIRCE, steers his ship close by Scylla to avoid the worse danger, Charybdis. Scylla, snatches six of Odysseus' men overboard, but the ship passes by, rowed by the surviving crew. Odysseus' adventure has given rise to the expression "Steering on Scylla to avoid Charybdis," meaning to choose the lesser of two evils.

Later writers described Scylla as having genitalia consisting of ferocious, snarling dogs' heads. This deformity was said to be the result of a magic spell. Scylla had once been a beautiful woman who became the lover of the sea god POSEIDON and was then hideously bewitched in a magical bath prepared by Poseidon's jealous wife, Amphitrite.

Scythia   See BLACK SEA.

Second Athenian League   The name given by modern historians to the alliance formed by ATHENS and various other Greek states in 378 B.C. and modeled after the DELIAN LEAGUE, which had been founded exactly 100 years before. The league arose in response to Spartan repression in the generation following SPARTA's victory in the PELOPONNE-SIAN WAR (404 B.C.) and particularly as a result of the unpopular Spartan-Persian treaty known as the KING's PEACE (386 B.C.).

In order to entice Greek allies into the league, Athens had to promise to avoid its previous imperialistic excesses of the Delian League, including the levying of tribute and the imposition of Athenian garrison colonies; the latter promise was not kept scrupulously. The most important ally in the league was THEBES. But, after defeating the Spartans at the Battle of LEUCTRA in 371 B.C., Thebes led other central Greek states in seceding from the league. Indeed, the rapid decline of Sparta after 371 B.C. removed much of the league's original reason for being.

The league received another blow in 357 B.C., when three major east Greek member states—CHIOS, RHODES, and BYZANTIUM—revolted. The league was dissolved by the Macedonian king PHILIP II, after he had seized mainland Greece in 338 B.C.

Seleuceia   See ANTIOCH; SELEUCID EMPIRE.

Seleucid Empire   The largest of several Hellenistic kingdoms that emerged from the Eastern conquests of the Macedonian king ALEXANDER THE GREAT (died 323 B.C.). At its greatest secure extent, circa 280 B.C., the Seleucid Empire occupied much of what had been Alexander's domain, from ASIA MINOR and the Levant to Afghanistan, but excluding EGYPT. The Seleucids' governing and soldiering classes came from a Greek and Macedonian minority based in the western cities and in military colonies throughout; these people ruled a population of Syrians, Persians, Phoenicians, Babylonians, JEWS, and others. Unfortunately, this unwieldy domain lacked a unifying identity and had trouble replenishing its Greco-Macedonian soldiery. For most of its 250-year history, the empire was losing territory.

The term *Seleucid Empire* is a translation of the kingdom's Greek name, Seleukis, which was derived from the name of the founding dynast, SELEUCUS (1), who lived circa 358–281 B.C. Seleucus began his career as a Macedonian nobleman and soldier under Alexander. After Alexander's death, he was one of several Macedonian generals, known collectively as the DIADOCHI (Successors), who seized portions of the conqueror's domain; Seleucus' share was by far the largest.

In 300 B.C. Seleucus built the Syrian coastal city of ANTIOCH, which later became the Seleucid capital, superseding the prior capital of Seleuceia-on-the-Tigris, in Mesopotamia. Brilliantly located to be a gateway between the Mediterranean and the East, Antioch became the seat of a lively Syro-Greek culture, personified for us by the poet and anthologist Meleager of Gadara (circa 100 B.C.). Antioch was named for Seleucus' son and eventual successor, Antiochus, who reigned 281–261 B.C. The names Antiochus and Seleucus (also Demetrius) became traditional for the Seleucid royal house.

Despite their Eastern holdings, the Seleucid rulers tended to look westward, being preoccupied with territorial conflicts against Ptolemaic Egypt. The six Syrian Wars (274–168 B.C.), fought over the two empires' shared frontier in the Levant, involved use of war elephants and huge phalanxes of heavy infantry. Meanwhile the city of PERGAMUM, revolting from Seleucid rule, established a rival domain in Asia Minor (circa 262 B.C.). Farther east, the hellenized kingdom of BACTRIA rebelled (circa 250 B.C.), and the non-Greek kingdom of Parthia emerged to deprive the Seleucids of territories in PERSIA and Mesopotamia (mid-200s–mid-100s B.C.).

ANTIOCHUS (2) III (reigned 223–187 B.C.), the greatest Seleucid king, re-created much of the old empire; but he came to grief against the overseas armies of the Italian city of ROME. The Romans defeated Antiochus in battle in Greece (191 B.C.) and Asia Minor (190 B.C.), and forced him to relinquish his holdings in Asia Minor (188 B.C.). Weakened by palace factions and by the Maccabean Revolt of the Palestinian Jews (167 B.C.), the Seleucid realm gradually shrank to the region that was called Syria (including modern Syria and Lebanon). The Seleucid kingship was dismantled in 64 B.C., when Syria became a Roman province.

The Seleucid Empire's significance for history is its role in hellenizing the Levant. This effect can be seen today in Greek-style ruins at such sites as Palmyra, in the Syrian desert. Long after the end of the Seleucid Empire, Greek was still the language of commerce, government, and higher learning in the Near East. Under Roman rule, in the first century A.D., the Bible's New Testament was written in Greek—rather than in Hebrew, Aramaic, or Latin—as a result of the Seleucid legacy.

(See also CELTS; HELLENISTIC AGE; WARFARE, LAND.)

Seleucus (1)   Founder and first king of the SELEUCID EMPIRE, which was named after him. Living circa 358–281 B.C., Seleucus was one of the most capable of the DIADOCHI (Successors), who fought over the dismembered empire of ALEXANDER THE GREAT. The kingdom Seleucus received, which was the largest of any Successor's, extended from the Levant to the Indus River valley.

This Oriental despot was born—neither Oriental nor royal—in MACEDON, as the son of a Macedonian nobleman in the service of the Macedonian king PHILIP II. At about age 24, Seleucus (Shining one) accompanied Philip's son and successor, Alexander, on his invasion of the Persian Empire (334 B.C.). Although not mentioned as a prominent commander, Seleucus may have been a close friend of the young king, who was his near contemporary.

Following Alexander's spectacular conquests and his death, Seleucus became the Macedonian governor at Babylon (321 B.C.). Coming into conflict with ANTIGONUS (1), who was based in ASIA MINOR, in 316 B.C. Seleucus fled to the protection of PTOLEMY (1), in EGYPT, but in 312 B.C. he returned to Babylon with an army and recaptured the city. Later Seleucus conquered eastward to seize an empire that nearly compared with Alexander's. Soon Seleucus, like the other Diadochi, was calling himself "king" (*basileus*). In 301 B.C. he and the Macedonian dynast LYSIMACHUS destroyed Antigonus at the Battle of Ipsus, in central Asia Minor. An essential element in the victory was Seleucus' 480 trained Indian war elephants, acquired from an Indian king in exchange for Seleucid territorial concessions in the Indus region.

The Ipsus victory left Seleucus with secure gains in Syria and southeastern Asia Minor. He then sought westward outlets; no doubt he saw that his domain could survive only by remaining a part of the Greek world and by attracting Greek immigration. Having established an eastern capital, Seleuceia, on the River Tigris (circa 312 B.C.), he then founded a western capital, the great city of ANTIOCH, near the Syrian seacoast (300 B.C.).

Antioch was named for Seleucus' son and eventual successor, Antiochus. Prince Antiochus' mother was Apama, a noblewoman of BACTRIA whom Seleucus had married under Alexander's supervision, in 324 B.C. In 298 B.C., without divorcing, the 60-year-old Seleucus took a second wife—Stratonicē, the 20-year-old daughter of his prior enemy, DEMETRIUS POLIORCETES (Antigonus' son). Later, when the dynamic but unstable Demetrius invaded Asia Minor, Seleucus captured him (285 B.C.) and chivalrously provided a comfortable captivity in which Demetrius ate and drank himself to death.

In 281 B.C. Seleucus took aim at what would be his last great acquisition—Asia Minor, most of which was held by his former ally, Lysimachus, now king of Macedon. For Seleucus, Asia Minor represented the crucial westward link to the central Greek world. Seleucus defeated Lysimachus at the Battle of Corupedium, near Sardis. Lysimachus's death in the fighting inspired the 77-year-old Seleucus with dreams of seizing the vacant Macedonian throne. Seleucus invaded Macedon and was on the point of capturing the kingdom when he was murdered by one of his followers, a son of Ptolemy who wanted the throne for himself. Seleucus was succeeded by Antiochus, who had been reigning as his father's partner since 292 B.C.

The Seleucid Empire continued under Seleucus' descendants for nearly another 220 years, but the vast conquests of Seleucus I gradually were eroded.

(See also WARFARE, LAND.)

Seleucus (2):   see Seleucid Empire

Selinus   Westernmost Greek city in SICILY. The site of ancient Selinus, now uninhabited, boasts one of the grandest collections of Greek temple ruins from the 400s B.C.

Founded circa 628 B.C. by Dorian-Greek colonists from the city of Megara Hyblaea (on Sicily's east coast), Selinus occupied a terrace of land overlooking the southwestern Sicilian coastline, just south of modern Castelvetrano. According to one tale, Selinus was named for local growths of wild celery (Greek: *selinon*). Selinus enjoyed access to rich coastal farmland and sea trade, but it also lay within the territory of the Greeks' traditional enemies, the Carthaginians, who occupied western Sicily. This menace was decreased by the immense Greek victory over the Carthaginians at the Battle of HIMERA (480 B.C.), after which the Selinuntines became allies of the preeminent Sicilian-Greek city, SYRACUSE.

It was during these years—late 500s–early 400s B.C.—that the prosperous Selinuntines constructed the eight Doric-style temples whose remnants grace the site today. Of these, the building now known as Temple G (probably a shrine of APOLLO) must have been planned as one of the largest buildings in the Greek world; it was left incomplete, circa 480 B.C. The temples all seem to have been toppled by earthquake in ancient times.

A traditional enmity existed between Selinus and the northwestern city of Segesta (inhabited by a non-Greek native people, the Elymi). This conflict took on international proportions in 415 B.C., when the Segestans appealed for help to the powerful city of ATHENS, in mainland Greece. During the subsequent, ill-fated Athenian invasion of Sicily, Selinuntine troops fought alongside their Syracusan allies, against the Athenians (415–413 B.C.). But soon Segesta had found a new ally, CARTHAGE, and in 409 B.C. Selinus was destroyed by the Carthaginians in their drive to reconquer Sicily.

Reinhabited by refugees, Selinus probably remained a Carthaginian vassal until 250 B.C., when it was again destroyed in the course of the First Punic War, between Romans and Carthaginians.

(See also ARCHITECTURE; DORIAN GREEKS; PELOPONNESIAN WAR; ROME.)

Semele   See DIONYSUS.

Semonides   Early Greek lyric poet, probably of the late 600s B.C. Semonides came from the island of SAMOS but emigrated—possibly because of social unrest—to Amorgos, an island of the CYCLADES.

Semonides' work survives in one apparently complete poem and one fragment, both written in iambic meter, a form associated with satire. The poem—a social satire on the nature of WOMEN—is typical of the misogyny of Greek male culture of the 600s–400s B.C. The gods (the poem explains) made women from different materials or animals: from mud, the changeable sea, the weasel, the donkey, and so forth. According to the poem, only one type is good to marry: the one made from the quiet, industrious bee.

Semonides should not be confused with the more famous SIMONIDES of Ceos, who lived a century later.

(See also LYRIC POETRY.)

Sestos   Small Greek city on the European shore of the HELLESPONT, midway along the strait, at the narrowest section. Sestos was the fortress of the Hellespont, with a hilltop citadel whose walls ran down to flank the best harbor in the region. Ideally situated to control shipping in the channel, Sestos served as a naval base for ATHENS in the 400s–300s B.C., protecting Athenian imports of precious grain from the BLACK SEA.

Sestos was founded by colonists from LESBOS in the 600s B.C. Around 512 B.C. Sestos was annexed by the Persian king DARIUS (1). The Persian king XERXES, in his campaign to conquer Greece, marched his vast army across the Hellespont on two pontoon bridges that reached the European shore near Sestos (480 B.C.). After the Persian defeat in Greece, Sestos was immediately captured and occupied by Athenian forces (479 B.C.). For nearly the next 75 years, Sestos was a member of the Athenian-led DELIAN LEAGUE.

Athenian-held Sestos played a prominent role in naval campaigns for the Hellespont in the later PELOPONNESIAN

WAR. After Athens' defeat (404 B.C.), Sestos was taken over by SPARTA. Sestos became Athens' subject again in 365 B.C. but soon rebelled. The Athenians crushed the rebellion, captured the city, sold the inhabitants as SLAVES, and repopulated the place with Athenian colonists (357 B.C.). In 334 B.C. the Macedonian king ALEXANDER THE GREAT brought his army to Sestos for his shipborne invasion of Persian territory across the Hellespont.

On the Asian shore opposite Sestos, one mile away, stood the Greek city of Abydos. In later Greek times there arose the legend of Hero and Leander, about a man of Abydos (Leander) who swam the Hellespont ever night to visit his girlfriend in Sestos.

(See also EUROPE AND ASIA; PERSIAN WARS.)

Seven Against Thebes, the   Well-known MYTH, part of the so-called Theban Cycle, about the legendary woes of the royal house of THEBES (a city in central Greece). By the 600s B.C. the myths of Thebes had been collected in an epic poem, now lost, called the *Thebaïd*. Like other episodes in the Theban Cycle, the tale of the Seven was presented onstage by the great Athenian playwright AESCHYLUS, in his tragedy *Seven Against Thebes* (467 B.C.).

According to the legend, the Theban king OEDIPUS had two sons, Eteocles (True Glory) and Polynices (Greek: Poluneikes, Much Strife). The brothers' destiny was not happy. After Oedipus' death, they argued as to who should be king—Eteocles was the elder, but the law of primogeniture did not apply among the Greeks—and they finally agreed to reign in alternate years. Eteocles drew the lot allowing him to rule first, and Polynices withdrew to the city of ARGOS, awaiting his turn.

With the year's passing it became obvious that Eteocles would not relinquish his throne. So Polynices enlisted the aid of Adrastus, king of Argos, whose daughter (Argeia) he had married. Polynices and Adrastus collected a mighty army, to be led by Polynices and six other champions, usually identified as Tydeus of Calydon; Amphiaraus of Argos; Capaneus of Argos; Hippomedon of Argos; Parthenopaeus of ARCADIA (son of the huntress ATALANTA); and, in most versions, King Adrastus.

Foremost among the Seven was Tydeus, a small but valiant man who had gone to Argos after being banished from Calydon for homicide. Like Polynices, Tydeus had married one of Adrastus' daughters, Deipyle. Their baby son, DIOMEDES, was destined to outshine even his father, as a hero in the TROJAN WAR.

Also notable among the Seven was Amphiaraus, a seer who foresaw that the expedition would be a disaster and that he himself would never return if he accompanied it. Amphiaraus knew that his wife, Eriphyle, would be approached to convince him to join the campaign, and he forbade her to accept any gift from Polynices. She disobeyed, and was bribed by the fabulous necklace that had once belonged to Polynices' great-grandmother Harmonia (wife of the hero CADMUS). As a result, Eriphyle successfully convinced Amphiaraus to join the doomed expedition—an odd concession by him, given his foreknowledge, but so runs the myth. In departing, Amphiaraus compelled his son ALCMAEON (1) to pledge to avenge his death by killing Eriphyle (i.e., Alcmaeon's own mother); he also made the boy vow to launch his own attack on Thebes someday.

The tale of Amphiaraus was a favorite among the Greeks, who liked stories, mythical or otherwise, about people choosing a course of certain death. Amphiaraus' fateful departure from Argos is the subject of one of the most beautiful surviving Corinthian-style vase paintings, circa 560 B.C.

The Seven's attack on Thebes was, as Amphiaraus had predicted, a failure. At each of the seven gates of Thebes, one of the Seven fought a Theban champion in single combat. Polynices and Eteocles killed each other, and the rest of the Seven died, with the exception of King Adrastus, who escaped on his superlative horse. Amphiaraus, attempting to flee in his chariot, was swallowed up in the earth.

In the next generation, Amphiaraus' son Alcmaeon, true to his vow, marched to Thebes with six other heroes, including Tydeus' son, Diomedes; this time the city fell to the attackers. Alcmaeon's exploit was known as the Expedition of the Epigoni (Descendants) and was described in a now-lost epic poem titled *Epigonoi* (circa 600 B.C.).

Because Greek myths often provide distorted reflections of events in the distant Mycenaean age (circa 1600–1200 B.C.), this tale may contain a kernel of historical truth. Thebes and Argos represent the two heartlands of Mycenaean Greek civilization, with Argos equivalent to the royal city of MYCENAE. The legends of the Seven and the Epigoni surely commemorate repeated attempts by the king of Mycenae to capture Thebes and its fertile plain, perhaps circa 1350 B.C.

(See also ANTIGONE; MYCENAEAN CIVILIZATION.)

Seven Sages, the   A list of seven men said to be the wisest in ancient Greece. Each of the sages (Greek: *sophoi*) was a real person, typically a statesman, active in the 500s or late 600s B.C. One or two were benign TYRANTS. The list first appears in PLATO's dialogue *Protagoras*, written circa 390 B.C.; but the tradition probably dates back another 200 years. The seven were: (1) THALES, a philosopher and scientist of MILETUS; (2) PITTACUS, an elected ruler of MYTILENE, on the island of LESBOS (3) Bias, a judge and diplomat of Priēnē (in IONIA); (4) SOLON, an elected ruler and lawgiver at ATHENS; (5) Cleobulus, tyrant of Lindus, on the island of RHODES; (6) CHILON, an EPHOR (chief official) at SPARTA; and (7) Myson of Chenae (in Trachis in central Greece), a rustic sage.

In other versions, the obscure Myson is replaced by PERIANDER, tyrant of CORINTH.

Seven Wonders of the World, the   By a popular tradition in the HELLENISTIC AGE (circa 300–150 B.C.), the Greeks counted seven monuments as preeminent in size or grandeur among all man-made works. In the most usual list, five of the seven wonders belonged to the Greek world; the other two—the oldest—were built by non-Greek civilizations. The seven were:

1. the pyramids of EGYPT, built between about 2700 and 1800 B.C.

2. the hanging gardens of Babylon, dating from the early 500s B.C.

3. the temple of the goddess ARTEMIS at EPHESUS, constructed over the period 550–430 B.C.

4. the giant cult statue of ZEUS fashioned circa 430 B.C. by the Athenian sculptor PHIDIAS for the god's temple at OLYMPIA.

5. the Mausoleum, or tomb of the ruler Mausolus, at HALICARNASSUS, built circa 350 B.C.

6. the Colossus of RHODES—a statue of the sun god, HELIOS, erected beside the harbor at Rhodes city circa 285 B.C.

7. the lighthouse at ALEXANDRIA (1), built on the isle of Pharos, outside Alexandria harbor, circa 270 B.C.

Of all these works, only the pyramids of Egypt survive today.

ships and seafaring   "We live around a sea like frogs around a pond," the Athenian philosopher SOCRATES is reported to have said (circa 410 B.C.), summarizing the ancient Greeks' reliance on seaborne TRADE and transport. Like the Phoenicians, but unlike many other Mediterranean peoples, the Greeks had a genius for seamanship. Seafaring was proverbially dangerous in ancient times, but it was also far faster, more efficient, and more lucrative than overland freighting; mule teams or ox-drawn carts could never compare with the speed and efficency of ships carrying cargo (or troops) under sail or oar. New cities were established regularly to take advantage of nearby natural harbors or waterways. The great expansion of the Greek world in 800–500 B.C. was largely the story of seaborne trade, COLONIZATION, and conquest, along ever-enlarging shipping routes. On the military side, sea power came to mean (by the mid-500s B.C.) something like what air power means to modern generals—the fastest way to bring harm to enemies at various points, including the ability to stop their imports and starve them. Sea power became the necessary condition for imperial strength among classical Greek states. It was by sea that ATHENS became great in the 400s B.C.

Seafaring was encouraged by the geography of mainland Greece—with its mountains, scarce farmland, and immensely long overall coastline, nearly 2,000 miles total. Many Greeks, such as the people of the island AEGINA, took to the sea to compensate for their home region's lack of space or fertility.

Aside from Athens and Aegina, major GREEK seagoing states in various eras of history included CHALCIS, CORINTH, MILETUS, PHOCAEA, SAMOS, CHIOS, LESBOS, and RHODES.

The Mediterranean Sea—including its northeastern corner, the Greeks' AEGEAN SEA—offered inducements to seafaring. Unlike the Atlantic Ocean, the Mediterranean has no tides and is broken by many islands and peninsulas, with a reliable "window" of calm weather in summer. Against these natural advantages, the ancient Greeks were burdened by primitive means of navigation. Lacking the compass and sextant, they depended on visible reckonings, such as coastal landmarks and position of the stars. This need for landmarks—along with a fear of straying too

A pirate ship, at right, intercepts a merchant vessel, in a black-figure scene on an Athenian cup, late 500s B.C. The painter has clearly distinguished the two ships' designs: the low-riding pirate bireme, built for speed, powered mainly by oars, carrying a bronze ram; and the heavier, taller, deeper-hulled freight ship, built to hold cargo. Note the merchantman's thick mast. This ship would rely mostly on its sail for power. The horizontal lines atop the merchant's hull probably represent a defensive fence.

far from shelter—explains the ancient seafarers' persistent reliance on coastal routing. A Greek colony such as COR-CYRA, on the Adriatic coast, long remained an important anchorage between Greece and ITALY, even though on a map it looks to be a northern detour.

Ancient vessels were made from TIMBER, and relied on two forms of power—wind and oars. Most ships carried a single mast, capable of hoisting one square sail typically made of patchwork linen (from the flax plant) or canvas (from Egyptian cotton). Unlike modern sailboats, ancient square-riggers could make direct progress only if the wind was fully or nearly astern; a wind from the side (abeam) required the ship to sail close-hauled, on a zigzag course of tacking; a wind forward of the beam tended to be unusable. Still, heavier ships, such as the larger merchant vessels, had to rely mostly on wind power. Smaller craft, such as warships, could make progress under oars alone if that was preferable to using the sail. War squadrons always rowed when moving into battle, for better control and uniformity.

Despite changes in ship design during the Greek epoch of 1600–100 B.C., these two basic categories persisted: merchant vessel and war vessel. The merchantmen were by far the larger type, designed to carry freight; such ships had deep drafts, wide beams, and heavy masts; their hulls were usually closed at top by a deck. They carried only a small crew. A war craft, by contrast, was designed for speed and was slender, shallow-drafted, and low-riding. Like a canoe or modern racing shell, the warship's hull was typically undecked (or only partly decked), and almost every foot of space was taken by oarsmen or shipboard soldiers.

The major difference in handling between warships and merchantmen was that war crews, sitting at their crowded benches, could not spend the night aboard ship easily. To rest or cook, they needed to pitch camp ashore. Merchant freighters, on the other hand, could sail day and night.

Sheltered under the top decking, the off-duty crew could rest on mattresses and could feed from supplies aboard. Under proper conditions, a freighter might leave the shore behind and course out over the open sea; with a favoring wind, such a ship might reach between four and six knots, traveling 100 or more miles in 24 hours.

Because a merchant ship was capable of long-range travel, ancient Greek merchant voyages tended to be ambitious and dangerous. Shipwrecks were common—as suggested by vase paintings, written references, and modern underwater ARCHAEOLOGY. Many harbors had temples where mariners went to pray and sacrifice for a safe voyage. The main patron gods of seafaring were POSEIDON, ATHENA, APHRODITE, and CASTOR AND POLYDEUCES.

For safety, shipping and naval operations normally were confined to the season from May to mid-September, when Mediterranean weather tends to be sunny and calm. But even this period seemed too long to HESIOD (circa 700 B.C.), whose epic poem *Works and Days* mentions that seafaring is safe for only the 50 days following the summer solstice— roughly June 21 to mid-August. Only the extremes of war or greed could induce ships to put to sea during autumn or winter. The hazard of winter seafaring lay partly in violent storms, but also in reduced visibility due to rain, fog, and short daylight. The apostle Paul's shipwreck of A.D. 57 (described in the New Testament book *Acts of the Apostles,* Chapter 27) occurred because the skipper had risked sailing from CRETE after the season's end.

(See also CYPRUS; GREECE, GEOGRAPHY OF; MASSALIA; MINOAN CIVILIZATION; MYCENAEAN CIVILIZATION; PHOENICIA; WARFARE, NAVAL.)

Sicyon Largest (9,860 square miles) island of the Mediterranean, lying just west of the "toe" of ITALY. Sicily is shaped roughly like an isosceles triangle, with its base facing east.

Renowned in ancient times for its fertile coastlands, Sicily attracted waves of Greek settlers at the outset of the great colonizing epoch (beginning after 750 B.C.). The island became a major part of the Greek world, producing a dozen or so noteworthy Greek cities, particularly the Corinthian colony of SYRACUSE, which grew to be the greatest Greek city of the West (400s–200s B.C.). Syracuse and other Sicilian-Greek cities supplied precious grain for CORINTH and other populous mainland Greek cities.

Despite prosperity, Greek Sicily had a tragic history, full of social unrest within cities and conflicts between cities inhabited by DORIAN GREEKS and those inhabited by IONIAN GREEKS. But worst of all were the repeated wars with the non-Greek, Carthaginian settlers of western Sicily.

The name Sicily (Greek: Sikelia) commemorates the Sicels—a native, non-Greek people of the island's east coast, whose prime land at Syracuse and on the plain of Catania was seized by the early Greek colonists. Other native peoples included the Sicani, in the island's west-central region; and the Elymi, in the west. The relatively unsophisticated level of these peoples no doubt helped to attract early Greek settlers. (The Greeks tended to plant colonies where they knew they could subdue local inhabitants.)

Sicily's earliest Greek colonies—NAXOS (2), Syracuse, CATANA, and Leontini—arose circa 734–728 B.C. along the

island's 200-mile-long eastern coast. Among the coast's distinctive geographic features are volcanic Mt. Etna (over 11,000 feet tall) and the plain of Catania (whose fertility is due in part to volcanic lime, washed down from Etna's slopes). Toward the coast's southern end is the promontory of Syracuse, with its superb natural harbor and nearby farmland.

Most of the eastern coast was Ionian Greek, with the exception of Dorian Syracuse. But a Dorian bloc soon arose on Sicily's southern coast, with the founding of GELA (circa 688 B.C.) and ACRAGAS (circa 580 B.C.). After Syracuse, Acragas became the second most important city of Greek Sicily (400s B.C.).

Sicily's western side, meanwhile, had been occupied by settlers from the African-Phoenician city of CARTHAGE (which lay only about 135 miles southwest of Sicily). By about 500 B.C. Greeks and Carthaginians had settled into a bitter conflict that lasted over 250 years and monopolized the energies of Greek Sicily. The constant Carthaginian threat largely shaped the authoritarian nature of Sicilian Greek politics. Long after the age of TYRANTS had passed away in mainland Greece, Sicilian Greek cities were still relying on military tyrants who could promise protection against the hated Carthaginians. Foremost among such powerful rulers were the Syracusan tyrants: GELON (reigned circa 490–478 B.C.), his brother HIERON (1) (478–467 B.C.), DIONYSIUS (1) (circa 400–367 B.C.), and AGATHOCLES (317–289 B.C.). Under these men, Syracuse dominated the other Greek cities and several times came close to driving the Carthaginians from the island. At other times leaders from mainland Greece were called in to help the beleaguered Sicilian Greeks. For example, the Corinthian commander TIMOLEON (345–340 B.C.) defeated the Carthaginians in battle and gave the Greek cities new governments. King PYRRHUS of EPIRUS arrived and beat the Carthaginians (279 B.C.), then hurried away before exploiting his advantage.

The conquest of Sicily remained an elusive and dangerous dream for Syracuse, for Carthage, and for the mainland Greek city of ATHENS, whose attempt to capture Syracuse during the PELOPONNESIAN WAR proved a disaster (415–413 B.C.). It took the emerging might of Italian ROME to conquer Greeks and Carthaginians alike. Sicily became a battlefield between Rome and Carthage in the First Punic War (264–241 B.C.), before it passed to Roman control. A defiant Syracuse was besieged and captured by the Romans in 213–211 B.C., during the Second Punic War. Sicily was then made a province of the Roman Empire.

(See also COLONIZATION; CYCLOPS; HIMERA; PERSEPHONE; SELINUS; ZANCLE.)

Sicyon Important city of the northeast PELOPONNESE, about 15 miles west of CORINTH. Sicyon was located two miles inland, on a fertile coastal plain beside the Corinthian Gulf, at the foot of a lofty hill that served as the city's ACROPOLIS. The city had a mixed Dorian and Achaean population, having been founded (probably) from Dorian ARGOS, circa 1000 B.C. Supposedly Sicyon was named for its local growths of cucumbers (*sikuai*).

Sicyon was one of the first Greek cities to be seized by TYRANTS. The dynasty created circa 660 B.C. by the tyrant Orthagoras lasted for over a century and made Sicyon into a great power. Orthagoras' descendant CLEISTHENES (2) ruled circa 600–570 B.C., leading the First Sacred War against PHOCIS and later celebrating his daughter's wedding with Homeric magnificence. This era saw construction of the Sicyonians' treasury house at DELPHI, prominently occupying the start of the Sacred Way up to APOLLO's temple.

Under Cleisthenes, wealthy Sicyon was a center for manufacturing and art, particularly SCULPTURE and PAINTING. A Sicyonian poet, Egigenes, is said to have been a pioneer in the writing of "tragic choruses" in the early 500s B.C. The city's schools of art remained important for centuries; Sicyon's most famous artist was the sculptor Lysippus (circa 330 B.C.).

The Sicyonian tyranny was extinguished circa 550 B.C. by the Spartans. Sicyon became an OLIGARCHY and a Spartan ally. Sicyonians fought alongside the Spartans in the PERSIAN WARS (480–479 B.C.) and PELOPONNESIAN WAR (431–404 B.C.). In the mid-200s B.C. Sicyon's most famous son was the statesman and commander Aratus.

(See also ACHAEA; DORIAN GREEKS; THEATER.)

siege warfare See WARFARE, SIEGE.

Sigeum See HELLESPONT.

Silenus Mythical semihuman creature, distinguished by his horse ears, horse tail, pot belly, shaggy hair, bald head, and pug nose. Like the SATYRS, whom he resembled, Silenus was associated with the wine god DIONYSUS. On vase paintings of the 500s–400s B.C., Silenus was portrayed cavorting in the god's retinue or lustily pursuing the NYMPHS. Sometimes he was shown as several creatures (called by the plural, Silenoi or Sileni). A widespread Athenian joke of the late 400s B.C. claimed that Silenus resembled the living philosopher SOCRATES.

silver Precious metal in both ancient and modern times. Silver traditionally has been less prized than GOLD, partly because silver ore is more common and less malleable for shaping.

Throughout antiquity, silverwork was used for luxury items such as plates, goblets, statuary, and jewelry; it was particularly favored for cups and plates with repoussé work. More important, silver was the prime substance for Greek COINAGE (first appearing just after 600 B.C.) Even before coinage, silver was being used in ingot form for high-level exchange, in the monetary unit known as the TALENT.

Unlike gold, silver existed as a natural mineral deposit in mainland Greece. The publicly owned silver mines at Laurium, 15 miles south of ATHENS, played a large role in Athenian greatness in the 500s–400s B.C. The Laurium mines helped finance naval fleets and the social programs of the DEMOCRACY.

But the main supplier of raw silver for the Greek world was the north Aegean coast (in the non-Greek land of THRACE) and particularly Mt. Pangaeus, near the lower Strymon River. From there—where silver seems to have been available by panning in local rivers—the precious ore reached Greek hands by TRADE and eventually by conquest. In the 600s–500s B.C., Greek traders began operating out of THASOS, SAMOTHRACE, ABDERA, and AENUS, acquiring raw silver from local Thracian kings. From the Thracian shore, this silver—typically in the form of large, bowtie-shape ingots—would be shipped to markets in the Greek world or to foreign markets such as EGYPT and PHOENICIA. In this early era (650–480 B.C.), raw silver was one of the few goods that Greek traders could offer to the sophisticated Near Eastern markets.

During the mid-400s B.C., Mt. Pangaeus seems to have come under control of imperial Athens, through the Athenian colony at AMPHIPOLIS. In the mid-300s B.C. the region fell to the cash-hungry Macedonian king PHILIP II. Other sources of raw silver included non-Greek Asian kingdoms such as LYDIA and Phrygia, fabled for their wealth. Another source, circa 600–500 B.C., was the Celtic kingdom in southern Spain known as Tartessus (the Tarshish of the Bible). To this distant domain sailed Greek traders from SAMOS and PHOCAEA.

In the HELLENISTIC AGE (300–150 B.C.), silver became more plentiful among the Greeks, due to the formerly Persian-owned mines and treasure hordes acquired by ALEXANDER THE GREAT. The silver mines of Thrace, Asia Minor, and Mesopotamia made possible the beautiful, large-denomination coins of the Hellenistic Greek kings.

Simonides Lyric poet (circa 556–468 B.C.) from the island of Ceos, in the CYCLADES. Over his long lifetime, Simonides enjoyed success with many genres of poetry. He was famous for his epitaphs written to commemorate the Greek dead in the PERSIAN WARS (490–479 B.C.). He developed the choral song known as the victory ode (epinikion), thereby in effect clearing the way for his younger and greater contemporary, the Theban poet PINDAR. The only poems by Simonides that survive complete are epigrams—short poems in elegiac verse, written to be carved in stone. Fragments of his victory odes and his dirges exist, but other categories are largely lost, including Simonides' dithyrambs—narrative poems on mythological topics, performed by choruses.

Simonides' work was admired in the ancient world for its clarity, word choice, and sympathy for human transcience and suffering. His simple language went right to the heart—particularly in its expressions of sorrow—and was considered more effective than the grandiose phrasings of other great poets such as AESCHYLUS.

Simonides was also the first poet to work for hire—that is, to compose poetry for a one-time fee from successive patrons rather than in a permanent position in the retinue of some wealthy man. Simonides was said to be fond of money and shrewd in business dealings. He seems to have had an affable, worldly personality.

Ceos—where Simonides, son of Leoprepes, was born into an upper-class family—was an Ionian-ethnic island, 15 miles off the Athenian coast. After gaining repute for his victory odes, Simonides was summoned to ATHENS (circa 525 B.C.) by Hipparchus, the brother and cultural minister of the Athenian tyrant HIPPIAS (1). There Simonides enjoyed high payments from Hipparchus, whose majestic court hosted another famous poet, ANACREON.

At Athens in these years, Simonides surely wrote some of his many dithyrambs, now lost. Late in life Simonides set up an inscription commemorating his 56 victories in dithyramb contests at Athens; the inscription mentions that he himself taught the choruses, which were composed of men.

Simonides left Athens around 514–510 B.C., as the tyranny crumbled. He traveled to THESSALY, and there found employ with the wealthy Aleaud and Scopad clans. But his stay ended after the Scopads were decimated by the collapsing roof of a banquet hall. The disaster later inspired Simonides to write a poem containing one of his much-admired reflections on the brevity of human happiness: "Since you are mortal, never say what tomorrow will bring nor how long a man may be happy. For the darting of the dragonfly is not so swift as change of fortune."

By the early 490s B.C., Simonides, then approaching 60, was back in Athens, his former intimacy with the tyrants apparently pardoned. Amid the great events of the Persian Wars he found a new calling as the poet laureate of Greece. After the Athenian victory at MARATHON (490 B.C.), the Athenians honored their dead with an epitaph by Simonides, chosen over one submitted by the young poet Aeschylus (himself an Athenian who had fought at the battle). According to the story, the Athenians decided that Simonides' poem conveyed a keener sympathy.

In 479 B.C., after the invasion by the Persian king XERXES had been repelled, Simonides was again commissioned to write patriotic verse. He produced choral odes about the sea battles at ARTEMISIUM and SALAMIS (1) and several much-admired epitaphs for the Greek dead.

In 476 B.C., at age 80, Simonides left Athens again, this time for the grand court of the tyrant HIERON (1) of SYRACUSE, in SICILY. Simonides' departure might have been related to the political downfall at Athens of his friend THEMISTOCLES. At Syracuse, Simonides—with his nephew and protégé, the poet BACCHYLIDES—is said to have indulged in a feud with Pindar, who was also in Sicily at that time. Another tale claims that Hieron's wife once asked Simonides which is better, to acquire wisdom or wealth. "Wealth," the poet replied. "For I see the wise sitting at the doorsteps of the rich."

Simonides died in Sicily in 468 B.C. and was buried at ACRAGAS.

(See also IONIAN GREEKS; LYRIC POETRY; THEATER; THERMOPYLAE.)

Sinope

Sinope Prosperous Greek city on the BLACK SEA. Founded circa 625 B.C. by colonists from MILETUS, Sinope (modern Sinop, in Turkey) was located halfway along the north coast of ASIA MINOR, where the coast bulges advantageously northward. The city was built at the neck of a lofty promontory with a fine double harbor—the only first-rate harbor on the Black Sea's southern shore.

Isolated by mountains inland, Sinope depended for its prosperity on seaborne TRADE. The city was probably an export center for goods shipped in from other Greek ports of the Black Sea. Such goods would include the metals of Asia Minor—GOLD, SILVER, IRON, and copper and tin for BRONZE-making—as well as "Sinopic earth" (cinnabar, or red mercuric sulfide, used for making a prized red dye).

Sinope lay 220 miles due south of the eastern Crimean peninsula, which was home to PANTICAPAEUM and other Greek seaports; the shipping run between Sinope and the Crimea was a vital link in the Greek navigation of the Black Sea.

Sinope founded its own colonies, farther east on the Black Sea coast. Chief among these daughter cities was Trapezus ("the table," named for a mountain landmark), which is now the Turkish city of Trabzon. Unlike mountain-girt Sinope, Trapezus had access to the Asia Minor interior and the land route to the Near East.

Sinope probably offered nominal submission to the Persian kings who had conquered Asia Minor by 545 B.C. The city was being ruled a Greek dictator in the mid-400s B.C., when an Athenian fleet under the commander PERICLES arrived on a Black Sea expedition. The Athenians established DEMOCRACY at Sinope and settled Athenian colonists there. The city may have henceforth had some trading agreement with ATHENS, but it never became a member of the DELIAN LEAGUE.

Occupied briefly by Persian troops in around 375 B.C., Sinope was liberated by ALEXANDER THE GREAT's conquest of the Persian Empire (334–323 B.C.). The city seems to have remained independent of the several Hellenistic kingdoms that subsequently dominated Asia Minor, but was captured by the Iranian-ethnic kingdom of Pontus in 183 B.C. and became the Pontic capital. After the Romans' conquest of Pontus (63 B.C.), Sinope became a city of the Roman Empire.

Sinope was a center of Greek culture in the East, with grand temples, markets, and a tradition of learning. Its most famous citizen was the Cynic philosopher DIOGENES (mid-300s B.C.).

Sirens

Sirens In Greek MYTH the Seirēnes were sea witches who lured sailors to their deaths. The sailors, hearing the Sirens' enchanting song, would land their ship and go ashore, where the Sirens would kill them.

The Sirens are first mentioned in book 12 of HOMER's epic poem the *Odyssey* (written down circa 750 B.C.). There they are two in number; their appearance is never described. The seafaring hero ODYSSEUS defies the Sirens by plugging his crewmen's ears with beeswax beforehand. However, wishing to hear the song himself, he has his men bind him to the ship's mast. As the crew rows past the Sirens' island, Odysseus is bewitched by the song and pleads, unheeded, to be untied. Eventually the ship passes out of earshot. The Sirens, whose name may mean "Scorchers" or "Binders," are among several female threats whom Odysseus enounters on his voyage home.

Later generations of Greeks named 11 Sirens and pictured them as half woman, half bird. These Sirens resemble other winged, malevolent, female creatures of Greek myth—the HARPIES and the FURIES.

Sisyphus

Sisyphus One of the three infamous sinners—betrayers of the gods' friendship and thus eternally damned—encountered by the hero ODYSSEUS in book 11 of HOMER's epic poem the *Odyssey*. In his visit to the Underworld, Odysseus observes Sisyphus' punishment, which is to roll a great boulder up a hill but, on nearing the top, to have it slip backward past him, back down the slope. Sisyphus must pursue this frustrating and exhausting labor forever. In theory, his punishment would end if he could ever reach the summit and push the boulder down the *far* slope, but the vindictive gods will never allow this to happen.

The *Odyssey* does not mention Sisyphus' original offense, but later writers describe him as the conniving founder of the city of CORINTH. In exchange for receiving a perpetual water source for his city's citadel, Sisyphus informed the god Asopus that the great god ZEUS had abducted Asopus' daughter. When angry Zeus sent the god HADES to fetch Sisyphus to the Underworld, the hero outwitted Hades and tied him up, thus unnaturally stopping all death in the world. Eventually the gods captured Sisyphus.

Sisyphus was a hero of the "trickster" type—a category that included the god HERMES, the Titan PROMETHEUS, and Odysseus himself (sometimes said to be Sisyphus' illegitimate son).

(See also AFTERLIFE; TANTALUS.)

Skepticism   Greek school of thought which believed that no positive knowledge is possible, since everything is in a constant state of flux. This notion appears early in Greek philosophy, in statements of HERACLITUS (circa 500 B.C.) and in the relativism of the SOPHISTS (latter 400s B.C.), who maintained that any argument could be opposed by an equally true counterargument. The Athenian philosopher SOCRATES (469–399 B.C.) was famous for his statement "All I know is that I know nothing." Socrates' younger contemporary Cratylus became convinced that all communication is impossible, since the original meanings of words are inevitably altered by changes in the speaker, the listener, and the words themselves. According to legend, Cratylus therefore refused to discuss anything, preferring to wiggle his finger when addressed.

The founding of a formal school of Skepticism was the work of Pyrrhon (circa 363–273 B.C.), a native of ELIS (in the western PELOPONNESE) who had accompanied ALEXANDER THE GREAT on his conquest of the Persian Empire (334–323 B.C.). Centered at Elis, the Skeptics (Skeptikoi, from the word Greek *skepsis:* "perception" or "doubt") withheld judgment on all matters, stating no positive doctrines but accepting tentatively the outward appearances of things for the sake of day-to-day living. This outlook was supposed to bring the Skeptic to the desired state of imperturbability (*ataraxia*).

Alongside STOICISM and EPICUREANISM, Skepticism became one of the major philosophies of the HELLENISTIC AGE (circa 300–150 B.C.). It had its greatest influence at the ACADEMY, the prestigious philosophical school founded at ATHENS by PLATO circa 385 B.C. Skepticism was introduced as a study at the Academy in the mid-200s B.C., and for nearly the next two centuries it provided the basis of much Academic thought. Rejecting many of their founder Plato's doctrines, the Academics of these years saw Skepticism as connecting back to Socrates' statement about knowing nothing. They sought to prove the impossibility of positive knowledge and also used Skepticism to attack their rivals the Stoics, whose beliefs placed faith in sensory perception.

slaves   Slave labor was a fundamental part of the ancient Greek economy. No less a thinker than ARISTOTLE (circa 330 B.C.) believed that the use of slaves, although lamentable, was unavoidable; to him, a slave was "a living tool." Only the mystical PLATO (circa 360 B.C.) imagined a society where slavery would be abolished (and where WOMEN would be equal citizens). Unfortunately, we know little about ancient Greek slavery; no extant ancient Greek writer discusses it at length, and modern scholars must rely on a patchwork of references in ancient Greek poetry, written history, stage comedy, and courtroom and political speeches. Archaeological evidence, such as tombstone inscriptions, add valuable details. Inevitably—as in all studies of ancient Greek society—the available information focuses on the rich and literate city of ATHENS, especially from the 300s B.C. onward.

Generally, a slave is a person without civil rights, owned as a possession, usually by another individual. The owner might have the power of life and death over the slave. (However, at Athens an owner could not legally kill a slave at will, but needed state permission.) To his or her master, the slave owes all labor and service—including, if required, sexual favors. In exchange, the master shelters, clothes, and feeds his slaves, just as he would be expected to care for his dogs or cattle. The origins of this brutal institution are lost in prehistory; certainly slavery was not confined to the Greeks. In HOMER's epic poem the *Iliad* (written down circa 750 B.C.), slaves are shown to be war captives; the proud Trojans' preordained fate is death or slavery at the Greeks' hands.

War was a major source of slaves. A defeated people would face slavery at the victors' discretion. These enslaved captives could be either Greeks or non-Greeks. To take one of many examples: After subduing the defiant Greek island of MELOS in 416 B.C., during the PELOPONNESIAN WAR, the Athenians put to death the entire adult male population and sold the women and children into slavery. Rather than being transported back to the conquerors' home city, such captives probably were sold on the spot to slave traders, who followed every Greek army. These traders were businessmen, with access to cash and transport, who would bring their newly purchased slaves to some major market for resale. The east Greek states of CHIOS and EPHESUS were important slave markets in the 400s B.C.; other commercial centers, such as Athens and CORINTH, played their roles.

The fate of war captives was surely ghastly. Families must have been broken up. The demand for adult male slaves (purchased for heavy labor) was far less than the demand for women, teenagers, and children (purchased for domestic duties). Children were especially prized as being pliant, physically pleasing, and long-term investments, but the mothers surely were often left behind on the auction block.

In times of peace, slaves might originate outside the Greek world. References in Homer, along with other documents, show Greek pirates of the 700s B.C. swooping down on the coast of ASIA MINOR or THRACE to carry away captives. Thracian slaves are mentioned regularly in Greek literature, and the Greek colonies founded on Thrace's Aegean coast—such as ABDERA and AMPHIPOLIS—probably were active in acquiring slaves. This was done with the help of the feuding Thracian chieftains of the interior, who would bring their war captives to the Greek town, to sell.

In Greek cities the "exposure" of unwanted infants, particularly girls, was a legal, common practice. Exposed infants—that is, babies abandoned outdoors by their parents—automatically assumed slave status and would become the property of whoever rescued them. However, Greek cities typically had laws forbidding, within the city, the enslavement of any recognized citizen, whether child or adult. The Athenian lawgiver SOLON (circa 594 B.C.) wrote famous legislation prohibiting the enslavement of any Athenian for debt.

Except for SPARTA—with its large numbers of HELOTS, or serfs—Greek cities tended to depend heavily on slave labor. The Athenian state-run SILVER mines at Laurium may have employed as many as 30,000 slaves in the 400s–300s B.C. Modern ARCHAEOLOGY has revealed the hellish work conditions at Laurium, where slaves, including children, worked 10-hour shifts in black crawl-tunnels with poor ventilation; it seems to have been cheaper to let the workers sicken and die than to improve conditions. Smaller and less gruesome were privately owned factories, where skilled slaves produced beds, knives, and other household goods. The largest such operation now known of was an Athenian shield factory, owned by the family of the orator LYSIAS, which employed 120 slaves.

Some Athenian slaves probably worked semiindependently of their owners. A slave might practice a trade or keep a shop, delivering the profits to his master; a slave might be bailiff of a country estate, overseeing the slave farmhands and selling produce for the absentee owner. Slaves might be educated men, serving as clerks or tutors. Such trusted workers might look forward to the day when their master would free them (perhaps in his legal last will). At Athens, a freed slave took on the status of a metic, or resident alien.

Slave-population numbers are difficult to guess. Modern estimates suggest that, at the outbreak of the PELOPONNESIAN WAR (431 B.C.), Athenian territory was home to slightly over 100,000 slaves; this figure is probably equivalent to the number of nonslaves living there at that time. The ratio of 1:1 implies that slave ownership went fairly far down the social ladder. At the bottom of the scale might be (for example) a cobbler owning one slave to assist him in the shop and to do domestic work in the evening. Purely domestic slaves, bringing in little or no income, were a sign of wealth; the richest Athenian families might have 50 household slaves. No doubt many Athenians were too poor to afford even one slave, but this was viewed as a hardship.

With a 1:1 ratio, the Athenian slave population seems ominously large; yet there never was a slave revolt comparable to that led by Spartacus against the Romans in 73 B.C. The closest we come to this is the Athenian historian THUCYDIDES' (1) statement that 30,000 skilled slaves ran away from Athens during the latter part of the Peloponnesian War (413–404 B.C.). Reasons for this relative lack of unrest include the diverse origins and languages of the slaves, and their piecemeal segregation by owners and duties. In fact, when a Greek army marched to war, each HOPLITE had a servant (probably a slave) to carry armor

and supplies. This would seem to provide a golden opportunity for revolt or escape, but the slaves lacked the motive and organization.

(See also METICS; NICIAS; PROSTITUTES.)

Smyrna   See ARCHAEOLOGY; IONIA.

Socrates   Athenian philosopher who lived 469–399 B.C. Although Socrates left no writings, he is of landmark importance in Western thought. By his example, PHILOSOPHY was turned away from its prior emphasis on natural SCIENCE and became directed more toward questions of ethics—that is, the right conduct of life. In the words of the Roman thinker Cicero (circa 50 B.C.), "Socrates was the first to call philosophy down from the sky."

Socrates profoundly influenced his pupil PLATO. Socrates' central conclusions—that happiness depends solely on living a moral life, and that moral virtue is equivalent to knowledge and is therefore teachable—became the spring-

Socrates' unhandsome appearance was a source of jokes among his contemporary Athenians, who compared him with the grotesque mythical figure Silenus. This portrait comes from a marble bust of the Roman era, thought to be copied from a bronze statue made by the renowned Athenian sculptor Lysippus, circa 330 B.C., 70 years after the philosopher's death.

board for Plato's elaborate theory of reality and system of ethics. Socrates' equation of virtue with knowledge led to the daring corollary that evil is ignorance and hence unintentional. According to Socrates, the evildoer acts mistakenly in harming his or her own soul.

Socrates himself taught no doctrine, claiming simply, "I know nothing." This professed ignorance was denoted by the Greek word *eironeia:* that is, the famous Socratic irony. Unlike other philosophers, he never founded a school or charged fees for lessons. At ATHENS he attracted a following of young, aristocratic men, with whom he would dispute ethical or political issues. Since he took no money, his goal was evidently to prepare these students for public office by teaching them to think for themselves. His "Socratic method" consisted of asking questions, particularly in pursuit of definitions. For example: "You say that this man is a better citizen than his opponent? Let us consider therefore what we mean by 'good citizen.' " This question-and-answer process forced the respondent to examine his own preconceptions, in a search for general truths.

Socrates' disputations and skeptical outlook led him to be associated—unfairly, from his viewpoint—with those well-paid teachers of intellectual skills, the SOPHISTS. One famous sophist, PROTAGORAS of ABDERA, who taught at Athens circa 455–415 B.C., is recorded as believing that expertise (Greek: *aretē*) in most fields is teachable. Protagoras surely inspired Socrates' similar but more profound view that moral virtue (likewise denoted by the Greek word *aretē*) is teachable.

Among Socrates' well-heeled students were two destined for great importance in Athenian politics: the brilliant but erratic ALCIBIADES and the extreme right-winger CRITIAS (who was killed in 403 B.C. while trying to abolish Athenian DEMOCRACY). The link with Critias was probably responsible for Socrates' death. In 399 B.C. the 70-year-old philosopher was prosecuted for corrupting the youth (a charge implicitly referring to Critias and Alcibiades) and for impiety. After making a flamboyantly nonconciliatory defense speech, Socrates was found guilty by the jury of 501 Athenians and was sentenced to die by being given poison. The famous prison scene, in which Socrates discusses the soul's immortality with his visitors before drinking the fatal hemlock, is recounted in Plato's dialogue *Phaedo.*

Information about Socrates comes mainly from two sources. Plato's fictional dialogues contain much biographical information about Socrates while also foisting onto him Plato's own more complex philosophical theories. Here the insoluble question arises: What aspects of Plato's Socrates show us the real Socrates, and how much is just a mask for Plato's own thought? Probably a more biographical Socrates is portrayed in Plato's early work (such as the *Crito* or *Euthyphro,*) while the Socrates in the *Republic* and later dialogues is a more fictionalized character, who discusses concepts that the real Socrates never explored. The other source is XENOPHON, a stolid Athenian soldier and historian who was one of Socrates' disciples and who wrote about him in three nonfiction memoirs, *Memorabilia, Symposium,* and *Apology.* (The latter two titles also belong to works by Plato.) That Socrates could be the beloved mentor of two such different people as Plato and Xenophon is itself revealing. Other information comes from ARISTOPH-

ANES' stage comedy *Clouds* (performed 423 B.C.), in which a crackpot scientist named Socrates operates a "Thinking Shop." Clearly the real Socrates was a dynamic personality who fascinated friend and foe alike. When one contemporary Athenian asked the oracle at DELPHI who was the wisest of all men, the answer came back "Socrates."

He was born into the Athenian middle class, the son of a stonecutter or sculptor named Sophroniscus. Socrates came of age during the political primacy of PERICLES, when Athens reached its zenith as a radical democracy and imperial naval power—twin developments that alienated many conservative Athenians. As a youth, Socrates supposedly studied under a disciple of the philosopher ANAXAGORAS, but became discouraged by the emphasis on physics and cosmology rather than ethics.

During the PELOPONNESIAN WAR between Athens and SPARTA (431–404 B.C.), Socrates served as foot soldier in the POTIDAEA campaign (432–430 B.C.), at the disastrous Battle of Delium (424 B.C.), and at AMPHIPOLIS (422 B.C.), by which time he would have been about 47 years old. On campaign, he distinguished himself by his physical endurance and courage. One anecdote describes Socrates striding calmly amid the Athenian retreat from Delium, defying the pursuing enemy CAVALRY.

In later life he repeatedly resisted the political hysteria of Athens in crisis. In 406 B.C., while serving a citizen's normal duty on the council panel to prepare the agenda for the Athenian ASSEMBLY, Socrates refused to go along with an illegal motion ordering a group trial for six commanders charged with negligence after the sea battle of Arginusae. In 403 B.C. Socrates defied his old pupil Critias, who had seized power in the coup of the THIRTY TYRANTS: Brought before the Thirty, Socrates refused to help them arrest a certain intended victim. No doubt Socrates himself would have become a victim of the Thirty, had not their reign of terror soon ended. Instead, Socrates was denounced by prominent accusers after the restoration of democracy.

That Socrates should have been prosecuted under the democracy is significant. An original thinker who defied convention, Socrates was known for his antidemocratic sentiments. As Xenophon's memoirs make clear, he criticized the democracy's inability to entrust its government to the most apt and expert people. Without advocating revolution or dictatorship, Socrates seems to have favored a meritocracy, with power entrusted to a worthy ruling class. Such beliefs—although purely theoretical—must have seemed damning after Critias' right-wing coup. Following the Thirty's downfall, the Athenians' wrath turned against Socrates.

Across the centuries, Socrates' eccentric personality communicates itself. Although magnetic in character, he was physically unattractive in middle age—balding, pug-nosed, and paunchy. His contemporaries humorously compared him to the mythical figure SILENUS. Socrates was famous for his austerity: Impervious to cold and fatigue, he almost always went barefoot, even over frozen winter ground at the siege of Potidaea.

He had three sons by his wife, Xanthippe (whom several sources describe as a bad-tempered shrew). Socrates may have practiced a stonecutter's trade, like his father, but he evidently spent most of his time at the Athenian sports grounds where educated men of leisure congregated. There he would conduct semipublic debates with his followers or rivals.

Socrates' disciples (all male) included several of the most glamorous youths of the day in the homosexual society of aristocratic Athens. A homosexual ambiance pervades many of Plato's dialogues, such as the *Symposium*, where the topic is love and where the mutual attraction between Socrates and Alcibiades is discussed. But as so much is said about his indifference to physical needs, it remains unclear whether Socrates actually was intimate with these young men.

(See also GYMNASIUM; HOMOSEXUALITY; LAWS AND LAW COURTS; SKEPTICISM.)

Solon   Athenian statesman who in the early 500s B.C. drafted a new code of law, which averted a revolution at ATHENS and laid the foundations for Athenian DEMOCRACY. Solon's democratic reforms came at a time of major class tension: between the nobles and the increasingly confident middle class, as well as between the country landowners and the tenant farmers who paid rent under onerous conditions. Solon alleviated the burdens of the poor farmers and, at the upper end of the social scale, broke the nobles' traditional monopoly on political power.

Lawgiver, poet, and patriot, Solon saved Athens from civil war and dictatorship, and laid the foundations for Athenian democracy, circa 594 B.C. His likeness here is based on a marble bust of the Roman era.

Later generations revered Solon as one of the SEVEN SAGES of Greece. The texts of his laws, carved into wooden tablets, were kept on display in the Athenian AGORA. These laws supplied the code at Athens for nearly 200 years, until the legal revisions of 410–400 B.C.; even afterward, the Athenians still called their code "the laws of Solon."

Solon was also a poet. A number of his verses are preserved in two later written works—ARISTOTLE's *Constitution of Athens* (circa 340 B.C.) and PLUTARCH's biography of Solon (circa A.D. 100). But because Solon is the earliest important figure in Athenian history, much of his life and work remain unclear to us.

Born around 630 B.C. into an aristocratic Athenian family, Solon first distinguished himself in a war against MEGARA (1). His patriotism won the respect of his fellow citizens, and they asked him to serve as arbitrator and lawgiver, to avert civil war. It was probably in 594 B.C., the year in which he served as chief ARCHON, that Solon instituted his famous reforms.

The most grievous social problem facing Athens at that time was the plight of the rural poor in ATTICA, the 1,000-square-mile district surrounding Athens. It seems that the rich landowners were crushing the tenant farmers who paid part of their produce as rent. The law allowed loans to be secured on the person of the borrower; that is, defaulting debtors were liable to be sold as SLAVES. Tenant farmers who forfeited on their rent (in bad harvest years, e.g.) were faced with catastrophe, for both themselves and their families.

Meanwhile, in the city, the better-off commoners had their own grievances, directed against the government. Citizens of the middle class—who supplied the backbone of Athens' army, serving as HOPLITE infantry—were chafing at being excluded from government. At this time, Athens was still an ARISTOCRACY. All political power was held by a few ancient, upper-class families (of which Solon was a member). Only aristocrats could hold executive posts or be admitted to the powerful decision-making council and supreme court known as the AREOPAGUS. All of the law courts, overseen by aristocrats, showed a strong upper-class bias; the existing law code, devised around 620 B.C. by the nobleman DRACO, was mainly repressive.

By the early 500s B.C. there was fear at Athens that these two aggrieved classes—the peasantry and the hoplite class—would join forces and place a dictator, or *turannos*, on the throne. TYRANTS had seized power at CORINTH and Megara, and Athens itself had seen a failed coup by a would-be tyrant named CYLON in around 620 B.C. In this volatile atmosphere Athens turned to Solon, whom all parties trusted. He could have exploited the situation to make himself tyrant; but he was a greater man than that.

Solon rescued the tenant farmers and other poor Athenians by forbidding that loans be secured on the borrower's person—henceforth no Athenian could be enslaved for debt—and Solon cancelled all such existing debts. "I plucked up the marker-stones," he declares in one poem, referring to the hated signs standing at repossessed farms. He also freed Athenians who had been enslaved, bringing home many who had been sold abroad. Solon's poverty-relief measures were known as the *seisachtheia*, "the shaking off of burdens."

Solon overhauled the crude Draconian law code and created political changes that broke the aristocrats' monopoly on power. He devised a new system of social ranking, with four citizen classes based entirely on income level. This new emphasis on income worked against the traditional emphasis on noble birth. The upper classes might still be full of rich aristocrats, but now other men—commoners—could be admitted to these classes. Since a man's social rank determined his eligibility for various political offices, this was a significant democratic change.

Solon enfranchised the lowest income class, the Athenian peasants, admitting them as citizens and allowing them to vote in the ASSEMBLY. He created a new deliberative COUNCIL, of 400 members, open to the upper three income classes; the council members served for one year, after being chosen by lot. This new council, very influential in that it helped prepare the agenda for the assembly, served to counterbalance the old aristocratic Areopagus. Also, it was probably Solon who set up the Athenian "people's court," to which any citizen had the right of appeal; this assured that a defendant could be heard by a jury of his peers rather than by a court consisting of nobles.

The principal beneficiaries of Solon's reforms were the rich commoners—nonaristocratic landowners, traders, and manufacturers who could now take their place in Athens' upper classes and enjoy greater political voice. Solon was not a complete democrat; he was more of a timocrat. As his poetry makes clear, he believed that the populace should be governed by a worthy, fair-minded ruling class.

Certain embittered verses by Solon indicate that his reforms came as a disappointment to both extremes: The nobles resented their losses, and the poorer classes were angry that Solon had stopped short of redistributing the land. Having made the Athenians promise to obey his laws unchanged for 10 years, Solon left Athens to travel (some say) to EGYPT and LYDIA. Returning home, he lived long enough to see his kinsman PISISTRATUS make himself tyrant in Athens (circa 561 B.C.)—the very outcome that Solon had tried to prevent. But Solon's laws and political apparatus survived in Athens (the tyrants did not) and set the stage for CLEISTHENES' (1) reforms (508 B.C.) and the radical democracy of the 400s B.C.

(See also LAWS AND LAW COURTS.)

sophists *Sophistai* (experts or professors) were itinerant teachers who, in the latter 400s B.C., went from city to city in the Greek world, tutoring young men in disputation and other intellectual skills. These lessons, for which the sophists charged hefty fees, were designed to help students achieve practical success as lawyers, politicians, speechwriters and so on. The visiting sophists caused a cultural sensation at the wealthy, intellectual city of ATHENS, but they also earned a reputation for amoral cleverness; the hallmark of a sophist was the ability to argue any question from two opposing sides. The modern English word *sophistry* (meaning "clever but false reasoning") retains the negative associations of this rationalistic movement.

Yet not all sophists were amoral. The best were genuine thinkers, breaking new intellectual ground and answering a need for "college-level" EDUCATION in their day—the sophist Hippias of ELIS, for instance, taught a method

of memory training, among many offered courses (circa 430 B.C.).

The earliest and most famous sophist was PROTAGORAS of ABDERA (circa 445 B.C.); another prominent one was Prodicus of Ceos (circa 430 B.C.). The orator GORGIAS of Leontini (circa 427 B.C.) was associated with the sophists, due to the ingenuity of the arguments he used in public speaking. And in the eyes of many Athenians, the philosopher SOCRATES (469–399 B.C.) was a sophist, on account of his question-and-answer method of inquiry.

Sophocles   Athenian tragic playwright who lived circa 496–406 B.C. Sophocles is reckoned among the three great classical tragedians (the other two being AESCHYLUS and EURIPIDES). His work has been seen as Greek tragedy's high point, wherein the separate requirements of plot and character are fused most successfully. He is said to have written 123 plays, of which only seven survive today;

Sophocles was—to modern taste, at least—the finest of the Athenian tragedians. In his day he was also a well-liked figure, elected several times by his countrymen to high office, including one or two generalships. His human insight and sophistication are suggested in this likeness, from a bronze bust of Hellenistic or Roman date.

among these is the play that the philosopher and critic ARISTOTLE admired most of any Greek tragedy, *Oedipus the King.*

SOPHOCLES ("famed for wisdom") was born the son of a rich manufacturer at the Athenian DEME of Colonus—the beauty of which he would commemorate in a famous choral ode in his tragedy *Oedipus at Colonus.* His life spanned the near century of Athenian greatness. Growing up during the PERSIAN WARS, he partook of the spirit of Athenian confidence following the miraculous victory over the Persians. After the Greek sea victory at SALAMIS (1) (480 B.C.), the teenage Sophocles was honored with the assignment of dancing and singing, naked and anointed, at the trophy monument. To win this commission he must have been a performer of considerable talent and beauty. Supposedly, in his earlier plays he occasionally appeared in roles onstage, but gave that up due to a weak voice.

At about age 28 Sophocles won his first tragedy-competition, at the major annual drama festival known as the City Dionysia (468 B.C.). We know that one of the playwrights whom he defeated this year was the well-established Aeschylus, but the centuries have not preserved the three Sophoclean tragedies (and one satyr-play) that comprised this winning entry. Sophocles went on to win a total of 24 victories in over 65 more years of writing. Of the seven times (only) when he failed to win first prize, he always took second prize, never third. This remarkable record shows that Sophocles was the most successful tragedian of his day; Euripides, by contrast, won first place only five times. Relatedly, Sophocles was highly popular as a social figure. Several ancient writings testify to his charming personality and many friends—who included the historian HERODOTUS and the Athenian statesman CIMON.

In the development of Greek THEATER, Sophocles is credited by ancient writers with making several changes in the way tragedy was performed. Most important, he raised the number of speaking actors from two to three—which greatly increased the possible number of speaking parts, since an actor could play multiple roles. Sophocles supposedly ended the custom of presenting tragedies as linked trilogies, in favor of presenting three tragedies on unrelated topics. And he is said to have increased the size of the chorus from 12 to 15 men and to have developed the use of painted backdrops as scenery.

Outside the theater, Sophocles played a substantial role in Athenian public life prior to and during the PELOPONNE-SIAN WAR (431–404 B.C.). He was devoted to ATHENS, and—unlike Aeschylus, Euripides, and other artists—he refused all lucrative invitations to visit other cities of the Greek world. In 443 B.C. Sophocles was elected to the office of treasurer of the DELIAN LEAGUE. In 441 B.C., reportedly in recognition of his play *Antigone,* he was elected for the following year as a general of the Athenian armed forces. Under PERICLES' senior command, General Sophocles served in the campaign against the rebellious island of SAMOS. Possibly (we do not know for sure) Sophocles was later elected as general a second time.

In 420 B.C. Sophocles was active in developing the god ASCLEPIUS' cult at Athens, which may mean that he helped establish a public hospital. In 413 B.C., amid the state emergency following the Athenian military disaster at SYR-ACUSE, the Athenians appointed Sophocles, age 83, to a special executive post.

Sophocles married twice and we hear of two sons. One of them became a successful writer of tragedies, as did one of Sophocles' grandsons. Like other Greek men of his era, Sophocles may have pursued a private life that we would call bisexual. An anecdote in the memoirs of the writer ION (2) describes Sophocles relaxing at a SYMPOSIUM during the Samian military campaign: Sophocles coaxed a kiss from a handsome slave boy, then commented to the other guests, "So you see, I am not so bad a strategist as Pericles believes." Another famous quotation is preserved in the philosopher PLATO's treatise *The Republic:* When Sophocles in old age was asked if he was still able to have sex with a woman, he replied that he had happily escaped from his sex urge, "as from a cruel and insane master."

In about 406 B.C., after Euripides died, the 90-year-old Sophocles presented his chorus dressed in mourning, to commemorate his dead rival. Soon afterward Sophocles died, and he was remembered in ARISTOPHANES' comedy *Frogs* (405 B.C.), which is set in the Underworld: "He was a good fellow up there and now he's a good fellow down here."

The first performance dates for most of Sophocles' seven existing tragedies are unknown. But the following sequence is plausible: *Ajax* (performed perhaps circa 450–445 B.C.), *Antigone* (perhaps circa 442 B.C.), *The Women of Trachis* (perhaps circa 429–420 B.C.), *Oedipus the King* (perhaps circa 429–420 B.C.), *Electra* (perhaps circa 418–410 B.C.), *Philoctetes* (409 B.C.), and *Oedipus at Colonus* (performed in 401 B.C., after Sophocles' death). These tragedies survived because they were chosen in later antiquity to be taught in schools. Of the lost plays, the titles of many are known and there exist some fragments of text; apparently about a third of them were drawn from legends of the TROJAN WAR. All of Sophocles' plays, in keeping with the custom of the day, retold tales already familiar from EPIC POETRY and other sources.

A brief description of a few of the plays must suffice here. *The Women of Trachis* presents the horrible death of the hero HERACLES, poisoned by a venom-smeared robe given to him by his innocent wife, Deineira (who wrongly believes the robe to be a magic charm to reclaim her husband's love). The play is named for the characters portrayed by the chorus: local women in the region of central Greece where Heracles legendarily met his end. The action emphasizes Heracles' agony in death and the tragic irony that the world's mightiest hero, vanquisher of monsters, should die at the unintending hands of his gentle, loving, naive wife.

Oedipus the King and *Antigone* are today among the most accessible and widely read of all existing Greek tragedies. *Oedipus* is often misunderstood as the tragedy of a man undone by arrogance, or *hubris.* But, like much of Sophocles' work, the play is really about the limits of human knowledge and power. The Theban king OEDIPUS, at the play's outset, seems as blessed as a human can be: young, wise, powerful, just, beloved by his people. By the play's end he is blind, accursed, and homeless; his prior happiness has been revealed as an illusion. Unlike certain other Greek tragic heroes, Oedipus onstage does not do anything evil or foolhardy to bring on the gods' wrath. Although he does show pride and anger early in the play, these do not lead to bad action—rather, Oedipus' destructive actions lie buried, unbeknownst to him, in the past. *Oedipus the King* presents his gradual discovery of his own calamity; ironically, it is Oedipus' intelligence and perseverance that bring about this discovery.

The tightly plotted play opens with King Oedipus' city of THEBES ravaged by plague and famine; the oracle at DELPHI has revealed that the land lies under a curse because the murderer of the prior king, Laius, has not been punished. Since the killer's identity is unknown, Oedipus vows to discover it. The blind seer TIRESIAS is summoned for questioning. The ensuing scene is perhaps the finest in all extant Greek tragedy. As Oedipus grows puzzled and enraged, Tiresias at first refuses to speak, then angrily replies that Oedipus himself is the defiler of the land; Oedipus himself is the murderer. Oedipus ignores the stated message and shrewdly assumes that Tiresias is trying to discredit him as king, perhaps in league with the ambitious nobleman Creon.

Tiresias, alone of all the characters, understands that Oedipus slew King Laius years ago, in a quarrel at a crossroads far from Thebes. Oedipus, traveling from CORINTH (where he had grown up as the son of the king and queen there), did not know the identity of the arrogant older man whom he killed. Worse, he did not know that Laius was his own father. Worst of all, Oedipus has since married Laius' widow, Jocasta, and had children by her—who is really Oedipus' mother. He had been taken from her at his birth, and she did not recognize him as a young man.

The tragedy moves toward its climax as Oedipus, like an ideal courtroom judge, gradually uncovers the truth by interrogating witnesses, including Jocasta and a Theban shepherd who is the sole survivor of Laius' fatal fight. At one point Oedipus realizes that it was he who killed Laius, but he holds onto the hope that at least Laius was not his father (and Jocasta his mother). When finally the whole truth is publicly revealed, Oedipus in horror gouges out his own eyes and Jocasta hangs herself (both offstage). The final scenes show the blind Oedipus departing into self-imposed exile, cursed by his revealed parricide and incest. The tragedy ends with the statement—appearing in the writings of Sophocles' friend Herodotus—that no human being should be called happy until he is safely dead. Sophocles' *Oedipus at Colonus* presents the hero's final days, when he finds sanctuary and divine forgiveness under protection of the mythical Athenian king THESEUS.

Antigone presents the classic conflict of public duty versus private conscience. In the aftermath of the destructive war of the SEVEN AGAINST THEBES, Oedipus' daughter ANTIGONE chooses to disobey an edict of Creon (who is now ruler of Thebes) in favor of her religious and familial obligations. Creon has forbidden anyone on pain of death to grant funeral rites to the slain attacker Polynices, Antigone's brother. In breaking this law, Antigone discards all happiness, including her betrothal to Creon's son, Haemon. But death comes as a triumph for her and a curse for Creon and his family. It is Antigone who has upheld the higher, unwritten law of social obligation.

The Sophoclean hero or heroine tends to be a splendid individualist, set apart from other people by a refusal to compromise. These protagonists are larger than life—stronger, wiser, or more pious than others—yet they inevitably succumb to circumstance or FATE. This two-sided view is essential to Sophocles' work: The hero may be called "godlike," but usually he fails due to his human flaws, such as anger or ignorance. Ignorance in particular interests Sophocles: He portrays Oedipus and Heracles each as violently undone by an imperfect, human understanding of the facts.

Above human beings stand the gods. Where Aeschylus' surviving tragedies convey a faith in divine wisdom and Euripides' show gods who are malicious and capricious, Sophocles' work falls somewhere in between. In Sophocles, the great god ZEUS controls mortal destiny, but Zeus' purpose may be mysterious to the onstage characters and to the audience. "All of these events are Zeus," the chorus announces at the end of *The Women of Trachis*, amid Heracles' gruesome death. Zeus' purpose seems needlessly cruel, except that Heracles will win blessed immortality after his suffering. Sophocles refuses to clarify or justify the workings of the gods. Rather, his plays mirror the religious questions of real life.

(See also AJAX [1]; DEMOCRACY; ELECTRA; HOMOSEXUALITY; HUBRIS; MYTH; ORESTES; PHILOCTETES; RELIGION.)

Sparta One of the greatest city-states of mainland Greece, often in rivalry with ATHENS. Located in the southern Greek region known as the PELOPONNESE, Sparta dominated southern Greece after 600 B.C. In 404 B.C. Sparta became the supreme Greek city, having defeated Athens in the PELOPONNESIAN WAR. But a declining birthrate among Sparta's citizens, poor relations with its subject cities, a constant fear of serf revolt, and a resistance to change all made the failure of the Spartan Empire inevitable. In 371–369 B.C. Sparta was unexpectedly defeated and crippled (although not captured) by its erstwhile ally THEBES. Thereafter Sparta confined itself mainly to intrigues in the Peloponnese, often in defense against armies of the kingdom of MACEDON. In 222 B.C., amid internal political convulsions, Sparta was defeated and captured by the Macedonian king Antigonus III. Within the next 80 years, however, both Macedon and Sparta surrendered to the armies of ROME.

Sparta was unique among Greek cities, because of its program of patriotic indoctrination and full-time military service for males. This program arose in the mid 600s B.C., probably at the hands of a Spartan statesman named LYCURGUS (1), who was revered as a hero by later generations of Spartans. Today nothing is known for sure about Lycurgus' life, but he evidently shaped Sparta into an authoritarian state, devoted to maintaining the bravest and most disciplined of all HOPLITE armies. Between about 600 B.C. and 371 B.C. the Spartans could justifiably claim to be the best infantry in the Greek world (also superior to the one foreign infantry they encountered, the Persians). Eventually, however, the Spartans' reliance on traditional battle tactics left them vulnerable to new tactics, developed by the Thebans and Macedonians.

The grim world of Sparta was the "other" Greece, in contrast to the exuberant life and literature of classical

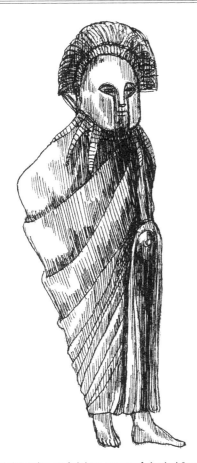

The austerity, valor, and sinister aspect of classical Sparta are apparent in this bronze figurine of a cloaked Spartan soldier, circa 400 B.C. Note the plaited hair beneath the helmet. Spartans were known for their long tresses. On the morning before their heroic last stand at Thermopylae (480 B.C.), the Spartan soldiers combed their hair.

Athens. The Spartans were secretive and anti-intellectual. They rarely let in visitors and left behind few writings. Most modern knowledge of Sparta comes from information preserved by ancient Greek writers who were not themselves Spartan—the historians HERODOTUS, THUCYDIDES (1), and XENOPHON, the philosopher ARISTOTLE, and the biographer PLUTARCH. Still, much remains mysterious about the Spartans today.

Although militaristic and austere, Sparta was not necessarily repulsive to all other Greeks. In a Greek world where ideals of DEMOCRACY (rule by the many) vied against those of OLIGARCHY (rule by the few), Sparta was the model oligarchy. It maintained its dominance over other Greek cities by supporting the ruling classes of those cities. In so doing, Sparta counterbalanced the appeal of Athens, which was trying to export democracy to the lower-income classes everywhere. In southern Greece, aristocrats and other wealthy people welcomed Spartan protection and leader-

ship. And many other Greeks admired Sparta's army and stable government.

Even Athens itself contained pro-Spartan individuals. Typically these Athenians were aristocrats. The best remembered of them is the gentleman-soldier-historian Xenophon (circa 428–354 B.C.). Similarly, Xenophon's contemporary, the Athenian philosopher PLATO, used Spartan government as inspiration for the authoritarian utopias imagined in his writings The Republic and The Laws.

Sparta ("sown land," or possibly "broom shrub") was located in the region called LACONIA, or Lacedaemon, in the southeastern Peloponnese. Nestled between lofty mountain ranges on the west and the east, the city sat at the northern tip of the Laconian plain, which fans out triangularly 25 miles southward to the sea. Just west of the city, the River Eurotas flowed southward through the widening plain. Nowadays a Greek provincial capital, Sparti, stands near the ancient site.

Long before the city of Sparta arose, the fertile and rain-nourished Laconian plain was home to pre-Greek inhabitants in the third millennium B.C. and to Mycenaean Greeks in the second millennium B.C. According to legend, this was the kingdom ruled by MENELAUS at the time of the TROJAN WAR (circa 1220 B.C.). Archaeological excavations reveal that the town of Amyclae, just south of the future site of Sparta, was a civic center containing a sanctuary of a pre-Greek god named HYACINTHUS. Later Amyclae became an important shrine of the Greek god APOLLO, one of the patron gods of the Spartan region.

Sparta itself was founded by descendants of the DORIAN GREEKS who overran most of the Peloponnese circa 1100–1000 B.C., after the collapse of MYCENAEAN CIVILIZATION. Circa 950 B.C. four local Dorian villages became amalgamated around a shared civic center. This multipart beginning probably explains the odd Spartan institution of dual kingship, whereby Sparta always had two coequal kings, drawn from two royal familes, the Agiads and Eurypontids. One reason the double kingship survived for the next 700 years was that Spartan kings were primarily military leaders, commanding armies in the field. Certainly by the 600s B.C.—and probably long before—the kings' power at home was being curtailed by other governmental branches, specifically the EPHORS (Greek: ephorai, "overseers") and the COUNCIL.

In appearance Sparta remained a sprawling village, interspersed with trees. Disdaining wealth and pomp, the Spartans of later centuries continued to make their houses out of wood and to build very few public stone monuments. Sparta at its height of power had no perimeter wall; the Spartans preferred to trust in their army and their protective mountains. Not until 318 B.C. did an enclosing wall finally go up, against the threat of a Macedonian invasion. Similarly, the Spartan ACROPOLIS was a puny, unwalled mound (very unlike the lofty citadels of other Greek cities), whose main job was to hold the temple of the city's patron deity, ATHENA. The building itself was known as the temple of Athena Chalkioikos ("Athena in Bronze"), so named because its walls were covered in BRONZE plates showing mythical scenes.

This temple and that of ARTEMIS Orthia, which stood to the west, by the Eurotas' bank, were Sparta's two main monuments. Thucydides, writing during the Spartan heyday (circa 400 B.C.), contrasted such physical simplicity with the elaborate grandeur of Athens. In a famous passage, Thucydides commented that if Sparta were to become deserted and only its empty structures viewed by future generations, people would never believe that the city had been so great a power.

The earliest events of Spartan history saw Sparta still governed as an old-style ARISTOCRACY, prior to Lycurgus' reforms. By about 700 B.C. this aristocratic Sparta had conquered Laconia (including the seaport of Gytheum, about 25 miles south of Sparta, to serve as the Spartans' maritime link).

The capture of Laconia and its inhabitants created three distinct social levels. At the top were the original Spartans, called Spartiatai (or "Spartiates"). Below them were the PERIOECI (Greek: *perioikoi*, "dwellers around"), second-class citizens who were descendants of the earliest-subdued Laconian villagers. As their name suggests, the perioeci lived in towns that roughly formed a circle around the Spartiates' prime land on the central plain. The perioeci were obligated to pay taxes and serve alongside the Spartiates in the army; they enjoyed legal protections, rights of ownership, and so on but were excluded from the political process. Spartiates and perioeci together comprised the people known as the Lacedaemonians.

Below these was another group, far inferior in status. They were the serfs, or HELOTS (Greek: *helotai*), supposedly named for the Laconian coastal village of Helos ("marsh"). It seems that the Spartans, at some point in their expansion, changed their policy toward the villagers they subdued: instead of admitting them as lesser citizens, they began to subjugate them as serfs. This brutal serf system existed elsewhere in the Greek world, but the Spartans used it the most.

The helot population increased enormously after the Spartan capture of the fertile Greek region called MESSENIA, in the southwestern Peloponnese. Invading across the high Tagytus mountain range that borders Sparta to the west, Spartan armies descended into the Messenian plain and fought a long war (circa 735–715 B.C.) to seize the farmlands and helotize the people. Sparta's victory in this First Messenian War is associated with a Eurypontid king, Theopompus, the earliest reliably real figure in Spartan history.

The annexation of Messenia made Sparta rich, with control of two-fifths of the Peloponnese. In a land where famine was a constant threat, Sparta alone had solved the food problem, with supplies from Messenia abundant to its needs: no other Greek state ever managed to subdue an entire Greek region and population. Yet the helots in Messenia and Laconia were also a source of fear. They outnumbered their Spartan masters—by the mid 400s B.C. the ratio would be seven to one. Fear of helot uprisings, which occurred periodically, kept Spartan armies close to home and created a mass neurosis in the Spartan mentality. Every year the ephors would formally declare war on the helots, thus allowing them to be killed with impunity; Spartan youths were enrolled in the Krypteia, or Secret Society, whose job it was to murder subversive helots. Conversely, the helots became a magnet for intrigues by Sparta's external enemies, such as Athens in the 400s B.C.

But helot freedom had to wait until 369 B.C., when the triumphant Theban leader EPAMINONDAS liberated the helots of Messenia (although not those of Laconia), setting up an independent Messenian state.

Meanwhile, Sparta came into conflict with the one southern Greek power that could challenge Spartan ambition—the city of ARGOS, in the northeastern Peloponnese. In 669 B.C. a Spartan army was defeated by an Argive army at Hysiai, on the road to Argos. Modern scholars believe that the battle involved the victory of organized hoplite tactics, as perfected by the Argive king PHEIDON, over the old-fashioned, individualistic fighting of the aristocratic Spartan army. Scholars further believe that the defeat fully discredited the aristocratic leadership at Sparta and brought on drastic changes in government, society, and military organization, through the reforms of Lycurgus.

Lycurgus changed Sparta from a narrow aristocracy to a broad-based oligarchy. That is, he brought middle-class Spartan men into the government as voters and soldiers, creating an enlarged citizen body of about 9,000 adult males. Henceforth, perhaps once a month, all citizens over age 30 gathered at the *apella*, or ASSEMBLY, to vote on proposals framed by a 30-man council called the *gerousia* ("the elders"), which included the two kings. The assembly could vote only "yes" or "no" and not initiate any business. But its voting included such duties as declaring war or peace, ratifying the appointment of military leaders, and electing ephors and council members aside from the kings. Council members had to be 60 or more years old; they held office for the rest of their lives. Although elected annually, ephors had immense power as chief legal officials and as monitors controlling the kings' conduct.

In theory any citizen could be elected to the council or ephorate, but in practice these offices probably tended to be filled by a few rich and prestigious families. Both the council and the ephorate were probably survivals of the old aristocratic government, now adapted to the Lycurgan government.

Most significant, Lycurgus' system created a large, full-time hoplite army, supported by Sparta's captured territories. The 9,000 full-rank citizens—the Spartiates—henceforth were barred from practicing any profession aside from soldiering; crafts and TRADE became solely the province of the perioeci. Instead, every male Spartiate (excepting perhaps the rich) received an allotment of public land in Messenia or Laconia. Farmed by helots overseen by state officers, the allotment produced food that supported the citizen and his family; the citizen was thus free to devote himself to lifelong military drill and campaigning.

Of all Greek city-states, only Sparta had a permanent soldiering class, free of the need to earn a livelihood as farmers or craftsmen. Spartan armies, for example, could campaign through late summer and autumn, when other states' farmer-soldiers might feel obliged to return home for their various sowings and harvests.

The Spartiates—the full-rank male Spartan citizens—sometimes called themselves *homoioi*, "equals." They were equal in that each man had a land allotment (although rich families undoubtedly kept their traditional estates in Laconia) and each had one vote in the assembly. But *homoioi* also means "those who are all the same," and this nuance reveals the essence of Lycurgus' reforms. Sparta became a city where concepts of the individual and the family were erased, in favor of a grim system of conformity and state service.

An individual Spartiate reached full citizenship by meeting three requirements: legitimate birth to Spartiate-rank parents, completion of a 13-year-long boyhood training program called the *agogē*, and election at age 20 to one of the communal dining messes that were the center of Spartan adult male life. The *agogē* process is described in the writings of Plutarch and Xenophon. At birth, boys (and girls) were examined for health and were accepted or rejected by state officials—not by the family father, as elsewhere in the Greek world. Those rejected were killed. At age seven, boys were taken from their mothers, to be brought up in "packs" under supervision of older boys who reported to a state officer. By age 12, boys lived in barracks, sleeping on mattresses of river rushes that they gathered themselves. Year round they went shoeless and were allowed only one outer garment, a kind of cloak. Their staple diet was a kind of pork-boiled porridge—the famous "Spartan broth"—which they were encouraged to supplement by stealing food from local storages and farms. If caught stealing, they were beaten for their clumsiness.

Boys received schooling in traditional Spartan musical art forms, such as competitive choral singing and dancing, but book-learning was minor. Their EDUCATION was mainly physical—combat-type sports and games. They exercised naked outdoors in all weather. They were subjected to routine hazing and abuse by the older boys, intended to toughen them. Homosexual pairings between older and younger boys were officially encouraged, as being helpful to patriotic esprit.

Foremost, boys were taught to obey orders and endure hardship without complaint. Scrutinized and judged by their elders, they grew up fearing disgrace more than death. Plutarch recounts how a Spartan boy somehow stole a fox cub and hid it under his cloak, only to have the animal start biting out his insides. Rather than cry out or otherwise reveal his theft, the child collapsed and died without a whimper.

The training program was designed to prepare boys for a soldiering life and to weed out anyone unsuitable for full citizenship. For each young male the reckoning came at age 20, when he sought admittance to one of the Spartan dining messes (Greek: *sussitia*). Each *sussition* probably consisted of about 15 men, who voted among themselves whether to admit or reject a candidate. Once selected, a new member remained part of the mess for life, barring expulsion, and he contributed a portion of his land's produce to help feed the group. (Their diet seems to have been far more ample and varied than the boyhood fare.) A man's mess-mates—not his family—were the center of his life and identity.

Thus, at Sparta, a man's most intense feelings were normally directed at other males. Men were still expected to marry citizen-rank WOMEN and breed children, but MARRIAGE was not a deeply emotional affair. Probably until age 30 a male Spartan continued to live with his mess-mates, visiting his wife only in secret. And Spartan law even allowed a husband to arrange for his wife to sleep with another suitable man, possibly at her request—a custom that other Greeks found outrageous.

The Spartan screening system inevitably created classes of citizens in between the Spartiates and perioeci. Spartiates who failed to win admittance to a sussition—or who were expelled because of cowardice or inability to provide a share of food—ceased to be Spartiates and descended to a rank known as Inferiors. Conversely, individual perioeci boys might be selected for the rugged Spartiate training program, but it is unclear whether such boys could ever attain full citizenship. A tendency to exclude groups on grounds of inferior birth was a deeply ingrained aspect of Spartan mentality: as early as 700 B.C. (probably before Lycurgus' reforms) a rejected group called "the sons of virgins" sailed off to found Sparta's only major colony, TARAS, in southern ITALY.

Sparta's extreme social conditions created an unusual life for women, as well. Sparta was unique among ancient Greek cities in the freedom it granted to its female citizens—this was partly due to reliance on women to manage estates while men were away at war. Somewhat similarly to boys, Spartan girls received training in choral singing, dancing, and gymnastics. Scandalously (as it seemed to other Greeks), Spartan girls exercised in public, naked or scantily clad. Like boys, Spartan girls apparently might experience homosexual love affairs in the course of their upbringing—as suggested in extant verses by the poet ALCMAN (circa 620 B.C.). And Spartan women had a unique reputation for heterosexual initiative and promiscuity. At least some of these conditions were intended to mold Spartan females into healthy and capable child-bearers, to supply future soldiers for the state.

Yet for reasons that are not clear, Sparta eventually faced a dwindling of its Spartiate population (as opposed to the perioeci or helots). Perhaps Spartan marriages were unproductive, with the problem worsened by the brutal screening system. The shrinkage reached crisis proportions after 464 B.C., when a catastrophic earthquake wiped out large numbers of Spartiates in the city center. By 425 B.C. the Spartiates numbered no more than 3,000—whereas Lycurgus in the mid-600s B.C. had made arrangements based on a population of 9,000.

In theory, Sparta's population problem could have been eased by promoting large numbers of perioeci up to Spartiate status. Although this drastic measure was proposed amid Sparta's political turmoil of the 200s B.C., it was never carried out. Spartiates viewed themselves as an ethnically distinct elite, raised from birth to dominate "lesser" peoples. Their mentality did not allow for mass enrollments of new citizens.

Another long-term result of Lycurgus' reforms was loss of trade and arts. Although the late 600s B.C. saw Sparta's cultural heyday—with verses being written by choral poets such as Alcman and TYRTAEUS, and Laconian perioeci bronzesmiths producing a valued metalwork for export—in the 500s B.C. Sparta's crafts declined, even as the city thrived. A major reason for this was Sparta's decision not to adopt COINAGE, an invention that revolutionized Greek trade soon after 600 B.C. Instead of using coins, Sparta retained a primitive, awkward currency of IRON rods, thereby assuring itself, intentionally, of economic and cultural isolation.

The 500s B.C. saw Sparta dominate the Peloponnese, to become the foremost mainland Greek city. After an attempt to conquer ARCADIA met with defeat (circa 570 B.C.), Sparta changed its policy toward its Peloponnesian neighbors: instead of seeking to crush and helotize them (which was certain to inspire fierce resistance), Sparta began offering them a place in a Spartan-led alliance that modern scholars call the Peloponnesian League. This "league policy" is sometimes associated with the Spartan ephor CHILON, circa 556 B.C. Eventually the league embraced most Peloponnesian states except Argos, which remained Sparta's enemy but was badly defeated in wars circa 546 and 494 B.C. Sparta's staunchest allies in the league included TEGEA, CORINTH, and ELIS.

Sparta reached its peak under its most capable king, the first CLEOMENES (1), who reigned circa 520–490 B.C. and tried to organize all of Greece against the coming Persian invasion. During the PERSIAN WARS (490–479 B.C.), Sparta led the land-army defense of mainland Greece, alongside the Athenian-led defense at sea. The final victory brought Sparta immense prestige—which it soon lost to Athens.

The years 478–431 B.C. saw a steady worsening of Sparta's relations with Athens. Thucydides relates that the Spartans feared the growth of Athenian power—specifically Athens' naval empire organized through the DELIAN LEAGUE. But Sparta also feared the appeal and aggressive export of Athenian democracy, so dangerous to Sparta's oligarchic friends in its allied cities. Spartan-Athenian hostility culminated in the huge Peloponnesian War (431–404 B.C.). A hard-fought victory left Sparta dominant over an exhausted Greece.

Sparta had by now acquired a navy and an important foreign ally, the empire of PERSIA, but Sparta's turn as an imperial power was destined to last barely a generation. By harsh rule in Greece and adventuring in ASIA MINOR, Sparta managed to unite several of its former allies and enemies, including Persia, Corinth, Thebes, Athens, and Argos, in a war against itself. This CORINTHIAN WAR ended with Spartan hypocrisy exposed by the shameful terms of the KING'S PEACE (386 B.C.): far from seeking to liberate the Greek cities of Asia Minor from Persian rule as they claimed, the Spartans just wanted to retain power in Greece.

Growing anti-Spartan anger fueled the emergence of a challenger state, Thebes. The Spartan king AGESILAUS, despite personal virtues, proved blind to the danger posed by the Theban leader Epaminondas. At the Battle of LEUCTRA (371 B.C.) the age-old myth of Spartan invincibility was shattered: a Spartan army was destroyed and Sparta thrown forever on the defensive. Invading Laconia for the first time in its history, Epaminondas decided not to attack Sparta itself. But he proceeded to dismantle the Spartan empire, by freeing Messenia and Arcadia from Spartan domination (369–368 B.C.). Messenia's liberation in particular was devastating to Sparta, since it removed the city's source of surplus food. With these events, the Peloponnesian League more or less dissolved.

Sparta remained resistant to Thebes and then to the Macedonians, who conquered Greece in 338 B.C. While the Macedonian king ALEXANDER THE GREAT campaigned through distant Persia, the Spartan king Agis III led a few Peloponnesian states in revolt. But he was defeated and killed at the Battle of Megalopolis, at the hands of the Macedonian regent ANTIPATER (331 B.C.).

By the mid-200s B.C. Sparta was a relatively poor state, its citizen body shrunken to a mere 700 Spartiates, vastly outnumbered by perioeci and helots. In foreign policy, Sparta lay on the defensive against the Achaean League, which was now the dominant Peloponnesian power. This era saw the final significant moments of Spartan history. Hoping to revive the city's prior greatness, the young king Agis IV tried to abolish debts, redistribute land, and enroll perioeci as new citizens. Opposed by conservative Spartiates, Agis died violently (241 B.C.), but his revolutionary plan inspired a new king, Cleomenes III.

After a few years on the throne, Cleomenes discarded constitutional kingship and seized absolute power (226 B.C.). He abolished the ephorate, redistributed the land into 4,000 lots, and enrolled perioeci as full citizens. Next, seeking to recover Sparta's military supremacy in the Peloponnese, he waged war with the armies of the Achaean League. But when the Achaean League leader Aratus invited the powerful Macedonian king Antigonus III to intervene, Sparta's revival was doomed. At the Battle of Sellasia, just north of Sparta, Antigonus destroyed a Spartan army (222 B.C.). Cleomenes fled into exile, soon to die, while Antigonus seized Sparta and canceled Cleomenes' reforms.

Of the Spartan kings who came later, Nabis was a noteworthy adventurer during and after the Second Macedonian War (220–197 B.C.). By 146 B.C., however, Sparta and all of Greece had passed into Roman hands. During the first century A.D., under the Roman Empire, Sparta enjoyed a revival as a tourist attraction. Spectators were regaled by the sight of such age-old endurance contests as Spartan boys running the gauntlet of whips at the altar of Artemis Orthia.

(See also ACHAEA; AGIAD CLAN; CIMON; EURYPONTID CLAN; HOMOSEXUALITY; LYSANDER; MUSIC; TYRANTS; WARFARE, LAND.)

Speusippus See ACADEMY; PLATO.

sport The ancient Greeks of the 700s B.C. and later revered competitive sports, especially for men and boys. Sport was seen as a character-building facet of a boy's EDUCATION and as a way of demonstrating the gods' favor for individual competitors. The Greeks associated sport with RELIGION. Their major competitions took place at festivals in the gods' honor; the most famous of these were the OLYMPIC GAMES, sacred to the great god ZEUS.

The Greeks overwhelmingly favored individual contests over team sports. Typical events at public competitions included foot races (200 yards, 400 yards, long distance, and the race in armor), field events (long jump, discus throw, and javelin throw), combative events (WRESTLING, BOXING, and PANKRATION), and the horse races and chariot races.

WOMEN and girls were not completely barred from sports. For instance, SPARTA maintained a vigorous program of girls' gymnastics, and the Olympic Games included a girls' foot race (held outside the main sanctuary where the males competed). However, the Greeks' love of sport specifically involved a glorification of male strength and beauty; in most public events, males competed naked or nearly so, their bodies anointed with oil. Such display was considered inappropriate for Greek women. (In the few events open to them, female competitors wore tunics.)

Every Greek city-state had its own schedule of festivals, where local athletes might compete in honor of the city's patron gods. In every city, the GYMNASIUM was an important local institution, where the wealthier men might pass the day in socializing and political discussions, as well as sports practice. The Greeks' serious approach to sports was an aspect of Greek culture that attracted many non-Greek peoples—including the ETRUSCANS, Romans, and certain of the JEWS—who came into contact with the Greeks in the centuries before Christ.

(See also CHARIOTS; HOMOSEXUALITY; ISTHMIAN GAMES; NEMEAN GAMES; PENTATHLON; PINDAR; PYTHIAN GAMES.)

statues   See SCULPTURE

Stesichorus   Important Greek lyric poet, active in the first half of the 500s B.C. and usually associated with the Sicilian-Greek city of HIMERA. Stesichoros, meaning "chorus master," may have been a title; according to one story, the man's real name was Tisias. Prolific and inventive, Stesichoras was the first west Greek literary celebrity, and he strongly influenced later generations of Greek poets. He was known for his long narrative poems on mythological subjects, perhaps 26 in number. Of these, much has been lost; the remnants survive mainly in quotations by later writers and in some recovered ancient papyrus fragments, published in A.D. 1973, containing portions of Stesichorus' poem *Geryoneis* (about the mythical creature Geryon, slain by HERACLES).

Writing in the Doric Greek dialect, Stesichorus told tales inspired by HOMER's verses and by other poems of the epic cycle. In the *Wooden Horse*, the *Capture of Troy*, and *Homecomings*, he described the TROJAN WAR and its aftermath. His *Oresteia*—about the murder of AGAMEMNON and the vengeance taken by his son, ORESTES—almost certainly later influenced the *Oresteia* stage trilogy by the Athenian playwright AESCHYLUS.

Stesichorus was both clever and verbose. The *Geryoneis* ran at least 1,300 lines (probably much longer) and featured a sympathetic portrait of the three-bodied Geryon, who traditionally had been presented as a fierce monster.

It is not known how Stesichorus' poems were performed. He usually is called a choral poet, meaning that his work typically would have been sung or chanted by a trained chorus at a public event. However, his more recently discovered verses seem to lack certain hallmarks of choral song, leading certain scholars to believe that at least some of Stesichorus' poems were written for a solo singer accompanying himself on the lyre. Perhaps this performer was the poet himself.

Stesichorus is traditionally credited with inventing the "triad"—a three-stanza metrical grouping that became an essential element in lyric verse and Athenian stage drama. The triad consisted of the *strophē*, or "turn," the *antistrophē*,

"counterturn," and the *epodos*, "after-song." This sequence was repeated throughout the poem. The strophe and antistrophe had to be metrically identical; the epode was different. Supposedly the names denote the chorus' motions in singing the parts—dancing rightward on the strophe, leftward on the antistrophe, and standing still for the epode.

One well-known story claims that Stesichorus wrote two different poems dealing with the mythical HELEN OF TROY. The first was a conventional treatment of Helen's adulterous elopement with the Trojan prince PARIS. The second poem, entitled the *Palinodia* (retraction), claimed that the first version was untrue: Helen had never left her Spartan husband, MENELAUS; rather, the gods had sent a phantom-Helen to TROY, so that the city's doom might be fulfilled.

The daring contrivance of this palinode was much admired in the ancient world and gave rise to a legend: Supposedly, after writing the first Helen poem, Stesichorus was struck blind. Only after publishing the retraction did the poet regain his sight.

(See also LYRIC POETRY; MUSIC.)

Stoicism   School of Greek PHILOSOPHY founded at ATHENS *circa* 300 B.C. by Zeno, a Cypriot of Phoenician-Greek descent. With its ideal of a virtuous life impervious to misfortune, and its assurance of an ordered universe in which the individual person played a role, Stoicism addressed certain feelings of change and doubt that accompanied the start of the HELLENISTIC AGE.

During Hellenistic times (circa 300–150 B.C.), Stoicism remained a modest influence, about equal to its major rival philosophy, EPICUREANISM. But once introduced at the non-Greek city of ROME circa 144 B.C., Stoicism captured the Roman mentality (more so than the Greek) and grew into the major intellectual movement of the early Roman Empire. Unlike Epicureanism, Stoicism encouraged its followers to engage in the public life of government, and many ruling-class Romans were Stoics, such as the statesman Seneca the Younger (circa A.D. 60) and the emperor Marcus Aurelius (circa A.D. 170).

Stoicism's long history is divided by scholars into three phases, called the Early, Middle, and Late Stoa. The Middle Stoa, circa 144–30 B.C., saw Stoicism transplanted to Rome, where it flourished as the Late Stoa, circa 30 B.C.–mid-200s A.D. Although finally submerged by the spread of Christianity, Stoicism helped to shape the ethical outlook of early Christian thinkers. Most modern knowledge of Stoicism comes from extant Greek and Latin writings of the late period. The early Stoic writings survive only in brief quotations or summaries by later authors.

Zeno, the Stoic founder, immigrated to Athens as a young man and probably studied the teachings of the Athenian CYNICS. By about age 33 he had created his own philosophy, borrowing Cynic ethical theories of self-sufficiency along with select teachings of PLATO and others. Zeno presented his new ideas in public lectures and disputations in a part of the Athenian AGORA known as the Stoa Poikilē, or Painted Colonnade. This locale gave the new movement its name.

Zeno died around 261 B.C., bequeathing his school to a disciple named Cleanthes. Cleanthes' successor was Chrysippus (president 232–207 B.C.), a highly important thinker: His writings (not extant today) clarified Zeno's teachings and fused Stoic ethics, scientific theories, and theories of knowledge into a coherent, interconnected system.

Although most ancient Greeks worshipped many gods, the Stoics inclined toward belief in a single divinity. They pictured a universe imbued with a divine purpose or intelligence, variously referred to as reason (Greek: *logos*), fire, breath, or FATE. Every human being, they believed, contained a small version of the divine purpose, which is demonstrated in the human ability to reason, plan and give speech (*logos*).

This idea of a shared divine spark is background to one of Stoicism's most appealing teachings: the essential brotherhood of all people. The Stoic was taught to ignore distinctions of weath and birth and to see all humans, including WOMEN and SLAVES, as being spiritually the same material.

Stoicism recognized only two classes of people: the virtuous and the wicked. Like SOCRATES and Plato, the Stoics described virtue (Greek: *aretē*) as a form of knowledge or wisdom. Courage, moderation, and other virtues were evidence of this wisdom; greed, fear, sensuality were symptoms of ignorance. Wisdom produced virtue and virtue produced happiness; the greedy or dishonest person could not, by definition, be happy. In life, virtue was to be exercised, not in the cloistered setting that Epicureanism favored, but in areas of social responsibility: earning a living, raising a family, holding public office.

Contrary to some popular belief, the Stoics did not seek out pain. But they believed that pain, poverty, and death were not to be feared, since those ills could not harm a person's virtue. Thus the Stoic could find consolation in adversity: Happiness dwelt within, unaffected by external misfortune or external success. "Only the wise man is rich," a Stoic proverb ran. The Stoic tried to emulate the calm and grandeur of the universe, by accepting all events in life with a serene mind. This state of mind the Stoics called *apatheia*, "absence of passion."

Stoicism involved many other beliefs in fields such as logic and SCIENCE, but it was its noble, reassuring ethical system that made Stoicism so popular in later antiquity. Today we still use the adjectives "stoic" and "stoical" to denote an indifference to pain or misfortune.

Styx   See AFTERLIFE.

Sybaris   Affluent Greek city on the Gulf of Taranto, on the "instep" of the southern coast of ITALY. Founded by colonists from ACHAEA in around 720 B.C., Sybaris grew rich from its fertile farmland and its TRADE with the ETRUSCANS of the north. The city's reputation for luxury has produced the English word *sybarite*, meaning "someone excessively devoted to pleasure."

Sybaris enlarged its territory at the expense of local non-Greeks and founded Italian colonies of its own, including POSEIDONIA (Paestum). But rivalry with the nearby Greek city of CROTON led to a war, in which Sybaris was defeated and obliterated (510 B.C.). Nearly 70 years later, the Athenians established the colony Thurii near the site of Sybaris.

symposium   Type of all-male, after-dinner drinking party. The symposium (Greek: *sumposion*, "drinking together"; plural: *sumposia*) played a vital role in ancient Greek aristocratic life. Only the rich could afford to host symposia; and the symposium's expense, its male homosexual or bisexual aspect, and its intellectual games were all part of a separate aristocratic identity.

The feasting of kings and their retainers goes back to prehistoric times. The poems of HOMER, written down circa 750 B.C. describe aristocratic warriors sitting at banquets. By the 600s B.C. the symposium had arisen, probably through Phoenician influence, as a new form of social gathering. Snacks such as sesame cakes might be served, but the symposium's central activity was the semiritualistic drinking of WINE. All the drinkers were men, of equal noble status. The servers and entertainers were typically young female and male SLAVES chosen for their beauty.

The symposium was the natural setting for the type of woman known as a *hetaira*, or courtesan; such women might be dancers or flute-girls, but they would also be obliged to give sexual favors. Similarly, according to ancient Greek aristocratic taste, the symposium would be the scene of various homosexual attractions, whether between guests or involving a guest and slave. One anecdote tells how the great Athenian playwright SOPHOCLES coaxed a kiss from a slave boy at a symposium (circa 440 B.C.). A surviving tomb painting from POSEIDONIA (circa 480 B.C.) shows a youthful guest warding off a caress from his couchmate, a slightly older man.

The symposium was governed by rules. The typical "symposiast" (reveler) did not sit but rather reclined on a couch, propped up on his left elbow, Phoenician style. There were usually between seven and 15 couches, with two men to each. One of the drinkers was appointed "king," or master of ceremonies, to decide on the sequence of activities.

Symposia had their own equipment, including many of the forms of Greek POTTERY that are known from ARCHAE-

A symposium scene, from an Athenian red-figure cup, circa 485 B.C. Tended by slave boys, the symposiasts recline on couches, drinking wine from the kind of shallow cup known as the kylix. The setting is a special room of the host's house, where walls are hung with wine pitchers and kylixes.

OLOGY. The men drank from cups such as the *kulix* (or *kylix*)—wide and shallow, for sipping on the recline. According to Greek custom, the wine was diluted with water, usually one part wine to two or three water. The mixture was prepared in a large bowl, the *kratēr,* and from there distributed by slaves to the drinkers' cups. During the festivities the wine-to-water ratio might be altered according to the wishes of the "king," but drinking undiluted wine was considered very unhealthy. Games included *kottabos* (in which wine dregs were flicked from the cup at a target) and competitive singing by individual symposiasts to flute accompaniment—the origin of the Greek verse form known as the elegy.

Undoubtedly events could grow wild as men got drunk—for example, more than one vase painting shows *hetairai* climbing onto couches to embrace guests. The party might end in a *komos,* a drunken torchlight procession in honor of DIONYSUS, the wine god.

But symposia were also the setting for philosophical and, especially, political discussion. The symposiasts were usually men of right-wing views, and the symposium was designed to foster a sense of exclusivity in an atmosphere of male bonding. At ATHENS and other democracies, such a strong minority could be subversive. The right-wing conspiracies that threatened democratic Athens in 457, 411, and 404 B.C. were surely hatched in gatherings such as symposia.

The symposium's dual intellectual-sexual nature is conveyed in idealized terms by the philosopher PLATO, in his dialogue titled the *Symposium.* In this fictional account, SOCRATES, ARISTOPHANES, ALCIBIADES, and other notable fifth-century-B.C. Athenians meet to drink and discuss the nature of sexual love.

(See also ALCAEUS; ANACREON; ARISTOCRACY; HOMOSEXUALITY; LYRIC POETRY; MUSIC; OLIGARCHY; PHOENICIA; POTTERY; PROSTITUTES.)

Syracuse   Preeminent Greek city of SICILY, and one of the grandest and most violent cities of Greek history. Under a series of military dictators in the 400s–200s B.C., Syracuse led the Sicilian Greeks in their constant struggle against the Carthaginians, who occupied Sicily's western corner. Syracuse played a major role in the downfall of ATHENS during the PELOPONNESIAN WAR, when the Syracusans totally destroyed an Athenian invasion force (413 B.C.). By the first half of the 300s B.C., Syracuse vied with North African CARTHAGE for control of the western Mediterranean, before falling to the expansionism of ROME (211 B.C.).

Syracuse (now the Sicilian city of Siracusa) was one of the earliest Greek colonies. Located on the south part of Sicily's east coast, it was founded circa 733 B.C. by shipborne Corinthian settlers who subdued the local native Sicels. The site combined fertile coastal farmland with the best harbor of eastern Sicily—a double harbor, formed by the inshore island Ortygia ("quail island"). The Greeks fortified Ortygia and the mainland opposite, eventually linking them with a causeway and bridge.

The Syracuse colony was undoubtedly intended as a breadbasket for its mother city, CORINTH. Syracuse's surplus harvest of barley and wheat was probably offered first for sale to the Corinthians.

Like Corinth, Syracuse in the 700s–500s B.C. was governed as an ARISTOCRACY. The descendants of the first settlers became a ruling class known as the Gamoroi, "landholders," who lived in the city and whose farms occupied the best land of the plain. Lower on the social ladder were the descendants of later Greek arrivals, who might be craftsmen in the city or have smallholdings in the hills. Lowest of all were the Sicel-ethnic serfs, who tilled the land for their Greek masters (and whose condition resembled that of the Spartan HELOTS). These distinctive social layers created class hatreds, which—when added to the external menace of the Carthaginians and native Sicilian tribes—were destined to have important political consequences. By the 400s B.C. Syracuse saw TYRANTS (*turannoi,* "dictators") arising, as champions of the common people and as promisers of military security.

The first tyrant was GELON; ruler of the nearby Greek city of GELA, who seized Syracuse under pretext of aiding the beleaguered Gamoroi (485 B.C.). Gelon transferred his capital to Syracuse and from there ruled as the most powerful individual in the Greek world. He led Greek Sicily to victory against the Carthaginians at the Battle of HIMERA (480 B.C.), and he extended the Syracusan empire westward, subjugating Carthaginians, Greeks, and natives across two-thirds of Sicily.

Gelon was succeeded by his brother HIERON (1), who ruled 478–467 B.C. and extended Syracusan power to Greek ITALY with his defeat of the Etruscans at the sea battle of CUMAE (474 B.C.). Under Hieron, Syracuse became a cultural capital, attracting literary artists of old Greece, such as AESCHYLUS, PINDAR, SIMONIDES, and BACCHYLIDES. The Greek amphitheater, ancient Syracuse's best-known surviving remnant, was first built under Hieron, quite possibly for the performance of Aeschylus' play *Women of Aetna* (476 B.C.). A Sicilian Greek playwright Epicharmus, probably a Syracusan, is said to have pioneered the writing of stage comedy in the early 400s B.C.

After Hieron's death, the tyranny was overthrown (466 B.C.). A Syracusan DEMOCRACY, based on the Athenian model, lasted for about 60 years. During this time Syracuse remained the foremost Dorian-Greek city of Sicily, in opposition to such local Ionian-Greek cities as Leontini. Eventually Syracuse's enemies appealed to the great city of Athens for help. The ambitious Athenians dreamed of capturing Syracuse's wheatfields and other riches, and in 415 B.C. they dispatched an ill-fated armada that eventually totaled perhaps 50,000 troops and 173 warships. The attackers besieged Syracuse but, after two years' fighting, were annihilated. The architects of this Syracusan triumph were the Spartan general Gylippus and the Syracusan statesman-general Hermocrates.

In 410 B.C. a new threat emerged, as the Carthaginians began a series of eastward campaigns in Sicily. Following so close after the Athenian attack, this crisis threw the Syracusan democracy into turmoil, and circa 405 B.C. there emerged a new dictator, DIONYSIUS (1), a military officer and former follower of Hermocrates (since killed in civil war). Seizing power, Dionysius married Hermocrates' daughter and embarked on a war that rolled the Carthaginians back from the very walls of Syracuse to Sicily's western corner. The ensuing peace (397 B.C.) left Greek Sicily securely under Syracusan protection and rule.

The prosperous years until Dionysius' death (367 B.C.) saw Syracuse as the magnificent capital of the western Greeks. Dionysius made Ortygia island his private citadel and fortified Syracuse's inland heights, called the Epipolae ("above the city"); still standing are the remains of one of his forts, now called the Castle of Euryalus. Like Hieron, Dionysius sought to attract poets and thinkers to his court. In 387 B.C. the Athenian philosopher PLATO made the first of his ill-fated visits to Syracuse. (The philosopher was unimpressed, complaining that in Sicily everyone overate twice a day and never slept alone.)

Dionysius' son and successor, Dionysius II, lacked his father's ability to rule successfully, and was ousted after 10 years. Greek Sicily relapsed into civil strife, and Syracuse's power declined.

The reorganization of Greek Sicily by the Corinthian commander TIMOLEON (345–circa 340 B.C.) left Syracuse with a moderate OLIGARCHY on the Corinthian pattern. Yet, once again, a dictator emerged: AGATHOCLES, who ruled 317–287 B.C. The hectic events of his reign saw Syracuse again besieged by the Carthaginians and again leading the defense of Greek Sicily.

After Agathocles' death, a new autocrat emerged from the ranks of military officers: Hieron II, who in 269 B.C. declared himself king and whose 54-year reign brought Syracuse to its final peak of glory. Hieron wisely made an alliance with the emerging power of Rome.

Under him, Syracuse was one of the three great Greek cities of the HELLENISTIC AGE, along with ALEXANDRIA (1) and ANTIOCH. Syracuse's most famous citizen of this era was the mathematician-scientist ARCHIMEDES.

Syracuse's downfall came amid the conflict between Rome and Carthage. After Hieron's death (215 B.C.), his successor made a foolhardy alliance with Carthage that soon brought Syracuse under attack by Roman forces. From 213–211 B.C. the city's huge fortifications withstood the Roman siege: According to legend, the aged Archimedes invented a giant glass lens, designed to focus sun rays on Roman warships in the harbor and set them afire. But eventually the city's outer wall fell to night assault and its inner wall to treason. The Romans captured Syracuse amid slaughter and looting. Among the booty shipped back to Rome were statues and other art objects that spurred the Romans' fascination with Greek culture. Later, Syracuse became the chief city of Roman Sicily and eventually lost its Greek identity.

(See also DORIAN GREEKS, THEATER.)

T

talent   Large monetary unit, equivalent to a certain weight (Greek: *talanton*) of SILVER, usually about 58 pounds. The talent measure was in use well before the beginnings of Greek COINAGE (circa 595 B.C.), and no talent coin existed. In ATHENS in the 400s to 300s B.C., a talent was considered equivalent to 6,000 of the silver coins known as drachmae.

Tantalus   In HOMER's epic poem the *Odyssey*, the hero ODYSSEUS visits the Underworld (book 11), and sees three great sinners there who are suffering eternal punishment for having betrayed the friendship of the gods. The sinners are the giant Tityus and the mortals SISYPHUS and Tantalus. Described as an old man, Tantalus is tortured by unrelieved thirst and hunger. He stands in a cool pond up to his neck, with the boughs of fruit trees hanging above his head; but when he lowers his head to drink, the water drains away instantly, and when he reaches up for fruit, the boughs are lifted away by the wind. Tantalus' fate has given rise to our English word *tantalize*, meaning "to cause torment by showing but withholding something desirable." In Greek the name Tantalus may have meant "sufferer."

Like certain other characters in Greek MYTH, Tantalus was described as a non-Greek; he was a wealthy king in ASIA MINOR and a son of the great god ZEUS. But Tantalus' good fortune brought on insane arrogance (HUBRIS). To test the omniscience of the gods, he invited them to a banquet, then he killed his own young son, PELOPS, and cooked him as the dish. But only the goddess DEMETER—distracted by grief for her lost daughter, PERSEPHONE—ate a few bites, from the shoulder. Zeus and the other gods detected the trick and brought Pelops back to life, replacing his shoulder's missing part with ivory. Tantalus was sent off to an eternal pain that mirrors his crime somewhat. Through Pelops, Tantalus was the ancestor of the mythical kings who eventually ruled MYCENAE, in Greece. This family of the Pelopidae included ATREUS, AGAMEMNON, and ORESTES; the misfortunes of this royal house can be understood partly as originating with Tantalus' crime.

(See also AFTERLIFE.)

Taras   Greek city founded by Spartan colonists in the late 700s B.C. on the "instep" of the southern coast of ITALY. Often known by its Latin name, Tarentum, this city is now the Italian seaport of Taranto, located beside the Gulf of Taranto.

As the only colony established by SPARTA, Taras maintained a Spartan form of government until switching to DEMOCRACY, circa 475 B.C. Taras thrived from FARMING, manufacturing (including POTTERY and jewelry), and Adriatic TRADE, despite the hostility of local Italian tribes. By the mid-400s B.C. it was the foremost Greek city of south Italy. The city's peak came in the 300s B.C., when it was producing such luminaries as the philosopher-engineer Archytas and the philospher–musical theorist Aristoxenus. But by midcentury Taras was being threatened by its Italian enemies—the nearby Lucanii and the more distant, expansionist city of ROME.

For help, Taras appealed to other Greek states. The last and best known of these episodes came in 280 B.C., when the dynamic King PYRRHUS of EPIRUS arrived with his army to fight the Romans. After early victories gave way to defeat, Pyrrhus withdrew.

Taras was captured by the Romans and became a Roman subject state (272 B.C.). Later it was an important port city of Roman Italy.

Tarentum   See TARAS.

Tartarus   See AFTERLIFE.

Tegea   City in the southeastern part of the plain of ARCADIA, lying along the main route between SPARTA, to the south, and ARGOS, to the northeast. Tegea was one of the two original Arcadian cities. (The other was MANTINEA, Tegea's rival.)

Tegea arose circa 600 B.C. from an amalgamation of local villages, to resist Spartan aggression. Renowned as fighters, the Tegeans defeated a Spartan invasion circa 585 B.C., but in the mid-500s B.C. they made peace and became staunch Spartan allies. Tegean troops had the traditional privilege of occupying the left wing of the battle line in a Spartan-led army.

Tegean troops played a prominent role alongside the Spartans in the PELOPONNESIAN WAR (431–404 B.C.). But after Sparta's defeat by THEBES in 371 B.C., Tegea turned against the crippled Sparta and fought on the Theban side at the Battle of Mantinea (362 B.C.). Later, however, enmity with Mantinea brought Tegea back to a treaty with Sparta.

The glory of ancient Tegea was its temple of the goddess ATHENA. Destroyed by fire in 390 B.C., this shrine was rebuilt as the largest and grandest temple in southern Greece. The site, three miles outside Tegea, was excavated by French archaeologists in the early 1900s A.D.; the later temple's foundations and column fragments are visible today.

Teiresias   See TIRESIAS.

Telemachus In MYTH, the son of King ODYSSEUS and PENELOPE. Telemachus' name, "distant battle," refers to his father's part in the TROJAN WAR, which began just when the boy was born. A subplot in HOMER's epic poem the *Odyssey* traces Telemachus' passage to maturity. At the *Odyssey's* opening, Telemachus, about 20 years old, is a dutiful but timid prince, overawed by the confident nobles who crowd his absent father's palace at ITHACA and compete for Penelope's hand in MARRIAGE. Unable to make them leave, Telemachus voyages by ship to the Peloponnesian courts of NESTOR and MENELAUS, to ask about the whereabouts of the father he has not seen since he was a baby. With the goddess ATHENA's help, Telemachus sails back to Ithaca (evading an ambush by the suitors en route) and encounters his father, who has returned in disguise. By now the boy is showing considerable confidence and initiative. In the climactic scene, where Odysseus slaughters the suitors (book 22), Telemachus fights bravely alongside his father, sustaining a wrist wound.

Other legends add a few details. Supposedly Telemachus later married his father's former paramour, CIRCE.

Teos See IONIA.

Terpander Lyric poet of the mid-600s B.C. Terpander came from the island of LESBOS but composed and performed at SPARTA. His name means "delight of man," and legend claims that his poetry soothed the Spartans at a time of civil crisis. Only a few lines ascribed to Terpander survive, and even these were probably not really written by him. He was apparently an important early figure in creating choral poetry as an art form and in making Sparta a center for that art. Almost certainly, he influenced the younger Spartan choral poet ALCMAN.

Terpander may have pioneered certain techniques in playing the lyre. However, the story crediting him with inventing the seven-stringed lyre (in place of four strings) is not true, as the seven-stringed type dates back to the second millennium B.C.

(See also LYRIC POETRY; MUSIC.)

Thales The first Greek thinker to try to explain the universe in nonreligious, rationalistic terms. As such, Thales can be considered both the first scientist and the first philosopher in the West. He lived between about 610 and 540 B.C. in MILETUS, in the flourishing Greek region called IONIA, in ASIA MINOR. Although he left no writings, he is best remembered for his theory that water is the fundamental constituent of all matter.

Thales and two of his followers, ANAXIMANDER and ANAXIMENES, comprise the first known philosophical movement: the Milesian School of natural philosophers. These men used physical observations to inquire about a primary substance in the universe. The significance of such thinkers is that they were the first to look for answers without reference to the traditional myths of the gods. Later generations considered Thales to be one of the SEVEN SAGES of Greece. He was famous in his lifetime, and took part in great events. In around 545 B.C., when Ionia was under attack by the Persian king CYRUS (1), Thales proposed the creation of a federated union of Ionian cities.

He established—probably on the basis of Babylonian or Egyptian learning—the studies of ASTRONOMY and geometry among the Greeks; he was believed to be the first Greek to accurately predict the year of a solar eclipse (probably 585 B.C.). Like other Greek wise men, he is said to have traveled to EGYPT, where he supposedly calculated a pyramid's height by measuring its shadow simultaneously with that of his walking stick and calculating the ratios.

He was of partial Phoenician descent, and Near Eastern influences may lurk behind his emphasis on water and his theory that the earth floats like a log in a cosmic watery expanse. (This resembles the Semitic myth of watery creation in the biblical book of Genesis.) But in Thales' mind such ideas became scientific.

(See also MATHEMATICS; PHILOSOPHY; PHOENICIA; SCIENCE.)

Thasos Wealthy island of the northern AEGEAN SEA, lying six miles offshore of the non-Greek mainland of THRACE. Thasos is a round island, about 13 miles in diameter, rising to a central peak. The Greek poet ARCHILOCHUS sourly described it as sticking up like a donkey's back, topped with forests (circa 670 B.C.). The main city was a seaport, also named Thasos (site of the modern Greek town of Limen); it lay at the north of the island, opposite the mainland.

As one of the very few Aegean sites to offer mineral deposits of GOLD, Thasos attracted Greek colonists at an early date, circa 700 B.C. These colonists—of whom Archilochus eventually was one—came from the island of Paros in the CYCLADES. Although Thasos' mines were soon exhausted, the island served as a base from which to pursue mining and panning on the nearby Thracian mainland. The most important mainland prospecting area lay on the eastern slopes of Mt. Pangaeus, at a site called Skaptē Hulē (dug-out wood), about 25 miles due northwest of Thasos.

But the Pangaeus fields existed amid a hostile native people—the warlike Thracians. Much of Archilochus' surviving poetry describes fierce fighting against the "mop-haired men of Thrace," and what these verses seem to portray is Greek military protection for miners and for convoys of raw gold and SILVER, moving from the slopes of Pangaeus to the safe anchorage at Thasos.

The island grew rich from its exports of precious ore, TIMBER, local marble, and, probably, SLAVES acquired as Thracian war captives.

Thasos had a renowned school of SCULPTURE in the 600s and 500s B.C. and was the birthplace of the painter Polygnotus (circa 475 B.C.).

The island surrendered to the advancing Persians under King DARIUS (1) in 491 B.C. After the Persian defeat in 479 B.C., Thasos joined the Athenian-controlled DELIAN LEAGUE, and, like most other Delian allies, reorganized its government as a DEMOCRACY.

But in 465 B.C. Thasos revolted from the Delian League, over Athenian interference in its crucial mining operations on the mainland. An Athenian war fleet defeated the Thasians in a sea battle, and besieged and captured the capital city (465–463 B.C.). Relatedly, the Athenians began colonizing the west foot of Mt. Pangaeus, at the site later known as AMPHIPOLIS.

The Athenians apparently now took over Thasos' mainland mines, at least temporarily. We know that in 454 B.C. Thasos was paying only three TALENTS of Delian tribute a year—a tiny assessment for that rich state, unless it was no longer rich. But by 446 B.C. the Thasian tribute had jumped to 30 talents a year, which may signify the Thasians' recovery of their mainland possessions.

In 411 B.C., amid the widespread Delian revolt against a beleaguered ATHENS in the PELOPONNESIAN WAR, Thasos rebelled again and went over to the Spartan side. But the common people resisted this defection, and the next years saw civil war on Thasos, followed by recapture by the Athenians (407 B.C.). In 404 B.C., at the war's end, the exhausted island's Athenian loyalists were massacred by the Spartan general LYSANDER.

In 389 B.C. the island joined the SECOND ATHENIAN LEAGUE, of which it remained a faithful member. Thasos was seized by the Macedonian king PHILIP II in 340 B.C.; by about 300 B.C. he and his successors had depleted the Pangaeus mines. Thasos remained a part of the Macedonian kingdom until 196 B.C., when it was freed by the Romans in their liberation of Greece.

As befits a rich capital, Thasos city boasted a number of grand buildings. Among the remnants visible today are parts of the AGORA and of a temple of HERACLES (400s B.C.). Most impressive is the partly surviving ancient city wall, dating back to the Thasians' preparation for revolt in 411 B.C.

(See also PAINTING; PERSIAN WARS; ROME.)

theater Many cultures have produced some original form of public performance that might be called drama or theater. It was the ancient Greeks, specifically the Athenians of the 400s B.C., who perfected the two genres known as tragedy and comedy, which defined European theater for centuries following. Shakespeare (circa A.D. 1600) wrote tragedies and comedies because those were playwriting's two principal forms, inherited from the Greeks.

Greek tragedy drew on tales from MYTH. This meant that in most cases the entire audience would be familiar with the story's plot beforehand (similar to an audience at a modern Easter pageant). The playwright's skill would lie in shaping the material so as to communicate a particular world view or character portrait.

Most Greek tragedy presents the downfall of a hero or other lofty protagonist. In the more sophisticated tragedies, this downfall is shown to be due to HUBRIS (arrogance): Having attracted the anger of the gods, the hero is destroyed by a disastrously arrogant decision of his own. The clearest example of this pattern is in AESCHYLUS' *Agamemnon*, where the hero displays his hubris by walking atop a priceless tapestry.

The philosopher ARISTOTLE, in a famous passage in his literary-critical *Poetics*, explains that tragedy's artistic goal is to arouse the audience's emotions of pity and fear in a way that purges these feelings and provides relief; this purging is called *katharsis*. Greek tragedy also strives to examine the nature—or absence—of divine justice, and the role of humankind in the universe.

Comedy, on the other hand, was always meant to be funny and riotous, with characters less noble and compli-

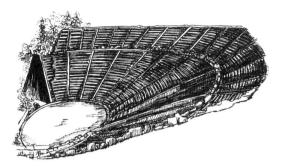

The theater at Epidaurus, in the Peloponnese, as it appears today. Built into the side of a hill, this structure dates from the mid-300s B.C. and is the best preserved of any ancient Greek theater, with excellent acoustics. Its 55 rows of limestone benches could seat 12,000. Actors and chorus would perform mainly on the 66-foot-wide, open disk of beaten earth, called the *orchēstra* (dancing floor). Behind the orchestra, at far left, there would have been a stage building, or *skēnē*, which provided storage, changing rooms, and a means of backdrop display. Also, characters such as gods could make an entrance by being winched down from the skene roof.

cated than those in tragedy or even real life. ARISTOPHANES' 11 surviving comedies, dating between 425 and 388 B.C., are farcical, fantastical works that celebrate the city's political life, while mocking specific individuals and institutions.

Ancient Greek theater was a form of poetry, with all dialogue being spoken or sung in verse. Theater was also mass culture, intended for an audience that included several social classes, and it thrived in democracies such as ATHENS (although it is unclear whether WOMEN, even female citizens, were allowed to attend). Because the theater audiences comprised much the same constituency as the democratic ASSEMBLY, Greek drama often conveyed strong political messages.

Tragedy apparently was invented at Athens in the 500s B.C. (although the city of SICYON claimed this honor, too). Comedy was developed at various Greek states, including SYRACUSE and other cities of SICILY, before being instituted most grandly at Athens. Both genres probably emerged from the public performances of choral singers at religious festivals in honor of DIONYSUS, the god of WINE and fertility, who was a favorite deity of the masses. Greek comedy, with its farce and obscenity, seems clearly derived from the riotous Dionysian procession known as the *komos*, held at many Greek states; *komoidia* means "song of the *komos*." Vase paintings show the *komos* as a parade of masked men costumed as SATYRS and carrying a log carved as a huge penis. The *komos* was probably an occasion for rude jokes exchanged with onlookers; out of this interplay there may have developed the *parabasis* (a direct choral address to the audience that was a hallmark of Athenian stage comedy). The belief that Dionysus could spiritually possess his worshippers probably led to individual speaking or singing roles in the god's character.

The origins of tragedy are less clear than those of comedy. According to Aristotle's *Poetics*, tragedy emerged from the narrative choral song known as the dithyramb. Like the *komos*, the dithyramb was performed at certain festivals of Dionysus, but was more solemn and rehearsed than the *komos*. The meaning of the word *dithyramb* is unclear now, but it is known, from extant dithyrambs written by the poet BACCHYLIDES (mid-400s B.C.), that these songs told tales from Greek myth, not necessarily relating to Dionysus. The chorus would sing or chant the story and probably dance interpretively.

Assuming that what Aristotle said was accurate, there must have come a time at Athens when certain types of performance broke away from the rules governing the dithyramb's poetic meter, size of chorus, and so on. Most significantly, individual performers began stepping out of the chorus, to sing or speak roles in the character of a mythical figure in the story. This step is traditionally credited to a shadowy genius named Thespis (circa 535 B.C.), who also may have introduced the single actor's wearing of a mask to signify character. Thespis' actor apparently delivered set speeches in between the chorus' presentations; the actor may have changed masks to assume multiple roles.

This new Athenian art form was called *tragoidia*, "goat song," perhaps referring to its presentation at festivals of Dionysus. (The sacrifice of goats was part of the god's cult.) By about 534 B.C., under the enlightened tyrant PISISTRATUS, tragedy performance was installed officially at the important Athenian early springtime festival called the City Dionysia. By 500 B.C. this festival had developed into the annual, publicly funded, three-way competition that was the famous occasion for all performances of new tragedy. Performances were held in a theater—first of wood or earth, later of marble—at the south base of the Athenian ACROPOLIS.

The Dionysia contest typically presented three authors' new work—in each case, a tragic trilogy and a satyr play (*saturikon*), for comic relief. The satyr play, an offshoot of comedy, featured a clownish chorus always represented as satyrs. In a typical plot, this gang would "wander into" one of the great myths, such as that of PERSEUS (1). Today only one complete satyr play survives: the *Cyclops* of EURIPIDES (circa 410 B.C.).

The three groups of plays performed at the Dionysia would have been selected previously, in written form, by an official who judged the applicants. Qualifying entrants were assigned a paying sponsor (*choregos*), who paid part of the cost out of pocket as a form of state service; the balance came directly out of state funds. At the festival a panel of judges, consisting of ordinary citizens chosen by lottery, awarded first, second, and third prize to the three playwrights. Sophocles is said to have won first prize 24 times, second prize seven times, and never third.

Comedy, less esteemed than tragedy, was installed as a competition at the City Dionysia only around 488 B.C. The entries were single plays, one by each playwright. By 440 B.C. a second contest had been introduced, at the Lenaea (a Dionysian festival in midwinter). Normally five comedies competed. The two earliest comedy-writers about whom any information exists are CRATINUS and Crates (mid-400s B.C.).

Comedy employed a chorus of 24 members; tragedy used 12 at first, later 15. Comic choruses tended to be more important to the play's action and message than were their tragic counterparts—at least by the time of Aeschylus (525–456 B.C.), who was remembered for having reduced the tragic chorus' speaking role. All Athenian actors and stage choruses were male, although the roles might be female.

The first Athenian tragedian about whom any information exists is PHRYNICHUS (circa 540–475 B.C.). His tragedies may have been a form of costumed oratorio, with a simple narrative. The story would unfold around a single speaking actor (the *protagonistes*), who might assume multiple roles by changing masks and who would deliver his speeches in alternation with the chorus.

Stagecraft, plotting, and characterization were improved by Aeschylus, whose *Persians* (472 B.C.) is the earliest extant tragedy. Emphasizing individual roles over the chorus, Aeschylus introduced a second speaking actor, which allowed for better-developed conflicts onstage and which greatly increased the number of available roles. Sophocles (circa 496–406 B.C.) introduced a third speaking actor, and he emphasized characterizations of his protagonists that tended to remove the chorus from the plot. His younger rival Euripides (circa 485–406 B.C.) produced innovations in plotting and in characterization of mythical characters that often seem intended to disturb the audience. These three tragedians—along with a fourth, AGATHON (late 400s B.C.)—were recognized in their own day as being the greatest practitioners of the art.

With the deaths of Euripides and Sophocles (both in 406 B.C.) and Athens' defeat in the PELOPONNESIAN WAR (404 B.C.), the great age of Athenian theater had passed. New tragedies were still performed—the Syracusan tyrant DIONYSIUS (1) wrote one that won a single-play prize at Athens in 367 B.C.—but in the absence of steady new talent, a tradition arose of restaging the plays of the three classic tragedians.

Comedy at Athens enjoyed a resurgence with MENANDER, Philemon, and other writers of "New Comedy," in the late 300s B.C. This socially satirical comedy of manners—so different from the directly political invective of Aristophanes or EUPOLIS—went on to influence the work of the Roman comedy-writers Plautus and Terence (100s B.C.).

Outside Athens, monumental theater buildings had arisen before circa 470 B.C., when the Syracusan tyrant HIERON (1) constructed a theater for the production of a tragedy by the visiting Aeschylus. By the HELLENISTIC AGE (300–150 B.C.), every major Greek city had a marble theater, seating as many as 24,000, where performances might consist largely of restaged plays of the three great Athenian tragedians. Today admirable ancient theaters have been reconstructed at EPIDAURUS, DODONA, PERGAMUM, and EPHESUS, among other sites.

Thebes　Major city of central Greece. Set in the eastern plain of BOEOTIA, seven-gated Thebes (Greek: Thēbai) enjoyed wide farmlands and control of overland routes both north and south. Today the ancient city's central fortress, the Cadmea (named for Thebes' legendary founder, King CADMUS) lies buried directly under the modern Greek town of Thivai.

Thebes was known for its first-rate army, which included a strong CAVALRY arm, and throughout its history the city usually dominated all of Boeotia. In the 300s B.C. Thebes became the foremost Greek power for a brief time, after defeating and displacing its former ally SPARTA.

Along with its neighbor and rival ORCHOMENUS, Thebes seems to have been preeminent in the earlier centuries of MYCENAEAN CIVILIZATION, circa 1600–1350 B.C. Archaeological excavations at Thebes, hampered by the site's modern town, have yielded portions of a Mycenaean palace as well as LINEAR B tablets and Near Eastern seal stones (which may add credence to the legend that King Cadmus originally came from the Levant). Thebes' importance in this era is reflected in the city's large role in Greek MYTH. The ruling caste's fortunes and misfortunes are recounted in the tales of HERACLES, OEDIPUS, and the SEVEN AGAINST THEBES. The legend of the Seven—with its sequel, the tale of the Epigoni—possibly commemorates Thebes' downfall at the hands of the rival Greek kingdom of MYCENAE, circa 1350 B.C.

By the 500s B.C. the tales of Thebes had been organized into three epic poems, the *Oedipodia*, the *Thebaïd*, and the *Epigoni*, collectively known as the Theban Cycle. These stories later became favorite material for the Athenian tragic playwrights.

In historical times Thebes' hegemony over the other Boeotian cities took the form of a federation—the Boeotian League, wherein Thebes supplied two or more of the 11 delegates, and every other represented state supplied one. Thebes shared an ill-defined, mountainous frontier with ATHENS, which lay about 40 miles southeast. The two cities were enemies in the late 500s–early 300s B.C., due largely to Athens' alliance with Thebes' defiant neighbor PLATAEA. The creation of the Athenian DEMOCRACY (508 B.C.) further alarmed the Thebans, whose government was an OLIGARCHY.

During the Persian king XERXES' invasion of Greece (480–479 B.C.), Thebes was the major Greek city to submit to the Persians, and it contributed soldiers and a base of operations for the Persian war effort. After the Persian defeat, Thebes fell into deep discredit. Stripped of its Boeotian hegemony by the vindictive Spartans, the city remained a minor power until the mid-400s B.C., when the Spartans revived it as an ally against their common enemy, Athens. As a staunch Spartan ally, Thebes again became the chief city of Boeotia. The Thebans' attack on Plataea precipitated the PELOPONNESIAN WAR (431–404 B.C.). In 424 B.C. the Thebans defeated an Athenian invasion at the Battle of Delium.

Victory in the war added to Thebes' prestige and territory, gained at the expense of its small Boeotian neighbors. But, alienated by Spartan arrogance, Thebes soon made alliance with Athens, ARGOS, and CORINTH against Sparta, in the CORINTHIAN WAR (394–386 B.C.).

The following decades saw the acme of Theban power, under the city's greatest statesman and general, EPAMINONDAS. He led his countrymen against the Spartans—supposedly the greatest soldiers in Greece—and defeated them at the Battle of LEUCTRA (371 B.C.). The Thebans then dismantled Sparta's empire, marching into the PELOPONNESE and freeing MESSENIA and ARCADIA from Spartan control. The Theban army of these years was distinguished by the Sacred Band (Hieros Lochos), an elite corps of 300 HOPLITES consisting of paired male lovers. Classical Thebes in general was known for its military male-homosexual society.

In the mid-300s B.C. Thebes was confronted with the emerging power of MACEDON. Initially siding with the Macedonian king PHILIP II, Thebes switched sides to join the Athenian-led alliance that opposed Philip. After taking part in the disastrous Greek defeat at CHAERONEA (338 B.C.), Thebes was stripped of power and garrisoned by Philip's vengeful troops. A Theban revolt after Philip's death brought the city to complete destruction at the hands of Philip's successor, ALEXANDER THE GREAT: 6,000 Thebans were supposedly killed and 30,000 sold as SLAVES (335 B.C.). Thebes was rebuilt in 316 B.C. by the Macedonian ruler CASSANDER but was never again a great power. By the first century B.C. it was little more than a village.

Greek Thebes had nothing to do with the magnificent ancient Egyptian city called Thebes (modern Luxor and Karnak). Thēbai was a hellenized name, given to the Egyptian site by Greek visitors. One ancient Egyptian name for the city was Apet; to the Greek ear, this apparently sounded enough like Thēbai for the two names to become assimilated.

(See also ANTIGONE; DIONYSUS; EPIC POETRY; HOMOSEXUALITY; PERSIAN WARS; WARFARE, LAND.)

Themistocles Athenian statesman and general who lived circa 528–463 B.C. In the history of ATHENS, Themistocles is second in importance only to PERICLES (who was his political successor). By urging the Athenians to create a powerful navy in the early 480s B.C., Themistocles provided his city and all of Greece with an effective defense against invasion in the PERSIAN WARS (480 B.C.). This Athenian navy then became the means by which Athens acquired and held its sea empire of 479–404 B.C. In domestic politics, Themistocles was a radical left-winger who helped broaden the base of the Athenian DEMOCRACY, in opposition to the rich and noble-born. He was also an inveterate enemy of SPARTA, foreseeing, as few Athenians did in the 470s B.C., that Sparta would be Athens' next great foe.

Themistocles remained a controversial figure long after his death. His deeds are described by the historian HERODOTUS (circa 435 B.C.), by the biographer PLUTARCH (circa A.D. 100), and briefly by the historian THUCYDIDES (1) (circa 410 B.C.). Herodotus and Plutarch show signs of having used anti-Themistoclean source material, which condemns the man for his greed and flawed patriotism. But Thucydides praises Themistocles' foresight and decisiveness, summarizing him with these words: "With his inborn genius and speed of action, he was the best for doing at a moment's notice exactly what the emergency called for" (book 1, 103).

Themistocles' father Neocles was of an aristocratic Athenian family. Themistocles' mother is sometimes described as a non-Athenian—which, if true, would have placed the future statesman in a relatively humble social category. Themistocles rose quickly as a left-wing politician in the newly created democracy, being elected chief ARCHON at about age 35 and organizing the development of PIRAEUS as Athens' harbor and naval base (493 B.C.).

The years after the Battle of MARATHON (490 B.C.) saw political turmoil at Athens, with at least five prominent

The hero of the Persian Wars. This portrait of Themistocles comes from a marble bust, titled with his name and found at Ostia, near Rome. The likeness is thought to be based on an original Greek portrait statue of circa 460 B.C. The figure's blunt, pugnacious features recall the fact that, however brilliant he may have been, Themistocles was basically a soldier and left-wing politician. In this face can be seen the hearty, outspoken man of the people.

politicians banished by OSTRACISM—but not Themistocles, who emerged as the city's leading statesman. It was then he made his great contribution to Athens' future. In 488 B.C. the publicly owned SILVER mines at Laurium, outside Athens, produced a bonanza yield. Although it was customary for such surpluses to be distributed as cash to each citizen, Themistocles convinced the Athenian ASSEMBLY to use the revenue to build new warships. His ostensible reason was Athens' current war against the nearby Greek state of AEGINA, but his real reason seems to have been his expectation of the Persian invasion. Within three years Athens had acquired the biggest navy in the Greek world—going from 70 warships to 200—and all its new vessels were the superior type of warship known as the trireme.

When the Greek states allied against the attack of the Persian king XERXES (480 B.C.), Themistocles served as a fleet commander and as one of the strategy-planning chiefs of staff. (He was not, however, the top-ranking Greek admiral; that honor went to a Spartan.) To Themistocles can be ascribed the strategy of confronting the southward-sailing Persian fleet inside certain narrow channels, where the invaders' superior numbers and seamanship would be canceled out. After moderate success at the sea battle of ARTEMISIUM, this strategy resulted in a total Greek victory at SALAMIS (1), inside a mile-wide channel not far from Athens, specifically chosen by Themistocles long before the event.

Even before the war was over, Themistocles foresaw that Sparta would be Athens' next enemy. Although the Spartans respected him, Themistocles began to steer his city against them. The walls of Athens, destroyed by the Persians, were rebuilt despite Spartan disapproval (479 B.C.), and alliances were formed with ARGOS and THESSALY, two enemies of Sparta.

But Themistocles' downfall soon followed. The creation of the DELIAN LEAGUE and the naval counteroffensive against the Persians brought new Athenian soldier-politicians to the fore, particularly the young, conservative, pro-Spartan CIMON. Circa 471 B.C. the Athenians voted to ostracize Themistocles, who was by then nearly 60. He spent the next years traveling around the PELOPONNESE, where his activities seem connected with the establishment of anti-Spartan democracies at Argos, at MANTINEA, and elsewhere. The alarmed Spartans appealed to Athens, claiming to have proof that Themistocles was conducting treasonous intrigues with the Persian king. Indicted by the Athenians for treason, Themistocles fled Greece for ASIA MINOR (circa 467 B.C.). Eventually making his way to the Persian court at Susa, he became a valued adviser to King Artaxerxes I (464 B.C.). For about the last year of his life, the hero of Salamis served as a local Persian governor at the city of Magnesia-on-the-Maeander, in Asia Minor. He died, probably of natural causes, at age 65.

Themistocles was married twice, to Athenian women; his second wife, Archippe, accompanied or followed him to Asia with the youngest of their children. Two of Themistocles' daughters had the unusual names Italia and Sybaris, which may indicate yet another of his foreign-policy visions—namely, the extension of Athenian influence westward to the Greek cities of southern ITALY.

(See also AESCHYLUS; ARISTIDES; ATTICA; SYBARIS; WARFARE, NAVAL; XANTHIPPUS.)

Theocritus   One of the best-known poets of the HELLENISTIC AGE. Born circa 300 B.C. in the Sicilian Greek city of SYRACUSE, Theocritus flourished at Egyptian ALEXANDRIA (1), at the wealthy and literary court of king PTOLEMY (2) II Philadelphus; there Theocritus seems to have been a friend of the great Alexandrian poet CALLIMACHUS. Theocritus wrote in several poetic genres, but his most influential verses were his innovative pastoral poems. It was Theocritus who bequeathed to future generations of Roman and European Renaissance poets the pretty literary convention of Sicilian shepherds and shepherdesses, pining for love or playing contentedly on panpipes. Of his work, 31 poems survive today; in addition to bucolic poems, these include mimes (Greek: *mimoi*, realistic or satirical scenes rendered into hexameters) and epyllia (little epics)—hexameter poems of several hundred lines presenting a heroic MYTH or love story.

Theognis   Lyric poet of the Greek city of MEGARA (1), of the mid-500s B.C. Theognis' work survives as a collection of nearly 700 elegiac couplets, many of which apparently were written by anonymous later poets in imitation of Theognis' poems. Within this collection (known as the Theognidia), modern scholars have tentatively identified a core of about 300 poems, which seem to reflect a consistent poetic personality and a composition date in the mid-500s B.C.

One reason why Theognis' poetry attracted imitators is that he spoke for an entire ancient Greek social class—the ARISTOCRACY, who by the 500s B.C. had lost their monopoly on wealth and political power, and whose very lives were threatened, in some cities, by the rise of violent popular leaders known as TYRANTS (*turannoi*). Theognis' verses angrily bewail the fact that noble families are intermarrying with wealthy families of lower social status. "Now blood is diluted by base wealth," the poet typically laments. Most of the poems of the Theognidia are drinking songs (*skolia*), written for musical recitation at the upper-class drinking party known as the SYMPOSIUM. These poems heartily reflect the symposium's intellectual and homosexual atmosphere. Nearly all of the authentic Theognis poems are addressed to a certain Cyrnus, who was the poet's boyfriend; in certain verses Theognis speaks candidly of his love and passion for Cyrnus.

(See also HOMOSEXUALITY; LYRIC POETRY.)

Theophrastus   Greek philosopher and essayist who lived circa 370–287 B.C. Born on the island of LESBOS, he was active at ATHENS, where he succeeded ARISTOTLE as head of the philosophical school known as the LYCEUM. Theophrastus maintained the school's broad range of study, and he eventually moved the location to a larger building complex, called the Peripatos.

Theophrastus wrote on a variety of scientific and philosophical subjects, but is best remembered today for his extant work titled *Characters*, a collection of 30 sketches of eccentric or abnormal personality types.

Thera   Greek island of the mid AEGEAN SEA, at the southern edge of the island group known as the CYCLADES. The island's alternative, Italian-derived name, Santorini, commemorates St. Irene of Salonika. Covering only 29 square miles, Thera consists of an irregular, westward-opening crescent that rises dramatically from the sea. This odd shape marks the remnant of an ancient volcanic cone, which—as geology and ARCHAEOLOGY show—erupted in about 1480 B.C., blasting itself in half.

Before the eruption, Thera was home to a branch of the pre-Greek MINOAN CIVILIZATION. Modern excavations at Akrotiri, in southern Thera, have uncovered the most important Minoan site known to us outside of CRETE, with remnants of streets and villas, and some fine frescoes. This settlement was preserved for millennia by being buried in lava after its inhabitants had fled.

Thera's cataclysmic eruption of 1480 B.C. probably resembled that of the Indonesian island Krakatoa in A.D. 1883.

The resultant tidal waves battered other islands, including Crete, 70 miles south. The disaster may have been the direct cause of a sharp social decline observable in Crete at that time, including depopulation of Crete's coastlines. Thera's destruction may possibly lie behind the later Greek legend of ATLANTIS.

Circa 1000 B.C., Thera was occupied by DORIAN GREEKS from the mainland, who founded Thera city, in the south mid-island. An impressive temple of Carnean APOLLO, datable to the 500s B.C., is among the city's early monuments revealed by excavation. Scratched onto rocks nearby are ancient Greek graffiti, many with jocular homosexual messages, which represent some of the earliest surviving examples of Greek alphabetic WRITING (600s B.C.).

Despite prosperity, early Dorian Thera was badly enough afflicted by drought to send out large numbers of its young men to found a colony in North Africa, circa 630 B.C. This colony was CYRENE (1), which became one of the foremost cities of the Greek world within just a few decades.

Although Dorian-Greek and not Ionian, Thera was a subject ally of ATHENS in the DELIAN LEAGUE (400s B.C.). In the 200s B.C. the island became a naval base for Ptolemaic EGYPT, before being annexed by the Romans in the first century B.C. Most of Thera city's physical remains, including the AGORA, colonnades, and temple of the god DIONYSUS, date from the Ptolemaic and Roman occupations.

(See also COLONIZATION; HOMOSEXUALITY.)

Theramenes   Athenian commander and right-wing politician of the late PELOPONNESIAN WAR and its aftermath. Theramenes was instrumental in arranging the Athenian surrender to SPARTA at the war's end (404 B.C.). More important, he was involved in both of the oligarchic coups at ATHENS in these years—that of the FOUR HUNDRED (411 B.C.) and that of the THIRTY TYRANTS (404–403 B.C.). As leader of the moderate faction within the Thirty, Theramenes lost his life for opposing the extremist leader, CRITIAS.

The contemporary Athenian historian XENOPHON, who knew Theramenes, portrays him as a cynical opportunist. But later writers (including ARISTOTLE in his *Constitution of Athens*) have seen Theramenes as a true moderate and patriot, trying to steer his city through disaster.

(See also OLIGARCHY.)

Thermopylae   Seaside mountain pass, connecting the frontiers of THESSALY and East LOCRIS, at the eastern edge of the Mt. Oeta range, in northeast-central Greece. In 480 B.C., during the PERSIAN WARS, Thermopylae was the site of a famous three-day battle in which 5,000 Greek HOPLITES, led by the Spartan king Leonidas, blocked a Persian army of perhaps 200,000, marching south under the command of King XERXES.

Long before the battle, Thermopylae was recognized as the strategic weak point on the main route into central Greece. Just under four miles long and less than 50 feet wide at its narrowest point, the pass was hemmed (to the west) by a wall of cliffs and (to the east) by the waters of the Gulf of Malis. Circa 600 B.C. the pass was further closed by a wall, built by inhabitants of the central Greek region of PHOCIS to block the southward incursions of their enemies, the Thessalians.

North of the pass, the River Spercheios flows into the gulf. The river's alluvial deposits have changed the coastline since ancient times, resulting in a seaward widening of the pass. No longer is Thermopylae the grim "catwalk" it once was. The name Thermopulai, "hot gates," refers to local sulfur springs. Ancient Thermopylae also served as a sanctified meeting place for the local peoples of the AMPHICTYONIC LEAGUE.

The Battle of Thermopylae was fought in the late summer of 480 B.C., simultaneous with the sea battle of ARTEMISIUM, 40 miles away. On the Greek side, the object of both battles was to stop the enemy at narrow points on land and sea, north of the Greek heartland. Unfortunately, the Thermopylae effort was undermined by the indecision of leaders at SPARTA, who sent an advance guard under Leonidas, but then declined to send the main army—in part because their religious festival of the Carneia offically forbade the dispatching of troops during that time. So Leonidas was left to hold Thermopylae with his small force.

The Persian infantry entered the northern mouth of the pass and charged against the Greek hoplites, who had formed up alongside and behind the stone wall. The Greek historian HERODOTUS, the main source for information on the Persian Wars, describes how the Persians and their countrymen, the Medes—unable to use their superior numbers in the narrow space—fell back repeatedly with heavy losses. Even Xerxes' elite legion of Immortals failed to push through. The invaders were disadvantaged by having shorter thrusting spears and lighter armor than the Greeks, and perhaps by having inferior morale and discipline. But, after two days, with the help of a traitorous local Greek named Ephialtes, the Persians found a mountain footpath that brought their troops down behind the Greek lines.

Leonidas, learning that he was being outflanked, sent most of the army south to safety. The battle's climax, on the third day, was the heroic last stand of Leonidas with his royal guard of 300 Spartans and 1,100 other Greek troops, from BOEOTIA. The Persian troops, lashed on by the whips of their commanders, attacked from both ends of the pass; in the crush, some fell into the sea or were trampled underfoot. The Greeks fought until their spears were broken, then fought on with their swords. Leonidas was killed, as were all his 300 Spartans—except for one man, who had been sent home ill. The Boeotians died, too, or surrendered. On the Persian side, the dead included two of Xerxes' brothers. But the invading hordes marched through, into central Greece.

Although in military terms Thermopylae was a Greek failure—with more men and better organization they might have seriously stalled the Persian land invasion—the battle became very significant in emotional and patriotic terms. Like other suicidal exploits, the Spartan defense at Thermopylae inspired strong reverence in the Greek mind. Monuments to the slain were erected at Sparta and in the pass itself, where the defenders were buried. The poet SIMONIDES wrote one of the epitaphs:

Here is the tomb of the renowned Megistias
Whom the Persians slew close by the River Spercheios.

A seer, he clearly saw the goddesses of death approach,
Yet could not desert his Spartan king.

But the most enduring Thermopylae epitaph is an anonymous elegiac couplet, from a commemorative column in the pass:

Go tell the Spartans, O passerby,
That here we lie, complying with their orders.

The Thermopylae pass remained a strategic bone of contention throughout Greek history. In 352 B.C. it was occupied by the Macedonian king PHILIP II, in a military-diplomatic maneuver against ATHENS. In 279 B.C. a united Greek army defended the pass—again unsuccessfully—against the southward invasion of the CELTS.

(See also LYRIC POETRY; PROPHECY AND DIVINATION.)

Theron   See ACRAGAS.

Theseus   Mythical Athenian hero and king. Whereas many Greek legendary heroes were connected with the cities of THEBES or MYCENAE, relatively few figures were attached to ATHENS. Theseus therefore came to be viewed as an Athenian national hero—not only a great warrior and lover, but a civilizer, who rid the countryside of brigands and who unified the villages of ATTICA into a single federation, centered at Athens. In historical times, he was honored at an annual festival, the Theseia, held in the fall.

Being an Athenian cultural treasure, the Theseus MYTH was reworked by generations of poets and storytellers. Several of Theseus' adventures seem specifically modeled on those of HERACLES, in an attempt to make Theseus as important as that greatest Greek hero. Some of this nationalistic myth-making perhaps occurred in the 500s B.C., under the Athenian tyrants PISISTRATUS and HIPPIAS (1).

The mythical Theseus probably commemorates some actual Athenian king of the Mycenaean era, perhaps circa 1300 B.C., whose lasting achievement was to consolidate the 1,000-square-mile region of Attica under his rule. Possibly this king's name really was Theseus (Settler). Alternatively, the king's accomplishments were eventually ascribed to an existing legendary hero. The historical essence of the Theseus legend appealed to PLUTARCH (circa A.D. 100), who wrote a biography of Theseus among his biographies of more strictly historical Greeks and Romans.

According to the myth, the Athenian king Aegeus, being childless, consulted the god APOLLO's oracle at DELPHI. He received the advice to return home but that, until arriving, he should not "loosen the wineskin's jutting foot." In fact this was a warning, not against alcohol, but against sexual intercourse; however, Aegeus, failing to understand, dallied with King Pittheus' daughter, Aethra, at the city of Troezen (in the northeastern PELOPONNESE). Departing from Troezen, Aegeus left behind a sword and a pair of sandals underneath a huge boulder; he secretly instructed Aethra that when their future son—whom Aethra was confident she had conceived—was strong enough to shift the boulder and recover the items of proof, he should go to Athens.

The son was born at Troezen and named Theseus. King Pittheus, to protect his daughter's reputation, claimed that

Theseus' father was the god POSEIDON, who supposedly had seduced Aethra. On reaching manhood, Theseus easily pushed the boulder away from the sandals and sword. Taking these tokens of identity, he went to find his father at Athens. Rather than use the quick sea route across the Saronic Gulf, Theseus chose to travel by land, around the top of the gulf, for adventure's sake.

On the journey, he encountered a series of sadistic brigands and slew them all. Reaching Athens, Theseus was acknowledged by his father, King Aegeus. Soon, however, Theseus came into danger from Aegaeus' paramour, the Colchian princess MEDEA, who feared Theseus' influence and right of succession. At Medea's prompting, Aegeus sent Theseus against the Bull of MARATHON, which was ravaging the countryside. (This adventure is clearly based on Heracles' Seventh Labor, against the Cretan Bull.) Theseus captured the animal and sacrificed it to Apollo.

Next came the hero's most famous adventure. Athens (according to the myth) was at this time a subject city of Crete, having been subdued by the Cretan king MINOS. The Athenians were compelled to pay a yearly tribute of seven youths and seven maidens, who were sent by Athenian ship to Crete to be locked up inside the maze of the LABYRINTH. There the young people would be devoured by the ferocious Minotaur (bull of Minos), who was the monstrous half-man, half-bull offspring of Minos' wife, Queen Pasiphaë. Theseus, deciding to put a stop to this oppression, volunteered to sail to Crete amid the next batch of young people.

Reaching Crete, he met the princess Ariadne, daughter of Minos and Pasiphaë. She fell in love with him and, to guide him through the dark Labyrinth, gave him a thread, one end of which he fastened near the entrance. Then he slew the Minotaur, escaped from the Labyrinth, and fled from Crete with Ariadne aboard the waiting Athenian tribute ship. But Theseus callously abandoned Ariadne on the island of Naxos, where she was later found and wed by the god DIONYSUS.

Theseus' ship sailed on toward Athens. The hero had arranged with his father that, if he were successful on Crete, he would substitute the tribute ship's black sail for another one, colored white. In the excitement of the return Theseus forgot this agreement, and Aegeus, seeing the ship approach under a black sail, assumed that his son had been killed. The remorseful Aegeus immediately threw himself into the sea and drowned. Supposedly, from this, the AEGEAN SEA was named.

Succeeding his father as king, Theseus brought about the unification of Attica. He then departed on a campaign against the distant-dwelling AMAZONS, the tribe of fierce female warriors. One version says that Theseus accompanied Heracles' Amazon expedition, another that Theseus went on his own, but in either case he brought back to Athens, as his captive, the Amazon queen, Hippolyta. In pursuit, the mass of Amazons marched to Athens and besieged the city, but were repulsed. (In classical times, the Amazonomachy, or Battle with the Amazons, was a favorite subject of monumental Athenian SCULPTURE and PAINTING.) Hippolyta died after bearing Theseus a son, HIPPOLYTUS. Later Theseus married Phaedra, the younger sister of Ariadne, and this young wife conceived an illicit

passion for her stepson, resulting in the tragic deaths of both.

One of Theseus' last adventures was his visit to the Underworld with his friend Pirithous, king of the Lapiths. Their ambitious goal was to carry off the goddess PERSEPHONE, to be Pirithous' wife. However, Persephone's husband, HADES, captured the two heroes by tricking them into sitting on an enchanted bench, which held them fast. Theseus eventually was rescued by Heracles, who managed to rip him out of his chair; but Pirithous remained in the nether world.

The end of Theseus' life was unhappy. Ousted from Athens by a rebellion, he voyaged to the island of Scyros, where he was murdered by the king, Lycomedes, who disputed Theseus' claim to a local estate.

The myth has a historical aftermath. In about 476 B.C. the Athenian commander CIMON brought back from Scyros a skeleton and relics said to be those of Theseus. The hero was reburied in a monumental tomb in the middle of Athens. The writer Plutarch mentions that the tomb became a sanctuary for runaway SLAVES and the needy, because, in his lifetime, Theseus was the champion of the oppressed.

(See also MYCENAEAN CIVILIZATION; PROCRUSTES.)

Thespis See THEATER.

Thessaly Large, northeasterly region of Greece. Thessaly, whose best-known landmark is Mt. OLYMPUS, consists of two wide and fertile plains, enclosed on four sides by mountains. To the south rises the range of Mt. Oeta, which—in ancient Greek geographical terms—separated Thessaly from PHOCIS and the rest of central Greece; the principal route through this barrier was the pass of THERMOPYLAE. On Thessaly's western and southwestern frontiers stood the Pindus mountain range, beyond which lay the Greek states of EPIRUS and AETOLIA. On the north, more mountains divided Thessaly from the kingdom of MACEDON. And, in the east, the north-to-south line of Mt. Olympus, Mt. Ossa, and Mt. Pelion occupied the Aegean coast and rendered the shoreline harborless and unusable for shipping.

The only suitable harbor in all Thessaly was located at the top of the Gulf of Pagasae (the modern Gulf of Volos), nestled behind the southward-jutting peninsula called Magnesia. There two seaports emerged in different phases of history: First was Iolcus (modern Volos), a major city of the MYCENAEAN CIVILIZATION (circa 1600–1200 B.C.), fabled as the home of the hero JASON (1). Later came nearby Pagasae, which flourished in the 400s and 300s B.C.

The name Thessaly commemorates the Thessaloi, a Greek people of the Aeolian ethnic group who subjugated the area circa 1100 B.C., soon after the Mycenaean collapse. The inhabitants retained an Aeolic dialect in ancient times. Thessaly's wealth lay in its wide plains, which provided grain, cattle, and—the region's hallmark—horses. The Thessalians were famous horsemen; their armies, unlike most Greek forces, consisted mainly of CAVALRY.

Isolated by its mountain perimeter, Thessaly developed as a self-contained, horse-ranching ARISTOCRACY. During the great centuries of Greek history (800–300 B.C.) it remained politically and culturally backward, with power and ownership concentrated in the hands of a few immensely rich families. One such family was the Aleudae, based at the city of Larissa, in the northern plain. These aristocrats resisted both kingship and DEMOCRACY, and it was not until about 374 B.C. that Thessaly became united under one leader, the tyrant JASON (2) of the city of Pherae.

In the 350s B.C. Thessaly fell under the sway of the Macedonian king PHILIP II, and Thessalian cavalry did important service in the army of Philip and of his son ALEXANDER THE GREAT. Valuable as a doorway into central Greece, Thessaly received a Macedonian garrison, which was housed (circa 293 B.C.) in a newly built fortress called Demetrias, adjoining Pagasae. The region remained under Macedonian control until the Romans broke Macedon's power, in 168 B.C.

(See also AEOLIAN GREEKS; GREECE, GEOGRAPHY OF; GREEK LANGUAGE; ROME; TYRANTS.)

Thetis   See ACHILLES; PELEUS.

Thirty Tyrants, the   Name commonly given to the 30-man committee that ruled in ATHENS as a dictatorial puppet government for the Spartans immediately after Athens' surrender in the PELOPONNESIAN WAR (404 B.C.). The Thirty ruled for over a year, from spring 404 until early autumn 403 B.C., in a reign of terror.

The 30 men were right-wing Athenians, elected by the Athenians at a rigged meeting of the ASSEMBLY under the watchful eye of the occupying Spartan general, LYSANDER. Elected ostensibly to draft a new law code, they seized the government, with Lysander's approval, and dismantled the Athenian DEMOCRACY. They disbanded the democratic COUNCIL, abolished the people's law courts, and convinced Lysander to install a Spartan garrison on the ACROPOLIS. With their private police force of 300 "whip-bearers," the Thirty conducted arrests and executions to eradicate opposition and raise funds by confiscation. As many as 1,500 citizens and METICS (resident aliens) are said to have lost their lives; many others fled.

Eventually there arose division within the Thirty, between the extremist CRITIAS and the more moderate THERAMENES. At length, Critias had Theramenes put to death.

When a resistance band under the exiled Athenian soldier Thrasybulus seized a fortress in the Attic countryside, the Thirty began preparing a refuge for themselves at the town of Eleusis, outside Athens. This led to their worst atrocity—the execution of 300 men of Eleusis—perhaps the town's entire adult male population.

But the despots' days were numbered. When Thrasybulus' rebels seized Athens' harbor town of PIRAEUS, the Thirty brought out an army against them and were defeated (winter 404–403 B.C.). Critias was killed in the fighting, as was his nephew and lieutenant Charmides. The remnants of the Thirty were deposed, and full democracy was restored by the autumn of 403 B.C. Individual members of the Thirty were executed thereafter.

Remarkably, the Spartans had made little effort to save their puppet government. This inactivity owed much to a political rift at Sparta, where King Pausanias was repudiat-

ing Lysander's policies. Pausanias soon came to terms with the new Athenian government.

The Thirty represent the worst of three different oligarchic attempts to subvert the Athenian democracy during the 400s B.C. The first of these was the plot to hand over the LONG WALLS to the Spartans in 457 B.C.; the second was the coup d'etat of the FOUR HUNDRED in 411 B.C. All three attempts were inspired by an upper-class desire to rid the government of its lowest-income class of citizens, the *thetes*. Such plots failed because they inevitably did harm to the middle class—the HOPLITE class—as well as causing patriotic outrage.

(See also OLIGARCHY; PLATO; SOCRATES; SYMPOSIUM.)

Thrace   Non-Greek land extending for about 300 miles across the top of the AEGEAN SEA and the Sea of MARMARA, with a further coastline on the southwestern BLACK SEA, south of the Danube River. This region is now divided among the modern nations of Greece, Turkey, and Bulgaria. Relevant geographical features include three large rivers that empty southward into the Aegean; these are (from west to east) the Strymon, Nestus, and Hebrus. The largely mountainous interior rises to the Rhodope chain, which runs east–west along southern Bulgaria and the modern Greek border.

The ancient Greek name Thraikē probably renders the sound of some native name for the homeland. The Thracians spoke a non-Greek language and possessed northern European physical features, such as red hair. They brewed beer but for WINE they depended on Greek imports; they craved many Greek goods. The Thracians were renowned for their ferocity in battle (they used heavy slashing swords) and for their drunken devotions to the god DIONYSUS (a deity who may have originally been a Thracian beer god).

Throughout most of their history the Thracians remained grouped into various warlike tribes, chief of which were the Odrysae, in the east. Only in the mid-400s B.C. did a united Thracian kingdom emerge, briefly, under the Odrysian king Sitalces and his successors. The Thracians lived in villages, with no cities until Roman times (after the mid-100s B.C.).

Although Greece and Thrace had no common border—being buffered by the kingdom of MACEDON, northeast of Greece—Greek traders and settlers gravitated to Thrace's Aegean coast early on, to acquire the land's precious resources. GOLD and SILVER deposits at Mt. Pangaeus brought the Greek colonists to nearby THASOS (circa 700 B.C.) and Maroneia (mid-600s B.C.), in defiance of hostile local tribes. Other Greek colonies in Thrace included BYZANTIUM (mid-600s B.C.), AENUS (circa 600 B.C.), Perinthus (circa 600 B.C.), the CHERSONESE region (mid-500s B.C.), ABDERA (545 B.C.), and AMPHIPOLIS (437 B.C.).

Besides resources for mining, Thrace offered wheat, TIMBER, and SLAVES to the Greeks. The slaves were often freeborn Thracian war captives, acquired in internal Thracian feuds and then sold to local Greek traders. Thracians might even sell their own children (according to the Greek historian HERODOTUS). Thracian slaves, particularly females, are mentioned periodically in writings from ancient Greece.

The internal history of Thrace consists mainly of the rise of the Odrysian state in the 400s B.C., followed by its collapse in the 300s B.C. The Macedonian kings PHILIP II and ALEXANDER THE GREAT invaded Thrace repeatedly (340s–330s B.C.), annexing the Strymon valley and other locales and subjugating the entire land. After Alexander's death, Thrace briefly became a sovereign power under the Macedonian dynast LYSIMACHUS (reigned 323–281 B.C.), before returning to Macedonian control. After the Roman conquest of Macedon in 167 B.C., Thrace became an uneasy section of the Roman province of Macedonia.

(See also COLONIZATION; ORPHEUS.)

Thucydides (1)   Athenian historian who left behind a detailed but unfinished account of the PELOPONNESIAN WAR (431–404 B.C.), which he had lived through. Thucydides' work is one of the most valuable and impressive writings surviving from ancient Greece.

Although he was not the first Greek to write history—his main predecessor was HERODOTUS—Thucydides was in many ways the first real historian, the first author to apply rationalistic standards in inquiring about the past. Unlike Herodotus, Thucydides keeps strict chronology and avoids fables, biographical anecdotes, and (usually) digressions, instead focusing austerely on the most important events. In Herodotus' work, war and politics can result from the gods, FATE, or sexual passion. In Thucydides there are no such fairy-tale causes of action; Thucydides, like a modern political scientist, explains events in terms of a fundamental human drive for power and self-advantage.

In modern terms, Thucydides was as much a journalist as a historian, because much of what he reported was current or very recent as he was writing. He was no mere library scholar; already an adult when the Peloponnesian War began, he served (briefly and unsuccessfully) as an Athenian general. He states in his opening sentence that he began writing as soon as fighting broke out, since he believed that the war would be bigger and more worth recording that any prior conflict. He says that, for all events described, he either witnessed them firsthand or carefully interviewed participants afterward. Also (implicitly contrasting himself with the crowd-pleasing Herodotus), Thucydides announces that his opus will be the last word on the subject, and that it contains only strictly relevant information: "My work is written not as a display piece for an immediate audience, but as a prize to last forever" (book 1)

Born in around 460–455 B.C., Thucydides belonged to a very distinguished Athenian family with wealth from GOLD- and SILVER-mining privileges in the Mt. Pangaeus region of THRACE. His father, although Athenian, bore the Thracian royal name Olorus. According to a plausible reconstruction of Thucydides' family tree, the eminent Athenian soldier and statesman CIMON was Thucydides' granduncle, while Thucydides' maternal grandfather was the right-wing politician THUCYDIDES (2), in whose honor the future historian was named. Yet the younger Thucydides at some point deserted his family's politics and followed the radical democrat PERICLES, the bitter enemy of both Cimon and the elder Thucydides. In his writing, Thucyd-ides the historian (normally sparing of praise) extolls Pericles' intelligence and leadership.

The young Thucydides probably heard the historian Herodotus give public readings in ATHENS, circa 445–425 B.C. The earliest episode in Thucydides' life that is known today comes from a rare autobiographical mention in his history. Early in the Peloponnesian War, probably in 430 B.C., Thucydides caught the deadly plague that was sweeping through Athens. Unlike many Athenians, he survived, and in one passage he describes with scientific detachment the bodily symptoms of the disease and its devastation of the city (book 2).

By 424 B.C. he had been elected as one of Athens' 10 annual generals. He was assigned to the strategically vital coast of Thrace, where he already wielded influence as a mining mogul, but there (as he coolly relates in his history) he failed to prevent the Spartan commander BRASIDAS from capturing the Athenian colony of AMPHIPOLIS. For this failure, Thucydides was banished by the Athenians and lived away for 20 years, returning only when the exiles were recalled in 404 B.C., after Athens' final defeat.

Ironically, it was exile that allowed him to produce so fine a history. As an independently wealthy member of the international ARISTOCRACY in the days before general suspicion of espionage, Thucydides was able to travel through the theaters of war. "Because of my exile, I saw what was happening on both sides, particularly on the Peloponnesian side," he relates (book 5). He may have made the Thracian mining region his base, but he journeyed to SPARTA, whose paltry physical monuments he comments on (book 1), and to SYRACUSE, which looms large in his written work. He must have been a relentless seeker of truth—observing battles, interviewing soldiers and politicians, consulting archives, collating notes, and rejecting items in a drive for accuracy. Much of his information is amazing in its detail, but he rarely allows the details to submerge his story.

According to a later writer, Thucydides was married and had children. Apparently he died in around 400 B.C., only a few years after his return to Athens. He never completed his history, which breaks off in midsentence describing events of 411 B.C. (The last seven years of the war are recounted by the historian XENOPHON, in his *Hellenica*.)

Thucydides' history was organized by later scholars into eight "books," but in content it can be broken down into four unequal sections: (1) books 1–5 (partial), on the Archidamian War and Peace of NICIAS, 431–421 B.C.; (2) book 5 (remainder), on the troubled years of temporary peace, 421–415 B.C.; (3) books 6 and 7, a beautifully polished section describing the calamitous Athenian invasion of Syracuse, 415–413 B.C.; and (4) book 8, describing naval events in the eastern Aegean and the right-wing coup of the FOUR HUNDRED in Athens, 412–411 B.C. Both book 5 and the unfinished book 8 are clearly unrevised drafts. The work's well-known set pieces include Pericles' Funeral Oration over the Athenian dead (book 2), the description of civil war and moral breakdown at the city of CORCYRA (book 3), and the Melian Dialogue, in which notions of Might vesus Right are debated prior to the Athenians' devastation of the helpless island of MELOS (book 5). Writing in his native Attic prose, Thucydides uses a uniquely clipped and condensed style, which is sometimes difficult to understand. He seems to want to fit as much meaning into as few words as possible.

The writer's intelligence and mastery of his material tend to disguise certain flaws or quirks. It may be that Thucydides overrates Pericles as a soldier and glosses over a major Periclean military setback, the failed siege of the Peloponnesian city of EPIDAURUS in 430 B.C. Conversely, Thucydides surely underrates the motives and abilities of the Athenian politician CLEON; Thucydides seems to have disliked him personally—perhaps Cleon proposed the edict banishing General Thucydides in 424 B.C. Also, Thucydides shows himself totally uninterested in finance, despite its importance for the Athenian empire and war effort. His treatment of Greek-Persian affairs is skimpy, insofar as it was PERSIA's funding of the Spartan navy, 413–404 B.C., that enabled Sparta to defeat Athens. But some of these shortcomings might have been corrected had the historian lived to complete his work.

Another idiosyncrasy is Thucydides' way of ignoring questions of emotional motive, such as patriotism or religious piety, as not being true causes of events. Modern historians believe that emotional issues were important in such gatherings as the Athenian democratic ASSEMBLY, where demagogues might whip up the citizens to get them to vote a certain way. But in Thucydides' world it is only the victims, such as the doomed Melians in the Melian Dialogue, who make emotional appeals to the gods or to justice; the winners always speak in rational terms of self-advantage and expediency.

Nevertheless, Thucydides stands as a monumental early figure in history-writing. The personal impression he creates is that of an Olympian intellectual, patterned after his hero, Pericles. An atheist and a loner, enamored of intelligence and power, Thucydides could combine icy objectivity with a fascination for human affairs. He was a cynical genius, well suited to recording the suicidal event that toppled the classical Greek world.

Thucydides (2)   Athenian politician who led the right-wing opposition to the radical democrat PERICLES in the 440s B.C. and was ostracized by Pericles' efforts. Thucydides' defeat brought on a 14-year period of Periclean supremacy in the Athenian DEMOCRACY. This Thucydides probably was the maternal grandfather and namesake of the historian THUCYDIDES (1).

The future politician was born circa 500 B.C. His father, Melesias, an Athenian nobleman and celebrated wrestler, was a friend of the poet PINDAR. Thucydides grew up in the cosmopolitan world of Greek aristocrats and married a sister of the great Athenian soldier CIMON. After Cimon's death (circa 450 B.C.), Thucydides succeeded him as leader of the conservative opposition. He organized a system whereby all his followers sat together in the ASSEMBLY, in order to create more noise and effect during public debate.

An able orator, in around 448 B.C. Thucydides attacked Pericles' public-building policy, whereby allied DELIAN LEAGUE funds, contributed for defense against PERSIA, were to be used instead to erect grand monuments in ATHENS (such as the PARTHENON). Thucydides may have been sin-

cerely offended by Athens' domination of other Greek states, as well as by Periclean domestic policies that opened up political opportunities to the Athenian lower-income classes.

But Pericles' support was overwhelming, and the Athenians voted to ostracize Thucydides (circa 443 B.C.). He seems to have returned to Athens after his term of exile ended, circa 433 B.C., but we hear of no more political activity.

(See also OSTRACISM; WRESTLING.)

Thurii   See SYBARIS.

timber   In ancient mainland Greece, thick forests flourished in the foothills and mountains, which were cooler and far less heavily farmed than the arable plains. Trees carpeted mountainous regions such as ARCADIA and the Ossa-Pelion massif of southern THESSALY. The wood of these trees was a crucial construction material for public buildings, private homes, furnishings, machinery, and ships.

Foothills and lower mountain slopes supported a natural growth of deciduous trees; the most common was the oak, in several varieties. The oak's strong, heavy wood was an important source of timber for building beams and furniture. A tall, majestic tree, the "king" of the Greek forests, the oak was from an early period associated with ZEUS, king of the gods.

Other timber-producing trees of the middle-altitude region might include cypress, elm, and ash. Ash provides a tough, flexible wood that early on was used for military purposes. In HOMER's poems, the warriors' spears are described as being of ash.

Above 4,000 feet over sea level, the mountain regions produced the tallest conifers—fir, juniper, and cedar—which as a group supplied much of the best building timber in the ancient Mediterranean. Cedars produce large, durable beams, prized for big constructions such as a temple's roof supports. The fir tree, which grew in several varieties, was the seagoing tree; its lengthy, flexible, lightweight wood was well suited to the building of warships. Alternatively, the shipwright could use pine or cypress, which grew at lower altitudes than fir and were more accessible throughout the Greek world, but which gave the disadvantage of somewhat heavier planking. Merchant ships usually were made of pine.

Like grain, timber was a crucial import for the populous, powerful cities of central and southern Greece in the classical period. For the imperial ATHENS of the 400s B.C., with its need to maintain a large war fleet, foreign policy was partly a matter of ensuring friendship with—or else conquering—those states that had access to valuable forests of fir trees (such as MACEDON or the CHALCIDICE region).

In RELIGION, the Greeks associated certain trees with the Olympian gods. As mentioned, the oak was linked to Zeus; similarly, the olive "belonged" to ATHENA, the laurel to APOLLO, the cedar and nut trees to ARTEMIS, and the myrtle to APHRODITE. DIONYSUS, the god of WINE and vegetation in general, was associated with the pine, the plane tree, and most fruit-bearing trees as well as with the grape and ivy vines. Despite these divine associations, such trees generally were not immune from being cut down. In most

Greek communities, however, there existed sacred groves dedicated to a god or local hero, where the trees were sacrosanct.

(See also DODONA; FARMING; SHIPS AND SEAFARING.)

Timoleon   Corinthian-born commander and statesman, who in the 340s B.C. became the political savior of Greek SICILY. Liberating the various cities from their dictatorial TYRANTS, Timoleon led the Greeks in resistance to Carthaginian invaders.

Timoleon was a soldier and aristocrat of middle age, living in CORINTH in 345 B.C., when the Corinthians sent him with a small mercenary force to Sicily, in response to a request for help from the aristocrats of SYRACUSE. (Syracuse was the foremost Sicilian Greek city, and a Corinthian colony and ally.) The Syracusans were seeking aid against the tyrant Dionysius II, who, after a period of exile, had reinstated himself as master of the city. By combining military strategy with diplomacy, Timoleon ousted Dionysius. Then he reorganized the Syracusan government, creating a liberal OLIGARCHY on the Corinthian model. Thereafter he began a campaign to oust the tyrants of the other Sicilian-Greek cities and reorganize those governments.

Amid these events, in 341 B.C., a seaborne Carthaginian invasion force landed in Sicily. Timoleon won an initial victory over the invaders at the Crimisus River, in northwestern Sicily, but he was forced to sue for peace with the Carthaginians, after the Greek tyrants joined the war against him. Having made this peace, he was then free to defeat the tyrants separately (circa 340–337 B.C.) and to complete his reorganization of the cities' governments. He spent his final few years as a revered private citizen at Syracuse and died in 334 B.C. His achievements were short-lived: Within a generation chaos had returned to Greek Sicily, and there arose a new Syracusan tyrant, AGATHOCLES.

(See also CARTHAGE.)

tin   See BRONZE.

Tiresias   In MYTH, a blind Theban seer, renowned for his wisdom and longevity; he was said to have lived for seven generations. In HOMER's epic poem the *Odyssey* (book II), the hero ODYSSEUS visits the Underworld to consult the ghost of Tiresias, who prophesies as to what FATE awaits the hero at home and mentions certain precautions to observe on the return voyage.

Tiresias was not born blind; the best-known story about him tells how he lost his sight. Out walking one day, he encountered two snakes mating and hit them with his walking stick, killing the female. Immediately he was transformed into a woman, and remained so until, some time later, he again encountered two snakes mating. This time he killed the male and so regained his prior gender. Because Tiresias had had this unique experience, the god ZEUS and his wife, HERA, asked Tiresias to settle their argument as to who gets more pleasure from sexual intercourse, men or WOMEN. Zeus claimed it was women, but Hera modestly insisted it was men. When Tiresias declared that women get nine times more pleasure than men, Hera

angrily blinded him. But Zeus, to compensate, gave him long life and the inner sight of prophecy.

(See also PROPHECY AND DIVINATION; SOPHOCLES.)

Tiryns   Ancient Greek city in the Argolid region of the northeastern PELOPONNESE, near modern Nauplion. With its spectacular fortifications, first excavated by archaeologist Heinrich Schliemann in A.D. 1884, Tiryns provides the best surviving example of a fortress city of the MYCENAEAN CIVILIZATION (circa 1300 B.C.).

Tiryns was ideally located, atop a rocky hill in the southeast Argive plain, beside the sea (which now lies a mile away, due to coastal changes since ancient times). The site was inhabited long before the Greek era; the name Tiruns was not originally Greek, for its ending resembles the distinctive *nth* sound found in such other pre-Greek names as CORINTH and OLYNTHUS. Archaeological evidence suggests that Tiryns was among the first sites in Greece to be taken over by Greek-speaking invaders. The Greeks' arrival probably is indicated in the destruction of the pre-Greek palace known as the House of the Tiles, at nearby Lerna (circa 2100 B.C.).

In the Mycenaean age (1600–1200 B.C.) Tiryns served as the port for the overlord city of MYCENAE, nine miles to the north. Tiryns received its famous encircling walls, at two separate levels of its terraced hill, after 1400 B.C. These fortifications, made of huge limestone blocks weighing as much as 14 tons each, rose about 65 feet, with a typical thickness of 20–30 feet. In the east there stood a tall gateway, protected by an enfilading wall, similar to the Lion Gate at Mycenae. Greeks of later centuries ascribed these works to the mythical giant creatures known as Cyclopes, and they coined the adjective *Cyclopean,* which still is used today to denote Mycenaean grand masonry.

Within the walls stood a city complex, ascending to the summit's two royal halls (east and west), built in different eras. These two palaces were made of limestone and wood; a bathhouse and remnants of frescoes throughout suggest a primitive luxury. Tiryns' prominence in this epoch is reflected in Greek MYTH, which claimed that the hero HERACLES was born there or that his family came from there.

Like Mycenae and other cities, Tiryns shows clear signs of having been destroyed by fire circa 1200 B.C., amid the collapse of Mycenaean society. Reinhabited on a reduced scale, the town survived into historical times. But by then the nearby city of ARGOS was the dominant power of the plain, and in around 470 B.C. the Argives destroyed Tiryns.

(See also ARCHAEOLOGY; CYCLOPS; GREEK LANGUAGE.)

Titans   In MYTH, the Titans were a race of primeval gods who preceded the Olympian gods. They were the offspring of the goddess GAEA (Mother Earth) and the god Uranus (Greek: Ouranos, Sky); the most important of their number was CRONUS, who ruled the universe prior to his son ZEUS.

The Titans represent the brutal era before Zeus' civilizing reign. As recounted in HESIOD's epic poem the *Theogony* (circa 700 B.C.), Zeus became king after leading his fellow gods in a 10-year war against Cronus and the other Titans. (But two Titans, PROMETHEUS and Themis, fought beside the gods, as did other supernatural beings—the Cyclopes and the Hekatoncheires, or "hundred-handed ones.") De-feated, the enemy Titans now lie shackled forever in the lowest level of the Underworld—all except ATLAS, whose immense strength is employed in holding up the sky.

If the name Titan (plural: Titanes) is actually a Greek word, it may mean "honored one." More probably it is not Greek, but derives from the lost language of the pre-Greek inhabitants of Greece. The legend of the defeated Titans may distortedly commemorate the Greeks' conquest of a native people, circa 2100 B.C.

(See also AFTERLIFE; CYCLOPS; GIANTS; OLYMPUS, MT.; ORPHISM; RELIGION.)

trade   The Greeks share with the Phoenicians the distinction of being the greatest traders and seafarers of the ancient Mediterranean. One important reason why the Greeks were able to make such a strong impression on other ancient peoples—ETRUSCANS, CELTS, Romans, Scythians—was that they sailed far and wide in search for new markets to trade in.

For the archaeologist, ancient Greek trade routes often are suggested by the presence, in non-Greek lands, of surviving Greek POTTERY and metalwork. Written references by such authors as the Greek historian HERODOTUS or the Roman geographer Strabo also help fill in the picture. It is known that as early as about 1300 B.C., long before the invention of COINAGE, Mycenaean-Greek merchants were spanning the Mediterranean, trading by barter. Archaeological evidence shows that these early Greeks had trade depots in the Lipari Islands (near SICILY) as well as in CYPRUS, western ASIA MINOR, and the northern Levant. During the Greek trading and colonizing expansion of circa 800–500 B.C., Greek merchants visited southern France and Spain and the farthest corners of the BLACK SEA. Circa 308 B.C. a Greek skipper, Pytheas of MASSALIA, explored the Atlantic seaboard, sailing around Britain and perhaps reaching Norway in a search for new trade routes.

What lured the Greeks along these amazing distances was the need to acquire certain valuable resources or luxury goods (depending on the locale). Southern Spain, for example, offered raw tin, a necessary component of the alloy BRONZE, a metal on which Greek society of all centuries strongly depended. In the elaborate trade network of the ancient Mediterranean, tin was quarried by Celtic peoples in British Cornwall and (possibly) in northwest Spain, and was brought to the Greek market, overland to the Mediterranean, by Celtic middlemen. Other prizes of the western Mediterranean included SILVER ore and lead. In exchange, the Greeks might offer metalwork, textiles, or WINE, brought from mainland Greece or from the Greek cities of Asia Minor.

Other lands offered more sophisticated commodities and different rules of trade. To acquire the carved ivories, metalwork, or textiles of EGYPT, the Greeks of 800–500 B.C. might have to offer SLAVES, silver ore, or other basic resources that the wealthy Egyptians lacked. Perhaps most desirable of all Egyptian goods was the grain surplus of the Nile valley, which Greek merchants could ship to hungry Greece for lucrative resale. Grain, along with TIMBER, was also a major attraction of Sicily, ITALY, THRACE, and the northern Black Sea coast. Among valuable Greek

Trade-borne influences from the Near East are embodied in the griffin, a dragonlike beast of Mesopotamian religion whose image the Greeks appropriated for their own art in the 700s and 600s B.C., during the "Orientalizing period." The Greeks saw griffins and other Eastern motifs on imported metalwork, textiles, and carved ivory, and Greek craftsmen then adapted these designs. This drawing shows a bronze cauldron attachment, cast on the Greek island of Rhodes, circa 600 B.C.

exports were the painted pottery of CORINTH (600s B.C.) and ATHENS (500s B.C.), and the woolens of MILETUS and other cities of IONIA.

The conquests of the Macedonian king ALEXANDER THE GREAT (334–323 B.C.) changed the trading map of the ancient world, flooding the Greek market with luxury goods. For instance, the availability of metalwork now snuffed out most of the demand for ceramic pottery.

(See also AEGINA; AL MINA; CARTHAGE; CHALCIDICĒ; CHALCIS; CHIOS; COLONIZATION; CRETE; GOLD; ILLYRIS; PITHECUSAE; PHOENICIA; RHODES; SAMOS; SHIPS AND SEAFARING; TROY.)

tragedy   See THEATER.

trees   See TIMBER.

tribes   See KINSHIP.

trireme   See WARFARE, NAVAL.

Troilus   Son of the mythical Trojan king PRIAM and his wife, HECUBA. As a handsome youth in the early days of the TROJAN WAR, Troilus was slain by the Greek champion ACHILLES.

Although Troilus had only a small role in Greek MYTH, he became important later, in the medieval European legend of Troilus and Cressida.

Trojan War   The legend of the Trojan War is today the best-known story from Greek MYTH. Amazingly rich in its many characters and events, the Trojan War legend describes how the allied Greeks—under the command of King AGAMEMNON of MYCENAE—sailed from Greece and laid siege to the non-Greek city of TROY (also called Ilium), located outside the mouth of the HELLESPONT sea channel, in northwest ASIA MINOR. The Greeks had come at Agamemnon's behest to avenge the abduction of the beautiful Helen—wife of Agamemnon's brother MENELAUS—by the Trojan prince PARIS. The Trojans, then sheltering Paris and the compliant Helen within their walls, had refused the Greeks' demand for Helen's return. This was the official reason for the war, although the Greeks also craved Troy's wealth.

The siege, consisting mainly of battlefield fighting on the plains outside the city, lasted for 10 years and saw the death of many heroes of both sides, including the Trojan prince HECTOR and the Greek champion ACHILLES. Finally Troy fell to a stratagem devised by the wily Greek hero ODYSSEUS. Pretending to abandon the siege, the Greeks sailed away, leaving behind a huge wooden horse they had constructed—the so-called Trojan Horse. Hidden within this hollow monument was a picked force of Greek "commandoes," but the unsuspecting Trojans, believing the horse to be a Greek offering to the gods, brought it into the city. After nightfall, the Greeks emerged from the horse and opened Troy's gates to the waiting Greek army (which had hurried back under cover of darkness).

Destruction of the rich and proud city followed, with the inhabitants all massacred or captured as SLAVES. However, the Greeks' arrogant and impious behavior at the sack of Troy angered the gods, who decreed that many of the surviving Greek heroes would be killed on the voyage home.

The immense saga—of which HOMER's *Iliad* and *Odyssey* present only a portion—was the product of Greek oral poetic tradition over several centuries, approximately 1200–550 B.C. The legend produced a body of EPIC POETRY, describing major episodes of the war. The earliest and greatest of the heroic epics were the two poems written down circa 750 B.C. and ascribed to the poet Homer— namely, the *Iliad*, or *Tale of Ilium*, recounting the "passion" of the Greek hero Achilles during the war's 10th year; and the *Odyssey*, describing the homecoming of the Greek hero Odysseus, with several back references to the last days of the war.

These two Homeric poems, however, were not the only epic poems dealing with the Trojan War. The classical Greeks (400s B.C.) knew at least six other Trojan-related epics, not ascribed to Homer. These poems did not survive antiquity, but their story plots are summarized by later writers. The lost Trojan War epics were: (1) the *Cypria* ("Tales from CYPRUS"), describing the war's causes and outset; (2) the *Aethiopis*, recounting Achilles' slaying of the Ethiopian king MEMNON (a Trojan ally) and Achilles' own death in battle; (3) *The Little Iliad*, describing the madness of the Greek hero AJAX (1) and the episode of the Wooden Horse; (4) the *Capture of Troy* (*Iliou Persis*), recording the Greeks' bloody capture of the city; (5) the *Homecomings*, recording the calamitous homeward voyages of the surviving Greek heroes other than Odysseus; and (6) the *Telegonia*, describing Odysseus' last days and the related adventures of Telegonus, who was his son by the witch CIRCE.

In A.D. 1870–1890 the pioneering German archaeologist Heinrich Schliemann discovered and excavated the ancient site of Troy, which—amid its various ancient strata— showed clear signs of having been destroyed by a great fire circa 1220 B.C. Since this epoch-making discovery, scholars have universally come to agree that the Trojan War of legend was based on some genuine event of the late Mycenaean age. Certainly the Mycenaean Greeks possessed the wealth, manpower, and organization to launch such an expedition, and they probably had sufficient cause; even if we dismiss the abduction of Spartan Helen as a fiction, there remains that fact that ancient Troy must have controlled the Hellespont waterway, and was probably preying on the Mycenaeans' vital imports of raw metals.

(See also AJAX (2); ARCHAEOLOGY; ANDROMACHE; BRONZE; CASSANDRA; DIOMEDES; HECUBA; HELEN OF TROY; LAOCOÖN; NEOPTOLEMUS; NESTOR; PHILOCTETES; PRIAM; TRADE; WARFARE, LAND; WARFARE, SIEGE.)

Troy   Ancient city of ASIA MINOR, usually described as being inhabited by a non-Greek people. In the late BRONZE AGE (circa 1300 B.C.), Troy was evidently one of the most powerful cities of the eastern Mediterranean. The site of ancient Troy—at the village of Hissarlik, in modern-day Turkey—was discovered by the great German archaeologist Heinrich Schliemann in A.D. 1870. But Troy had been famous for 3,000 years prior, immortalized in the ancient Greek epic cycle of the TROJAN WAR, of which the two greatest poems are HOMER's *Iliad* and *Odyssey*. Schliemann's epoch-making discovery revealed that the historical Troy had achieved affluence in the early second millennium B.C., before being destroyed in an immense fire, at the archaeological level known as Troy VIIa (circa 1220 B.C.). Modern scholars tend to believe that this destruction marks the same event commemorated in the mythical Trojan War.

The name *Troy* comes to us from the poet Homer and other Greek writers who called the city Troia and Ilion. These names seem to have no meaning in the Greek language, and may simply preserve the ancient Trojans' names for their city. Greek MYTH mentions two Trojan founding fathers—Tros and his son Ilus—who gave the city its two names; but this sounds like a later rationalization. The first founder of Troy, according to Greek myth, was Tros' grandfather, named Dardanus.

Troy is situated at the very northwestern corner of Asia Minor, about four miles south of the western mouth of the HELLESPONT waterway and about four miles inland of the AEGEAN SEA. Set on a height commanding the seaside plain, ancient Troy could raid or toll the merchant shipping in the Hellespont without itself being blockaded inside the strait; its inland site left it safe from surprise raids by sea. Troy's control of the Hellespont must have been a crucial factor in the city's prosperity and was probably the reason why the real Trojan War was fought: The Mycenaean Greeks of the mid-1200s B.C. may have decided to destroy Troy because it was blocking their badly needed imports of metals from Asia Minor.

Schliemann's excavations uncovered no less than nine levels of habitation at Troy, dating from circa 2500 B.C. to just after the birth of Christ. The significant levels for our purpose begin with Troy VI (about 1900–1300 B.C.), which marks the arrival of certain invaders—an accomplished people, with horses and superior building techniques, who enlarged and refortified the city. These Trojans may have been Luwians, displaced from interior Asia Minor by the Hittites. Or these Trojans may have been kinfolk of the first Greeks, who in the same centuries were descending through the Greek peninsula, overrunning or assimilating the prior inhabitants there.

This impressive Troy VI was devastated by an earthquake circa 1300 B.C. Troy VIIa represents the survivors' rebuilding in the wreckage, along the plan of the preceding city. This Troy was destroyed by fire circa 1220 B.C., in what may have been the Trojan War.

Scholars have always noted that the small size of Schliemann's Troy VIIa seems at odds with Homer's picture of a mighty and defiant fortress city. Until archaeologists can find convincing evidence of wider ancient city limits, it must be assumed that the Trojan War legends greatly exaggerate the grandeur of the real Troy of the 1200s B.C.

(See also ARCHAEOLOGY.)

Tydeus   See SEVEN AGAINST THEBES.

Typhon   One of several mythical monsters that arose to challenge the might of ZEUS soon after the beginning of the world. Like the rebellious GIANTS, Typhon (or Typhoeus) was a son of the earth goddess, GAEA. The epic poet HESIOD, in his *Theogony* (circa 700 B.C.), vividly describes Typhon as having a vaguely human form with 100 serpents' heads that sparked fire and made the deafening noise of many different beasts. This grotesque creature tried to take over the world, but was incinerated by Zeus' thunderbolts. Being immortal, Typhon could not die, and was imprisoned for eternity in Tartarus (the lowest abyss of the Underworld).

Like other hybrid creatures described in Hesiod, Typhon probably represents a mythological borrowing from the Near East. Greek legend often associated Typhon with the southeastern ASIA MINOR region called Cilicia, and perhaps Typhon was originally a spirit of Cilician volcanoes.

As Greek exploration opened up SICILY and southern ITALY in about 800–600 B.C., Typhon became "reassigned" to that new frontier (as did other Greek mythical figures). At that time he was said to be imprisoned under Mt. Etna, in Sicily, where his fire and rage were the cause of that volcano's eruptions.

In surviving artwork, Typhon is sometimes shown as a snake-footed man in combat with Zeus. For the Greeks, the battle provided a picturesque emblem of savagery versus civilization.

(See also PINDAR.)

tyrants   The Greek tyrants were dictators who first arose at various Greek cities on a wave of middle-class anger in the mid-600s B.C. and seized the government from the aristocrats who had hitherto ruled. The Greek title tyrant (*turannos*) did not at first denote the cruel abuse of power, as it does now; rather, it had a neutral meaning—"usurper with supreme power." The word *turannos* apparently was imported to Greece from the Near East, where it had been used to describe the usurping Lydian king Gyges (circa 670 B.C.). The point of this newly minted Greek word was that, for the first time in Greek memory, these despots were coming from outside the narrow ruling circles.

What brought the first tyrants to power was a growing Greek middle class that was ready for political and social privileges that the aristocrats had denied them. By the mid-600s B.C., CORINTH and other cities had been active in seaborne TRADE for probably 200 years. This trade had created a class of merchants and manufacturers with wealth but no prestige or political voice. When a revolution in military tactics brought these middle-class men into the army to serve as HOPLITES, their potential power increased greatly. There followed, throughout the greater Greek cities, a wave of tyrants' revolutions.

The first Greek *turannos* now known is PHEIDON of ARGOS (circa 670 B.C.). Other famous tyrants include CYPSELUS of Corinth (and his son PERIANDER), CLEISTHENES (2) of SICYON, PISISTRATUS of ATHENS (and his son HIPPIAS (1)), and POLYCRATES of SAMOS. Tyrants also held power at MEGARA (1), MILETUS, and many other Greek cities. These rulers spanned the period from about 670–510 B.C. Their dynasties rarely lasted for more than two generations, since it was impossible to maintain or repeat constructively the popular discontent that had raised the tyrant to power in the first place.

Like other popular dictators throughout history, the tyrants sought to bring amenities to the poor and to relieve unemployment with public works. Tyrants such as Polycrates were known for improving local water supplies as well as for their monumental building programs, which glorified themselves and their cities. Tyrants might also be known for their unbridled passions and sexuality.

The enemy of the tyrants was the panhellenic class of the ARISTOCRACY, who had most to fear from revolution. But the tyrants also had an enemy in the Greek city of SPARTA, which by the 500s B.C. had developed into a kind of Greek police force, sending out troops in response to appeals from displaced aristocrats of Samos, Athens, and elsewhere. In 510 B.C. the Spartans ejected the last important tyrant of mainland Greece, Hippias of Athens; in his place, the Athenians soon established the first Greek DEMOCRACY.

The great supporter of the tyrants was the Eastern kingdom of PERSIA, which used Greek tyrants as puppet rulers in its conquest of Greek ASIA MINOR. The Persians also negotiated in secret with independent tyrants in mainland Greece, in hopes of winning collaborators.

Tyrants played a major role in the history of Greek SICILY, particularly at the preeminent city of SYRACUSE. This was due in part to bitter class divisions within Sicilian-Greek society. But another factor was the abiding external menace of the Carthaginians, who inhabited the western corner of Sicily and who periodically launched massive campaigns to subjugate the island's Greek cities. There thus arose a demand for capable Greek military dictators who could organize defense. The early 400s B.C. saw a series of grand Sicilian tyrants, culminating in GELON of Syracuse (circa 480 B.C.), his brother HIERON (1) (circa 470 B.C.), and Theron of ACRAGAS (circa 480 B.C.), all of whom were known for their wealth and magnificent court.

Although Syracuse saw periods of democracy, conditions there remained ripe for tyrants down through the 200s B.C., long after tyranny had faded away elsewhere in the Greek world. The most famous or notorious of the later Syracusan tyrants were DIONYSIUS (1) (circa 390 B.C.) and AGATHOCLES (circa 300 B.C.); Agathocles was the first tyrant to assume the title king.

(See also PERSIAN WARS.)

Tyre See PHOENICIA.

Tyrtaeus Spartan lyric poet of the later 600s B.C. who wrote verses encouraging his countrymen in their difficult fight in the Second Messenian War. According to tradition, Tyrtaeus was a Spartan general and his poems were sung by soldiers in competitions at the evening meal. There is also a late, absurd tale claiming that Tyrtaeus was originally a lame Athenian schoolmaster.

Only fragments of Tyrtaeus' work survive today, in several dozen lines of elegiac verse. (The elegy is a form intended for recital to flute accompaniment.) Tyrtaeus' poems were patriotic and instructional—reminding his listeners, for example, how beautiful it is to die for one's country, and urging them to adhere to the specific tactics of HOPLITE warfare. His poetry of propaganda belonged to a larger program by which SPARTA transformed itself in those years into a militaristic society, with the best army in Greece.

Tyrtaeus is said to have composed marching songs (now lost) in the Spartan Doric dialect, but he wrote his elegies in Ionic Greek, following the literary convention of his day. His verses contain epic-style language with many echoes of HOMER. Depending on how late in the 600s B.C. Tyrtaeus lived, he may have been influenced by the Ionian poet CALLINUS of EPHESUS, who also developed the elegy's use for patriotic themes.

(See also GREEK LANGUAGE; LYRIC POETRY; MESSENIA.)

U

Ulysses   See ODYSSEUS.

Underworld   See AFTERLIFE; HADES.

Uranus   See CRONUS; GAEA.

V

vase-painting   See POTTERY.

vines and viticulture   See FARMING; WINE.

voting   See DEMOCRACY.

W

warfare, land The famous land battles of ancient Greece were primarily collisions of heavy infantry, who met on open ground by mutual consent. CAVALRY remained secondary, partly due to the mountainous Greek terrain and partly due to technical matters, such as the small size of Greek horses and the absence of stirrups. It took the tactical genius of the Macedonian king PHILIP II and his son ALEXANDER THE GREAT (mid-300s B.C.) to make cavalry at least partly effective against infantry.

It is less obvious why light-armed foot soldiers were underemployed until the 400s B.C. Commanders in mountainous Greece might have been expected to develop guerrilla tactics using projectile troops—javelin men, archers, and slingers. However, for social and psychological reasons, such tactics did not arise among the major Greek states until the PELOPONNESIAN WAR (431–404 B.C.). Instead, the Greeks (a sporting people) tended to think of war as a manly and consensual contest of strength. "Whenever the Greeks declare war on one another, they go find the most smooth and level piece of ground and fight their battle there," states an observer cited by the historian HERODOTUS (circa 435 B.C.). In classical Greece, as in Europe of the 18th century A.D., brutal warfare was conducted along certain gentlemanly guidelines.

Greek military history falls into three major phases: (1) Mycenaean and post-Mycenaean warfare, circa 1600–750 B.C., (2) the age of the HOPLITE, or heavily armed infantryman, circa 650–320 B.C.; and (3) the era of the Macedonian-developed PHALANX, perfected by Alexander the Great and employed by his successors. The HELLENISTIC AGE (circa 300–150 B.C.) saw giant phalanx armies, commanded by absolute monarchs, battling for vast tracts of land in the eastern Mediterranean and using such innovative war "machines" as elephants. In the end, phalanx and elephant fell to the superior maneuverability of the legions of Republican ROME (100s B.C.).

To understand Mycenaean warfare, modern scholars rely on such archaeological evidence as arms and armor from burial sites and artistic depictions of soldiering on surviving artwork. Also helpful if approached cautiously are battle descriptions in HOMER's *Iliad* (written down circa 750 B.C. but purporting to describe the TROJAN WAR, fought circa 1220 B.C.).

Mycenaean warfare (somewhat like medieval European warfare) revolved around armored noblemen who would take the field at the head of their kinsmen and retainers. These warlords are commemorated in such Homeric heroes as ACHILLES and DIOMEDES. In battle, such champions would seek out their social equals on the enemy side, to duel it out with javelins, jabbing spears, and stabbing swords. As IRON was yet unknown, the choice metal for war was BRONZE. The most dramatic Mycenaean armament—the body-covering shield of oxhide, stretched on a wooden frame, such as AJAX (1) carries in the *Iliad*—was obsolete by about 1450 B.C., replaced by wooden shields faced with bronze. CHARIOTS were used for war—perhaps to convey champions across the plain to the fighting, or perhaps for chariot battles, on the model of contemporary Egyptian and Hittite warfare. The rough terrain of Greece does not generally lend itself to chariots, but the plains of ARGOS and BOEOTIA would have sufficed.

The depressed years of the DARK AGE (1100–900 B.C.) continued the Mycenaean pattern on an impoverished scale. War was still a job for aristocrats and their followers. Bronze armor became scarcer then, but iron—more plentiful than bronze—made its first appearance, in swords and spear-points.

The emergence of the hoplite (after 700 B.C.) banished the old, individualistic approach to war. Henceforth battles were decided not by dueling champions but by large con-

This battle scene, painted on a Corinthian wine pitcher circa 650 B.C., is the best surviving illustration of the hoplite tactics that dominated Greek warfare between 700 and 350 B.C. The armies collide in orderly rows, with the front-rank men jabbing overhand with spears. (An extra spear is held in the shield hand.) The presence of a flute-player to keep the men in step may identify the left-hand army as Spartan. The scene accurately shows the hoplites' armor and round shields. The battle ranks, cleverly foreshortened by the anonymous ancient painter, would have in fact contained several hundred men each.

centrations of armored hoplites, arrayed in tight rows, who fought by pushing with their spears and shields in an organized effort to break the enemy formation. The hoplite era includes the most famous conflicts of mainland Greece: the PERSIAN WARS and Peloponnesian Wars (400s B.C.), and the wars of SPARTA and THEBES (300s B.C.).

The precise origins of hoplite warfare are unclear. It is known that in 669 B.C. the army of ARGOS decisively defeated a Spartan force at Hysiae in the eastern PELOPONNESE; evidence suggests that the Argives at this battle were the first Greeks to use large-scale hoplite tactics, against Spartans who were still fighting in the disorganized old manner.

The hoplite's name came from his new-style shield, the *hoplon*, made of bronze-faced wood. The *hoplon* was round, wide (about three feet in diameter), heavy (about 16 pounds), and deeply concave; in battle it enclosed the soldier's torso while extending toward his neighbor on the left. Other hoplite armament included a bronze helmet and breastplate, a six- to eight-foot-long jabbing spear, and a stabbing or slashing sword of forged iron, for use after the spear had broken. A hoplite's armor, weighing about 60 pounds, would not be worn on the march, but would be carried in wagons or by personal SLAVES or servants.

One difference between the hoplite and previous Greek warriors was that the hoplite was nearly helpless on his own. He remained an effective fighter so long as he stayed grouped with his fellows. Should soldiers leave the battle formation—whether by turning and fleeing from the rear ranks or by breaking ranks in front to chase an enemy—the whole structure was endangered. This obligation to stand fast in battle shaped the classical Greek values of steadfastness, calmness in danger, and the ability to endure fatigue and pain.

Another difference between the hoplite and the armored warrior of prior centuries was that the hoplite was probably not an aristocrat. (Aristocrats comprised the cavalry at this time.) The hoplite was a middle-class citizen, levied in defense of his city-state and fighting against analogous citizens in the enemy army. Cities henceforth relied for their defense on large numbers of uniformly equipped citizens, not on a few noble heroes; the coming of the hoplite thus saw the democratization of warfare.

Ancient writers use the word *othismos*, the "push," to describe hoplite battle. Down to the 300s B.C., the battle line typically was formed six to eight rows deep, with a front of several hundred men. The men in the first three rows advanced with spears leveled over their shoulders; behind them, the soldiers held their spears pointing upward. As the two armies collided, sometimes at a full run, the front ranks of both sides met the enemy spear-points while thrusting overhand with their own spears. But at the same time, the rear ranks kept pushing forward—each man actually leaning his shield into the back of his countryman ahead and shoving him toward the enemy. The armies tried to push each other apart.

For the front hoplites, battle must have been hellish and exhausting. There are tales of soldiers dying of suffocation, pinned upright by the press of men. More usually, of course, soldiers died of wounds—possibly to the neck or genitals (areas not always protected by shield or breast-

plate), or possibly to the head or chest (the armor splitting under the spear point). When a hoplite fell, the man behind him took his place with leveled spear, and most men who went down alive would be very lucky not to be trampled to death.

The heart of the battle, the excruciating *othismos*, lasted probably less than an hour. As one army started to get the worst of it, soldiers on that side would begin fleeing (rear rows first), and suddenly the entire losing army might be reduced to a chaotic rout as every man dropped his shield and spear, running in panic. Then the cavalry might come into play, either in slaughtering a fleeing enemy or in covering its own side's retreat.

Unlike modern armies, the Greeks did not usually make war all year long. The campaign season lasted from March until October, when weather conditions were right for encamping and moving large numbers of men. Furthermore, since most Greek soldiers were farmers by trade, the end of summer usually saw a consensus to stop campaigning and go home for the autumn sowings and vintage. One reason for the military superiority of SPARTA in the 500s to 400s B.C. was that its citizens were professional soldiers; they had no job but war. (Their fields at home were worked by a society of serfs, the HELOTS.)

In strategy, hoplite warfare was very simple, and relied on an element of cooperation between antagonists. The aggressor army would march into enemy territory, and the defending army would march out to meet it. Defenders did not like to stay confined behind their city walls—the Athenian statesman PERICLES' strategy for the Peloponnesian War was unique in its passive defense. Rather, defending armies would come out to protect the farms of the countryside, upon which the city's food supply might depend.

The size of hoplite armies could vary greatly. At the Battle of PLATAEA, against the Persians (479 B.C.), the allied Greek force was said to number over 38,000 hoplites. At the Battle of MANTINEA (418 B.C.), the opposing armies had about 3,600 hoplites each, plus light-armed troops. Other armies, fielded in local disputes, might be much smaller.

By the late 400s B.C. military minds had begun adjusting hoplite tactics. It had long been observed that an army's right wing tended to outperform its left wing—partly because the better troops were stationed on the right, but partly because the battle line itself would drift rightward on the approach to battle, as each man leaned right to gain the protection of his neighbor's shield; this rightward drift meant that each army advantageously outflanked the other on the right. To increase this advantage, the Boeotians at the Battle of Delium used a fortified right wing, 25 rows deep, and defeated an Athenian army (424 B.C.).

Similarly, the Spartans' superior tactics involved speedily gaining the upper hand on their right wing and then wheeling the right wing leftward, rolling up the enemy from the side. However, at the Battle of LEUCTRA (371 B.C.), the Theban general EPAMINONDAS beat the "invincible" Spartans by stacking his *left* wing 50 men deep and crushing the 12-man-deep Spartan right wing before it could destroy him.

Theban triumphs partly inspired the innovations of King Philip II of MACEDON (reigned 359–336 B.C.), who brought land warfare into its third stage with his development of the formation that modern scholars call the phalanx. To make his Macedonian peasantry effective against Greek hoplites, Philip forged a new-style heavy infantry—lighter-armored than hoplites and equipped with an innovative, 13- to 14-foot-long pike, the *sarissa*. The phalanx formation consisted of about 9,000 such infantry, arrayed 16 rows deep, with the first five rows presenting their pikes forward. On the model of Spartan organization, Philip's phalanx was articulated into 1,500-man battalions, for maneuverability. A well-trained phalanx enjoyed advantages over a hoplite army in terms of its weapons' reach and probably its level of fatigue. (The phalanx men were not crowded together as closely as the hoplites, nor were they so heavily armored.)

In battle Philip employed the phalanx mainly for defense—to halt and punish an enemy attack—while using his cavalry to charge against any gap that opened in the enemy formation. The phalanx was the anvil; the cavalry was the hammer. The superiority of Philip's tactics was proven at the Battle of CHAERONEA (338 B.C.), where his troops totally defeated a hoplite army of allied Greeks. The hoplite age was passing, 330 years after the Battle of Hysiae.

Philip's innovations helped produce the spectacular victories won by his royal son, Alexander the Great (reigned 336–323 B.C.). In military history, Alexander opened the door to further development of cavalry, under Persian influence and using larger Persian horse breeds. More important, Alexander's conquests changed the social-political basis of ancient warfare, by creating several large and wealthy Greco-Macedonian kingdoms around the eastern Mediterranean. The incessant warfare of these Hellenistic kingdoms—particularly Ptolemaic EGYPT against the Levantine SELEUCID EMPIRE (274–168 B.C.)—saw the use of huge, unwieldy phalanxes, upward of 20,000 men. These kingdoms were constantly trying to perpetuate a Greco-Macedonian soldiering class, so as to reduce reliance on mercenaries.

The most dramatic aspect of Hellenistic warfare was its use of war elephants, which Alexander first encountered in his Indus Valley campaigns (327–325 B.C.). Later generations of Greeks acquired elephants from Africa as well from India. Typically ridden by a handler and an archer or javelin man, the war elephant provided a kind of live "tank," used especially by the early Seleucid armies. At the Battle of Ipsus (301 B.C.), the 480 elephants of King SELEUCUS (1) helped to destroy his enemy, ANTIGONUS (1). Deployed usually to screen the phalanx and charge ahead, elephants were effective mainly as weapons of terror, to scare horses and soldiers not accustomed to them. But use of these unmaneuverable beasts had diminished by the mid-200s B.C., as commanders learned to deflect their charge with arrow or javelin volleys, or to let them pass harmlessly through by having the troops open corridors in their path.

(See also CRETE; DEMOSTHENES (2); LELANTINE WAR; PHEIDON; PHILIP V; PYRRHUS.)

warfare, naval　In the earliest centuries of Greek history (circa 1600–700 B.C.), warships served primarily as troop

transports—the troops in question were the oarsmen, who would leave their benches to go ashore as infantry. Eventually the sea itself became the scene of fighting, as defending states learned to send out ships to oppose an oncoming enemy fleet on the water. The historian THUCYDIDES (1) writes that the earliest remembered sea battle was fought circa 664 B.C. between the navies of two Greek states, CORINTH and CORCYRA. Thucydides mentions another early naval battle, circa 600 B.C., between Phocaean Greeks and Carthaginians in the western Mediterranean.

Such early sea fights, tactically crude, were probably conducted as infantry battles on water—that is, the opposing fleets would crowd together, allowing boarding parties of spearmen to fight it out hand to hand. But naval warfare was changed by two developments circa 700–430 B.C.: the invention and gradual spread of the superior Greek warship type known as the trireme; and the acceptance of ramming tactics over boarding tactics, as a more effective way to destroy the enemy without sustaining harm oneself. The famous Greek sea battles of the 400s B.C.—such as the Battle of SALAMIS (1) (480 B.C.)—featured trireme warships maneuvering to ram and sink the enemy.

The trireme was invented in response to a specific challenge: how to fit as many oarsmen as possible into a vessel that would still be seaworthy. Throughout Greek history, the oar was the main power source for any warship. Most war vessels carried one midship mast, capable of hoisting a single square sail; but the mast was not always used and typically could be removed. It was the oarsmen who powered the ship through battle and in passage through contrary winds or calms.

The more oarsmen, the greater the power—up to a point. The practical limit in length for an undecked wooden ship is about 100 feet; beyond that, the hull is liable to break apart. In a simple ship design, this 100-foot limit confined the total number of rowers to about 50—whence the Greek term *pentekontoros*, or pentecanter, meaning a 50-oared, single-leveled vessel. Images in vase paintings and other surviving art show pentecanters as resembling Viking longboats, with the oarsmen seated along one level in the open air. There was no deck—that is, no layer of planking across the hull's top. The rowers sat in double file—two men side by side on each bench, each man handling his own oar, which projected out (left or right) through thole-pins above the gunwale.

Circa 900–700 B.C., Greek shipwrights—probably copying Phoenician designs—learned to fit more oarsmen into a 100-foot hull. They did so by laying the benches at two different levels (still without any deck) and providing oarports below the gunwales for the lower row of oars.

This two-leveled type of Greek warship is known by modern scholars as the bireme. But the real breakthrough came circa 700 B.C., with the Greeks' development of a three-leveled warship (again, probably based on a Phoenician model). This was the ship that the Greeks called the *triērēs* (three-rowing or three-fitted) and that is now called the trireme—the ancient Greek warship par excellence.

However, the trireme caught on slowly. Pentecanters, cheaper and easier to build, were still being used by some Greek states as late as the PERSIAN WARS (490–479 B.C.). The universal change to trireme navies came after 479 B.C.

A trireme typically carried 160 to 170 oarsmen, far more than prior designs could hold. The oars emerged in three rows on each side—one above the gunwale and two below. The added power meant greater speed, hence greater maneuverability in battle. The ample power also meant that triremes could take on more weight; therefore, they carried such array as partial decking fore and aft, vertical defensive screens, and an overhead central catwalk running the length of the vessel. These structures created room for a contingent of archers and HOPLITES, who did not row but served purely as ship's soldiers, to aim projectiles in battle and fend off enemy boarding attempts. By the time of the Peloponnesian War, the number of shipboard hoplites had settled at 10. Including crew, officers, and soldiers, the trireme might carry 215 men in all.

With its partial decking, the trireme hull could be built to about 120 feet long. The design was narrow, with a width at the gunwales of only 12 to 16 feet. There was scant room for passengers or any cargo aside from drinking water—most food supplies had to come from shore or from supply ships. A trireme had no accommodations for eating or resting. Confined to their crowded benches, the crew could not easily spend a night at sea; to cook and sleep, they had to camp ashore every night.

This basic restriction applied to all ancient warships and influenced all Greek naval strategy. A navy could conduct operations only within range of a friendly harbor or beaching place. To fight an offensive naval war, a state would have to create and maintain forward naval bases (as SPARTA did against Athenian interests in western ASIA MINOR in the later PELOPONNESIAN WAR, circa 413–404 B.C.). Relatedly, naval blockades of enemy harbors tended to be faulty, since fleets could not ride off the coast day and night.

Ramming tactics favored the faster and more skillful ship or fleet. The Greek ship's ram was a wooden post—sheathed in BRONZE, often styled as a boar's head—jutting forward of the prow at water level. The challenge in ramming was to avoid a head-on collision (which could sink both ships) and instead strike the enemy vessel abeam or astern. The classic ramming maneuver was called *diekplous*, "going through and out." When two opposing fleets moved to battle, each side would typically deploy in rows abreast. In *diekplous*, a fleet would suddenly shift from row-abreast to single-file formation, with ships prow to stern, and then veer inward, perhaps by squadrons, to penetrate the enemy's row-abreast formation. Proceeding through the enemy line, the attackers would come around to ram from behind.

Because the *diekplous* required sea room, a commander wishing to defend against this tactic could seek to offer battle inside a confined area—as the Greeks did at Salamis, against a superior Persian fleet. A way to equalize terms further was to try to compel a battle of boarding tactics—as the Syracusans did in their three victories over the Athenians inside SYRACUSE's harbor (414–413 B.C.). A commander intent on boarding tactics might outfit his ships beforehand with raised platforms to hold more soldiers. Generally, the superior-skilled fleets in Greek naval history sought to force battle on the open sea, where there was room for ramming by *diekplous*.

A fleet's skill and speed depended on crews' training and ships' maintenance (since wooden hulls need periodic drying out, caulking, etc.). The top Greek naval power of the 400s–early 300s B.C. was the city of ATHENS, with its standing fleet of 200 triremes (circa 431 B.C.) and its elaborate shipbuilding and drydocking facilities at PIRAEUS. The creator of this navy was the Athenian statesman THEMISTOCLES, circa 488 B.C. The heir to Themistocles' program was the statesman PERICLES (active circa 462–429 B.C.). Unlike many Greek states that employed foreign mercenary oarsmen, Athens employed its lower-income citizens as rowers. This military reliance on large number of poorer citizens effectively increased their political power in the DEMOCRACY.

Athens aside, the important navies in Greek history down to the late 300s B.C. belonged to Corinth, Corcyra, SAMOS, PHOCAEA, AEGINA, CHIOS, LESBOS, and Syracuse. Sparta, not originally a sea power, developed a navy with Persian funding in order to defeat Athens in the Peloponnesian War. Among non-Greek peoples, the Phoenicians (ruled by PERSIA by the mid-500s B.C.) were the Greeks' most dangerous enemies at sea. Farther west, the Greeks' naval opponents included the ETRUSCANS and those Phoenician colonists, the Carthaginians.

New navies and naval tactics arose in the later 300s B.C. Partly as a result of ALEXANDER THE GREAT's studious contact with powerful Phoenician fleets (332 B.C.), Greek shipwrights began building warships larger than the trireme. There are types called "four-rowing" (*tetrērēs*), "five-rowing" (*pentērēs*), and others, eventually up to "16," and even "30" and "40." Modern scholars believe that these names describe three-leveled ships containing multiple oarsmen per oar at one or more levels. The "five" type, usually called the quinquereme, may have employed two men per oar on the upper two rows, with one man per oar on the lowest row. The quinquereme was favored by Greek and Roman navies of the HELLENISTIC AGE (300–150 B.C.).

The late 300s–200s B.C. saw two Hellenistic empires battling for control of the eastern Mediterranean—Ptolemaic EGYPT and the dynasty of ANTIGONUS (1) (based first in Asia Minor, then in MACEDON). The best-known sea battle of this era is also called the Battle of Salamis, fought near a different Salamis, on the island of CYPRUS, in 306 B.C. There a fleet of 108 warships under Antigonus' son DEMETRIUS POLIORCETES destroyed 140 ships of PTOLEMY (1). This era also saw the rise of RHODES as a naval and mercantile power.

Ramming remained the primary battle tactic, but a more remote means of attack emerged in the form of shipborne catapults, shooting arrows. Too bulky for a trireme or quinquereme, a catapult might be fitted onto a merchant ship or onto two warships lashed together. Historians report the first use of such naval artillery at Alexander the Great's siege of Tyre. Demetrius Poliorcetes used naval arrow-catapults in his Battle of Cyprian Salamis and at his siege of Rhodes (305–304 B.C.). Later navies of the Hellenistic era probably also employed rock-throwing catapults.

The deadly use of fire against wooden ships is at least as old as the Peloponnesian War, when the Syracusans sent out a fire-ship against Athenian vessels in Syracuse harbor (413 B.C.). Later, circa 190 B.C., Rhodian warships carried fire-pots—containers of pitch, set ablaze and then slung by long poles onto nearby enemy ships. But the more fiendish tactic of shooting burning naphtha ("Greek fire") across the water at enemy vessels was not invented until the late 600s A.D., by the medieval Byzantines.

In the second half of the 200s B.C., naval control of the Mediterranean was won by the Romans, who had copied and adapted the designs and tactics of Hellenistic and Carthaginian navies.

(See also AEGEAN SEA; AEGOSPOTAMI; ARTEMISIUM; BOSPORUS; CARTHAGE; CIMON; CONON; CORINTHIAN WAR; CYZICUS; DELIAN LEAGUE; HELLESPONT; HIERON (1); IONIAN REVOLT; LYSANDER; PHOENICIA; POLYCRATES; ROME; SHIPS AND SEAFARING; TIMBER; WARFARE, SIEGE.

warfare, siege   Siege warfare entails the capture of forts and fortified cities. For much of Greek history, this process remained crude. An attacking army might try to take a site by storm—that is, by massed assault using scaling ladders. Alternatively, there was siege—the attackers would encircle the enemy walls with earthworks (a procedure known as circumvallation) and wait to starve out the defenders or to win treasonous help from within. The legend of a 10-year-long siege of TROY surely reflects the frustrations of primitive siege warfare.

By the late 700s B.C. the armies of Near Eastern empires (well in advance of the Greeks) were using machines and scientific methods to reduce enemy fortifications. The Greeks, impressed by Persian siegecraft in the era 546–479 B.C., began copying these tactics. These included use of battering rams to tear open an enemy wall, siege mounds to bring attackers to the top of a wall, and miners tunneling under walls. Yet the PELOPONNESIAN WAR (431–404 B.C.) saw only a few successful sieges, such as at PLATAEA or BYZANTIUM. Siege was still largely a waiting game, and a fortress city with a harbor (such as ATHENS) could almost never be captured without being completely blockaded, by both warships at sea and troops on land.

A breakthrough came circa 399 B.C., with the Greeks' development of the catapult. Credit goes to the engineers of the Syracusan dictator DIONYSIUS (1), who probably were copying the machines used by their enemies, the Carthaginians. The earliest type of Greek catapult resembled a giant medieval crossbow, set atop a stand. This wooden device shot a single, six-foot-long arrow and was typically aimed at troops visible at the parapet of the enemy wall. Although unable to knock down walls, the arrow could easily pierce a man's armor, hence the Greek name *katapeltēs*, "shield-piercer."

Volleys from multiple catapults provided valuable "covering fire" for troops conducting siege operations. Typically the besiegers' catapults would be perched inside of siege towers. The siege tower was a wooden structure, built as tall as the enemy wall and used as a kind of multistory armored car, with catapults set on internal parapets and sighted through portholes. Pushed forward on wheels, the tower approached the enemy wall gradually, while engineers prepared a roadbed ahead. Some towers were apparently designed to be pushed right up to the city wall,

in order to bring up attacking troops on internal ladders or to employ a ground-level battering ram.

The first recorded use of Greek catapults and siege towers was at Dionysius' capture of the Carthaginian stronghold of Moyta, in western SICILY (397 B.C.). Dionysius' dramatic successes brought swift imitation and improvement by other Greek commanders. A more powerful type of arrow-shooting catapult arose, perhaps under the Thessalian dictator Jason of Pherae (reigned circa 385–370 B.C.). This new design used the principle of torsion. Instead of a horizontal, bending wooden bow, the torsion catapult featured two vertical cylinders of taut skeining (composed of human hair or animal sinew), set on either side of the front of a long wooden stock. Into each skein was slotted one wooden arm, extending outward; the arms' outer ends were attached to a bowstring. Winched back, the bowstring brought great tension from the twisting skeins to the arrow waiting in the groove of the stock.

Siegecraft in the Greek world reached its mature stage under the Macedonian king PHILIP II (reigned 359–336 B.C.), who successsfully coordinated the use of tower, catapult, and battering ram. Philip's catapults were torsion-powered arrow-shooters. It was Philip's son ALEXANDER THE GREAT who (among other achievements) pioneered the use of rock-firing catapults. Alexander's "stone-throwers" (*lithoboloi* or *petroboloi*) could hurl 170-pound boulders more than 190 yards, to batter apart enemy walls. Mounted aboard ships, these deadly machines helped Alexander to capture the island fortress of Tyre, in one of history's monumental sieges, conducted simultaneously by land and sea (332 B.C.).

Stone-throwing catapults were made of wood and were torsion-powered, looking much like the foregoing arrow-shooting type. This design remained the basic form for Greek catapults. (A different design, with one vertical arm, has been popularized by medieval European artwork and now represents what most people think of as a catapult. Although probably invented by the Greeks, this type was used later, by Roman armies.)

Alexander and his successors of the HELLENISTIC AGE (circa 300–150 B.C.) were the most ambitious besiegers the world had yet seen. The Macedonian prince DEMETRIUS POLIORCETES won his surname (Poliorkētēs means "city besieger") from his huge—but unsuccessful—siege of RHODES in 305–304 B.C. Demetrius' armament included two massive battering rams (iron-clad treetrunks, perhaps 130 feet long, hung inside mobile sheds and worked by hundreds of men) and an armor-plated siege tower called the Hēlēpolis, or "taker of cities," containing nine levels of stone-throwers and arrow-catapults.

Tactics of defense also improved in this era—with catapults on city walls shooting flaming projectiles against wooden siege machines—but generally the advantage had now swung to the besiegers. The Romans of the late 200s B.C. adopted Hellenistic siege tactics and brought them to new technical heights in conquering the Mediterranean. In 213–211 B.C. the Romans besieged and captured the Greek fortress city of SYRACUSE, which 200 years before had defied and destroyed a besieging Athenian army.

(See also ROME; SCIENCE; THESSALY; WARFARE, LAND; WARFARE, NAVAL.)

wine The making of wine—the alcoholic beverage produced by controlled fermentation of grapes—was practiced in the eastern Mediterranean long before the first Greek-speakers arrived, circa 2100 B.C. Greeks probably learned wine-making from the pre-Hellenic inhabitants of mainland Greece. By the Mycenaean era (circa 1600–1200 B.C.), wine played an important role in the economy and recreations of the Greeks. The Greeks' development of wine-making skills may be reflected in legends describing the arrival of a newcomer god, DIONYSUS, lord of viticulture and wine.

By the 500s B.C., the Greeks had perfected their wine production to the point where Greek wines were an important export item, prized throughout the Mediterranean. The Greeks exported wine to such advanced Eastern kingdoms as EGYPT, while Greek traders in THRACE, southern Gaul, and elsewhere used wine to exploit the native peoples and to acquire local goods cheaply (much as European fur traders used brandy on the northeast American Indians in the 1600s A.D.).

The hilly terrain of Greece was (and is) apt for vine-growing, and renowned wines were produced in particular by some of the islands, including THASOS, CHIOS, LESBOS, RHODES, Lemnos, and Cos. But wine was made throughout the Greek world and was cherished by both the peasantry (as a mode of riotous release, on festival days sacred to Dionysus) and by the upper classes (as an object of ritualized consumption, at the type of male drinking party known as the SYMPOSIUM).

In Greece, grapes were harvested in September. Juice was produced by workers first treading the grapes in vats, then crushing the remaining pulp in wine presses. The juice was stored indoors in tubs and allowed to ferment for six months; then it was filtered through cloth and sealed inside storage jars (*amphorai*). Unlike modern wine-makers, the Greeks could not halt the natural fermentation. Therefore, Greek wines had to be consumed within three or four years. These wines had more natural sugar than modern wines, and hence more alcohol, perhaps 18 percent (versus 12.5 percent for most modern consumer wines).

Not surprisingly, the ancient Greeks customarily mixed water into their sweet, potent wine just before drinking—the typical ratio was two or three parts water to one part wine. Such distinctive Greek POTTERY forms as the *psuktēr* (cooler) and *kratēr* (mixer) were developed expressly for the chilling and diluting of wine. Once cooled, the straight wine would be poured into a krater, mixed with water, and ladled out. Undiluted wine was considered unhealthy, but watered wine, if used moderately, was viewed as medicinal—as wine is still viewed today in some Mediterranean countries.

(See also CELTS; FARMING; MASSALIA.)

women The inferior role of women in ancient Greek society reminds us that the Greeks remained in some ways a primitive people. Even in classical ATHENS, at its height of democratic enlightenment (mid-400s B.C.), women were considered second-class citizens at best. A female Athenian citizen, protected by law, was far better off than a slave or a metic (resident alien); but the citizen woman also was forbidden to own much property, to inherit in her own name, to vote, or to attend political debate in the ASSEMBLY.

Women might practice humble trades such as street-cleaning, but this was a sign of hardship, and very few skilled or lucrative trades were open to women. Instead, a woman was considered to be the ward of a man—her husband, her father, or her guardian (such as a brother).

Female SLAVES might run errands in public, but a respectable woman's place was in the home—specifically, in the house's interior and secluded "women's chambers." There the wife or mature daughter was expected to perform—or, if the household was wealthy, to oversee—such domestic duties as child care, cleaning, and spinning and weaving. The only crucial public role of citizen women was to give birth to young citizens for the state.

Of all the major Greek city-states, only warlike SPARTA granted its citizen women any degree of freedom, allowing them to own quantities of property and encouraging such male-imitative pastimes as girls' gymnastics. The unusual freedom of Spartan women probably arose from their roles as estate managers during the absences of their soldiering husbands and kinsmen. Spartan women also had a unique reputation for promiscuity. The philosopher ARISTOTLE (mid-300s B.C.) criticized Spartan society for allowing its women too much freedom and influence. Of all Greek thinkers, only PLATO, in his dialogue *The Republic* (circa 360 B.C.), could imagine a utopian society where women and men would be equally eligible for roles in government.

As with all other social topics from ancient Greece, the existing evidence for women's lives comes overwhelmingly from Athens in the 400s–300s B.C. This evidence includes extant stage drama, courtroom speeches, and archaeological remains such as tombstone inscriptions.

Woman as worker. A woman places clothing or bedding in a storeroom chest, in a terra-cotta relief from the Greek city of Locri, in southern Italy, circa 460 B.C. This woman is probably a slave or servant, but even upper-class Greek ladies might spend their days on certain domestic duties, such as spinning and weaving.

Woman as entertainment. A young woman plays a double flute, in a Greek marble bas-relief, circa 460 B.C. A flute-girl would generally be the kind of slave known as a *hetaira* (companion). She would provide music at male drinking parties, often accompanying the guests' poetry recitals, and would also be obliged to give sexual favors. This carving appears on one side of the marble Ludovisi Throne—probably in fact an altar to the goddess Aphrodite—now in a museum in Rome.

Nothing is known for certain about the role of women during the era of MYCENAEAN CIVILIZATION (circa 1600–1200 B.C.). But a cautious reading of Greek MYTH and particularly HOMER's poems suggests that Mycenaean baronial society did allow considerable power to a few highborn ladies. For example, the queens PENELOPE and CLYTAEMNESTRA in the *Odyssey* are each shown as managing a kingdom in her husband's absence.

The segregation and devaluation of women in Greece began sometime in the era 1100–700 B.C. and may be connected to two related changes: the emergence of the Greek city-state, with its wide, citizen-based military organization; and the idealization of male strength and beauty, as expressed most fully in institutionalized male HOMOSEXUALITY. The misogyny expressed by the poets HESIOD (circa 700 B.C.) and SEMONIDES (late 600s B.C.)—in contrast with Homer's often-charming portrayal of women—surely indicates this social shift.

In archaic and classical Greece, circa 800–300 B.C., women were seen as the opposites or subjugated opponents of men. Male Greek society valued rational discourse, military courage, and physical endurance and self-restraint. Women were believed to be irrational, fearful, and ruled by physical desires. One reason why women were kept secluded at home is that they were thought liable to sexual

seduction (or other mischief) if they ventured out unescorted. "The highest honor for a woman is to be least talked about by men, whether in praise or criticism," declared the Athenian statesman PERICLES in his famous Funeral Oration of 431 B.C.

Only in RELIGION were Greek women allowed to participate in public life to any degree. Holy days, such as the autumn sowing festival of the Thesmophoria, provided occasions when women were expected to leave the house and congregate for religious ceremonies. Also, certain priesthoods were reserved for women, such as the office of Pythia or priestess of APOLLO at DELPHI. These religious duties probably date back to a prehistoric belief in the magical properties of female fertility. Similarly, the large

Woman as ideal beauty. A statue of an aristocratic maiden (*korē*), carved in marble circa 515 B.C. and set up as an offering on the Athenian acropolis. Such *korai* statues were the female counterpart to the male *kouroi* of this era.

role played in Greek mythology by such goddesses as ATHENA or HERA may represent vestiges of a non-Greek religion, adopted by the first arriving Greek tribes circa 2100 B.C.

There is some evidence that female infanticide was regularly practiced at classical Athens and elsewhere. A father could choose whether to officially accept a child or not, and many men might prefer to raise sons, who could help with the farmwork, inherit the estate, and so on.

Girls had a narrow upbringing. A girl of the middle and upper classes grew up in the women's chambers of the house, perhaps rarely seen by her father. At age seven, she might start attending a girls' school, but only long enough to acquire literacy and numeracy. In various Greek cities, she might be considered ready for MARRIAGE by age 14 or even 12. The poet SAPPHO (circa 600 B.C.) has some poignant verses on the plight of an aristocratic girl who must go from the beautiful security of childhood to the strangeness and anxiety of marriage.

Marrying young, women bore children young and died young. Medical examination of extant skeletons from ancient Greece suggest that women typically died around age 36, having borne four children. The estimated average age for men at death was 45, but (since husbands might be 20 years older than their wives) many wives must have survived their husbands and remarried. At classical Athens and elsewhere, a woman's inheritance would legally pass to her new husband's hands at her remarriage, and so heiresses and widows were in great demand.

The oppression of women seems to have lightened somewhat in the changed world of the HELLENISTIC AGE (circa 300–150 B.C.). The royal courts at ALEXANDRIA (1), ANTIOCH, and PELLA created a breed of rich, ruling-class women who were able to influence public and cultural life. These royal examples probably created new opportunities for other women—at least for wealthy citizen women. A surviving public inscription from CYMĒ honors a certain Archippe for her public donations (100s B.C.), while papyrus documents from Ptolemaic EGYPT show women to have been active as lessors, creditors, and debtors much more so than at Athens in prior centuries.

Relatedly, Hellenistic culture placed a new, greater value on female intelligence and sexuality. The Athenian philosopher Epicurus (circa 300 B.C.) is said to have admitted women to his school on equal terms with men. Female beauty reemerged as an ideal for painters and sculptors—most famously in the Athenian sculptor PRAXITELES' celebrated nude statue of the goddess APHRODITE (mid-300s B.C.). In literature, poets such as APOLLONIUS (circa 270 B.C.) showed a new interest in female psychology and male-female romance.

(See also ALCMAN; AMAZONS; EPICUREANISM; ERINNA; EURIPIDES; FUNERAL CUSTOMS; MAENADS; METICS; POLIS; PROSTITUTES; SCULPTURE.)

wrestling   Among the sports-loving Greeks, wrestling was a highly popular and well-organized event. Less brutal than BOXING and PANKRATION, the other two major Greek combat sports, wrestling was considered a valuable element in a boy's EDUCATION and military training as well as

Two wrestlers, from a bas-relief scene on a marble Athenian statue base, circa 510 B.C. The man on the right grips his opponent's left wrist and forearm, perhaps working for an arm-drag. Note the two men's difference in size: The ancient Greeks observed no weight classes, and size could be a distinct advantage. This statue base was probably part of a young aristocrat's gravestone, showing one of his favorite pastimes in life.

an appropriate exercise for well-bred adult men. Most sizable Greek towns of the classical age contained at least one *palaistra* (enclosed wrestling court).

Wrestling was among the most prestigious events at great athletic festivals such as the OLYMPIC or PYTHIAN GAMES. In addition to separate competitions for men and boys, there were wrestling contests that served as the final round in the five-event PENTATHLON.

The patron deity of wrestlers was the god HERMES, who was said to have invented the sport. In fact, wrestling predates the Greek world, having been practiced in the ancient Near East. The Greeks adopted the sport early in their history, maybe in the Mycenaean era (1600–1200 B.C.). Wrestling is described in HOMER's poems—in the *Iliad;* for example, the heroes ODYSSEUS and AJAX (1) engage in a friendly match (book 23). Other mythical wrestlers included the hero HERACLES, who in the course of his 12th Labor had to grapple the giant Antaeus to death.

In its rules, the classical Greek sport was much like modern collegiate free-style wrestling, only tougher. There were no weight classes for the ancient Greeks—advantage favored size and weight. Punching was forbidden, but other harmful moves, such as strangleholds, shoulder-throws, or breaking an opponent's finger, were allowed.

Like other Greek athletes, wrestlers competed naked and were typically slicked down with olive oil (which prevented abrasions but also had a ritualistic significance). They competed atop soft ground; practice sessions were generally held in a mud pit, and formal matches took place on the *skamma,* a special bed of fine sand. At grand events, the matches might be held in a stadium full of spectators.

The bout began with the two competitors standing, facing each other, and ended with a "fall," when one man was forced down in such a way that his back, his shoulders, or his chest and stomach touched the ground. (Alternatively, a man could lose by being thrown off the wrestling ground.) To win in an official contest, a man had to gain three falls against his adversary; therefore, a single match could run to as many as five bouts.

(See also GYMNASIUM; SPORT.)

writing   The use of written symbols to convey words or ideas predates the Greeks by many centuries. In the third millennium B.C., well before the start of Greek civilization, the Sumerians and other Mesopotamian peoples had developed a script called cuneiform. The Egyptians of this era had several forms of writing, including the famous hieroglyphic pictograms that can still be seen on inner pyramid walls and the like. The Mycenaean Greeks had by 1400 B.C. adapted a form of writing from Minoan CRETE. Modern scholars call this Mycenaean script LINEAR B.

The use of Linear B ended with the collapse of MYCENAEAN CIVILIZATION circa 1200 B.C. Thereafter, the invention of the versatile Greek ALPHABET, circa 775 B.C., brought widespread literacy to the Greek world and allowed the Greeks to produce a great literary culture. The emergence of the first Greek literature—HOMER's epic poems *Iliad* and *Odyssey* is clearly a result of the invention of the alphabet, which allowed such orally developed stories to be written down (circa 750 B.C.).

The earliest extant specimen of Greek alphabetic script is a verse inscription scratched onto a Geometric cup, found in a grave at the Greek colony of PITHECUSAE, in western ITALY, and dated to about 725 B.C.: *I am the cup of Nestor and this I say: whoever drinks from me will instantly be smitten by lovely Aphrodite.* This inscription, coming from what was then the Greek world's western frontier, is striking evidence of the spread of the alphabet among the Greeks within one or two generations. General literacy also is indicated by extant graffiti and public inscriptions of the latter 600s B.C., from THERA, CHIOS, and elsewhere. But the most dramatic specimen of early Greek writing is the graffito scratched onto the left leg of a colossal statue of the Egyptian pharaoh Ramses II at Abu Simbel, 700 miles up the Nile. Written in about 591 B.C. by Greek mercenary soldiers in the service of Pharaoh Psamtik II, the message, still visible today, records the names of the expedition's leaders. It is the earliest known announcement that "Kilroy was here."

More typical of early Greek writing materials were clay tablets or the skins of animals, which could be pumiced smooth and stitched together to form a roll. For scratching in clay, a stylus was used, but animal skins took pen and ink. (The pen was merely a quill or the like, and the ink often was a vegetable mixure.) By the 600s B.C., papyrus—cheaper and plentiful—had replaced animal skins for Greek writing. The papyrus plant, which grew only in the Egyptian delta, had a pith that, when cut into strips, could be arranged and pressed so as to create a sheet of paperlike material. These sheets would then be glued together to form a continuous roll, normally of 30–35 feet. When two wooden pins were fastened to the ends of the roll, the result was a scroll, which could be rolled back and forth between the pins. The papyrus scroll was the ancient Greeks' "book" (*biblion*), the premier tool for reading and writing. Long works were produced in multiple scrolls, or "books." Most lengthy writings from the Greco-Roman world—such as those of Homer or Vergil—are still divided editorially into different books, even if the whole work is now contained in one modern volume.

The drawback of papyrus was that it came exclusively from Egypt. After the Greek-Egyptian king Ptolemy V discontinued papyrus exports circa 200 B.C.—supposedly to hamper the rival book-collecting of King Eumenes II of PERGAMUM—the Pergamenes responded by inventing parchment (Greek: *pergamēnē*). Parchment (or vellum, as it is now known) was made from cattle, goat, or sheep skin processed in an improved way so as to smooth it down to papyruslike quality. Today important documents, such as college diplomas, still are printed on vellum, hence the nickname "sheepskin."

(See also BYBLOS; EPIC POETRY.)

X

Xanthippus Athenian soldier and politician who lived circa 525–475 B.C. and was active in the PERSIAN WARS.

Xanthippus (Yellow Horse) was born to an aristocratic family at ATHENS. In the days after CLEISTHENES' (1) democratic reforms (508 B.C.), Xanthippus began his political career by marrying Cleisthenes' niece Agariste. Uncle and niece both belonged to the noble and ambitious Alcmaeonid clan. Agariste and Xanthippus had three children, the youngest of whom was the future left-wing leader PERICLES, born in 494 B.C.

With family wealth and connections, Xanthippus rose to political prominence in 489 B.C., when he prosecuted the soldier-statesman MILTIADES on a charge of deceiving the people. With Miltiades' downfall, Xanthippus briefly became the foremost politician in Athens, but was himself soon on the defensive, probably at the hands of the left-wing leader THEMISTOCLES. In 484 B.C. Xanthippus was ostracized by the Athenians—one of five important OSTRACISMS in the 480s B.C.

Although the normal term of banishment in an ostracism was 10 years, Xanthippus was recalled early, in the state emergency created by the Persian king XERXES' invasion of Greece (480 B.C.). Elected as a general for the year 479 B.C., Xanthippus commanded the Athenian contingent at the land battle of MYCALE, where the Greeks liberated IONIA. Elected general again, for 478 B.C., he led a Greek fleet against the Persian-held fortress of SESTOS, on the HELLESPONT; after a grueling siege, Xanthippus captured the city and crucified the hated Persian governor. Xanthippus returned to great acclaim at Athens, but died within a few years, perhaps from injuries received at Sestos. By 472 B.C. the young Pericles had inherited his father's estate (the other son had died) and was embarked on his own political career.

(See also ALCMAEONIDS.)

Xenophanes Greek poet and philosopher, born circa 570 B.C. at Colophon, in ASIA MINOR, but active in Greek SICILY and southern ITALY. There he traveled from city to city, presenting his PHILOSOPHY in verses (some of which have survived as quotations in later writers' work). Xenophanes apparently lived into his 90s. He is said to have founded the philosophical school at the Italian-Greek city of Elea and to have tutored there the student destined to be the most famous Eleatic philosopher, PARMENIDES.

It is known that Xenophanes left Colophon at age 25—probably to escape the invading Persians under King CYRUS (1). Like his contemporary PYTHAGORAS, Xenophanes brought to the western Greeks the rationalism and sophistication of his native IONIA, and he seems to have caused an intellectual sensation with his attack on traditional Homeric theology. "HOMER and HESIOD," Xenophanes wrote, "have attributed to the gods everything that is shameful and disgraceful among human beings—theft and adultery and deceiving each other." Xenophanes also expressed the enlightened theory that humans have created gods in their own image: The Ethiopians say that their gods are black and snub-nosed; the Thracians make their gods blue-eyed and red-haired. "But if cattle or horses or lions had hands," Xenophanes wrote, "then horses would portray their gods as horses, and cattle as cattle." Rather, said Xenophanes, there is one god, who is in no way like humans, either in form or thought. Xenophanes' concept of God—as a single, unmoved mover—may have inspired Parmenides' more elaborate concept of a unified, motionless Reality.

Remarkably, Xenophanes' also intuited the nature of fossils. Observing the impressions of fish and seaweed in rock quarries near SYRACUSE, Xenophanes supposedly guessed that that area had once been under water and that the earth's land in general is created from, and returns to, the sea.

A brilliant, dilettantish observer rather than a deep thinker, Xenophanes stands as an embodiment of Ionian rationalism and as an intellectual "pollenizer" for Greek Sicily and Italy. His lifetime saw the violent end of the Ionian Enlightenment and the emergence of new intellectual centers, among the mainland and western Greeks. One poignant fragment by Xenophanes gives a brief self-portrait of a wanderer, dispossessed by the Persians' conquest of his native land: "In winter, as you lie by your fire after dinner, drinking wine and cracking nuts, speak thus to the wayfarer at your door: 'What is your name, my friend? Where do you live? What is your age? How old were you when the Persians came?' "

(See also PERSIAN WARS; RELIGION.)

Xenophon Athenian historian, soldier, and gentleman, who lived circa 428–circa 354 B.C. Xenophon wrote several histories and treatises, but is best remembered for producing the most exciting memoir from the ancient world—the *Anabasis* ("expedition to the interior"), describing his adventures in leading 10,000 beleaguered Greek mercenary soldiers out of the heart of the Persian Empire (401–400 B.C.). Among Xenophon's other surviving work is his valuable but biased history titled *Hellenica* (Greek history). Beginning at the point where THUCYDIDES' (1) history of the PELOPONNESIAN WAR abruptly breaks off, with the events of 411 B.C., Xenophon's *Hellenica* recounts the turbulent events of his own lifetime, from the later years of the war to the rise of THEBES and the destruction of Spartan hegemony in Greece (411–362 B.C.). In terms of breadth, objectivity, and analysis, Xenophon as a historian is far inferior to his predecessor Thucydides.

Born into a rich, aristocratic family at ATHENS, Xenophon was a contemporary of the philosopher PLATO. Like Plato, the young Xenophon, although not a deep thinker, became a disciple of the Athenian philosopher SOCRATES. Today our most important source of information about the real-life Socrates (as opposed to the Socrates of Plato's scheme) is Xenophon's memoir titled *Memorabilia*.

The Peloponnesian War was being waged throughout Xenophon's entire childhood and youth, and—like other Athenian aristocrats—Xenophon was to show strong pro-Spartan sympathies during his life. He probably participated in the war's last years—perhaps in the naval battle at Arginusae (406 B.C.), which looms large in his *Hellenica*, and perhaps in CAVALRY patrols outside the city. Also in these years, he married an Athenian woman, Philesia, and had two sons, Gryllus (named for Xenophon's father) and Diodorus.

In 401 B.C., after Athens' defeat in the war and the disastrous reign of the THIRTY TYRANTS, Xenophon left his native city for what was fated to be an absence of 35 years. As a member of the discredited Socratic circle, he probably felt uncomfortable in the restored DEMOCRACY. (And, in fact, within two years the Athenians would condemn and execute Socrates.) Xenophon went to ASIA MINOR as one of about 10,000 Greek mercenary HOPLITE soldiers in the service of the Persian prince Cyrus but, as it turned out, Cyrus used this force in his attempt to seize the Persian throne from his brother, Artaxerxes II. After Cyrus was killed and his army defeated at the Battle of Cunaxa, near Babylon (401 B.C.), the frightened and demoralized surviving Greek troops elected Xenophon to lead them the 1,500 miles out of hostile territory. Four months later, the Greeks finally emerged from the Persian interior, at the Greek colony of Trapezus, on the southeast coast of the BLACK SEA. These exploits are recounted in the *Anabasis*.

Circa 399 B.C., during Xenophon's absence, the Athenians declared him exiled forever; the probable causes were Xenophon's pro-Spartanism and prior friendship with Socrates. The following years saw Xenophon doing military service under the Spartan king AGESILAUS. During the CORINTHIAN WAR (in which Sparta and Athens were enemies, 395–386 B.C.), Xenophon probably served against his fellow Athenians. Xenophon remained a close associate of Agesilaus, whose deeds are recounted in the *Hellenica* and in Xenophon's laudatory biography *Agesilaus*.

In around 388 B.C. Xenophon and his family were settled by their Spartan friends at an estate near OLYMPIA. There Xenophon devoted himself to writing and to the pursuits addressed in his treatises *On Hunting* and *On Household Management*. In a spirit of gratitude toward Sparta, he wrote a laudatory account of the Spartan governmental system, the *Lakedaimonion politeia*. Other works of the 380s and 370s B.C. include the treatise *On Horsemanship* (our only surviving full account from ancient Greece on this subject) and the *Education of Cyrus*, a historical novel that imagines the ideal tutoring received by the old-time Persian

ruler CYRUS (1) (not the Cyrus of the *Anabasis*). Some of these works seem to have developed out of Xenophon's notes toward the EDUCATION of his two sons.

In 371 B.C., after Sparta's defeat at Theban hands at the Battle of LEUCTRA, the people of ELIS (near Olympia) rose in defiance of Sparta and reclaimed local lands, including Xenophon's estate. Xenophon, then nearly 60, was eventually allowed by the Athenians to return.

At Athens he lived his last decade or so, finishing the *Hellenica* (which ends with a description of the Theban victory over the Spartans at the second Battle of MANTINEA in 362 B.C.). Xenophon's own son Gryllus was killed at this battle, fighting on the Spartan side. On receiving the tragic news, Xenophon is said to have replied, "I knew my son was mortal."

Xenophon rewards modern study because he is the complete Athenian gentleman. He embodied many of the values and interests of his social class—soldiering, horsemanship, estate management, pro-Spartanism (exaggerated, in Xenophon's case), respect for education, and so on. He had verbal skill (his prose is plain and workmanlike) and a strong interest in right and wrong. However, his youthful dabbling in PHILOSOPHY clearly had more to do with Socrates' dynamic personality and the intellectual milieu of late-fifth-century B.C. Athens than with any genius of Xenophon's.

His flaws as a historian are apparent in his failure to present a full, unbiased account in his magnum opus, the *Hellenica*.

Xerxes Persian king who led the failed invasion of GREECE in 480 B.C. Our knowledge of Xerxes comes mainly from the ancient Greek historian HERODOTUS, whose viewpoint is hostile; he portrays the king as sometimes reflective and aesthetic-minded, but also intoxicated by power and capable of great lust, cruelty, anger, and cowardice. "Xerxes" is the Greek form of the name, which in Persian sounded like Khshah-yar-shan and meant "king of kings." In the biblical book of Esther, Xerxes is called King Ahasuerus and is pictured favorably.

As son and heir of the brilliant king DARIUS (1), Xerxes was about 32 years old when he came to the throne in late 486 B.C. Soon he turned his attention westward, to resume his father's conflict with the mainland Greeks. Various Persian inscriptions of Xerxes' reign make it clear that he was a pious worshipper of Ahura Mazda, the Zoroastrian supreme god, and he may have thought he was on a divine mission to conquer Greece.

After four years' preparation, including the spanning of the HELLESPONT with elaborate twin bridges of boats, Xerxes led a mighty host—perhaps 200,000 troops and 600 warships—to Europe. Descending through THRACE and MACEDON, he subdued northern and central Greece, but his navy was first eroded due to storms and a sea battle, and then destroyed when Xerxes overconfidently decided to attack the Greek fleet inside SALAMIS (1) channel. After the Salamis defeat in late summer 480 B.C., Xerxes hurried back to Asia with most of his force, leaving behind a Persian army, which the Greeks smashed at PLATAEA the following summer.

Little is known of Xerxes' life afterward. He apparently

devoted himself to construction of royal buildings at Persepolis, the empire's summer capital, and was assassinated in a palace intrigue around 465 B.C. He was succeeded by his son Artaxerxes I.

To the Greeks, Xerxes supplied the prime living example of the sin of HUBRIS—insane pride that leads to divinely prompted self-destruction. The abiding picture of him in Western tradition (whether true or false) is a vainglorious emperor who, after a Hellespont storm had wrecked his boat-bridges, ordered his men to punish the channel by lashing its waters with whips.

(See also PERSIA; PERSIAN WARS.)

Z

Zanclē Greek city of northeast SICILY, located beside the three-mile-wide Strait of Messina, which separates Sicily from the "toe" of ITALY. Located on a crescent-shaped peninsula enclosing a fine harbor, Zanclē (now the modern Sicilian city of Messina), was founded circa 725 B.C. by Greek settlers from CUMAE and CHALCIS. Its sister city was RHEGIUM, across the strait.

Zanclē's original setters were of the Ionian-Greek ethnic group, but circa 490 B.C., Zanclē was repopulated by settlers of Dorian-Greek identity, commanded by the powerful tyrant Anaxilas of Rhegium. Chief among these newcomers were refugees from the Peloponnesian region of MESSENIA, which was suffering under Spartan domination. Anaxilas, whose ancestral home was Messenia, then renamed Zanclē as Messana (in the Doric dialect) or Messene (in Ionic form).

Zanclē-Messana eventually became an ally of Syracuse against ATHENS and the Carthaginians in the latter 400s and early 300s B.C. In 264 B.C. the city was captured by the Carthaginians—an episode that eventually brought on the titanic First Punic War between CARTHAGE and ROME (264–241 B.C.). After the Roman victory, Messana thrived as a Roman ally.

(See also DORIAN GREEKS, IONIAN GREEKS.)

Zeno (1) See STOICISM.

Zeno (2) See PARMENIDES.

Zeus King of the gods, spiritual father of gods and men, and dispenser of divine justice in the universe, according to Greek RELIGION and MYTH. Zeus' name appears on Mycenaean Greek LINEAR B tablets dated to 1400 B.C., but his cult is probably much older than that. Unlike many of the classical Greek gods, Zeus was truly Greek in origin. Probably he was originally a Sky Father—a weather god and chief deity—worshipped by the Greek tribes who first came southward from the Balkans into the land of Greece circa 2100 B.C. In name and function, this primitive Zeus seems related to celestial father gods of other ancient Indo-European peoples, such as the Roman Jupiter (*Zeu-pater*) and the Germanic Tiu. The name *Zeus* is also related to the Greek word *dios*, "bright." Throughout antiquity Zeus never lost his function as a weather god. "Sometimes Zeus is clear, sometimes he rains," writes the poet THEOCRITUS (circa 265 B.C.). Zeus is portrayed as sending thunderstorms against his enemies in HOMER's epic poem the *Iliad* (written down circa 750 B.C.), and in art he is often shown hurling a thunderbolt.

But it was Zeus' moral dimension as orderer of the universe that made him so important to Greek civilization. During the Mycenaean age (1600–1200 B.C.) Zeus was the supreme king over a human society organized around kings; from his cloud-shrouded palace atop Mt. OLYMPUS, in Thessaly, Zeus ruled the subordinate gods and oversaw human events in the world below.

As the age of Greek kings passed away during the 1100s–900s B.C., Zeus retained his preeminence, developing into a kind of chief judge, peacemaker, and civic god. Myths describe how he had destroyed various primeval monsters and forged peace in place of violence. The poet HESIOD (circa 700 B.C.) invokes Zeus as the lord of justice, and the god's other epithets include Kosmetas (orderer), Polieos (overseer of the *polis*—the city), Soter (savior), and Eleutherios (guarantor of political freedoms). He maintained the laws, protected suppliants, instituted festivals, gave prophecies (such as at his important oracle at DODONA), and in general oversaw the fruits of civilized life. This high moral

The Artemisium Zeus: a 6.5-foot-tall bronze statue, sculpted circa 455 B.C. and recovered in the 1920s from the sea-channel off Cape Artemisium, at the northern tip of Euboea. This most magnificent of surviving Greek bronzes stands in the National Museum in Athens. Previously identified as Poseidon, the figure is now thought to show Zeus hurling a thunderbolt (since lost). With such bolts, Zeus vanquished the Giants, the monster Typhon, and other enemies of civilization and peace.

The head of the Artemisium Zeus, with its plaited hair and beard. The eye sockets, which in ancient times would have been inlaid with onyx or another material, now stand empty, revealing the statue's hollow core. This work, beautifully conveys the power and grandeur of the king of the gods.

conception of Zeus reaches its epitome in certain choral odes in the tragedies of the great Athenian playwright AESCHYLUS—for instance, in *The Suppliants* (performed 472 B.C.) and *The Eumenides* (458 B.C.). By the 200s B.C. the Stoic philosophers tended to see Zeus as the single, universal deity.

Zeus' central myths—as recorded particularly by Hesiod in his *Theogony*—tell how the young Zeus usurped the heavenly kingdom from his father, CRONUS, then reordered this kingdom and defended it against attacks by monstrous demigods. In the myth, Cronus, king of the race of TITANS, always ate each of his newborn children, but baby Zeus was spirited away by his mother, Rhea, and brought up on the island of CRETE. Returning, Zeus led a revolt against his father, banished him, and installed himself as king of a new race of immortals, many of whom he fathered. As king of the gods, Zeus ruled the sky; his brothers, POSEIDON and HADES, ruled the sea and Underworld, respectively.

In defending their kingdom, Zeus and the other gods withstood three separate assaults by the violent offspring of GAEA (Mother Earth). The three rebellious parties were the GIANTS, the multiserpent-headed TYPHON, and the twin brothers called the Aloadae, who piled Mt. Ossa atop Olympus and Mt. Pelion atop Ossa in their attempt to storm heaven. Originally such mythical battles may have commemorated the first Greeks' conquest of mainland Greece and the subjugation of the prior inhabitants' religion by the invaders' cult of Zeus.

During the TROJAN WAR (as described in Homer's *Iliad*), Zeus sided with the aggrieved Greek hero ACHILLES and brought misfortune to the Greeks, until Achilles' quarrel with AGAMEMNON was resolved. Yet even Zeus had to yield to FATE, and so was unable to save his mortal son Sarpedon from preordained death in the fighting at TROY (*Iliad*, book 16).

However, Zeus had a second, more grotesque mythological dimension, which certain Greek thinkers found puzzling or repugnant. For "the father of gods and men" (as the poet Homer calls him) was quite literally that, insofar as his numerous love affairs produced many offspring, both human and immortal. His wife and sister, the goddess HERA, bore him the gods ARES, HEPHAESTUS, and Hebe, but Zeus' liaisons with other goddesses and mortal women (often involving rape or deception) produced the deities ATHENA, APOLLO, ARTEMIS, HERMES, and DIONYSUS, the hero HERACLES, and others. Among the humans whom Zeus raped or seduced were: the Spartan queen Leda (whom he approached in the form of a swan and who gave birth to two pairs of twins—CASTOR AND POLYDEUCES and HELEN OF TROY and CLYTAEMNESTRA), the Argive princess Danaë (whom he visited as a shower of gold and who bore him the hero PERSEUS [1]), the Phoenician princess EUROPA (whom he abducted as a bull and who bore him MINOS and Rhadamanthys), and the Trojan prince GANYMEDE (who was abducted by an eagle, perhaps Zeus in disguise, to become Zeus' lover and cupbearer atop Olympus).

The legends of Zeus' sexual exploits with human women probably arose individually throughout Greece during the Mycenaean age, in an attempt to connect the great god with some local noble family's genealogy. But the unsavory discrepancy in these myths—the god of justice descending to earth to commit rape and adultery—was commented on by intellectuals such as the Ionian philosopher XENOPHANES (latter 500s B.C.) and was exploited in the tragedies of the innovative Athenian playwright EURIPIDES (latter 400s B.C.).

In art, Zeus was often shown as a bearded, kingly figure in vigorous middle age. His weapons were the thunderbolt and the aegis (a magic cloak or shield, originally imagined as a stormcloud). Of his innumerable shrines throughout the Greek world, probably the most magnificent was his Doric-style temple built in the mid-400s B.C. at OLYMPIA, at the site of the great sports festival held in his honor—the games of Olympian Zeus. Inside the temple was an immense GOLD-and-ivory statue of the enthroned god, sculpted by PHIDIAS and reckoned as one of the SEVEN WONDERS OF THE WORLD for its size and grandeur.

(See also OLYMPIC GAMES; PROMETHEUS; STOICISM.)

Zeuxis See PAINTING.

BIBLIOGRAPHY

Adcock, F. E. *The Greek and Macedonian Art of War*. Berkeley: University of California Press, 1957.

Anderson, J. K. *Xenophon*. New York: Charles Scribner's Sons, 1974.

Andrewes, Anthony. *Greek Tyrants*. London: Hutchinson University Library, 1974.

Austin, M. M., ed. *The Hellenistic World from Alexander to the Roman Conquest: A Selection of Ancient Sources in Translation*. New York: Cambridge University Press, 1981.

Avery, Catherine B., ed. *The New Century Classical Handbook*. New York: Appleton-Century-Crofts, 1962.

Barber, Robin. *Blue Guide: Greece*. New York: W. W. Norton, 1987.

Barnes, Jonathan. *Aristotle*. New York: Oxford University Press, 1982.

Bickerman, E. J. *Chronology of the Ancient World*. New York: Thames and Hudson, 1968.

Biers, William R. *The Archaeology of Ancient Greece: an Introduction*. Ithaca, N.Y.: Cornell University Press, 1980.

Blanchard, Paul. *Blue Guide: Southern Italy: From Rome to Calabria*. New York: W. W. Norton, 1990.

Boardman, John. *Greek Art*. New York: Thames and Hudson, 1987.

———. *The Greek Sculpture: The Classical Period*. New York: Thames and Hudson, 1985.

———. *The Greeks Overseas*. Rev. ed. New York: Thames and Hudson, 1980.

Boardman, John, and Hammond, N. G. L., eds. *The Cambridge Ancient History: The Expansion of the Greek World, Eighth to Sixth Centuries B.C.*, vol. 3, part 3. 2nd ed. New York: Cambridge University Press, 1982.

Boardman, John, et al., eds. *The Cambridge Ancient History: Persia, Greece, and the Western Mediterranean c. 525–479 B.C.*, vol. 4. 2nd ed. New York: Cambridge University Press, 1988.

Boardman, John; Griffin, Jasper; and Murray, Oswyn, eds. *The Oxford History of the Classical World*, chaps. 1–15. New York: Oxford University Press, 1986.

Bowra, C. M. *Greek Lyric Poetry: From Alcman to Simonides*. New York: Oxford University Press, 1936.

———. *Homer*. London: Gerald Duckworth and Company, 1972.

———. *Pindar*. New York: Oxford University Press, 1964.

Bright, John. *A History of Israel*. 2nd ed. Philadelphia: Westminster Press, 1972.

Buck, Carl Darling. *Comparative Grammar of Greek and Latin*. Chicago: University of Chicago Press, 1933.

Burkert, Walter. *Ancient Mystery Cults*. Cambridge, Mass.: Harvard University Press, 1987.

———. *Greek Religion*. Trans. John Raffan. Cambridge, Mass.: Harvard University Press, 1985.

Burn, Andrew Robert. *The Lyric Age of Greece*. New York: St. Martin's, 1960.

———. *The Penguin History of Greece*. Rev. ed. New York: Penguin Books, 1985.

———. *Persia and the Greeks*. London: Edward Arnold, 1970.

Bury, J. B., Cook, S. A., and Adcock, F. E., eds. *The Cambridge Ancient History: Athens 478–401 B.C.*, vol. 5. 1st ed. New York: Cambridge University Press, 1964.

———. *The Cambridge Ancient History: Macedon: 401–301 B.C.*, vol. 6. 1st ed. New York: Cambridge University Press, 1964.

Casson, Lionel. *Ships and Seamanship in the Ancient World*. Princeton, N.J.: Princeton University Press, 1971.

Cawkwell, George. *Philip of Macedon*. Boston: Faber & Faber, 1978.

———. Lectures presented at Oxford University ("Thucydides" and "Persia and Greece"), 1977–1978.

Ceram, C. W. *Gods, Graves, and Scholars: The Story of Archaeology*. Trans. E. B. Garside. New York: Alfred A. Knopf, 1952.

Childe, Gordon. *What Happened in History*. Rev. ed. Foreword and footnotes Grahame Clarke. Baltimore: Penguin Books, 1964.

Cook, R. M. *Greek Painted Pottery*. London: Methuen and Co., 1960.

Cotterell, Arthur, ed. *The Encyclopedia of Ancient Civilizations*. New York: Mayflower Books, 1980.

Davies, J. K. *Democracy and Classical Greece*. Atlantic Highlands, N.J.: Humanities Press, 1978.

Dover, K. J. *Aristophanic Comedy*. Berkeley: University of California Press, 1972.

———. *Greek Homosexuality*. Cambridge, Mass.: Harvard University Press, 1978.

Easterling, P. E., et al., eds. *The Cambridge History of Classical Literature*. New York: Cambridge University Press, 1989.

Edwards, I. E. S., et al., eds. *The Cambridge Ancient History: The Middle East and the Aegean Region, circa 1380–1000 B.C.*, vol. 2, part 2. 3rd ed. New York: Cambridge University Press, 1975.

Edwards, Paul, ed. *The Encyclopedia of Philosophy*, vol. 1–8. New York: Macmillan, 1967.

Ehrenberg, Victor. *Sophocles and Pericles*. Oxford: Basil Blackwell, 1954.

Ellis, Walter M. *Alcibiades*. New York: Routledge, 1989.

Evans, J. A. S. *Herodotus*. Boston: Twayne Publishers, 1982.

Finley, M. I. *Early Greece: The Bronze and Archaic Ages*. Rev. ed. London: Chatto and Windus, 1981.

Fornara, Charles W., ed. and trans. *Archaic Times to the End of the Peloponnesian War*. Baltimore: Johns Hopkins University Press, 1977.

Fornara, Charles W., and Samons, Loren J. *Athens from Cleisthenes to Pericles*. Berkeley: University of California Press, 1991.

Forrest, W. G. *The Emergence of Greek Democracy*. New York: World University Library, 1966.

———. *A History of Sparta: 950–192 B.C.* London: Hutchinson University Library, 1968.

Fox, Robin Lane. *The Search for Alexander*. Boston: Little, Brown; 1980.

Fuller, J. F. C. *The Generalship of Alexander the Great*. New Brunswick, N.J.: Rutgers University Press, 1960.

Gagarin, Michael, *Early Greek Law*. Berkeley: University of California Press, 1986.

Gomme, A. W. *A Historical Commentary on Thucydides*, vol. 1. New York: Oxford University Press, 1945.

Gomme, A. W., Andrewes, A., and Dover, K. J. *A Historical Commentary on Thucydides*, vol. 4. New York: Oxford University Press, 1970.

Graves, Robert. *The Greek Myths*, vols. 1 and 2. Baltimore: Penguin, 1955.

Green, Peter. *Alexander of Macedon, 356–323 B.C.* Berkeley: University of California Press, 1991.

———. *A Concise History of Ancient Greece*. London: Thames and Hudson, 1979.

Griffin, Jasper. *Homer on Life and Death*. New York: Oxford University Press, 1980.

Guthrie, W. K. C. *Socrates*. New York: Cambridge University Press, 1971.

Halperin, David. *One Hundred Years of Homosexuality*. New York: Routledge, 1990.

Hamilton, J. R. *Alexander the Great*. Pittsburgh: University of Pittsburgh Press, 1974.

———. *Plutarch: Alexander: A Commentary*. New York: Oxford University Press, 1969.

Hammond, N. G. L., and Scullard, H. H., eds. *The Oxford Classical Dictionary*. New York: Oxford University Press, 1970.

Hanson, Victor Davis. *The Western Way of War: Infantry Battle in Classical Greece*. New York: Alfred A. Knopf, 1989.

Hare, R. M. *Plato*. New York: Oxford University Press, 1982.

Harris, H. A. *Greek Athletes and Athletics*. Bloomington: Indiana University Press, 1966.

Hornblower, Simon. *Thucydides*. Baltimore: Johns Hopkins University Press, 1987.

How, W. W. and Wells, J. *A Commentary on Herodotus*, vols. 1 and 2. New York: Oxford University Press, 1975.

Hussey, Edward. *The Presocratics*. London: Gerald Duckworth and Company, 1972.

Janson, H. W. *History of Art*. Englewood Cliffs, N.J.: Prentice-Hall, 1969.

Jones, A. H. M. *Athenian Democracy*. Oxford: Basil Blackwell, 1975.

———. *Sparta*. Cambridge, Mass.: Harvard University Press, 1967.

Kirk, G. S. *Homer and the Oral Tradition*. New York: Cambridge University Press, 1976.

———. *The Songs of Homer*. New York: Cambridge University Press, 1962.

Kirk, G. S., and Raven, J. E. *The Presocratic Philosophers*. New York: Cambridge University Press, 1957.

Knox, Bernard. *The Oldest Dead White European Males and Other Reflections on the Classics*. New York: W. W. Norton, 1993.

Lefkowitz, Mary R. *The Lives of the Greek Poets*. Baltimore: Johns Hopkins University Press, 1981.

Levi, Peter. *Atlas of the Greek World*. New York: Facts On File, 1984.

Lewis, David, et al., eds. *The Cambridge Ancient History: The Fifth Century*, vol. 5. 2nd ed. New York: Cambridge University Press, 1992.

Liddell, H. G., ed. *An Intermediate Greek-English Lexicon* (abridgement of the 7th ed. of Liddell and Scott's Greek-English Lexicon). New York: Oxford University Press, 1889.

Lloyd, G. E. R. *Aristotle: The Growth and Structure of His Thought*. New York: Cambridge University Press, 1968.

———. *Early Greek Science: Thales to Aristole*. London: Chatto and Windus, 1970.

———. *Greek Science after Aristotle*. London: Chatto and Windus, 1973.

Long, A. A. *Hellenistic Philosophy: Stoics, Epicureans, Sceptics*. London: Gerald Duckworth and Company, 1974.

Luce, J. V. *An Introduction to Greek Philosophy*. New York: Thames and Hudson, 1992.

Macadam, Alta, ed. *The Blue Guide: Sicily*. New York: W. W. Norton, 1988.

MacDowell, Douglas M. *The Law in Classical Athens*. Ithaca, N.Y.: Cornell University Press, 1978.

MacKendrick, Paul. *The Greek Stones Speak: The Story of Archaeology in Greek Lands*. New York: W. W. Norton, 1962.

Martin, Roland. *Greek Architecture*. New York: Electa/Rizzoli, 1988.

McDonagh, Bernard. *Blue Guide: Turkey: The Aegean and Mediterranean Coasts*. New York: W. W. Norton, 1989.

McLeish, Kenneth. *The Theatre of Aristophanes*. New York: Taplinger Publishing Company, 1980.

Meiggs, Russell. *The Athenian Empire*. New York: Oxford University Press, 1972.

———. *Trees and Timber in the Ancient Mediterranean World*. New York: Oxford University Press, 1982.

Meiggs, Russell, and Lewis, David, eds. *A Selection of Greek Historical Inscriptions*. New York: Oxford University Press, 1969.

Morrison, J. R., and Williams, R. T. *Greek Oared Ships: 900–322 B.C.* New York: Cambridge University Press, 1968.

Murray, Gilbert. *Euripides and His Age*. New York: Henry Holt and Company, 1913.

Murray, Oswyn. *Early Greece*. 2nd ed. Cambridge, Mass.: Harvard University Press, 1993.

———. Lectures presented at Oxford University ("Greek Poetry and Greek History"), 1978–1979.

———. "Sweet Feasts of the Grape." *The Times Higher Education Supplement*, July 6, 1990, pp. 13–17.

Murray, Oswyn, and Price, Simon, eds. *The Greek City from Homer to Alexander*. New York: Oxford University Press, 1990.

New York Times Atlas of the World, The. New York: Times Books, 1993.

Ostwald, Martin. *From Popular Sovereignty to the Sovereignty of Law: Law, Society, and Politics in Fifth-Century Athens*. Berkeley: University of California Press, 1986.

Pickard-Cambridge, A. W. *Dithyramb, Tragedy, and Comedy*. New York: Oxford University Press, 1962.

Podlecki, A. J. *The Life of Themistocles*. Montreal: McGill-Queen's University Press, 1975.

Poliakoff, Michael B. *Combat Sports in the Ancient World*. New Haven: Yale University Press, 1987.

Pollitt, J. J. *Art in the Hellenistic Age*. New York: Cambridge University Press, 1986.

Pomeroy, Sarah B. *Goddesses, Whores, Wives, and Slaves: Women in Classical Antiquity*. New York: Schocken Books, 1975.

Race, William H. *Pindar*. Boston: Twayne Publishers, 1986.

Renault, Mary. *The Nature of Alexander*. New York: Pantheon Books, 1975.

Rhodes, P. J. *A Commentary on the Aristotelian Athenaion Politeia*. New York: Oxford University Press, 1981.

Richter, Gisela, M. A. *A Handbook of Greek Art*. London: Phaidon Press, 1959.

Robertson, Alec, and Stevens, Denis, eds. *The Pelican History of Music*, vol. 1. Baltimore: Penguin Books, 1960.

Robertson, Martin. *A History of Greek Art*, vols. 1 and 2. New York: Cambridge University Press, 1975.

Rose, H. J. *A Handbook of Greek Literature*. New York: E. P. Dutton, 1934, 1961.

———. *A Handbook of Greek Mythology*. New York: E. P. Dutton, 1959.

———. *Religion in Greece and Rome*. New York: Harper and Row, 1959.

Ross, W. D. *Aristotle*. London: Methuen and Co., 1949.

de Ste. Croix, G. E. M. *The Origins of the Peloponnesian War*. London: Gerald Duckworth and Company, 1972.

Salmon, J. B. *Wealthy Corinth: A History of the City to 338 B.C.*. New York: Oxford University Press, 1984.

Scodel, Ruth. *Sophocles*. Boston: Twayne Publishers, 1984.

Sherratt, Andrew, ed. *The Cambridge Encyclopedia of Archaeology*. New York: Crown Publishers/Cambridge University Press, 1980.

Singer, Charles. *Greek Biology & Greek Medicine*. New York: Oxford University Press, 1922.

Snodgrass, A. M. *Arms and Armour of the Greeks*. Ithaca, N.Y.: Cornell University Press, 1967.

Snowden, Frank M., Jr. *Blacks in Antiquity: Ethiopians in the Greco-Roman Experience*. Cambridge, Mass.: Belknap Press/Harvard University Press, 1970.

Stewart, Andrew. *Greek Sculpture: An Exploration*, vols. 1 and 2. New Haven: Yale University Press, 1990.

Stillwell, Richard, ed. *The Princeton Encylcopedia of Classical Sites*. Princeton, N.J.: Princeton University Press, 1976.

Stockton, David. *The Classical Athenian Democracy*. New York: Oxford University Press, 1990.

Stone, I. F. *The Trial of Socrates*. Boston: Little, Brown; 1988.

Tarn, W. W. *Hellenistic Military and Naval Developments*. New York: Cambridge University Press, 1930.

Taylour, Lord William. *The Mycenaeans*. 2nd ed. New York: Thames and Hudson, 1983.

Wade-Gery, H. T. "Thucydides the son of Melesias." *Journal of Hellenic Studies*, vol. 52, 1932, pp. 205–227.

Walbank, F. W. et al., eds. *The Cambridge Ancient History: The Hellenistic World*, vol. 7, part 1. 2nd ed. New York: Cambridge University Press, 1984.

———. *The Cambridge Ancient History: The Rise of Rome to 220 B.C.*, vol. 7, part 2. 2nd ed. New York: Cambridge University Press, 1989.

———. *The Cambridge Ancient History: Rome and the Mediterranean to 133 B.C.*, vol. 8, 2nd ed. New York: Cambridge University Press, 1989.

Walker, Steven F. *Theocritus*. Boston: Twayne Publishers, 1980.

Weidman, Thomas. *Greek and Roman Slavery*. Baltimore: Johns Hopkins University Press, 1981.

Wellesz, Egon. *The New Oxford History of Music. Vol. 1: Ancient and Oriental Music*. New York: Oxford University Press, 1957.

Winnington-Ingram, R. P. *Sophocles: An Interpretation*. New York: Cambridge University Press, 1980.

Wood, Michael. *In Search of the Trojan War*. New York: Facts On File, 1985.

Zimmerman, Bernhard: *Greek Tragedy: An Introduction*. Trans. Thomas Marier. Baltimore: Johns Hopkins University Press, 1991.

Ancient authors in Greek and in translation

Aeschylus. *Agamemnon, Libation-bearers, Eumenides, Fragments*. Greek text, trans. Herbert Weir Smyth, ed. Hugh Lloyd-Jones. Cambridge, Mass.: Harvard University Press (Loeb Classical Library), 1971.

———. *Prometheus Bound, The Suppliants, Seven Against Thebes, The Persians*. Trans. and intro. Philip Vellacott. Baltimore: Penguin Books, 1961.

———. *Septem quae supersunt tragoediae*. Greek text, 2nd rev. ed. Denys Page. New York: Oxford University Press, 1972.

Archilochus et al., *Greek Lyric Poetry*. Ed. and trans. Willis Barnstone. New York: Schocken Books, 1967.

———. *Greek Lyrics*. Ed. and trans. Richmond Lattimore. Chicago: University of Chicago Press, 1981.

———. *The Penguin Book of Greek Verse*. Greek text, ed. and trans. by Constantine A. Trypanis. New York: Penguin Books, 1971.

Aristophanes. *The Complete Plays of Aristophanes*. Ed. and intro. by Moses Hadas. New York: Bantam Books, 1962.

Aristotle. *The Athenian Constitution* et al., Greek text, trans. H. Rackham. Cambridge, Mass.: Harvard University Press (Loeb Classical Library), 1952.

———. *Ethica Nicomachea*. Greek text, ed. I. Bywater. New York: Oxford University Press, 1890.

———. *Nicomachean Ethics*. Trans., intro., and notes Martin Ostwald. Indianapolis: Bobbs-Merrill Company, 1962.

——. *On the Art of Poetry*. Ed. and trans. Lane Cooper. Ithaca, N.Y.: Cornell University Press, 1947.

——. *Politics*. Ed. and trans. Ernest Baker. New York: Oxford University Press, 1946.

Arrian. *The Campaigns of Alexander*. Trans. Aubrey de Sélincourt, intro., and notes J. R. Hamilton. New York: Penguin Books, 1971.

Euripides. *Bacchae*. Greek text, ed. and notes E. R. Dodds. New York: Oxford University Press, 1960.

——. *The Complete Greek Tragedies*, vols. 3 and 4. Trans. David Grene and Richmond Lattimore. Chicago: University of Chicago Press, 1959.

——. *Hippolytos*. Greek text, ed. and notes W. S. Barrett. New York: Oxford University Press, 1964.

——. *Medea*. Greek text, ed. and notes Denys L. Page. New York: Oxford University Press, 1938.

Herodotus. *Historiae*, vols. 1 and 2. Greek text, ed. Charles Hude. New York: Oxford University Press, 1927.

——. *The Histories*. Trans. Aubrey de Sélincourt, intro. and notes A. R. Burn. New York: Penguin Books, 1972.

Hesiod. *Theogony* Trans. Apostolos N. Athanassakis. Baltimore: Johns Hopkins University Press, 1983.

——. *Works and Days*. Trans. Apostolos N. Athanassakis. Baltimore: Johns Hopkins University Press, 1983.

Homer. *The Iliad*, vols. 1 and 2. Greek text, ed. and trans. A. T. Murray, Cambridge, Mass.: Harvard University Press (Loeb Classical Library), 1939, 1942.

——. *The Iliad*, trans. Alston Hurd Chase and William G. Perry, Jr. New York: Bantam Books, 1960.

——. *The Iliad*. Trans. Robert Fitzgerald. Garden City, N.Y.: Anchor Press/Doubleday, 1975.

——. *The Odyssey*, vols. 1 and 2. Greek text, ed. W. B. Stanford. New York: St. Martin's Press, 1965.

——. *The Odyssey*. Trans. Robert Fitzgerald. Garden City, N.Y.: Anchor Press/Doubleday, 1961.

Menander. *The Dyskolos of Menander*. Greek text, ed. and intro. E. W. Handley. Cambridge, Mass.: Harvard University Press, 1965.

Pausanias. *Guide to Greece*, vols. 1 and 2. Trans. and intro. Peter Levi. New York: Penguin Books, 1979.

Pindar. *The Odes of Pindar*. Trans. Richmond Lattimore. Chicago: University of Chicago Press, 1947.

——. *Pindari carmina cum fragmentis*. Greek text, ed. C. M. Bowra. New York: Oxford University Press, 1947.

Plato. *Euthyphro, Apology, Crito*. Trans. and intro. F. J. Church. Indianapolis: Bobbs-Merrill Company, 1948.

——. *Gorgias*. Greek text, ed. and notes E. R. Dodds. New York: Oxford University Press, 1959.

——. *Gorgias*. Trans. and intro. W. C. Helmbold. Indianapolis: Bobbs-Merrill, 1952.

——. *Protagoras*. Trans. and intro. Gregory Vlastos. Indianapolis: Bobbs-Merrill Company, 1956.

——. *The Republic of Plato*. Trans. and intro. Francis Macdonald Cornford. New York: Oxford University Press, 1941.

——. *Res Publica*, in vol. 4 of *Opera* (complete works). Greek text, ed. John Burnet. New York: Oxford University Press, 1903.

——. *The Symposium*. Trans. and intro. Walter Hamilton. Baltimore: Penguin Books, 1951.

Plutarch. *The Age of Alexander*. Trans. Ian Scott-Kilvert, intro. G. T. Griffith. New York: Penguin Books, 1973.

——. *Plutarch's Lives*, vols. 1–7, 9. Greek text, trans. Bernadotte Perrin. Cambridge, Mass.: Harvard University Press (Loeb Classical Library), 1967.

——. *Plutarch on Sparta*. Trans., intro., and notes Richard J. A. Talbert. New York: Penguin Books, 1988.

——. *The Rise and Fall of Athens*. Trans. and intro. Ian Scott-Kilvert. New York: Penguin Books, 1960.

Sappho, et al., *Greek Lyric*, vol. 1. Greek text, ed. and trans. David Campbell. Cambridge, Mass.: Harvard University Press (Loeb Classical Library), 1982.

Sophocles. *The Complete Plays of Sophocles*. Trans. Richard Claverhouse Jebb, intro. Moses Hadas. New York: Bantam Books, 1971.

——. *Oedipus Rex*. Greek text, ed. R. D. Dawe. New York: Cambridge University Press, 1982.

Stesichorus, et al., *Greek Lyric*, vol. 3. Greek text, ed. and trans. David Campbell. Cambridge, Mass.: Harvard University Press (Loeb Classical Library), 1991.

Thucydides. *Historiae*, vols. 1 and 2. Greek text, ed. Henry Stuart Jones and Enoch Powell. New York: Oxford University Press, 1960, 1963.

——. *The Peloponnesian War*. Trans. and intro. Rex Warner. Baltimore: Penguin Books, 1954.

Xenophon. *Conversations of Socrates: Socrates' Defence, Memoirs of Socrates, The Dinner Party, The Estate-manager*. Trans. Hugh Tredennick and Robin Waterfield, ed. Robin Waterfield. New York: Penguin Books, 1990.

——. *A History of My Times (Hellenica)*. Trans. Rex Warner, intro. and notes George Cawkwell. New York: Penguin Books, 1979.

——. *The Persian Expedition*. Trans. Rex Warner, intro. and notes George Cawkwell. New York: Penguin Books, 1972.

INDEX

Main essays are indicated by **bold** page numbers.